SNAKES

of North America

Eastern and Central Regions

SNAKES
of North America
Eastern and Central Regions

Revised Edition

Alan Tennant

Contributing Authors

Gerard T. Salmon
Dr. Richard B. King

Maps by Gerard T. Salmon

Lone Star Books

SNAKES
of North America
Eastern and Central Regions

Published by Lone Star Books
A Member of the Rowman & Littlefield Publishing Group
4501 Forbes Boulevard, Ste. 200
Lanham, MD 20706

Distributed by National Book Network

Library of Congress Control Number: 2002113489
ISBN: 1-58907-003-8 (alk. paper)

∞™ The paper used in this publication meets the minimum requirements
of American National Standard for Information Sciences—Permanence of
Paper for Printed Library Materials, ANSI/NISO Z39.48-1992.
Manufactured in the United States of America.

Book design by Roxann L. Combs.
Cover painting by Ed Acuña. To purchase a fine art print of the cover painting,
contact Ed Acuña, calebra97@aol.com or (512) 330-0655.

Dedication

For the late Jozsef Laszlo,

former Curator of Herpetofauna at the San Antonio Zoo—

the most empathetic guy toward reptiles and

amphibians I've known, and the least elitist.

Without Joe's enthusiastic encouragement,

I'd never have started this two-decade-long series of

books on snakes.

Alan Tennant

CONTENTS

SPECIES ACCOUNTS

TYPHLOPIDAE

---

*According to both *The Chicago Manual of Style*, 14th ed., and *Scientific Style and Format*, 6th ed. (Council of Biology Editors), family and subfamily names such as LEPTOTYPHLOPIDAE and COLUBRIDAE should be capitalized rather than italicized. Yet in the herpetological literature these terms are italicized about as often as not—as I have done here.

COLUBRIDAE

Small Burrowing Snakes, 37

Crowned, Flat, and Black-Headed Snakes, 37

Tantilla, 37

Red-Bellied and Brown Snakes, 53

Storeria, 53

Earth Snakes, 67

Virginia, 67

Ring-Necked Snakes, 74

Diadophis, 74

Ground Snake, 84

Sonora, 84

Worm Snakes, 86

Carphophis, 86

Pine Woods Snakes, 90

Rhadinaea, 90

Short-Tailed Snakes, 92

Stilosoma, 92

Lined, Garter, and Ribbon Snakes, 95

Lined Snake, 95

Tropidoclonion, 95

Garter and Ribbon Snakes, 96

Thamnophis, 96

Aquatic Snakes, 130
Water and Salt Marsh Snakes, 130

Nerodia, 130

Swamp Snakes, 165

Seminatrix, 165

Crayfish Snakes, 169

Regina, 169

Mud and Rainbow Snakes, 178

Farancia, 178

Kirtland's Snakes, 186

Clonophis, 186

Patch-nosed Snakes, 188

Salvadora, 188

Green Snakes, 193

Liochlorophis and *Opheodrys,* 193

Whipsnakes, Racers, and Indigo Snakes, 198

Whipsnakes, 198

Masticophis, 198

Racers 330

Coluber, 330

Indigo Snakes, 347

Drymarchon, 347

Speckled Racer, 353

Drymobius, 353

Brown-blotched Terrestrial Snakes, 355
Hog-Nosed Snakes, 355

Heterodon, 356

Pine, Gopher, and Bullsnakes, 367

Pituophis, 367

Glossy Snakes, 382

Arizona, 382

Rat and Fox Snakes, 387

Elaphe, 387

Trans-Pecos Rat Snake, 410

Bogertophis, 410

Mexican Hook-Nosed Snake, 414

Ficimia, 414

Western Hook-Nosed Snake, 416

Gyalopion, 416

Kingsnakes, Milk, and Scarlet Snakes, 418

Lampropeltis, 418

Scarlet Snakes, 457

Cemophora, 457

Long-nosed Snakes, 463

Rhinocheilus, 463

Mildly Venomous Rear-fanged Snakes, 466
Night Snakes, 466

Hypsiglena, 466

Cat-Eyed Snakes, 469

Leptodeira, 469

Rattlesnakes, 509

Pigmy Rattlesnakes and Massasaugas, 510

Sistrurus, 510

Rattlesnakes, 523

Crotalus, 523

Note on Contents Listing

The arrangement of snakes in the table of contents follows the now universal system of Latin and Greek genus, species, and subspecies nomenclature devised nearly two hundred and fifty years ago by Swedish botanist Carl con Linne', better known as Linnaeus. Beyond this convention, however, to facilitate field identification, snakes that look alike and/or share similar habitat are grouped together.

This grouping sometimes parallels these animals' genetic affinities. Yet, confusingly, snakes that look alike and behave similarly may not be closely related. (Their similarities are often due to the demands of a particular habitat, often referred to as parallel evolution.) On the other hand, snakes which look and behave differently may still be closely related.

In fact, the best way to determine kinship is through molecular comparisons of snakes' body proteins, combined with morphological data. This work has called into doubt many traditional ophidian classifications, but, following the most recent authoritative reference (Carl H. Ernst, and Roger W. Barbor 1989, *Snakes of Eastern North America*), the genetic relationships of North American snakes are currently thought to be as follows:

Family *Typhlopidae*
- Genus
  - *Ramphotyphlops*

Family *Leptotyphlopidae*
- Genus
  - *Leptotyphlops*

Family *Colubridae*
- Subfamily *Colubrinae*
  - Genus
    - *Coluber*
    - *Drymarchon*
    - *Drymobius*
    - *Masticophis*
    - *Opheodrys*
    - *Liochlorophis*
    - *Salvadora*
- Subfamily *Natricinae*
  - Genus
    - *Nerodia*
    - *Seminatrix*
    - *Regina*
    - *Storeria*
    - *Thamnophis*
    - *Tropidoclonion*
    - *Virginia*
    - *Clonophis*
- Subfamily *Lampropeltinae*
  - Genus
    - *Lampropeltis*
    - *Cemophora*
    - *Rhinocheilus*
    - *Elaphe*
    - *Bogertophis*
    - *Pituophis*
    - *Arizona*
    - *Stilosoma*
- Subfamily *Xenodontinae*
  - Genus
    - *Diadophis*
    - *Carphophis*
    - *Farancia*
    - *Rhadinaea*
    - *Tantilla*
    - *Sonora*
    - *Ficimia*
    - *Gyalopion*
    - *Heterodon*
    - *Hypsiglena*
    - *Leptodeira*
    - *Coniophanes*
    - *Trimorphodon*

Family *Elapidae*
- Genus
  - *Micrurus*

Family *Viperidae*
- Genus
  - *Agkistrodon*
  - *Sistrurus*
  - *Crotalus*

ACKNOWLEDGEMENTS

Authors frequently write that they could not have completed a particular work without the help of colleagues. Yet rarely is this as true as is the case with *Snakes of North America: Eastern and Central Regions*. This geographic area is so vast and diverse in climate and topography that only those long familiar with particular regions—through residency or repeated field work there—are truly qualified to speak of its unique habitats. For this reason, this volume could have only been produced with the help of many such people, who generously offered hard-won knowledge of their particular regions. Yet, within the herpetological community, this generosity is typical. Those who share an enthusiasm for reptiles and amphibians (both professionals and people whose reward is entirely personal and intellectual) are almost unfailingly willing to pass on the insights into habitat and behavior they have gained from years in the field, offer their breeding and captive-maintenance skills (often earned by decades of meticulously kept herpetocultural data), and share the fruits of lifetimes of academic research—all so that others with the same enthusiasms might benefit from what they have learned.

No one has been more generous with his time and unflagging enthusiasm than Craig McIntyre. Map-maker, editor, consultant, and critic—as well as my longest-time field partner—Craig's help over the years cannot be overstated. He has contributed slides, extensive journal and literature sources, and notes on his long-term captive-maintance of rare species such as *Cemophora coccinea copei*. The same support came from Connie, Jeff, and Jonathan McIntyre.

Richard D. Bartlett worked long and diligently on the first edition of this volume and his contributions, as well as his excellent photographs, occur throughout.

Also among this group of major-league supporters are Jim Stout, who long ago introduced me to field herpetology, and to Craig and Linda Trumbower, who went out of their way to re-involve me in Florida's herpetological community.

Other contributors from this nation-wide community of enthusiasts who made the book possible are Jim and Barb Costabile, whose support, both herpetological and emotional, proved invaluable; Joseph E. Forks has devoted a major part of his life to unraveling the mysteries of the very secretive lifestyle of the Gray-banded Kingsnake, *Lampropeltis alterna*—the search for which, every spring and summer, brings hundreds of reptile enthusiasts to West Texas—and he has brought to this volume extensive field work and careful library research.

Without Kenneth L. Krysko's energy and enthusiasm, backed by years of field collecting in Florida's marshes and pinewoods, sawgrass prairies, cypress domes, and offshore Keys, this volume would have been infinitely poorer; as it would wihout the unfailing support, interest, and hospitality of Kenney's dad, Len Krysko.

That is also the case with Kevin Enge. His familiarity with the Southeast's myriad natural community types and their ophidian populations, combined with his familiarity with herpetological literature, provided a great deal of the research and collaborative editorial input upon which this volume relies.

Dr. Paul E. Moler, as administrator of the Wildlife Research Laboratory of the Florida Game and Fresh Water Fish Commission, is a busy guy with great responsibilities, yet with enormous generosity he took a tremendous amount of time to meticulously examine parts of this text. Using both his long experience in the field and his comprehensive knowledge of the pertinent scientific literature—as well as great patience—he carefully steered a major portion of this manuscript onto firmer herpetological ground.

Barry Mansell's ability to come up with superlative color photographs of snakes so rare that, like *Tantilla oolitica* and *Nerodia clarkii taeniata*, they have almost never been found in the wild—let alone photographed—is supported by his broader skills as woodsman and field biologist.

Bill and Kathy Love offered both excellent photographs and the sort of hospitality and encouragement that only comes from people who share one's lifelong fascination with reptiles and amphibians.

John Decker is one of those rare naturalists motivated only by a love of the natural world—in this case the subtropical lower Florida peninsula whose native ecology is so rapidly disappearing—who devote themselves both to its study and the conservational propagation of its vanishing reptiles and amphibians.

Kathryn Vaughan, James R. Dixon, Jonathan Campbell, and David Sinclair shared their academic/governmental perspectives.

Dr. Craig Rudolph shared his research into the lesser-known ophidian fauna of East Texas, while Terry, Troy, and Toby Hibbitts, who comprise perhaps Texas' most eminent family of herpetologists, were extremely generous in sharing their careful, authoritative observations of ophidian natural history.

The same is true of field biologist and photographer Damon Salceies, who took the first photographs of a neonate *Trimorphodon biscutatus vilkinsonii* in the wild and added many pertinent observations. Andrew Sansom, Executive Director of the Texas Department of Parks and Wildlife and noted natural-history author, has long been a friend and staunch supporter of these books; his department's nongame biologist, Dr. Andrew Price, contributed references for hard-to-find data, the current legal standing of a number of species and subspecies, and research supporting their classification.

Other important contributors to this volume are Jack Joy, former director of both the Dallas and Abilene zoos, who dipped into his wealth of field experience to fill in observations of previously unreported ophidian habitat utilization or behavior whenever an account lacked sufficient library references; Billy Griswold, whose photographic skill resulted in excellent color plates; and Billy's dad, Bill Griswold, who provided most of the information on the southern hog-nosed snake, *Heterodon simus*.

David Auth gave access to the collection of the Florida Museum of Natural History in Gainesville, where Kenney Krysko spent weeks of research. Kenny Wray and Brice Noonan were invariably quick to offer help with field notes, library research, digging up fossorial snakes in the midst of rainstorms, and poking fun at undue seriousness. Kenny was also the author of two significant herpetological firsts: first to hatch *Masticophis schotti* in captivity, and first, with Dick Bartlett, to find *Ramphotyphlops braminus* in a radically new range in subtropical Texas. Tim Walsh of the Central Florida Zoo generously shared his collected data and insight on one of the state's rarest snakes, *Lampropeltis calligaster occipitolineata*. Jeff Barringer cheerfully provided computer consultation and on-line searches for information and color slides, while Dr. Kelly McCoy, of Angelo State University, added his observations of *Tantilla rubra cucullata*. Augustus Rentfro brought me up-to-date on Texas lyre snake reproduction, John Caspers edited some *Elaphe* accounts, and William B. Montgomery offered dozens of beautifully shot slides as well as both esthetic and herpetological perspective. Tim Cole, by e-mail, has kept me constantly updated on both local lore and periodic valuable new field observations.

Still others in the herpetological/medical/natural history community who contributed freely of their time and knowledge include: Dr. Joseph M. Abell, Jim Ashcraft, Bob Binder, Johnny Binder, the late W. F. Blair, Bryan Blake, Dave Blody, Hugh Brown, Mark Brown, Kelly Bryant, Jim Bull, Patrick Burchfield, Tim Cole, Bill Degenhardt, Jim Dunlap, David Easterla, Rowe Elliott, Richard Etheridge, Mollie and David Francis, Jerry Glidewell, Charles Goodrich, Harry Greene,

Ed Guidry, Ron Gutberlet, Tom Harding, Dr. David M. Hardy, Linda Hedges, Richard Hix, Erik Holmback, Richard Hudson, J. P. Jones, John Jones, Tim Jones, Alan Kardon, Robert E. Kuntz, Greg Lasley, *Thamnophis* enthusiasts Bill and Donna Marvel, Ray Meckel, Dennie Miller, Susie and S. I. Morris, Dr. Andrew Price, Rick Pratt, Hugh Quinn, Francis Rose, Dr. Findlay E. Russell, Neils Saustrup, Barbara Scown, Dean Singleton, Larry and Marlene Smitherman, Steve Spangle, U.S. Fish and Wildlife Service, Tom Tining, Jeannie Taylor, Luke Thompson, Earl Turner, Thomas Vermersch, Russ Walker, Brett Whitney, Michael A. Williamson, Sherri Williamson, Larry David Wilson, Tom Wood, Richard Worthington, Jim Yantis, and David Alan Zlatkin.

It is also important to acknowledge my debt to Roger Conant and Joseph T. Collins' *A Field Guide to Amphibians and Reptiles of Eastern and Central North America* (Houghton Mifflin, 1991) as the source of several of the record lengths cited in this volume. Further, beyond the inspiration this volume provided, one of its authors, Joe Collins, discussed at length with me speciation theory and ophidian evolution, for which I offer my thanks.

My sincere thanks, also, to those who graciously and laboriously read, corrected, and commented at length on several of the preliminary manuscripts leading to this volume's predecessor, *The Snakes of Texas* (Texas Monthly Press, 1984), *A Field Guide to Snakes of Florida* (Gulf Publishing, 1997), and the most recent edition of *A Field Guide to Texas Snakes* (Gulf Publishing, 1998). These include: Neil B. Ford, University of Texas at Tyler; William W. Lamar, University of Texas at Tyler; Dave Barker; Jim Stout; A. J. Seippel; Joe Forks; and especially Gerard T. Salmon.

Corrections and amendments to the first edition of *Snakes of North America: Eastern and Central Regions* were submitted by, among others, Bart Bruno and Brian Gray, while biographical/historical references were checked against those offered by the excellent website of Ellin Beltz (http://ebeltz.net).

Final proofreaders were Ed Acuña, John MacGregor, D. Craig McIntyre, and Gerard T. Salmon.

Visually, this book is indebted to the fine drawings of Artists John Lockman and David Moellendorf; to the extreme realism of Ed Acuna, who created the cover painting; to photographers Michael Allender, Dave Barker, Richard D. Bartlett, Michael J. Bowerman, Ted L. Brown, Jim Costabile, Doug Durre, James H. Evans, Paul Freed, Billy Griswold, James H. Harding, M. Higgrer, Laura Jarrell, Richard E. King, Kenneth L. Krysko, Katherine Love, William B. Love, John MacGregor, J. V. Maldonado, Donna Marvel, D. Craig McIntyre, John McGregor, William B. Montgomery, Rick Reed,

Damon Salceies, Gerard T. Salmon, Tom Tyning, and Robert Wayne Van Devender. Also to Chicago Herpetological Society editor Mike Dloogatch, to researcher Melody Lytle, and to Tim Cole.

I also want to thank my skillful (and very patient) editors at Lone Star Books, Rick Rinehart and Stephen Driver.

Alan Tennant
Marathon, Texas
August, 2002

The production of the maps in this book were no easy task. They provide the reader with a general idea of where each species or sub-species is currently found although these ranges are subject to constant change. We relied heavily on the published works on the herpetofauna of the various states and regions and, in part, on data supplied from several of the amphibian and reptile atlas projects currently being conducted. Also, countless hours were spent in museum collections looking at specimen tags and records which helped form a basis of our knowledge for areas where we had not spent time in the field. Special thanks go to Jonathan A. Campbell of the University of Texas–Arlington, James R. Dixon and Kathryn Vaughan of the Texas Cooperative Wildlife Collection at Texas A&M University and Todd Hunsinger of the New York State Museum for allowing nearly unlimited access to the collections. William H. "Marty" Martin was especially helpful in supplying maps and data for several species of snakes which he is intimately familiar, particularly for the timber, canebrake and eastern diamondback rattlesnakes.

The following people assisted us by sharing their field notes, knowledge and/or specimens which were used in compiling the data for the preparation of the range maps: Lee Abbott, Edward Acuña, Mitch Allen, Charles Annicelli, Ralph W. Axtell, Jeff Barringer, Geb Bailey, Paul Bailey, David Barker, James Bear, John Behler, Doug and Nancy Beckwith, Lance Benton, Ric Blair, David A. Blody, Elizabeth A. Bonnen, Robert Bowker, Craig Boyd, Steve Boyd, Tom Boyden, Alvin R. Breisch, Joe Branham, Bill Brown, Bartholomew B. Bruno, Steve Cade, John Caspers, Pat Cherryhome, Peter Chimel, Heyward Clamp, Jr., Al Coffee, Henry Cohen, David Cook, Henry Dean, John Decker, Dan Dellatorre, Vincent DeMarco, Robert Deptula, Walter Deptula, Richard Deuel, Ben Dial, Michael Dloogatch, David Doherty, Douglas Duerre, Robert G. Dunning, Jason Edwards, David Eldien, Kevin M. Enge, Kevin Enright, Richard Evans, Michael Faircloth, Robert Fengya, Bruce Finley, David Finley, Mary Finley, Joseph E. Forks, John Fraser, Katherine L. Freeman, Steve Fuller, Steve Garnett, Alan

Garry, Todd Gdula, Michael Geiger, Bill Griswold, Werner "Buck" Gros, Michael Harazim, David Heckard, Martyn Hess, Troy Hibbits, Craig R. Hodgson, Tim Hoffnagle, John Hollister, William F. Holmstrom, Jr., Wayne Howell, Les Hughey, Matthew J. Ingrasci, Steve Jensen, Glenn Johnson, David Justice, Paul Kaiser, John Kemnitzer, Gerald Keown, Bonnie Key, Erik Kiviat, Larry Krajkowski, Kenneth Krysko, Bill Lamoreaux, Christopher J. Lechowicz II, Fred Ledermann, Greg Lepera, Brian Levenson, Jamie Levis, David B. Long, Clive Longden, Howard Lynn, Paul Lynum, Frank Maccarrone, Dan Martin, Brian Mason, Jeff McAdoo, Jim McLean, Richard McNabb, John Meltzer, Gerold Merker, Dennis J. Miller, Charles D. Montfort, Peter Montfort, Doug Moody, Jeff Mourning, Norman Nunley, Lou Parotti, Mike Patterson, Bill Perron, H. William Peterson, Steve Phillips, David Powell, Ray Queen, Scott Quint, Brian Radenburg, Christopher J. Raithel, Eric Richter, Howard Riley, Jeff Ross, Damon Salceies, Hunter Salmon, Greg Savino, Marlon Sawyer, Jon C. Seifer, Christopher J. Sheldon, David Sheldon, Howard Sherman, James Sirch, King Smith, Don Soderburg, Randy Stechert, Adam Sweetman, Gary Swinford, Scott Swormstedt, Kamuran Tepedelen, Eric Timaeus, Bruce Timmerman, Michael Tkacz, Ron Tremper, Craig Trumbower, Rick Van Dyke, Russ Walker, Joseph Wadagnolo, Thomas Warner, Doug Wenzel, Jess Whitfield, Pete Wright, Tommy Yarbrough, Robert T. Zappalorti, Bill Zovickian, and Richard Zuchowski.

Published material used in compiling the distribution areas of the maps includes Gerald G. Raun and Frederick R. Gehlbach, *Amphibians and Reptiles in Texas* (Dallas: Dallas Museum of Natural History, 1972); *Herpetological Review*, vols. 3–13; Jerry Glidewell, *Southwestern Naturalist* 19 (2):213–23, 1974; Dennie Miller, "A Life History Study of the Gray-banded Kingsnake, *Lampropeltis mexicana alterna*, in Texas" (master's thesis, Sul Ross State University, 1979); John E. Werler, *Poisonous Snakes of Texas and the First Aid Treatment of Their Bites* (Austin: Texas Parks and Wildlife, 1978); Roger Conant/Joseph T. Collins, *A Field Guide to Amphibians and Reptiles of Eastern and Central North America* (Boston: Houghton-Mifflin, 1991); *Journal of Herpetology* 11 (2):217–20, 1977; Charles J. Cole and Lawrence M. Hardy, *Bulletin of the American Museum of Natural History*, vol. 171, (New York, 1981); J. S. Mecham, *Copeia* (1956, 51-52); and Alan Tennant, *The Snakes of Texas* (Austin, Texas Monthly Press, 1984), *A Field Guide to the Snakes of Florida* (Houston, Gulf Publishing Co., 1997), and *A Field Guide to Texas Snakes*, second edition (Houston: Gulf Publishing Co., 1998).

Gerard T. Salmon
Rhinebeck, New York

PREFACE

In the end
We will preserve only what we love,
We will love only what we understand,
We will understand only what we have been taught.
> —Senegalese Conservationist Baba Dioum

Paleontologist Robert T. Bakker once observed that only with considerable difficulty had he been able to gain a perspective from which a thecodont—a stubby little Jurassic reptile—seemed as beautiful as a cheetah. The thecodont just had a different environment. An environment to which it adapted by squatting on the shores of ancient mud pans, gobbling down smaller creatures and living in the same tentative give-and-take with its neighbors that, extrapolated across the great panoply of living beings, reveals an infinitely complex system of delicately counterweighted balances. The system is so intricate that only a bit of its circuitry is yet available to our understanding, but its essence is clear. Cosmologically intermingled sets of opposing hungers and wills-to-live suspend each life form in a tenuous balance between dominance over its environment and extinction. In this unconscious genetic struggle, each species' capacities contribute to the natural forces massed against its prey, its predators, and often, its neighbors. Collectively asserted, the efforts of those neighbors/competitors—for a while, at least—manage to oppose the species' own drive for biological success just enough for both sides to co-exist, balanced in communities ranging from those swarming through a drop of water to others carpeting the continents' great plains.

Although periodically re-shuffled by evolutionary changes typically brought about by environmental upheaval, over long spans of time these communities appear to generally be relatively stable, dropout species quickly replaced by variations of neighboring organisms which venture evolutionary tendrils into every newly vacated environmental space.

As little more than blinking spectators to this mortal process, the least we can do is respect the contenders. Yet nothing could be further

from our historical record: wildlife of all kinds has always been something for mankind to overcome, to exploit, to eliminate.

Shedding the opacity of the cultural biases which, for thousands of years, have fueled this drive for dominance is the first step toward respecting our fellow beings. But this is far from easy, for the most difficult step in learning anything meaningful about the natural world is to overcome the slanted human perspectives that determine so many of our biological empathies.

This is especially true where snakes are concerned. In the prevailing cultural context serpents are so scary and repugnant that, even to people who would hesitate to harm any other vertebrate, it has long seemed proper to kill a snake.

Yet with the disappearance of so many formerly abundant animals that viewpoint is changing. Gradually, we are starting to see how much we have lost in ridding ourselves of the bears and wolves, mountain lions and rattlesnakes that threatened first our lives, then our livestock.

Too late, for the most part, awareness is dawning of the fundamental ignorance of seeing such creatures as villains. It has been a mistake to filter their appearances and actions through our provincial human perspectives of good and evil, beauty and ugliness—as though such narrow criteria could set standards for a system of harmonies that preceded our existence by billions of years and will certainly outlast us by an equivalent span. Culturally ingrained as it is, to choose certain striking beings—cheetahs, swallows, or redwood trees—to grace with our eccentric notion of beauty is to ignore how meager are our recently acquired cultural concepts when judged against a cosmic order whose structure binds the stately parade of stars and planets, shapes the flow of the tectonic currents that mold the continents, and has wrought the symmetry of serpents no less than that of tigers.

Moreover, assigning malfeasance to creatures we perceive as psychologically alien creates in us an illusion that our species is different: a higher sort of creature.

It is this unconsciously arrogant notion that obscures from us our essence. We are but one minuscule thread in the planet's great organic tapestry—a thread, moreover, entirely dependent upon neighboring threads to maintain its place in the weave of life. In this intricate matrix every single species of us is bound to our neighbors by myriad dovetailing pacts. These pacts of mutual dependency are supremely complex pacts, pacts not of our choice nor over which we exercise control, but mutually dependent pacts, nevertheless, on which our joint survival ultimately depends.

SNAKES
of North America
Eastern and Central Regions

Area covered by this book.

where they were less likely to fall prey to saurian predators poorly equipped for digging.

But learning to live permanently beneath the earth's surface would have been painfully procrustean. There's not much room below ground, even for burrowers, so this group of swiftly adapting lizards had to become very small. At the same time, deep in their subterranean burrows, their senses were limited to, primarily, a combination of smell and taste. (The neurological pathways connecting these sensory organs were already linked in the ancestral monitors, which had originated a sensitive forked tongue whose sticky surface gathered scent particles from the air and soil, then carried those particles to a paired vomeronasal gland located in the roof of their mouths.) Thus the olfactorily active tongues of these new burrowers became a significant advantage for lizards embarking on a new life below the surface.

In a similar way, the great lateral flexibility of the monitors lent itself to their fossorial descendants' need to squirm through tight subsurface milieus.[2] Wriggling worked better than walking in narrow subterranean tunnels, and in the course of the millions of years during which the post-monitors' bodies became ever-smaller and slimmer, their limbs shrank into fetus-like stubs and, as they gradually assumed a serpentine form, little by little these creatures ceased to be lizards at all.

This elaborate process—one of the triumphs of adaptive evolution—entailed almost complete internal restructuring: to exclude the press of soil, these nascent snakes' eyes grew scale-cap goggles (transparent eyelids are still found on some contemporary burrowing monitors). Then, since vision was useless in the darkness below ground, those rigid eye-caps hardened into an unbroken armor of facial scales covering eyes that ultimately atrophied into dots of vestigial ocular pigment. At roughly the same time, the dirt-gathering orifice of the ear permanently closed, presumably because it could be so easily damaged from sudden pressure changes in the constricted airspace of subterranean passages, and with it the lizard's delicate eardrum also vanished. At the same time, the auditory bones (that in other reptiles transmit airborne sounds from the eardrum to the aural nerves) fused to the lower jaw, leaving the evolving serpents deaf to all but a narrow range of earth-borne vibrations. The monitors' big carnivore's

---

[2]Throughout their history many lacertilian species have shown a tendency to lose their legs. Within a single genus, South African snake-lizards show several intermediate stages of limb reduction: one has four fully developed legs, each with a five-toed foot; another has four rudimentary limbs with only two toes each; a third has vestigial hind legs bearing but one toe each and no external front limbs.

teeth were sacrificed as well, in favor of scaled-down dentition—adequate for the little subsurface-living lizards' minuscule new prey of annelids and insect larvae.[3] Tiny teeth were, of course, a further adaptation to the slender snouts with countersunk lower jaws these small reptiles developed to probe through soil without scooping up mouthfuls of terrain.

Posteriorly, equally radical adjustments occurred, but only at the expense of significantly impaired metabolic efficiency. Among the most costly change was proto-snakes' loss of the powerful lizard heart. Only a slender, considerably less-muscular heart—which suffers more backwash between its poorly divided chambers than the better-segmented hearts of lizards—could fit into these creatures radically thinned bodies. Moreover, the corollary loss of a rigid lower thoracic shield left their fragile cardiovascular chambers vulnerable to external blows, and makes all serpents prone to serious injury in a fall. Respiratory efficiency also suffered as snakes, evolutionarily striving for the smallest possible diameter, adopted a single long lung. (This prompted the development of subsidiary pulmonary capacity in other organs: the alveolar lining at the rear of most snakes' tracheas evolved some capillary-oxygen exchange capability, while the posterior end of the lung developed into a nonvascular air-storage sac which enlarges the lung's capacity by some 20 percent.)

For those nascent snakes to so completely restructure their bodies was a risky evolutionary strategy—but over the long term it has proven to be a superior one. When the first Cretaceous monitors began their subterranean life reptiles dominated the earth, with more varieties than all species of amphibians, birds, and early mammals combined. Then things changed: by the beginning of the Cenozoic era, environmental cataclysms had eliminated the remaining small dinosaurs—on land no animal heavier than about 50 pounds survived—and cut the number of reptile species to less than a third of those that had flourished during the previous era.[4] The supple, miniaturized bodies that this group of chthonic lizard-snakes had evolved to evade their surface-living predators now allowed them to withdraw from the climatic vagaries that extirpated so many other terrestrial vertebrates and, as the most recently developed of the rep-

---

[3]Like most of their lizard forebears, all snakes are carnivores: no known serpent has ever opted for a herbivorous diet.

[4]By far the most likely hypotheses for this mass extinction now seems to be that a middle-sized asteroid, probably the Alvarez Comet, struck the earth some 65 million years ago, detonating a dense cloud of dust that enveloped the planet for years, dimming the sun enough to eliminate most plant life and thus starving every terrestrial animal too large either to subsist on the remaining scraps of seeds and lichens, or to get by on the limited prey offered by the few creatures that could.

tile groups, slide relatively unharmed through the bottleneck of Cretaceous/Tertiary extinction.[5]

By the dawn of the Cenozoic some 68 million years ago, a different surface prevailed—one well suited for genetic expansion. Almost all of the old dinosaur hunters were gone, but for those now thoroughly miniaturized, deaf and blind fossorial serpents, returning to life above ground presented immense problems.[6] One of the most pressing was the widely fluctuating surface temperature.[7]

Other reptiles faced the same problem, but snakes were uniquely suited to cope with it. Avoiding falling air temperature or burning sun was mostly a matter of returning to the far more temperate cosm beneath the surface, a realm their hard-won tubular shape and new flexibility now let them access better than most other reptiles. To make use of both worlds, however, snakes had to adopt new behavior—actively avoiding the surface's temperature extremes while still making selective use of solar radiation to maintain the narrow range of temperature their increasingly sophisticated metabolisms required. This new strategy was thermoregulation, and for species active in daylight it took the form of basking (at high altitudes, as well as in northerly latitudes where little of the sun's energy remains at the surface after dark, serpents are mostly diurnal). Heat-avoidance thermoregulation was even simpler, entailing, for the most part, avoiding the sun by withdrawing either into water, the shade, or into the cool realm below ground.

Of equal importance for these little subterranean reptiles was the need, once again, to see. So, with the genetic flexibility typical of snakes (which are comparatively resistance to the lethal gene combinations that cause most mutations of warm-blooded creatures to die), those formerly blind, burrowing Paleocene serpents re-evolved the sense of sight. As the opaque scales covering their now-vestigial

---

[5]No more than 40 kinds of monitors are still found in restricted tropical ranges, while today snakes are by far the most widespread reptile, with over 2,000 species occupying a broader range of habitats than any other cold-blooded land animal.

[6]After the archeosaurian hunters vanished, snakes still faced a world dominated by equally formidable mammalian and avian predators—hunters whose big new brains required a stable internal climate, provided by a metabolic thermostat that meant most could forage well in cool weather when snakes were too slow-moving to afford being abroad.

[7]As legless creatures unable to use even the lizards' ploy of raising their bellies to tip-toe across hot sand, terrestrial snakes are constantly in total contact with a surface substrate which heats and cools much more rapidly than the more temperate subterranean biological province. And no amount of physical reorganization could shield snakes—which like all reptiles lack an active temperature-regulating mechanism—from having to closely reflect the thermal level of their surroundings . . . and to die if that temperature varied more than forty degrees Fahrenheit in either direction.

eyes once more gradually cleared into transparent lens caps, their retinal cells began to regenerate.[8] Physical reshaping has its limits, though, and—genetically adaptable as snakes had proven themselves to be—they were still unable to fully re-evolve their old lizard eyes.

Part of the problem was the rigid lens cap they had developed underground to keep particles out of their eyes. It was there to stay. What this meant was that without the pliant, focal-length-altering optical lenses that lizards share with birds and mammals, snakes can focus an image only by the relatively crude tactic of moving the entire, rigid lens further from or closer to the retina—which has itself been unable to regenerate the high-resolution central focal zone enjoyed by even the earliest reptiles. The result is that snakes seem to have a sort of peripheral vision generalized across their entire field of view: sight that's quick to pick up movement but lacks sharp definition of detail.[9] (In contrast, the old contractile iris of the lizards **was** able to re-form, and even develop entirely new morphology: in advanced genera such as the vipers a long, slit-like pupil allows the widest possible nocturnal aperture, while still narrowing enough for daylight vision.)[10]

Among the first primitive snakes to emerge from highly restricted underground environments, moving further than a few feet at a time presented equally complex problems. But to expand their range into the newly available biological territory of the surface—much less grow large enough to exploit the wealth of warm-blooded prey now living there—serpents had to be able to get around . . . preferably with speed and agility. No sizable terrestrial creature had ever managed this without legs and feet but, as serpents have done throughout their history, snakes once more developed their own unique solution.

Without fore- and hind-limbs, serpents were no longer restricted to a short, mechanically effective distance between pelvis and shoulders, and, over time, snakes were able to turn this freedom to their advantage. But first they had to evolve skeletal modifications far more elaborate than merely folding their limbs within their skins.[11] The most

---

[8]Although, unlike those of the diurnal ancestral monitors, in an elongate, rod-like configuration better adapted to night vision.

[9]Because snakes, as limbless animals, are unable to groom themselves, shield their eyes from twigs or clean them with a paw, the protection of that eye-armoring lens cap may be worth the loss of visual acuity brought about by its rigidity.

[10]North of the Rio Grande, all venomous snakes except the coral snake, *Micrurus fulvius*, are pitvipers with vertically positioned, slit-like pupils. In other areas, in species such as the arboreal, sight-hunting African twig snakes and the Asian whip-snakes, the pupilar slits grew horizontally.

[11]Some of the earliest to evolve of presently living snakes are the giant boids, pythons and boas, which are characterized by both vestigial internal rear legs and tiny male-to-female claspers—the toe-tip remnants of long-vanished hind feet—that protrude from their flanks.

important was to create an extremely supple spinal column, which could be accomplished only by proportionately further miniaturizing the vertebrae. This made room for many more vertebral ball-and-socket joints, which—among some snake species—ultimately produced a spine sufficiently flexible to literally tie itself into a knot.[12] Ultimately, that suppleness allowed snakes to move so well that they developed two entirely new methods of terrestrial locomotion.

One of these is the gait serpents use most of the time. Called lateral undulation, it is the mysterious, biblical "way of the serpent upon the rock" that allows snakes, without a visible means of propulsion, to slide almost magically across uneven terrain. For centuries, this sur-real-seeming slither mystified—and often threatened—mankind, although it's actually no more than a simple, efficient biomechanical process that seems effortless only because it's so different from the way mammals and birds stride or scurry around on legs and feet. Again, as does so much in ophidian biology, this gait builds on the mechanics of the ancestral lacertilians. In this case, the monitors' side-to-side, head- and body-swinging walk (in which the head and body bend to the right as the right foreleg moves back and the right hind leg simultaneously moves forward) is reflected in serpents' sinuous alternate flexing of its right- and left-side flank muscles. This draws big, S-shaped loops of its trunk forward and outward on either side of the snake's line of travel. Pressing rearward against protruding objects and surface irregularities, these loops move gracefully rearward along the snake's body, imperceptibly levering the animal ahead. In extremely agile genera like those of whipsnakes and old-world mambas, these alternating right-side left-side leveraging loops are thrown to the side and then slid rearward so rapidly—and so smoothly—that these swift snakes seem almost to fly along an inch above the surface.

When traction is poor, the lateral loops of all snakes become proportionately larger as the serpent extends more and more of its belly-length into the sideways search for something to press backward against. Extreme cases, on loose sand, call for "sidewinding." Here, the only way to move in any direction is by extending the foremost body loop (which includes the neck) well to the side and digging it in to scoop up a little ridge of sand to pull inward against. Anchored by this granular berm wedged up by its neck, a series of posterior body loops then reach out to scoop up their own tiny ridges of sand to pull themselves toward; as muscular contractions sweep down the sidewinder's trunk its body is drawn sideways across these notched

---

[12]The blind, burrowing *Typhlopidae* have 180 vertebrae, while the more advanced colubrids have as many as 435. (Mammals have 33.)

depressions—which, after it has passed, remain as the sidewinder's distinctive, scalloped desert track. (Worldwide, many other sand-dwelling serpent species use this form of locomotion, though all snakes employ an approximation of it by throwing out radically enlarged lateral coils when fleeing a pursuer or trying to negotiate slippery surfaces.)

The other of the two primary forms of ophidian locomotion is more subtle. Called rectilinear, or concertina, movement, it involves snakes' thin, flexible ribs, each pair of which is linked to one of the mid-trunk spinal vertebrae. The relatively loose architecture of serpents' bodies means that these ribs—which are controlled by more finely articulated muscles than those which initiate the larger movements of lateral undulation—are to some degree free to move fore and aft beneath the skin.

This barely perceptible "rib-walking"—one of the more fascinating attributes of ophidian morphology—is the slowest but most energy-efficient ophidian gait. Attached to the ends of each pair of ribs, a single, belly-wide ventral scale angles rearward like a shingle. When pressed down and back, its rearward edge digs in to give serpents' bellies a toe-hold for their trunk's lengthwise muscular ripples to push back against. Flowing back and forth along their bodies, these subtle contractions let serpents swing successive pairs of ribs forward, then press them back in minuscule increments (not unlike the movements caterpillars use to hitch their multiple pairs of legs ahead), slowly sliding themselves forward by inching ahead over successively anchored patches of ventral scales. Used on the surface primarily for straight-line travel, below ground this gait allows serpents to move through rodent tunnels too narrow for them to negotiate by extending lateral loops to press backward against.[13]

Among tree-climbing serpents, both gaits—straight-ahead concertina-creeping and backward-shoving lateral loops—may be used at the same time. As one of the sideways coils levers the snake forward against twigs and stems, other body segments often find traction by lengthwise inching along a branch. Some snake species can even dig in their belly scales firmly enough to creep straight up a rough-barked trunk. This calls for both a very muscular mid-section (the three major epaxial muscles, M. semispinalisspinalis, M. longissimus dorsi, and M. iliocostalis, are

---

[13]Rectilinear movement's minimal apparent motion can also enable snakes to approach wary food animals . . . as long as they maintain a directly head-on perspective. From this angle—a telephone pole looks small when only seen end-on—their quarry may perceive nothing but a flat disc apparently too small to be dangerous.

highly developed in most arboreal snakes),[14] as well as for great flexibility: tree-dwelling North American *Elaphe* have about 50 percent more vertebrae than most aquatic and terrestrial serpents.

Having learned to get around without the traditional vertebrate's stiff skeletal platform, then, serpents became mobile creatures with rope-like suppleness possessed by no other land animal. This gave them the unique predatory advantage: being able to strike. (Being able to reach out to suddenly snatch a food animal had long been an optimal hunting technique: very early, frogs, toads, and then a few lizards evolved projectable, jack-in-the-box tongues to snatch prey from a distance. But to catch anything larger than an insect, they still had to jump on it.)

Snakes had a better way, becoming the only contemporary reptile to develop a forebody so flexible and neuromuscularly sophisticated that it could instantly thrust the head and jaws well away from the animal's compact, inconspicuous body coil to seize prey or—mouth agape—threaten an intruder. But even with this ability to seize comparatively large prey from a distance, snakes have never been able to dismember it. During the millions of years their subterranean prototypes fed only on soft invertebrates, the chewing teeth of serpents' lizard forebears were lost forever. But when their emergent descendants began to tackle chunkier prey, swallowing more sizable animals became a problem. And by that time serpents needed the big blocks of caloric energy they got from larger prey because ingesting them would then let them spend most of their time hiding and digesting—thus minimizing their exposure to the dangerous world of surface-living predators.[15]

This meant taking bigger vertebrate prey. Yet fish and frogs (as well as birds and small mammals) were frequently larger in diameter than the snakes themselves, and devouring them called for a radical feeding physiology.

Snakes simply had to expand. And now without the limits of either a limb-supporting thoracic cage or a rib-confining sternum, there was no structural reason that snakes could not do so, eventually developing the capacity to flex their ribs so far outward that serpents were able to balloon themselves into shapes unattainable by

---

[14]A corollary characteristic developed by most arboreal serpents is bodies light and wiry enough to allow them to span branch-to-branch gaps at least half as great as their total length; a majority of terrestrial and aquatic serpents, in contrast, collapse across horizontal distances no more than a fifth their body length.

[15]Again, the seeds of this strategy lay with the ancestral varanids. Monitors are typically great body-distenders, swelling their bellies with big chunks of prey so as to—especially in the case of group-living species like *V. komodoensis*—keep it away from rivals.

any other vertebrate. Snakes' rib cages couldn't unfold this much without a very stretchy covering, but here, too, an endowment of singularly elastic skin remained from serpents' voracious monitor ancestors. Like other *Squamata*, in a process called ecdysis snakes shed their skins as they grow (young snakes shed more frequently, but fully grown individuals still shed).[16]

The result of both morphological changes was a singular biological success. Soon, these swiftly developing, newly expandable serpents enjoyed the ability to slip the largest possible bodies through narrow crevices in pursuit of lizards and rodents; then, having nosed its way down a burrow to seize a sleeping rat, such a snake could distend like a stretchy sock to draw itself over its plump prey and—safe from conventionally shaped carnivores—coil quietly to digest its meal in a space no larger than that which had sheltered its prey.

Before engulfing big creatures, though, serpents had to fit them through their narrow skulls and jaws. But their attenuated heads—an essential part of their ancestors' tight-places survival strategy—made this almost impossible. The only way to get a small skull over a large carcass is for the skull to come apart, at least temporarily, and once again, snakes' evolutionary answer lay in the biology of their monitor forebears. The old cephalic expansion joints that had let ancient varanids partially dislocate their jaws to gulp down big chunks of meat gradually evolved, among serpents, into more elaborate sutures. Connected by elastic, cartilaginous hinges, these joints were eventually able to separate far more than those of the monitors ever had. Stretchy ligament bands allowed snakes' lower skulls to disjoint each lateral half of their long lower mandibles, independently pivoting each side forward on its own linkage of loosely connected quadrate bones joined by a flexible band of cartilage at the chin. Ultimately,

---

[16]Shedding is also a factor in replenishing the reptilian skin's moisture-impervious lipid barrier and is a mechanism of pheromone dispersal. Sheds occur at variable times in the ophidian life cycle, including a few days after birth or hatching, after emergence from dormancy, prior to parturition, and following an injury or seasonal climatic change. For a few days before shedding, a bluish cast dulls a snake's pattern and clouds its eyes. Then, when the animal's newly formed underskin is sufficiently developed, its old epidermis is nudged free, separating first from the lips. As the snake crawls forward, pushing against irregularities in its surroundings, its thin outer skin is turned inside out as the serpent slips forward out of its old vestment. This leaves an opaque, keratinous stocking—which includes the transparent eyecaps, or brille—imprinted with the species' typical scale pattern.

The highly elastic ophidian epidermis also explains the giant rattlesnake skins proudly displayed on so many honky-tonk walls. When the rattler's very stretchable between-scale skin is pulled out to its absolute maximum (indicated by scales separated by a scale-width or more of taughtly drawn, paper-thin skin), these hides can measure over a third longer and wider than the actual snake. Some of the biggest skins, however, turn out to be Burmese or reticulated python hides, bleached and then artfully re-patterned with rattlesnakes' dorsal diamonds.

aided by recurved teeth able to slip forward in ratchet-like steps over inward-bound prey, serpents' alternately advancing right- and left-half jaw segments could draw a snake's head over a rat or rabbit several times thicker than the unhinged skull itself.

Ingesting comparatively large masses of flesh and bone impacted other aspects of snakes' metabolism as well. This included their breathing, for the buccal passage of a big carcass can take over an hour, during which every layer of soft tissue in a snake's throat is compressed to the utmost. That includes its airway, and since even reptiles have trouble holding their breath this long, a non-collapsible respiratory passage became mandatory; the trachea of contemporary snakes is stiffened by closely spaced rows of cartilaginous rings that nevertheless retain sufficient articulation to preserve the neck's delicate flexibility.[17]

But pressing the swallowing mechanism to such biological lengths meant that getting food into their stomachs was a slow process for snakes—a procedure which left them immobile and helpless for long periods, as well as vulnerable to injury inflicted by mammals capable of counterattack during the time it took to get them down. For this reason, being able to immobilize a biting, struggling victim before starting the slow process of swallowing it whole became a major biological incentive to small ophidian carnivores.

Immobilizing a prey animal, however, meant either paralyzing it or killing it outright—new predatory ground for snakes, who had formerly swallowed most large prey alive, and this meant more innovation. Among the earliest methods snakes evolved to subdue food animals was suffocation. Some species evolved powerful constrictive coordination, developing the same basic musculature that let arboreal species hang tightly onto tree branches in order to rapidly cinch lengths of their ropy bodies around food animals. Then, each time its captive exhaled the snake's coils could be drawn tighter until, unable to expand its lungs at all, its victim suffocated. For larger prey this process could still require several minutes, though—during which time the snake's coils were directly exposed to its prey's teeth and claws.

But by approximately the middle Miocene, according to the fossil record, other serpents had begun to develop a faster way of killing. Forced into shallow wounds by the teeth, toxic saliva had already proven effective among some species in minimizing the struggles of smaller prey. Longer, heavily grooved upper teeth that let this rudi-

---

[17]Higher vertebrates have cartilage-ringed tracheae, but because snakes typically swallow disproportionately large, solid food items, the difficulty of keeping their airway open is greater.

This requires its airway, or trachea, to be stiffened (more than that of other creatures) with closely spaced rows of cartilaginous rings that still retain enough articulation to preserve the serpent neck's delicate flexibility.

mentary venom penetrate deeper were the next development.[18] But more elaborate systems were soon to follow.

The first family to develop hollow hypodermic fangs from those grooved teeth was the *Elapidae*. But, despite having very powerful and intricate neurotoxic venom produced by separate venom glands, elapids, for the most part, still use the bite-and-squeeze venom delivery of more primitive groove-toothed serpents.

Members of the viper family went further, evolving not only tubular anterior teeth, but long, articulated ones (even the biggest cobras have comparatively minuscule fangs because as rigid, non-folding pegs they have to fit within the animal's mouth when it is closed). Viper fangs, in contrast, fold back like the blades of a pocketknife into bony slots in the roof of the snake's mouth when its jaws are closed. When the viper is ready to strike they can be erected, swinging forward on hinged maxillary bones that rotate individually within sockets in the upper jaw. Therefore, viper fangs can be quite long: those of the largest tropical bushmasters are capable of delivering venom over an inch below the surface.

Exposed by jaws that can gape open a full 180 degrees, forming a nearly flat oral wall, the angle of attack of viper fangs can be adjusted in mid-strike, giving their owners the choice of stabbing rather than biting large animals. (This option is solely a defensive one, though, since—except for the occasional misjudgment of juveniles new to hunting—no creature too big to be swallowed whole is ever attacked.)

As bite-and-squeeze envenomaters, even the powerfully venomed elapids expose themselves to counterattack by (even briefly) holding onto their quarry; early viperids evolved a more sophisticated system of venom transfer. Delivered by a flashing strike and instantly forced into prey by big *compressor glandulae* muscles that surround the toxin storage glands and swell the rear of vipers' heads into their distinctive triangular shape, viperids' venom is injected so quickly that prey animals have no time to retaliate.[19] Nor do they usually any inclination, due to the immediate, intense pain these toxins almost always cause.

Most sophisticated of all is the vipers' final delivery mechanism—hypodermic fangs not only articulated but, in their erect position,

---

[18]Many species pursued the strategy no further: today the saliva of the Southwest's rear-fanged lyre, cat-eyed, night, and black-striped snakes constitutes a comparatively mild venom lethal only to the small creatures on which they feed.

[19]The pitviper strike has been measured at a speed of up to 11 feet per second. These snakes must be able to deliver their bite so rapidly because their small mammal prey typically reacts quickly enough to dodge anything slower. (Elapids, in contrast—which feed largely on less agile reptilian prey—make do with strikes only about half as fast. This lack of striking speed makes even deadly-venomed cobras fairly sure prey for quick, aggressive predators like the mongoose. But a mongoose confronted with a big, fast-striking rattlesnake aided by its heat-sensors would be envenomated before it managed its first feint.)

hydraulically pressurized to jet dollops of venom through a victim's skin and muscle during the fraction of a second the snake's mouth is pressed against it. This far quicker and safer (for the snake) way of injecting venom into agile, warm-blooded prey was paralleled by the development of an equally sophisticated venom. Generated almost entirely from a pair of parotid, salivary-derived glands— hyper-developed into complex lumens capable of generating 12 to 31 separate toxic proteins—vipers eventually evolved a complex blend of tissue-disintegrating proteases, each directed toward a specific part of a prey animal's circulatory and/or nervous system.

At roughly the same time, the vipers' already refined sensory skills were further developed by a new ophidian subfamily, the *Crotalinae*, or pitvipers. These highly evolved reptiles' new strike-guidance system centered on a pair of small depressions—the pits for which they are named—located on either side of the head between eye and nostril. The inner surface of these pits is lined with a thin membrane, sensitive to heat radiation and dotted with neural receptors. Collectively, these nerves signal the pitviper's brain along a sensory pathway so closely integrated with the optic tectum that impulses both from the eyes and from the sensory pits join to generate a single, thermally enhanced optical image . . . or an optically enhanced thermal image.

This neurological combination compensates so well for the loss of sight that from the heat of a prey animal's small body a pitviper's overlapping, right-left stereoscopic infrared scan so effectively delineates its image that even in total darkness the snake can locate and lethally strike its prey: rattlesnakes deprived of vision with eyecaps suffer almost no loss of predatory efficiency. (Moreover, pitvipers' thermal pits are sensitive enough for them to distinguish newly slain prey from quiescent live animals—only living creatures are ever struck[20]—while these organs also seem to be used by both rattlesnakes and moccasins in seeking the warmer recesses of hillside caves for brumation, or winter dormancy.)[21]

---

[20]All living animals, including "cold-blooded" ectotherms, generate at least some radiant heat energy, but pitvipers' targets are most often warm-bodied endotherms.

[21]The distance at which these pits are effective sensors has not been formally measured, but they are probably sensitive at a distance of at least 12 feet. Coasting down a Caldwell County incline on a bicycle, I drew an instantaneous angry whir and raised-forecoil defensive posture from a 4-foot-long *C. atrox* as I passed its hiding place in roadside Johnson grass—a reflexive response that was repeated on subsequent passes. My narrow-tired bike was nearly vibrationless on the smooth pavement and these encounters took place well after dark, with a slight breeze blowing my scent away from the rattler's visually shielded niche, so it almost certainly detected only the large block of my body heat suddenly passing through its thermal perceptual field. Another rattlesnake in my experience, an adult *C. molossus*, could perceive through the plateglass front of its cage the tiny glow of heat from a lighted cigarette held up to a foot away . . . the back and forth movements of which it would accurately track with its snout.

But using their stereoscopic infrared scan to locate and accurately strike living prey involves only the initial phase of the pitviper's hunting strategy. Although a large amount of its toxins can kill in seconds any animal it is able to swallow, a pitviper's effectiveness as a small carnivore operating well beyond the conventional limits of its modest size depends largely on its venom not acting too quickly. This is because in order to take full advantage of viperid toxin's digestive function, the venom's more lethal peptide enzymes must not shut down its victim's circulatory system until the venom's tissue-dissolving components have had time to disperse throughout the creature's body. There, even before it dies, these digestive proteases have so rapidly disintegrated a prey animal's muscles and organs that what the viper swallows a few minutes later is an already partially predigested carcass—a condition which substantially reduces the time the snake must spend in a vulnerable state of post-meal lethargy.

Ultimately, both the ancestral viper's long, erectile fangs and the later-to-evolve heat-sensing organs of the *Crotalinae* brought this group of snakes such predatory success that they came to enjoy the luxury of thick-girthed trunks much less athletic than those of non-venomous serpents that still had to pursue, capture, and wrestle food animals into submission.[22] Yet, the corpulent bodies that pitvipers' sedentary, ambush-style predation permitted may, for a time, have prevented them from moving into every habitat they might otherwise have been able to occupy.

One such potential environment was the North American prairie. In the Pliocene, Nearctic vipers probably spent most of their time near aquatic environments or within stands of cover for, it is thought, herds of ungulates would have made the continent's vast grasslands a dangerous place for inconspicuous, slow-moving, non-burrowing serpents. Yet the plains' rich supply of rodents and ground-nesting birds would surely have presented a major attraction to any ophidian predator that could solve the problem of foraging without fear across open country. The cottonmouth, the only aquatic pitviper living north of Mexico, could rely to some extent on its ability to gape open-mouthed in threat toward other animals. But backing up its "Don't tread on me" with an excruciating bite was of limited value as long as the snake died delivering it to the first bison

---

[22]In addition, like other advanced ophidian genera, vipers are able to enhance their offspring's chances for survival in cool or extremely dry climates—environments which are dangerous to desiccation-prone reptilian eggs—by retaining the developing young within the more stable milieu of the female's body. Among such species the embryo is encased in a thin, water- and salt-permeable membrane that (in a metabolic antecedent to the placental nutrition of fetal mammals) may allow the unborn young to draw some sustenance from it's mother's blood diffusing through the walls of the oviduct pressed against it.

that thundered over. What these ancestral vipers may have needed was a way to warn the grazing herds to avoid them in the first place.

The problem seems to have been solved when several genera of viperids amplified the fear-threat response of the many other serpents that twitch their tails in agitation by developing on their caudal tips a loose-fitting column of hollow scales. Swollen like hard-shelled kernels of puffed rice, these scale segments, when shaken by the vipers' high-speed tail-twitch, created the earliest-known aposematic buzz. Used first among *Sistrurus* and later among *Crotalus*-genus rattlesnakes, that distinctive reverberating whir taught predators as well as grazing mammals to stay clear. Its success may be inferred from the fact that today the western plains are the home to more than a dozen rattlesnakes species, while no rattleless pitviper is common there.

Nevertheless, in the last hundred years the warning signal that allowed rattlesnakes to colonize the prairie has been their downfall, for the human attention it attracts now almost always means the death of the snake. For much the same reason, after millennia of biological success snakes are now in worldwide decline as man's domination of the planet has driven species after herpetological species to the brink of extinction. The formerly profuse reptile fauna of the southeastern United States has been decimated by commercial and residential development, lumbering, chemical effluent, the invasion of South American fire ants, and commercial collecting for the pet trade.

Yet, among the few reptiles that survive even in the heart of the urban world are a number of small serpents. Brown, earth, and ringneck snakes can still be found in parks and vacant lots, are usually not harmed by limited, gentle handling, and if not allowed to become overheated may be observed for a few days and then released undamaged by the experience. In the meantime, where most other vertebrate wildlife can only be observed from a distance, these little snakes can serve as touchable points of reference: connecting threads leading back to that vast, biological world from which most of us have lost the sense of our own vital continuity.

SNAKE VENOM POISONING

With their bright, unblinking eyes that seem to reflect a preternatural serenity, their apparent ability to rejuvenate themselves by casting off their aged skins, and their uncanny agility—"the way of the serpent upon the rock"—snakes are distinctly different from other animals. For millennia, men have seen in these animals both intimations of transcendence (the serpent that tempted Eve was part of a long historical line of supernatural snakes) and the manifestation of supernatural power.

Throughout the world, early cultures placed great emphasis on both projected elements of serpents' nature. In the Toltec-Aztec-Maya civilizations of Middle America an early rattlesnake god—ultimately evolved into the feathered serpent Quetzalcoatl—became the deity whose potency sanctified the priesthood's control over the secular population. The same seemingly transcendent ability to kill with a pinprick inspired the Egyptian priesthood, from the time of earliest dynasties, to deify *Naja haje*, the Egyptian cobra, as the serpent-god Uraeus. Over the centuries Uraeus gradually rose among the celestial pantheon to a position second only to that of Ra, the sun king; later, *Naja haje* became the symbol of imperial authority, and the bejeweled face of a cobra glared from the brow of every royal headdress—whose flared neckpiece was itself designed to emulate the snake's spreading hood.

Not much was known about the snakes themselves; however, priests, postulating that mortal cobras derived their lethal virulence from Uraeus himself, sometimes cut open the limbs of bitten individuals to release the supernatural vapors assumed to have been implanted there.[1] Because no other explanation for the destructive

---

[1]In pre-columbian North America, however, the affinity of snake venom for living protoplasm was widely recognized among native peoples, and stood as the rationale behind the most common American Indian antidote for snakebite, which was to slice through the fang marks and press the freshly opened body of a bird against the wound in the hope that some of the still un-bonded serum within might be drawn up into the unsaturated avian tissues. Although venom could not actually be drawn out in this way, the approach was rational enough for variations to be recommended by turn-of-the century medical officers looking for a better means of extraction than the

power of venomous snakebite existed, this belief persisted, largely unchallenged, until renegade physician Francesco Redi opposed the medical doctrines of seventeenth-century Florence (where it was believed that the virulent symptoms of envenomation were caused by the rage of the serpent, somehow passed, like the madness of a rabid dog, into its victim by means of its saliva). Redi maintained, instead, that the "direful effects" of snakebite were the result of a lethal poison held in the snake's "great glands," but apparently no one paid much attention.

Even with the much later advent of chemical analysis there was still little to support his point of view, however. Late-nineteenth-century chemists were unanimous in finding that vipers' big buccal glands held no identifiable poison—at least not any substance, like the toxic alkaloids or burning acids, that they could recognize as a poison. Quite the opposite: snake venom seemed to be an apparently commonplace protein, so nearly indistinguishable from egg white in structure that in 1886 R. Norris Wolfenden, speaking for the Commission on Indian and Australian Snake Poisoning, reported: "It is quite impossible to draw any deductions as to the nature of the poison. It is merely a mixture of albuminous principles."

The first real clue to how this particular assemblage of reptilian body fluids could bring about the immediate physical deterioration of other animals came six years later, with French physician John de Lacerda's conceptualization of the tissue-disintegrating biological catalysts he termed *enzymes*. And indeed, much like the enzymes of stomach acid, harmless to the gut that contains them yet able to break down devoured flesh into its constituent amino acids, most components of North American pitviper venom have evolved to enzymatically disintegrate the internal tissues of the snake's prey. For contemporary victims of pitviper poisoning this is an important concept, since it emphasizes the progressive tissue-death aspect of venom poisoning over the commonly held belief that envenomation typically poses an immediately fatal threat.

W. C. Fields liked to tell people he always kept a bottle of whiskey handy in case he saw a snake—which he also kept handy. Few people still rely on Fields' remedy, but almost no one is aware that following

---

dangerous and ineffective cut-and-suck regimen. But, except for including thin sheets of latex to place between mouth and wound in some army snakebite kits, no improvement on the old method was developed until the 1920s, when Dudley Jackson (1929) slightly refined the old extraction approach by placing a series of heat-transfer suction cups over incisions both across the fang marks and around the perimeter of the expanding mound of edema that surrounds most serious pitviper envenomations. Although probably the best of the incision therapies, Jackson's approach was still unable to prevent the disabling tissue necrosis associated with severe crotalid envenomation and was entirely useless against the peptide-based venom of the coral snake.

most of the widely recommended "in the field" first-aid procedures is nearly as dangerous. For example, cutting open a snakebite wound in the field is probably worse than doing nothing at all because attempts to suck or syringe out venom are inevitably futile and the preliminary incision, even if it is not large, can cause significant harm.

And there may be no need to do anything: the chances are good, in fact, that the snake may not be venomous. The great majority of the several thousand snakebites that occur annually in the United States involve non-venomous serpents and require nothing more than reassurance and a tetanus shot.[2] Then, because venomous snakes have control over whether or not they inject their toxins during a bite, envenomation doesn't always occur; punctures by pitvipers are entirely free of toxins about 15 percent of the time, and superficial envenomation is much more common than severe poisoning. Probably less than half of coral snake bites result in severe poisoning, and with either pitviper or elapids like the coral, unless heavy poisoning has been established it is irresponsible to destroy irreplaceable nerve and muscle tissue by following invasive first-aid procedures.

Many properties of snake venom, moreover, weigh heavily against a person cutting into the fang marks left by a bite. One of these is the tendency of reptilian toxins to suppress the body's bactericidal and immune responses, particularly the action of its white blood cells, and without the leukocytes' prophylactic intervention an exceptionally receptive environment awaits the host of pathogens introduced by every deep field incision. In addition, rapid local dispersal of infective agents is ensured by the seepage of contaminated plasma and lymphatic fluid that, following envenomation, is suffused through tissues made more permeable by the fiber-dissolving effect of hyaluronidase.

An even more pressing reason to avoid incision in the field is that the anticoagulant effect of pitviper venom on plasma fibrinogen so impairs the blood's ability to clot that opening an envenomated limb is likely to produce much more profuse bleeding than one would expect. It is always dangerous to risk bleeding in people whose level of fibrinogen is low, and following severe envenomation taking a chance on setting off heavy bleeding is particularly chancy because when people die of snakebite (which happens in less than 1 percent of poisonings inflicted by native species), loss of circulating blood volume is what kills them.

Therefore, maintaining sufficient circulating blood volume is crucial in the initial management of critical snakebite poisoning, and cutting open a limb which may bleed profusely is not the way to

---

[2]Most envenomations occur in the southwestern states, and less than a dozen a year are fatal.

maintain blood volume. Avoiding dehydration by having the victim drink as much as he is comfortable with is a good idea, however.[3]

Fortunately, in-the-bush surgery is usually out of the question anyway, because getting bitten by a venomous snake is such a terrifying experience that then being able to execute this classically prescribed procedure is impossible for most people. (It is also almost unbearable to be cut open after a pitviper bite because the digestive dissolution of blood within the subcutaneous tissue releases bradykinin from its disintegrating plasma and serotonin from its serum platelets, and both substances produce burning pain—which makes the skin so sensitive that the prospect of crude pocketknife incisions becomes nearly unthinkable.)

---

[3]After severe envenomation, some internal bleeding always takes place. Except in the most severe poisonings, or in the case of a small child, it ordinarily takes hours to lose a mortally significant quantity of blood internally because leakage through enzyme-perforated arterioles and venules normally only comparatively gradually allows the vascular fluids to pool in the interstitial spaces of an envenomated limb. (Eventually, though, a seemingly minimal amount of such swelling—Findlay E. Russell, dean of U.S. snake venom toxicology, estimated as little as a 2-centimeter increase in the circumference of a thigh—could account for the loss into the tissue spaces of nearly a third of the body's circulating blood volume, dropping vascular pressure enough to put a patient into shock.)

Ironically, the swelling of edema seldom threatens the limb itself. While huge serosanguinous blisters may bulge up around pitviper bites, the distension is usually soft and limited to the epidermal and outer cutaneous layers. As this fact has become widely known, the formerly common practice of surgically opening such swollen limbs—a technique long assumed to be widely necessary to relieve hydraulic pressure built up by swelling which might cause necrosis from restricted circulation—is now employed much less often, even in the most severe envenomations. (In treating some 200 venomous snakebites, Ken Mattox and his team at Houston's Ben Taub Hospital have used fasciotomy to relieve hydraulic tourniqueting less that a half-dozen times, while Russell, in treating more ophidian envenomations than anyone in North America, has never had to perform a fasciotomy due to excessive intra-compartmental pressure.)

Finally, sophisticated surgical techniques for dealing with another, particularly pernicious type of deep pitviper envenomation have been developed by Dr. Thomas G. Glass, professor of surgery at the University of Texas Medical School in San Antonio. Although most pitviper toxins reach only subcutaneous levels, occasionally a large rattlesnake accomplishes a much deeper penetration, sinking its fangs through skin, subcutaneous fatty layers, and the outer muscle fascia to deposit an infusion of venom within the muscle belly. While a rattler's toxins are much more destructive here, even a large amount of venom this far below the surface may produce few external symptoms because such areas are poorly supplied with nerve endings. (In subcutaneous tissues great pain, swelling, and discoloration accompany venom poisoning, but with deeper envenomations the toxins' proteolytic enzymes may be temporarily encapsulated within the underlying layers of muscle, and give few symptomatic indications of how severe the bite actually is. The trick, of course, is to be able to tell a real subfascial poisoning of this sort from the far more common, largely symptomless superficial snakebite in which little or no envenomation has occurred, and being able to do it in a hurry. If such a bite is accurately diagnosed, however, a considerable amount of the venom infusion can sometimes be removed by deep incision and debridement, although only in this unusual sort of poisoning is a major surgical campaign widely advised by medical authorities—and then only if it is executed by one of the handful of those experienced in the delicate excision of this sort of deep-lying lacunae.

Therefore it is infinitely better to avoid wrestling with the agony of such archaic procedures and to instead apply one's efforts to getting proper medical management. In the field, all one need remember is to immobilize an envenomated extremity, remove rings or shoes before swelling makes that difficult, then wrap the limb firmly but not tightly in a splinted elastic bandage. The important part is getting the victim to a good hospital.

All the old field-guide therapies—binding the limb with thin, circulation-cutting cords, packing it in ice, or cutting open the punctures—are dangerous procedures, treatments that invariably go awry because they are founded on a basic misunderstanding of the complex process that begins when a venomous snake bites a human being. The most common misconception is that a strike by a pitviper can be expected to result in the injection of a lethal fluid which then oozes through the veins toward the heart. If this were the case one should probably do anything possible to arrest the venom's progress, but it isn't what happens at all.

Instead, from the moment it enters the body venom is almost instantly incorporated into the tissues surrounding its entry punctures. Here, after only a few seconds, it is no more removable than ink dripped on a wet sponge. That is why cut-and-suck, or cut-and-pull with a syringe, or any other snakebite-kit extraction technique, is not a viable therapy for serious envenomation. More than 60 years ago, in experiments with cats and rabbits, F. M. Allen (1939) demonstrated that no benefit resulted even when, within five minutes, a large section of surrounding tissue was entirely removed from the site of an injection of either a western diamondbacked rattlesnake or eastern cottonmouth venom. During even this brief time between injection and tissue removal, Allen's laboratory animals had so thoroughly absorbed the venom's most lethal peptide components that every victim that had received a large enough dose to kill a surgically untreated control, also died. This led Allen to conclude that large infusions of crotalid venom spread so quickly throughout a large mass of local tissue that even when an extensive excision immediately follows, the seemingly normal tissue outside the excised area still contains enough venom to cause the animal's death.

These experiments illustrate the futility of trying to remove venom from a snakebite victim, but they also demonstrate that in most cases, after its initial rapid bonding to local tissue, most of the components of pitviper toxin are no longer free to circulate. Thus, beyond the general vicinity of the bite they tend to disperse rather slowly throughout the rest of the body. This means that, to a considerable extent, temporarily localizing these toxins can be accomplished with the mild pressure of an elastic bandage.

Although at great odds with most prevailing popular concepts of snakebite poisoning, this concept is consistent with the pattern of dispersal required by the predatory role that venom plays in a pitviper's life. For example, a majority of the 12 to 30 separate toxic peptides and enzymes these reptiles generate are not designed to kill large animals. Instead, their primary function is to pre-digest small but chunky vertebrate prey so that it is easier for a small-throated viper to swallow.

To accomplish this, the toxins do not have to move very far from the general region of a bite, so *crotalid* venom disperses only gradually throughout the body of a large victim such as a human being. But it methodically digests tissues as it goes. And, like all digestion, the process is complicated, since most of the venom's diverse proteases and kinases have a separate metabolic function, often a different target organ, and frequently a different way of getting there.[4] These toxins include hyaluronidase, collagenase, thrombin-like enzymes, L-amino oxidase (which gives venom its amber tint), phosphomonoesterase, phosphodiesterase, two kinds of kinases (both of which are similar to pancreatic secretions and, like pancreatic secretions, prepare soft tissue for more extensive breakdown by analogous solutions in the reptile's stomach), nucleotidase, at least one phospholipase, arginine ester hydrolase, and various proteolytic enzymes.[5]

Within the bodies of human beings bitten by pitvipers these enzymes gradually, and with great pain to the victim, disintegrate living tissues. Hyaluronidase, for example, breaks down connective fibers in the muscle matrix, allowing various proteases and trypsin-like enzymes to penetrate the limbs directly. Meanwhile, in concert with several endothelial cell-specific thrombin-like enzymes, other peptides simultaneously perforate the vascular capillary walls, allowing the seepage of plasma thinned by the simultaneous assault of another set of venom enzymes: phospholipase A

---

[4]Many of these venom enzymes, moreover, operate most powerfully in complementary combinations.

[5]In poisoning by most pitvipers (although envenomations by western—Type A venom—populations of the Mojave rattlesnake, *Crotalus scutulatus*, may entail a large complement of neurotoxically-active peptides) the venom's ultimate target is not the heart but the lungs. Among the snakebite's few fatalities, pulmonary embolism is a nearly universal finding postmortem, but congestive pooling of blood in the lungs seldom has time to accumulate enough fluid to interfere with respiration before fatal shock from loss of circulating blood volume has occurred.

combines with lipids in the blood to inhibit their coagulative function, toxic fibrinolytic and thrombin-like enzymes disintegrate the hematic fibrinogen also required for clotting, and a pair of related hemolysins, specifically keyed to the destruction of red blood cells, attack the erythrocytes directly.[6]

Although nothing short of antivenin (which can be administered only in a hospital) is able to stop this process, besides wrapping the limb in an elastic bandage, mildly cooling the limb may offer a slight numbing of the pain. An icepack on the forehead can also mitigate the intense nausea often associated with venom poisoning, and because toxin-induced intestinal spasms have sometimes been violent enough to provoke hemorrhage of the trachea, any reduction in their severity is of importance. (Severely chilling a bitten limb, however, is deadly to it. While the cell-disintegrating action of enzymes is to some degree slowed by extreme cold, it would take freezing a limb to achieve sufficient chilling to deactivate its infused venom enzymes.)[7]

By taking the conservative approach of simply wrapping the bitten limb or digit in an elastic bandage, splinting it to keep it immobile, then rewrapping the entire area, one allows essential oxygen exchange via the bloodstream, while the broad pressure of an elastic bandage—which moderately compresses the lymph vessels—slows the mostly muscular contraction-pumped flow of venom-saturated lymphatic

---

[6]The relative proportion of these elements in the venom mix varies considerably. Determined by the varying output cycles of each of more than a dozen secretory cells that release their separate toxins into a viper's paired storage bladders, or lumens, snake venom's composition varies from day to day. This makes it one of the most complex of biological substances and to some extent accounts for the disparity in potency observed between similarly sized snakes of the same species taken from the wild at the same time. (Since, at any given time, different venom ingredients are present in variable concentrations, their relative effect on each of a victim's organs may also be somewhat different.)

Outside the lumen, venom will even digest itself, for catalytic agents pumped into the serum from secondary secretory glands located downstream from the primary storage bladder metabolically break down venom's peptide components—which are themselves easily digested proteins.

[7]The worst of the cold-treatment therapies was ligature-cryotherapy. This regimen received popular attention during the 1950s as a way to avoid the obvious perils of incision and suction, but it instead combined two extremely destructive procedures: putting tourniquets around a limb or extremity, then radically chilling the constricted part by immersing it in ice, sometimes for hours. As might be expected, tissue deprived of the oxygen exchange and waste dispersal of normal blood flow and subjected to the cell membrane-cracking effect of lengthy chilling—while simultaneously being exposed to a concentrated dose of corrosive venom enzymes—died so frequently that amputations following ligature-cryotherapy became almost routine.

Although this procedure is no longer followed in medical circles, a legacy of its erroneous concepts remains, and some literature still in print, as well as recent public-service television commercials, still refer to the option of packing envenomated limbs in ice.

fluid.[8] This singularly safe and effective field treatment dovetails with the medical consensus that now prevails concerning subsequent hospital management of severe reptile envenomation—an approach that relies heavily on the intravenous administration of antivenin, sometimes combined with antihistamines or epinephrine to stifle allergic reaction.

Although antivenin is still viewed with suspicion by both doctors and laymen—largely as a result of the poor reputation of earlier, less

---

[8]The most numerous components of pitviper toxin, its enzymatic venom fractions, are dispersed primarily through the lymph system. In contrast, the mostly neurotoxically targeted peptide components of *elapid* venoms, including those of all three North American coral snakes, disperse primarily through the bloodstream, where they are not subject to any mechanical constraint short of a total tourniquet. Only antivenin is effective in treating this sort of envenomation, and only in poisoning by such peptide-based venoms might employing a temporary total arterial tourniquet be appropriate because, cinched down for more than a few minutes, a tourniquet is likely to cause permanent injury to the limb, sometimes severe enough to require amputation. Applying a tourniquet is, in fact, such a dangerous procedure that binding a strap or cord around any envenomation, except perhaps that of a severe coral snake poisoning or of a toddler deeply envenomated by a big rattlesnake, is now decried by almost everyone involved in treating snakebites. (The neurotoxically active polypeptides of coral snake venom are particularly dangerous. Because they evolved to quickly paralyze the other snakes—and potential adversaries—on which many *elapids* feed, these polypeptides can effect the same paralysis in human victims of coral snakebite. Similar neurotoxically destructive proteins are also present, in smaller proportions, in nearly all snake venom, even that of genera such as the *viperids* (whose venom is principally comprised of hematoxic, or blood-targeted components). But in the peptide-based venom of new world coral snakes these enzymes seem to be particularly targeted toward the neural membranes branching from the upper spinal cord, where they block acetylcholine receptor sites in the junctions between adjoining nuchal ganglia, impairing neuromuscular transmission and, by shutting down the autonomic triggering of respiration, can sometimes cause death by suffocation.

Other components of *elapid* venom are hemolytic, or blood- and circulatory-system directed. While generally less potent than the venom's neurotoxic elements, these cardiotoxically active components can be lethal in high doses. Neither Wyeth's equine-derived coral snake antivenin (Antivenin, *Micrurus fulvius*, Drug Circular, Wyeth, 1983) nor Savage Laboratories' new CroFab *crotalid*, or pitviper, antivenin is reported to neutralize these hemolytic elements, however. At a median dose of 6.5 vials, Wyeth reports that 35 percent of patients treated with its coral snake antivenin experienced side-effects; in 50 percent of those cases, the side effects were severe, resulting in anaphylactic shock or serum sickness.

Another type of coral snake antivenin, with reportedly about the same dosage requirement, effectiveness, and problematic side effects, is manufactured by the Instituto Butantan in Sao Paulo, Brazil. Manufactured from antibodies generated by a mixture of the venom of two South American coral snake species, *M. corallinus* and *M. frontalis*, it may at some point be joined by a new, ovine-based *Micrurus* antivenin reportedly under development at St. Bartholomew's Hospital, Medical College, London, and the Liverpool School of Tropical Medicine, Liverpool, U.K. This antivenin is purported to neutralize both neurotoxic and cardiotoxic components of *Micrurus* venom—which, in preliminary trials, it reportedly did so with a fourfold reduction in dosage. Because this antivenin is derived from sheep antibodies, the negative side effects of prior sensitization to equine-based serums used in previous inoculations are likely to be largely absent. (Antivenin from the same company—CroFab™ North American pitviper antivenin—is produced at the Protherics manufacturing facility in Blaenwaun, Wales, which also produces ViperaTab®, a European viper antivenin.)

well-prepared serums[9]—administered by an experienced physician with immediate access to intensive care facilities, the newer antivenins (particularly, according to initial reports, the recently released Cro-Fab™ serum)[10] seem to be fairly safe, although they must be administered with extreme care. Medical proponents of antivenin therapy maintain that not only are the life-threatening systemic failures that may follow heavy envenomation best offset by antivenin antibodies, but that these serums offer the only significant means of mitigating the often extensive local necrosis caused by pitviper toxins.[11]

Nearly as biologically complex as the venom it is cultured to neutralize, antivenins have long been known to sometimes trigger allergic histamine shock, or anaphylaxis—a much more serious manifestation of the ordinary allergic response elicited by sensitizing agents from feathers to pollen. Therefore they should never be used outside a hospital because, like any other immunization, antivenin therapy depends on establishing a protective titer of antibodies in the entire bloodstream. This normally requires far more antigen-bearing serum than conventional immunization—and once this sizable volume of foreign protein has been infused into the blood, there is no getting it out.[12] Any allergic reaction that develops therefore must be mitigated with pharmaceutical intervention available only in a hospital—even intensive care—setting,

---

[9]In particular, the old Institute Pasteur globulin often caused adverse responses because so much was asked of it by European doctors using it under primitive conditions in the bush to treat the devastatingly toxic bites of African and Indian cobras, mambas, and vipers.

[10]This new *crotalid* antivenin, CroFab™ (Crotalidae Polyvalent Immune Fab was introduced in late January, 2001. Its U.S. distributor is Savage Laboratories, a pharmaceutical division of Altana Inc., 60 Baylis Road, Melville, N.Y. 11747, (800) 231-0205. Altana Inc. is itself the U.S. subsidiary of Byk-Gulden, a multi-national pharmaceutical company based in Konstanz, Germany.

   According to literature released by Savage (http://www.savagelabs.com) on Feb. 18, 2001, "The majority of adverse reactions to CroFab™ reported in clinical studies were mild or moderate in severity—primarily rash, urticaria and pruritus. CroFab™ should not be administered to patients with a known history of hypersensitivity to papaya or papain unless the benefits outweigh the risks and appropriate management for anaphylactic reactions is readily available. . . . Adverse events involving the skin and appendages were reported in 14 of 42 patients. Three of the 25 patients who experienced adverse reactions experienced severe or serious adverse reaction. All adverse reactions resolved during the course of treatment."

   An older source of both North American pitviper and coral snake antivenin is Wyeth Laboratories of Philadelphia, (610) 688-4400, whose *Crotalinae* and *Elapid* serums have been in use since 1954.

[11]"The administration of an antivenin is important not just for saving lives, but for avoiding serious tissue and bleeding complications," according to Richard Clark, M.D., director of Medical Toxicology, University of California San Diego Medical Center, and medical director, San Diego Division, California Poison Control Systems.

[12]This is why antivenin must never be injected directly into an envenomated extremity: you can't build up immunity in a finger alone.

because serum anaphylaxis could cause enough swelling to obstruct the respiratory passages, and even coronary attacks have occurred.[13]

Yet, administered by an experienced physician with immediate access to intensive-care facilities, both current antivenins can save lives. The most critical aspect of their use lies in the need for immediate intervention to offset any incipient allergic response, usually with antihistamines or epinephrine. This sort of reaction is relatively unlikely, though, since before antivenin can be administered each patient's sensitivity to its foreign proteins is determined by an allergic-reaction skin-test trial.[14]

If no allergic reaction occurs, antivenin can result in a marked decrease in the pain of ophidian venom poisoning. The reason lies in the way antivenin acts to prevent the proteolytic, fibrinolytic, and hemolytic

---

[13]Anaphylaxis could perhaps be largely avoided if animals other than horses were used to make antivenin but, until recently, only horses—the traditional source animals for all types of immunization vaccines—have been bled for the serum antibodies they produce in response to small, periodic injections of snake venom. These antibodies are so nearly the same for all North American pitvipers that Wyeth distributes a single antivenin, *Crotalinae*, for use against the bites of copperheads, cottonmouths, and all indigenous rattlesnake species. For coral snake envenomation, Wyeth has a separate antivenin, *Micrurus*.

The problem is that horses have been used to produce so many antigen-bearing vaccines that people who have been inoculated against typhoid, tetanus, and diphtheria bacilli have often become sensitized to equine cellular matter. This does not create a problem when they receive the very small dose of foreign protein involved in subsequent conventional immunizations, but when the far larger volume of equine proteins required for treatment of severe venomous snakebite is suddenly dumped into their systems, they sometimes experience allergic anaphylaxis.

Until the recent release of Savage Laboratories' ovine-based CroFab™ antivenin, other experimental animals had only been used to produce plasma antigens on a small scale, although some of these, such as sheep and goats, reportedly produced milder reactions than the earlier equine vaccines because few people have been sensitized to sheep and goat proteins. Antivenin has even been derived from western diamond-backed rattlesnake blood—to which no one is pre-sensitized. This antivenin has reportedly afforded laboratory animals a high level of protection from the effects of pitviper envenomation, especially when combined with goat antibodies.

Human beings could also generate reaction-free antibodies if anyone were willing to undergo the misery of periodic minimal venom poisoning. Understandably, no commercial human-globulin antivenin has ever been produced, but William E. Haast, who for many years operated the Miami Serpentarium, has injected small, antigen-producing amounts of elapid venom into himself for decades. As a probable result, he has survived a number of what in all likelihood would otherwise have been fatal cobra bites, and has even transfused his own presumably antigen-bearing blood into other victims of elapid poisoning, perhaps mitigating the effects of their envenomations. (Haast, incidentally, is now in his mid-eighties and remains amazingly vigorous.)

[14]Individuals vary so widely in their sensitivity to antivenin infusion that some people need nearly twice as long as others to build up the same blood level of antibodies, but if it can be tolerated, several vials of the vaccine may be given during the first hour. Infusion is then likely to be maintained at two or three vials per hour until an adequate plasma titer is established. According to literature released by Savage Laboratories, "The availability of CroFab™ presents a safe treatment option for victims of venomous snakebite," said Richard C. Dart, MD, PhD, Director, Rocky Mountain Poison and Drug Center, Denver Health Authority and Associate Professor of Medicine, Surgery and Pharmacy, University of Colorado Health Sciences Center.

action of snake venom. Introduced into the bloodstream, its antibody clusters are drawn to reptile venom's large, variably shaped toxic peptides and enzymes. (Venom enzymes are usually spherical; peptides may be tubular, coiled, or globular, but all of venom's toxic proteins are spiked externally with sharp-edged, key-like protuberances that work by penetrating the serum's target cells and disintegrating their structure.)

To inhibit this process, antivenin antibodies physically encrust these protrusions so thickly that the toxins can no longer penetrate their target cells. Eventually, enough of their protective frosting is built up to attract the body's particle- devouring macrophagocytes— cleaner cells which, like giant amoebas, eventually engulf and digest most of the conglomerate specks of alien protein.

But they don't do it without potential problems. As the last of these deactivated antibody-antigen complexes precipitate out of the blood, up to two weeks after treatment, they may lodge in vascular vessel walls throughout the body, causing the skin rashes, hives, and temporary kidney impairment that collectively are known as serum sickness. Moreover, even after recovery from snake venom poisoning a small cadre of the body's own antigens (spawned both by venom proteins and by the antivenin's foreign serum antibodies) may remain in the bloodstream, sensitizing the individual to any subsequently encountered foreign globulins—or, it is thought, to another snakebite.

Although neither the Wyeth *Crotalinae* and *Micrurus* antivenin nor the newer Savage Laboratories CroFab™ pitviper antivenin is kept on hand by many major hospitals, an emergency source is the producers:

New *crotalid* (pitviper) antivenin:
CroFab™ (Crotalidae Polyvalent Immune Fab—Ovine)
Savage Laboratories Inc.
60 Baylis Road
Melville, New York, 11747
(800) 231-0205
(631) 454-9071

For North American pitviper and coral snake antivenin (*Crotalinae* and *Elapid* serums): Wyeth Laboratories of Philadelphia, (610) 688-4400. Coral snake antivenin: (*Micrurus fulvius*, Drug Circular, Wyeth, 1983).

Another option is to contact the Antivenin Index, compiled by the Arizona Poison Center, which offers a comprehensive array of data on venomous snakebite and a list of all the antivenins currently stored in the United States, including those for foreign species. Their 24-hour emergency number is (602) 626-6016.

Finally, some authorities on envenomation by both native and exotic reptiles are as follows:

Arizona Poison Control System
Coagulation Research Laboratory
Department of Pediatrics,
University of Arizona Health Sciences Center
Tucson, Arizona

Richard Clark, M.D.,
Director of Medical Toxicology
University of California San Diego Medical Center
Director, San Diego Division
California Poison Control Systems
San Diego, California

Richard C. Dart, M.D., Ph.D.
Director, Rocky Mountain Poison and Drug Center and Associate
   Professor of Medicine, Surgery and Pharmacy
University of Colorado Health Sciences Center
Denver, Colorado

James L. Glenn, M.D.
Western Institute for Biomedical Research
Salt Lake City, Utah

L.H.S. Van Mierop, M.D.
Department of Pediatrics (Cardiology)
University of Florida Medical School
Gainesville, Florida 32611

Damon C. Smith
Therapeutic Antibodies, Inc.
St. Bartholomew's Hospital Medical College
Charterhouse Square
London, EC1, U.K.

Venom Potency Table

Species	High	Low	Mean
Western Diamond-backed Rattlesnake, *Crotalus atrox*	4.07	8.42	6.25
Western (Prairie) Rattlesnake, *Crotalus viridis*	2.00	2.37	2.19
Mojave Rattlesnake, *Crotalus scutulatus* (Type A) Yuma, Arizona	0.13	0.54	0.34
Mojave Rattlesnake, *Crotalus scutulatus* (Type B) unknown	2.29	3.80	3.05
Timber Rattlesnake, *Crotalus horridus*	2.69	3.80	3.25
Pigmy Rattlesnake, *Sistrurus miliarius*	6.00	10.29	8.15
Copperhead, *Agkistrodon contortrix*	7.80	16.71	12.26
Cottonmouth, *Agkistrodon piscivorus*	4.88	5.82	5.35
Coral Snake, *Micrurus fulvius*	0.53	0.73	0.63

BLIND SNAKES
Family Typhlopidae

Typhlopidae is a primarily tropical family consisting of three genera and more than 160 species. All are blind—as is indicated by the Greek *Atyphlos*, (blind), and *Ops*, (eye)—and all are so small, writes Harry Greene, (1997), that they are resistant to the stares of biologists: "We ignore these shy little creatures, periodically look again, and are frustrated by the lack of resolution; we literally cannot see them very well."

All blind snakes are tiny, primitive burrowing serpents whose maxillary bones are toothed and, unlike those of other snakes, are not fused to the skull. Also unlike more evolutionarily advanced serpents, the lower jawbones bear no teeth. None of the *Typhlopidae* are native to the United States, but one genus, *Ramphotyphlops*, occurs here in the form of a single, artificially introduced species, the Brahminy blind snake.

BRAHMINY BLIND SNAKE
Genus Ramphotyphlops

Brahminy Blind Snake, *Ramphotyphlops braminus*

The only member of the parthenogenetic, oviparous genus *Ramphotyphlops*, the Brahminy Blind Snake is the single serpent known to be able to reproduce without males. Members of this all-female genus have a high number of chromosomes but, as might be expected of near-clonal animals, little variability in individual morphology. Like other Blind snakes, they lack the large laterally elongate ventral scales of more advanced ophidian families, and though formerly thought to be radically different from other serpents, Blind snakes are now believed to be closer to the mainstream of ophidian evolution and may even be crucial to understanding the evolution of modern snakes from their subterranean forebears.

1   BRAHMINY BLIND SNAKE

Ramphotyphlops Braminus

Nonvenomous The Brahminy blind snake is too small to bite humans.

Abundance This primitive serpent, perhaps reminiscent of the subterranean late Cretaceous snakes from which all modern serpents are descended, is native to Southeast Asia. Yet, in southern Florida (where its progenitors probably first arrived in the soil of imported house plants) *R. braminus* is now common from Pinellas County and Lake Okeechobee south to the upper Keys.

During the spring of 1997, the Brahminy blind snake—which is often referred to as the flowerpot snake—was found to have invaded new terrain when it was recorded for the first time in Brownsville, Texas, the US' other subtropical biotic community, by Richard Bartlett and Kenny Wray.

Size *Ramphotyphlops braminus* is adult at about 5 inches in length. Though it may reach 6.5 in., this minuscule serpent is not much thicker than coathanger wire.

Habitat In residential areas of well-watered sod and rich garden humus the Brahminy blind snake is often abundant, occurring most often in flower beds.

Prey Primarily the eggs, larvae, and pupae of ants and termites.

Reproduction Both egg-laying and live-bearing. Large groups of Brahminy Blind Snakes—an all-female species in which the ova begin cell division without spermatozoa—often live together in soil or rotting vegetation. This produces up to eight genetically identical offspring which, between April and June, may be either born alive or deposited as eggs. These may hatch in less than a week, with the 2-inch-long newborns being among the smallest of living serpents.

Coloring/scale form Brahminy blind snakes resemble shiny black or dark brown earthworms (like worms, *R. braminus* is sometimes washed onto pavement by heavy rains). Its blunt head and tail seem nearly identical—there is no narrowing of the neck and the lower jaw is barely visible—while its vestigial eyes are no more than dots of black pigment. The Brahminy blind snake's non-tapering posterior end is tipped, however, by a tiny spur. Unlike the transversely widened ventral scales of other serpents, the same size scales occur in 14 rows that completely cover the blind snake's back, sides, and belly. Also unlike other snakes, there is no anal plate, for its vent is surrounded by minuscule scales.

Similar snakes   The **plains blind snake** (2) is a pale, fleshy color.

Behavior   The specialized spur on the Brahminy blind snake's tail tip is dug into the earth to obtain purchase for pressing its tiny body through soft soil. Then the tail tip is brought forward, planted, and used to once more lever the body ahead.

SLENDER BLIND SNAKES
Family Leptotyphlopidae

Worldwide, *Leptotyphlopidae*—"Leptos" is "slender" in Greek— is a large, oviparous family characterized by untoothed maxillary bones which are fused solidly to the skull. Because of a bilateral intra-mandibular hinge on the lower jaw (the only place the tiny teeth are found), this animal's dentition is arranged semi-transversely. First scientifically described by L. J. F. Fitzinger in 1843, this family is comprised of 2 genera—only a single genus, *Leptotyphlops*, divided into 2 species (both found west of the Mississippi River), occurs in the United States—containing nearly 80 species.

AMERICAN BLIND SNAKES
Genus Leptotyphlops

Plains Blind Snake, *Leptotyphlops dulcis dulcis*
New Mexico Blind Snake, *Leptotyphlops dulcis dissectus*
Trans-Pecos Blind Snake, *Leptotyphlops humilis segregus*

Unlike the vast majority of serpents, members of the genus *Leptotyphlops* lack both enlarged ventral scutes (their belllies are covered with the same small scales as their backs) and functional eyes. These tiny, primitive snakes are constant burrowers that surface only occasionally, mainly in the spring and fall, or when summer rains flood their burrows. American blind snakes are thought to feed largely on the larvae and pupae of ants, but subterranean termites and the burrowing larvae of some beetles are also accepted by captives.

2 PLAINS BLIND SNAKE

Leptotyphlops dulcis dulcis

Nonvenomous This miniature reptile is much too small to bite humans.

Abundance Locally common, but unevenly dispersed across a broad section of the southern Great Plains. This 350-mile-wide band stretches from the Tamaulipan thorn woodland of the Rio Grande Valley north across Texas' Edwards and Stockton Plateaus to the grasslands/crosstimbers interface of northern Texas and southern Oklahoma.

Before South American fire ants invaded the southern part of this range, where *L. d. dulcis* was most abundant, plains blind snakes were often easy to find in areas of soft, loamy soil—especially in early spring before summer's drying and hardening of the ground's upper layers forced it deeper into the earth.

Size Slender, and but 2½ to 11 inches in length, *L. d. dulcis* looks much like a large earthworm.

Habitat This predominantly subterranean snake is sometimes found at the surface beneath leaf and plant litter or under decaying logs. Plains blind snakes also often inhabit the well-watered sod and rich garden humus of residential neighborhoods where they are turned up by those weeding gardens or planting flower beds.

Prey Blind snakes feed primarily on the eggs, larvae, and pupae of ants and termites. The adults of soft-bodied insects, usually commensals in ant and termite colonies, are reportedly taken as well. Harry Greene (1997) reports that "in feeding, L. Dulcis first grasps a termite's abdomen, then breaks off its head by pressing it against the substrate, and finally swallows the soft hindparts. In contrast, that species arches its anterior over ant larvae and pupae, then forces its mouth down over the intact prey."

Reproduction Egg-laying. During late June and early July, female blind snakes deposit 3 or 4 thin-shelled, ½-inch-long eggs (sometimes in a nest cavity used by as many as a half-dozen females) hollowed from decaying vegetation or within loose, sandy soil. More than forty eggs have been located in a single such site, with old broken shells indicating that these nests were used for a succession of breeding seasons.

Coloring/scale form *Leptotyphlops dulcis dulcis* is much the same shape, size and color as a large earthworm. Unlike Blind snakes such as *Ramphotyphlops Braminus*—which spends brief periods on the surface—the almost entirely fossorial plains and New Mexico blind snakes lack most external pigmentation. This little snake seemingly has no facial features, for its vestigial eyes are no more than dots of non-functional pigment barely visible beneath its enlarged, translucent ocular scales. Each of these ocular scales extends to the mouth and, in the plains subspecies, is preceded by a single upper labial scale. Unlike those of other North American snakes, blind snakes' ventral scales are not transversely widened into long plates (14 rows of smooth scales encircle the whole trunk), and the tail is tipped with a tiny spur.

Similar snakes   The **New Mexico blind snake (3)** is distinguished by the 2 upper labial scales that occur just forward of the lower portion of each of its ocular scales. **See Illustration: New Mexico Blind Snake.** The **Brahminy blind snake (1)**, now found in the lower Rio Grande Valley, is a darker brown color.

Behavior   If they are recognized as reptiles at all, blind snakes are usually taken to be the newborns of larger snakes. Where soil conditions are ideal, several *L. d. dulcis* (which are often found in close proximity) are commonly mistaken for a "nest of baby snakes."

The specialized spur on the blind snake's tail tip is dug into its tunnel walls to obtain purchase in pressing through the soil; as might be expected of so vulnerable a creature, on open ground these animals never cease wriggling in search of cover in which to burrow.

The slippery scales of *Leptotyphlops Eptotyphlops*, as well as the viscous fluid this genus excretes when attacked, serve not only to protect it from the assaults of the ants and termites on which it feeds, but probably also makes it difficult for larger predators to grasp. Frederick Gehlbach of Baylor University has documented blind snakes escaping from the talons of screech owls trying to carry the snakes back to feed their young—snakes which then survived on the insect larvae found in the owls' nest cavities . . . and even laid eggs there. Though not a beneficial situation for the snakes, their predation on the owls' insect parasites allowed owlets in nests populated by blind snakes to suffer lower mortality and grow faster than owlets whose nest holes lacked resident *Leptotyphlops*.

3   NEW MEXICO BLIND SNAKE

Leptotyphlops dulcis dissectus

Like other *Leptotyphlops*, the New Mexico blind snake resembles a pale, shiny earthworm, particularly since adult specimens are no more than 6½ inches in length and not much thicker than coathanger wire. (Blind snakes also resemble earthworms because they lack the distinctly serpentine belly-wide ventral scales of other snakes. Since there is no narrowing of either the neck

Trans-Pecos blind snake
(L. h. segregus)

Plains and New Mexico
blind snakes
(L. dulcis)

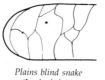

Plains blind snake
(L. d. dulcis)

New Mexico blind snake
(L. d. dissectus)

or tail, blind snakes' blunt heads and tails seem nearly identical, for their vestigial eyes are almost invisible and their mouths and lower jaws are barely discernible. The blind snakes' posterior end is distinguished, however, by its minuscule tail-tip spur.)

The New Mexico blind snake inhabits a curiously dissected range. One population (probably a relic group remaining from the area's wetter Pleistocene climate) inhabits the scattered grasslands of Texas' Trans-Pecos, while another group occupies the uniformly grassy plains of the Texas and Oklahoma panhandles and west-central Oklahoma.

Leptotyphlops dulcis dissectus is differentiated from the **Trans-Pecos blind snake (4)**, which shares most of its Trans-Pecos Chihuahuan Desert range, by the 3 small scales—the Trans-Pecos has only 1—that separate the tops of the ocular plates that cap its crown. The **plains blind snake (2)**, a subspecies of the New Mexico race, is distinguished by the presence of 2 narrow upper labial scales—*dissectus* means "cleft," in reference to their shared central suture—between the lower extension of the ocular plate and the nasal scale. The plains blind snake has but 1 such intervening scale. In other respects these two races are identical, and intergrades between them are common. (Because these two races so closely resemble each other, no distinguishing characteristics are visible in a photograph; the New Mexico blind snake's two narrow upper labial scales are so small as to be visible only in an enlarged drawing).

Behavior Preyed upon by a host of small carnivores, including desert scorpions, the New Mexico blind snake's ecology is probably almost identical to that of its subspecies, the plains blind snake. This may include a tendency for several females to deposit their egg clutches in the same nest cavity. Of necessity, in arid country where the substrate is loose enough for burrowing, *L. d. dissectus* descends quite deeply to avoid desiccation; individuals have been unearthed from several feet below the surface by road-grading machinery working the extremely dry, sandy terrain along the Rio Grande near Castolon, Texas.

4 TRANS-PECOS BLIND SNAKE

Leptotyphlops humilis segregus

Nonvenomous   This animal is much too small to bite humans.

Abundance   Widely but spottily dispersed over its arid range in Texas' northern Chihuahuan Desert, the Trans-Pecos blind snake is so inconspicuous that it is seldom noticed, although it can be fairly common in areas of moist soil.

Size   Slightly larger than the plains and New Mexico blind snakes, *L. h. segregus* reaches a maximum length of 13 inches.

Habitat   Trans-Pecos blind snakes—*segregus* refers to this animal's "distantly set-off" range, as assumed by L. M. Klauber, who described this subspecies in 1939—are recorded from a variety of terrestrial communities, but are seldom if ever found in severe desert terrain. Their preferred habitat is the slightly more mesic, richer-soiled conditions of the Trans-Pecos grasslands such as those in Presidio and southern Jeff Davis counties.

Prey   *Leptotyphlops humilis segregus* apparently feeds almost exclusively on the eggs and pupae of ants and termites, which it reportedly finds by following these insects' pheromone trails.

Reproduction   Egg-laying. See **Plains Blind Snake.**

Coloring/scale form   The shiny, flesh-colored back may have a brown tinge on 5 to 7 of its vertebral scale rows; the venter is pale pink. Along with 95 other species and subspecies of *Leptotyphlopidae* (many of them abundant in the American tropics), the Trans-Pecos blind snake has a cylindrical head and a tail almost the same diameter as its mid-section, so that both its ends look remarkably alike. The head has tiny dots of vestigial ocular pigment, however, while the tail is distinguished both by the tiny spur at its tip and by its tendency to wriggle back and forth when the animal is disturbed, smearing musky cloacal fluid over the rest of the body. (Enhancing the protection afforded by the blind snakes' small, tightly overlapping scales, this musk functions as an olfactory armor by discouraging the bites and stings of ants, whose nests blind snakes must enter for food.)

Fourteen rows of small scales encircle these blind snakes' entire trunk, for the elongation of the ventral scales into the transverse plates of most serpents is absent, as is the anal plate (the vent of *L. h. segregus* is surrounded by small scales).

Similar snakes Only other *Leptotyphlopidae* are similar. The **plains (2)** and the **New Mexico (3) blind snakes** are distinguished by the 3 small scales present in the center of the crown between the right and left ocular plates; a single mid-crown scale separates the ocular scales of the Trans-Pecos blind snake. See **New Mexico Blind Snake.**

Behavior L. M. Klauber (1940) noted that this little serpent "progressed with less lateral undulation than other snakes. On smooth surfaces it employed the tail spine to aid in its motion. When placed in loose or sandy soil it burrowed immediately. It is never peaceful or quiet when above ground."

COLUBRID SNAKES
Family Colubridae

Although studies in the future will almost certainly divide this unwieldy biologic assemblage—the snakes in this family vary so widely in appearance and lifestyle that many are probably only distantly related—*Colubridae* is the vast and diverse family to which most North American snakes are currently assigned. This family is divided into four subfamilies, *Colubrinae*, *Natricinae*, *Lampropeltinae*, and *Xenodontinae*.

Most North American colubrids are harmless to humans, but a number of the species in the two subfamilies *Natricinae* and *Xenodontinae* are characterized by mildly toxic saliva and/or enlarged teeth at the rear of the upper jaw.

SMALL BURROWING SNAKES
Crowned, Flat, and Black-Headed Snakes
Genus Tantilla

Southeastern Crowned Snake, *Tantilla coronata*
Peninsula Crowned Snake, *Tantilla relicta relicta*
Central Florida Crowned Snake, *Tantilla relicta neilli*
Coastal Dunes Crowned Snake, *Tantilla relicta pamlica*
Rim Rock Crowned Snake, *Tantilla oolitica*
Flat-headed Snake, *Tantilla gracilis*

Plains Black-headed Snake, *Tantilla nigriceps*
Southwestern Black-headed Snake, *Tantilla hobartsmithi*
Mexican Black-headed Snake, *Tantilla atriceps*
Black-hooded Snake, *Tantilla rubra cucullata*

First described in 1853 in their famous "Catalog of North American Reptiles"—by the team of Smithsonian Institute Secretary Spencer Fullerton Baird and Frenchman Charles Frederich Girard—this oviparous genus is contained in the subfamily *Xenodontinae*. In the east, these diminutive burrowers are called crowned snakes. Farther west, they are larger, but equally secretive reptiles known as flat-headed, black-headed, or black-hooded snakes. Most are characterized by a black crown and, sometimes, a black nape, which may or may not be separated from the rest of the back by a light collar.

The uni-colored dorsum is often the color of the substrate—typically sandy and well drained—on which that particular species is found. *Tantilla* vary by species from common and fairly well known, despite their persistent secrecy—most occasionally turn up beneath flat stones and building debris—to rare and poorly understood.

Tantilla—a name drawn from a gypsy dance, presumably because of the lively struggles of this genus' members to escape when handled—is characterized by 15 rows of smooth dorsolateral scales. The anal plate is divided, and there is no loreal scale—an important fact when trying to distinguish the flat-headed snake, a *Tantilla* species with muted head and nape colors, from the grayish phases of the ground snake, *Sonora*.

Possessing both saliva toxic to their small, mostly invertebrate prey, as well as a pair of enlarged (but still tiny) teeth at the rear of each upper jaw with which to deliver this fluid, most *Tantilla* species are, nevertheless, too small and reluctant to bite to harm mankind.

5 SOUTHEASTERN CROWNED SNAKE

Tantilla coronata

Nonvenomous   All *Tantilla* have enlarged, but still tiny, grooved teeth in the rear of their minuscule upper jaw. The southeastern crowned snake is unable to harm humans, however.

Abundance   Generally common throughout a range that stretches from the Mississippi, Alabama, and Florida panhandle north to west-central Kentucky and Virginia, then down the Atlantic seaboard to southern Georgia.

One isolated individual was collected in eastern Tennessee by Sherman Minton. In the southern part of this range, populations of *Tantilla coronata*, like those of other small terrestrial reptiles, have been heavily impacted by the recent invasion of South American fire ants.

Size   Adult southeastern crowned snakes reach a maximum of 13 inches in length.

Habitat   Seldom found at the surface except beneath rocks, boards, or leaf litter, *T. coronata* is partial to dry microhabitats and prefers loose, silica-based soil in which to burrow. It occupies both wooded and grass/brushland communities, occurring most often in pine or oak forest—although it has also been reported from mesic meadows, hardwood hammocks, and even swamps.

Prey   This species' prey is primarily tenebrionid beetle larvae; also snails, centipedes, termites and their larvae, spiders, and cut- and wireworms. Vertebrates such as ground skinks are also reportedly taken.

Reproduction   Egg-laying. Reproduction in this species is complicated. First, for such a small reptile *Tantilla coronata* requires a long period of maturation, with females reaching sexual maturity only in the spring of their third year at about 21 months of age. Second, recent study indicates that both male and female *T. coronata* store sperm.

This is necessary because the two genders' procreative cycles differ markedly: males' spermatogenesis occurs in late summer, while females ovulate during June and July. For autumn breeding this is fine, but in order for viable sperm to be present at the time of early springtime copulation—which also occurs—it must remain active in the males' vas deferens throughout the winter. Then, to fertilize the ova female *T. coronata* produce only in midsummer, this spermatozoa must continue to remain viable in seminal receptacles within the female's oviduct for 2 or 3 additional months.

Delayed fertilization is also reflected in the southeastern crowned snake's morphology: the left oviduct serves as an auxiliary sperm-storage receptacle. The 2 to 5 oval, whitish eggs are laid in a cup-shaped cavity amid moist woodland debris, hatching into neonates no more than 3 inches long.

Coloring/scale form   The southeastern crowned snake's back and sides are solid rusty-brown or tan, while its blackish head is crossed posteriorly by a cream-colored band that also occupies the nape. Behind this pale collar is a broad black band, 3 to 5 scales in width, that extends well back onto the neck; the venter is white to yellowish-pink.

Similar snakes   The **central Florida crowned snake (7)** has little or no light crossbanding between its crown and neck. Neither the **midland**

brown snake (20) nor its relative the **Florida red-bellied snake (16)** has a dark band behind its pale nape; both brown and red-bellied snakes also have keeled dorsal scales.

Behavior Named *T. coronata* for its black-crowned head, the crowned snake's skull is no wider than its neck and is flattened from above and below into a penetrating wedge to facilitate burrowing.

6 PENINSULA CROWNED SNAKE

Tantilla relicta relicta

Nonvenomous This little reptile does not bite larger animals.

Abundance Most common of Florida's endemic *T. relicta*, the peninsula crowned snake may be the most abundant of all snakes in this state's dry, sandy-soiled upland communities. (It is seldom noticed, however, because its small size and cryptic microenvironment beneath vegetative ground cover enable it to escape human attention.) This habitat is believed to be a remnant, or relic, of the Leistocene desert that during glacial advances bordered the northern shore of the Gulf of Mexico—hence the name "relicta."

  Tantilla relicta relicta is found from Marion Co. in northern Florida south to Highlands County in central Florida; disjunct populations occur both on Cedar Key and in Sarasota, Charlotte, and Lee counties along the Gulf Coast.

Size Adults are 7 to 8½ inches long; the record is 9½ in.

Habitat Within the xeric interior scrub of central Florida (as well as among a small strip of coastal dunes just north of Tampa), the peninsula crowned snake's sole microhabitat seems to be a thin subsurface layer where fallen vegetative litter meets the sand below. In the sandy-soiled pine scrub of the Ocala National Forest, peninsula crowned snakes were found to be most abundant in previously burned or clearcut areas currently supporting second-growth vegetation, but they were also present in mature pine forest.

Prey One study of food resource partitioning found roughly 90% of this animal's prey to consist of tenebrionid beetle larvae, with snails and centipedes making up the remainder.

Reproduction Egg-laying. No other reproductive data is recorded.

Coloring/scale form Most peninsula crowned snakes have a pale neck ring interrupted by a dark patch of pigment along the spine.

Like other crowned snakes, to penetrate soil *T. r. relicta* has evolved a pointed rostral scale, beneath which its lower jaw (unlike that of most snakes) is recessed; one basal hook occurs on each hemipenis.

Similar snakes   The **central Florida crowned snake (7)** has a black head and neck with little or no pale nuchal crossband. The **Florida brown snake (19)** has a speckled dorsum and keeled scales, and the **southern ring-necked snake (27)** has a black dorsum and a black-spotted, orange-to-red venter.

Behavior   Adept at prying its way through the tiniest soil crevice with its hard, flattened snout, *Tantilla relicta* has been observed burrowing or sand-swimming through loose grains of silicaceous soil just below the surface.

7   CENTRAL FLORIDA CROWNED SNAKE
Tantilla relicta neilli

Nonvenomous   Rarely seen or photographed, the secretive little central Florida crowned snake is unlikely to ever encounter a human being, much less bite one.

Abundance   Locally, not uncommon. First described by S. R. Telford in 1966, and named for Florida herpetologist W. T. Neill, *T. r. neilli* is found only in north-central Florida, where it occurs from Madison County south to Hillsborough and Polk counties.

Size   *Tantilla relicta* is the smallest of the state's three *Tantilla* species: adults are no more than 7 to 9 inches in length.

Habitat   The central Florida crowned snake's primary habitat is well-drained sandhills, with most of the few individuals that have been found turning up on the eastern side of the state's north-central uplands. According to state biologist Kevin Enge, "Central Florida crowned snakes apparently prefer areas with at least partial shade and a thin to moderate layer of leaves or pine needles in sandhills and xeric and mesic hammocks. Crowned snakes have [also] been found in pocket gopher and gopher tortoise mounds."

Prey   See **Peninsula Crowned Snake.**

Reproduction   Egg-laying. See **Southeastern Crowned Snake.**

Coloring/scale form   This small, glossy brown snake has a mostly black head and neck whose pigment reaches 3 to 8 scale rows behind its cephalic parietal plates. Its only other marking is a pale blotch below the eye which shades into a light-hued lateral area on its neck; its venter is yellowish-white. One basal hook occurs on each hemipenis, and the lower jaw is slightly less inset within the upper than is the case with Florida's other races of *T. relicta*.

Similar snakes The **peninsula crowned snake (6)** has an interrupted, light-hued crossband between its head and neck.

Behavior It is reported that when *T. relicta* occupies the mounds of sandy dirt piled around the mouths of pocket gopher burrows it sometimes basks beneath a layer of sand, extending only its head above the surface.

8   COASTAL DUNES CROWNED SNAKE

Tantilla relicta pamlica

Nonvenomous Like other crowned snakes, *T. r. pamlica* is harmless to humans.

Abundance Rare. *Tantilla relicta pamlica* is found only along Florida's south-central Atlantic Coast. This strip of land—known geologically as the Pamlica Terrace—is made up of extremely valuable ocean-front real estate, and in such a development-prone area the coastal dunes crowned snake's future seems certain to be increasingly jeopardized.

Size Adults are tiny: no more than 8½ inches in length.

Habitat A littoral reptile whose primary habitat is the grassy barrier dunes that line the Atlantic between Brevard and Palm Beach counties, *T. r. pamlica* is also reported from inland hardwood hammocks and pinelands.

Prey Unknown in the wild, but like other races of *Tantilla relicta*, the coastal dunes race probably preys on subterranean insects and their larvae.

Reproduction Egg-laying; otherwise unknown.

Coloring/scale form The shiny brown body—more reddish than that of other Florida *Tantilla*—is separated from the dark crown by a pale band across the rear of the skull followed by a broad black nuchal collar, 3 or 4 scale rows in width. The coastal dunes subspecies has more white on its head than other crowned snakes, with both a pale snout and light-hued labial scales; its venter is yellowish- to pinkish-white. Consistent with this animal's sand-burrowing lifestyle, grit is excluded from its mouth by its lower jaw being sunk well within the downturned overlap of its upper labial scales. One basal hook occurs on each hemipenis.

Similar snakes   The **rim rock crowned snake (9)** has less light cephalic pigment than *T. r. pamlica*. It may have an interrupted pale collar, and male rim rock crowned snakes possess two basal hooks on each hemipenis. The **Florida brown snake (19)** has a speckled, grayish-brown dorsum and keeled scales. The young of **southern ring-necked (27)** and **earth snakes (24, 25)** appear similar to crowned snakes, but juvenile ring-necks are dark gray above and have black-speckled yellow-to-red venters; both species of earth snakes lack a sharp delineation between their dark crowns and paler backs.

Behavior   Florida's *Tantilla* are the northeastern-most branch of a family of predominantly tropical serpents that ranges through Central and western South America: all three of the state's *Tantilla* species are former members of an ancient, xeric-adapted fauna that once occupied a dry corridor joining the desert southwest to the Florida peninsula. After this community was split by the cooler, wetter Gulf Coast climate brought about by the advance of late Pleistocene glaciers, crowned snakes survived as relict populations—the source of the coastal dunes crowned snake's species name, *relicta*—in Florida's central sandhills and coastal dunes.

9   RIM ROCK CROWNED SNAKE

Tantilla oolitica

Nonvenomous   Rim rock crowned snakes do not bite humans.

Abundance   Endangered. Protected by the state of Florida. *Tantilla oolitica* is one of the rarest snakes in North America: less than 10 individuals are known, most associated with the low pine ridge called the Miami rim rock, or Oolitic Limestone Terrace, that parallels the state's southeastern coast. (*Tantilla oolitica* has also been found on Grassy Key, Marathon Key, and upper Matecumbe Key, while a lone individual was reported from Key West.)

Because this limited range includes some of the nation's most valuable real estate it has become a virtual Ground Zero for non-mobile wildlife: according to U.S. Fish and Wildlife, 99% of Dade County's natural upland areas has been destroyed. The designation of a portion of Key Largo as a federal and state refuge and parkland may provide a vestigial habitat, however.

Size   Adults are 6 to 9 inches; the record is 11½ in.

Habitat   Even before commercial development spread over its habitat of hardwood hammocks and pine rocklands (the type specimen is from a long-vanished Miami vacant lot), the rim rock crowned snake was probably a rare animal, thought to have seldom emerged from crevices within the porous oolitic limestone, overlain with a thin layer of pine needles, that makes up the subterranean oolitic formation for which it is named.

Prey   The primary prey of this very rare reptile is not known. However, it is probable that, like Florida's other crowned snakes, *Tantilla oolitica* feeds largely on tenebrionid beetle and termite larvae, snails, centipedes, spiders and smaller snakes. Herpetologist John Decker, who specializes in south Florida and Keys herpetofauna, believes that the rim rock crowned snake may share the predatory orientation of western *Tantillas* which feed on large chilopods and arachnids. One *T. oolitica* he discovered in a grassy lot on Marathon Key was scarred on its head, nape, and anterior back in a way that resembles the scarring typically inflicted on Chihuahuan Desert–living *Tantilla* by the big Scolependra centipedes and scorpions they prey upon, and Decker reports a rim rock crowned snake feeding on small scorpions.

Reproduction   Egg-laying; nothing else is recorded.

Coloring/scale form   The dorsum is tan or slightly pinkish posterior to the neck—Decker reports that among conifer needles this tiny reptile looks like a short strand of rope—with each dorsolateral scale's posterior edge minimally edged with an off-white wash. The rim rock crowned snake's snout is also pale tan or off-white, its venter creamy. The only contrasting coloration is this animal's dark brown to blackish head and neck, whose dusky pigment extends below the rear corner of its mouth. Two basal hooks occur on each hemipenis.

Similar snakes   The **coastal dunes crowned snake** (8) has a light-hued band between its head and neck, white pigment on its head, and only one basal hook on each hemipenis.

Behavior   Presumably much like that of other southeastern species of *Tantilla*.

10   FLAT-HEADED SNAKE, *Tantilla gracilis*

Nonvenomous   Although technically a rear-fanged opisthoglyph serpent with very mild salivary toxins that presumably help to immobilize its diminutive prey, the flat-headed snake is too small to harm humans.

Abundance   Formerly common. Historically among the most abundant of the little soil-colored serpents turned up in flower beds and gardens within a broad range stretching, along the Rio Grande, from the Gulf Coast to the Pecos River, then north across the eastern ⅔ of Texas and Oklahoma to southeastern Kansas, southern Missouri, and western Arkansas and Louisiana.

In the southern part of this range *Tantilla gracilis* has now become less common. This is apparently due primarily to the impact of invading South American fire ants which, in the last few years, have decimated the nests of small, egg-laying terrestrial reptiles.

Size   Adult *T. gracilis* reach a length of 10 inches; hatchlings measure only about 3 in.

Habitat   The flat-headed snake prefers loose, slightly damp soil in which to burrow; it consequently occurs most often in well-watered deciduous woods and grass/brushland communities.

Prey   Flat-headed snakes' primarily arthropod and annelid prey seems to be at least partly partitioned through species-specific predation among the several other small fossorial serpents that share their semi-subterranean microhabitat. The stomach contents of most *Tantilla gracilis* examined in one study consisted of centipedes and earth-dwelling insect larvae such as cutworms and wireworms, while ground snakes were found to eat mainly arachnids; ring-necked snakes, mostly earthworms.

Reproduction   Egg-laying. Reproduction among most *Tantilla* requires a long period of maturation, especially for a small reptile: females reach sexual maturity only in the spring of their third year. In one study, copulation was found to take place during the first half of

May, with clutches of 1 to 4 oblong eggs being deposited in either shallow subsurface hollows or within decaying vegetation during the latter part of June. Depending on the temperature, these eggs hatched after about 60 days into neonates—which exactly resemble their parents—no more than 3 inches long.

Coloring/scale form   Dorsolateral color is uniformly grayish-tan except for the darker crown whose rear border is slightly concave. Flattened from top and bottom, the snout appears rounded from above; the venter is whitish to pale salmon. Although too small to note easily with the naked eye, there is a single postocular scale and no loreal (the second of the 6 upper labial scales touches, or almost touches, the prefrontal).

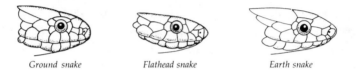

Ground snake   Flathead snake   Earth snake

Similar snakes   The **plains black-headed snake (11)** has 7 upper labial scales, a distinct black skullcap that stretches back to a point on its nape 3 to 5 scale rows behind its crown and a whitish-edged pink venter. **Earth snakes (25–26)** have a loreal scale and 17 rows of dorsal scales, with faint keels on the scales of at least the mid-dorsal rows. (The rough earth snake also has 5 upper labial scales and more grayish coloration.) **Ground snakes (33)** living in the flathead snake's range usually have a yellowish or reddish-tan ground color as well as a partially crossbanded back and undertail; there is also both a loreal and paired postocular scales.

Behavior   Secretive and nocturnal, *T. gracilis* is active mainly between April and early November because temperature and soil moisture are the major factors determining the presence of *Tantilla* at the surface (their small bodies, which are adapted to the comparatively constant temperature below ground, have little resistance to the pronounced fluctuations of atmospheric temperature).

Summer heat induces a period of aestivation, while low winter temperatures often force these animals to withdraw several feet into the ground by insinuating themselves through tiny crevices in the earth (to facilitate this the flat-headed snake's skull is no wider than its neck and is compressed from above and below into a penetrating wedge).

11 PLAINS BLACK-HEADED SNAKE

Tantilla nigriceps

Nonvenomous   The plains black-headed snake is too small and non-aggressive to harm humans.

Abundance   Moderately abundant in an extensive range that encompasses primarily the southern Great Plains, but stretches from the Tamaulipan thorn woodland along the Rio Grande northwest through Texas' Chihuahuan Desert, north across the Texas and Oklahoma panhandles into western Kansas and southwestern Nebraska. In both the thorn brush of the Rio Grande plain and the shortgrass prairie of the Texas and Oklahoma panhandles, *T. nigriceps* is often common, although seldom noticed because its small size and cryptic home beneath vegetative ground cover enable it to escape human attention.

Size   Adults are 7 to 14¾ inches in length.

Habitat   This snake's microhabitat is the thin subsurface layer where fallen vegetative litter meets the harder substrate below; it is most often found at the surface on the slightly damp soil beneath rocks and debris.

Prey   The plains black-headed snake's prey is primarily tenebrionid beetle larvae, centipedes, and small scorpions—the arthropods envenomed by the toxic saliva forced into their bodies by the enlarged upper rear teeth of the *Tantilla*. Less vigorous prey (typically found in semi-subterreanean locations) such as snails, worms, spiders, and insect larvae are also taken.

Reproduction   Egg-laying. See **Flat-headed Snake.**

Coloring/scale form   The dark skullcap—"nigriceps" is "blackheaded" in Latin—is longer than that of other southwestern *Tantillas*, stretching back 3 to 5 vertebral scale rows to end in a point

Underchin: plains black-headed snake

Underchin: southwestern black-headed snake

on the nape; there is a ruddy flush along the plains black-headed snake's midventral line. A single postocular and 7 upper labial scales (the second of which, due to the absence of a loreal, touches the prefrontal plate just ahead of the eye) are characteristic of this species. The anterior lower labial scales generally touch beneath the chin.

Similar snakes   The **flat-headed snake (10)** has 6 upper labial scales and a short brown skullcap whose slightly concave rear border extends rearward no more than 2 scale rows beyond its parietal plates. The straight rear-bordered skullcap of the **southwestern black-headed snake (12)** reaches no more than a single dorsal scale row onto its nape (where it may be edged with a faint pale line), its rostral scale is a bit more pointed, and its first pair of lower labial scutes do not touch under its chin. The **ground snake (17)** has a loreal scale and a pair of postocular scales.

Behavior   See **Flat-headed Snake.**

---

12   SOUTHWESTERN BLACK-HEADED SNAKE, *Tantilla hobartsmithi*

Nonvenomous   See **Flat-headed Snake.**

Abundance   Probably moderately abundant. Named for venerable herpetologist Hobart M. Smith, this fossorial reptile occupies a primarily northern Chihuahuan Desert biotic community that reaches northward from Laredo on the Rio Grande to Texas' northern Stockton Plateau, as well as westward across the Trans-Pecos into southern New Mexico. Here, *T. hobartsmithi* is seldom noted because its range is sparsely populated by human beings and its almost exclusively underground home enables it to escape their attention, but after heavy summer rain it is not uncommon as a roadkill.

Size   Maximum adult length is no more than 9½ inches.

Habitat   *Tantilla hobartsmithi* is a burrowing reptile usually found on the surface only where moisture has condensed under flat stones, or moving about after rainfall.

Prey   The stomachs of 37 southwestern black-headed snakes contained only butterfly, moth, and beetle larvae even though many other suitably sized invertebrates were to be found in the immediate vicinity.

Reproduction   Egg-laying. One female carrying a single egg was discovered on the first of June in Texas' Big Bend area.

Coloring/scale form   The southwestern black-headed snake, *Tantilla hobartsmithi*, owes its current identity to studies of the morphology of the tiny spines covering the hemipenes of these animals by Charles Cole and Lawrence Hardy (1981). Their work revised the classification of the **Mexican black-headed snake (13)**, *T. atriceps*, into two different species. These authors believe the Mexican black-headed snake to be confined to a small range in south Texas, while the *Tantillas* once thought to make up this animal's western population—a population which lives northwest of Kinney, Edwards, and Sutton counties—are now believed to represent a separate species, the southwestern black-headed snake, *Tantilla hobartsmithi*).

Within this species' large range, however, individual *T. hobartsmithi* display several types of head color. Each of these variants was once carefully charted since the different configuration were thought to define different species. Now, however, it is believed that local populations of *Tantilla hobartsmithi* include individuals with both short black cephalic caps and long ones—caps either bordered or not bordered with a pale nuchal collar—as well as specimens with either all-black or white-spotted snouts.

The shiny brown back and sides of the southwestern black-headed snake are perhaps slightly more reddish than those of other *Tantillas*, an orangeish streak often lines the center of its forebelly, and its undertail is salmon-colored. There are 7 upper labial scales, and the anterior lower labial scales usually do not meet beneath its chin.

Similar snakes   The cap of the **plains black-headed snake (11)** tapers to a point on the nape 3 to 5 scale rows behind the cephalic parietal scales; the first pair of lower labial scales meets under its chin.

Behavior   Where *Tantilla hobartsmithi* lives below ground during most of the year is not known; it has only been found—foraging, or perhaps seeking a mate, for most recorded specimens are male—during moist periods in spring and summer.

13   MEXICAN BLACK-HEADED SNAKE

Tantilla atriceps

Nonvenomous   See **Flat-headed Snake.**

Abundance   In the Bulletin of the American Museum of Natural History (1981), Charles J. Cole and Lawrence M. Hardy revised the classification of the Mexican black-headed snake, *Tantilla atriceps*, into 2 separate species. These are: (1) the *Tantilla* population found northwest of Kinney, Edwards, and Sutton Counties of Texas, which is now defined as a different species, the **southwestern black-headed snake (12)**, *T. hobartsmithi*; (2) a population of rare, predominantly sub-tropical snakes whose range lies primarily in the northern Mexican state of Tamaulipas, which retains the name Mexican black-headed snake, *Tantilla atriceps*. This species is known in Texas only from a pair of specimens collected over 100 years ago in Duval and Kleberg counties; whether it still occurs north of the Rio Grande is unknown. Nothing is known of its natural history in this country, and no photograph of a Texas specimen exists (the animal pictured here is from Nuevo Leon, Mexico).

Size   Maximum adult length is probably no more than 11 inches.

Habitat   In Mexico, *Tantilla atriceps* reportedly occupies both wooded and grassland/thorn brush communities.

Prey   The Mexican black-headed snake's food preferences are unknown, but like other *Tantillas*, it probably preys on subterranean insects and their larvae.

Reproduction   Egg-laying. One to 3 eggs are deposited in early summer; reproduction is otherwise unknown.

Coloring/scale form   Based on specimens from Tamaulipas, this snake displays its genus' typical brownish or grayish dorsolateral hue, slightly darker along the mid-dorsal line. Its black crown (*Tantillas* are also known as crowned snakes) reaches no further rearward than the posterior border of its parietal scutes and does not touch the posterior corner of its mouth, which is bordered on each side by 7 upper labial scales. The Mexican black-headed snake's pale orange venter reddens beneath its tail.

Similar snakes   The **flat-headed snake (10)** has a brown skullcap with a slightly concave rear border, a lighter-hued undertail, and 6 upper labial scales.

Behavior   The *Tantilla* of the southwestern US are a northern branch of a family of predominantly tropical snakes that reaches through Central America into western South America.

14 BLACK-HOODED SNAKE

Tantilla rubra cucullata

Nonvenomous   The only *Tantilla* that grows large and assertive enough to nip a human being, the black-hooded snake is harmless to humans, despite its technical classification as a rear-fanged opistho-glyph snake. (All *Tantilla* have enlarged, though still minuscule, grooved teeth in the rear of their upper jaws and bear mild salivary toxins to help immobilize their small prey.)

Abundance   Threatened. Protected by the state of Texas. This rare fossorial serpent, endemic to Trans-Pecos Texas, was until recently known only from a few specimens. It was thought to almost never emerge from its subterranean microenvironment except when surface conditions were optimal, for as many as 8 individuals have been found in a small area within a few days during humid weather when soil moisture levels were high.

Yet, during the severe drought summer of 1998 2 individuals were found near Jose Maria Spring in Val Verde County by Bill Armstrong, manager of the Devil's River State Natural Area. One of these was a hatchling discovered shortly after dawn on a dry, ash juniper/oak–covered slope where one would never have expected to find such a tiny snake moving about in the open. (There had been rain earlier in the week, however.)

Size   The black-hooded snake is a giant when compared to other *Tantillas*: the few individuals on record have measured 8½ to 17¼ inches in length; a single neonate was reported by Terry Maxwell and Kelly McCoy of Angelo State University.

Habitat   Black-hooded snakes are known from 2 principle habitats: (1) Elevations between 1,300 and 5,000 feet in the Chisos and Davis mountains; (2) Both broken and flat terrain in the low desert of Terrell and Val Verde counties. (This easterly, desert-living population was for years known as the Devil's River blackhead snake, *Tantilla rubra diabola*.)

Prey   According to Trans-Pecos *Tantilla* expert Troy Hibbitts, of the University of Texas at Arlington, the black-hooded snake's prey is primarily centipedes, particularly members of the genus *Scolependra*. Extremely abundant in the black-hooded snake's range, these formidable invertebrates reach 9 to 10 inches in length and, armed with the prominent fangs and toxic saliva for which centipedes are noted, are powerful adversaries for black-hooded snakes sometimes barely longer than themselves. (The predatory power of these big centipedes toward small snakes is not merely theoretical, for in 1975 David Easterla observed a big *Scolependra heros* devouring a Texas long-nosed snake approximately as long as the centipede itself.)

A series of photographs shot by Hibbitts south of Alpine shows how diminutive *Tantillas* regularly manage to overcome this agressive prey, however. After seizing a centipede at midbody, Hibbitts' *T. r. cuculatta* hangs on with determination, chewing on the chilopod's midsection despite its attempts to twist around and counterattack. (The black-hood's comparatively heavy skull, armored with rimmed eye sockets, enables it to withstand the centipede's fangs, but adult *T. r. cuculattas* still tend to have scarred heads and necks from encounters of this kind.)

Eventually, the black-hooded snake's mildly paralytic saliva—which is worked into the chilopode's body by its grooved rear teeth—apparently overcame this particular centipede, which at last allowed the snake to swallow it. (In another instance, T. J. LaDuc, et al., report a road-killed desert kingsnake in whose stomach was a freshly swallowed black-hooded *Tantilla*, which itself contained a *Scolependra* centipede.)

Reproduction   Egg-laying. A single captive-laid clutch, of 3 elongate eggs, has been recorded for *T. r. cucullata*. It was deposited June 13, while a female found dead in Big Bend National Park on July 16 contained a pair of eggs whose stage of development suggests that they would have been laid before August. The neonate—an age never before seen or photographed, but whose picture appears here—found by Armstrong appeared similar to most adults except that its pale nuchal collar was less clear in both contrast and definition.

Coloring/scale form   The most distinctive marking of *T. r. cucullata* is its generally solid black head and anterior neck. There are several different nuchal-cephalic patterns, however. In one, except for some pale spots on the lower jaw, the head and neck are wrapped in a uniformly black hood; in another, the dark hood is interrupted across the nape by a light collar sometimes split with blackish pigment over the spine, with white spots occurring on the snout and upper labial scales. (*T. r. cucullata* from the Chisos Mountains often have light collars, while most of those from northern Brewster, Jeff Davis, and Presidio counties have solid dark hoods.)

Among the more easterly population, there is often a prominent white collar, a white-tipped snout, and a pronounced oval or irregularly shaped white spot just below and behind the eye. For 40 years this difference in coloring caused this eastern population to be classified as the Devil's River blackhead snake, *Tantilla rubra diabola*, until it was found that color morphs typical of both populations some-times occur together in the same area. Both the author (Tennant) and Damon Salceies have found disparate color phases in close proximity in Terrell County road cuts and in small canyons near Sanderson. The venter of all color patterns is off-white.

Similar snakes Previously known as the Devil's River blackhead snake, *Tantilla rubra diabola*, the black-hooded snake is apparently again about to be re-named. A 1997 paper by Dixon, Vaughn, and Wilson, of Texas A & M University, proposes that the black-hooded snake be accorded full species status as *T. cucullata* (reserving *T. rubra* for a more southerly ranging group of exclusively Mexican snakes), and the authors expect this nomenclature to be adopted in the near future.

The dark crown of the **plains black-headed snake (11)** is pointed or convex along its rear edge, is not followed by a light collar, and does not extend onto the lower jaw. The **southwestern black-headed snake (12)** has an abbreviated dark skullcap that extends laterally only as far as the middle of its upper labial scales; its lower labials and chin are whitish. Although a narrow pale line is occasionally evident just behind the black cap, this area is not followed by a black band. Both animals also have pinkish venters.

Behavior Little is known of the subterranean habits of West Texas' predominantly fossorial snakes, some of which were discovered only recently—Sherman Minton first described the black-hooded snake in 1956 (current authorities on these *Tantilla* species are Hibbitts, Kathryn Vaughn and James Dixon of Texas A & M University, as well as Buzz Ross of Fort Davis' Rattlesnake Museum).

The sporadic above-ground forays of *T. r. cucullata* apparently occur mostly in June and July, almost always during humid conditions following recent precipitation: each of 6 individuals found on the roads, as well as 2 specimens collected in the field, turned up immediately after rainy periods.

BROWN AND
RED-BELLIED SNAKES
Genus Storeria

Northern Red-bellied Snake, *Storeria occipitomaculata occipito-maculata*
Florida Red-bellied Snake, *Storeria occipitomaculata obscura*

Black Hills Red-bellied Snake, *Storeria occipitomaculata pahasapae*
Northern Brown Snake, *Storeria dekayi dekayi*
Florida Brown Snake, *Storeria dekayi victa*
Midland Brown Snake, *Storeria dekayi wrightorum*
Texas Brown Snake, *Storeria dekayi texana*
Marsh Brown Snake, *Storeria dekayi limnetes*

The viviparous genus *Storeria*—whose name honors physician David H. Storer, author of the 1839 "Ichthyology and Herpetology of Massachusetts"—is contained in the colubrine subfamily *Natricinae*. It is thus closely reated to the water and garter snakes, yet its two North American species, *S. occipitomaculata* and *S. dekayi*, are entirely terrestrial. Like their water and garter snake relatives, both these species are are apt to void musk and smear feces on an aggressor, but unlike aquatic snakes they are secretive little animals that seldom, if ever, bite even when grasped.

Storeria have keeled dorsal and lateral scales and a divided anal plate. Except for **the Florida brown snake (19)**, *S. d. victa*, which has 15 dorsolateral scale rows, other brown snake species have 17 dorsolateral scale rows. Most red-bellied snakes, in contrast, have 15 such rows, but John MacGregor, of Nicholasville, Kentucky, has found what appears to be a first-generation *dekayi/occipitomaculata* hybrid, and it is possible that some of Louisiana's and East Texas' largely dark gray *Storeria* also carry genes from both species.

Brown and red-bellied snakes also usually lack the loreal scale, present in many other snake genera, located between the preoculars and the posterior nasal scale. (Like the handful of other serpents among whom mortality brings about an immediate change in pigmentation, red-bellied snakes tend to turn very dark after death.)

15   NORTHERN RED-BELLIED SNAKE

Storeria occipitomaculata occipitomaculata

Nonvenomous   This tiny snake is entirely harmless to humans.

Size   The smaller of the two U.S. species of *Storeria*, adult northern red-bellied snakes measure from 8 to 10 inches; the record is 16 in.

Abundance   Formerly locally common. Ranging from the Canadian Provinces of

Nova Scotia, New Brunswick, southern Quebec, and the Thunder Bay region of Ontario south to western North Carolina, northern Georgia and eastern Oklahoma, the northern red-bellied snake now occurs in noticeably diminished numbers. It is still more common than the closely related brown snakes, however, at higher elevations, in areas of acidic, boggy, soils, and in dense woodlands.

Habitat   *Storeria occipitomaculata occipitomaculata* favors a microhabitat of rocks and logs in both wooded areas and at the edges of forest clearings. Since these little reptiles apparently do not wander far in search of food, red-bellied snakes are typically closely associated with areas which, while not wet, retain the moisture necessary for the existence of their primarily shell-less mollusk prey.

Prey   In predatory orientation the red-bellied snake is a slug specialist (in captivity, some specimens refuse all other prey, though others will accept earthworms). Interestingly, there are reliable reports of red-bellied snakes eating small snails which they have managed to extract from their shells.

Reproduction   Live-bearing. Where low ground temperatures and a short activity season prevail, red-bellied snakes may take 2 or even 3 years to attain maturity. Breeding occurs both autumn and spring, with vernal couplings documented in both North Carolina and Massachusetts. (These specimens were taken captive in April and May, and then bred repeatedly, giving birth in July and August; parturition in the wild seems to occur between mid-June and August with southern specimens from lower elevations giving birth earlier in the year than those from northern and high-elevation locales.) Litters consist of 5 to more than 15 neonates averaging 3½ inches in length. Although at birth red-bellied snakes are darker and more obscurely marked than adults, females of either the dark or light color phases may give birth to neonates of the opposite phase.

Coloring/scale form   Dorsal pigmentation is variable: tan to russet hues are most common, but a dark gray ground color is seen frequently in northern specimens, and nearly black specimens have been recorded. In all phases a wide, often quite pale mid-dorsal stripe (which tends to be most prominent anteriorly) is normally present, bordered by a thin dark line. Dark-phase northern red-bellied snakes bearing a broad tan to russet mid-dorsal stripe have been reported, however. A dim light lateral line is also sometimes present, especially on pale-phase specimens.

Characteristically, a single light-hued blotch occurs on the nape, flanked by a pair of pale nuchal blotches, which are the source of this snake's scientific name *occipitomaculata* or "spotted back of the head;" these spots may fuse into a light-hued collar. Another whitish spot on the fifth supralabial scale occurs below and slightly to the rear of each eye.

The venter is usually an intense orange-red, but gray- and black-bellied individuals have often been found. An irregular darker stripe may also occur along the outer edges of the ventral scutes. There are 15 rows of dorsolateral scales.

Similar snakes   Among the most beautifully-hued North American serpents, the northern red-bellied snake's dark dorsum and intense red-orange venter is reflected by many other serpents worldwide. The uncommon **Kirtland's snake (95)** has prominent large dark paravertebral and lateral blotches and a prominent row of black dots on each side of its orange venter. The **pine woods snake (37)** has smooth scales and a white belly, while none of the four species of **earth snake (23–26)** found in this animal's range has a red-orange venter.

Behavior   As might be expected, this little reptile is seldom found away from cover, although individuals—perhaps males in search of mates—are sometimes abroad on warm, rainy spring and early summer nights.

Here, unable to defend itself—for this tiny reptile can be overcome by a predator as small as a shrew or bluejay—*S. o. obscura* can only hide its head beneath a body coil. Alternatively, like other *Storeria*, it may employ a death-feigning display: rolling over, mouth agape, and flattening its body and head as though partially crushed. Then, in a strange and enigmatic behavioral pattern, an occasional individual may draw back its upper labial scales, exposing its teeth in a sort of miniature snarl. (John MacGregor reports that this behavior is especially prevalent among gravid females.)

16   FLORIDA RED-BELLIED SNAKE

Storeria occipitomaculata obscura

Nonvenomous   This shy little woodland animal does not bite humans.

Abundance   Locally common. Throughout much of the southeastern U.S. range—which stretches from the Atlantic coasts of northern Florida and southern Georgia, along the Gulf

coasts of the Florida panhandle, most of Alabama, southern Mississippi and Louisiana into eastern Texas—*S. o. obscura* is fairly abundant in damp woodland. In northern Florida it is less common, while at the western boundary of its range in Texas it is rare and quite restricted in distribution.

Size   Most adults are 8 to 10 inches in length, with *S. o. obscura* reaching a maximum of 16 in.

Habitat   The Florida red-bellied snake's favored habitat includes moist, heavily-vegetated hardwood forest; this little reptile is less often found in either upland or flat-country pine forest. Its microhabitat is most often leaf litter and the underside of decaying logs.

Prey   Slugs are the Florida red-bellied snake's primary prey. Richard D. Bartlett has fed newborns on bits of both common garden slugs and snails, and while earthworms are also taken, and as the soil dries during summer, *S. o. obscura* follows its mollusk and annelid prey deeper into the earth along a soil-moisture gradient.

Reproduction   Live-bearing. Litters of *S. o. obscura* number up to 23, with the 2¾- to 4-inch-long young being born between early June and August. Grayer than adults and usually lacking their dark dorsal spots, neonates are marked with a pale band across the nape.

Coloring/scale form   The Florida red-bellied snake is characterized by the three big pale spots behind its head which often form a light-hued collar. Another prominent, black-bordered white spot occurs beneath the eye. A double row of dark flecks usually runs along both sides of the speckled back which, in the southern part of its range, is cinnamon or blue-gray, with faint nuchal spots. Usually, the venter is red.

Yet *S. o. obscura* varies widely in color. Several individuals from East Texas were yellowish above with yellow venters and barely visible nuchal spots (the white spot marking the upper labial scales beneath the eye was present, but lacked a black lower border); another specimen from the same area had a solid dark-brown back and blackish lower sides whose color extended onto the outer edges of its russet ventral scales. A third individual was brown-bellied, and also lacked the black border below its white subocular spot.

Similar snakes   Florida, Texas, and **midland brown snakes (19–21)** have a dark subocular spot, pale cheeks, bellies, and 17 midbody scale rows.

Behavior   See **Northern Red-bellied Snake.**

17   Black Hills Red-bellied Snake

Storeria occipitomaculata pahasapae

Nonvenomous   This little snake is entirely harmless to humans.

Size   Adult at from 8 to 11 inches in length, the Black Hills red-bellied snake only rarely exceeds 15 in.

Abundance   In its pure form, the Black Hills red-bellied snake is currently known to occur only in central western South Dakota and adjacent Wyoming—an area once inhabited by the Pahasapae Tribe, for which this reptile is named. The current size of its population is unknown, but undoubtedly small.

Habitat   This diminutive serpent has a curiously disjunct range probably caused by the expanses of exposed, unsuitable grassland habitat that now separates the *Storeria* populations of the northern Great Plains. (An intergrade population intermediate between the Black Hills and northern red-bellied subspecies of *S. occipitomaculata* occurs from southern Manitoba and Saskatchewan south to northwestern Iowa, and a disjunct population of this intergrade group lives in south-central Nebraska.)

It is thought that these populations were once more uniformly spread across the formerly wooded terrain that prevailed here during the late Pleistocene, for this sort of microenvironment is the Black Hills red-bellied snake's habitat in the mesic uplands where this subspecies remains in relic residency, sheltering beneath both natural cover and human-generated debris.

Prey   Slugs and earthworms are this red-bellied snake's preferred prey but, like other *S. occipitomaculata*, this race also consumes small snails which it removes from their shells.

Reproduction   Live-bearing. The Black Hills red-bellied snake bears 5 to 12 (rarely a few more) neonates averaging about 3½ inches in length.

Coloring/scale form   Even in its pure form, this subspecies seems poorly differentiated from the northern red-bellied snake (like other *S. occipitomaculata*, both dark and light color phases are known). The Black Hills red-bellied snake lacks the northern red-bellied snake's pale nape and nuchal blotches, as well as its characteristic light spot on the upper lip beneath the eye.

However, of the half dozen specimens from central-western South Dakota seen by Richard Bartlett, half had either relatively prominent light-hued neck blotches or blotches fused into a distinct pale collar. All had at least a vestige of the whitish labial spot as well, and two had well-developed labial spots.

Ventral coloration may be yellowish, orange-red, or on occasion dark gray.

Similar snakes   None: within its range, this is the only small woodland snake with a red, yellow, or orange venter and 15 midbody rows of dorsal scales.

Behavior   This serpent's natural history is not well known: it is reportedly active both by day (especially following showers) and on warm spring nights, when males—presumably seeking female pheromone scents—seem most prone to leave cover.

18   NORTHERN BROWN SNAKE

Storeria dekayi dekayi

Nonvenomous   Despite their small size brown snakes may present a formidable bluffing display, raising their flattened foreparts and even making harmless mock strikes.

Abundance   Formerly very common. In bygone years, *S. d. dekayi* was not only a snake of the countryside, but an urban dweller as well. Even in the midst of large towns it seemed to be present under nearly every piece of discarded newspaper, plank, or garden stone in backyards and urban parks.

It was particularly common beneath debris on the sunny banks of urban drainage ditches, and throughout its eastern Ohio and West Virginia, New York and most of New Hampshire, southern Vermont and southeastern Maine range, and was probably the snake most commonly encountered by city dwellers. *Storeria dekayi dekayi* also occurs southward to the Piedmont provinces and the coastal plain North Carolina, but everywhere in its range is absent at higher elevations.

Burgeoning expanses of sterile concrete paving, as well as suburban pressures such as the greatly expanded use of pesticides, have now taken their toll on brown snake populations, and today, in either town or country it is necessary to make a concerted search to find a northern brown snake.

Size   *Storeria dekayi dekayi* reaches adulthood at from 10 to 14 inches in length; the record is just over 19 in.

Habitat   Northern brown snakes have been found beneath flat rocks at the edges of woodland clearings, along fencerows, and beneath natural and manmade surface debris. These secretive little reptiles occur in lowlying areas—including riparian bottomland near water—in open deciduous forest, and high on rocky slopes. They are most common, however, where surface rocks or leaf litter offer cover.

Prey   The primary food of the northern brown snake seems to be slugs, but earthworms, caterpillars, and other such fare may be eaten by a hungry individual.

Reproduction   Live-bearing. This tiny snake most often produces litters of between 3 and 10, although sometimes as many as 20 offspring sometime during the summer months. (More northerly populations or those living at higher and cooler elevations in the south bear their young later in the year than northern brown snakes inhabiting warmer climates.) Neonates are usually between 3 and 4 inches in length, and because they have a prominent whitish neck ring and are often largely unmarked above, they may be mistaken for young ring-necked snakes.

Coloring/scale form   Although the common name is descriptive of this animal's dorsolateral coloring, the shade of brown varies from dark to yellowish, reddish, or olive; more rarely to gray. A clearly defined lighter-hued vertebral stripe is often present, bordered by a row of well-separated black dots. Among the intergrade population inhabiting the Carolinas these dots may be connected over the back, however, by thin dark lines, and may or may not also be present on the lower sides.

The interstitial skin between the northern brown snake's scales is whitish and may be easily visible when the snake inflates or flattens itself in fright. Ventral coloring varies from yellowish to pale brown, whitish, or pinkish, with dark dots at the outermost edges of the ventral scales. A dark diagonal streak usually occurs behind each eye, with a heavier streak normally marking each side of the nape. (Gerry Salmon reports a melanistic northern brown snake found in Dutchess County, New York.)

Similar snakes   Across most of southeastern North Carolina and all of South Carolina the northern brown snake intergrades with its subspecies, the **midland brown snake (20)**, which may be distinguished by its dark cross-dorsal lines. The related **red-bellied snakes (15–17)** also closely resemble brown snakes, although red-bellied snakes lack a dark diagonal marking posterior to the eye and have brilliant red-orange (rarely slate-gray or nearly black) venters.

Behavior All brown snakes inhabit loose, well-drained soils—where they move about among soil crevices and earthworm burrows—although they are equally apt to secrete themselves beneath surface debris. They are occasionally found behind the loose bark on decaying stumps, and a few individuals have been discovered well above ground level in shrubs and vines. This species' activity peaks on warm spring nights—when it may even be found crossing roads. At this time there seems to be a preponderance of males abroad, and it is assumed that they are searching for females.

19 FLORIDA BROWN SNAKE, *Storeria dekayi victa*

Nonvenomous *Storeria dekayi victa* is small and entirely harmless, but if threatened or frightened, it may put on an impressive defensive display, flattening its body, pulling its neck into the same threatening, elevated S-curve as larger serpents, and striking repeatedly (often with its mouth closed). When grasped, it typically squirms about, smearing the contents of its cloaca over the source of its distress.

Abundance The Florida brown snake is common throughout most of peninsular Florida and a bit of southeastern Georgia. The population living in the lower Keys (like much of the other herpetofauna of Florida's Caribbean islands) is considered to be threatened, however.

Size Most adults measure 7 to 10 inches, while *S. d. victa* probably does not get larger than 13 in.

Habitat Macrohabitat includes riparian bottomland, open deciduous woodland and overgrown pastures, but not swampland. The Florida brown snake is rare in sawgrass marshes and often-inundated areas like the Everglades, but it is common in the slightly elevated hardwood hammocks and pinelands scattered among these open wetlands. In microhabitat preference, Florida brown snakes are burrowers partial to the moist conditions often found beneath decaying logs and other woodland debris.

Prey Small terrestrial serpents such as brown, earth, and ring-necked snakes are also drawn to the planks and sheets of corrugated iron that litter abandoned rural outbuildings, for these sheltering planes provide optimal habitat for slugs and earthworms—the principal prey of

Storeria—as well as for the arthropods, annelids, and larval insects that constitute their secondary prey. Here, brown snakes are themselves preyed upon by larger ophiophagous burrowers such as king and coral snakes (it was from the stomach of a coral snake that, in 1892, the type specimen Florida brown snake was recovered, giving rise to this race's designation as "victa," for "victim").

Reproduction   Live-bearing. Most births occur from July to September, with litters consisting of 8 or 9 young, 3½ to 4½ inches in length. Neonates have an unmarked gray-brown dorsum and a pale collar.

Coloring/scale form   Considered by many researchers to be a full species, *Storeria victa* (unlike other brown snakes, it has 15 midbody rows of dorsal scales), most individuals are faintly speckled cinnamon to blue-gray above. There is an indistinct light-colored vertebral stripe bordered by a row of dark spots or smudges, while a wide pale band crosses the rear of the head, followed by a darker band across the nape. Directly below the eye is a pronounced brown spot. The tan or pinkish venter is unmarked except for black dots along its outer edges, and the 15 midbody rows of dorsal scales are strongly keeled.

Similar snakes   The **midland brown snake (20)** has 17 midbody rows of dorsal scales, while the paired dark spots flanking its vertebral stripe are often linked by dark pigment across the spine. The **Florida red-bellied snake (16)** has pale bars occurring on the nape instead of the rear of the skull, a light spot on the fifth upper labial scale, and a red venter.

Behavior   See **Midland Brown Snake.**

20   MIDLAND BROWN SNAKE

Storeria dekayi wrightorum

Nonvenomous   Named for the famous team of Albert Hazen and Margaret Wright, authors of *A Handbook of Snakes of the United States and Canada*, this reptile does not bite human beings. See **Florida Brown Snake.**

Abundance   Well studied over most of its broad eastern range, *S. d. wrightorum* ranges southward from southern Michigan and northern Indiana to southern Georgia, the Florida panhandle, and northeastern

Louisiana. Here, it is often a suburban, backyard snake. According to Robert H. Mount it is numerous in the Alabama highlands, but is less common in the southern part of its range—it is an uncommon snake in Florida—where it has been adversely impacted by two species of South American fire ants. (These exotic insects have proven to be voracious predators of small terrestrial herpetofauna, although live-bearing snakes such as *Storeria* seem to be less heavily predated than egg-laying species.)

Size Although most individuals are much smaller, measuring 9 to 15 inches in length, the record midland brown snake is 20¾ in.

Habitat A resident of damp fields and open woodlands, this race of brown snake is associated with moist microhabitats. Yet, though it is often found along the edges of ponds, marshes, and canals, it does not inhabit truly wet areas, and is instead found most often beneath moisture-retaining natural and manmade debris such as fallen logs (especially pines), newspapers, tarpaper, and discarded lumber lying on higher ground.

Prey The primary prey of *Storeria dekayi* is slugs, but earthworms are a secondary food source. Arthropods, insects, small salamanders, tiny fish, and newly metamorphosed frogs are also sometimes taken.

Reproduction Live-bearing. Breeding takes place both spring and fall, with spermatozoa from autumn pairings being retained in the female's oviducts until her late spring ovulation. Born in mid- to late summer, most litters of the 3- to 3½-inch-long young vary between 5 and 20—although one Alabama female deposited 31 offspring; another, 41.

Coloring/scale form First described by H. Trapido in 1944, the midland brown snake is similar in dorsolateral coloring to other *S. dekayi*, varying from tan through light brown to olive or reddish-brown above. A dorsolateral row of darker spots is present, and though most descriptions stipulate that these dark spots are connected by dark lines across the spine, this is not always the case: in actuality the various races of brown snakes are difficult to identify and, especially in the Carolinas where this subspecies intergrades with the northern brown snake, their differentiating characteristics may overlap.

Among *S. d. wrightorum*, the crown of the head is slightly broader than that of other small serpents found in woodland leaf litter, and normally darker than the body. A light vertebral line is usually present between its sometimes-linked dark dorsolateral spots, and its venter is cream to pinkish-white. A dark subocular blotch on the pale cheeks makes the eye appear quite large, while larger dark temporal and nuchal spots are the midland brown snake's most distinctive marking. The dorsal scales lack apical pits and are arranged in 17 rows. The anal plate is divided.

Similar snakes   The midland brown snake intergrades extensively with the **northern brown snake (18)**, which tends to have a less strongly cross-lined dorsum, along the eastern periphery of its range. Intergrades also occur where the ranges of these two races abut the territory of the **Texas brown snake (21)**, whose dark nuchal spot occupies the entire side of its neck.

The **Florida red-bellied snake (16)** has a pale spot beneath its eye, 15 midbody dorsal scale rows, and a red to black venter. The **pine woods snake (37)** has smooth scales and a white-bordered black line through its eye.

Behavior   Because midland brown snakes find favorable conditions in the soft soil of well-watered suburban yards, they are sometimes found while gardening. Although generally secretive little animals, during cool, damp weather they may move about in the open, even in daylight; in the hottest months brown snakes are nocturnal.

21   TEXAS BROWN SNAKE, *Storeria dekayi texana*

Nonvenomous   See **Marsh Brown Snake.**

Abundance   Common. Texas brown snakes are in no way limited in range to the state for which they are named. In a 200- to 300-mile-wide swath, their range extends from the Rio Grande straight up the Great Plains as far as north-central Minnesota.

In the southern part of this range, Texas brown snakes, as live-bearers, are apparently less susceptible than small egg-laying serpents to attacks by South American fire ants because their newborns seem to be sufficiently vigorous to slip away from these newly introduced insect predators.

Size   Most adults are 9 to 12 inches in length; the record is 18 in.

Habitat   Along the intricate north/south intersection of North America's eastern woodlands and Great Plains, this animal's macrohabitat includes both riparian bottomland and most open deciduous forest. Texas brown snakes also occur in grassland, including overgrown pastures, but they are not as common there as in places where leaf litter offers cover.

Prey Brown snakes' primary prey is slugs, while earthworms are a secondary food source; arthropods, salamanders, minnows, and newly metamorphosed frogs are also occasionally taken.

Reproduction Live-bearing. Breeding may take place both spring and fall, with spermatozoa from autumn pairings remaining in the female's oviducts until her spring ovulation. Most births occur between mid-June and the first week in August: one central Texas female found in late April devoured slugs and small earthworms until late May, by which time she had become too swollen with developing young to continue feeding. (Brown snakes exhibit the evolutionarily advanced trait of placental nourishment of their offspring during the latter stages of fetal development.)

On June 12 this female gave birth to 11 very active, 4-inch-long young. After their first shed at 9 to 11 days of age, these neonates were offered Q-tips swabbed with the scents of fish, tadpoles, and worms, but only the scent of slugs and snails elicited a feeding response. Other litters have contained 3 to 27 young, measuring from 3½ to 4½ inches.

Coloring/scale form Dark-speckled reddish brown above, with a pale vertebral stripe, adult Texas brown snakes have bold white posterior labial scales. Below and behind the eye the fifth through seventh upper labial scales are blotched with one or more big brown spots; another large brown marking occupies the side of the neck. The creamy venter has a few black dots along its sides. Neonates have dark-speckled gray-brown backs and sides, dark brown heads with little white on their cheeks, and a pale band across their napes. This race's dorsal scales lack apical pits, are arranged in 17 rows, and its anal plate is divided.

Similar snakes Along the eastern periphery of its range the Texas brown snake intergrades with its subspecies, the **midland brown snake (20)**, a race distinguished (often with difficulty) by its often cross-dorsally dark-lined back. Another subspecies, the **marsh brown snake (22)**, has a small, dark horizontal bar that lines its light-hued temporal and postocular scales and generally unmarked pale labial scales.

Behavior See **Midland Brown Snake.**

Storeria dekayi limnetes

Nonvenomous When threatened, this little reptile can present a formidable coil-and-strike demeanor, lunging forward, mouth closed, in pseudo-strikes. Despite its small stature, the abruptness of its vigorous mock defense is sometimes enough to deter a not-very-determined predator.

Abundance *Storeria dekayi limnetes* is a somewhat uncommon inhabitant of the northwestern Gulf's coastal prairie. Here, in a 60- to 80-mile-wide strip of the seaside plain it replaces other brown snake races, inhabiting marshy estuarine grasslands and inland savannahs, where it hides in grassy hummocks.

Size Adult size is 9 to 13 inches; the record is 16 in.

Habitat Marsh brown snakes also shelter in the high-tide flotsam of the Texas coast's barrier islands—the type specimen from which this subspecies' description is drawn was collected under driftwood on Galveston Island—where *S. d. limnetes* is the predominant small "garden snake" found around houses.

Prey Away from the coast, the marsh brown snake feeds mostly on slugs. On the saline barrier islands where slugs cannot survive, *S. d. limnetes* presumably preys on the earthworms, arthropods, small salamanders, minnows, and newly metamorphosed frogs that also constitute part of the diet of inland populations.

Reproduction Live-bearing. Most small serpents are so short-lived that they must reproduce rapidly, and although nothing is recorded of reproduction in this race, it is probably as prolific as other *S. dekayi*. See **Texas Brown Snake.**

Coloring/scale form All five U.S. brown snakes are also referred to as DeKay's snakes in reference to James Ellsworth DeKay who, early in the early nineteenth century, first recorded the northern race along the Atlantic seaboard. (The marsh brown snake's subspecies designation, *limnetes*, refers to the slim horizontal bar or line marking its temporal and postocular scales.) Its faintly dark-speckled back is brown, usually with a paler vertebral stripe; its sometimes partially speckled venter is off-white.

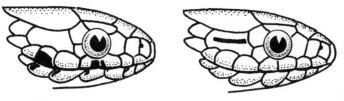

Texas brown snake   *Marsh brown snake*

Similar snakes   A horizontally lined temporal scale and unmarked upper and lower labial scales differentiate this race from its more inland subspecies, the **midland** and **Texas brown snakes (20, 21)**. Similarly pale-collared as a newborn, the **southern ring-necked snake (27)** has a solid dark gray back and a black-spotted yellow to reddish-orange venter.

Behavior   Like their relatives the garter and water snakes, brown snakes' defensive behavior includes excreting musk from anal glands located in the cloaca, then squirming about to smear musk and feces over the source of their distress. Sometimes this species also flattens its body and rolls over, mouth agape, as if injured.

Although not popular as captive animals, brown snakes thrive in terrariums—although as devoted burrowers they are almost never seen—living as long as 7 years.

EARTH SNAKES
Genus Virginia

Eastern Earth Snake, *Virginia valeriae valeriae*
Mountain Earth Snake, *Virginia valeriae pulchra*
Western Earth Snake, *Virginia valeriae elegans*
Rough Earth Snake, *Virginia striatula*

Both species, *V. valeriae* and *V. striatula,* are contained in the colubrine subfamily *Natricinae,* most of whose members are water snakes. *Virginia,* however, is an entirely terrestrial genus characterized, in part, by dorsolateral scales that occur in either 15 or 17 rows. All three subspecies of *Virginia valeriae* have weakly keeled dorsolateral scales, at least posteriorly, while the dorsal—and particularly, the vertebral—scales of *Virginia striatula* are prominently keeled.

Because a preocular scale is absent in this genus a horizontal loreal scale touches the anterior edge of the eye, and the anal plate is divided. Neither species of earth snake has prominent dorsal markings, but either may be finely peppered with tiny dark dots—appropriate coloration for these flat snouted little snakes which spend most of their time burrowing into loose soil and are usually found at the surface beneath rocks and debris in moist woodland, forest edges, and clearings.

23   EASTERN EARTH SNAKE

Virginia valeriae valeriae

Nonvenomous   Eastern earth snakes are too small to bite humans, but often smear their cloacal contents on their captor if they are picked up.

Abundance   This little reptile's name honors Valeria Blaney, the 19th-century collector of the type specimen. It is sporadically dispersed, but sometimes locally common throughout a broad southeastern range that reaches from the Gulf Coast of Alabama and Florida panhandle (where it is rare), northeast through Georgia, the Carolinas, and Virginia, to Maryland, Delaware, southeastern Pennsylvania and the entire state of New Jersey. The eastern earth snake is not found at high elevations, but in less montane terrain west of the Appalachians a more westerly population lives in parts of Tennessee, Kentucky, West Virginia, and southern Ohio.

Size   Most adults measure 7 to 13 inches in length; occasional individuals reach as much as 15 in.

Habitat   Primarily pine forest. This subspecies also occurs in upland hardwood forest, sandhills, pine flatwoods, and second-growth scrub habitat, however; its microhabitat is most often the damp soil beneath tree litter, logs, and human-generated debris.

Prey   Eastern earth snakes feed mainly on earthworms, but small snails and insects are also sometimes taken.

Reproduction   Live-bearing. Neonates are 3¾ to 4 inches long, and number 2 to 15 per litter; one 11½-inch-long female *Virginia valeriae* deposited 7, 4-inch-long charcoal-gray neonates on August 20.

Coloring/scale form   The dorsum is unmarked rusty-brown, more reddish in color laterally, and a vaguely defined pale collar may even be present. In most cases the venter is white, although it may be dark brown, tan, or grayish, sometimes with a yellowish wash. The smooth dorsolateral scales are arranged, most often over the entire length of the snake, in 15 (rarely, 17) rows. Although faint keels may appear on the scales along the posterior spine, in general only hairline seams that resemble keels mark the mid-line of the scales. There is no preocular scale, the loreal scale is horizontally elongated, and there are both a pair of small postocular scales and 6 supralabials. The snout is rounded rather than pointed.

Similar snakes   The **rough earth snake (26)** is grayer, without a russet lateral cast. It has a more pointed snout, only 5 supralabials and several vertebral rows of strongly keeled dorsal scales. The **crowned snakes (5, 6)** living in this animal's range have chocolate-capped heads, pinkish bellies, no loreal, and a single postocular scale.

Behavior   Eastern earth snakes are burrowers, appearing at the surface only when conditions are optimal—usually beneath flat rocks, fallen tree trunks, and human-generated debris. When exposed in these hiding places, this tiny reptile's only defense is to hide its head beneath a body coil, although a threatened individual may occasionally make little feinting strikes. During hot weather the lack of moisture in the upper layers of the soil brings about subterranean aestivation, and in the southern part of its range *V. v. valeriae* is more likely to be seen on the surface during the cooler months.

24   MOUNTAIN EARTH SNAKE

Virginia valeriae pulchra

Nonvenomous   This tiny, harmless snake is reluctant to bite, but when disturbed it may make numerous feinting strikes or, alternatively, hide its head beneath a body coil.

Abundance   Population statistics of the mountain earth snake are unknown, but it is not currently protected by either of the states (Pennsylvania and West Virginia) in which it occurs.

Size   Adult at 7 to 9 inches in length, the mountain earth snake rarely exceeds 11 inches.

Habitat   This race of the smooth earth snake occurs in a narrow, north/south band that runs through western Pennsylvania and eastern West Virginia's uplands. Neil Richmond (1954) defines this habitat as "unglaciated Allegheny high plateaus and the Allegheny Mountain section of the Appalachian Plateau."

Here, *V. v. pulchra* occupies grassy hillsides, stream edges, the edges of deciduous forests, or where pastures and woodland abut. Its microhabitat includes the sheltered space beneath flat rocks, fallen trees, and other such natural forest debris as well the cover offered by manmade trash.

Prey   This little reptile seems to feed almost entirely on earthworms. Some authors report that slugs, cutworms, grubs, and other insect larvae are also eaten, but these do not seem to constitute preferred prey.

Reproduction   Female mountain earth snakes produce between 3 and 7 live young in mid- to late summer. Neonates average 4 inches in length and are often darker and even more drab than the adults.

Coloring/scale form   Dorsally and laterally the mountain earth snake varies from gray to reddish, its color often closely matching the soil and rocks on which it is found. (When that soil has reddish iron pigments, this small snake's Latin designation, "pulchra," or "pinkish," is particularly apt.) Its dorsal scales, which are often keeled, occur in 15 rows anteriorly, 17 rows from midbody rearward. There are 6 upper labial scales, and the venter is whitish, sometimes with a greenish sheen.

Similar snakes   The **eastern earth snake (23)** usually has 15 scale rows along its entire body length. **Brown snakes (18, 20)** have preocular scales, but lack a loreal, have strongly keeled body scales and a more bluntly rounded snout. The **northern red-bellied snake (15)** has a red, orange, or rarely, gray or black belly; the **eastern worm snake (34)** has only 13 rows of midbody scales, the lowermost lateral row or two of which, as well as its venter, are pink.

Behavior   Although they can be common in places, mountain earth snakes are so secretive that sizable populations may go unnoticed. Because these snakes burrow in times of drought, during dry periods even diligent turning of rocks in prime habitat may disclose none, despite the fact that many individuals may be found when turning the same rocks following a heavy spring or summer rain. In wet weather earth snakes may even be encountered moving about in the open both day and night: during one torrential summer rain Richard Bartlett found a number of mountain earth snakes attempting to cross an interstate highway in northern West Virginia, although traffic caused most to fail in their attempt.

WESTERN EARTH SNAKE

Virginia valeriae elegans

Nonvenomous   Western earth snakes do not bite humans.

Abundance   Generally locally common, although the western earth snake seems to be less abundant in the eastern part of its range. *Virginia valeriae elegans* occupies a complex and somewhat bifurcated territory, however. East of the Mississippi valley (which, for the most part it does not inhabit) this snake occupies a long north-south stretch of low-lying terrain reaching from the Gulf Coast of Mississippi and eastern Louisiana north through western Tennessee and Kentucky into parts of central Indiana.

West of the Mississippi valley the western earth snake is found, in a much broader range, from central Texas' Edwards Plateau (in whose oak/juniper savannah *V. v. elegans* can be locally abundant), northeast through northern Louisiana, most of Arkansas, western Oklahoma and Missouri to southern Illinois, and even south-central Iowa.

Size   Adult western earth snakes measure 7 to 13 inches in length.

Habitat   Microhabitat is most often the damp soil beneath tree litter, the underside of logs, and the often humid layer of topsoil and detritus found beneath human-generated debris.

Prey   Western earth snakes feed mainly on earthworms, but small snails and insects also sometimes constitute prey.

Reproduction   Live-bearing. One 11-inch-long North Texas female gave birth on August 20 to 7, 4-inch-long charcoal-gray neonates.

Coloring/scale form   The uniformly reddish-tan dorsum is unmarked except for a pale, dimly defined vertebral stripe, and the dark hairline seams (that resemble keels) found in the centers of some of the scales adjacent to the faintly keeled vertebral scales found on the posterior portion of the back; otherwise, the 17 midbody rows of dorsal scales are smooth. The venter is unmarked white, sometimes with a yellowish wash, the forward edge of the eye is touched by a horizontally lengthened loreal scale while a pair of small postoculars borders the rear of the eye. There are usually 6 upper labial scales, and the anal plate is divided.

Similar snakes   The **rough earth snake (26)** is grayer, without a russet cast; it has 5 supralabial scales and several rows of keeled vertebral

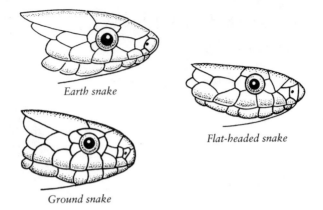

Earth snake

Flat-headed snake

Ground snake

scales. The **flat-headed snake** (10) has a slimmer body with a flat-tened, dark-capped head, a salmon-pink venter, no loreal scale, a single postocular, and 15 rows of smooth dorsal scales. The **ground snake** (33) has 15 or fewer rows of smooth dorsal scales, a small preocular separating its eye from its loreal scale, and a faintly braided appearance due to its lighter-hued scale borders.

Behavior   Although primarily fossorial, western earth snakes appear at the surface when the soil is cool and moist on a summer night. (Among sumac-covered limestone ledges in eastern Kansas, Abilene Zoo director Jack Joy found *V. valeriae* only on two or three April days, when they appeared under nearly every large stone. In exactly the same spot, during the summer he turned up numerous worm and ring-necked snakes but never another western earth snake.)

In hot weather the lack of moisture in surface soil brings about subterranean aestivation, and *V. valeriae* is more likely to emerge during spring and fall: as late as December in central Texas these animals may be active beneath boards and sun-warmed sheets of fallen metal siding.

26   ROUGH EARTH SNAKE, *Virginia striatula*

Nonvenomous   This little snake is not big enough to bite humans.

Abundance   Formerly, much more common. The rough earth snake is another species with separate eastern and western populations separated by the

Mississippi valley. (This riparian corridor's ancient embayment as an inland-reaching finger of salt water is thought by some herpetologists to explain the continued absence there of certain reptiles and amphibians.)

East of this low-lying strip of land, *Virginia striatula* was formerly abundant in northeastern Louisiana, most of Mississippi, southern Alabama, Florida's panhandle and southern Georgia, but throughout this area its numbers have declined in recent years due to the infestation of newly established South American fire ants. This decline is less evident in the rough earth snake's eastern Carolinas and southeastern Virginia range.

West of the Mississippi corridor, *Virginia striatula* is found in most of Louisiana and Arkansas, southern Missouri, and eastern Oklahoma, as well as in the eastern half of Texas—where its range stops abruptly at the edge of the state's arid western rangeland. This demarcation has also halted the spread of fire ants, which cannot tolerate dry soil, but to the east these insects have taken over much of the rough earth snake's microhabitat beneath surface debris. In sheltered sites where, until recently, during damp spring weather dozens of rough earth snakes could be found in a few hours, nothing now exists but myriad fire ant swarms.

Size *Virginia striatula* may reach 12½ inches in length, but even at this size it is no thicker in diameter than a pencil.

Habitat Macrohabitat is primarily open woodland, either pine or deciduous. Here, rough earth snakes are largely fossorial, generally appearing at the surface only when the soil is moist from recent rain. Microhabitat is the sheltered, semi-subterranean layer found beneath fallen leaves, pine needles, and the rusting roofing metal that litters abandoned farms.

Prey The stomachs of 45 *V. striatula* contained only earthworms.

Reproduction Live-bearing. According to J. K. Stewart, "*Virginia striatula* represents a stage in . . . evolution in which placental nourishment supplements yolk nutrition [with a consequent] enhancement of newborn quality."

Sixteen litters ranged in number from 3 to 8 young, measuring 3 to 4½ inches in length.

Coloring/scale form Rough earth snakes are unmarked grayish brown above (newborns have a pale collar) with slightly darker pigmentation around the eyes and on the upper labial scales; the belly is creamy white. There are 17 midbody rows of dorsal scales—several of the vertebral rows are keeled, hence the "rough" of its common name, as well as the "striatula," or "striped" of its Latin designation. A horizontally elongate loreal scale touches the front of the eye, and there are 2 small postocular scales, typically 5 upper labials, and usually a divided anal plate.

Similar snakes Most similar is the **eastern earth snake (23)**, which has a more rusty-hued back and lower sides, 6 upper labials, and entirely smooth dorsal scales. **Crowned, flat-headed, and black-headed snakes (5–13)** have tan dorsums, dark-crowned heads with no loreal scale, a single postocular, and smooth dorsal scales.

Behavior The rough earth snake's lightly shielded head is less effective in rooting through hardened soil than the hooked or armored rostral scutes of larger burrowing serpents, but its pointed snout allows it to penetrate the moist loam where its annelid prey is most plentiful. (Since *V. striatula* tends to be a rather shallow burrower, even a few warm midwinter days bring these little reptiles to the surface.)

RING-NECKED SNAKES
Genus Diadophis

Southern Ring-necked Snake, *Diadophis punctatus punctatus*
Northern Ring-necked Snake, *Diadophis punctatus edwardsii*
Key Ring-necked Snake, *Diadophis punctatus acricus*
Mississippi Ring-necked Snake, *Diadophis punctatus stictogenys*
Prairie Ring-necked Snake, *Diadophis punctatus arnyi*
Regal Ring-necked Snake, *Diadophis punctatus regalis*

The genus *Diadophis*, known scientifically since Carolus Linneaus' classification of the natural world in 1766, is part of the colubrine subfamily *Xenodontinae*. It is characterized by smooth dorsolateral scales, a loreal scale, and a divided anal plate. It is restricted to the U.S., Canada, and northern Mexico, and contains only a single species, *D. punctatus*, which occurs in a number of races, all of which intergrade with geographically adjacent groups. All, except for the Florida Keys ring-neck and the regal ring-neck of the Southwest, among which the pale nuchal collar may be muted or lacking, can be identified by their yellowish-cream to brilliant orange to orange-red nuchal collars.

Harmless to humans and traditionally classed as nonvenomous, ring-necked snakes actually have a mildly toxic saliva to aid in overcoming their small prey. The eastern members of this genus occupy woodlands, plains, prairies, and, often, backyards. When startled, members of these species elevate their posterior bodies to display their often bright undertail coloring. This an aposematic display that may signal danger to avian carnivores by suggesting the coral snake's bright hues. Or, it may indicate unpalatability, for small mammalian hunters sometimes regurgitate ring-necked snakes or even release them after a single bite, wiping their mouths against the ground as if trying to rid themselves of an unpleasant taste. Ophidian predators such as coral and kingsnakes generally eat ring-necked snakes without distress, but John MacGregor reports some fatalities among captive *Lampropeltis* that had just eaten a ring-neck.

27   SOUTHERN RING-NECKED SNAKE

Diadophis punctatus punctatus

Nonvenomous   Ring-necked snakes are members of the uneven-toothed subfamily *Xenodontinae*, which is characterized by slightly longer (but still minuscule) posterior teeth. The salivary glands of this group secrete enzymes that slowly immobilize their tiny prey, but ring-necks almost never bite when handled and are not dangerous.

Abundance   The southern ring-necked snake is generally very common throughout the Southeast's Gulf and Atlantic coastal plains, occupying all of Florida, southeastern Alabama and Georgia, and the eastern Carolinas and Virginia. Yet in the southern part of this little reptile's range many of its sheltered microhabitats are now infested with South American fire ants—exotic predators that threaten to extirpate much of the region's small herpetofauna, especially egg-layers like the ring-necks.

Size   Adults average 6 inches, with a maximum size of 10 in.

Habitat   Damp meadows and woodlands are the favored habitat, where several ring-necked snakes may share the lower layers of a rotting log or live beneath the same piece of discarded roofing material. Dry hardwood forest, pinelands, and residential areas are also occupied, and individuals are sometimes found trapped in swimming pools.

Prey   Southern ring-necked snakes feed mainly on earthworms and slugs, located by scent, as well as on small vertebrates. The latter, which may include salamanders, ground skinks and other terrestrial lizards, smaller snakes, and newly metamorphosed frogs, are also located by scent beneath woodland ground cover.

Reproduction Egg-laying. Two to 8 elongate, ¾-inch-long eggs are laid during summer in moist soil or within rotting logs; the 3- to 4-inch-long young can emerge in as little as 5 weeks.

In contrast to the activity pattern of most serpents, among which the males move about most widely, female *Diadophis punctatus*, which are also larger than males, travel farthest beyond their home territory on journeys to their (sometimes communally used) nesting sites.

Coloring/scale form The southern ring-neck's gray-black dorsum is punctuated by a broad, usually unbroken yellow nuchal ring; darker pigment occurs on its crown and supralabials. The golden venter orange-red under the tail is marked with a prominent row of large half-moon-shaped dark spots along its centerline. These spots are the punctuation—"punctatus" in Latin—of this animal's scientific name. There are 15 (sometimes 17) forebody rows of dorsal scales.

Similar snakes The **Key ring-necked snake (29)** lacks a distinct neck ring, and the **Mississippi ring-necked snake (30)** has a narrower neck ring, often interrupted by black pigment over its spine, and a double row of much smaller black crescents lining its venter.

Behavior Like other brightly under-tailed *Diadophis*, the southern ring-neck employs a defensive combination of color and posture that includes hiding its head beneath a body coil, twisting its caudal section over to expose its orange-red underside, and voiding musk and feces.

28 NORTHERN RING-NECKED SNAKE

Diadophis punctatus edwardsii

Nonvenomous Northern ring-necked snakes do not corkscrew the undertail as a defense mechanism, and when captured seldom bite, although they freely void feces, urates, and musk on one's hands.

Abundance Common (although, like all *Diadophis* the northern ring-necked snake is so secretive it is seen less often than its numbers would suggest) throughout a very large range that extends south from Nova Scotia and southeastern Ontario to the mountain counties of northern Alabama and Georgia. Its subspecies name honors 18th-century ornithologist and author of *The Natural History of North Carolina*, George Edwards.

Size *Diadophis punctatus edwardsii* is the largest ring-neck subspecies east of the Mississippi. Typically between 10 and 14 inches in length, occasional specimens may exceed 18 in.; the record is just under 28 inches.

Habitat Everywhere in its territory, *D. p. edwardsii*, is primarily a woodland animal, yet it is also associated with fencerows, forest openings, and pond edges. Here, it dwells beneath rocks, logs, leaf mats, and other terrestrial debris. Northern ring-necked snakes seem to be especially common in logged areas where stumps are left in the ground to decompose, and in such situations they may congregate behind the loosened bark. These little snakes are also found in roadside trash dumps—tarpaper and shingle piles provide an ideal habitat—as well as beneath garden and lawn ornaments in suburban settings. (Human detritus left in moist areas is a magnet for snakes. In a southern Ohio woodland, beneath a discarded wooden door, D. Craig McIntyre found a northern ring-neck and a northern brown snake, as well as an eastern milk snake seeking these smaller serpents as food, and a northern copperhead taking shelter in a spot also frequented by its rodent prey.)

Prey Most northern ring-necked snakes seem to prefer salamanders as prey, but where these amphibians are difficult to find, *D. p. edwardsii* may prey on small frogs, snakes, skinks, and, occasionally, worms (one large captive female from Massachusetts readily consumed nightcrawlers).

Reproduction Almost all ring-necked snakes deposit eggs that hatch in 7 to 9 weeks, depending on the temperature of the medium in which they are laid. Clutches vary dramatically in size, with eggs numbering from one to a dozen; the hatchlings are 5 to 6 inches long and darker than adults, though they have a paler collar.

Coloring/scale form Whether slate, blue-gray, or olive in color, the northern ring-neck's smooth dorsolateral scales have a satiny luster. The neck ring is nearly always complete (not broken mid-dorsally) and may be yellow, golden, or orange. The yellow to yellow-orange venter (the subcaudal scales beneath the tail are of the same hue as the belly) most often entirely lacks black markings. If present, these markings will be small, located in a single midventral line, and missing from many scutes. There are usually 15 forebody rows of dorsal scales.

Where intergradation with the southern ring-neck occurs in the Carolinas and Georgia, individual snakes may have heavier ventral spotting, however, richer orange bellies, and a broken nuchal collar (intergradation with the Mississippi ring-necked snake in central Alabama, western Tennessee, and western Kentucky also produces snakes with variable characteristics).

Similar snakes   **Northern and midland brown snakes (18, 20)** have a whitish collar, a pinkish belly, and keeled scales. The **northern red-bellied snake (15)** has three light-hued, but not bright yellow or orange, spots on its nape and posterior crown, keeled scales, and (usually) a vivid red-orange venter.

Behavior   The northern ring-necked snake is adept at remaining hidden, but seldom actually burrows. Under cover of darkness, especially on rainy spring and summer nights, it may emerge from hiding and wander rather extensively.

29   KEY RING-NECKED SNAKE

Diadophis punctatus acricus

Nonvenomous   Tiny *D. p. acricus* does not bite humans.

Abundance   Rare. Legally protected by the state of Florida, where it is endemic, *D. p. acricus* is threatened by human encroachment into its restricted Florida's Keys range. Small serpents are often able to adapt to residential areas, but the Keys are now so thoroughly covered with paving, commercial development, and human housing (which brings with it the threat to small serpents of myriad canine and feline domestic carnivores) that the native race of ring-necked snake has lost most of its limited natural environment.

Size   The few observed adults have been 6 or 7 inches in length.

Habitat   The primary habitat of *D. p. acricus* is the sparsely vegetated hardwood hammocks and pinelands of the lower Keys, particularly Big Pine and the Torch Keys—tiny scraps of land that still sustain many of Florida's other imperiled island-living animals.

Prey   Herpetologist John Decker, who has studied *D. p. acricus* in the wild, found this subspecies' favored food species to be the tiny Cuban greenhouse frogs now plentiful on the Keys. Other small frogs and their tadpoles (taken from rain-filled limestone depressions), earthworms, anoles, and geckos also constitute prey.

Reproduction   Egg-laying. A single clutch of 3 very small, elongate white eggs has been reported for the Key ring-necked snake. After incubation in moistened vermiculite these eggs hatched into 3-inch-long newborns, one of which showed signs of albinism; the others resembled their parent. All fed on mouse tails and, after a few weeks, were released.

Coloring/scale form   The Key ring-neck's dorsum is slate gray, with slightly darker pigment occurring on its crown and labial scales; the yellow collar of the mainland and upper Keys–living southern ring-neck is absent or indistinct. The venter is yellow, shading to orange-red beneath the tail, and there are 15 forebody rows of dorsal scales.

Similar snakes   The **southern ring-necked snake** (27) has a much darker back and sides, a bright yellow nuchal collar, and darker pigment on its supralabial scales; the **midland brown snake** (20) has keeled dorsal scales.

Behavior   Like other ring-necked snakes, *D. p. acricus* burrows into leaf litter—which is often scarce in its barren habitat, for in many places the small, low-lying offshore keys where this snake is still found are devoid of ground cover. Here, in an exceptionally harsh, largely saline, mangrove- and exposed-limestone habitat, Decker reports that *D. p. acricus* seeks shelter beneath washed-up chunks of reef-coral rock.

---

30   MISSISSIPPI RING-NECKED SNAKE
Diadophis punctatus stictogenys

Nonvenomous   See **Southern Ring-necked Snake.**

Abundance   Abundant in much of the northern part of its range—a divided territory that, in the East, includes northeastern Texas and Louisiana, southeastern Arkansas and Missouri, all of Mississippi, and western Kentucky, Tennessee, and Alabama—*D. p. stictogenys* is less numerous in its disjunct southwestern territory along the Texas and western Louisiana Gulf Coast.

Much of this area is treeless grass- and marshland, which is not optimal habitat for the primarily woodland-living Mississippi ring-neck, but its scarcity here is more likely due to the fact that many of its sheltered microhabitats are now infested with South American fire ants. These fierce little insects are especially destructive of oviparous snakes like the ring-necks, whose eggs are vulnerable to the ants' depredations.

Size   Adult Mississippi ring-necked snakes are 10 to 12 inches in length.

Habitat   Throughout its range *D. p. stictogenys* is primarily a woodland animal, though it is often found along the forested borders of damp meadows and in overgrown fields near water. As with most semi-fossorial snakes, the principal factor determining its presence is the availability of cover: either the natural shelter of fallen logs and plant detritus or human-generated debris such as discarded sheets of metal siding.

Prey   Ring-necked snakes are scent hunters which search woodland ground cover for smaller snakes as well as for salamanders, skinks, small frogs, earthworms, slugs, and insect larvae. The Mississippi ring-neck is itself a mid-level hunter in the ophiophagous predatory pyramid, however, for in the wild it has been found in the stomachs of larger serpent-eaters such as the coral snake, and in captivity kingsnakes feed readily on ring-necks.

Reproduction   Egg-laying. See **Southern Ring-necked Snake**.

Coloring/scale form   The Mississippi ring-neck's slate-gray dorsum, separated from its black head by a bright-yellow nuchal collar, is unmistakable. Its venter, cream beneath the snout, shades to yellow at midbody and darkens to orange under the tail. Among eastern specimens the belly and underchin—referred to by the Greek "stiktos" for "spotted"—are patterned with a double row of tiny black scallops; in the Texas population most individuals have scattered black ventral crescents. There are usually 15 forebody rows of dorsal scales.

Similar snakes   The Mississippi ring-neck is a race poorly differentiated from both its easterly subspecies, the southern ring-neck, and its western subspecies, the prairie ring-neck. In fact, the Mississippi ring-neck may be only an intergrade form between these two races. The **southern ring-necked snake (27)** has a single midbelly row of large black half-moons, however, while the **prairie ring-necked snake (31)** has small, scattered black ventral crescents and (usually) 17 forebody rows of dorsal scales and a reddish undertail.

Behavior   See **Southern Ring-necked Snake**.

Diadophis punctatus arnyi

Nonvenomous   See **Southern Ring-necked Snake.**

Abundance   Variable. In the southern part of a huge range that stretches from central Texas north across Oklahoma and most of Kansas and Missouri to southern Iowa and eastern Nebraska, *D. p. arnyi* is uncommon in many places. Yet in other parts of the Great Plains the prairie ring-necked snake can outnumber all other serpents: herpetologist H. S. Fitch once captured 279 individuals beneath two dozen pieces of sheet metal in a single hilltop field in eastern Kansas.

Ring-necked snakes apparently follow one another to such communal shelters using the scents left by their musky dermal pheromones; when 40 individuals were released in an enclosure containing 12 evenly spaced plates, the four plates under which the first 5 snakes hid subsequently attracted the whole group, leaving the other, non-scented shelters unoccupied.

Size   Adults are 10 to 14 inches long; the record is 16½ in.

Habitat   Despite its name, the prairie ring-neck often occurs beneath an open canopy of tree branches; in the western part of its range it also occupies open grassland and mountain slopes, however.

Prey   See **Mississippi Ring-necked Snake.**

Reproduction   Egg-laying. See **Southern Ring-necked Snake.**

Coloring/scale form   Separating this subspecies' black head from its dark-gray back is a golden neck ring which, in only 17 of the 220 individuals examined by Troy Hibbitts, of the University of Texas at Arlington, was interrupted over the spine by dark pigment. The gray lips, chin, and throat are speckled with black, while both the yellow venter and the orange-red undertail are randomly marked with little black half-moons. The dorsal scales occur in 15 or 17 forebody rows (about half the population has 15 rows, the other half, 17).

Similar snakes   The **Mississippi ring-necked snake (30)** usually has 15 anterior rows of dorsal scales and a row of small, dark, paired half-moons lining the center of its belly. According to Hibbitts, an expert on *D. punctatus*, throughout Texas' Trans-Pecos the prairie ring-neck intergrades with its western subspecies, the **regal ring-necked snake (32)**, a slightly larger, lighter-gray race that often lacks a pale neck ring; it has 17 dorsal scale rows on its forebody and an orange venter whose color extends 1 or 2 scale rows up onto its lower sides. (In the Guadalupe Mountains some ring-necks are prairie type, some are intermediate between it and the regal ring-neck, and some are pure examples of the western subspecies.)

Behavior   Prairie ring-necked snakes, whose name honors Samuel Arny, a 19th-century Kansas collector who recorded this race's type specimen, are very localized reptiles. Marked specimens may be re-captured as much as a year after their release, and so close to the same spot that this animal's usual range is thought to be no more than 400 feet in diameter. Travel beyond this distance probably rep-resents only a seasonal movement between winter brumation and summer egg-laying sites. If adequate refuge from low winter tempera-tures is not available within its small summer range, *D. p. arnyi* may venture several hundred yards in search of high, rocky ground with deep crevices to provide the subsurface drainage necessary for suc-cessful dormancy. Flooded dens cause considerable mortality among snakes which, due to cold weather, are unable to relocate to drier quarters.

32   REGAL RING-NECKED SNAKE
Diadophis punctatus regalis

Nonvenomous   When threatened, even large regal ring-necked snakes usually do no more than evert the brightly colored undertail.

Abundance   Common. Widely distributed (mostly as an intergrade with the prairie ring-necked snake) throughout Texas' Trans-Pecos and Stock-ton Plateau regions, *D. p. regalis* is seldom seen because it keeps to the cover of shrub or cactus roots and rock crevices.

Size   *Diadophis punctatus regalis* is named for its comparatively statuesque—if not quite regal—proportions. Troy Hibbitts, who has studied these animals intensively in their natural habitat, has recorded nine specimens from the Trans-Pecos which measured more than 19½ inches in length while, in Santa Fe County, New Mexico, herpetologist William B. Love photographed the 32½-inch record-length regal ring-neck whose picture is included here.

Habitat   In northwestern Texas the regal ring-necked snake (which occurs here primarily as an intergrade with its more easterly prairie subspecies) occupies both prairie and mesquite brushland. In the Trans-Pecos this animal inhabits environments ranging from the evergreen-covered slopes of the Davis and Guadalupe Mountains to the limestone-floored desert of Terrell and Val Verde counties. Other varied microhabitats include the spaces beneath large rocks and fallen yucca logs, as well as the interior and shriveled roots of dead agaves, often those situated near sporadically flowing streambeds.

Prey   Like other ring-necked snakes, *D. p. regalis* feeds primarily on reptiles, principally smaller snakes. These are grasped and chewed vigorously until immobilized by the salivary toxins that flow into the punctures made by the ring-neck's enlarged upper rear teeth.

Reproduction   Egg-laying. Two to 5 proportionately large, elongate eggs are laid in early summer.

Coloring/scale form   Regal ring-necked snakes vary in dorsal coloring. Some are unmarked light gray above, while others exhibit a full or partial pale nuchal band. Hibbitts has found that pale-collared *D. p. regalis* are most likely to be found in the contact zone with the golden neck-ringed prairie subspecies, although individuals with light-hued nuchal bands occur throughout areas where solid-hued individuals predominate, such as Texas' Trans-Pecos and eastern New Mexico.

The yellowish lower labial scales are marked with tiny black spots which extend rearward within the band of yellowish-orange ventral pigment that extends 1 or 2 scale rows upward from the venter onto the lower sides. Randomly placed black half-moons spot the yellow to dark gray forebelly; posteriorly, the venter is less heavily spotted as it darkens to red under the tail. There are usually 17 rows of dorsal scales on the forebody.

Similar snakes   An intergrade with the regal race throughout West Texas, the **prairie ring-necked snake (31)** is slightly smaller and darker, with a prominent yellow neck band and a black crown. Its yellowish-orange ventral coloring does not extend as far up its sides (only ½ scale row) as that of the regal ring-neck.

Behavior   See **Prairie Ring-necked Snake.**

GROUND SNAKES
Genus Sonora

Ground Snake, *Sonora semiannulata*

As part of the colubrine subfamily *Xenodontinae*, the genus *Sonora*, whose type specimen, described in The Catalog of North American Reptiles in 1853, came from Sonora, Mexico. This genus is characterized by a blunt, rounded head only moderately wider than its neck, smooth dorsal scales that occur in either 13 or 15 rows, 6 or 7 upper labial scales, and a divided anal plate. In color and pattern combinations, few snakes in North America rival the variability of *Sonora*. Individual *S. semiannulata* may be uniformly russet, buff, greenish-buff or gray (often with a slightly darker crown), or sharply banded with contrasting shades of its dorsal hues or at least two tones of gray or pink. There may be a prominent terra-cotta colored vertebral stripe, sometimees broken by broad black saddles, while each light-hued dorsolateral scale may have a dark central spot.

This highly variable coloration makes it difficult to distinguish ground snakes from other small snake species, but this genus' most important identifying characteristic is the loreal scale (usually distinct but sometimes partially fused to another scute) that separates the second upper labial scale from the prefrontal.

A secretive, oviparous group of small serpents, *Sonora* is usually associated with well-drained plains, prairies, semi-deserts, and desert-edge habitats; here, *S. semiannulata* may be numerous where flat surface rocks are abundant. Using their weakly toxic saliva, ground snakes feed on arthropods and, occasionally, tiny geckos and their eggs, but they pose no danger to humans.

33   GROUND SNAKE, *Sonora semiannulata*

Nonvenomous   *Sonora semiannulata* does not bite humans.

Abundance   Widely distributed and locally fairly common throughout a broad range that stretches from southern Kansas and Missouri to southwestern Texas.

Size   Most adults measure less than 12 inches; the record is 16⅜ in.

Habitat   Ground snakes inhabit a wide range of terrestrial milieus: mountain slopes to low-lying desert, juniper brakes to High Plains grassland. *Sonora semiannulata* seems to be most abundant, however, in the oak-juniper savannah of Oklahoma and north/central Texas and in the succulent- and shrub-desert of the latter state's Trans-Pecos; it is present but less numerous on most of the Great Plains and in the thorn woodland of the Rio Grande valley. Ground snakes are also found in suburban areas, especially in disturbed sites such as dumps or empty lots piled with debris.

Prey   *Sonora semiannulata* preys principally on invertebrates, mainly spiders, as well as on centipedes and scorpions.

Reproduction   Egg-laying. Most female ground snakes deposit their clutches of 4 or 5 eggs during early to mid-summer.

Coloring/scale form   A variety of dorsolateral color and pattern characterize *S. semiannulata*. In fact, several different combinations may be found among the small population inhabiting a single rocky bluff.

Yet geographic variations also exist: individuals from central Texas are most often uniformly yellowish tan above, with a small dark band across the nape. In the northwestern part of the range a majority of ground snakes exhibit up to 35 dark vertebral crossbars; these bars may completely encircle the tail and are the source of this reptile's Latin name, for *semiannulata* means "partially-ringed." Individuals from the Trans-Pecos area are often a beige/salmon above, sometimes accentuated with an orange-red vertebral stripe broken by dark crossbars. These snakes' lower sides are typically a lighter pinkish or yellowish tan, with tiny blocks forming a dashed lateral line.

All *Sonora* have light-hued venters, often boldly crossbarred beneath the tail, but usually without markings forward of the vent. Dorsolaterally, ground snakes' pale, dark center-lined scales give this species a woven or textured appearance.

Similar snakes   Flat-headed (10) and black-headed (12–14) snakes have smaller, ventrodorsally flattened, dark-crowned heads, unmarked backs, salmon-colored midbellies, and no loreal scale. Earth snakes (25, 26) have 17 rows of dorsal scales that lack the ground snake's two-toned pigmentation; unlike the ground snake, earth snakes' loreal scale touches the eye.

Behavior   Like most small serpents, *S. semiannulata* is unable to tolerate the daily surface-temperature variations of its Great Plains and desert habitat. The author has seen these animals, taken from subterranean sites, die after only a few minutes, even in deep shade, when the air temperature was above 100°F. (This means that within most of this species' range, during late spring and summer ground snakes can function above ground only at night.)

Some *S. semiannulata* exhibit a head-hiding, tail-waving defensive posture called a flash display because the animal suddenly everts, or flashes, its bold undertail patterning. This behavior may have evolved in imitation of the defensive display of the similarly subcaudally banded coral snake.

WORM SNAKES
Genus Carphophis

Eastern Worm Snake, *Carphophis amoenus amoenus*
Midwestern Worm Snake, *Carphophis amoenus helenae*
Western Worm Snake, *Carphophis amoenus vermis*

The oviparous genus *Carphophis* is classified in the colubrine subfamily *Natricinae*. Here, according to researchers, this genus may contain either one full species with three subspecies or two full species (the latter view is perhaps more widely accepted, with the eastern species, *Carphophis amoenus*, being divided into two subspecies).

Worm snakes are small burrowing serpents with smooth, shiny scales which—except when their colors are muted by approaching ecdysis—display a beautiful opalescent sheen. The head is small and pointed and the eyes are tiny. The dorsal scales are arranged in only 13 rows, the tail terminates in a tiny spine, and the anal plate is divided.

34 EASTERN WORM SNAKE
Carphophis amoenus amoenus

Nonvenomous *Carphophis amoenus* does not bite when held, nor do most individuals smear their cloacal contents about. Instead, worm snakes typically attempt to escape by prodding between one's fingers with both the pointed nose and tail.

Abundance Common. This is a fairly abundant but seldom seen snake that ranges southward and westward from Massachusetts and southeastern New York to West Virginia and northern Georgia and Alabama.

Size   At a record size of 13¼ inches, this is one of the smallest snakes of the eastern U.S. Most individuals are considerably smaller than the record, becoming full-sized adults at between 8 and 10 inches in length.

Habitat   The eastern worm snake is a backyard, vacant lot, field, meadow, and open woodland serpent. When surface soil moisture levels are high, worm snakes are to be found beneath flat rocks, man-made debris, in compost piles, or under or within rotting logs (they seem to prefer pines). Dryness causes these little reptiles to burrow—at which they are adept, in part due to their small, pointed heads and the traction/leverage afforded by their sharply pointed tail tips.

Prey   The primary prey of *Carphophis amoenus* is earthworms, but cutworms and grubs are also supposedly eaten. See **Midwestern Worm Snake**.

Reproduction   Egg-laying. Worm snakes lay small numbers (normally 1 to 5; rarely as many as 9) of thin-shelled eggs. The 3½-inch-long hatchlings emerge following 7 to 9 weeks of incubation.

Coloring/scale form   The eastern worm snake's shiny dorsum is brown to nearly black, with an opalescent sheen, except when approaching ecdysis turns its back a bluish-gray. On its sides, the low-ermost row or two of lateral scales are the same pink color as its venter—its antiquated common name is "pink-bellied snake."

Among members of the eastern race, at least one of the pair of pre-frontal scales (and usually both) is not fused with the internasal scales.

Similar snakes   Along the western edge of the eastern subspecies' range it intergrades with its midwestern relative, the **midwestern worm snake (35)**, whose prefrontal scale is fused with the adjacent internasal. Otherwise, this is the only small eastern snake with smooth scales in 13 rows and pink ventral color extending upwards onto the first row or two of lateral scales.

Behavior   Worm snakes are truly fossorial animals. Adept at burrowing, during droughts they may burrow deeply, following the receding moisture in the soil, while heavy rains bring these little reptiles to the surface.

At this time *Carphophis amoenus* seems to be more crepuscular than either diurnal or nocturnal, moving about most often in late afternoon and evening: on a rainy afternoon in Massachusetts Richard D. Bartlett watched worm snakes crawl erratically about 50 yards across a yard from one fencerow to another. During these excursions robins investigated but did not feed on the little snakes, although a bluejay grasped and flew off with one.

Carphophis amoenus helenae

Nonvenomous Like its eastern relative, *C. a. hele-nae* is an innocuous creature that cannot be made to bite.

Abundance Common. Perhaps less abundant today than in years past, the midwestern worm snake is still to be found throughout much of its range, which reaches southward from central Ohio and Illinois to western Georgia and eastern Louisiana.

Size This race's adult measures 8 to 11 inches in length.

Habitat The midwestern worm snake inhabits open woodlands, rock-strewn hillsides and fields, mostly where sheltering ground cover is available. As with many shelter-seeking snakes, *C. a. helenae* also frequents trash dumps.

Prey Earthworms are the preferred prey, but soft-bodied insect larvae are reportedly also consumed. Midwestern worm snakes' predators include larger serpents: having found milk snakes near *Carphophis* colonies in Ohio, Roger Conant (1940) suggested that these small kingsnakes may be a major predator on worm snakes.

Reproduction Egg-laying. One to 6 (rarely as many as 8) thin-shelled eggs are laid in or beneath moisture-retaining logs or plant debris. The incubation period is between 7 and 9 weeks, and the hatchlings average 3½ inches in length.

Coloring/scale form This creature's coloring is similar to that of the eastern worm snake and the two races are so similar that they are scarcely worth differentiating. (John MacGregor maintains that this situation is a case of two alleles, with intermediate heterozygote forms erroneously being called intergrades.) However, the midwestern worm snake has its prefrontal scales fused with the corresponding internasal scale. Intergrade individuals between this race and the eastern form occur across broad areas where the ranges of the two abut or overlap.

Similar snakes Throughout its range *C. a. helenae* is the only small snake with 13 rows of smooth scales on which the pink belly color extends upward onto the lowermost row or two of lateral scales. The **eastern worm snake (34)** has at least one (usually both) of its pair of prefrontal scales separated from its internasal scales. The **western worm snake (36)** has a nearly black, or blue-black dorsum (its internasal and prefrontal scales are also separate), and its pinkish ventral coloring may extend upward to the third row of lateral scales.

Behavior See **Western Worm Snake**.

Carphophis amoenus vermis

Nonvenomous   The western worm snake is harmless to humans.

Abundance   As the westernmost race of an essentially eastern forest serpent, *C. a. vermis* occupies almost all of Missouri and Arkansas, as well as eastern Kansas and Oklahoma. Yet its small size and secretive behavior may make *C. a. vermis* very difficult to find, despite the fact that it is often abundant enough to occur in small colonies.

Size   Adults are 7½ to 11 inches long.

Habitat   In its relatively dry (for a worm snake) western milieu, *C. a. vermis* is restricted to damp areas similar to its species' primary eastern habitat of mesic woodland, well-vegetated stream banks, brushy meadows, and overgrown farmland. Usually discovered in spring beneath stones, rotting logs, vegetative debris or leaf mold, the western worm snake seeks moisture during the drier months by withdrawing to depths of as much as 6 feet.

Prey   Western worm snakes feed primarily on earthworms, slugs, grubs, and soft-bodied invertebrates.

Reproduction   Egg-laying. In late summer, about 7 weeks after they are deposited in an earthen cavity, the 1 to 8 thin-shelled eggs (which measure 1¼ by ⅝ inch) hatch into 3- to 4-inch-long young.

Coloring/scale form   Named "beautiful worm" in Latin, this creature's distinctive dorsolateral coloring results from the striking longitudinal demarcation which separates its salmon-hued venter and lower sides from its iridescent, purplish-black back. Like that of other burrowing snakes, the western worm snake's head is no wider than its neck, while its sharply pointed terminal caudal scute is similar to the pointed tail tip of the unrelated *Leptotyphlopidae*, which also use their tail tips as anchoring pins to press through the soil.

Similar snakes   None: *C. a. vermis* is the only small burrowing snake with a horizontal black-and-salmon color demarcation along its sides.

Behavior   In spring, when the organic foodstuff of decomposing leaves draws earthworms to the surface, *Carphophis* is active in the upper layers of the soil, and when both air and ground temperature reach 58 to 78°F and the soil is damp, these animals may even forage abroad during the day. Later in the year, as midday heat dries the surface, annelids retreat deeper into the earth and worm snakes go down with them.

When restrained, *C. a. vermis* tries to thrust itself forward, suddenly pressing either its pointed snout or its sharp tail tip between one's fingers. This produces a startling sensation so much like the prick of a tooth that one's reflexive response is to drop the snake. Less often, the western worm snake may expel a yellowish musk from its anal glands, spreading the unpleasant-smelling mucus about in its efforts to escape.

PINE WOODS SNAKE
Genus Rhadinaea

Pine Woods Snake, *Rhadinaea flavilata*

Although well represented in Latin America, only a single species of the genus *Rhadinaea* (a part of the Colubrine subfamily *Xenodontinae*, whose mildly toxic saliva helps its members overcome their small lizard and amphibian prey) occurs in the U.S.

This is the pine woods snake, a small, secretive, and oviparous southeastern serpent most often found in pine flatwoods and abandoned fields. Here, it hides beneath or within decomposing logs, forest floor vegetation, and roadside debris, although it also turns up beneath litter in damp urban backyards.

The pine woods snake's smooth scales lack apical pits and are arranged in 17 rows; its anal plate is divided.

37 PINE WOODS SNAKE, *Rhadinaea flavilata*

Nonvenomous Although pine woods snakes do not bite when picked up, *Rhadinaea flavilata* is characterized by progressively longer posterior teeth—the most rearward pair of which is separated from its anterior dentition to allow these demi-fangs to puncture the small lizards, frogs and salamanders on which pine woods snakes  feed. These tiny punctures (for all this happens on a very small scale) introduce a few droplets of the pine woods snake's saliva, which carries toxins produced in its well-developed Duvernoy's glands.

Although these toxins eventually immobilize small vertebrates enough for them to be swallowed, the pine woods snake's saliva is so minimally paralytic that it can take more than two hours to overcome even very small frogs or lizards, and poses no threat to humans.

Abundance   *Rhadinaea flavilata* is secretive, and if not rare seems to be generally uncommon. In an unusual distribution pattern, it is thought to occupy three disjunct ranges: the largest of these encompasses peninsular Florida (including the Gulf barrier islands) from Lake Okeechobee northward past the Georgia state line. Further up the Atlantic seaboard, coastal North and South Carolina constitute a second range, while another population of pine woods snakes lives well to the west, mostly in southern Louisiana, Mississippi, and Alabama.

A great deal of seemingly ideal habitat occurs between these widely separated ranges, and at least some of this apparent distributional hiatus may be due to a lack of herpetological scrutiny in the intervening terrain.

Size   Most adults are between 10 and 12 inches in length; the record is 15¾ in.

Habitat   As its name indicates, the pine woods snake's principal environment is lowland pine flatwoods (slash, loblolly, and longleaf pine woodlands are all occupied). Here, its favored microhabitat is rotting logs, the damp ground litter of well-shaded fallen pine needles, and the often humid spaces found within piles of pine bark shingles. *Rhadinaea flavilata* is also occasionally found in the wetter, lowland portions of mixed hardwood and scrub environments.

Prey   Pine woods snakes feed on salamanders, small frogs (especially hylids), small lizards (especially ground skinks) and possibly small snakes. Prey is often, but not invariably, immobilized by its weak venom before being swallowed.

The pine woods snake's salivary toxins are no defense against the ophiophagous eastern and scarlet kingsnakes, though, which frequent the same rotting pine stumps as *R. flavilata*, feeding on it along with other small serpents.

Reproduction   Egg-laying. No natural nests are known, but this species reportedly produces 2- to 4-inch-long eggs between May and August; very few of the 5-inch-long hatchlings have been observed.

Coloring/scale form   This satiny little reptile's yellowish- to reddish-brown dorsum has a polished appearance. Its lower sides are considerably lighter, and on some individuals the upper back darkens into a vertebral stripe. The crown is also darker than the back, while a horizontal black ocular stripe, which broadens behind the eye, is thinly bordered above by a whitish line. Below, this stripe defines the upper margin of the prominent pale yellow labial scales—scales from which this species' antiquated common name, "yellow-lipped snake," is drawn.

The venter is unmarked whitish- or greenish-yellow. Like that of the related mud and rainbow snakes, the pine woods snake's tail tip ends in a small spine thought to aid in burrowing through soft soil.

Similar snakes   Several other small, brownish woodland snakes occur within the range of the pine woods snake, but neither the **red-bellied and brown snakes (15–22)**, the **earth snakes (23, 25)**, nor the **crowned snakes (5–9)** have a distinct dark eye-stripe bordered above with a pale line and below with yellowish labial scales.

Behavior   *Rhadinaea flavilata* is most active at the surface during its March to early May breeding season. During summer it may briefly emerge from below ground after warm rain or during flooding, but usually only as far as the underside of natural debris like decomposing logs or moisture-retaining human detritus such as discarded newspaper, plastic, boards, and tin. Like most small serpents, pine woods snakes are not long-lived: just over 3 years is the longest recorded captive lifespan.

SHORT-TAILED SNAKE
Genus Stilosoma

Short-tailed Snake, *Stilosoma extenuatum*

The genus *Stilosoma* is part of the colubrine subfamily *Lampropeltinae* and therefore akin to both the kingsnakes, *Lampropeltis*, and the scarlet snakes, *Cemophora*. *Stilosoma* is a strange genus, whose Greek-derived name, which means "stiff," refers to the unusually wide, inflexible vertebral column. *Stilosoma* contains but a single species, the short-tailed snake, *Stilosoma extenuatum*, a small, oviparous, caudally attenuate animal with 19 midbody rows of smooth dorsal scales and an undivided anal plate.

Little is known about the life history of the short-tailed snake, a rarely seen burrowing animal found only in the sandy pinelands of Florida's north/central region and its central Gulf Coast. What is known is that the preferred (and perhaps only) prey of *S. extenuatum* is crowned snakes of the genus *Tantilla*, which share its restricted range (captive short-tailed snakes have steadfastly refused to feed on tiny snakes of several other species, yet immediately constricted and ravenously eaten crowned snakes).

38   SHORT-TAILED SNAKE, *Stilosoma extenuatum*

Nonvenomous   This excitable but harmless little snake vibrates its tail if startled, and will hiss and strike when further annoyed.

Abundance   Rare. Legally protected by the state of Florida, *Stilosoma extenuatum* is an endemic found only from Suwanee and Columbia counties south to Hillsborough, Orange, and Highlands counties. Because this singular reptile is the only species in its genus, protecting it is particularly important: if the short-tailed snake were to vanish, the entire genus *Stilosoma*—unique in the strange shape of its vertebra, which are short and wide, with a long condylar neck and a condyle wider than it is high—would disappear forever.

Size   Adult short-tailed snakes are usually no more than 14 to 20 inches in length and pencil thin; the record is 25¾ in.

Habitat   *Stilosoma extenuatum* is another of the rare, relict inhabitants of old "Island Florida"—the dry interior uplands of the Florida peninsula which, due to elevated sea levels during interglacial periods, was for long periods in fact an island. Here, the short-tailed snake's primary habitat is sandhill environments, including early successional sand pine scrub and xeric hammocks. But the prevailing sandy-soiled, longleaf pine/turkey oak woodland typical of this biome is rapidly being depleted of its remaining woodland by timber management. Other parts of this reptile's range are, at an even greater rate, being converted to citrus groves, residential subdivisions, and golf courses. The Ocala National Forest is the most extensive area still containing large tracts of the short-tailed snake's original habitat.

    Yet to survive *Stilosoma* may not require pristine woodland. According to Campbell and Moler (1990):

> In areas subject to unavoidable development, *S. extenuatum* may be able to coexist with man as long as development is not too intense . . . homesites which retain the native plant and animal species . . . may [suffice, but] care should be taken to preserve the invertebrate and small vertebrate fauna on which this species depends.

Prey   In captivity this small quasi-constrictor seems to be almost entirely ophiophagous, refusing skinks and taking only small, smooth-scaled snakes. (Serpentine motion is the triggering factor in eliciting the short-tailed snake's predatory response, for only wriggling snakes are attacked—dead specimens are ignored, while live individuals of the same species quickly taken.)

Further, although no predation in the wild has been recorded, the almost exclusive preference of captives for crowned snake prey suggests that snakes of the genus *Tantilla* may be the exclusive prey of *S. extenuatum.*

Tantilla relicta is the crowned snake species most prevalent in the short-tailed snake's range, and smaller individuals are seized near the head and swallowed while larger specimens are constricted. They are not killed by this constriction, however, for the body coils of *Stilosoma* seem capable only of temporarily restraining prey; its powerful jaws and side-to-side, kingsnake-like chewing motions are its principal ingestive strategy.

Reproduction   Egg-laying. No reproductive behavior is recorded.

Coloring/scale form   The short-tailed snake's slender, cylindrical body has a medium gray ground color. This is patterned along the spine with a broad, often indistinct orangish stripe broken by 50 to 80 dark vertebral blotches. A dark brown Y with a yellow-orange center marks the short-tailed snake's crown, and its internasal and prefrontal scales are often fused.

Its white venter is blotched with dark brown and, as its common name implies, the short-tailed snake's tail is indeed attenuated, comprising less than 10 percent of its total length.

Similar snakes   Externally, *S. extenuatum* resembles the kingsnakes, particularly the mole kings, and current immunological albumin-sequencing techniques suggest that this species is, in fact, a Pliocene evolutionary radiation of the kingsnake line, falling somewhere between the scarlet kingsnakes, the mole kingsnakes, and the scarlet snakes of the genus *Cemophora*. (Fossils from this period found near Gainesville show that *Stilosoma* was already present in the area, which it has evidently continuously occupied since its origin.)

The short-tailed snake's close relationship to the **mole kingsnake (148)** is evident in its similar Y-shaped cephalic marking, but the mole king is a stockier snake with a brownish ground color which lacks an orangish vertebral stripe.

Behavior   Even in areas of prime habitat short-tailed snakes are almost never seen because they so seldom appear above ground, emerging mainly at night during either April or October. While primarily a burrower, in a surprising attribute for a fossorial snake *S. extenuatum* also climbs well.

LINED SNAKE
Genus Tropidoclonion

Lined Snake, *Tropidoclonion lineatum*

Like others in its colubrine subfamily *Natricinae*, the mostly grassland and prairie-living genus *Tropidoclonion* (first scientifically described by dinosaur fossil hunter Edward Drinker Cope in 1860) is closely related to both the water snakes and to the garter and ribbon snake genus, *Thamnophis*. Its only U.S. species, the lined snake, is often mistaken for a small garter snake.

Tropidoclonion lineatum is most easily distinguished from its garter snake relatives, however, by its belly markings: a double row of black half-moons extends from neck to tail tip. Its keeled dorsal scales occur in 19 rows at midbody (in 17 rows just anterior to the vent), there are 5 or 6 upper labial scales, and its anal plate is undivided.

39   LINED SNAKE, *Tropidoclonion lineatum*

Nonvenomous   Lined snakes do not bite humans, but if threatened a large specimen may flatten its neck and engage in bluffing strikes.

Abundance   Common. From the Gulf of Mexico to southern Wyoming, throughout much of the Great Plains *T. lineatum* is a familiar snake often seen in areas of altered and softened soil near rural houses.

Size   Adults are between 8 and 12 inches, but J. P. Jones, former reptile director of the Fort Worth Zoo, recorded one gravid Tarrant County female of 21½ inches.

Habitat   Despite its kinship to aquatic snakes, *Tropidoclonion lineatum* is an entirely terrestrial, semi-fossorial inhabitant of grasslands; even in wooded areas it lives mostly in open meadows. Its primary microhabitat above ground is the narrow spaces found beneath rocks lying on the surface.

Prey   Prey is primarily earthworms, but *T. lineatum* is one of the few vertebrates to also be able to feed on the toxic little crustaceans known as sow bugs, which frequent lined snakes' damp retreats.

Reproduction   Live-bearing. In Oklahoma, 23 broods of 4- to 5-inch-long newborns were deposited between August 9 and 31.

Coloring/scale form   The lined snake's slender, gray to olive ground-colored (often dark-speckled) dorsum bears a pale vertebral stripe. Midway down its side, a pale stripe, often ill-defined, is bordered both above and below by dark checks that resemble another pair of stripes. The throat and belly are creamy (the midventral region may have a yellowish cast) with a double row of rearward-arched black half-moons; the pointed head, no wider than the neck, is adapted for burrowing.

Similar snakes   Lined snakes formerly differentiated into the separate subspecies, the **Central Lined Snake**, *T. l. annectens*, and the **New Mexico Lined snake**, *T. l. mertensi*, are now rejoined with the race formerly called the **Texas Lined Snake**, *T. l. texanum*, to form a single species, the **Lined Snake**, *Tropidoclonion lineatum*. Lined snakes' relatives the **garter snakes (40–53)** have heads twice the width of their necks when seen from above and 8 upper labial scales vertically edged with black along their sutures; none has a double row of black ventral half-moons.

Behavior   Lined snakes are seldom seen in the open, typically remaining coiled beneath cover during the day, emerging mainly at night during damp weather. A favored prey of milk- and kingsnakes, *T. lineatum* is detected in these places by its musk scent. In suburban areas, lined snakes often hide in the sunken concrete cylinders that house residential water meters, and meter readers may see more *T. lineatum* than any herpetologist.

GARTER AND RIBBON SNAKES
Genus Thamnophis

Eastern Garter Snake, *Thamnophis sirtalis sirtalis*
Maritime Garter Snake, *Thamnophis sirtalis pallidulus*
Blue-striped Garter Snake, *Thamnophis sirtalis similis*
Chicago Garter Snake, *Thamnophis sirtalis semifasciatus*
Red-sided Garter Snake, *Thamnophis sirtalis parietalis*
Texas Garter Snake, *Thamnophis sirtalis annectens*
Short-headed Garter Snake, *Thamnophis brachystoma*
Butler's Garter Snake, *Thamnophis butleri*
Wandering Garter Snake, *Thamnophis elegans vagrans*
Eastern Plains Garter Snake, *Thamnophis radix radix*

Western Plains Garter Snake, *Thamnophis radix haydeni*
Checkered Garter Snake, *Thamnophis marcianus marcianus*
Western Black-necked Garter Snake, *Thamnophis cyrtopsis cyrtopsis*
Eastern Black-necked Garter Snake, *Thamnophis cyrtopsis ocellatus*
Eastern Ribbon Snake, *Thamnophis sauritus sauritus*
Northern Ribbon Snake, *Thamnophis sauritus septentrionalis*
Peninsula Ribbon Snake, *Thamnophis sauritus sackeni*
Blue-striped Ribbon Snake, *Thamnophis sauritus nitae*
Western Ribbon Snake, *Thamnophis proximus proximus*
Red-striped Ribbon Snake, *Thamnophis proximus rubrilineatus*
Gulf Coast Ribbon Snake, *Thamnophis proximus orarius*
Arid Land Ribbon Snake, *Thamnophis proximus diabolicus*

The genus *Thamnophis* is contained in the colubrine subfamily *Natricinae*. Greek for "bush serpent," the term *Thamnophis* was coined by L. J. F. Fitzinger in 1843, and both garter and ribbon snakes are indeed at home in the brushy environs of lake and stream shorelines. Both garter and ribbon snakes are closely allied to the water snakes and, like them, are musky, smelly animals when threatened or captured. Formerly, some biologists believed that water and garter snakes should be classified together in a single genus; a view is that garter snakes are ancestral to *Nerodia*-genus water snakes.

Almost all garter and ribbon snakes share a pale vertebral line and light-hued side stripes, which quickly identifies them as *Thamnophis*, although determining their particular species can be difficult, especially where melanistic populations occur (in some places most *Thamnophis* are black). In fact, a number of *Thamnophis* species are distinguishable only by the position of the scale row on which their pale lateral line occurs, the overall number of dorsal scale rows, the labial scale count, and whether the labial scales are barred or unmarked. (The keeled scales of garter and ribbon snakes occur in 17 to 21 rows, though this number varies not only by species but individually and, usually, an undivided anal plate.)

Most small garter snakes are reluctant to bite, but if grasped some of the larger ones can nip vigorously, and all *Thamnophis* are likely to smear musk and feces about in defense—making themselves as unpalatable as possible to a predator. Another tactic is to flatten and laterally expand their bodies, which not only makes them appear larger but displays the often bright red skin between their scales. (Though garter snakes are nonvenomous, bites have caused mildly adverse reactions.)

40   EASTERN GARTER SNAKE

Thamnophis sirtalis sirtalis

Nonvenomous   Wild-caught individuals may emit musk, flatten their necks and feign strikes, sometimes bumping one's hands with their snouts, but those that choose to bite can hang on tenaciously. Very rarely, slight toxic reactions have been noted in humans as a result of bites by this subspecies, and, while not dangerous, *T. s. sirtalis* should probably be handled with care.

Abundance   Common. In areas of suitable habitat—particularly along heavily vegetated waterways crossing prairie, meadow, and marshland—eastern garter snakes can be abundant anywhere in their broad range. This includes almost the entire eastern U.S., from the middle Texas Gulf Coast north almost to Hudson's Bay, then east across Canada to Upper New York state and Cape Cod and south to the tip of peninsular Florida.

Size   Average adult length is 20 to 28 in., although the largest recorded eastern garter snake measured 49 inches.

Habitat   Primarily open or semi-open lowland, especially stream banks and suburban ditches containing water. In the North, both evergreen woodland and bottomland forest are also inhabited, while in the South, pinelands, stands of cypress and melaleuca, and even Everglades swale are home to eastern garter snakes.

Prey   *Thamnophis sirtalis sirtalis* will prey on almost any smaller creature, but a majority of its diet consists of aquatic or semi-aquatic life: small fish, frogs and salamanders. Terrestrial food animals such as toads and earthworms are sought by scent and seized with the aid of sight, but aquatic prey is often taken without using either of these senses. For example, as an eastern garter snake moves along the margins of a shallow pond, in response to movements in the water it may thrust its foreparts below the murky surface, wagging its open mouth from side to side as it gropes for fish or tadpoles.

Reproduction   Live-bearing. Most litters are born during May, along the Gulf Coast and in Florida, during June, and July, and number from 6 to nearly 60. This great range in litter size generally reflects the size of the mother, with large females giving birth to many more young.

Coloring/scale form   Garter snakes are named for men's old striped sock garters ("sirtalis" also means "striped" in Latin), and although *T. s. sirtalis* is somewhat variable in both color and pattern (individuals found along the Gulf Coast sometimes have red markings amid the dark pigment separating their straw-colored vertebral and lateral stripes), a distinct light brown to yellowish-green vertebral stripe is always evident. A similarly-colored lateral stripe occupies the second and third scale rows above the pale venter at least among the most commonly pigmented color phase. However, a considerable population of melanistic eastern garter snakes—entirely black animals except for white chin and lip mottling—occurs near Lake Erie. In Ohio's Erie and Ottawa counties, where enthusiasts often search for fox snakes, pure black eastern garter snakes that suggest a non-glossy black race are found with some frequency. Melanism may even be the dominant color morph among *T. sirtalis* from this area, for a wild-caught Erie County female taken May 23 by D. Craig McIntyre deposited 23 young on August 16—15 of which were pure black, while the remaining 8 exhibited ordinary eastern garter snake pigmentation.

   T. s. sirtalis has 19 midbody rows of dorsal scales and the anal plate is undivided.

Similar snakes   The **maritime garter snake (41)** is a less boldly patterned—its dorsolateral spots may be smudged brown rather than black—northern race which often lacks a complete or well-defined vertebral stripe. In a little-understood anomaly of coloration, along Florida's upper Gulf Coast the eastern garter is replaced by the **blue-striped garter snake (42)**, a race distinguished by its pale blue vertebral and lateral stripes and bluish dorsal flecks. **Ribbon snakes (54–61)** are slimmer, with proportionately longer tails, a rearward-curved white spot in front of the eye, and a pale side stripe on the 3rd and 4th scale rows above the belly.

Behavior   On land, *T. s. sirtalis* is a deliberate, scent-trail forager. Individual ranges are generally about 2 acres, with the average activity area found in one 3-year study being about 600 by 150 feet; the greatest distance traveled by any of the project's subject snakes was less than ⅙ mile. Few small serpents reach old age in the wild but, as the most-studied snake in confinement, captive eastern garter snakes have lived for as long as 14 years.

41 MARITIME GARTER SNAKE
Thamnophis sirtalis pallidulus

Nonvenomous When provoked or captured, some maritime garter snakes will coil, strike and bite. Others may merely hide their head beneath their coils and lash their tails.

Abundance The relative abundance of this subspecies remains uncertain, but it is probably not rare. Its far northern range seems to extend south from central Quebec and southern Newfoundland only to central Vermont, New Hampshire, and Maine, but garter snakes showing characteristics of the maritime race are reported as far south as northeastern Massachusetts.

Individuals from this region often exhibit characteristics mingled with those typical of the eastern garter snake. As Tom Tyning reports, some *Thamnophis sirtalis* from both this area and southern New England are similar to the maritime subspecies both in the dimming and shortening of their vertebral and lateral stripes and their tendency toward stoutness—a tendency that seems to be especially pronounced among the population inhabiting Tuckanuck Island near the east side of Nantucket.

Size This rather poorly understood subspecies is adult at from 18 to 28 inches in length, and proportionately thick-girthed; the largest examples may attain a length of 3 ft. Neonates are about 8 in. long.

Habitat The maritime garter snake is primarily an inhabitant of mature hardwood and mixed hardwood-fir forests in southeastern Canada and northern New England.

Prey Frogs and earthworms comprise the majority of the maritime garter snake's prey, but salamanders and small fish are also accepted by captives.

Reproduction Live-bearing. Little is known about the reproductive biology but it is thought that breeding occurs both as groups gather at hibernacula in the autumn and when they emerge en masse in the spring. One large female gave birth to 10, 7½-in.-long babies—which were very like the adult in appearance—during early September.

Coloring/scale form Ground color varies from olive-gray and olive-green to warm brown, overlaid, along each side, with two alternating rows of black or brown spots in a checkerboard pattern. This dorsal coloring is sometimes split by a vertebral stripe (which varies from gray to yellow, but is most often tan) which can be entirely absent, absent only posteriorly, or complete and well defined.

The lateral stripes, from which both the Latin "sirtalis" or "striped," and "pallidulus" or "pale" are drawn, occupy the second and third scale rows above the light-hued venter, and are usually more distinct than the vertebral stripe. They are strongest along their dorsal aspect, however, and may merge with the ventral color along their lower edge. The pale belly darkens toward the tail.

Dorsal scales occur in 19 rows and the anal plate is undivided; like other subspecies of *T. sirtalis*, there are usually 7 upper labial scales.

Similar snakes The southerly-ranging **eastern garter snake** (40) has a more sharply contrasting dorsolateral patterning, with bolder dorsolateral checkering and a more clearly delineated, complete vertebral stripe. The **northern ribbon snake** (55), sympatric only in northern New England, is a more slender reptile which lacks dark dorsolateral checks.

Behavior See **Eastern Garter Snake.**

42 BLUE-STRIPED GARTER SNAKE

Thamnophis sirtalis similis

Nonvenomous Some individuals do no more than flatten the head and body, feign strikes, and emit musk when cornered, but when picked up, most garter snakes can bite sharply.

Abundance Common, but very restricted in range: found only along Florida's northern Gulf Coast, the blue-striped garter snake replaces its subspecies the eastern garter from eastern Wakulla County in the panhandle to Hernando County in central Florida.

Size Adults are the same size as the eastern garter snake.

Habitat See **Eastern Garter Snake.**

Prey Blue-striped garter snakes prey on earthworms, small fish, frogs, and toads. Vision is used for capturing prey, but sight is less important in garter snake predation than scent, and the instinctually recognized smell of appropriate prey species such as earthworms, anurans and fish is what most often elicits predation.

Reproduction Live-bearing. See **Eastern Garter Snake.**

Coloring/scale form Except for its pale blue vertebral stripe and uniformly blackish-brown dorsum, *T. s. similis* is identical to the eastern garter snake.

Similar snakes   The similarly-colored **blue-striped ribbon snake** (57) is slimmer, has a rearward-curved white spot in front of its eye, and a pale lateral stripe on the 3rd and 4th scale rows above its belly. It also lacks black labial scale sutures.

Behavior   Blue-striped garter snakes are active all day during even during the hottest summer months, almost always in some sort of watery milieu, especially wet prairie hammocks and tall-grass marshes. Confronted with danger, *T. s. similis* can partially alter its normally dark appearance by inflating its lungs to spread its ribs, splaying its dorsolateral scales to reveal previously unseen patches of light-hued skin along its sides that make it look larger and more formidable.

43   CHICAGO GARTER SNAKE
Thamnophis sirtalis semifasciatus

Nonvenomous   See **Eastern Garter Snake.**

Abundance   Taxonomically, *T. s. semi-fasciatus* is a somewhat controversial form of the estern garter snake: a study in the Chicago Herpetological Society Bulletin by Michael Benton discounts the Chicago  garter as a distinct subspecies. Yet—though it is seen as a problematic race by most authorities—James H. Harding includes it in his 1997 *Amphibians and Reptiles of the Great Lakes Region.* In (its questionable) pure form, the Chicago garter is found only within 50 miles or so of the southern tip of Lake Michigan, however, as well as in southeastern Wisconsin, northeastern Illinois, and adjacent Indiana. Here, depending on the quality of its habitat, the Chicago garter snake may vary from uncommon to fairly common. Intergrades with the eastern garter snake occur in a broad periphery around this range.

Size   With an average adult size of no more than 18 to 26 inches and a record of only 35⅝ in. this is one of the smaller races of *Thamnophis sirtalis.*

Habitat   The Chicago garter snake is a reptile of open woodlands and, in urban areas, city parks and undeveloped sanctuaries such as weedy vacant lots. Utilizing boards, logs, woodpiles, mats of vegetation, and rocks as refugia, it is most abundant in areas where surface litter offers extensive ground cover. Like other garter snakes, *T. s. semifasciatus* favors wetlands, particularly the edges of swamps, ponds, and ditches where its prey is abundant.

Prey   Amphibians and worms seem to be this animal's primary natural prey, but small fish are also eagerly accepted by captives.

Reproduction   Live-bearing. Little is published about the reproductive biology of *T. s. semifasciatus*, but in late summer captive females have produced 7 to 18 young about 8¼ in. long.

Coloring/scale form   This race of *Thamnophis sirtalis* has recently been recognized by several researchers in spite of the fact that the characteristics which most reliably define the Chicago garter are also found on garter snakes living well outside of the Chicago area—while within the Chicago garter's supposed range, typical eastern garter snakes also turn up periodically.

Nevertheless, the primary characteristic ostensibly distinguishing *T. s. semifasciatus* from the eastern garter snake is that anteriorly its pale lateral stripe (and, more rarely, its vertebral stripe) is broken by 6 to 8 downward extensions of the black spots that occupy its rather dark dorsolateral ground color. This is the "semifasciatus" or "partially banded" part of its scientific name. In addition, several dark spots intrude from below into this lateral stripe, which occupies scale rows 2 and 3 above its belly line. Its dorsal scales occur in 19 rows and its anal plate is undivided.

Similar snakes   See **Eastern Garter Snake.** The **western ribbon snake (58)** is much more slender, with a proportionately longer tail and a pale side stripe that occupies the 3rd and 4th scale rows above its belly. It usually has an orange vertebral stripe and a dark face with a rearward-curved light vertical bar immediately anterior to its eye.

Behavior   See **Eastern Garter Snake.**

44   Red-sided Garter Snake
Thamnophis sirtalis parietalis

Nonvenomous   Unlike some of the smaller garter and ribbon snakes, the red-sided garter typically does not hesitate to bite if provoked or carelessly re-strained, as well as to discharge musk and feces on a captor. A bite from this snake has caused local redness and pain (probably from orally-infused bacteria), but no overt symptoms of envenomation.

Abundance   Variable. The range of this hardy, open-country garter snake extends northward from northeastern Texas to western Ontario and the southern part of Canada's Northwest Territory. Within this vast sweep of the Great Plains *T. s. parietalis* varies from uncommon (in marginally suitable habitats it may only seldom be seen) to immensely abundant near some of its hibernation sites, or hibernacula.

Size This is a large—the record is 48⅞ inches—rather heavy-bodied subspecies. Individuals between 18 and 30 inches long are fully adult, however, while neonates measure about 8½ in.

Habitat Throughout its often arid territory the red-sided garter snake is almost always found in areas (whether on the prairie or in open woodland) characterized by at least the intermittent presence of water. Most commonly, these are also areas where either natural or manmade ground litter offers shelter.

Particularly in the drier, westward part of its range where moisture is more intermittent and ephemeral, *T. s. parietalis* typically hunts along creeks, ditches, potholes, and marshes.

Prey This large garter snake seeks a wide variety of prey: frogs, salamanders, worms, lizards; even nestling birds and small rodents are opportunistically eaten.

Reproduction Live-bearing. Large litters are characteristic: clutches of 30 to 50 babies, having a length of about 8 in., are not uncommon.

Coloring/scale form The red-sided garter snake is among the most colorful serpents in eastern and central North America. Its dorsolateral ground color can be black or dark to olive-brown, patterned with a series of prominent red and black bars or a bold red and black checkerboard (for which the animal is named), split by a bold, dark-edged yellow vertebral stripe. On its sides, a broad yellow lateral stripe (which covers all of scale rows 2 and 3, and sometimes both the bottom of scale row 4 and the top of scale row 1) can be more indistinct since the partial scale row beneath this stripe may not clearly separate it from the olive to bluish belly. The dorsal scales occur in 19 rows and the anal plate is undivided.

Similar snakes This is the only striped snake within its range that, along its sides, has narrow alternating bars (or a checkerboard) of red and black.

Behavior The red-sided garter snake is primarily diurnal during cool weather and at northern latitudes, although in warm weather it becomes crepuscular or nocturnal. *Thamnophis sirtalis parietalis* is the famous garter snake race that, in parts of Manitoba, is often filmed for nature documentaries as it gathers by the thousands at its hibernation sites.

45 TEXAS GARTER SNAKE

Thamnophis sirtalis annectens

Nonvenomous   When first picked up, Texas garter snakes generally choose to emit musk and bump aggressively with the snout rather than bite; a large one can nip with determination, however.

Abundance   Uncommon, but still fairly numerous in scattered locales. According to ecologist Frederick R. Gehlbach of Baylor University, populations of *T. s. annectens* were historically highest in the original tall grass prairies of Texas and Oklahoma. Over 95% of this narrow strip of blackland clay—whose ecosystem of successively maturing grasses reached 7 feet in height by mid-summer—has now been cleared for agriculture. But before tractors smoothed its pocked surface into cotton and sorghum fields, that prairie's vegetation concealed millions of pothole ponds, each a little wetland harboring its own springtime complement of frantically breeding anurans . . . and the Texas garter snakes that fed on them.

Size   Adult Texas garter snakes average 18 to 30 inches in length.

Habitat   In addition to its primary tall-grass prairie habitat, open woodland and riparian bottomland are also inhabited, for the author (Tennant) has found Texas garter snakes in shady juniper canyons along the eastern edge of the Edwards Plateau.

Prey   Like other eastern U.S. garter snakes, this race will take any moving prey small enough to swallow. Earthworms, minnows, tadpoles, frogs and small toads are reported as its main food, however.

Reproduction   Live-bearing. See **Eastern Garter Snake.**

Coloring/scale form   With its dark back split by a broad orange stripe that occupies the vertebral scale row as well as more than half of each adjacent row, *T. s. annectens* is a visually striking reptile (when threatened, by spreading its ribs the Texas garter snake can splay its lateral scales to reveal the bright red skin hidden along its sides).

On the forward third of its trunk, its yellowish lateral stripe occupies most of the second, all of the third, and about half of the fourth scale row above the whitish or light green venter. There are 19 midbody rows of dorsal scales and the anal plate is undivided.

Similar snakes   Within its range, only *T. s. annectens* has pale side stripes that involve the fourth lateral scale row above the belly (in the eastern [40], checkered [51], and **black-necked garter snakes** [52, 53], these stripes do not touch the fourth scale row). The **red-sided garter snake (44)** is also distinguished by its lack of a pale lateral stripe occupying the entire 4th scale row.

Behavior   During the hot summer months Texas garter snakes are active morning and evening, and their lack of wariness makes *T. s. annectens* an interesting animal to watch. One individual marked by the author came regularly to a limestone pool among cedar brakes lining the Pedernales River. This 20 inch-long serpent sometimes attacked anurans much too large for it to swallow and once hung on to a leopard frog for 20 minutes, never managing to engulf more than a single hind leg.

46   SHORT-HEADED GARTER SNAKE

Thamnophis brachystoma

Nonvenomous   This little reptile, although excitable, is not prone to bite and is harmless to humans.

Abundance   Locally common. *Thamnophis brachystoma* is an inhabitant of the meadows, fields and hillsides of the Allegheny High Plateau. Its main population is restricted to western Pennsylvania and adjacent New York, while a small, disjunct group occurs in the vicinity of Tioga County, N.Y. In suitable habitat within this small area the short-headed garter snake can be abundant. In a 1992 paper, "The Snakes of Pennsylvania," William B. Allen stated, "It is not unusual to lift debris and find several dozen or more at one time."

Size   Most specimens of this slender little garter snake measure but 14 to 17 inches and the record is only 22 in.

Habitat   The favored microhabitat of *Thamnophis brachystoma* is areas of herbaceous growth, rockpiles, and other sheltered sites such as fencerows and thickets.

Prey   This species feeds almost exclusively on earthworms. Rarely, slugs, some insects, frogs and salamanders may be accepted by captives.

Reproduction   Live-bearing. Broods of up to 14 (more often 4 to 10) young, each about 5¾ in. long, are born in mid- to late summer.

Coloring/scale form   The short-headed garter snake in fact has a short, narrow head, as described by its Greek-derived name, "brachystoma." Barely wider than its neck, the head may be somewhat paler than the dorsum. Its dorsolateral ground coloring is dark, though not quite black, and there may or may not be still-darker spots within it. Both its typical pale vertebral and lateral stripes may be whitish to pale yellow, with its clearly defined lateral stripes—which are bordered above and below by thin black lines—being restricted to scale rows 2 and 3 above its belly line. (On some individuals this lateral stripe may also involve the bottom of scale row 4.) There are usually 17 rows of dorsal scales and the anal plate is undivided.

Similar snakes   The similarity of the short-headed garter snake to other garters is evident from the fact that it has, at one time or another, been classified as a subspecies of the plains garter, *T. radix*, Butler's garter, *T. butleri*, and the eastern garter, *T. sirtalis*. Identifying it can still be difficult, but both the **eastern garter snake (40)** and the **Butler's garter snake (47)** have proportionately larger heads and 19 rows of dorsal scales.

Behavior   When grasped, like other *Thamnophis* the short-headed garter snake thrashes about, smearing musk and feces on its captor.

47   BUTLER'S GARTER SNAKE, *Thamnophis butleri*

Nonvenomous   Although a nervous species, this small garter snake is not prone to bite and is harmless to humans.

Size   Most Butler's garter snakes are between 15 and 20 inches long (among garter snakes of the eastern U.S., only the short-headed garter is smaller), and few *T. butleri* exceed 25 in. The record is 27¼ inches.

Abundance   Locally common in only a few areas, Butler's garter snake (which is named for 19th-century Indiana naturalist Amos Butler) seems curiously variable in numbers. Typically, it is abundant in places—where one is found, others are likely to turn up nearby—yet in other areas of seemingly ideal habitat it may be scarce or absent.

This species' main range includes central, western and northern Ohio, central and eastern Indiana, eastern Michigan and adjacent southern Ontario. Yet, according to Harding (1997), the identity of the Ontario specimens is questionable. This population apparently contains a preponderance of individuals more similar to the short-headed garter snake, while others appear to be intermediate between the Butler's and short-headed garter snakes. There is also a disjunct population in southeastern Wisconsin.

Habitat   *Thamnophis butleri* is a species of open wetlands—of stream, swamp, and marsh edges occurring in meadows, fields, and pastures (records abound for the southern and western shores of Lake Erie and for the area around Buckeye Lake in central Ohio). Butler's garter snake can also be abundant in litter-strewn urban lots for, like other *Thamnophis*, it takes refuge beneath mats of grass or other vegetation, stones, paper, and boards.

Prey   Although earthworms are favored, leeches, amphibians and, reportedly, some insects are also taken as prey.

Reproduction   Live-bearing. This species bears from 3 to 16 (most often, 6 to 12), 6-inch-long young.

Coloring/scale form   Similar in appearance to the short-headed garter snake, *T. butleri* exhibits somewhat richer pigmentation: its dorsolateral ground color varies from olive-brown to black, upon which in some individuals appears a checkerboard pattern of darker spots. Both vertebral and lateral stripes may be bright yellow or even orange, while the light lateral stripe includes all of scale row 3, the bottom of scale row 4 and the top of scale row 2. The dorsal scales occur in 19 rows and the anal plate is undivided.

Similar snakes   The **short-headed garter snake (46)** has a narrower head, less intense coloring, and only 17 rows of dorsal scales. The **eastern garter snake (40)** has a proportionately broader head and a light side stripe which does not involve lateral scale row 4.

Behavior   *Thamnophis butleri* is typically abroad only in late afternoon and early evening, and seldom found far from cover. When surprised at these times, or when uncovered in hiding, its tendency to erratically throw loops of its body from side to side is well known. If grasped, in defense it squirms even more excitedly and smears an unpleasant mixture of musk and feces over its body.

48   WANDERING GARTER SNAKE

Thamnophis elegans vagrans

Nonvenomous   When uncovered in hiding, wandering garter snakes may attempt to flee, or they may simply hide their heads in their coils and remain stationary. If roughly restrained, this animal may not only bite, but smear itself as well as its captor with a pungent mixture of musk and feces.

Abundance   Generally common over much of a range that reaches southward from western Saskatchewan and central British Columbia to western Nevada and central New Mexico.

Size This is an active garter snake of moderate girth and length. Adults vary from 20 to 30 inches in length, with the record being 37 in.

Habitat *Thamnophis elegans vagrans* occurs in most damp habitats (and some dry ones) at elevations up to 10,500 feet. It may be found along the edges of streams, ponds, and marshes, in mountain and lowland meadows, in forested areas, forest edges and clearings, in fields and along fenceline pasture borders, and in almost all habitats intermediate between these, including sites both higher in elevation and further from water than any other garter snake.

Prey The wandering—"vagrans" in Latin—garter snake is a prey generalist, opportunistically consuming amphibians, lizards, worms, leeches, slugs, and nestling birds. Harry Greene (1997) reports that some populations of this reptile "eat rodents, subduing them by constriction."

Reproduction Live-bearing. From 4 to 20, approximately 8¼ in.-long offspring are produced during July, August and September.

Coloring/scale form *Thamnophis elegans vagrans* is one of the less brilliantly and precisely patterned garter snakes. Many individuals are dusty or dingy in appearance, for example, with a ground color that may be almost any shade of brown or gray, often with a greenish tinge. This is overlaid with a double row of alternating, often rounded, blackish spots.

Both the wandering garter snake's vertebral and lateral stripes (which occupy scale rows 2 and 3 above its belly) also vary in color, but are usually whitish to yellowish. Its pale vertebral line is particularly straight and well defined posteriorly, yet due to the encroachment of its uppermost anterior lateral black spots, its dorsal line appears to zigzag and lose definition toward its neck.

On the wandering garter's crown and nape there may be an extensive area of darker pigment; its venter can be grayish or greenish and, especially posteriorly, is often dusted with darker pigment. There are usually 8 upper labial scales, the dorsal scales occur in 19 or 21 rows, and the anal plate is usually undivided, but may occasionally be divided.

Similar snakes In the area covered by this book, only two other garter snakes share the wandering garter's range: the **red-sided garter snake (44)**, which has red dorsolateral markings, and the **western plains garter snake (50)**, whose lateral stripe is restricted to scale rows 3 and 4 above the belly.

Behavior Congregations of wandering garter snakes have been found in exhumed rodent burrows, including muskrats' bankside tunnels.

Thamnophis radix radix

Nonvenomous   Although they normally try to flee when surprised, if restrained, *T. r. radix* will, like other garter snakes, smear musk and feces on the hand of a captor, and some individuals may even bite vigorously.

Abundance   Common to abundant in areas of prime habitat, but uncommon in the marginal environments that now make up most of its range, *T. r. radix* has suffered extensive habitat degradation from the intensive agricultural exploitation of its small Illinois/Iowa/southern Minnesota range.

Size   The eastern plains garter snake can attain considerable size: although most adults measure only 20 to 30 in., the record is 43 inches. This makes for a large snake because *T. r. radix* is only slender when it is young; with advancing age and length it becomes proportionately bulky.

Habitats   *Thamnophis radix radix* is a creature of open spaces, but usually not truly exposed prairies. It is most often associated with moisture-retaining lowlands and prairie potholes, but farm country meadows, fields, and pastures, as well as city parks and even vacant lots, may harbor sizable populations.

Prey   Worms are this little carnivore's preferred prey, but amphibians and occasional nestling rodents are also taken.

Reproduction   Live bearing. Breeding usually occurs soon after emergence from hibernation, while parturition occurs in mid- to late-summer. Litters of the 6½ inch-long neonates average between 6 and 25, but on occasion number more than 50; the verified record brood is 92.

Coloring/scale form   The eastern plains garter snake is less variable in appearance than many garters. Nevertheless, its ground color may be brownish, olive, reddish, greenish, or charcoal, with overlaying black spots in either a single row or an alternating double row (on snakes with the darkest ground color, these spots may be almost entirely obscured).

This dark pattern is split by a well-defined olive to yellow vertebral stripe. Among both races of *Thamnophis radix* the pale lateral stripe is higher on the side than that of any other garter snake, occupying scale rows 3 and 4 above the belly—which allows room for another row of dark spots below the lateral line.

The venter is bluish, greenish, or yellowish, with an irregular row of dark markings along each side. There are prominent black vertical bars on the upper labial scales, the dorsal scales occur in 19 to 21 rows, and the anal plate is undivided.

Similar snakes   Other garter and ribbon snakes within the range of the eastern plains garter snake have their characteristic pale side stripe on scale rows 2 and 3 above the belly, and many lack black bars on the upper labial scales.

Behavior   This is an alert snake that moves quickly to safety if circumstances allow. In autumn, it may congregate in large numbers in the vicinity of good hibernation sites. A good hibernaculum should be deeply creviced for protection from the cold, and well drained to escape late winter flooding; to the dismay of homeowners, plains garter snakes often find these qualities in the stone foundations of houses.

50   WESTERN PLAINS GARTER SNAKE

Thamnophis radix haydeni

Nonvenomous   This animal will not bite unless handled, when it may snap abruptly in its own defense.

Abundance   Common. From the tip of the Texas panhandle north along the Rockies' front range to Alberta, Saskatchewan and Manitoba, through eastern Minnesota and Iowa to northeastern Missouri, *T. r. haydeni* is a common snake where good habitat prevails.

Size   Adults average 20 to 28 inches in length; the record is 40 in.

Habitat   This subspecies' popular name suggests a grassland range, but within most of its huge central and northern Great Plains range, its microenvironment is more likely to involve the borders of streams, washes, and gullies that cross the prairie, where it is sometimes locally abundant. This is more in keeping with the focus of its namesake, frontier geologist Ferdinand V. Hayden.

Prey   Amphibians and other small vertebrates as well as insects (especially grasshoppers and, among the young, earthworms) are the principal prey of *T. r. haydeni*.

Reproduction   Live-bearing. Litters average 29 offspring.

Coloring/scale form   Dorsally, the western plains garter snake resembles a checkered garter snake: its white or very light yellow vertebral stripe is flanked with a closely spaced double row of black squares. Below these checkers, a prominent pale yellow lateral stripe occupies the third and fourth scale rows above the belly—a position higher on the sides than that of any other garter snake and one unique to *Thamnophis radix*. Below it another row of squarish black spots appears.

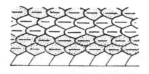

Lateral stripe marking: western plains garter snake

With 21 rows of dorsal scales, *T. r. haydeni* also has more numerous dorsal scales than any other garter snake but the checkered. Its off-white to pale-greenish ventral scales often bear a line of dark distal spots and its anal plate is undivided.

Similar snakes   This is a difficult animal to distinguish from the **checkered garter snake (51)**, whose range overlaps that of the western plains garter in the Texas and Oklahoma panhandles. The checkered garter's light yellow, posteriorly black-bordered neck crescent is more prominently defined, however, and its light-hued side stripe does not reach the fourth scale row above its belly line. **Ribbon snakes (54–61)** are more slender, with proportionately longer tails, unspotted backs, unmarked whitish lips and bellies, a prominent, recurved white spot just ahead of the eye, and 19 rows of dorsal scales.

Behavior   Seasonally active from March to November, western plains garter snakes retire below ground during the hottest weeks of summer, for they are quite sensitive to high temperatures, becoming overheated at more than 90°F. *Thamnophis radix* is relatively hardy in cool weather, though, for on sunny autumn days too chilly for most reptiles to be abroad large numbers of western plains garter snakes sometimes crawl onto asphalt roads where they remain, absorbing warmth from the blacktop, until many are slain by traffic.

51 CHECKERED GARTER SNAKE

Thamnophis marcianus marcianus

Nonvenomous   Large checkered garter snakes may nip if handled roughly.

Abundance   *Thamnophis marcianus marcianus* is often abundant in the southern part of its U.S. range—the western two-thirds of both Texas and Oklahoma and southern Kansas—but is far less common elsewhere. In past years, during its late spring and early summer foraging period, checkered garter snakes were by far the most numerous terrestrial serpents observed in rural South Texas. By the late 1990s, however, only a handful of these animals could be seen in a night's drive over roads which, ten years earlier, had produced sightings of as many as 80 *T. m. marcianus* in an evening. Habitat has not changed appreciably in this area, so the checkered garter's decline here may be due to increased traffic.

Size   Adult *T. m. marcianus* average 15 to 28 inches in length; the record specimen measured 42½ in.

Habitat   In North Texas, the Trans-Pecos, and Oklahoma, the checkered garter snake seems to prefer grassy areas near water, where it is widespread but, most often, is not particularly numerous. In the dry Tamaulipan thorn brush of the Rio Grande plain, checkered garters are much more common. Here, their periods of activity are more closely tied to rainfall, for when the soil is moist from recent precipitation the annelid and anuran prey of *T. m. marcianus* is abroad on the surface and the humid air allows this olfactory predator to follow their scent.

Prey   Captive checkered garter snakes feed voraciously on worms, tadpoles, frogs, and small mice. A variety of other small vertebrate, insect, and annelid prey is undoubtedly taken in the wild, while *T. m. marcianus* is also among the handful of serpents that sometimes feed on carrion. See **Eastern Black-necked Garter Snake.**

Reproduction   Live-bearing. Most checkered garter snakes give birth between late May and September. The Oct. 6 deposition of 38 newborns, averaging just over 7¾ inches in length, by a 28-inch-long southern Texas female is the latest date on record. (In a somewhat unusual ophidian developmental process, young checkered garter snakes are partially nourished through their mother's placenta.) Following their birth, the young, which exactly resemble their parents except with more vivid coloring, tend to be relatively sluggish in the wild, and throughout the Rio Grande brush country it is not unusual to find healthy neonates lying full length in the middle of mesquite-shaded cow paths.

Coloring/scale form The checkered garter snake's white or very light yellow vertebral stripe is flanked, on each side of its pale, gray-green back and sides, with a double row of black squares. (Checkered garter snakes from Texas' Edwards Plateau have a tendency toward melanism: two melanistic *T. m. marcianus* from this area were displayed at the San Antonio Zoo, and other all-black specimens have come from Kerr and Medina counties.)

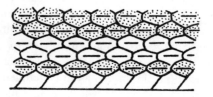

Lateral stripe marking: checkered garter snake

The checkered garter snake's most distinctive marking, however, is the prominent pale-yellow crescent behind its jaw, posteriorly bordered by a large black nuchal spot. Laterally, a light-hued stripe occupies only the third row of scales above the belly on the foreparts, but widens to include the second scale row over the rest of the body; the otherwise unmarked whitish-yellow ventral scales sometimes have blackish edges. The dorsal scales are arranged in 21 rows at midbody; the anal plate is undivided.

Similar snakes Texas (45) and both **black-necked garter snakes (52, 53)** lack a prominent yellow crescent behind the jaw and have only 19 midbody rows of dorsal scales. The **western plains garter snake (50)** has a less prominent yellow nuchal crescent, while its anterior lateral stripe occupies the third and fourth scale rows above its venter.

Behavior Named *T. m. marcianus* for Captain Randolph B. Marcy, who in 1852 delivered to the Smithsonian Institute the original type specimen obtained during an expedition along the Red River, the checkered garter snake ranges from Kansas to Belize. It is also an ancient animal: the fossilized remains of a snake thought to be *T. marcianus* were recovered in Hardeman County, Texas strata dating from the Wisconsin Glacial Period of 50,000 to 100,000 years ago.

Marcy's garter snakes follow the typical ophidian pattern of foraging at dawn and dusk in spring and fall, then becoming both nocturnal and less active during the hottest months; with cooler autumn weather checkered garters appear once more. In the manner of ring-necked, ground, and other subcaudally red or banded snakes, occasional specimens exhibit a defensive posture (first photographed by Donna Marvel beside a Rio Grande irrigation ditch) in which the tightly curled yellowish underside of the posterior third of the trunk is suddenly everted.

52 WESTERN BLACK-NECKED GARTER SNAKE, *Thamnophis cyrtopsis cyrtopsis*

Nonvenomous   Western black-necked garter snakes nip humans only if they are molested or handled roughly.

Abundance   Common. In scattered well-watered habitats (which are sparsely distributed across Texas' Northern Chihuahuan Desert), this reptile may be abundant. In Brewster County, Sherman Minton (1959) found, "In late July, almost every pool in the little canyon below Boot Spring was occupied by 2 to 6 of these snakes. They were sunning on rocks or swimming in pursuit of *Hyla arenicolor* [canyon treefrog] tadpoles, which were found in the stomachs of all those collected."

Size   Adults average 16 to 28 inches; the largest western black-necked garter on record measured 41¾ in.

Habitat   Due to the presence of water there, *T. c. cyrtopsis* is more often a mountain-canyon dweller than a resident of low-lying desert, but near desert valley springs it may be common.

Prey   See **Eastern Black-necked Garter Snake**.

Reproduction   Live-bearing. Broods of 3 to 25 young have been recorded.

Coloring/scale form   On the forebody, a broad, pale orange vertebral stripe divides a single row of large black dorsolateral squares; posteriorly, this row of black markings splits into a double, checkerboard-like row. The crown is bluish gray, strikingly set off from the big black neck patch that is the source of both this subspecies' common name, and, from "cyrto" or "curved," its scientific name as well. The western black-necked garter snake's whitish side stripe occupies the second and third scale rows above its venter throughout its length, and its chin is also white, with dark-edged labial scales. Its venter is white as well, sometimes with a greenish or yellowish-brown cast, there are 19 rows of dorsal scales at midbody, and its anal plate is undivided.

Similar snakes The subspecies **eastern black-necked garter snake (53)** (with which the western race intergrades throughout the western Edwards Plateau and eastern Trans-Pecos) has a single row of much larger, rounded or V-shaped dark anterior dorsolateral blotches, the lower tips of which reach downward into its wide yellow lateral stripe, giving this stripe a wavy look. The **checkered garter snake (51)** is not usually found in the dry, upland locales where the western black-necked garter most often occurs, but is distinguished by the prominent yellow crescent located just behind its jaw, by the anterior restriction of its pale side stripe to the third row of scales above its belly, and by its 21 midbody rows of dorsal scales. **Ribbon snakes (54–61)** are more slender, with proportionately longer tails, unmarked white upper labial scales, and a white, half-moon-shaped spot just forward of the eye. Ribbon snakes also lack the garter snakes' black-blotched back.

Behavior *Thamnophis cyrtopsis cyrtopsis* is frequently encountered basking on creekside rocks from which, if disturbed, it flees by swimming across the surface to the opposite bank. Here it typically seeks shelter under overhanging rocks or vegetation. If cornered, this little animal may flatten its body against the ground and writhe as menacingly as possible.

   Such a strategy is of no use against large ophidian predators, however, for a freshly devoured, 22-inch-long western black-necked garter was disgorged by a Sonoran gopher snake captured south of Fort Stockton by the author (Tennant).

53 EASTERN BLACK-NECKED GARTER SNAKE, *Thamnophis cyrtopsis ocellatus*

Nonvenomous *Thamnophis cyrtopsis ocellatus* generally defends itself only by discharging feces and musk, but a large individual may nip if molested.

Abundance Common. Endemic to Texas, the eastern black-necked garter snakes' range is confined to this state's central hill country. Here, due to its vivid colors and diurnal foraging, it is often noticed in the residential neighborhoods spreading westward from San Antonio, New Braunfels, San Marcos, and Austin.

   In these new housing developments, homes are often built during the winter over the brumation crevices of *T. c. ocellatus*, and when these beautiful little serpents emerge in spring they find themselves literally on the new residents' doorsteps—often causing consternation since in popular mythology a bright orange and black snake, however small and innocuous, means danger.

Size   Adults average 16 to 20 inches in length; the record is 43 inches.

Habitat   The eastern black-necked garter snake's primary habitat is moist, wooded ravines and streamside bottomland; heavily foliaged residential neighborhoods approximate this environment and support sizable populations of *T. c. ocellatus*.

Prey   In an extensive study of predation in this and two other *Thamnophis* species in Travis County, Texas, M. J. Fourquette (1954) found that the eastern black-necked garter takes mainly tadpole prey during spring and early summer, then adult frogs the rest of the year. (Along the Balcones Fault west of Austin, Fourquette found that its anuran prey was primarily the locally abundant cliff frog, although slimy salamanders, red-spotted toads, and ground skinks were also noted.)

   In this area, the eastern black-necked garter snake competes for food mainly with the red-striped ribbon snake, which also favors amphibian prey. The garter snake takes primarily amphibians it finds on land, however, while the predominantly aquatic ribbon snake seeks frogs and salamanders in water.

Reproduction   Live-bearing. The average brood is 9 young, 8 to 10½ inches in length.

Coloring/scale form   First described by C. B. R. Kennicott in 1860, the eastern black-necked garter snake takes its name from the Greek *cyrto*, "curved," and *Aopsis*, "appearance"—a reference to the hemispherical black blotch located just behind its jaw. Flanking this snake's orange vertebral stripe, a row of large black dorsolateral blotches, separated by tiny light-and-dark bars, encroaches downward into the forward portion of its broad yellow side stripe (which occupies the second and third scale rows above its venter), giving this stripe a wavy appearance. Posteriorly, these blotches diverge into a double row of staggered black spots. The dorsal scales are arranged in 19 rows at midbody and the anal plate is undivided.

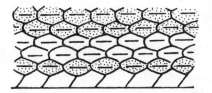

Lateral stripe markings: eastern and western black-necked garter snakes

Similar snakes No other *Thamnophis* occurring within the range of *T. c. ocellatus* has a single row of very large black blotches on either side of its neck. The **western black-necked garter snake (52)** (with which the eastern race intergrades throughout the western Edwards Plateau and eastern Trans-Pecos) has black checkerboard dorsolateral patterning on the rear of its body, the **checkered garter snake (51)** has three staggeered rows of small, black dorsolateral squares. The pale side stripe of the **Texas garter snake (45)**, unlike that of *T. c. ocellatus*, occupies part of the fourth scale row above its belly.

Behavior Both eastern and western black-necked garter snakes are diurnally active during even the hottest summer months, but almost always remain near some sort of aquatic habitat. Vision is used for capturing elusive nearby prey, but sight is less important than scent in locating food animals, for the instinctually recognized smell of appropriate prey species such as earthworms, anurans and fish is what usually allows garter snakes to find their prey.

Despite its gaudy appearance, the eastern black-necked garter's bright vertebral stripe apparently functions as sophisticated camouflage: as *T. c. ocellatus* slides away from danger, its black dorsal spots and orange vertebral pigment flash intermittently through intervening leafy undergrowth, focusing a predator's visual attention on what seems to be a flickering but stationary ribbon of orange.

---

54 EASTERN RIBBON SNAKE

Thamnophis sauritus sauritus

Nonvenomous Ribbon snakes are gracile, small-headed serpents that do not bite humans unless they are seized, but they can nip firmly.

Abundance Known since 1776, when Linneaus named both garter and ribbon snakes "sauritus" for their supposed resemblance to lizards, the eastern ribbon snake is common in good habitat throughout much of its very broad range, which runs from the Gulf coastlines of Louisiana, Mississippi, Alabama, and the Florida panhandle north along the Mississippi valley to southern Indiana. East of the Appalachians, its range extends along the Atlantic seaboard as far north as central New Hampshire, Vermont, and southern Maine.

Size   Adult *T. s. sauritus* average 20 to 32 inches in length, but are so slender that full-sized individuals generally weigh less than 5 oz. The record is 38 inches.

Habitat   The eastern ribbon snake inhabits an enormous variety of both wooded and grass- and marshland environments, as well as agricultural areas and urban parks, but it is seldom found far from water.

Prey   Most often a creature of creek, lake, and pond margins, *T. s. sauritus* typically ranges along marshy shorelines taking whatever small prey—crustaceans, frogs, and fish—it encounters; only when movement on the surface attracts its attention does it ordinarily make forays into the water. On land, *T. s. sauritus* uses scent-tracking to locate fossorial food species such as earthworms, but relies on the movement of prey to ferret small toads and frogs from beneath grass and leaf litter.

Reproduction   Live-bearing. Gravid individuals appear as early as April, while by July the majority of adult female *T. s. sauritus* are pregnant. See **Northern Ribbon Snake.**

Coloring/scale form   Like many other fast-moving snakes worldwide, ribbon snakes are prominently striped with bright colors. The extremely slender body and tail are black or dark olive above, with a pale yellow, orange, or greenish-tan vertebral stripe. Two tiny white dashes often punctuate the rear of the dark crown, a prominent white spot is visible in front of the eye, and the pale upper labial scales are unmarked. The light tan lateral stripe occupies the 3rd and 4th scale rows above the yellowish-green belly.

Like other ribbon snakes, there is sometimes a white spot on the rear of each parietal scale as well as a vertical white spot immediately in front of each large eye. The dorsal scales are arranged in 19 rows at midbody and the anal plate is undivided.

Similar snakes   Four races of *Thamnophis sauritus* occur from the Great Lakes to the Florida Keys: in northern New York state and the Midwest, *T. s. sauritus* is replaced by the **northern ribbon snake (55)**, a slightly smaller, proportionately shorter-tailed race whose dorsum appears darker because its vertebral stripe is often suffused with melanin. In Florida, the eastern ribbon is replaced by the **peninsula ribbon snake (56)**, whose dorsum is dark brown to tan rather than black, and whose pale lateral stripe is yellow.

The **western ribbon snake (58)**, *Thamnophis proximus*, which has a wider dark lateral band than the eastern ribbon, was long thought to be a subspecies of the eastern ribbon snake—*proximus* means "neighboring"—until Douglas Rossman (1963b) demonstrated that in the few regions where these animals occur together the two do not recognize each other as potential mates. (Because of this, Rossman concluded that western and eastern ribbon snakes are separate species whose differentiation occurred when the range of their common ancestor was split by the cold pushed southward by the advance of late Pleistocene glaciers.)

Garter snakes (40–53) are stockier, shorter-tailed (among garter snakes the tail is less than ⅓ of total length), less precisely patterned, and generally lack a prominent white spot in front of the eye.

Behavior   *Thamnophis sauritus sauritus* is fond of basking on bankside elevations such as logs and fallen fence posts, where it may remain motionless despite being approached very closely then quickly dashing into a crayfish burrow or thick vegetation. See **Peninsula** and **Blue-striped Ribbon Snakes**.

---

55   NORTHERN RIBBON SNAKE
Thamnophis sauritus septentrionalis

Nonvenomous   If grasped, *T. s. septentrionalis* will wriggle energetically in an attempt to escape, but it seldom bites. Yet like most natricines, it will attempt to make itself unpalatable to a predator by smearing copious amounts of pungent musk and fecal material on itself and its assailant.

Abundance   This ribbon snake is generally common in suitable habitat in the heart of its range—which extends westward from the Atlantic Coast of southern Maine, through central New Hampshire and Vermont, most of New York state, to Michigan, and in disjunct populations, eastern Wisconsin. Yet it is uncommon in what seem to be equally suitable locations in more outlying parts of this territory.

Size   This northernmost race—"septentrionalis," or "northerly," in Latin—of *Thamnophis sauritus* is adult at 20 to 34 inches in length.

Habitat   Because of their dietary preferences (including heavy reliance on tadpole prey during spring), ribbon snakes are tied to watercourses more closely than the related garter snakes, and are most often found along the edges of bogs, ponds, lakes, canals, wet ditches, swamps and marshes.

Prey   Amphibians and small fish are the primary prey of the northern ribbon snake (unlike garter snakes, ribbon snakes seldom feed on earthworms).

Reproduction   Live-bearing. *Thamnophis sauritus septentrionalis* produces an annual (occasionally biennial) litter of about 10 off-spring; occasionally, nearly twice that number are born. The young are 8 to 8½ inches long and are slightly paler versions of the adults.

Coloring/scale form   The ground color of the northern ribbon snake is black or a very dark brown. Its whitish- to butter-yellow or green-ish-white vertebral stripe may be partially suffused with dark pigment, while its identically hued lateral stripe occurs on scale rows 3 and 4 above its belly, being separated from the venter by a dark stripe on both scale rows 1 and 2 and the outer edge of each belly scale.

The unmarked venter is almost the same color as (sometimes a lit-tle greener than) the lateral stripes. Like other ribbon snakes, there is usually a white spot on the rear of each parietal scale as well as a ver-tical white spot immediately in front of each large eye. There are 19 rows of dorsal scales and the anal plate is undivided.

Similar snakes   The **eastern garter snake (40)** is stockier, shorter-tailed (among garter snakes the tail is less than ⅓ the total length), and less precisely patterned. It has a pale lateral stripe on scale rows 2 and 3 above its belly line. The **eastern ribbon snake (54)** is larger and proportionally longer-tailed, with a brighter and more clearly defined vertebral stripe. Most **western ribbon snakes (58)** have an orange rather than a yellow vertebral stripe.

Behavior   First described by *Thamnophis* authority Douglas Ross-man in 1963, in the manner of other ribbon snakes this shy but alert serpent often carries its head well above ground like a racer. See **Peninsula** and **Blue-striped Ribbon Snakes.**

56   PENINSULA RIBBON SNAKE

Thamnophis sauritus sackenii

Nonvenomous   See **Northern Ribbon Snake.**

Abundance   *Thamnophis sauritus sackenii* is named for Carl R. von der Osten-sacken, a Russian entomologist who in 1859 collected the type specimen for the Smithsonion In-stitute. This subspecies is common throughout southeastern Georgia and peninsular Florida south to the lower Keys (where it is threatened by commercial development). In areas of good habitat (luetic bodies of water with heavily vegetated banks) peninsula rib-bon snakes can be extremely abundant. When these areas are disturbed, as they often are, by plowing or clearing for subdivi-sions, newly exposed *Thamnophis sauritus* suffer heavy predation by carnivorous herons.

Size   Most adult *T. s. sackenii* are 20 to 28 inches long; the record is 40 in.

Habitat   See **Eastern Ribbon Snake.**

Prey   See **Eastern Ribbon Snake.**

Reproduction   Live-bearing. Breeding takes place from April through June. Litters of up to 20 are deposited between July and September.

Coloring/scale form   The dorsum is dark brown to tan, with both a yellowish-tan vertebral stripe and a whitish lateral stripe on the 3rd and 4th scale rows above the yellowish venter (the lips, light lateral stripes, and bellies of individuals living along the lower Gulf Coast have a bluish cast, however).

Like other ribbon snakes, there is usually a white spot on the rear of each parietal scale as well as a vertical white spot immediately in front of each large eye. There are 19 rows of dorsal scales and the anal plate is undivided.

Similar snakes   In mysterious anomaly of coloration, along Florida's upper Gulf Coast the peninsula ribbon snake is replaced by the **blue-striped ribbon snake (57)**, a race identical except for its black dorsum and striking blue lateral stripe. (In the same area the eastern garter snake is also replaced by a bluish race).

Behavior   Ribbon snakes are easily observed because they are diurnally active, though they also forage at dusk and during the night. In most of its southern range, *T. s. sackenii* is abroad year-round, occupying a home territory of several acres—much of which may be seasonally flooded. Although these snakes hunt throughout their territories, they seem to prefer canal banks to almost any other microenvironment—where they can be ubiquitous immediately after warm summer rains when frogs and toads are active.

57   BLUE-STRIPED RIBBON SNAKE

Thamnophis sauritus nitae

Nonvenomous   Like most *Thamnophis*, an adult can deliver a sharp nip if picked up roughly.

Abundance   Endemic to Florida, the blue-striped ribbon snake is common from eastern Wakulla County in the Florida panhandle down the Gulf Coast to Hernando County.

Size   Small even for a ribbon snake, most adult *T. s. nitae* measure less than 23 inches in length; the record is 30 in.

Habitat   This coastal plain serpent is seen most frequently in open marshes, prairies, and prairie hammocks; pine flatwoods and bottomland forest are also occupied.

Prey   Ribbon snakes' prey is seasonally variable. During late spring tadpoles constitute much of the diet; at other times, adult frogs and toads, lizards, and fish are principal food animals.

Reproduction   Live-bearing. Recorded broods range from 5 to 27.

Coloring/scale form   The blue-striped ribbon snake is identical to the subspecies peninsula ribbon snake except for its sooty black dorsum (usually devoid of pale vertebral line) and its striking, bright to pale-blue lateral stripe.

Similar snakes   The **blue-striped garter snake (42)** is heavier-bodied and proportionately shorter-tailed. It generally lacks both the pair of white spots found on most ribbon snakes' posterior crown and the rearward-curved white spot in front of the ribbon snake's eye. The blue-striped garter's pale side-stripe is located on the 2nd and 3rd scale rows above its belly. The **peninsula ribbon snake (56)** is similar, but has yellowish-tan vertebral and lateral stripes.

Behavior   Like other ribbon snakes, *T. s. nitae* is preyed upon by larger serpents such as racers, kingsnakes, and coachwhips, as well as by mammals and carnivorous birds. So many of these predators manage to grab only ribbon snakes' fragile tail tip—which is easily broken off, thus perhaps satisfying a small carnivore—that it is not unusual to find otherwise healthy *T. sauritus* which lack complete tails.

58   WESTERN RIBBON SNAKE

Thamnophis proximus proximus

Nonvenomous   See **Red-striped Ribbon Snake.**

Abundance   Western ribbon snakes are generally common in areas of suitable habitat throughout both the southern Great Plains and its complex interface with the eastern woodlands. *T. p. proximus* inhabits a long sweep of this terrain stretching from central Louisiana and northeastern Texas to northern Kansas and Missouri, then upstream along the Missouri and Mississippi River corridors to, respectively, northern Nebraska and southern Minnesota; other subspecies range as far south as Costa Rica.

Size   Adults are 20 to 34 inches long, with such slender bodies that 3 female western ribbon snakes between 27 and 34 inches in length—as with all *Thamnophis*, females are the larger gender—averaged less than 6 ounces in weight.

Habitat   As the old forest of the eastern U.S. woodlands thins toward the open country of the plains, agricultural lands now prevail, but these are not as hostile to ribbon snakes as to larger snake species. The drainage ditches bordering crop fields offer an approximation of ribbon snakes' natural creekside microenvironment, and *T. p. proximus* may occur near any strip of fresh water—natural or man-made—with vegetative cover along its banks. It is also often found in arid brush country, but seldom far from a source of water.

Prey   Western ribbon snakes' prey varies with the seasons: 92 percent of the stomach contents of one central Texas sample trapped during late spring consisted of tadpoles. At other times frogs and toads (whose digitaloid skin toxins garter snakes are metabolically equipped to digest), lizards, and small fish may be this snake's principal prey. Besides mammalian and avian carnivores, ribbon snakes are themselves devoured by big, fast-moving snakes like racers and coachwhips.

Reproduction   Live-bearing. One female *T. p. proximus* captured near Stanford, Oklahoma, gave birth to 21 young on Aug. 8, while three litters from northeast Texas were deposited July 10 and 18, and Aug. 20.

Of these three, the two smaller females each gave birth to 18 young, the larger one to 23. All the neonates were about the same size: between 9½ and 10 inches in length, slimmer than a pencil at midbody, and about ¹⁄₁₀ ounce in weight.

As with most snake species, mortality among first- and second-year juveniles is high. Donald Clark (1974) reports heavy winter die-offs among juvenile western ribbon snakes, presumably because their smaller ratio of bulk-to-surface area renders them more vulnerable to desiccation during their critical November-through-February brumation period.

Among Clark's East Texas population, sufficient rainfall before and during denning appeared to be the primary factor determining survival of juvenile *T. p. proximus*, for dry autumn weather limited the abundance of small frogs and resulted in low fat levels among the young about to enter winter dormancy. Little precipitation later in the year, combined with very cold winter weather, then resulted in an estimated mortality of 74% of this vulnerable age group during brumation.

Coloring/scale form   The western ribbon snake's unmarked dark gray-brown dorsum is split by a broad orange vertebral stripe. Like that of all ribbon snakes, its yellowish lateral stripe occupies the third and fourth scale rows above its yellowish-green venter. Its white upper labial scales are unmarked, although the lips, lateral stripe, and belly of individuals living north and east of Dallas often have a bluish cast. Two tiny white dashes punctuate the rear of its blackish crown and a rearward-curved white spot occurs just in front of each eye. The dorsal scales are arranged in 19 rows at midbody and the anal plate is undivided.

Similar snakes   Of the several races with which the western ribbon snake intergrades, the **Gulf Coast ribbon snake (60)** typically has a brownish- to olive-green back and sides and an olive-tan to dull gold vertebral stripe, and the **red-striped ribbon snake (59)** has a dark gray back, a wine-red vertebral stripe, and gray-green lower sides. The **arid land ribbon snake (61)** usually has a gray-brown back (although individuals from the Canadian and Cimarron River drainages sometimes have a darker ground color), with both a distinctive thin black ventrolateral seam and a broad orange vertebral stripe that lightens to gold on the nape.

Behavior   During late August and September newborn ribbon snakes can sometimes be found sheltering in tall creekside grass or under planks; in taller brush of lake and stream shorelines these juveniles are sometimes somewhat arboreal; near the Red River nine small western ribbon snakes were observed basking the branches of a brush-filled gully.

59   RED-STRIPED RIBBON SNAKE

Thamnophis proximus rubrilineatus

Nonvenomous   Like most *Thamnophis*, ribbon snakes, if seized roughly, can nip and hang on tenaciously despite their small heads.

Abundance   Common. Endemic to Texas, the red-striped ribbon snake is found primarily in the oak-juniper savannah of the state's central Edwards Plateau; intergrade individuals combining characteristics of the three ribbon snake races whose range surrounds that of *T. p. rubrilineatus* occur in a wide margin around this range.

Size   Most adults are 24 to 36 inches long. Typically, the red-striped ribbon snake is quite slender, but three-way intergrades between it and the Gulf Coast and arid land ribbons snakes (the latter the longest *Thamnophis proximus*) can grow much larger. Such animals inhabit South Texas' Tamaulipan thorn woodland and may attain more than twice this species' usual girth, becoming so thick-bodied that they resemble the similarly-colored Texas garter snake.

Habitat   Like other ribbon snakes, *T. p. rubrilineatus* is almost always found near water, where it is easily observed because of its diurnal activity pattern: when not actively foraging, it basks on rocks, logs, and the raised cypress knees that occur along watercourses.

Such individuals typically remain motionless until approached very closely, or even touched, when they streak away across the water's surface to hide beneath overhanging rocks or vegetation on the opposite bank. During late August and September newborn red-striped ribbon snakes can often be found sheltering under creekside limestone flags.

Prey   Ribbon snakes' prey is seasonally variable, but is almost always obtained from aquatic environments. In spring, tadpoles constitute much of the diet; at other times, small fish, salamanders, and adult frogs and toads—whose digitaloid skin toxins ribbon snakes are metabolically equipped to digest—are principal food animals.

On land, ribbon snakes use scent-tracking to locate fossorial food animals such as earthworms, as well as to ferret lizards and small anurans from beneath grass and litter.

Reproduction   Live-bearing. Breeding takes place from April through June. Litters of up to 20 are deposited between July and September.

Coloring/scale form   The narrow vertebral stripe splitting the dark gray back of this subspecies can vary from deep wine red (*rubrilineatus* means "red-striped") near the tail to bright orange at the nape, although entirely orange-striped specimens turn up throughout the range.

Like other ribbon snakes, there is usually a white dot on the rear of each parietal scale as well as a larger vertical white spot immediately in front of each large eye. There are 19 rows of dorsal scales and the anal plate is undivided.

Similar snakes   The 4 geographical races of *Thamnophis proximus* interbreed to produce clinal variations intermediate between the red-striped ribbon, the **Gulf Coast ribbon snake (60)**, which typically has a brownish- to olive-green back and sides and an olive-tan to dull gold vertebral stripe, the **arid land ribbon snake (61)**, whose orange vertebral stripe bisects an olive-brown to gray back and tan lower sides, and the **western ribbon snake (58)**, whose dark gray-brown back is split by a broad orange vertebral stripe.

Behavior   Ribbon snakes' conspicuous vertebral stripe is believed to help them evade predators. Seen through thick vegetation, as the snake moves away from a viewer this bright line between its unmarked dark sides appears to remain stationary (but gradually narrowing) as the snake slides deeper into the bushes.

Even knowing that such a partially hidden snake is moving away, it is still a surprise to see its tail tip suddenly slip from view, and predators may get the same surprise because so many manage to catch only the ribbon snake's tail tip—which is easily twisted off—that nearly 20 percent of the *Thamnophis proximus* in one Kansas study lacked complete tails.

60 GULF COAST RIBBON SNAKE

Thamnophis proximus orarius

Nonvenomous   See **Red-striped Ribbon Snake.**

Abundance   Common. Although to the north and west of its primary range *T. p. orarius* intergrades with the three ribbon snake races whose territories border its own, its principal distribution is along, and up to a hundred miles inland from, the Texas and Louisiana Gulf Coasts.

Size   See **Red-striped Ribbon Snake.**

Habitat   *Thamnophis proximus orarius* inhabits coastal marshes, moist prairie, and low dikes and roadbeds that rise a few inches above the surrounding wetlands (in Texas, a favored microhabitat is the levees that impound rice field irrigation lakes). Nearer the Gulf Coast, these reptiles are also found in grassy dunes no more than 30 yards from breaking surf, but wooded inland terrain is occupied as well.

Prey   Ribbon snakes typically forage along marshy shorelines, taking insects, crustaceans, and small vertebrates. Nearly as aquatic as the water snakes to which they are related, ribbon snakes rely on diving into water for protection. Without this refuge they seem to be quite vulnerable, for the author (Tennant) has seen small Gulf Coast ribbon snakes heavily preyed upon by cattle egrets in the drying bed of the Nueces River, Texas.

Reproduction   Live-bearing. Breeding begins early in the year: gravid *T. p. orarius* have been discovered as early as April, and by July, 88 percent of females examined in one study were found to be pregnant. Recorded broods for *Thamnophis proximus* have ranged from 5 to 27.

Coloring/scale form   First delineated as a subspecies in 1963 by *Thamnophis* specialist Douglas Rossman, this race is notable for its mint-green upper labial scales, chartreuse venter, and a less contrasting dorsal pattern than inland-living ribbon snakes. *T. p. orarius* has a brownish-green back whose pale vertebral line is almost the same color as its olive-tan side stripes. (*T. p. orarius* from South Texas often have cream-colored vertebral stripes, however, while those from East Texas and Louisiana may have a golden spinal stripe and backs and sides nearly as dark as those of the western ribbon snake.)

There is usually a white spot on the rear of each parietal scale, a vertical white spot immediately in front of each large eye, 19 rows of dorsal scales and an undivided anal plate.

Similar snakes The 4 races of *Thamnophis proximus* interbreed freely, producing intermediate forms which vary clinally as the range of each subspecies merges with that of adjoining races. In their pure forms, however, the **western ribbon snake (58)** has a darker back and a broad orange vertebral stripe, the **red-striped ribbon snake (59)** has a slightly narrower vertebral stripe (which can vary from wine-red near the tail to bright orange at the nape) that splits a dark gray back, and the **arid land ribbon snake (61)** has a gray-brown back with both a thin black ventrolateral seam and a broad orange verte-bral stripe that lightens to gold on its nape.

Behavior In studying a woodland population of Gulf Coast ribbon snakes on the Sarpy Wildlife Refuge, a cypress-gum swamp north-west of New Orleans, Donald Tinkle (1957) established that in this subtropical climate ribbon snakes are active almost year-round—although their most extensive foraging occurred immediately after warm summer rains when frogs and toads were abroad.

Tinkle found that his marked snakes occupied home territories sev-eral acres in extent although, because they foraged throughout the study area, he encountered them most frequently on earthen ridges extending into a swamp. Here, in cool spring weather, they basked in the sunny upper layers of blackberry vines; in summer they sought the protection of the wooded parts of the ridges.

61 ARID LAND RIBBON SNAKE

Thamnophis proximus diabolicus

Nonvenomous Ribbon snakes nip only if they are molested.

Abundance Common. The arid land ribbon snake's ability to penetrate westward along river courses and to subsist around even small bodies of water al-lows this westernmost race of *T. proximus* to oc-cupy large areas of West Texas and (as an intergrade with the western ribbon snake) parts of western Okla-homa and Kansas. Another population exists as far upstream on the Pecos River as Artesia, New Mexico.

In large measure this is because of man. Since the late 19th century, ranchers have been pumping water from panhandle aquifers into stock tanks—artificial ponds which provide frogs and toads an aquatic reproductive niche and provide them with flies drawn to the manure-covered banks. As a result, these anurans' ribbon snake predators, which were previously restricted to the heads of narrow creeks on the dry prairie, have now colonized the newly manmade waterholes scattered across the High Plains.

Size The longest of Texas' ribbon snakes, *T. p. diabolicus* has been recorded to just over 4 feet in length. See **Red-striped Ribbon Snake**.

Habitat See **Red-striped Ribbon Snake**.

Prey Any small vertebrate (or even suitably sized invertebrate, although annelids are not eaten) moving about within a ribbon snake's sight may constitute prey, but pond-dwelling frogs and toads seem to be the major component in the diet of many *T. p. diabolicus*. (Like their relatives the garter snakes, ribbon snakes are able to feed on toads because enlarged adrenal glands allow them to partially neutralize toads' toxic epidermal secretions. These secretions contain the digitaloid poisons which cause dogs that have bitten a toad to gag and froth at the mouth, and can slow or even stop the heartbeat of small predators not metabolically equipped to counter their neurologically suppressive effect.)

Reproduction Live-bearing. See **Gulf Coast Ribbon Snake**.

Coloring/scale form Because the type specimen was taken near the Devil's River, this snake owes its subspecies name to the Greek *diabolikos*. Its back is usually gray-brown—though individuals from the Canadian and Cimarron river drainages sometimes display a darker ground color—with a broad orange vertebral stripe that lightens to gold on the nape and a distinctive thin black ventrolateral seam.

Like other ribbon snakes, there is usually a white spot on the rear of each parietal scale as well as a vertical white spot immediately in front of each large eye. There are 19 rows of dorsal scales and the anal plate is undivided.

Similar snakes Throughout the Texas and Oklahoma panhandles *T. p. diabolicus* intergrades with the **western ribbon snake** (58), which generally has a darker back and a slightly narrower vertebral stripe. Likewise, on the Stockton and western Edwards plateaus the arid land ribbon snake intergrades with the **red-striped ribbon snake** (59), the latter having a ruddier vertebral stripe than the arid land race. As far northwest as Laredo on the Rio Grande plain, the arid land ribbon snake's range overlaps that of the olive-backed, vertebrally greenish-tan striped **Gulf Coast ribbon snake** (60), although in this area the genetic influence of the red-striped ribbon snake is also sometimes evident. See **Red-striped Ribbon Snake.**

Behavior   The arid land ribbon snake's behavior, although partially adapted to the drier conditions of its range, is fundamentally similar to that of other subspecies of *Thamnophis proximus.*

AQUATIC SNAKES
Genus Nerodia

Northern Water Snake, *Nerodia sipedon sipedon*
Lake Erie Water Snake, *Nerodia sipedon insularum*
Midland Water Snake, *Nerodia sipedon pleuralis*
Carolina Water Snake, *Nerodia sipedon williamengelsi*
Red-bellied Water Snake, *Nerodia erythrogaster erythrogaster*
Copper-bellied Water Snake, *Nerodia erythrogaster neglecta*
Yellow-bellied Water Snake, *Nerodia erythrogaster flavigaster*
Blotched Water Snake, *Nerodia erythrogaster transversa*
Banded Water Snake, *Nerodia fasciata fasciata*
Broad-banded Water Snake, *Nerodia fasciata confluens*
Florida Water Snake, *Nerodia fasciata pictiventris*
Gulf Salt Marsh Snake, *Nerodia clarki clarkii*
Atlantic Salt Marsh Snake, *Nerodia clarki taeniata*
Mangrove Salt Marsh Snake, *Nerodia clarki compressicauda*
Florida Green Water Snake, *Nerodia floridana*
Mississippi Green Water Snake, *Nerodia cyclopion*
Brown Water Snake, *Nerodia taxispilota*
Diamond-backed Water Snake, *Nerodia rhombifer rhombifer*
Brazos Water Snake, *Nerodia harteri harteri*
Concho Water Snake, *Nerodia harteri paucimaculata*

A part of the colubrine subfamily *Natricinae*, the aquatic genus *Nerodia* is named after the Greek sea nymph, Nereis (female *Nerodia* are usually larger than males, and are so fertile that when pregnant large individuals may reach comparatively immense girths.) Perhaps because they live in predator-filled surroundings, water snakes are adept at self-defense. If restrained they almost always try to bite and are inclined to smear a combination of musk, feces and urates on their assailant. Moreover, as with many snakes possessing a Duvernoy's gland, the saliva of *Nerodia* contains complex proteins which, along with the host of microorganisms present in their mouths, can produce inflammatory reactions around the site of their bite.

All American water snakes are live-bearing, with some giving birth to very large litters (one Florida green water snake just under 5 ft. long contained 128 well-developed young). In lifestyle, water snakes vary from semi-aquatic to almost exclusively aquatic. Most are dark, heavy-bodied serpents that fishermen, boaters, and hikers confuse with the venomous cottonmouth. This often brings about the death of the water snake, but before human intervention the resemblance of large *Nerodia* to the cottonmouth may have conferred some protective benefits as a mimic of the big aquatic pitviper.

Warm spring and rainy summer nights are the peak activity period for water snakes, and on such nights vehicles can take a terrible toll of *Nerodia* since they often linger on roads where frogs and toads tend to congregate.

In cooler weather, water snakes often bask all day if it is sunny, although this exposes them to predators such as man. Consequently, at this time *Nerodia* tend to be especially wary, usually dropping into the water and diving at the first sign of disturbance. They may surface quickly, however, either sculling slowly in place or swimming parallel to the shore to assess the danger, but if frightened again these reptiles tend to submerge and remain hidden for long periods.

Water snakes have heavily keeled scales whose rough surface tends to collect a thin film of mud, obscuring these animals' sometimes colorful dorsolateral patterns. The intricacy of these markings is usually most evident only when aquatic snakes are wet or have recently shed their skins.

In nearly all instances, *Nerodia* have a divided anal plate, although occasionally an undivided anal plate occurs among members of the several races of *N. erythrogaster*.

62 NORTHERN WATER SNAKE

Nerodia sipedon sipedon

Nonvenomous   Although juvenile northern water snakes will sometimes allow themselves to be handled without biting, this is not usually the case with the adults, which can be vigorous biters. These snakes have bacterial oral components that may have given rise to the Greek name

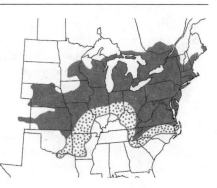

sipedon, or "infectious." Like other water snakes, to defend themselves members of this species may flatten their heads and bodies to approximate the look of a venomous cottonmouth, regurgitate their stomach contents, and excrete musk and feces.

Abundance *Nerodia sipedon sipedon* is one of the most common snakes in north-central and northeastern North America. Its broad range extends up the Atlantic seaboard from Virginia to northern Maine, across southern Canada to Lake Superior, northern Wisconsin and central Minnesota. To the west this adaptable reptile's range extends upstream along riparian corridors through Kansas and Nebraska into Colorado and south as far as northeastern Oklahoma.

Size Adults vary between 2 and 4½ ft. in length, while neonates measure about 9¼ in.

Habitat Within its range *N. s. sipedon* may be found in almost any suitable habitat—pond and lake shores, oxbows, the edges of rivers and streams (including those with considerable current), marshes, swamps and temporarily flooded areas. It may be encountered either in tiny, ephemeral ponds (when these dry up, northern water snakes disperse in search of new homes) or in large, permanent water systems that vary from spruce-edged Canadian lakes to mountain streams in western North Carolina and eastern Tennessee to the dry Rocky Mountain foothills bordering the headwaters of the Arkansas River.

Prey Amphibians—especially ranid frogs—and bottom-dwelling fish are northern water snakes' primary prey (reports also exist of adults eating crayfish and juveniles taking earthworms).

Reproduction Live bearing. *Nerodia sipedon sipedon* is as fecund as most large water snakes, producing litters numbering between a dozen and three dozen neonates (anecdotal accounts exist of litters numbering more than 90). Parturition usually takes place in late summer, but early fall births also occur.

Coloring/scale form Perhaps the most outstanding attribute of the northern water snake is the variability of its appearance. Its ground color may be gray, buff, tan or brown, anteriorly overlain with broad darker bands. Among juveniles (the northern water snake does not undergo extensive ontogenetic changes with age), these dorsolateral bands are blackish, as are those of some adults, while on others the bands may be reddish, with or without a black border. Posterior to midbody this banding often becomes irregular and may change to a combination of dorsal saddles and lateral blotches (occasional specimens are regularly banded for their entire length), while the caudal bands may be regular or irregular, but are usually incomplete.

The belly is usually strongly patterned, typically with large, dark-bordered half-moons or irregular triangles whose apex is directed posteriorly. It may be sparsely pigmented, with markings confined to the edges of the ventral scutes, or unpatterned except for a dusting of dark dots sprinkled along each side of a light mid-ventral line. (What is most confusing is that any northern water snake may combine any or all of these colors and patterns.) Most individuals lack a dark, horizontal ocular streak, and have 21 to 25 scale rows and a divided anal plate.

Similar snakes   Across a broad, roughly east-west band from eastern Oklahoma and Arkansas, through Missouri, Illinois and Indiana to Kentucky, Tennessee and North Carolina, the northern water snake intergrades with its southern race, the **midland water snake** (64). This duller, often grayish ground-colored subspecies is distinguished by its fewer and darker dorsolateral bands, by the dark vertical rectangles on its posterior sides, and by its more strongly and regularly marked belly. **Banded** and **broad-banded water snakes** (70, 71) usually have regular bands along their entire length and a dark, horizontal, postocular stripe. **Red-bellied, copper-bellied, yellow-bellied, and blotched water snakes** (66–69) have unmarked venters.

Behavior   In spring, when northern nights are still cold, *N. s. sipedon* basks during most of the daylight hours, sometimes in small, loose groups, foraging only occasionally. This post-winter warming is so important that a snake seeking to bask will utilize almost any fairly dry, sunlit spot, including bridge and dam abutments, rocks, beaver and muskrat lodges, and exposed snags and limbs.

Juveniles are at greater risk than adults on land and are less apt to come ashore to bask, but if the only available sunny spot is a patch of exposed bank, they will utilize it. As the seasons warm, the northern water snake is able to maintain a stable body temperature which allows it to forage extensively.

63   LAKE ERIE WATER SNAKE

Nerodia sipedon insularum

Nonvenomous   Lake Erie water snakes of all ages exhibit vigorous defensive behavior that includes flattening the head and body, excretion of musk and feces, and regurgitation of recent prey.

Abundance   Threatened. Protected by the Canadian province of Ontario. Formerly of questionable subspecific status, this Great Lakes race is now under review for federal protection in the United States. The distribution of *Nerodia sipedon insularum* is limited to islands in western Lake Erie (including those of Ohio's Put-in-Bay archipelago) and peninsular segments of the mainland. This includes parts of Essex County, Ontario, and Erie and Ottawa counties in Ohio—a total area less than 25 miles in diameter.

According to contributing author Dr. Richard B. King, of Northern Illinois University (1997), *N. s. insularum* remains locally abundant. Yet its highly limited distribution, together with population declines in this century (including extirpation form several smaller islands), make this taxon vulnerable to extinction.

Size   King (1986), who is both the preeminent authority on the Lake Erie water snake and who has taken the only extensive measurements of this subspecies, found adult males to range from 22 to 43 inches in total length, averaging about 32 inches; adult females ranged from 28 to 57 inches, averaging about 39 inches.

Habitat   The Lake Erie water snake is found along exposed limestone and dolomite shorelines and near-shore waters of the island region of western Lake Erie. It seems to be most common where piles of jumbled boulders and jetties exist, but neonates and juveniles are most often found under cover (when approached, these animals typically flee toward water).

Prey   *Nerodia sipedon insularum* forages on bottom-dwelling fish and amphibians in Lake Erie. King found that percid fish are important prey for younger snakes; catfish and mudpuppies are major prey species among adults. Round gobies, which were inadvertently introduced into the Great Lakes in the early 1990s, are also consumed. (The ranid frogs frequently preyed upon by the subspecies northern water snake are rare on most of these islands and appear not to be important prey for Lake Erie water snakes.)

Reproduction   Live-bearing. Courtship and mating occur in May and June and the young are born in August and September. Litter size ranges from 6 to 50, but averages about 23, with neonates measuring about 9½ inches in total length.

Coloring/scale form   The Lake Erie water snake is, in general, of lighter ground color and is less distinctly patterned than the northern water snake—whose range entirely surrounds that of *N. s. insularum*. Old accounts describe the water snakes of Put-in-Bay as a lighter, gray to gray-green form with less contrasting or absent dorsal and ventral patterns compared to individuals from the mainland, although the dorsal markings of both insular and mainland forms are of similar shape.

Yet the Lake Erie water snake's color and pattern are highly variable. Its ground color ranges from uniformly gray and unpatterned to clearly marked with regularly spaced dark gray-brown dorsal and lateral blotches. Intermediately patterned individuals have irregularly shaped blotches, or posterior dorsal blotches and anterior lateral blotches—sometimes of reduced height, which gives the appearance of a gray lateral stripe.

There is also a reduced belly pattern among *N. s. insularum*. Ventral ground color varies from cream to yellowish orange, and may be patterned with dark stippling, half-moons, or have heavily pigmented ventral scale margins. These markings may be restricted to the tail and cloacal region or may extend all the way to the chin.

The Lake Erie water snake's color and pattern variations have been studied by King, who found them to be maintained by a combination of natural selection and gene flow. Natural selection occurs because paler-hued individuals with reduced dorsal patterning are better camouflaged from visual predators along barren island shorelines, and consequently have higher survivorship than do more strongly patterned snakes.

However, immigration of heavily patterned northern water snakes from well-vegetated habitats on the mainland (where dorsolateral patterning is more cryptic) results in a constant exchange of genetic material between *N. s. insularum* and the darker water snakes of the mainland, accounting for the persistence of dark dorsolateral ground colors and strongly contrasting patterns in island populations. (Neonates are more contrastingly patterned than most adults.)

Roger Conant and Clay Conant (1937) found scale counts of *N. s. insularum* to be similar to those of the surrounding population of northern water snakes; its dorsal scales are heavily keeled and its anal plate is divided.

Similar snakes   Regularly patterned neonate and juvenile Lake Erie water snakes are similar in appearance to like-aged **northern water snakes (62)**. However, adult northern water snakes often become quite dark dorsolaterally, and can appear nearly black, whereas adult Lake Erie water snakes retain the gray juvenile ground color of the northern race. Entirely unpatterned Lake Erie water snakes are superficially similar in appearance to the **queen snake (89)**, which is also found in the island region of western Lake Erie, but which has a reddish venter marked with a double row of dark spots that converge to form a single line beneath its chin and tail.

Behavior   Adults emerge from hibernation about mid-May and at that time may be encountered basking and courting among rocks and vegetation of island shorelines. They begin foraging in the near-shore waters of Lake Erie soon after emergence and can be seen swimming or coming ashore to swallow prey; by mid-summer, *N. s. insularum* may be most active at night.

64   MIDLAND WATER SNAKE

Nerodia sipedon pleuralis

Nonvenomous   When cornered, *N. s. pleuralis* may flatten its head and body, void musk from its cloaca, vibrate its tail, and strike repeatedly in self-defense. In Alabama, herpetologist Robert H. Mount reports that this reptile "is considered venomous and killed on sight by a large segment of the populace, who designate it "water moccasin." [Yet] in spite of relentless persecution, the midland water snake persists in considerable numbers throughout nearly all its range."

Abundance   In the clear, sand-bottomed steephead streams which originate in the Appalachian uplands and empty into the Choctawhatchee, Yellow, and Escambia rivers, *N. s. pleuralis* can be more numerous than any other aquatic snake. Further south in its range, as the only race of the northern water snake group, *Nerodia sipedon,* to reach the Gulf Coast, the midland water snake is less numerous than the red-bellied and banded water snakes typical of the coastal lowlands.

To the north, across a broad, roughly east-west band from eastern Oklahoma and Arkansas through Missouri, Illinois, and Indiana on to Kentucky, Tennessee, and North Carolina, *N. s. pleuralis* intergrades with its more northerly race, the northern water snake.

Size   Most adults are 24 to 48 inches long; the record is 59 in.

Habitat   Like that of the ubiquitous northern water snake this subspecies' habitat can be almost any aquatic milieu: pond and lake shores, oxbows, the edges of rivers and streams, marshes, and flooded areas.

Prey   Midland water snakes prey mostly on small, bottom-feeding fish, but ranid frogs, tadpoles, and salamanders are also taken. In the manner typical of most *Nerodia*, larger prey is brought ashore to be overcome and swallowed.

Reproduction   Live-bearing. Newborn *N. s. pleuralis*, litters of which number from 12 to 30, appear from July to early September.

Coloring/scale form   The gray to rusty-brown dorsal ground color is marked with dark-edged brown anterior crossbands which, from midbody to tail, are replaced with dark vertebral blotches (crossbands and vertebral blotches total fewer than 30).

On its posterior sides, squarish vertical bars extend upwards from the midland water snake's belly line. Its venter is yellow, with a double row of rearward-facing brown crescents, while this snake's 21 to 25 midbody rows of dorsal scales are keeled, and its anal plate is divided.

Similar snakes   The **cottonmouth (179–181)** has a dark pit between its vertically slit pupil and nostril, as well as a single row of subcaudal scales. The **banded water snake (70)** has dorsal bands all the way to its tail, its yellow belly displays dark, squarish markings, and a dark stripe extends from its eye to its last supralabial scale. **Red-bellied, copper-bellied, yellow-bellied, and blotched water snakes (66–69)** have unmarked venters. See **Northern Water Snake.**

Behavior   A mostly nocturnal forager, the midland water snake searches stream bottoms for the small fish it captures in its nighttime shelters beneath overhanging banks and submerged logs.

65   CAROLINA WATER SNAKE

Nerodia sipedon williamengelsi

Nonvenomous   See **Northern Water Snake.**

Abundance   Uncommon to rare. *Nerodia sipedon williamengelsi* is restricted to the coastal shores of central North Carolina and to the Outer Banks of that state. Here, bearing the name of University of North Carolina's emeritus zoology professor, William L. Engels, it is listed as a species of special concern. Moreover, the Carolina water snake's limited range falls mostly within the boundaries of the Cape Hatteras National Seashore Preserve where, unlike many other coastal-island reptiles, it seems to be well protected.

Size   Average adult size varies between 30 and 40 inches; the record is 48 inches. (Females seem to be, at least marginally, the larger sex.)

Habitat   The Carolina water snake inhabits salt, brackish, and freshwaters, and it seems to be most common where salt grasses such as spartina and juncus grow thickly along canals, ditches, salt marshes, creeks and freshwater ponds.

Prey In its predatory behavior, the Carolina water snake follows the typical *Nerodia* pattern: feeding primarily on amphibians, fish, and sometimes carrion. See **Northern Water Snake.**

Reproduction The individual pictured here—a gravid female—was photographed by R. W. Vandevender; from such females, up to 27 neonates (a low number for members of this prolific genus), each about 9 inches long, have been reported.

Coloring/scale form The validity of the Carolina water snake as a separate subspecies has long been argued, but most researchers now accept it as a bona fide race.

Neonates are prominently patterned with up to 30 dark dorsolateral bands against a variable gray ground color. With growth and age, a suffusion of melanin gradually darkens the dorsum until the lighter ground color—1½ to 2 (rarely to 3) scale rows in width—that separates the dorsolateral bands is largely filled with blackish pigment. Especially along the spine, some individuals are almost solid black.

The belly is marked with solid black half-moons, with those on the forebody sometimes having lighter-hued centers.

Similar snakes The **banded water snake (70)** is lighter and more reddish or orangish in ground color and, along its entire body, has well defined dark bands with regular borders. Juvenile **red-bellied water snakes (66)** have an almost uniformly pale venter and adults have an unmarked red or orange-red belly. See **Northern Water Snake.**

Behavior See **Northern Water Snake.**

66 RED-BELLIED WATER SNAKE

Nerodia erythrogaster erythrogaster

Nonvenomous If this species is unable to escape, in self-defense it will often flatten its neck and body and make false strikes. If pressed further it will bite—and large *Nerodia* are strong enough to do so with vigor—void musk and feces, and sometimes regurgitate recently swallowed prey.

Abundance Common. *Nerodia erythrogaster erythrogaster* is a locally abundant resident of both

Gulf and Atlantic coastal plains from Florida's panhandle to tide-water Delaware and Maryland.

Size Most adults are between 28 and 48 inches in length. The record is 62 inches—an animal which would almost certainly have been female since males do not reach more than ¾ the length of the largest females, nor attain their thickness of girth.

Habitat The red-bellied water snake spends a majority of its life in and around rivers, lakes, and ponds, most often in those occurring in bottomland forest. Cypress swamps are another prime habitat.

These aquatic environments are chosen because they are rich in both food sources and shelter (murky water is a good place to hide), although there is nothing in the biology of water snakes to limit them to a wet environment. If food is available and predators are not present—captives often ignore their pools except just before shedding—all species of *Nerodia* are able to thrive without an aquatic habitat.

In fact, when optimal shelter (and therefore safety) is available some distance from a pond or waterway, all races of *N. erythrogaster* will spend the daylight hours there, moving to a more exposed aquatic milieu only after dark. Similarly, in search of breeding frogs and toads adult water snakes may be found in moist bottomland or flooded fields more than a mile from a permanent watercourse.

Prey Most reptiles partition habitat; snakes usually partition prey. The diverse population of sympatric water snake species in the southeastern United States tend to partition their food resources, and for *N. e. erythrogaster* that share of aquatic prey generally consists of fish and frogs, ranids in particular, although almost any small vertebrate can constitute prey.

Reproduction Live-bearing. Like their relatives the garter snakes, water snakes are characterized by large numbers of offspring. *N. e. erythrogaster* fits this pattern, depositing, after a 3½-month gestation period, litters containing from 11 to well over 30 young ranging from 9 to 11½ inches in length. After their birth in late summer, these neonates are often extremely numerous in farm ponds and other shallow bodies of water—where their mortality to wetland-foraging predators such as raccoons is very high.

Coloring/scale form Red-bellied water snakes are stout-bodied, short-tailed serpents with necks much narrower than their broad heads which, when flattened in threat, heighten their resemblance to pitvipers. Dorsolateral ground color is unmarked reddish brown to dark chocolate (some individuals have gray-green sides).

The venter of adults, although usually not quite red (despite the Greek *erythrogaster*, or "red-bellied"), is bright orange. Juvenile *N. e.*

erythrogaster are quite different in appearance. Their faintly pinkish ground color is conspicuously patterned over the forebody with dark dorsal bands that, posteriorly, become dark saddles alternating with vertical lateral bars. The belly of juveniles is paler, sometimes with a bit of dark pigment lining the forward edges of the ventral scutes. The dorsal scales occur in 23 rows at midbody and the anal plate is usually divided.

Similar snakes Juveniles are difficult to distinguish from those of the **midland water snake (64)**, while in the Florida panhandle *N. e. erythrogaster* intergrades with its olive-backed subspecies, the **yellow-bellied water snake (68)**, whose venter, in pure form, is unmarked lemon yellow, although intermediately colored individuals with pale yellow bellies occur throughout this area. Snakes more characteristic of the western race prevail to the west of Panama City, however.

Yet water snakes' heavy bodies and dark coloring most often cause them to be mistaken for the **cottonmouth (179–181)**. Water snakes have rounded heads and circular pupils, however, eyes visible from directly above, and lack a sunken heat-sensing pit between eye and nostril. They also swim much more vigorously than cottonmouths, their bodies drooping below the surface when they stop (the cottonmouth's entire body is usually buoyantly suspended on the surface). Cornered water snakes may strike, but they do not gape motionless in threat as the cottonmouth commonly does.

Both **Florida** and **Mississippi green water snakes (72, 77)** have a row of subocular scales between the eye and the upper labial scales.

Behavior During temperate weather red-bellied water snakes are daytime foragers, but during the hottest months they are active mainly in the early morning, evening, and at night.

67 COPPER-BELLIED WATER SNAKE

Nerodia erythrogaster neglecta

Nonvenomous Although water snakes are nonvenomous, people have occasionally reacted unfavorably to their bites—probably as a result of oral pathogens carried into the wound. See **Red-bellied Water Snake**

Abundance **In decline.** In spite of being protected by state law over much of its small and fragmented range (the major portion of which lies near the juncture of the Ohio and Mississippi rivers), this handsome snake is diminishing and is currently under consideration for listing as a Federally Endangered Species.

In part, this is because the copper-bellied water snake is a particularly vulnerable subspecies. Although in early postglacial times it was probably more generally distributed, due to the ever-growing human presence within its range *N. e. neglecta* now remains only in tiny pockets of suitable habitat in northwestern Tennessee, northwestern Kentucky and adjacent Indiana and Illinois, south-central Indiana, west-central Ohio, and south-central Michigan and adjacent Indiana and Ohio. (If the inhabitants of any of these small habitat pockets should be killed or seriously depleted, the natural process of re-colonization by neighboring populations would be difficult since no adjacent *N. e. neglecta* live nearby.)

Size   Although females (the larger sex) can near 4½ feet in length, they are usually somewhat smaller: 25 to 40 inches is the more commonly seen adult size. Neonates average 9 inches in total length.

Habitat   The most terrestrial of all *Nerodia*, the copper-bellied water snake is also associated with ponds, sloughs, swamps, oxbows, and river edges (or even water-retaining depressions) in or near deciduous woodlands. Occasionally it may be seen in much drier, more open areas. There is also evidence that *N. e. neglecta* tends to inhabit ephemeral waters in the spring, moving to permanent water sources as these shallow ponds dry (Harding 1997).

Prey   Amphibians, especially ranid frogs and salamanders—especially *siren* and *ambystoma* larvae—seem to be the most commonly taken prey, but fish and crayfish are also readily eaten. Large prey animals are dragged ashore to be overcome and swallowed.

Reproduction   Live-bearing. From 5 to more than 30 young are born in late summer or early autumn—sometimes even when seasonal cooling is well advanced (the largest females produce the largest litters, but not necessarily the largest babies).

Coloring/scale form   Considerable ontogenetic changes in appearance occur during the lifetime of almost all *N. erythrogaster*. Neonates are pale-bellied, prominently blotched or irregularly banded above with brown on a russet to gray ground color. As they mature, their dorsolateral contrasts fade, and with adulthood they have a nearly unicolored dark brown to blackish dorsum with a yellowish to coppery venter, most intensely pigmented along its midline. (On many individuals, dark dorsolateral tints extend onto the outer edges of the ventral scutes.) The dorsal scales occur in 19 to 23 rows at midbody and a majority of, but not all, individuals have a divided anal plate.

Similar snakes   A more westerly and southerly subspecies, the **yellow-bellied water snake (68)** is very similar but with a paler venter.

Both the **northern water snake (62)** and the **queen snake (89)** have a patterned belly with a pale ground color.

Behavior   In early spring, the copper-bellied water snake spends most of the daylight hours basking; as temperatures warm it increases its foraging activity and with the long days of summer may hunt primarily at night.

68   YELLOW-BELLIED WATER SNAKE

Nerodia erythrogaster flavigaster

Nonvenomous   Often after a preliminary display in which it typically discharges feces and foul-smelling musk excreted by glands within its cloaca, the yellow-bellied water snake will bite in self-defense. This behavior is usually accompanied by a flattening of the neck and head and preliminary false strikes—but large *Nerodia* can ultimately be nasty biters, causing long scratches as they quickly jerk their heads away from their assailant.

Abundance   Common. With a range that joins the territories of this race's adjacently ranging subspecies, the red-bellied race to the east and the blotched water snake to the west, *N. e. flavigaster* is found along the Gulf coasts of western Florida, Alabama, Mississippi, Louisiana, and eastern Texas north through Arkansas and western Tennessee, then upstream within the Mississippi valley to eastern Iowa and northern Illinois.

Size   Most adults are 30 to 48 inches in length. The record is just over 59 in. Because large *N. erythrogaster* are very heavy-bodied, an individual this massive would be almost certain to be mis-identified as a cottonmouth. (Actually, the majority of "moccasins" found around rural and suburban ponds within this animal's range are really yellow-bellied or banded water snakes.)

Habitat   Yellow-bellied water snakes are found in most rural wetland environments, more often in wooded than in open areas; they seem, however, to be most numerous in swamps, the luetic water of oxbow river segments, bayous, and the marshy verges of floodplain lakes and ponds. See **Red-bellied Water Snake.**

Prey Juvenile *N. e. flavigaster* eat small fish, tadpoles, and aquatic insects; adults feed primarily on fish, frogs, and other amphibians. One instance of predation was noted by Bill Marvel:

> At 2 p.m. on March 16 I was standing beside a roadside ditch when a 36-inch yellow-bellied water snake backed out of the water with a 10-inch lesser siren grasped about mid-body. The snake crawled up the embankment, where it began "walking" its jaws along the siren's body toward the head. The siren attempted to escape by burrowing among the grass roots and by twisting movements that forced the snake to turn on its back. Although the snake crawled across my boots during this struggle it did not seem to notice my presence. After it had swallowed the siren it raised its head, flicked its tongue, then crawled back into the ditch and swam away under water. The whole operation took about 45 minutes.

It is characteristic of water snakes, particularly *N. erythrogaster*, to drag large fish or other prey animals out of the water, gaining traction against the ground as leverage in overcoming the struggles of their prey. See **Blotched Water Snake**.

Reproduction Live-bearing. See **Red-bellied Water Snake**.

Coloring/scale form *Flavi*, which is Latin for "yellow," combined with *gaster*, Greek for "belly," aptly describes this yellow-bellied western race of *N. erythrogaster*. (*Erythro* means "red," the belly color of the eastern subspecies.)

Slightly paler on its lower sides, the dark unpatterned dorsum of the yellow-bellied water snake varies from entirely gray-green backed, orange-red bellied individuals found from the Florida panhandle to northern Georgia—to Texas specimens resembling the vertebrally pale-barred, laterally dark-blocked western subspecies, the blotched water snake, *N. e. transversa*.

In appearance, juvenile *N. e. flavigaster* differ greatly from adults: their faintly pinkish ground color is conspicuously patterned over the forebody with dark dorsal bands which break up posteriorly into dark saddles alternating with vertical lateral bars.

The lips are yellow, with dark labial sutures; there are 23 midbody rows of dorsal scales and the anal plate is usually divided.

Similar snakes The albumin proteins of water snakes indicate that they are close relatives of the garter and ribbon snakes. (*Nerodia* are thought to be a Pliocene evolutionary departure toward aquatic life on the part of some members of the much older, more terrestrially adapted garter snake genus *Thamnophis*.) See **Red-bellied Water Snake**.

Behavior   See **Blotched Water Snake**.

69   BLOTCHED WATER SNAKE

Nerodia erythrogaster transversa

Nonvenomous   When restrained, like other reptiles attempting to discourage a predator by making themselves unappetizing, *N. e. transversa* often forcibly discharges the contents of its cloaca, accompanied by musk discharged from glands located within the cloacal cavity.

Abundance   Common. Across the eastern ⅔ of Texas, all of Oklahoma, southeastern Kansas, and western Missouri, *N. e. transversa* is the predominant water snake.

Size   Most adults are 2 to 3 feet in length; the record is 58 inches.

Habitat   The chocolate-blotched newborns of this race are often found in more shallow, more dappled microenvironments—both small streams and the inlets of larger bodies of water—than are the more uniformly colored adults.

At the mouth of such inlets, the young often lie for hours, anchored against the bottom. With their snouts pressed into the incoming flow, they may be anticipating small prey washed downstream—although perhaps, like dogs with their noses pressed out of moving-car windows, these little water snakes are simply savoring the onrushing stream of scent flowing past.

Prey   Most reptiles partition habitat; snakes usually partition prey species. Like other diverse ophidian populations, the several sympatric water snake species in eastern Texas, Louisiana, and Oklahoma to some degree partition their food resources, with *Nerodia erythrogaster* taking mostly fish and frogs.

How they take large examples of this prey is remarkable. On three occasions, the author has seen blotched water snakes drag catfish too large and vigorous to be swallowed (or even gripped by their jaws for long in the water) out onto the nearly level banks of stock ponds. Here, all three snakes actively searched for an embedded stick or rock around which to anchor a body coil, thus preventing the frantically flopping fish from dragging them both back into the water. After their prey expired (which took up to half an hour out of the water), each of these snakes pulled its catfish back toward the pond's edge and slowly began to engulf its head.

Reproduction   Live-bearing. Breeding takes place on land, in spring. Like their relatives the garter snakes, water snakes are characterized by large numbers of offspring, and *N. e. transversa* fits this pattern. After a 3½-month gestation period, litters containing from 5 to 27 young, ranging from 7½ to 10½ inches in length, are born in late summer.

Coloring/scale form   Blotched water snakes are gray-brown above, often with a hint of olive. Over the spine, short, dark-edged pale bars are evident, while dimly defined dark vertical bars mark the sides. (The most westerly *N. e. transversa* live in shallow, rocky streambed channels like those frequented by eastern juveniles. Here, strongly contrasting dorsolateral patterning is more cryptic, and to benefit from this camouflage adults retain the distinct dorsal patterning of juveniles throughout their lives.)

Among both groups the belly is yellow, with the edges of larger animals' ventral plates lightly tinged with brown. There are 23 to 27 midbody rows of dorsal scales and the anal plate is divided. (The young are indistinguishable from juveniles of other races of *Nerodia erythrogaster*.) See **Copper-bellied Water Snake.**

Similar snakes   Intergrades between the blotched and **yellow-bellied water snake (68)** occur in East/Central Texas, but the typical yellow-belly is unmarked above, with light yellow posterior edging on its ventral scales.

Because blotched water snakes are stout-bodied, short-tailed serpents which darken with age, they superficially resemble the **western cottonmouth (181).** But the cottonmouth has a vertically slit pupil unlike the circular pupil of all water snakes. As a pitviper, the cottonmouth also has a dark heat-sensing pit between its eye and nostril and an angular head whose flat, undercut cheeks abruptly intersect its crown.

Behavior   For the most part *Nerodia* (the current genus name for North American water snakes previously classified as *Natrix*) have not made a radical physical accommodation to aquatic life. Instead, they have taken advantage of the benefits of life in the water by behavioral adaptations. Most important is their technique for gaining heat in cooler aquatic milieus by basking. Frequently seen draped along tree limbs overhanging water (like most aquatic serpents *N. e. transversa* is a good climber), blotched water snakes are also encountered crossing roads in the evening, especially following rainstorms that bring out breeding frogs.

During temperate weather blotched water snakes are crepuscular or diurnal foragers, but during the hottest months they are active mainly at night. Like other *Nerodia*, these reptiles are far more mobile than is commonly supposed by those who speak of the water snakes which "live" in their lakes or ponds. Individuals marked by the author have shown that at least some blotched water snakes are fairly wide-ranging, moving along intermittent stream beds and periodically visiting several different stock ponds.

70 BANDED WATER SNAKE
Nerodia fasciata fasciata

Nonvenomous If cornered, *N. f. fasciata* may discharge odorous musk from its cloaca, flatten its forebody and strike repeatedly in self-defense. Yet, like other large, dark-bodied water snakes that to some extent resemble the cottonmouth, it is harmless to humans unless harassed.

Abundance Common in suitable habitat throughout its broad range—which encompasses both the Gulf coastal plain of Mississippi, Alabama and Florida and the Atlantic coastal plain as far north as the southeastern tip of Virginia.

Size Adult length is 22 to 40 inches; the record is 60 in.

Habitat Banded water snakes occur in and around permanent bodies of luetic water—forest-bordered ponds, lakes, and small streams as well as coastal wetlands. In the southern part of its range, wet marl prairie and hydric hardwood hammocks are also occupied.

Prey See **Broad-banded Water Snake.**

Reproduction Live-bearing. See **Broad-banded Water Snake.**

Coloring/scale form The ground color of *N. f. fasciata* ranges from yellowish- to reddish-gray, while its very numerous (often more than 40) dark-edged dorsolateral crossbands—*fasciata* is Latin for "banded"—are even more variable, and can be any shade between bright russet and black.

As with most *Nerodia*, considerable ontogenetic change in appearance occurs during the lifetime of most banded water snakes: juveniles are paler and more boldly patterned with dark crossbands than adults, while very old individuals (as well as some dark-phase younger specimens) are often nearly solid dark brown above, with lighter scales on their lower sides.

A distinct blackish stripe, diagnostic of the banded water snake group, extends from the eye through the last supralabial scale. The yellow venter is ordinarily marked with squarish brown blotches, but some individuals have bright red ventral blotches and even crossbars. The dorsal scales are arranged in 21 to 25 rows at midbody and the anal plate is divided.

Similar snakes   Among the banded water snake's two subspecies, the western **broad-banded water snake** (71) has fewer (usually less than 20), much wider and darker dorsolateral bands on a golden brown ground color, while the more southerly ranging **Florida water snake** (72) has a dark lateral blotch between each of its dorsal crossbands and dark brown to red posterior borders on its ventral scutes. All water snakes' oval heads and snouts, round pupils, and lack of a sunken heat-sensing pit between eye and nostril set them off from the venomous **cottonmouth** (179–181), as does their more gradually tapered tail, whose undersurface bears a double row of scales.

The true relationship between the banded water snake, *N. f. fasciata*, and other water snakes is problematical. In 1963, *Nerodia fasciata*, a complex of southern water snakes, was taxonomically separated from the northern water snake complex, *Nerodia sipedon*, by Roger Conant. This re-classification was based on both the morphological and habitat disparities observed between different populations of northern water snakes—which in the Carolinas inhabited distinctly different habitats and seemed not to interbreed.

Then, during the 1980s, because of the same evident lack of genetic intermingling between different groups within this newly split-off population, the southern water snake complex was itself split. This formed a new, salt marsh snake species, *N. clarkii*.

Yet interbreeding has since been reported between members of the southern banded water snake complex and several races of the northern water snake, as well between the banded water snake group and the newly separated salt marsh snake complex.

This has produced unusual combinations of animals once thought to have entirely different habitats and life histories. For example, one of the northern water snake races, the **midland water** snake (64) is an inland, freshwater stream-living reptile. The **Gulf salt marsh snake (73)** inhabits the Gulf Coast's brackish marshes. Yet in the western Florida panhandle—where the ranges of both these animals overlap that of the banded water snake—three-way genetic crosses combine the midland water snake's vertically dark-barred posterior sides, the longitudinal stripes of the salt marsh snake, and the multiple dorsolateral crossbands of the banded water snake.

Behavior   See **Broad-banded Water Snake.**

71   BROAD-BANDED WATER SNAKE

Nerodia fasciata confluens

Nonvenomous   See **Banded Water Snake.**

Abundance   Uncommon in much of its extensive East Texas, Louisiana, Arkansas, and western Mississippi range, *N. f. confluens* follows the Mississippi valley as far north as southern Illinois. It is most abundant, however, along the upper Gulf Coast: in the marshes of Texas' Chambers and Jefferson counties and the adjacent Louisiana parishes it is the predominant water snake.

Size   Adult length averages 20 to 30 inches; the record is 45 in.

Habitat   Inland, broad-banded water snakes occur around woodland lakes, ponds and slow-moving bayous. They seem to be most common, though, in brackish coastal wetlands (often just inland of barrier dunes and breaking Gulf surf), as well as in seasonally flooded prairies.

Prey   *Nerodia fasciata* preys primarily on fish, frogs, toads, salamanders, and crayfish taken on both diurnal and nocturnal forays. One predatory technique involves slowly nosing across the bottom of shallow ponds.

Reproduction   Live-bearing. Mating has been reported to occur in April followed, after 70 to 80 days of gestation, by litters of up to 50 young. Only the largest *Nerodia fasciata* deliver this many offspring, however, and most broods are closer in number to the 15 young—all between 8½ and 9 inches in length and about ⅕ ounce in weight—deposited July 20 by a 32½-inch-long female captured in Smith County, Texas.

Coloring/scale form   Ground color is sulphur yellow to yellowish-brown or -gray, with (usually less than 20) very wide, dark-edged gray-brown to black dorsolateral crossbands. This is by far the most handsome of all *Nerodia*. Juveniles are more boldly patterned, while very old individuals may be almost entirely dark brown.

A prominent blackish eye stripe, which is characteristic of all banded water snakes, extends from the eye across the gray-brown cheeks through the last supralabial scale. The dappled yellow venter is generally marked with squarish brown blotches or, occasionally, crossbars. There are 21 to 25 midbody rows of dorsal scales and the anal plate is divided.

Similar snakes   The eastern **banded water snake** (70) has much more numerous (sometimes more than 40) narrower, sometimes russet-colored dorsolateral bands on gray-brown ground color. Its yellow venter sometimes also bears reddish blotches or bars. See **Banded Water Snake**.

Behavior   On sunny days, broad-banded, banded, and Florida water snakes spend hours basking on partially submerged logs or on overhanging tree limbs (like most water snakes, *N. fasciata* is a good climber), but in wintry weather these animals retire to bankside dens or burrow beneath vegetative debris.

Also like other water snakes, *N. fasciata* is more of a traveler across dry land than one might suspect. During anurans' breeding season, drawn by the congregations of frogs and toads that gather to deposit their eggs in ditches, temporary puddle-filled depressions, and flooded prairies, any of these subspecies may venture a mile or more from a permanent body of water.

72   FLORIDA WATER SNAKE

Nerodia fasciata pictiventris

Nonvenomous   Florida water snakes will bite only if molested. Because this animal has a stout body that becomes darker and more heavily proportioned with age (and since individuals often flatten their heads and strike repeatedly in self-defense) large *N. fasciata* are frequently mistaken for the venomous cottonmouth.

Abundance   Common. Except for a tiny corner of southeastern Georgia, *N. f. pictiventris* is a Florida endemic, and in parts of peninsular Florida north of the Everglades it is the most abundant water snake. These habitats include wet marl prairie and its incorporated hardwood hammocks, cypress swamps, and the sawgrass swale of the Everglades.

In a distant, equally semi-tropical ecosystem on the far side of the Gulf of Mexico, *N. f. pictiventris* has become established at the mouth of the Rio Grande. Texas' colony of Florida water snakes owes its existence to the live-animal business operated in Brownsville by W. A. "Snake" King, which between 1907 and 1956 imported and sold thousands of wild creatures to zoos, circuses, and snake charmers.

To provide food for King's large cobras, hundreds of water snakes were imported from the Southeast and held in ramshackle cages, many of which were torn open by a violent hurricane in September 1933. In addition, rather than maintaining these expendable "food snakes" during slack seasons, King's firm annually released large numbers of southeastern water snakes in the local resacas and parks—from which, it was hoped, they might be recaptured when business improved. That not all King's *N. f. pictiventris* were recovered is evident from the appearance here of newborn Florida water snakes a half-century after their predecessors' introduction.

Size Most adults measure between 22 and 40 inches. The record length is much larger, however, at 62½ inches.

Habitat Aquatic habitats include the margins of lakes, ponds, rivers and streams. Here, a favored microenvironment is the shelter provided by floating vegetation such as lily pads, hyacinths, and other aquatic plants. During hunting forays, Florida water snakes are also found in flooded terrestrial prairies, inundated stands of melaleuca, and even saline estuarine wetlands.

Prey *Nerodia fasciata* takes a variety of aquatic life, including crayfish, salamanders, frogs, and fish.

Reproduction Live-bearing. Following a mid-winter breeding season, females from southern Florida give birth in late spring; by June, baby Florida water snakes are often abundant in bankside vegetation. In the northern part of the state breeding takes place from April to June, with the young being born between July and September. Litters usually number 20 to 30 young 5 to 9 inches long, but as many as 57 offspring can be deposited by very large females.

Coloring/scale form The Florida water snake's grayish cheeks are paler than its dark crown and are marked, behind the eye, with a chocolate-colored stripe that extends posteriorly through the last supralabial scale. Otherwise, this animal's dorsal coloring is variable: its ground color ranges from tan to dark brown, with reddish-brown to black crossbands and dark intervening lateral blotches; other (often older) individuals may be so heavily pigmented as to appear entirely black.

If its back is both variable and nondescript the Florida water snake's belly is its signature. Named for its painted stomach (*pictum*, in Latin), *N. f. pictiventris* is distinguished by the bold—red to dark brown to black—wavy markings that border its yellowish ventral scales. The young have a light beige ground color, with contrasting dark dorsolateral crossbands. There are 23 to 27 rows of dorsal scales at midbody and the anal plate is generally divided.

Similar snakes The Florida water snake's subspecies, the **banded water snake (70)** has a more blotched or even dark-checked venter; it lacks lateral blotches between its dorsolateral crossbands. The **Florida green water snake (76)** has a speckled back, a unique row of subocular scales, and an unpatterned venter.

Unlike any water snake, the **cottonmouth (179–181)** has a triangular, slab-sided head, a dark pit midway between its nostril and its vertically slit pupil, and a single row of scales beneath its tail, where water snakes have a double row.

Behavior See **Broad-banded Water Snake.**

---

73 GULF SALT MARSH SNAKE
Nerodia clarki clarkii

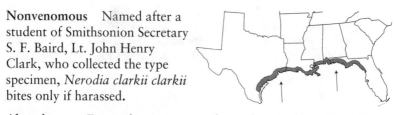

Nonvenomous Named after a student of Smithsonion Secretary S. F. Baird, Lt. John Henry Clark, who collected the type specimen, *Nerodia clarkii clarkii* bites only if harassed.

Abundance Formerly numerous along the northern Gulf Coast from north-central Florida to Corpus Christi on the central Texas coast, the Gulf salt marsh snake is now less common due to commercial development and pollution of tidal wetlands.

Size Adults are 15 to 30 inches long; the record is 36 in.

Habitat Salt marsh snakes live in brackish and saltwater tidal estuaries and salt grass meadows (*N. c. clarkii* is seldom found in freshwater). Favored microhabitats include the shelter of littoral debris, crayfish and fiddler crab burrows, and matted vegetation in the salt grass-lined margins of tidal mud flats.

Prey   *Nerodia clarkii* preys primarily on fish, especially shallow-living species such as killifish and small mullet (which are often taken when they become trapped by the falling tide), as well as crayfish and shrimp.

Reproduction   Live-bearing. Little else is known, but the 9- to 10½-inch-long young which, except for slightly bolder dorsolateral striping, resemble the adults, weigh only ¼ to ⅓ oz. at birth.

Coloring/scale form   On each of the Gulf salt marsh snake's upper sides, a pair of dark brown dorsolateral stripes stands out against its pale, grayish ground color. Its venter is reddish-brown, with a central row of cream-colored oval blotches often flanked by a lateral row of pale spots. The dorsal scales occur in either 21 or 23 rows at midbody, there is a double row of subcaudal scales, and the anal plate is divided.

Similar snakes   Salt marsh snakes were once classified as a sub-species of the freshwater-living banded water snake, *Nerodia fasciata*. Because salt marsh snakes have morphological differences and rarely enter freshwater, they are presently classified as a separate species, but where there ranges overlap, intergrade animals that may exhibit both the pale cheeks and lateral blotches of the **banded, broad-banded,** and **Florida water snakes (70, 71, 72)** and the longitudinal gray dorsolateral stripes of the salt marsh snakes occur. See **Broad-banded Water Snake.**

The subspecies **mangrove salt marsh snake (75),** found only in coastal peninsular Florida, largely lacks dorsolateral stripes (there is often a short, dark nuchal line). Its back ranges from almost solid black, to gray-green with dark crossbands, to unmarked orange. The **striped crayfish snake (85)** has a uniformly colored venter, the **glossy, delta,** and **gulf crayfish snakes (86–88),** as well as the **queen snake (89)** have dark, unstriped backs and 19 or fewer rows of dorsal scales.

Behavior   See **Atlantic Salt Marsh Snake.**

74   ATLANTIC SALT MARSH SNAKE
Nerodia clarkii taeniata

Nonvenomous   The Atlantic salt marsh snake bites only in self-defense.

Abundance   Threatened. Protected by both the federal government and the state of Florida. *Nerodia clarkii taeniata* is a rare reptile found only along a narrow strip of Florida's mid-Atlantic coast. It occurs primarily in

Volusia County, where much of its habitat has been lost to commercial development of the area's limited, and very valuable, ocean frontage.

Size   The smallest of Florida's water snakes, most adult *N. c. taeniata* are less than 20 inches long. The record is almost 24 inches.

Habitat   See **Gulf Salt Marsh Snake.**

Prey   See **Gulf Salt Marsh Snake.**

Reproduction   Live-bearing. See **Gulf Salt Marsh Snake.**

Coloring/scale form   Against a light grayish-tan ground color, the Atlantic salt marsh snake's anterior back and sides are dark-striped—*taeniata* is "striped" in Latin. Posteriorly, these stripes become dark blotches or even crossbands. Its venter, like that of other salt marsh snakes, is reddish brown with a central row of large yellowish blotches. There are 21 (sometimes 23) midbody rows of dorsal scales, a double row of subcaudal scales, and the anal plate is divided.

Similar snakes   The subspecies **Mangrove salt marsh snake (75)** largely lacks dorsolateral stripes (there is often a dark nuchal bar, however); its dorsum ranges from dark greenish gray, sometimes with black crossbands, to unmarked orange. The **striped crayfish snake (85)** has light and dark stripes running the length of its dorsum and a uniformly colored venter.

Behavior   The fluid conservation difficulties faced by marine reptiles—such as the sea turtles, sea snakes and, to a lesser extent, brackish water-living species like the salt marsh snakes—are as severe as those confronting desert-dwellers. Not only is freshwater absent from their environment, but seawater—which is saltier than their body fluids—exerts an osmotic draw on their tissues' electrolyte balance.

Scaly reptilian skin is a good barrier against external dehydration but, because intestinal membranes are salt-permeable, if seawater is ingested it draws the less-salty fluid of blood and body tissues into the stomach. Among North American snakes only *N. clarkii* has established itself in an entirely saline niche. A metabolic feat, salt marsh snakes manage by drinking rainwater when it is available, and at other times by swallowing nothing but prey animals—whose body fluids are as dilute as their own.

Nerodia clarkii compressicauda

Nonvenomous   Mangrove salt marsh snakes bite only in self-defense.

Abundance   Common, although infrequently seen, along both Florida's Gulf and Atlantic coastlines from mid-peninsula to Key West.

Size   Adults are 14 to 28 inches. The record is 36¾ in.

Habitat   *Nerodia clarkii compressicauda* primarily inhabits inundated estuarine forests of buttonwood and red mangrove. In this brackish-to-saline environment, competition with Florida's numerous freshwater natricines (whose more-inland habitat intersects the inshore margins of the mangrove salt marsh snake's strip of tidal wetland) is minimized. This small coastal serpent is also found on entirely saline offshore islands along both coasts as well as among the Florida Keys, where its laterally compressed tail—the "compressicauda" of its Latin name—aids in swimming.

Prey   In a study at Placido Bay, near Tampa, of the predatory behavior of the mangrove salt marsh snake, sheepshead minnows were found to be the most abundant of its small, estuarine prey.

Under captive conditions these snakes turned out to be quite sedentary predators: by far the largest amount of their time was spent resting, and only ripples caused by small fish swimming within a few inches of their bodies triggered predatory behavior (following an unsuccessful capture attempt, the snakes sometimes submerged and tongue-flicked along the sand, perhaps in an attempt to capture prey hidden in the upper layers).

This tendency toward minimal foraging except under the optimal conditions of maximum prey density and/or proximity is confirmed by field observations of herpetologist John Decker, who reports feeding behavior among free-ranging *N. c. compressicauda* which actively sought small fish and crayfish only when they were concentrated in shallow water by the falling tide.

Reproduction   Live-bearing. Little is known of courtship or breeding, but 22 young were recorded in one litter, and 15 in another. Salmon reports litters averaging 8, with differently color-patterned individuals present in the same brood.

Coloring/scale form   Mangrove salt marsh snakes are one of the most variably colored of reptiles. *N. c. compressicauda* ranges from reddish-orange, to tan, to almost black, although there are 2 primary color phases.

One phase has a dark-crossbanded olive gray dorsum (some individuals have partial lateral striping on the forebody) with a clouded, gray-green venter. The other variant is orange—its striking hue perhaps an adaptation to the russet-orange arching prop roots of the red mangrove.

Adults of this phase have an unmarked orangish back and sides; juveniles are orange with dark dorsal crossbands. Of interest is the fact that both color phases may occur in the same litter: a wild-caught female taken by D. Craig McIntyre near the Flamingo, Florida, entrance to Everglades National Park gave birth to 15 offspring—one a red-orange color phase individual, the rest dark-hued. Among both these color phases, the venter of adults and juveniles is pale yellow, the dorsal scales are arranged in 21 to 23 rows at midbody, and the anal plate is divided.

Similar snakes   The subspecies **Gulf salt marsh snake** (73) has full-length dark-brown dorsolateral stripes on a light grayish-tan ground color and a pale-spotted reddish-brown venter. The **Atlantic salt marsh snake** (74), also a subspecies, is dorsally striped on its forebody; posteriorly it is blotched. The **striped crayfish snake** (85) has stripes running the length of its dorsum and a uniformly colored belly.

The **cottonmouth** (179, 180) has a stouter body, an unstriped back, a flat-sided head with vertically slit pupils, and a single row of subcaudal scales.

Behavior   Sometimes seen crossing canal-side roads at night, *N. c. compressicauda* is also fond of basking on mangrove limbs during the day. When approached, instead of splashing head first into the water like other natricines, mangrove salt marsh snakes typically slip gently backward off the limb, silently disappearing tail first into the water or wet mangrove litter below. See **Atlantic Salt Marsh Snake**.

76   FLORIDA GREEN WATER SNAKE

Nerodia floridana

Nonvenomous   See **Mississippi Green Water Snake**.

Abundance   *Nerodia floridana* is widespread and fairly common throughout Florida, southern Alabama and Georgia, with a disjunct population living on the coast of South Carolina. In flooded marl prairie and Everglades saw-grass swale, however, the Florida green water snake may be the most abundant aquatic serpent.

Size Adult *N. floridana* are usually 30 to 55 inches long; the record is 74 in.

Habitat The Florida green water snake's optimal habitat is open wetland filled with herbaceous vegetation. This includes reed- and cattail-filled marshes, hyacinth-choked waterways, inundated saw-grass prairies, and brackish estuaries. *Nerodia floridana* is abundant in the mesic Payne's Prairie Preserve near Gainesville, in the Everglades, and in marshes along the St. Johns River.

Prey Unlike the Mississippi green water snake, which feeds mostly on fish, an examination of 75 Florida green water snake stomachs indicated that *N. floridana* preys more heavily on frogs: one individual contained 10 frogs, 4 fish, and a single large salamander. The young take tadpoles and small fish.

Reproduction Live-bearing. Breeding occurs from March to June, with litters deposited between June and September. These average 20 to 30, although the largest females sometimes give birth to extra-ordinary numbers of offspring: at Kissimmee Prairie, Flavio Morissey took more than 128 young from a 5-foot-long gravid female slain by traffic.

Coloring/scale form Dorsolateral color is dark olive green, with juveniles being somewhat more distinctly dark- and pale-speckled. The Florida green water snake's most distinctive characteristic, however, is the row of small subocular scales that separates the lower half of its eye from the supralabial scales. (See **illustration: Mississippi Green Water Snake.**) Also distinctive is this animal's pale, almost unmarked venter. Its dorsal scales are arranged in 27 to 29 rows at midbody and its anal plate is divided.

Similar snakes Similar in dorsolateral coloring, the **Mississippi green water snake** (77) has a patterned venter: yellowish white on its forebelly, darkening posteriorly to gray, heavily infused with pale yellow half-moons. All other water snakes lack these two species' distinctive row of subocular scales.

Behavior Like the Mississippi green water snake *Nerodia floridana* is a largely nocturnal forager probably most often observed crossing roads in the evening, especially after rain.

MISSISSIPPI GREEN WATER SNAKE
Nerodia cyclopion

Nonvenomous The Mississippi green water snake is often confused with the venomous cottonmouth—especially since, as a dark, thick-bodied aquatic serpent *N. cyclopion* may flatten its head and body and strike if molested. When handled, many individuals discharge an odorous musk from the cloaca, and may disgorge recently taken prey.

Abundance Along the northern Gulf Coast from the tip of the Florida panhandle—where it has been found in cypress swamps—to Corpus Christi Bay on the Texas coast, the Mississippi green water snake is an uncommon reptile. It also occurs sporadically throughout Louisiana and northward up the Mississippi River valley as far as southern Illinois.

Size Most adults measure between 30 and 45 inches; the record is 50 in.

Habitat For the most part, the Mississippi green water snake inhabits inundated lowland forest and tree-lined sloughs. Unlike its subspecies, the Florida green water snake, which is a snake of open marshes, *Nerodia cyclopion* is scarce in the brackish coastal estuaries favored by its more easterly relative, and seems to be found more often in cypress swamps.

Prey Robert H. Mount reports that in Alabama "fish appear to be by far the most important food. Amphibians are eaten infrequently."

Reproduction Live-bearing. Reproduction is much the same as that of the Florida green water snake: unlike the adults, the 6- to 8-inch-long newborns (litters average 15 to 25) are distinctly spotted and crossbarred.

Coloring/scale form The dorsum is dark olive green, both dark- and pale-speckled among younger animals, more uniformly colored, with a darkly pebbled appearance among older adults. The definitive characteristic of *Nerodia cyclopion*, however, is the row of small subocular scales that separates the eye from the supralabial scales.

The venter of the Mississippi green water is also distinctive. Its pale yellowish forebelly darkens posteriorly to gray, where it

Mississippi Green and Florida Green
water snakes: Row of subocular scales

All other water snakes: No row
of subocular scales

becomes heavily infused with yellow half-moons. This animal's dorsal scales occur in 27 to 29 rows at midbody and its anal plate is divided.

Similar snakes The **Florida green water snake (76)** has an unpatterned yellow belly except for dark marks and smudges beneath its tail. **All other water snakes (62–72, 75–95)** lack subocular scales.

Behavior Mississippi green water snakes are occasionally seen during the day basking at the water's edge, but this species is a largely nocturnal forager most often observed—both in the water and on shore—by spot-lighting after dark.

78 BROWN WATER SNAKE, *Nerodia taxispilota*

Nonvenomous As a dark, heavy-bodied aquatic serpent, *N. taxispilota* is often confused with the venomous cottonmouth, especially since if harassed it may flatten its head in threat and strike and bite vigorously in defense.

Abundance Very common. Throughout the southeastern Atlantic and Gulf coastal plains (including the entire state of Florida) from tidewater Virginia to Mobile, Alabama, the brown water snake is a locally abundant animal: in the most favorable habitats, a dozen or more may sometimes be seen within a few acres of wetland.

Size Most adults are 30 to 55 inches long, with the record being 69½ in. Any brown water snake this big would almost certainly be a female, for males do not reach the size of the largest females.

In one Virginia sample, males averaged 23¾ inches; females, at nearly 32 in., were almost a third longer. In weight, males averaged only 6½ ounces, non-pregnant females almost 11 oz. Gravid females, however, averaged an amazing 35 ounces—more than five times as heavy as males.

Habitat   Within its range, most aquatic environments can support brown water snakes if they contain fallen trees or branches suitable for basking, for *Nerodia taxispilota* is not primarily an animal of open marshes, although along both the Atlantic and Gulf coasts it is found in wet prairies as well as near the tree-bordered margins of brackish tidal wetlands. It is perhaps most common around waterways through bottomland forest, among flooded hardwoods, and in cypress swamps. In Florida, brown water snakes also inhabit canal banks, the hammocks of saw-grass marshes, and flooded stands of melaleuca.

Prey   Brown water snakes prey primarily on frogs and fish, but they also regularly take carrion: in one study, much of the food obtained by *N. taxispilota* was scavenged fish. The necessity for obtaining food anywhere it is available is central to water snake ecology, for giving birth to several dozen offspring places a great burden on the ability of the female to nourish her developing embryos.

Since fetal reptiles are nourished primarily by the fat yolks deposited within their membranous egg shrouds, female *N. taxispilota* have to acquire considerable reserves of fat well in advance of their pregnancies. Building up these lipid reserves by some 50% (only females that acquire this amount of body fat ovulate) occupies the winter prior to breeding, leaving them so much larger than their mates as to almost appear to be a different species. At this time, slowed by the weight of their burgeoning fat reserves, female *N. taxispilota* are limited in their hunting strategies but, still needing to acquire calories wherever they can, may come to rely on scavenging.

Reproduction   In southern Florida, brown water snakes begin breeding in late February; in the northern part of their range, breeding may not occur until May or June. Therefore the 7- to 11-inch-long neonates appear over a long period from June to October.

Coloring/scale form   Dorsolateral ground color is light brown, marked with widely separated big brown (usually light-edged), squarish vertebral blotches and similarly colored lateral blotches that occur along the length of its body. The several-scale-row-wide separation between both its vertebral and lateral blotches is the brown water snake's most distinctive characteristic, referrenced by its scientific name, *spilos*, Greek for "spotted."

Its pale yellow venter is heavily pigmented with both dark blotches and black crescents, its dorsal scale rows vary in number from 25 to 33, and its anal plate is divided.

Similar snakes   At least five species of *Nerodia* occur within the range of *N. taxispilota*, all with the same general shape, and sometimes, mud-obscured coloring. But there are distinct differences: **red-bellied** and **yellow-bellied water snakes (66, 68)** have unpatterned backs, sides, and venter; the **midland water snake (64)** has dark brown cross-bands on its neck, forebody, and tail, and squarish brown bars along its sides. **Banded** and **Florida water snakes (70, 72)** have dark cross-bands across their entire bodies and a distinct dark postocular stripe that extends from the eye through the posterior supralabial scale.

The **cottonmouth (179, 180)** has a triangular, slab-sided head with a dark pit midway between its nostril and its slit-pupiled eye. Unlike any water snake, there is a single row of scales under its tail.

Behavior   Like most other water snakes, *N. taxispilota* is a good climber as well as swimmer: in early spring it can be seen basking on either partially submerged or exposed overhanging tree limbs. During the hottest part of the summer it turns to primarily nocturnal activity, however.

79   DIAMOND-BACKED WATER SNAKE
Nerodia rhombifer rhombifer

Nonvenomous   If cornered, large diamond-backed water snakes can be vigorous biters, with an extraordinary ability to excrete and spew musk.

Abundance   Variably abundant across a great variety of environments that stretch from the desert banks of the Pecos River in western Texas to wooded swamps in eastern Alabama—and from the northwestern Gulf Coast across most of Texas, Oklahoma, and southeastern Kansas (with a gap occurring in both the Ozarks and Missouri hill country), then north along the Mississippi valley. *N. rhombifer* is very common in the large swamps of western Kentucky—to Iowa and Illinois.

The diamond-backed water snake's variable population density ranges from the central and northeastern parts of its range, where it is not numerous—*N. r. rhombifer* seems to almost never occur in upland terrain—to the southern Gulf coastal plain and Rio Grande valley, where it is the most common aquatic serpent.

Size   Most adults are 20 to 34 inches; the record is just over 60 in.

Habitat   Within its range, *N. r. rhombifer* may be found in or around almost any rural body of water, including small, temporary ponds (everywhere, manmade objects left along the banks are a frequent source of shelter). During rainy periods, however, diamond-backed water snakes often forage in moist grassland a considerable distance from water.

The same sort of overland travel occurs in southwestern Texas, where *N. r. rhombifer* inhabits more arid terrain than almost any other aquatic snake. Because waterways in this area are prone to seasonal drying, diamond-backed water snakes are often forced to make long journeys to permanent water holes, and at this time the young are particularly vulnerable to predation. With newborns at their most numerous during the seasonal droughts of late summer, the author has seen great blue herons and several species of egrets plucking neonates from shrinking pools in the Nueces River.

Yet, extensive overland travel is a basic part of the diamond-backed water snake's ecology, and no sooner have autumn rains refilled these rivers and ponds than adult *N. r. rhombifer* (usually traveling at night) reappear in their home territories among outlying stock tanks and the headwaters of small streams.

These temporary pools typically harbor a great many tadpoles and frogs, which are ideal prey for adult *N. r. rhombifer*—but the reason anurans are able to prosper here is that these ponds' periodic evaporation means predatory fish cannot survive. In permanent waterways such fish exact a heavy toll on both juvenile anurans and neonate water snakes—a toll presumably heavier than that taken by terrestrial predators during young water snakes' forced migrations to more permanent aquatic environments.

Prey The diamond-backed water snake's prey varies considerably with locale, but in most situations it feeds primarily on frogs and rough fish (few game fish, which are too fast for water snakes to capture, are taken). One predatory technique involves swimming parallel to the shore, then seizing the frogs that, flushed from their bankside resting places, sometimes leap directly into the snake's path.

As with other water snakes, carrion also seems to be an important part of the diet; drawn by both scent and vibrations in the water, *N. r. rhombifer* is often seen nosing around the dead and dying fish held by fishermens' stringers or, after dark, coming ashore in search of fish heads and offal at fishing camps such as those at Tennessee's Reelfoot Lake.

Reproduction Live-bearing. Twenty-two litters, all deposited between the first of August and mid-October, averaged just over 37 young; these neonates were 8¼ to 10¼ inches in length.

Coloring/scale form Blackish-brown lines form a diamond- or chain link fence–shaped network (the *rhombos*—"rectangular"—of its Latin species name), which crosses the diamond-backed water snake's olive to grayish-brown back; these lines also intersect dark vertical bars along its sides. The yellowish venter is randomly marked with small black crescents, there are 25 to 31 midbody rows of dorsal scales, and the anal plate is divided.

Similar snakes   The diamond-backed water snake's heavy body and indistinct dark coloring (especially when its pattern is obscured by mud) often cause it to be mistaken for the **western cottonmouth (181)**. This aquatic pitviper is distinguished by its slit-pupiled eye and the sunken, heat-sensing pit located between its eye and its nostril. Unlike the rounded heads of water snakes, the cottonmouth's angular head has flat, undercut cheeks which abruptly intersect its crown.

Nerodia water snakes typically swim and dive vigorously, moreover, while the cottonmouth's entire body is buoyantly suspended on the surface. (The aggregations of aquatic snakes often seen in shrinking water holes during late summer are almost always nonvenomous *Nerodia* rather than the "nest of cottonmouths" they are commonly taken for.)

Behavior   One predatory strategy involves sensitive lateral areas spaced along this animal's trunk; when these spots are touched, *N. rhombifer* snaps sideways in an automatic strike response that, as it swims parallel to pond and river banks, increases its chances of seizing prey trapped between its body and the shore.

Another such strategy is moving constantly from one water source to another as each pond's prey is exhausted; stocking a big batch of hatchery-bred sunfish (some of which are sure to be in poor condition and die) will often draw a visit from several scent-hunting diamond-backed water snakes already present in the general vicinity.

80   BRAZOS WATER SNAKE, *Nerodia harteri harteri*

Nonvenomous   Brazos water snakes will nip only if seized or molested.

Abundance   Threatened. Federally protected, and protected by the state of Texas. *Nerodia harteri* is the only species of snake unique to Texas, and while it is restricted in range, it is not close to extinction.

Size   Most adults measure 16 to 32 inches; the record is just over 35 in.

Habitat   *Nerodia harteri* typically hides under stones in shallow water or shelters beneath lakeshore or riverbank rocks. Until the late

1980s this species had almost never been reported from any other environment than stony-bottomed shallows located sporadically along the upper Brazos River and its tributaries. This habitat is so limited, with long stretches of the river planned for deep-water reservoir impoundments, that both *Nerodia harteri harteri* and its subspecies, the Concho water snake, *Nerodia harteri paucimaculata*, were thought to be in danger of extinction.

The ecological attention this situation received resulted in an intensive investigation by James Dixon and others, of Texas A & M University. When Dixon's 5-year-long study of both races of *N. harteri* appeared in 1992, it maintained that, although only a few thousand individuals of both races had been thought to exist, their numbers were probably in the tens of thousands.

This disparity was explained by the A & M group's finding that both Brazos and Concho water snakes—perhaps originally almost exclusively riffle-dwellers—had adapted to life in the newly constructed lakes that replaced much of their original shallow streambed habitat, and that the Brazos race is now found along rocky shorelines in both Lake Granbury and Possum Kingdom Lake.

Prey The opportunity to seize small fish as they become momentarily vulnerable in rocky riffles has historically been the primary factor determining the Brazos water snake's microhabitat. How it manages, over long periods, to forage and evade predation and human intrusion in environments far removed from these shallow rapids remains to be seen.

Reproduction Live-bearing. The September and early October parturition of 4 females captured while gravid resulted in the birth of 7 to 22 young that measured 7¼ to 9 inches in length.

Coloring scale/form The type specimen of *N. h. harteri*—captured in 1940 by veteran Palo Pinto County reptile fancier Phillip "Snakey" Harter—is defined by its medium brown vertebral stripe, flanked by a double row of brown spots (each row has 58 to 65 spots, more than any other indigenous water snake). Its ground color is tan, its throat is pale yellow, and its venter carrot-colored, with the ends of the ventral scales spotted or darkened.

The posterior chin shields are separated by 2 rows of small scales, the dorsal scales occur in 21 to 25 (usually 23) midbody rows, and the anal plate is divided.

Similar snakes The subspecies **Concho water snake (81)** has less-prominent ventral markings and a single row of small scales between its posterior underchin shields.

Behavior *Nerodia harteri* is a frequently diurnal forager whose exposed habitat requires it to hide from predators under submerged rocks—where it can remain without breathing for more than an hour—and to move fast when necessary. Exposed in these hiding places, Harter's water snakes typically streak diagonally downstream toward the opposite bank.

81 CONCHO WATER SNAKE

Nerodia harteri paucimaculata

Nionvenomous See **Brazos Water Snake.**

Abundance **Endangered. Federally protected, and protected by the state of Texas.** The only snake species unique to Texas, *Nerodia harteri* has always been restricted in range, with the subspecies Concho water snake inhabiting even narrower geographic boundaries than the Brazos race.

Recently, these boundaries have been narrowed still further. Since 1968, nearly half the Concho water snake's original streambed-shallows habitat has been inundated by the construction of Coke County's Spence Reservoir; this has left just 69 miles of the Concho water snake's original Concho and upper Colorado River habitat. Here, some 41 riffle sites in Tom Green, Concho, Coleman, and McCulloch counties were long thought to contain almost the entire world population of an estimated 330 to 600 Concho water snakes.

Moreover, since Stacy Dam is scheduled to flood at least 24.8 additional miles of this habitat and severely cut downstream flow during dry weather, Concho water snakes were expected to be confined to less than 22 miles of sparsely riffled and sometimes dried-up streambed—a remnant environment also vulnerable to development, for these shallows are the only spots to build low-water road crossings, to preserve the race from extinction.

Yet a 1992 study by James Dixon and others of Texas A & M University indicates that both the Brazos and Concho water snake races may have successfully adapted to the newly constructed lakes that have replaced much of their streambed habitat, for Concho water snakes are now found along rocky portions of the banks of Lakes Spence, Ivy, and other impoundments, and are reportedly under consideration for declassification as a threatened animal.

Size Adult length ranges from 16 to 32 inches.

Habitat   Some 135 miles southwest of the Brazos River headwaters where *N. h. harteri* is found, the same sort of fast-flowing upper Colorado and Concho river riffles are home to Texas' even more range-restricted, endemic race of the Harter's water snake, *N. h. paucimaculata* (still waters in this area are inhabited by the quite different blotched water snake, *N. e. transversa*).

Prey   See **Brazos Water Snake.**

Reproduction   Live-bearing. See **Brazos Water Snake.**

Coloring scale/form   Not discovered until 20 years after its Brazos subspecies, the Concho water snake has a paler dorsum and less conspicuous ventral spots—hence its designation *paucimaculata*, or "fewer-spotted." A single row of small scales separates its posterior underchin shields, its dorsal scales occur in 21 to 25 (usually 23) rows, and its anal plate is divided.

Similar snakes   The subspecies **Brazos water snake** (80) has a double row of small scales between its underchin shields. The **blotched water snake** (69) has vertebral crossbars and dark lateral blocks.

Behavior   See **Brazos Water Snake.**

SWAMP SNAKES
Genus Seminatrix

North Florida Swamp Snake, *Seminatrix pygaea pygaea*
South Florida Swamp Snake, *Seminatrix pygaea cyclas*
Carolina Swamp Snake, *Seminatrix pygaea paludis*

The rather strange genus *Seminatrix* is contained in the same colubrine subfamily *Natricinae* as the larger *Nerodia* water snakes—to which its close relationship is evident from its name "*Seminatrix*" (*Natrix* is the older term for the North American water snakes now known as *Nerodia*.)

Seminatrix contains but a single species, *S. pygaea*, a small serpent restricted to the southeastern Atlantic and eastern Gulf coastal plains, including all of Florida except the Keys and western panhandle. *Seminatrix pygaea* is itself divided into three subspecies—all of which favor plant-choked luetic habitats, where they can be very common.

Swamp snakes have smooth dorsal scales (although the dark scales of their lowest lateral rows contain a light-hued longitudinal line that appears to be a keel), arranged in 17 rows at midbody, and a divided anal plate.

Seminatrix pygaea pygaea

Nonvenomous *Seminatrix pygaea pygaea* does not bite humans.

Abundance Locally abundant from South Carolina across the northern half of the Florida peninsula to southeastern Alabama.

Size Adults measure only 10 to 15 inches in length; the record is 18½ in.

Habitat North Florida swamp snakes inhabit fresh, brackish, and sometimes even saline wetlands, including hyacinth-filled canals, sphagnum bogs, saw-grass prairies, cypress stands, marshes, temporary ponds and sloughs, and bayheads.

Prey Foraging is mostly nocturnal. See **South Florida Swamp Snake**.

Reproduction Live-bearing. See **South Florida Swamp Snake**.

Coloring/scale form The north Florida swamp snake's dorsum is shiny black, with its pigment continuing onto the outer sutures of the (generally) 118 to 125 red ventral scales.

Similar snakes The **South Florida swamp snake (83)** has fewer than 117 ventral scales.

Behavior It is often assumed that reptiles with restricted, clearly de-fined habitats—such as water snakes inhabiting small ponds—simply "live" there. Yet these bodies of water regularly dry up, forcing even partially fossorial reptiles like *S. p. pygaea* (which can retreat from drought by burrowing into wet mud) to find their way to more per-manent aquatic environments.

Success in making the journeys to these areas is therefore crucial to their survival. But travel over land exposes swamp snakes to both physiological stress and increased predation, and studies have shown that they do not set out on these odysseys at random. For example, during Florida's severe drought of the late 1980s, *S. p. pygaea* were found to travel directly from several small Putnam County ponds, that periodically dried up, to a pair of nearby permanent lakes.

Since the only adults captured at the pond (9 out of 10 migrants were juveniles) were gravid females, it became evident that these fe-males had purposely chosen those intermittently filled ponds. Being free of predatory fish, which are eliminated by drying, these shallow pools are able to support a great many tadpoles and small aquatic invertebrates on which young swamp snakes feed, and such temporary ponds are now thought to serve as a sort of nursery—or as biologists would say, developmental habitat—for juvenile swamp snakes.

Thus when these seemingly inconsequential, ephemeral little pools are eliminated by human development, larger lakes in the vicinity suffer. Without these ponds' juvenile re-colonization of species such as *S. pygaea*, larger lakes are likely to become biologically depauperized, depleted of their resident ophidian fauna.

83   SOUTH FLORIDA SWAMP SNAKE

Seminatrix pygaea cyclas

Nonvenomous   South Florida swamp snakes do not bite humans.

Abundance   This indigenous Florida race can be locally abundant from the state's central peninsula south to the tip of its mainland.

Size   See **North Florida Swamp Snake.**

Habitat   Swamp snakes' primary habitat is heavily vegetated wetlands: hyacinth-filled canals and ponds as well as inundated stands of cypress. *Seminatrix pygaea cyclas* has also been reported from wet marl and saw-grass prairie habitats as well as from brackish estuaries, and in the Everglades it is common in both hardwood hammocks and canals.

Prey   In brackish tidal bays *S. p. cyclas* feeds mainly on small fish, including mosquito fish and sailfin mollies. In freshwater environments, worms, leeches, and other aquatic invertebrates, along with frogs and tadpoles, salamanders, sirens, and amphiumas are taken.

Reproduction   Live-bearing. Like most water snakes, females are longer and weigh more than males, but they are still so small that litter size ranges from only 2 to 11. On August 1, a 15-inch-long captive female gave birth to 7 offspring which averaged just over 5¼ inches in length.

Coloring/scale form   The south Florida swamp snake is almost identical to its northern subspecies, *S. p. pygaea*. Its elongate head is only slightly wider than its neck; its crown, back, and upper sides are shiny black (pale lateral streaks occur on its lower lateral scale rows); and its venter is red, with black pigment edging the distal margins of its fewer than 117 ventral scutes.

Similar snakes   The **north Florida swamp snake (82)** has 118 or more ventral scales.

Behavior   Swamp snakes are adapted to enduring long periods of sparse rainfall by burrowing (often by descending crayfish burrows) into the mud beneath drying ponds. *Seminatrix pygaea* is so well suited to dealing with this extremely low-energy environment that in this sort of damp subterranean refugia it can survive prolonged shortages of water, food, and oxygen that would kill almost any other non-amphibious vertebrate: if the subsurface soil retains enough moisture for them to avoid desiccation, swamp snakes are able to remain underground for 6 to 8 months, emerging unharmed when the wetland above them refills.

84   CAROLINA SWAMP SNAKE

Seminatrix pygaea paludis

Nonvenomous   Although it may wriggle energetically when captured, this mild-mannered little snake seldom, if ever, attempts to bite.

Abundance   Common. Within a range which includes the Atlantic coastal plain south of Albemarle Sound, North Carolina, through most of eastern South Carolina to the Georgia–South Carolina state line, *S. p. paludis* is often locally abundant in suitable habitat. Like other swamp snakes this race is so secretive, however, that its presence may be unsuspected even where it is common.

Size   Adult at from 10 to 12 inches in length, the largest *S. p. paludis* slightly exceed 19 in.

Habitat   The Carolina swamp snake can inhabit almost any rural body of plant-choked luetic water. This includes stands of cypress, swamps, and riverain oxbows. Although it is most common in freshwater, *S. p. paludis* (*paludis* is Latin for "swampy") is also at home in tidewater bays and estuarine marshes with considerable saline content.

Carolina swamp snakes have been reported to seclude themselves within mats of vegetation at the water's edge, while others have been found burrowed deeply into sphagnum moss or decomposing pondside vegetation. Although *S. p. paludis* is primarily a mainland species, individuals have been found on the saline verges of offshore barrier islands.

Prey Invertebrates such as oligochoaete worms, tadpoles, salamanders (including dwarf sirens), and some small fish are the usual prey of *S. p. paludis*.

Reproduction Live-bearing. Gravid female Carolina swamp snakes attain a comparatively immense girth before depositing litters of up to 14, 5-inch-long young that are virtually identical in appearance to the adults.

Coloring/scale form In a color combination echoed by numerous snakes worldwide, *S. p. paludis* has evolved an unmarked shiny black dorsum and a brilliant orange-red venter. Although smooth, the scales in the lowermost lateral rows have a faint, longitudinal midscale line that gives the impression of a keel; a short black bar occupies both anterior corners of each red ventral plate. The Carolina swamp snake's dark head is narrow, but somewhat wider than its neck, and it generally has 127 or more ventral scales.

Similar snakes The Carolina swamp snake is very similar to its more southerly relative, the **north Florida swamp snake (82)**, which usually has but 118 to 125 belly scales. The larger, **red-bellied water snake (66)** has heavily keeled scales; juveniles are dorsally patterned and adults have an orange to orange-red belly and a dark russet dorsum.

Behavior Rainy nights tend to induce overland movement among Carolina swamp snakes, and at such times large numbers of these small snakes are sometimes encountered crossing wet, lowland roadways bordered by canals or flooded ditches. In contrast, when droughts shrink or eliminate many ponds, like its southerly subspecies, the Carolina swamp snake seeks refuge in deeply subterranean wet mud, which it reaches by descending crayfish burrows. See **South Florida Swamp Snake**.

CRAYFISH AND QUEEN SNAKES
Genus Regina

Striped Crayfish Snake, *Regina alleni*
Glossy Crayfish Snake, *Regina rigida rigida*
Delta Crayfish Snake, *Regina rigida deltae*
Gulf Crayfish Snake, *Regina rigida sinicola*
Queen Snake, *Regina septemvittata*
Graham's Crayfish Snake, *Regina grahamii*

Part of the colubrine subfamily *Natricinae*, the genus *Regina*—"Queen"—contains four species. Of these, only the striped crayfish snake, *R. alleni*, has smooth scales; the other three species, *R. rigida*, *R. septemvittata*, and *R. grahami*, have keeled scales. All four species have 19 midbody rows of dorsal scales, however, and a divided anal plate. The striped and the glossy crayfish snakes are stout, shiny reptiles; the Graham's crayfish and queen snakes are rather slender and dull-scaled.

In behavior, the striped crayfish snake is almost entirely aquatic, while the other three species of *Regina*, especially the queen snake, are typically found in aquatic milieus but often leave the water to bask and hide beneath shoreline litter and rocks. In this wetland environment *Regina* has developed a strong predatory adaptation to feeding on crayfish. The queen snake and Graham's crayfish snake are specialists, preferring soft-shelled (freshly molted) crayfish, while the other two crayfish snake species, the striped and the glossy, are less discriminating, taking both hard- and soft-shelled crayfish. (Studies have recently disclosed that some component in the saliva of the glossy crayfish snake renders crayfish immobile and thus easily swallowed.)

85   STRIPED CRAYFISH SNAKE, *Regina alleni*

Nonvenomous   The striped crayfish snake seldom, if ever, bites humans even when handled.

Abundance   Almost entirely endemic to Florida (it is also found just over the state line in Georgia), *Regina alleni* is common from the eastern panhandle south throughout the state.

Size   Most adults are 14 to 20 inches long; the record is just under 26 in.

Habitat   Named for venom collector, field researcher, and reptile showman E. Ross Allen, *Regina alleni* occupies heavily vegetated aquatic environments, especially hyacinth-filled canals. It is also common in wet saw-grass prairies and cypress sloughs, sphagnum bogs, and inundated stands of melaleuca.

Prey   Like other *Regina*, this species preys almost entirely on crayfish—a food animal unavailable to other small serpents due to its hard, spiny carapace. *Regina alleni* avoids the forward-pointed spines of this crustacean's armor, however, by swallowing it tail first. Small fish and dragonfly naiads, or nymphs, are also taken.

Reproduction   Live-bearing. See **Delta Crayfish Snake.**

Coloring/scale form   The striped crayfish snake's dark brown dorsum is marked with both a single black stripe along the spine and a dark upper lateral stripe; a pale yellow or rusty-brown stripe occupies each of the lower sides. Its yellow belly is unpatterned or midventrally marked with brownish spots.

Its cephalic scutellation is unique, however: *Regina alleni* has only one internasal scale, while—unusual in a genus whose other species all have keeled scales—its dorsal scales are smooth except above the cloaca.

Similar snakes   The **glossy crayfish snake (86)** is not distinctly striped, while its venter is marked with a double row of brown crescents. All other dark-backed **water snakes (66, 73, 78, 82, 83, 86)** living in the range of *R. alleni* lack its pale lateral color demarcation.

Behavior   This muscular, stiff-bodied little reptile forages at night during the summer but is more crepuscular in spring and fall, when it is sometimes seen crossing low-lying dirt roads.

86   GLOSSY CRAYFISH SNAKE, *Regina rigida rigida*

Nonvenomous   *Regina rigida rigida* seems to seldom bite humans, even when first captured, unless it is handled roughly. The saliva of this species apparently has some toxic qualities, at least to crustaceans, but it does not appear to be dangerous to humans.

Abundance   Uncommon. Apparently unevenly distributed across the Gulf Coastal plain from the Florida panhandle through south/central Florida and north along the Atlantic seaboard as far as southern Virginia, *R. r. rigida* is reportedly abundant in some areas. Yet long days may be spent searching this snake's swampy woodland habitat without seeing one.

Size   Most adults measure 14 to 23 inches in length; the record is 31 in.

Habitat   The glossy crayfish snake is both aquatic and fossorial, inhabiting partially flooded stands of cypress and wooded sloughs, where its primary microhabitat seems to be the burrows of the crayfish on which it feeds. *Regina rigida rigida* may also burrow deeply beneath rotting stumps, logs, or planks at the water's edge. (Perhaps because neither this semi-subterranean lifestyle nor predation on slow-moving crayfish calls for agility, crayfish snakes are decidedly stiff-bodied—feeling taut to the touch—an attribute from which their species name, *rigida*, is derived.)

Prey   The teeth of the glossy crayfish snake are highly unusual: stout and chisel-like, and hinged at the base (Dundee and Rossman 1989). This characteristic helps *R. r. rigida* ingest the large, keratinous carapaces of crayfish; the stomachs of a number of these snakes contained only freshly molted crayfish, but dragonfly nymphs may also be taken.

Reproduction   Live-bearing. See **Delta Crayfish Snake.**

Coloring/scale form   The back and upper sides of this race are shiny chocolate brown, usually dimly dark-striped. Along the belly line, the 2 lowest rows of dorsal scales are yellowish, split by a dark seam, while the pale sides of the throat are lightly streaked with brown. On most of the dark yellow venter, a double row of big brown half-moons is clearly evident. The dorsal scales are keeled, there are usually a pair of prefrontal scales per side and, among females, 54 or fewer subcaudal scales, 62 or fewer among males.

Similar snakes   The subspecies **Gulf crayfish snake (88)** has more numerous subcaudal scales (55 or more in females, 63 or more in males) as well as an unstriped throat.

Behavior   Although amphiumas constitute the prey of most adult *natricine* water snakes, these giant salamanders can also be snake predators: one 40-inch-long two-toed amphiuma trapped by Kevin Enge of the Florida Game and Fresh Water Fish Commission disgorged an only slightly shorter glossy crayfish snake.

---

87   DELTA CRAYFISH SNAKE, *Regina rigida deltae*

Nonvenomous   Some *R. r. deltae* will bite when captured, as well as smear copious musk and feces on their captor.

Abundance   Because of its secretive habits, the abundance of this snake is difficult to assess. Within its small, Mississippi River delta range a search of favorable habitat will usually bring a specimen or two to light, and fair numbers have been found crossing roadways traversing or paralleling marshes or closely connected bodies of luetic water on rainy spring and summer nights.

Size   The delta race is large for a crayfish snake, with adults measuring a stout 18 to 25 inches in length, while some delta crayfish snakes slightly exceed 30 in.

Habitat   Near the mouth of Mississippi, *R. r. deltae* may be found almost anywhere along the bayous, canals, and flooded ditches that traverse this low-lying terrain. It also occurs, further inland, around the numerous lakes, ponds, and marshes that dot western Mississippi and south-central Louisiana. In both areas the delta crayfish snake's microhabitat includes floating mats of hyacinth, water lettuce, and pennywort, while on these waterways' banks *R. r. deltae* shelters beneath logs, boards, and mats of vegetation.

Prey   Although physically well adapted to capture and eat difficult-to-ingest crustaceans, the delta crayfish snake apparently also occasionally preys on amphibians and fish.

Reproduction   Live-bearing. Heavily gravid females sometimes attain a proportionately immense girth before depositing litters of from 4 to 14 young, about 8 inches in length, in mid- to late summer.

Coloring/scale form   The delta crayfish snake is distinguished from the Gulf subspecies, whose range surrounds its territory, by its single prefrontal scale per side. Among *R. r. deltae* the dorsal coloring is a shiny dark olive-brown to brown, often with thin dark paravertebral and paler dorsolateral stripes. The dorsal scales are keeled, the unmarked throat is yellowish (darkest on old snakes), as is the venter, which bears two rows of bold, regularly sized semicircles.

Similar snakes   A subspecies, the **gulf crayfish snake (88)**, has a pair of prefrontal scales on each side. **Graham's crayfish snake (90)**, which shares this subspecies' range, is less shiny, more slender, and has both predominantly smooth scales and a broad yellowish lateral stripe above russet-colored lower sides.

Behavior   *Regina rigida deltae* is most active after dark; in daylight, this stout snake will often remain quietly in place even when the object beneath which it is sheltering is removed.

---

88   GULF CRAYFISH SNAKE, *Regina rigida sinicola*

Nonvenomous   Like all crayfish snakes, this shy little reptile seldom bites human beings even if it is handled.

Abundance   Probably uncommon. Certainly *Regina rigida sinicola* is not

often or easily found throughout most of its two broad ranges. The more westerly of these includes eastern Texas and Oklahoma, southern Arkansas and northwestern Louisiana; then, and after a gap across the Mississippi delta where only the subspecies delta crayfish snake is found, this subspecies' eastern range covers southwestern Georgia, the Florida panhandle, southern Alabama and southeastern Mississippi.

Size   Adults average 20 inches in length; the maximum size recorded for *R. r. sinicola* is 31½ in.

Habitat   The Gulf crayfish snake seems to be found most often in cypress sloughs and waterways through bottomland forest. Yet, in places where crayfish are common, it also occurs—in open country—in irrigation ditches, wet marl prairies, and muddy pastures.

Prey   *Regina rigida sinicola* preys primarily crayfish, lesser sirens, small fish, frogs, and aquatic insects such as dragonfly nymphs.

Reproduction   Live-bearing. Eleven newborns measured between 7 and 8½ inches in length.

Coloring/scale form   The Gulf crayfish snake's back is shiny chocolate brown, sometimes with dimly darker-striped sides above a yellowish-tan lateral stripe (split by a thin black seam) that occupies the first and second scale rows above its belly line.

Among *R. r. sinicola* the dorsal scales are keeled and there are two prefrontal scales per side. Both its labial scales and the unpatterned sides of its throat are yellowish, and its pale yellow venter (which, among females has 55 or more subcaudal scales, 63 or more among males) is marked with a double row of rearward-arced dark crescents that form a single line beneath its chin and tail.

Similar snakes   An easterly subspecies, the **glossy crayfish snake** (86) is distinguished by the thin brown stripes along its throat, as well as by its fewer subcaudal scales: 54 or fewer in females and 62 or fewer in males. Another subspecies, the **delta crayfish snake** (87), has a single prefrontal scale per side. The **queen snake (89)** has a dull brown dorsum, a prominent yellowish lateral stripe above russet-colored lower sides and (except for its lower back) smooth dorsal scales.

Behavior   Crayfish snakes are predominantly nocturnal, although Paul E. Moler of the Florida Game and Fresh Water Fish Commission has observed diurnal foraging in this subspecies. Because of its semi-subterranean lifestyle, *R. r. sinicola*—which is active mainly between March and early November—is sometimes able to subsist in suburban ponds and creeks where larger, more visible water snakes would soon be killed.

89 QUEEN SNAKE, *Regina septemvittata*

Nonvenomous   Like many snakes attempting to discourage a predator, *Regina septemvittata* may void the odorous contents of its cloaca when handled, but it seldom bites even when first picked up in the field. (Once past their initial fear, queen snakes adapt well to confinement and, when their specialized diet of crayfish was provided, have lived as long as 19 years in captivity.)

Abundance   Generally somewhat un-common, but locally abundant in places. John MacGregor once found 28 queen snakes hidden within a rusty automobile door discarded near Central Kentucky Creek. The queen snake occupies an exceptionally broad north/south distribution, ranging from the Alabama and Florida Gulf coasts to a small, disjunct range in northern Michigan. On an east/west axis, it is nearly as cosmopolitan, ranging from Chesapeake Bay to southern Illinois and central Arkansas.

Size   A moderately slender reptile with a slim head no wider than its body, adult *R. septemvittata* average 14 to 23 inches in length, reaching a maximum of just over 36 in.

Habitat   In the South, the queen snake is a flooded bottomland forest and cypress dome dweller, preferring aquatic habitats with sandy or hard-substrate bottoms to the muddy, open marshes favored by its *Regina* relatives. In Appalachia and the Midwest, less heavily wooded stream and riverbanks are occupied while, as far north as the Canadian shoreline, *R. septemvittata* is even found in the near-shore waters of the ocean-like Great Lakes. Everywhere within this broad range the local abundance of crayfish seems to be the crucial factor in determining which lake, pond, swamp, or flooded ditch the queen snake will occupy; along such shorelines it shelters beneath rocks or vegetative debris.

Prey   Freshly molted, soft-bodied crayfish are almost the queen snake's only prey. So strong is its instinctive orientation to this food source that newborns presented with an array of different odors taken from potential prey species react only to the scent of just-molted crayfish.

Reproduction   Live bearing. The young, numbering 10 to 12 per litter, are born in mid-summer.

Coloring/scale form   The queen snake's slender back and upper sides vary from grayish-brown to black. On lighter-hued individuals 3 dark dorsolateral stripes are dimly defined above a prominent yellowish-tan lateral stripe. Individuals from the Gulf Coast tend to be darker, and these stripes are hard to see except on the sides of the neck.

Among *R. septemvittata*, the brown-marked creamy venter—whose color extends to the lowermost pair of lateral scale rows—is marked with a double row of dark spots that converge to form a single line beneath its chin and tail, but very old individuals may have predominantly dark bellies. The dorsal scales are keeled.

Similar snakes   Except for the **Florida green water snake (76)**, which has an unstriped, dark-speckled gray-green dorsum, all other **water snakes** living within the range of *R. septemvittata* have patterned backs and lack the sharply defined color demarcation between the queen snake's yellowish-tan lateral stripe and its russet-hued lower sides.

Behavior   Both a diurnal and a nocturnal forager, the queen snake does not occur in the open estuarine marshes where larger *Nerodia* are numerous. In its more inland, streamside environment, *R. septemvittata* is often somewhat arboreal, climbing onto bankside bushes or overhanging limbs—from which, when approached, it drops into the water and dives.

90   GRAHAM'S CRAYFISH SNAKE

Regina grahamii

Nonvenomous   This slender, unagressive snake seldom if ever bites human beings even if it is handled.

Abundance   Uncommon. With a range that stretches from arid mesquite brushland along southern Texas' Nueces River, around the Gulf Coast to the mouth of the Mississippi, then northward up that broad riparian corridor as far as the southern tip of Lake Michigan and westward to northern Iowa, eastern Nebraska, and central Kansas (where *R. grahamii* follows river courses upstream onto the Great Plains), the Graham's water snake inhabits an exceptional variety of aquatic habitats. Few North American water snakes exhibit this sort of habitat diversity, yet Graham's crayfish snakes are not generally dispersed, and throughout this huge territory *R. grahamii* is locally abundant only in scattered places.

Size Small and slender, most adult Graham's crayfish snakes measure only 18 to 30 inches in length; the maximum size is 47 inches.

Habitat On the Gulf coastal plain, *R. grahamii* inhabits sloughs, rice field irrigation ditches and, where crayfish are abundant, muddy bottomland pastures. The aquifer-fed headwaters of rivers emerging from Texas' Balcones Fault constitute another habitat—Graham's crayfish snakes are common in the headwaters of the San Antonio River—while in the westernmost part of its range, *R. grahamii* occupies riparian valleys through agricultural fields, dry prairie, and even thorn desert.

Prey The first to report on this animal's diet was John K. Strecker (1926), who wrote that *Regina grahamii* "feeds largely on crayfish and a small species of fresh-water prawn." Recent studies have found the stomachs of Graham's crayfish snakes to contain only freshly molted crayfish, but frogs and snails may also be taken.

Reproduction Live-bearing. Lawrence Curtis and R. J. Hall (1949) first observed courtship, which occurs early in May, at night, in the water. At this time, a group of pheromone-drawn male Graham's crayfish snakes may entwine themselves around a female, forming a compact mass—within which only one copulation evidently occurs. More often, however, breeding pairs are solitary, floating wrapped together, their tails hanging downward.

Deposited in August and September, recorded litters have ranged from 6 to 39 (26 broods averaged just over 17 young, 7 to 9½ inches in length). Strecker also reported finding 4 or 5 newborns sheltering together under flat rocks at the water's edge. Males may breed as early as their second spring, females not until their third year.

Coloring scale/form Among *Regina grahamii* the back and upper sides are dark grayish brown, except for a pale vertebral line. A wide, yellowish-tan lateral stripe—edged by a serrated black seam—occupies the first three scale rows above this animal's yellowish venter. On its belly, a midventral row of brown dots is better defined toward its tail, while the belly's distal margin is delineated by a line of angular black spots. The dorsal scales are keeled.

Similar snakes The **delta** and **Gulf crayfish snakes** (87, 88) have shiny, chocolate-colored backs and bellies marked with a double row of dark brown crescents. The **Gulf salt marsh snake** (73) has a gray-striped back and sides, at least 21 rows of dorsal scales, and a dark venter whose mid-line bears a row of cream-colored ovals.

Behavior   Named for soldier, engineer, and naturalist James Duncan Graham, a member of the 1852–53 Mexican Border Survey that first described much of Texas' herpetofauna, *Regina grahamii* forages at night during the summer months but engages in more crepuscular activity in spring and fall. Because of its reclusive temperament, the Graham's crayfish snake is able to subsist in urban park ponds where its presence is often something of a surprise: on rainy spring nights Graham's crayfish snakes are sometimes found crawling across suburban lawns in Waco, Texas—the only time *R. grahamii* is ever seen in this area.

MUD AND RAINBOW SNAKES
Genus Farancia

Eastern Mud Snake, *Farancia abacura abacura*
Western Mud Snake, *Farancia abacura reinwardtii*
Rainbow Snake, *Farancia erytrogramma erytrogramma*
South Florida Rainbow Snake, *Farancia erytrogramma seminola*

The genus *Farancia* is contained in the rear-fanged, mildly venomed colubrine subfamily *Xenodontinae*. The two species in this genus—*F. abacura* and *F. erytrogramma*—are very specialized reptiles with moderately thick girths and heavy necks, rather small heads, and tails that terminate in spine-like tip. Their shiny black ground-colored backs and upper sides contrast sharply with their bright red or carmine bellies (the mud snakes are carmine-banded only along their lower sides while the rainbow snakes are dorsolaterally striped and speckled with red and pink flecks). The predominantly smooth scales of both species are arranged in 19 midbody rows and the anal plate of both species is usually divided.

These specialized bodies are the mud and rainbow snakes' adaptation to swampy or entirely aquatic environments where, when adult, both species are narrowly focused predators which feed, in the case of the mud snakes, mostly on large salamanders although some captives accept frogs; rainbow snakes take only eels.

Female mud and rainbow snakes can attain more than 5 feet in length (males are noticeably smaller) and when gravid, to shelter their eggs, dig burrows in the soil or beneath vegetative debris. These cavities are often comparatively sizable, for female mud snakes typically coil atop their large clutches during the eggs' entire incubation period.

Farancia abacura abacura

Nonvenomous *Farancia abacura abacura* does not bite humans. See **Rainbow Snake.**

Abundance   Common throughout Florida, the eastern mud snake is generally less abundant, although not uncommon in southeastern Georgia, the coastal Carolinas, and southeastern Virginia. Despite its secretive, aquatic/burrowing habits, *F. a. abacura* can be among the most numerous serpents found on roads through wetlands: in a 4-year-long survey of Payne's Prairie Preserve near Gainesville, Richard Franz of the Florida Museum of Natural History found this subspecies to be one of the five snakes that most often appeared after dark on the section of U.S. 441 that crosses the preserve. (In this area a small percentage of mud snakes have white rather than pinkish-red venters.)

Size   Although the record eastern mud snake measured 81½ in., few adults are more than 50 inches long.

Habitat   *F. a. abacura* may be found in and around most freshwater environments, but it seems to especially favor turbid bodies of water with swampy margins and profuse aquatic vegetation. Marshes of all kinds are usually good mud snake habitat, while these reptiles also occupy wet saw-grass prairies, irrigation canals, cypress stands, and both flooded hardwoods and, in Florida, inundated stands of melaleuca. Its microhabitat includes the underside of logs and debris on hummocks in flooded bottomland forest.

Prey   Identical to that of the **Western Mud Snake.**

Reproduction   Egg-laying. Like other large aquatic serpents, mud snakes are extremely prolific, with clutches/litters made all the more numerous because *farancia* offspring are proportionately so small. The 7- to 9½-inch-long hatchlings emerge from their eggs in early autumn. Particularly in northern parts of their range, however, neonate mud snakes may remain in their nest cavity for months, perhaps until the following spring. (This could enhance their chances for survival since their aquatic habitat is at its driest during autumn, when the amphibian prey of neonate *F. abacura* is both scarce and simultaneously being sought by large numbers of newborn natricine water snakes.) See **Western Mud Snake.**

Coloring/scale form   The bluish-black dorsum of adult eastern mud snakes is marked along its lower sides with 53 or more carmine-colored

AQUATIC SNAKES

bars. (Anerythristic, dorsolaterally black-and-white individuals entirely lacking red pigment have also been found.) Among juveniles, the pink lateral bars extend well up the sides. Black rectangles checker the pinkish-red venter except beneath the tail, where this rectangular pattern becomes black crossbands. There is no preocular scale and, like all *Farancia*, the terminal caudal scale is enlarged and stiffened into a point. This adaptation may aid traction in the mud snake's viscous environment but, judging from the behavior of captives, is primarily a grip-enhancing prong that helps *F. abacura* maintain control of its large, slippery amphiuma and siren prey.

The dorsal scales are smooth, except for keeled scales (among both sexes) on the lower back above the anal plate, which is usually divided.

Similar snakes The **western mud snake (92)** has fewer (52 or less) red lateral bars which do not extend as far up the sides as those of the eastern subspecies. Both the **rainbow snake (93)** and the **Florida swamp snakes (82, 83)** lack pink lateral blotches and the mud snake's checkered belly. The **red-bellied water snake (66)** has a reddish-brown to dark olive back and side, keeled scales, and an unmarked orangish venter.

The **cottonmouth (179–181)** has a triangular head with a dark pit between its nostril and its slit-pupiled eye.

Behavior *F. a. abacura* typically responds to restraint by curling the rear of its body around one's hands and wrists, pressing its hardened, horn-like tail tip inward so firmly that it was once believed that this spur could deliver a mortal sting. When mud snakes' habit of lying in a circular coil was factored into the story, the legend arose of the horn-tailed hoop snake that could take its tail in its mouth, roll down a fleeing man, and tail-sting him to death with venom powerful enough to kill a tree. See **Western Mud Snake**.

---

92   WESTERN MUD SNAKE

Farancia abacura reinwardtii

Nonvenomous This big, docile serpent seems to be entirely unwilling to bite, even when first handled in the field. See **Rainbow Snake**.

Abundance Common but seldom seen. In suitable habitat (which occurs only intermittently) the western mud snake occurs sporadically throughout a broad range that stretches from Corpus Christi Bay on the Texas Gulf Coast to the Florida panhandle, and up the Mississippi valley at least as far north as St. Louis.

Formerly, this animal was abundant in most marshes just inland from the Texas and Louisiana coasts. The last 20 years' industrialization of this area has reduced the western mud snake's numbers dramatically, but along Highway 87 in Chambers and Jefferson counties *F. a. reinwardtii* is still numerous in roadside bar ditches and luetic grassland a few hundred yards behind the Gulf beaches.

Elsewhere in its range this animal is seen less often. Scattered populations occur throughout inland East Texas (including one in Panola County at the north end of Toledo Bend Reservoir), Louisiana, Mississippi, Arkansas, western Tennessee, and Kentucky. Here, despite mud snakes' secretive, aquatic/burrowing habits they can be among the most numerous serpents that appear crossing low-lying roads on rainy spring nights.

Size   Slightly smaller than the eastern race, adult western mud snakes may reach over 6 feet in length—most measure between 30 and 48 inches—although at hatching the young may be as small as 6¾ in.

Habitat   Similar to that of the **Eastern Mud Snake**.

Prey   A prey-specific predator, *F. a. reinwardtii* has a heavily muscled neck, jaws, and trunk adapted to overpowering the giant salamanders—sirens and amphiumas—that are its principal prey. (Its horny tail tip may have evolved to help the mud snake overcome these vigorous, difficult-to-hold animals by giving it a point of purchase on the amphibians' slippery sides.) Captives also rarely accept other salamanders, frogs, tadpoles, and fish as food.

Reproduction   Egg-laying. Western mud snakes deposit eggs during July and August and, like the eastern race, do so prolifically: one clutch numbered 60, another 104. The eggs are parchment-like in texture, and adherent, forming a glued-together mass. They are typically laid in a moist subsurface cavity, inside which the female may remain coiled about her clutch throughout its 8- to 12-week incubation period. (Here, her respiration may aid in maintaining the chamber's humidity.)

At least 5 mud snake nests, 1 in northern Florida and 4 in Louisiana, have been located within the nests of American alligators. The big piles of composting vegetation that alligators amass to warm their eggs with the heat of decay also benefit the eggs of *Farancia abacura*—whose incubation period is similar to that of alligator eggs.

Mud snakes also benefit from this commensal nesting because female alligators defend their nests from raccoons and other carnivores, while the elevation of their nest mounds minimizes the chance of damage by flooding. See **Eastern Mud Snake.**

Coloring/scale form   Western mud snakes may live on wet soil, but they are anything but muddy in color. Their backs and upper sides are glossy blue-black, marked along the belly line with 52 or fewer round-topped, reddish-pink blotches; among juveniles, these carmine blotches extend up the sides as far as the lower back. The venter has a bright, red-and-black checkerboard pattern that, beneath the tail, becomes a series of similar-hued crossbands. The dorsal scales are smooth, except for the vertebral rows above the vent, where they may be keeled. There is no preocular scale, the terminal caudal scale is enlarged and hardened into a point, and the anal plate is usually divided.

Similar snakes   The **eastern mud snake (91)** has more numerous (53 or more) reddish bars along its lower sides; these are taller than those of the western mud snake and have sharply pointed tops. The **rainbow snake (93)** has a colorfully striped dorsum, and both it and the **Florida swamp snakes (82, 83)** lack pink lateral blotches and the mud snake's checkered belly.

Behavior   Western mud snakes are aquatic, nocturnal animals, and often burrowers. Unlike their relatives the rainbow snakes, which ascend cypress knees, mud snakes do not climb. The horny tail tip (which captured *F. a. reinwardtii* typically press against one's hands), besides helping grip slippery prey, may have also evolved to offer mud snakes a point of purchase in viscous mud. See **Eastern Mud Snake.**

93   RAINBOW SNAKE

Farancia erytrogramma erytrogramma

Nonvenomous   Like other members of the genus *Farancia*, rainbow snakes have a Duvernoy's gland—a mucous-secreting organ often associated with some degree of salivary toxicity. Rainbow snakes also have enlarged posterior maxillary teeth, perhaps in order to introduce this saliva into the eels on which they prey—or perhaps simply to help hold onto eels' very slippery bodies. In either case, these teeth are not used in defense, for few snakes are more unwilling to bite their captors than the *Farancia*, among which even newly captured adults can be handled with impunity.

Abundance   Uncommon to rare. *Farancia erytrogramma erytrogramma* is seldom seen across its broad range that stretches along the Gulf and Atlantic coasts from Louisiana to northern Virginia and inland as far as the Alabama uplands and southern Appalachians (isolated populations occur in Florida as far south as Pinellas and southern Pasco counties).

This spotty distribution may be the result of the rainbow snake's restriction to unaltered woodland swamps, although even in the optimal milieu of the spring-run streams of northern Florida, southern Alabama and Georgia, *F. e. erytrogramma* usually goes unnoticed, for the rainbow snake's secretive behavior and largely subterranean lifestyle make it extremely difficult to find. Yet when conditions are right, these animals are regularly encountered.

Size   Although most rainbow snakes are considerably smaller—between 40 and 54 inches in length—the record is a heavy-bodied 66 in. Hatchlings vary from 7 to 10 inches in length.

Habitat   This fossorial and aquatic species is principally associated with the clear, unpolluted moving water of springs, lakes, and cypress swamps. Here, rainbow snakes' microhabitat is often either floating vegetation or the shelter of shoreline debris such as mats of Spanish moss, the trunks of fallen trees, and manmade detritus like newspapers and plywood. In both freshwater and brackish tidal marshes along the southeastern coastal plain *F. e. erytrogramma* is also found beneath logs and planks washed onto estuarine mudflats.

Out of several hundred individuals observed in South Carolina, Georgia, and Florida by W. T. Neill, who first described the rainbow snake's southern race,

> Only one was not in the water or immediately beside it. . . .
> In the southern part of its range, this species is among the most aquatic of snakes.

Prey   Of the rainbow snake's predation in the wild, Neill wrote:

> Among rural residents it is well known that the rainbow snake eats *Anguilla*. The snake is vernacularly known as "eel moccasin" [because] upon catching an eel, the rainbow snake climbs out of the water, usually into the exposed roots of a bald-cypress tree, but sometimes into stream-side shrubs.

Here, the eel is swallowed head first, after which the *F. e. erytro-gramma* often rests with the eel's tail tip dangling from its jaws.

In captivity, juvenile rainbow snakes' preferred prey are tadpoles and both larval and adult salamanders. These young snakes will thrive for a year or more on this prey, plus an occasional small fish or frog, but they gradually become more reluctant to accept tadpoles—somehow apparently knowing instinctively that their proper prey species are eels. Even when their tadpoles are scented with eel, maturing juveniles eventually hold out for a real *Anguilla*, and adults cannot be induced to accept any other prey.

Reproduction   Egg-laying. Although little is known about the courtship or reproductive biology of the rainbow snake, from the many nests that have been found clutch size is known to vary from as few as 10 eggs or as many as 52.

Rainbow snakes' nest cavities are usually excavated in moist, sandy soils, and it is likely that in at least some cases the female remains with her clutch during incubation, as do the related mud snakes.

Coloring/scale form   As multi-hued as its namesake, the rainbow snake is one of North America's most beautiful serpents. In ground color, its back is deep olive-brown to black or purplish-black, with bright dorsolateral pigments separated by dark areas that set off isolated spots of color. There is a red vertebral stripe, while another pinkish stripe occupies each of the dark upper sides. The Greek *erytrogramma* refers to these red markings. Below these lateral stripes, the lower sides are yellow, with each scale containing a red dot.

A pair of black spots flank each yellowish-pink ventral scute, between which the midbelly is brighter red; posterior to the yellow chin a row of smaller black midventral dots, which terminates several scutes anterior to the anal opening, may also be present. The 19 rows of big dorsal scales are smooth (except on the lower back and sides, where they may be weakly keeled); the tail is tipped with an enlarged, pointed terminal scute and the anal plate is usually divided.

Similar snakes   As members of the Colubrine subfamily *Xenodontinae*, Florida's rainbow and mud snake races are the only North American serpents possessing their unusual dental morphology—not to mention their unique suite of dorsolateral colors. The one or two preserved specimens of the extremely rare (perhaps even extinct) **South Florida rainbow snake (94)** have almost entirely black venters and lower sides. The **eastern** and **western mud snakes (91, 92)** lack dorsal striping.

Behavior   Rainbow snakes usually emerge from their submerged daytime retreats only after sundown, then seek seclusion again around midnight; during the low barometric pressure of a passing weather front, however, rainbow snakes may be active both earlier and later in the day than usual. Warm rainy days are also times of peak activity, and heavy rains can bring rainbow snakes to the surface at any time. (This emergence is probably due more to increased foraging opportunities than to their being flooded out like other serpents, for *F. e. erytrogramma* is so well adapted to aquatic conditions that it can sustain long periods of total immersion that would displace many terrestrial snakes.)

Rainbow snakes can sometimes be found by quietly canoeing after dark among inundated cypress, scrutinizing boles along the water's edge, where *F. e. erytrogramma* often lies with only its head protruding from submerged crevices. (Success in capturing a rainbow snake is often followed by the animal curling its muscular tail around one's hand or arm, pressing inward with its hardened, horn-like tip—behavior thought to reflect the rainbow snake's manipulation of its slippery eel and amphibian prey into a better swallowing position. See **Eastern Mud Snake.**

94 SOUTH FLORIDA RAINBOW SNAKE

Farancia erytrogramma seminola

Nonvenomous   The only *Farancia erytrogramma seminola* ever collected were taken at night, and according to their captor, W. T. Neill, "made no attempt to bite."

Abundance   Extremely rare or possibly extinct, this endemic Florida subspecies is the least-known snake in North America: only 3 specimens have been recorded. *Farancia erytrogramma seminola* was first described in 1952 by Wilfred T. Neill, a field researcher and collegue of Ross Allen, who termed this rainbow snake race *seminola* for the Seminole tribe who once inhabited the vicinity of Lake Okeechobee, where he captured the type specimen.

Since the discovery of this adult female, only 2 other south Florida rainbow snakes—both also female—have been reported; no males have been found. The size of the population remains unknown, if indeed *F. e. seminola* still exists, for a number of specific searches for it have failed.

Size   The largest of the three recorded specimens was a heavy-bodied 51½ inches in length.

Habitat   Neill's two specimens were taken in Fisheating Creek, which flows into the west side of Lake Okeechobee. The third female, now in the collection of the late reptile showman E. Ross Allen, was taken from the same area.

Prey   Like its northern subspecies, the south Florida rainbow snake probably feeds on freshwater eels and sirens.

Reproduction   Egg-laying. See **Rainbow Snake.**

Coloring/scale form   Neill's type specimen (now preserved in the Florida Museum of Natural History in Gainesville) resembles a partially melanistic rainbow snake: dark pigment obscures most of the red-spotted yellow scales of this individual's lower sides and occupies the majority of its venter—where both a well-defined black patch posterior to its throat and the black spots beneath its tail are narrowly ringed with red. Scutellation is the same as that of the rainbow snake: 19 midbody rows of smooth dorsal scales (except for very weak posterior carination on both the vertebral row and adjacent rows 6 through 9). The tail is tipped with a pointed terminal scute and the anal plate is divided.

Similar snakes   The **rainbow snake (93)** has less dark pigment on both its sides and its predominantly pinkish-red belly. The **eastern mud snake (91)** lacks dorsolateral stripes and has a black-checked reddish-pink venter.

Behavior   Everything about this animal is enigmatic, but its life history is probably similar to that of its northern subspecies, *F. e. erytrogramma.*

KIRTLAND'S SNAKE
Genus Clonophis

Kirtland's Snake, *Clonophis kirtlandii*

Part of the colubrine subfamily *Natricinae*, the genus *Clonophis*, which is closely related to the *Nerodia* water snakes, is made up of only the single species, *C. kirtlandii*. Named by Robert Kennicott in honor of Jared Potter Kirtland, founder of the Cleveland Museum of Natural History, this small serpent is sometimes found along the edges of streams and marshes, but it is not aquatic, and instead inhabits moist terrestrial habitats such as damp, low-lying meadows and prairies. Its scales are keeled, arranged in 19 midbody rows, and its anal plate is divided.

95 KIRTLAND'S SNAKE, *Clonophis kirtlandii*

Nonvenomous Kirtland's snake is non-venomous and harmless to humans.

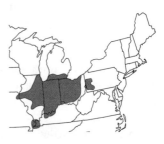

Abundance **Endangered in some areas; threatened and/or protected in others.** Although this is such a secretive animal that meaningful population assessments are difficult, Kirtland's snake seems to have formerly been far more common.

Because it is the only member of its genus, preservation of *Clonophis kirtlandii* is especially important, and it is now classified as **endangered** in its remaining Michigan and Pennsylvania range, **threatened** in Indiana and Illinois, and **protected** in Ohio. It is not specifically mentioned in regulations for Kentucky and Iowa (if indeed it continues to exist in the latter state). Nevertheless, small populations of Kirtland's snakes still turn up in urban and suburban areas, their widely separated locations contributing to the enigma of this snake's true status.

Size *Clonophis kirtlandii* is adult at only 16 to 18 inches in length; the record is 24½ in.

Habitat In urban and suburban settings Kirtland's snakes are often found beneath rocks, planks, and even discarded cardboard. In natural situations *C. kirtlandii* is equally secretive, utilizing flat stones, decomposing tree trunks, and the burrows of rodents and crayfish for shelter.

Prey Earthworms are this animal's primary prey, but slugs may also be taken.

Reproduction Live-bearing. Female Kirtland's snakes usually produce from 3 to 10 (rarely, up to 15), 5¾-inch-long young in late summer or early autumn.

Coloring/scale form Except for a single rarely seen variation, this beautiful little snake's ground color varies from olive tan to dark brown, with (often) a tan or brown vertebral stripe. A row of large, alternating dark spots occupies each side of the spine, while another row of dark spots runs along each side. In the less common dorsolateral variation the vertebral stripe is wider and better defined and the dark spots on either side of the spine are reduced.

PATCH-NOSED SNAKES

In both forms, the crown is blackish, the chin is white, brightening to pale orange beneath the neck and intensifying to a vivid reddish-orange on the remainder of the venter. A distinct black dot (by which this species may be definitely identified) is present on the distal margin of each ventral scute.

Similar snakes   Both the **northern red-bellied snake (15)** and the **copper-bellied water snake (67)** lack a well-defined black dot on the outer edge of each ventral scute.

Behavior   A startled Kirtland's snake may engage in any of several defensive ploys: it may writhe energetically in an attempt to escape, flatten its body and become rigid, or even strike and bite. Like many aquatic snakes, *Clonophis kirtlandii* will also smear musk, urates, and feces on its captor.

PATCH-NOSED SNAKES
Genus Salvadora

Mountain Patch-nosed Snake, *Salvadora grahamiae grahamiae*
Texas Patch-nosed Snake, *Salvadora grahamiae lineata*
Big Bend Patch-nosed Snake, *Salvadora deserticola*

The genus *Salvadora* is a part of the colubrine subfamily *Colubridae*. It contains two species of moderately sized, primarily terrestrial oviparous snakes characterized by an enlarged, free-edged, wrap-around rostral scale, 17 midbody rows of smooth scales (occasionally weakly keeled near the vent), and a divided anal plate. Both species are sandy brown to buff in dorsolateral ground color, with varying combinations of dark and light vertebral and lateral striping (the mid-dorsal area is the most richly hued, and is separated from the lighter sides by prominent dark stripes). The venter is whitish, but may be clouded with darker pigment.

Salvadora are swift-moving relatives of the racers (*Coluber constrictor*) which, like the racers, are active throughout the day even in the hottest weather, relying on their acute vision both for hunting and for quickly noting potential danger. Lizards (which patch-nosed snakes sometimes pursue up into shrubs) are these reptiles' primary prey, but amphibians, smaller snakes, and nestling rodents are also taken opportunistically.

Salvadora grahamiae grahamiae

Nonvenomous   The upper rear teeth of *Salvadora grahamiae* are slightly enlarged, a characteristic of many colubrids whose saliva is somewhat toxic to their small prey, but this beautiful little animal poses no danger to humans. In the field, when first handled mountain patch-nosed snakes may flail about, and even give a single panicky nip. If treated gently, however, these animals calm down quickly, and are unlikely to bite again.

Abundance   Common. Widely distributed throughout its Trans-Pecos range, in suitable habitat *S. g. grahamiae* occurs from low-lying desert floor to montane elevations over 7,000 feet.

Size   Slightly smaller than the closely related Texas patch-nose, adult *S. g. grahamiae* usually measure 18 to 30 inches in length. The record is 37½ in.

Habitat   Named for James Duncan Graham, astronomer and biological field collector on the 1852–53 Mexican Border Survey, *Salvadora grahamiae grahamiae* occupies a variety of stony and/or brushy northern Chihuahuan Desert habitats. In the stony desert west of the Devil's River, it is often found in the heart-root cavities under decaying agaves and sotol, or beneath yucca logs. Near the top of Mt. Locke and Guadalupe Peak, however, the author (Tennant) has also found it in alligator juniper/dwarf oak woodland.

Prey   This snake's primary prey is lizards, but smaller serpents, reptile eggs, and mice are also eaten; its lightly armored snout is presumably an aid to pressing into the subsurface nooks where these creatures sometimes shelter.

Reproduction   Egg-laying. See **Texas Patch-nosed Snake**.

Coloring scale form   The mountain patch-nosed snake's delicate form and subtle coloring make it one of the most attractive reptiles in North America, making it the author's favorite North American snake.

Its broad (usually 3 full scale rows in width), yellow to faintly peach-hued vertebral stripe is flanked by contrasting brownish-black stripes that set off its silvery-tan to pinkish-beige sides.

An enlarged rostral scale overlaps its adjacent nasal scales and folds back over the snout, giving the patch-nose its distinctive squared-off profile as well as its common name. There are usually

8 upper labial scales, and the posterior chin shields beneath its jaw either touch or are separated by a single small scale.

Similar snakes   The more easterly ranging subspecies **Texas patch-nosed snake (97)** has a narrower more richly hued vertebral line. This is bordered by a pair of wider, blackish-brown dorsolateral stripes. Its buff-colored sides are split by a thin dark seam along the third scale row above its belly. A separate species, the **Big Bend patch-nosed snake (98)** is distinguished by a line of dark hash marks along the fourth lateral scale row above its peach-colored venter, by its 9 upper labial scales, and by the 2 or 3 small scales that separate its posterior underchin shields.

Behavior   Quick and elusive in brush or near cover, the mountain patch-nose must still rely on ambush to obtain most of its even faster-moving prey. This may entail a deliberate process of advancing, in a series of short glides, each time its lizard quarry becomes preoccupied with its own foraging.

Once in striking range, the author has seen a medium-sized *S. g. grahamiae* seize a crevice spiny lizard larger than its own diameter, hanging on doggedly as its victim dragged it back and forth. After nearly half an hour, the patch-nose had worked its way along the tiring lacertillian's body to its snout. (The snake's saliva may or may not have exerted a partially paralytic effect.) Then, stretching its delicate head and jaws over the larger skull of the lizard, the patch-nose somehow squeezed its prey into its throat.

97   TEXAS PATCH-NOSED SNAKE
Salvadora grahamiae lineata

Nonvenomous   See **Mountain Patch-nosed Snake.**

Abundance   Common. The U.S. range of *S. g. lineata* is limited to central and southern Texas. Here, it can occur in almost every well-vegetated, rural terrestrial habitat, but it is probably most abundant in the interspersed open woods and farmland of the state's central crosstimbers.

Size   Almost all adults are between 20 and 34 inches long; the authors have seen many dozens of these animals, but never one approaching the record size of nearly 4 feet.

Habitat   The Texas patch-nosed snake's most likely microhabitat is probably the shelter it finds beneath flat rocks and fallen sheet metal/building materials in overgrown pastureland and along woodland/meadow boundaries. *Salvadora grahamiae lineata* occupies a similar habitat in the oak-juniper savannahs of Texas' Edwards Plateau, while it is present, but less abundant, in the thorn brush ecosystem of the Rio Grande valley.

Prey   As captives, most Texas patch-nosed snakes seem to prefer lizard prey. Yet, from the stomach contents of wild individuals mice, frogs, smaller snakes, and buried reptile eggs—the latter presumably rooted from their buried nest cavities with the aid of the enlarged rostral scale at the tip of the snout—are also reported.

Reproduction   Egg-laying. Reproduction was first recorded by Roger Conant in 1940: a Palo Pinto County female laid 10 adhesive-shelled, yellowish-white eggs 1⅛ inches in length and ⅜ inch in diameter on April 1—a time when many other serpents in central Texas have just begun courtship. Two other clutches of 5 and 7 eggs were deposited during the first week in May by a pair of Travis County females; these hatched 88 days later into young slightly paler than the adults, with whitish sides. The neonates were very active, vibrating their tails in excitement and striking about at random.

Coloring/scale form   As an adult, *S. g. lineata* has a blackish-brown back split by a prominent, golden-yellow stripe along the spine which occupies the vertebral scale row plus half of each adjacent row. The Texas patch-nosed snake's sides are buff to olive-brown, bordered below by a thin brown line: the *lineata* of its Latin name. On its foreparts, this line seams the third row of scales above its belly; on its posterior trunk, the line occupies the second lateral row of scales above the belly. An enlarged, slightly elevated rostral scale tips this animal's snout like a patch, and gives it its common name. (Its Latin species name, *grahamiae*, refers to James Duncan Graham, a naturalist member of the 1852–53 Mexican Border Survey that first systematically cataloged much of the southwest's herpetofauna.) There are 7 or, sometimes, 8 upper labial scales.

Similar snakes   In northeastern Terrell County the Texas patch-nose begins to intergrade with its western subspecies, the **mountain patch-nosed snake (96)**. This race has pastel gray to pinkish sides, a yellow to faintly peach-hued vertebral stripe 3 scale rows in width and, usually, 8 upper labial scales. **Garter (45, 51–53)** and **ribbon snakes (58–61)** have darker backs and sides, lack a large flat rostral snout, and have at least 19 midbody rows of keeled dorsal scales and an undivided anal plate.

Behavior   Despite its enlarged rostral *S. g. lineata* is not a fossorial animal: rather than diving into a hole when flushed from hiding beneath rocks, boards, or corrugated siding around old farms, like a racer this fast-moving serpent typically streaks away into tall grass. Partly because its diurnal orientation means it is abroad during the warmest part of the diel cycle, the Texas patch-nosed snake seems to be active in unusually cool weather: these animals forage in central Texas as late as mid-December and, after brief brumation, as early as mid-February.

98   BIG BEND PATCH-NOSED SNAKE
Salvadora deserticola

Nonvenomous   Slender, delicate *Salvadora deserticola* generally does not bite even when first handled in the field.

Abundance   This predominantly Mexican reptile is somewhat uncommon within its restricted U.S. range northeast of the Rio Grande from El Paso to Big Bend.

Size   A majority of adults are 20 to 45 inches in length.

Habitat   The Big Bend patch-nose inhabits low-lying shrub desert, tobosa/grama grassland, and catclaw/creosote/blackbrush flats, as well as a variety of broken upland terrain. One individual was found by the author in a cholla/sotol/alligator juniper savannah at over 5,000 ft. in the western Davis Mountains.

Prey   Lizards, snakes, reptile eggs, and small rodents are reported as the primary prey of *S. deserticola*—all but the latter thought to be often rooted from sand-filled depressions with the aid of the enlarged rostral scale.

Reproduction   Egg-laying. Little is known, but reproduction may be similar to that of the single *Salvadora* species, the mountain patch-nosed snake, which shares the Big Bend patch-nosed snake's range.

Coloring/scale form   This attractive serpent has yellowish-gray sides separated from its wide, peach-colored dorsal stripe by a flanking pair of dark-brown dorsolateral stripes. Its sandy-beige sides are marked with a line of dark-hued hash marks along the fourth scale row above its pinkish-orange venter. The Big Bend patch-nosed snake's enlarged rostral scale (which overlaps the adjacent nasal

Underchin: Texas and mountain
patch-nosed snakes

Underchin: Big Bend
patch-nosed snake

scales) covers the tip of the snout in a distinctive flat patch from which its common name is derived. Its lips and throat are unmarked white—there are 9 upper labial scales, and either 2 or 3 small scales separate its posterior underchin shields.

Similar snakes   The **mountain patch-nosed snake (96)** has 8 upper labial scales and posterior underchin shields that either touch or are separated by a single scale.

Behavior   Like many diurnal, desert-living serpents, the Big Bend patch-nose is inclined to midday basking in cool weather: Sherman Minton (1959) found it abroad as early as March 6 in Brewster County. In contrast, during the heat of July, August, and September, *S. deserticola* adopts a predominantly crepuscular activity pattern but (unlike many arid terrain snakes which retire into subsurface aestivation during summer) it remains abroad, although at this time it more often forages in the artificially moist environments of riparian canyons or even irrigated areas because diurnal hunters like patch-nosed snakes transpire more water than nocturnal/fossorial serpents.

Its daylight hunting also makes *S. deserticola* susceptible to avian predators. Minton found the remains of a Big Bend patch-nose in the nest of a red-tailed hawk, and a roadrunner has been photographed offering one of these slender colubrids to its fledglings.

GREEN SNAKES
Genus Liochlorophis* *and* Opheodrys

Smooth Green Snake, *Liochlorophis vernalis*
Rough Green Snake, *Opheodrys aestivus*

Both *Liochlorophis* ("smooth green snake" in Greek) and *opheodrys* (also Greek, for "forest-living snake") are members of the

*The smooth green snake has recently been placed by systematists in the genus *Liochlorophis*.

colubrine subfamily *Colubrinae*. While distantly related, the members of these two oviparous genera are rather different in morphology—the scales of the rough green snake are keeled and arranged in 17 midbody dorsolateral rows; those of the smooth green snake are smooth and set in 15 rows, though the anal plate of both is divided—as well as in both habitat and lifestyle.

Both *Liochlorophis* and *Opheodrys* share the acute vision of insect predators, similar slender bodies, and a unique bright green dorsolateral and whitish- or yellow-green ventral coloring, but the rough green snake is an agile arborealist that feeds on caterpillars, crickets, and spiders. (Most often an inhabitant of low trees, shrubs, and tall grasses, rough green snakes have also been found high in the canopy: Kevin Enge, of the Florida Game and Fresh Water Fish Commission, saw a swallow-tailed kite pluck one of these snakes from the topmost branches of a large live oak.)

In contrast, the smooth green snake can climb, but it ascends branches less readily than the rough green snake and is almost always found on the ground, where it hunts its prey of insects and spiders and hides beneath surface debris such as matted vegetation, flat rocks, newspapers, or boards.

99 SMOOTH GREEN SNAKE, *Liochlorophis vernalis*

Nonvenomous This small snake is harmless to humans.

Abundance Common in much of its range, yet **endangered** in some areas and **protected by the state of Texas**. In the Northeast, smooth green snake populations have deteriorated markedly during the last 50 years. While this little snake remains common in some places, in most parts of its range it has completely disappeared from

areas where it was formerly abundant. The reason is not known, but its abrupt decline may be partially due to the increased mechanized cultivation of crop fields. More likely, this little snake's dwindling numbers parallels the decline of many other insect-eating animals whose prey is now saturated with pesticides.

Largely because of this, like a drying puddle shrinking into disparate droplets, the smooth green snake's formerly broad range has fragmented into numerous small, disjunct pockets scattered across the Northeast and northern Great Plains (pockets typically too tiny and diverse to be accurately shown on a small map encompassing its entire range). The smooth green snake therefore now has the most complex distribution configuration of any snake in eastern and central North America.

An extremely isolated population may also occupy the coastal plain of Texas, where *L. vernalis* is known from fewer than 10 specimens, all collected in the coastal grassland of Austin, Chambers, Harris, and Matagorda counties. (Arnold Grobman of the Florida State Museum, an expert on this species, has suggested that rather than constituting a natural population these individuals may have been escaped captives, although that would seem to be less likely than their being a relictual group still living in a pocket of what was once a much broader range.

Size Most adults are 12 to 21 inches long; the record is 26 in.

Habitat In the northern and western portions of its territory *L. vernalis* is a resident of upland meadows—especially the periphery of grassy areas and open woodlands. It is also found in damp woodlands, shrubby clearings and overgrown orchards. (When preparing to shed, smooth green snakes are likely to hide beneath boards, newspapers, and other human-generated debris.) Although able to climb, this species is less likely to do so than the predominantly arboreal rough green snake.

Prey Almost exclusively sight-hunters, smooth green snakes are active only during daylight, foraging through dense grass and sometimes like the predominantly arboreal rough green snake, climbing into low bushes where John MacGregor has seen as many as 10 individuals basking in close proximity. Like the similarly sight-hunting rough green snake, the smooth green snake has a slightly concave channel lining each side of its snout just ahead of its eye. This enhances its forward vision and even gives each eye a small zone of overlapping vision with its opposite that presumably provides a narrow window of depth perception. As with other reptilian, avian, or mammalian sight-hunters, this three-dimensional focal zone helps *L. vernalis* more accurately gauge the distance to quick-moving insect prey. However, unlike the tree- and shrub-living rough green snake, the smooth green species typically forages deliberately along the ground, searching for grass-living insects such as crickets, grasshoppers, caterpillars and other larvae. See **Rough Green Snake**.

Reproduction Egg-laying. During the summer months up to 12 (usually 3 to 6) eggs are deposited in decaying wood or vegetation—in

Missouri, G. T. Hillie found 3 newly hatched young buried beneath a decomposed wooden fence post. There are reports from the northern part of the smooth green snake's range of communal nesting, as well as of an exceptionally short incubation period of as little as 4 days. (If accurate, this abbreviated period of external incubation is probably due only to a particular female retaining her eggs for most of their gestation.) Many of the 5- to 6-inch-long hatchlings have an olive- to light-brown dorsal hue.

Coloring/scale form *Liochlorophis vernalis* is the new scientific name of the smooth green snake which, until recently, was known as *Opheodrys vernalis*. Both green snakes formerly shared the genus *Opheodrys*, but the smooth green snake's smooth scalation, along with its distinct body configuration and different ventral scale count, has prompted Hobart M. Smith and the late Jonathan C. Oldham, to offer a new genus designation for this animal.

Smooth green snakes are bright green above with lighter hues, typically yellow or white, ventrally. The lips and chin are also whitish. Texas specimens and several upper midwest populations retain their gray to olive-brown juvenile coloration into adulthood. (Dead specimens lose their bright green dorsolateral color and turn blue shortly after death.) This snake's smooth dorsolateral scales are arranged in 15 midbody rows, its nostril lies across the juncture of adjacent nasal scales, and its ventral scales range widely in number, varying between 116 and 154.

Similar snakes The smooth green snake is the only uniformly leaf-green (rarely, olive) colored serpent living in the northeastern and north-central United States. The **rough green snake (100)** is slimmer and more wiry, has 17 rows of keeled dorsal scales, and 144 to 171 ventral scales. The **eastern yellow-bellied racer (115)** is a much larger, gray-green serpent that at the length of the adult smooth green snake still exhibits a contrasting, dorsally brown-blotched juvenile pattern. Each of the racer's nostrils is centered in a single nasal plate.

Behavior This unobtrusive little serpent relies on camouflage rather than flight to avoid detection. If startled, it most often ceases all movement, but at times may gape when threatened, displaying the dark interior of its mouth.

Large aggregations of smooth green snakes sometimes assemble for winter brumation (in Michigan, 148 individuals were found hibernating together), but during warm weather, like other snakes these animals are solitary.

Nonvenomous The rough green snake (which is also known in the South as "vine snake"—a tropical family to which it is not related) is unlikely to bite humans.

Abundance Abundant. With the exception of the higher elevations of the Appalachians, *Opheodrys aestivus* is widespread through-

out the southeastern ⅔ of the United States, where it is common in a variety of moist woodland habitats.

Size Adults average 22 to 32 inches; the record is 45⅝ in.

Habitat Thickly foliaged trees and shrubs are the preferred environment because their closely spaced stems allow *O. aestivus* to move about easily, well off the ground. This microhabitat is most prevalent along the sunlit edges of woods bordering ponds, meadows, and dirt roads, and this small reptile's abundance here makes it so easy to capture that until recently thousands were taken every year for the pet trade.

Prey Plucked from leaves and stems, most of the rough green snake's prey are insects. In one Arkansas study, 85% of its diet consisted of caterpillars, spiders, grasshoppers, crickets and odonates. Of these insects, caterpillars are the preferred food, and are positively selected for since they constituted more than twice as large a percentage of the total as their prevalence in the sample area would suggest. See **Smooth Green Snake**.

Reproduction Egg-laying. Spring and summer rainfall influences reproduction among rough green snakes because the more abundant insect prey available in wet years increases females' body fat, and thus their egg-laying capacity. One clutch of 15 *O. aestivus* eggs taken from a central Texas stone wall was incubated by Tim Cole; on July 2 these eggs hatched into 8-inch-long young, all of which immediately began feeding on small crickets.

Rainfall enhances the survival of such clutches—most of which are laid in plant litter between April and July—since the small size of the eggs makes them susceptible to dessication. The slender, gray-green hatchlings (like most temperate-zone snakes) can reach adult size in a year but do not breed until their second spring.

Coloring/scale form   Often called "grass snake," emerald-bodied *O. aestivus* is color-adapted, instead, to the verdant hue of tree leaves. (After death, these little snakes soon turn a dull blue.) The lips, chin, and belly are yellow, and the nostril lies across the juncture of adjacent nasal scales. The keeled dorsal scales are arranged in 17 rows at midbody.

Similar snakes   The **smooth green snake (99)** shares only a small amount of territory with the more southerly ranging rough green; it has 15 rows of smooth dorsal scales. The **eastern yellow-bellied racer (115)** is a much more robust, gray-green serpent with smooth scales; each of its nostrils is centered in a single nasal plate.

Behavior   For protection, slow-moving, unwary *O. aestivus* depends almost entirely on camouflage: when approached it may freeze, swaying with the wind to match the movement of surrounding foliage. Occasionally, a rough green snake may also indulge in a brief, mouth-gaping defensive display, but these little animals are very reluctant to bite.

During warm weather this diurnal forager sleeps at night in a loop draped along a branch, its head resting either on the branch or on a body coil. Here, its luminous venter reflects the beam of a flashlight so clearly that in places where rough green snakes are numerous they are easily found by scanning vegetation along forest roads. Despite the Latin name *aestivus*, or "summer," rough green snakes are abroad well into autumn, often in very cool weather, as long as foliage remains on the trees. Later in the year, *O. aestivus* spends the leafless months below ground where, in hardened clay several inches beneath the surface, Robert Webb reported finding one brumating Oklahoma individual.

WHIPSNAKES
Genus Masticophis

Eastern Coachwhip, *Masticophis flagellum flagellum*
Western Coachwhip, *Masticophis flagellum testaceus*
Desert Striped Whipsnake, *Masticophis taeniatus taeniatus*
Central Texas Whipsnake, *Masticophis taeniatus girardi*
Schott's Whipsnake, *Masticophis schotti*
Ruthven's Whipsnake, *Masticophis ruthveni*

Masticophis is part of the colubrine subfamily *Colubrinae*, where it is genetically allied to the racers, genus *Coluber* (only whipsnakes and racers, for example, lay eggs with both granular shells and a star-shaped indentation on one end). Like wiry-bodied—*mastix* is Greek for "whip"—big eyed, diurnal snakes the world over, coachwhips actively pursue lizards. The narrow, yet blunt-snouted head is distinctly set off from the slim neck; there are 15 to 17 (the number can be important in identification) midbody rows of smooth dorsolateral scales, and a divided anal plate.

Whipsnakes are alert serpents that sometimes hunt by periscoping their heads above tall grass and ground plants to make use of their acute vision—upon which *Masticophis* seem to rely almost as much they do on the chemical cues most snakes use when seeking prey. Watching their surroundings so closely also lets whipsnakes keep track of avian activity: this helps them avoid hawks, one of their major predators, and may enable them to spot arboreal bird nests beyond the scent-locating range of terrestrial snakes. Other prey includes lizards and smaller snakes, including their own kind, as well as mammals—all of which are seized and immobilized by the strong jaws but not constricted.

101 EASTERN COACHWHIP
Masticophis flagellum flagellum

Nonvenomous If cornered, this long, wiry serpent vibrates its tail and doesn't hesitate to strike and bite—often 2 or 3 times in succession. Instead of hanging on to an aggressor, however, *M. flagellum* typically pulls away quickly, its sharp teeth leaving shallow scratches.

Abundance Common. The eastern coachwhip is one of the most numerous large terrestrial serpents in its broad range. This territory encompasses the Southeast as far north as Virginia and Tennessee west to the Mississippi valley—which is not occupied—then north to Missouri and west to eastern Kansas, Oklahoma, and Texas. (One theory holds that the geologically recent submersion of the Mississippi River corridor in a saltwater embayment has not allowed time for snake species such as the eastern coachwhip, eastern coral snake and corn snake to re-colonize the area. Given the rapidity with which ophidian species typically move into suitable nearby habitat, however, this notion seems doubtful.

Size   The record eastern coachwhip measured 102 inches in length, but an individual this size would be very unusual: the majority of adult *M. f. flagellum* are between 50 and 72 in.

Habitat   Coachwhips occur in virtually every rural environment: forest, marsh, pastureland, borders of cultivated fields, the banks of both inland and estuarine watercourses, and sandy coastal strands. Probably because of the abundant rodent, lizard, and smaller snake prey usually to be found there, eastern coachwhips seem to be particularly abundant around abandoned farms.

Prey   The eastern coachwhip's prey can include almost any smaller vertebrate. Spiny and tree lizards probably comprise much of its diet, but the droppings of wild individuals have contained the remains of other snakes, mammals, birds, frogs, and even small turtles. Insects are probably the primary prey of juveniles. Serpentine greyhounds adapted for sight-hunting, coachwhips have evolved their specialized bodies only after giving up other adaptations. J. A. Ruben's research suggests that *M. flagellum*, like other whipsnakes, has gained speed and agility but lost some constrictive ability by evolutionarily lengthening the segment spacing of its three major epaxial muscle groups. (Whipsnakes are able to employ what is perhaps an evelutionary precursor of constriction, pressing a prey animal against the ground with a body coil rather than suffocating it in muscular loop like a true constrictor.)

Yet, despite these adaptations for sight-hunting and speed, the coachwhip's final feeding response is determined by vomerolfaction: only if a prey animal smells right do coachwhips bite down. For example, hatchlings with no prior exposure to their natural prey react instinctively to the scents of potential food species, snapping vigorously at cotton swabs rolled over the skin of lizard and snake species abundant within their range.

Reproduction   Egg-laying. Little is known about courtship and nesting among free-ranging *M. f. flagellum*. The 10- to 15-inch-long hatchlings, which emerge in July and August, have dimly defined brown anterior dorsal crossbars on their tan backs, and whitish, anteriorly spotted venters. This patterning is so different from the adults that in spite of their large yellowish eyes, pronounced supraocular scales, and cross-hatched tails (all of which they share with their parents), young coachwhips are frequently assumed to belong to another species.

Coloring/scale form   Adult *M. f. flagellum* exhibit unique two-toned coloring: the unmarked dark forebody gradually fades to progressively lighter shades of brown and tan on the posterior ⅔ of the trunk, and even the occasional entirely black individual usually has a russet-tinted tail.

Some local populations, such as the eastern coachwhips living east of Gainesville, Florida, harbor occasional uniformly light-colored individuals, however, while others display narrow brownish crossbands. A few miles east, on the Atlantic coastal ridge (home to other members of an ancient, xeric-adapted ophidian fauna that once occupied a dry corridor joining the desert southwest to the Florida peninsula), some eastern coachwhips exhibit the reddish-brown dorsolateral hues of *Masticophis* from the western United States.

The eastern coachwhip's ventral color matches that of its dorsum, while the dark bordered scales of its tail create a cross-hatched, braided whip-like pattern from which its common name is derived. See **Western Coachwhip**.

Coachwhips' heads are also distinctive: elongate yet wider than the wiry neck, with big eyes (shielded above by projecting parietal scale plates) bordered along their forward edges by a pair of small preocular scales. The dorsal scales are arranged in 17 rows at midbody, in 13 rows just ahead of the vent.

Similar snakes   Where the ranges of the eastern and **western coachwhips (102)** overlap, intergrades are common. To the west of this zone, the western race is distinguished by its lighter-hued, beige to brownish dorsolateral color, often barred with wide light and dark crossbands. Its venter resembles that of the juvenile eastern coachwhip: creamy, with a double row of dark dots beneath the neck. Adult **southern black, Everglades, and brown-chinned racers (108, 110, 111)** lack the eastern coachwhip's dark-anterior, lighter-posterior color demarcation, as well as its cross-hatched tail; racers also have 15 rows of dorsal scales just ahead of the vent.

Behavior   Like other whipsnakes, *M. f. flagellum* is exceptionally alert, perhaps even curious. To get a better look at an intruder, an adult surprised in the field may, like a slim-necked cobra, raise its head and forebody well off the ground; the author has noticed himself being observed in this way by coachwhips which had fled a short way, then paused to look back over tall grass—their direct gaze a startling contrast to the absence of long-distance vision in most snakes.

Because *M. flagellum* can traverse open ground more swiftly than any other North American serpent—and, when pursued, streak up into low trees—coachwhips are able to evade predators well enough to forage in comparatively unsheltered environments. Nevertheless, this diurnal movement across open terrain leaves *M. flagellum* vulnerable to predation by raptors, and both red-tailed and red-shouldered hawks are commonly seen in flight with a still-writhing coachwhip in their talons.

The nervous energy that fuels this vigorous, dangerous, open-terrain-searching lifestyle generates in coachwhips a constant need to move about, however, and as a result they tend to be frustrated cage-pacers in confinement—though they are such tough, resilient captives that individuals have lived for nearly 17 years in confinement.

102   WESTERN COACHWHIP

Masticophis flagellum testaceus

Nonvenomous   Western coachwhips are agile biters: cornered by a human being, a large individual may strike past its assailant's hands at his face or body. See **Eastern Coachwhip**.

Abundance   Among the most common large non-venomous serpents in terrestrial rural environments throughout the western ¾ of Texas, western Okla-homa, and southwestern Kansas, *M. f. testaceus* is particularly abundant in late summer/early autumn, when its dimly brown-banded, big-orange-eyed hatchlings seem to appear on every dirt road.

Size   Most adults are between 4 and 5½ feet in length, although the record is 6 feet 8 in. The young are 12 to 14 inches long at hatching.

Habitat   *Masticophis flagellum testaceus* occupies almost every ter-restrial, non-urban habitat within its range.

Prey   See **Eastern Coachwhip**.

Reproduction   Egg-laying. The 10- to 15-inch-long hatchlings, which emerge in July and August, are slender, pale-earth-colored lit-tle snakes notable for their speed, their proportionately large, orange-irised eyes, pronounced supraocular scales, and the cross-hatch-patterned tails they share with their parents. See **Eastern Coachwhip**.

Coloring/scale form   Although its head and neck are often slightly darker than its trunk, this animal's coloring to some extent follows the prevailing ground color of the terrain that various populations inhabit, and within its range individual *M. f. testaceus* are paler-hued as one moves westward (in all areas the young are tan, with thin, dim brown vertebral bars).

Many individuals living in the east/central part of the Texas range have broad light and dark gray-brown dorsolateral crossbands, while on the limestone of the Edwards Plateau unmarked silvery-tan coach-whips predominate. West of the Pecos River, brick red (the Latin

Brahminy Blind Snake,
Ramphotyphlops braminus

2   **Plains Blind Snake,**
Leptotyphlops dulcis dulcis

New Mexico Blind Snake,
Leptotyphlops dulcis dissectus

4   **Trans-Pecos Blind Snake,**
Leptotyphlops humilis segregus

5   **Southeastern Crowned Snake,**
Tantilla coronata

6   **Peninsula Crowned Snake,**
Tantilla relicta relicta

Central Florida Crowned Snake,
Tantilla relicta neilli

8 **Coastal Dunes Crowned Snake,**
Tantilla relicta pamlica

Rim Rock Crowned Snake,
Tantilla oolitica

10a **Flat-headed Snake,**
Tantilla gracilis

10b **Flat-headed Snake,**
Tantilla gracilis

11 **Plains Black-headed Snake,**
Tantilla nigriceps

M. J. Bowerman

12   Southwestern Black-headed Snake,
Tantilla hobartsmithi

K. Świak

13   Mexican Black-headed Snake,
Tantilla atriceps

T. L. Brown

14a   Black-hooded Snake,
Tantilla rubra cucullata

14b   Black-hooded Snake,
Tantilla rubra cucullata

15a   Northern Red-bellied Snake,
Storeria occipitomaculata occipitomaculata

5b Northern Red-bellied Snake,
Storeria occipitomaculata occipitomaculata

16a Florida Red-bellied Snake,
Storeria occipitomaculata obscura

16b Florida Red-bellied Snake,
Storeria occipitomaculata obscura

R. W. VanDevender

17 Black Hills Red-bellied Snake,
Storeria occipitomaculata pahasapae

18 Northern Brown Snake,
Storeria dekayi dekayi

9 Florida Brown Snake,
Storeria dekayi victa

20a Midland Brown Snake,
Storeria dekayi wrightorum

20b Midland Brown Snake,
Storeria dekayi wrightorum

211

M. J. Bowerman

21   Texas Brown Snake,
Storeria dekayi texana

John MacGregor

22   Marsh Brown Snake,
Storeria dekayi limnetes

23   Eastern Earth Snake,
Virginia valeriae valeriae

John MacGregor

24 Mountain Earth Snake,
Virginia valeriae pulchra

R. W. VanDevender

25 Western Earth Snake,
Virginia valeriae elegans

M. J. Bowerman

26 Rough Earth Snake,
Virginia striatula

27   Southern Ring-necked Snake,
Diadophis punctatus punctatus

R. D. Bartlett

28   Northern Ring-necked Snake,
Diadophis punctatus edwardsii

29   Key Ring-necked Snake,
Diadophis punctatus acricus

0   Mississippi Ring-necked Snake,
Diadophis punctatus stictogenys

31a   Prairie Ring-necked Snake,
Diadophis punctatus arnyi

31b   Prairie Ring-necked Snake,
Diadophis punctatus arnyi

M.J. Bowerman

32a **Regal Ring-necked Snake,**
Diadophis punctatus regalis

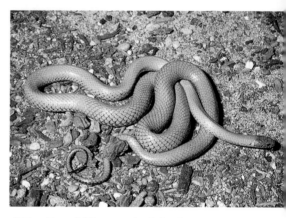

D. C. McIntyre

32b **Regal Ring-necked Snake,**
Diadophis punctatus regalis

33a **Ground Snake,**
Sonora semiannulata

3b   Ground Snake,
Sonora semiannulata

3c   Ground Snake,
Sonora semiannulata

34a   Eastern Worm Snake,
Carphophis amoenus amoenus

34b   Eastern Worm Snake,
Carphophis amoenus amoenus

35a   Midwestern Worm Snake,
Carphophis amoenus helenae

35b   Midwestern Worm Snake,
Carphophis amoenus helenae

36   Western Worm Snake,
Carphophis amoenus vermis

37   Pine Woods Snake,
Rhadinaea flavilata

38a   Short-tailed Snake,
Stilosoma extenuatum

38b   Short-tailed Snake,
Stilosoma extenuatum

39   Lined Snake,
Tropidoclonion lineatum

40 Eastern Garter Snake,
Thamnophis sirtalis sirtalis

41a Maritime Garter Snake,
Thamnophis sirtalis pallidulus

41b Maritime Garter Snake,
Thamnophis sirtalis pallidulus (albino)

42 Blue-striped Garter Snake,
Thamnophis sirtalis similis

43 Chicago Garter Snake,
Thamnophis sirtalis semifasciatus

14   Red-sided Garter Snake,
Thamnophis sirtalis parietalis

45   Texas Garter Snake,
Thamnophis sirtalis annectens

46a   Short-headed Garter Snake,
Thamnophis brachystoma

46b **Short-headed Garter Snake,**
Thamnophis brachystoma

47 **Butler's Garter Snake,**
Thamnophis butleri

48 **Wandering Garter Snake,**
Thamnophis elegans vagrans

49   Eastern Plains Garter Snake,
Thamnophis radix radix

50   Western Plains Garter Snake,
Thamnophis radix haydenii

51   Checkered Garter Snake,
Thamnophis marcianus marcianus

52a Western Black-necked Garter Snake,
Thamnophis cyrtopsis cyrtopsis

52b Western Black-necked Garter Snake,
Thamnophis cyrtopsis cyrtopsis

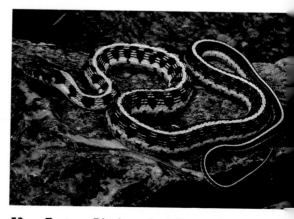

53a Eastern Black-necked Garter Snake,
Thamnophis cyrtopsis ocellatus

3b **Eastern Black-necked Garter Snake,**
Thamnophis cyrtopsis ocellatus (sub-adult)

54 **Eastern Ribbon Snake,**
Thamnophis sauritus sauritus

5 **Northern Ribbon Snake,**
Thamnophis sauritus septentrionalis

56   Peninsula Ribbon Snake,
Thamnophis sauritus sackenii

57   Blue-striped Ribbon Snake,
Thamnophis sauritus nitae

58   Western Ribbon Snake,
Thamnophis proximus proximus

59   Red-striped Ribbon Snake,
Thamnophis proximus rubrilineatus

Gulf Coast Ribbon Snake,
Thamnophis proximus orarius

61   Arid Land Ribbon Snake,
Thamnophis proximus diabolicus

62   Northern Water Snake,
Nerodia sipedon sipedon

63a   Lake Erie Water Snake,
Nerodia sipedon insularum

3b   Lake Erie Water Snake,
Nerodia sipedon insularum

64   Midland Water Snake,
Nerodia sipedon pleuralis

65   Carolina Water Snake,
Nerodia sipedon williamengelsi

66a   Red-bellied Water Snake,
Nerodia erythrogaster erythrogaster

B. Mansell

66b   Red-bellied Water Snake,
Nerodia erythrogaster erythrogaster (juvenile)

67a   Copper-bellied Water Snake,
Nerodia erythrogaster neglecta

R.W.VanDevender

7b Copper-bellied Water Snake,
Nerodia erythrogaster neglecta

M.J. Bowerman

68a Yellow-bellied Water Snake,
Nerodia erythrogaster flavigaster

R. D. Bartlett

8b Yellow-bellied Water Snake,
Nerodia erythrogaster flavigaster

M.J. Bowerman

69a Blotched Water Snake,
Nerodia erythrogaster transversa

69b Blotched Water Snake,
Nerodia erythrogaster transversa

M.J. Bowerman

69c Blotched Water Snake,
Nerodia erythrogaster transversa (juvenile)

234

R. D. Bartlett

70a   Banded Water Snake,
Nerodia fasciata fasciata

R. D. Bartlett

'0b   Banded Water Snake,
Nerodia fasciata fasciata (juvenile)

M. J. Bowerman

71   Broad-banded Water Snake,
Nerodia fasciata confluens

72a **Florida Water Snake,**
Nerodia fasciata pictiventris

72b **Florida Water Snake,**
Nerodia fasciata pictiventris

73 **Gulf Salt Marsh Snake,**
Nerodia clarkii clarkii

B. Mansell

74   Atlantic Salt Marsh Snake,
Nerodia clarkii taeniata

R. D. Bartlett

75a   Mangrove Salt Marsh Snake,
Nerodia clarkii compressicauda (red color phase)

W. B. Love

75b   Mangrove Salt Marsh Snake,
Nerodia clarkii compressicauda
(black color phase)

75c Mangrove Salt Marsh Snake,
Nerodia clarkii compressicauda (juvenile)

R. D. Bartlett

76a Florida Green Water Snake,
Nerodia floridana

76b Florida Green Water Snake,
Nerodia floridana

M.J. Bowerman

7   Mississippi Green Water Snake,
Nerodia cyclopion

W.B. Love

78   Brown Water Snake,
Nerodia taxispilota

M.J. Bowerman

79a   Diamond-backed Water Snake,
Nerodia rhombifer rhombifer

D. C. McIntyre

79b **Diamond-backed Water Snake,**
Nerodia rhombifer rhombifer (juvenile)

80 **Brazos Water Snake,**
Nerodia harteri harteri

M. J. Bowerman

81 **Concho Water Snake,**
Nerodia harteri paucimaculata

82   North Florida Swamp Snake,
Seminatrix pygaea pygaea

83a   South Florida Swamp Snake,
Seminatrix pygaea cyclas

83b   South Florida Swamp Snake,
Seminatrix pygaea cyclas

84 **Carolina Swamp Snake,**
Seminatrix pygaea paludis

85 **Striped Crayfish Snake,**
Regina alleni

86 **Glossy Crayfish Snake,**
Regina rigida rigida (gravid female)

87a **Delta Crayfish Snake,**
Regina rigida deltae

87b   Delta Crayfish Snake,
Regina rigida deltae (juvenile)

M. J. Bowerman

88   Gulf Crayfish Snake,
Regina rigida sinicola

89a   Queen Snake,
Regina septemvittata

R. D. Bartlett

89b **Queen Snake,**
Regina septemvittata

M. J. Bowerman

90 **Graham's Crayfish Snake,**
Regina grahamii

R. D. Bartlett

91a **Eastern Mud Snake,**
Farancia abacura abacura

R. D. Bartlett

91b **Eastern Mud Snake,**
Farancia abacura abacura

M. J. Bowerman

91c **Eastern Mud Snake,**
Farancia abacura abacura (anerythristic color phase)

92a **Western Mud Snake,**
Farancia abacura reinwardtii

92b   Western Mud Snake,
Farancia abacura reinwardtii

93a   Rainbow Snake,
Farancia erytrogramma erytrogramma

93b   Rainbow Snake,
Farancia erytrogramma erytrogramma
(hatchling)

94 South Florida Rainbow Snake,
Farancia erytrogramma seminola

R.W.VanDevender

95a Kirtland's Snake,
Clonophis kirtlandii

95b Kirtland's Snake,
Clonophis kirtlandii

M.J. Bowerman

96   Mountain Patch-nosed Snake,
Salvadora grahamiae grahamiae

R.D Bartlett

97a   Texas Patch-nosed Snake,
Salvadora grahamiae lineata

M.J. Bowerman

97b   Texas Patch-nosed Snake,
Salvadora grahamiae lineata

98a **Big Bend Patch-nosed Snake,**
Salvadora deserticola

98b **Big Bend Patch-nosed Snake,**
Salvadora deserticola

99 **Smooth Green Snake,**
Liochlorophis vernalis

M. J. Bowerman

100 Rough Green Snake,
Opheodrys aestivus

M. J. Bowerman

101a Eastern Coachwhip,
Masticophis flagellum flagellum

D. C. McIntyre

101b Eastern Coachwhip,
Masticophis flagellum flagellum
(juvenile)

102a Western Coachwhip,
Masticophis flagellum testaceus

M.J. Bowerman

102b Western Coachwhip,
Masticophis flagellum testaceus (juvenile)

102c Western Coachwhip,
Masticophis flagellum testaceus
(red color phase found in
West Texas' Trans-Pecos)

M.J. Bowerman

103   Desert Striped Whipsnake,
Masticophis taeniatus taeniatus

M.J. Bowerman

104   Central Texas Whipsnake,
Masticophis taeniatus girardi

M.J. Bowerman

105a   Schott's Whipsnake,
Masticophis schotti

105b Schott's Whipsnake,
Masticophis schotti (hatchling)

106   Ruthven's Whipsnake,
Masticophis ruthveni

107a Northern Black Racer,
Coluber constrictor constrictor

107b **Northern Black Racer,**
Coluber constrictor constrictor (juvenile)

08a **Southern Black Racer,**
Coluber constrictor priapus

108b **Southern Black Racer,**
Coluber constrictor priapus (juvenile)

109a Blue Racer,
Coluber constrictor foxii

109b Blue Racer,
Coluber constrictor foxii

109c Blue Racer,
Coluber constrictor foxii (juvenile)

110 Everglades Racer,
Coluber constrictor paludicola

R. D. Bartlett

111   Brown-chinned Racer,
Coluber constrictor helvigularis

112   Black-masked Racer,
Coluber constrictor latrunculus

M. J. Bowerman

113   Buttermilk Racer,
Coluber constrictor anthicus

114 Tan Racer,
Coluber constrictor etheridgei

15 Eastern Yellow-bellied Racer,
Coluber constrictor flaviventris

116a Mexican Racer,
Coluber constrictor oaxaca

116b Mexican Racer,
Coluber constrictor oaxaca

M. J. Bowerman

116c Mexican Racer,
Coluber constrictor oaxaca (hatchling)

117a Eastern Indigo Snake,
Drymarchon corais couperi

17b Eastern Indigo Snake,
Drymarchon corais couperi

117c Eastern Indigo Snake,
Drymarchon corais couperi (hatchling)

18a Texas Indigo Snake,
Drymarchon corais erebennus

261

118b Texas Indigo Snake,
Drymarchon corais erebennus (juvenile)

119   Central American Speckled Racer,
Drymobius margaritiferus margaritiferus

120a Eastern Hog-nosed Snake,
Heterodon platirhinos

120b Eastern Hog-nosed Snake,
Heterodon platirhinos (defensive tail-coiling and
neck-spreading)

20c Eastern Hog-nosed Snake,
Heterodon platirhinos (black color phase)

120d Eastern Hog-nosed Snake,
Heterodon platirhinos (defensive head/
neck-spreading)

121   Southern Hog-nosed Snake,
Heterodon simus

122   Plains Hog-nosed Snake,
Heterodon nasicus nasicus

123a   Dusty Hog-nosed Snake,
Heterodon nasicus gloydi

23b **Dusty Hog-nosed Snake,**
Heterodon nasicus gloydi (hatchling)

124 **Mexican Hog-nosed Snake,**
Heterodon nasicus kennerlyi

25a **Northern Pine Snake,**
Pituophis melanoleucus melanoleucus

125b Northern Pine Snake,
Pituophis melanoleucus melanoleucus (juvenile)

126a Florida Pine Snake,
Pituophis melanoleucus mugitus

126b Florida Pine Snake,
Pituophis melanoleucus mugitus

127a   Black Pine Snake,
Pituophis melanoleucus lodingi

27b   Black Pine Snake,
Pituophis melanoleucus lodingi (intergrade with
Florida pine snake [126])

128a   Louisiana Pine Snake,
Pituophis ruthveni

128b Louisiana Pine Snake,
Pituophis ruthveni (juvenile)

L.Jarrell

129a Bullsnake,
Pituophis catenifer sayi (pale, Southwestern
Plains form)

129b Bullsnake,
Pituophis catenifer sayi (russet, Central
Plains form)

J. H. Evans

29c Bullsnake,
Pituophis catenifer sayi (dark, Northern Plains
form)

M. J. Bowerman

130a Sonoran Gopher Snake,
Pituophis catenifer affinis

J. V. Maldonado

30b Sonoran Gopher Snake,
Pituophis catenifer affinis (intergrade with
bullsnake [129])

131 Kansas Glossy Snake,
Arizona elegans elegans

132 Texas Glossy Snake,
Arizona elegans arenicola

133 Painted Desert Glossy Snake,
Arizona elegans philipi

34a   Black Rat Snake,
Elaphe obsoleta obsoleta (dark-hued)

134b   Black Rat Snake,
Elaphe obsoleta obsoleta (pale-hued)

34c   Black Rat Snake,
Elaphe obsoleta obsoleta (intergrade with yellow
rat snake [135])

D. C. McIntyre

135a Yellow Rat Snake,
Elaphe obsoleta quadrivittata

135b Yellow Rat Snake,
Elaphe obsoleta quadrivittata (Gulf hammock variant)

R. D. Bartlett

135c Yellow Rat Snake,
Elaphe obsoleta quadrivittata

135d Yellow Rat Snake,
Elaphe obsoleta quadrivittata (upper Florida Keys variant)

136a Everglades Rat Snake,
Elaphe obsoleta rossalleni

136b Everglades Rat Snake,
Elaphe obsoleta rossalleni

137a **Gray Rat Snake,**
Elaphe obsoleta spiloides

137b **Gray Rat Snake,**
Elaphe obsoleta spiloides ("white oak"
color phase)

138a **Texas Rat Snake,**
Elaphe obsoleta lindheimerii

138b Texas Rat Snake,
Elaphe obsoleta lindheimerii (juvenile)

39a Baird's Rat Snake,
Elaphe bairdi

139b Baird's Rat Snake,
Elaphe bairdi (juvenile)

140a Corn Snake,
Elaphe guttata guttata (typical color phase)

140b Corn Snake,
Elaphe guttata guttata (northeastern Florida
dark red phase)

140c Corn Snake,
Elaphe guttata guttata ("Miami" color phase)

40d Corn Snake,
Elaphe guttata guttata (southern Florida olive color phase)

40e Corn Snake,
Elaphe guttata guttata (Florida Keys rosy color phase)

140f Corn Snake,
Elaphe guttata guttata (anerythristic color phase)

140g Corn Snake,
Elaphe guttata guttata (amelanistic color phase)

41a Great Plains Rat Snake,
Elaphe guttata emoryi (East and North Texas
dark phase, large-blotched form)

141b Great Plains Rat Snake,
Elaphe guttata emoryi (South and West Texas
paler, smaller-blotched form)

42a Eastern Fox Snake,
Elaphe gloydi

279

142b Eastern Fox Snake,
Elaphe gloydi

J. H. Harding

143   Western Fox Snake,
Elaphe vulpina

144a Trans-Pecos Rat Snake,
Bogertophis subocularis

44b Trans-Pecos Rat Snake,
Bogertophis subocularis (pale or "blonde" color phase)

144c Trans-Pecos Rat Snake,
Bogertophis subocularis (hatchling)

44d Trans-Pecos Rat Snake,
Bogertophis subocularis

144e Trans-Pecos Rat Snake,
Bogertophis subocularis

M. J. Bowerman

145 Mexican Hook-nosed Snake,
Ficimia streckeri

146a Western Hook-nosed Snake,
Gyalopion canum

146b Western Hook-nosed Snake,
Gyalopion canum

147 Prairie Kingsnake,
Lampropeltis calligaster calligaster

148a Mole Kingsnake,
Lampropeltis calligaster rhombomaculata

W. B. Love

148b **Mole Kingsnake,**
Lampropeltis calligaster rhombomaculata (juvenile)

149a **South Florida Mole Kingsnake,**
Lampropeltis calligaster occipitolineata

R. D. Bartlett

149b **South Florida Mole Kingsnake,**
Lampropeltis calligaster occipitolineata (juvenile)

A. Tennant

150a Eastern Kingsnake,
Lampropeltis getula getula

A. Tennant

150b Eastern Kingsnake,
Lampropeltis getula getula (Apalachicola,
Florida, lowland variant)

R. D. Bartlett

150c Eastern Kingsnake,
Lampropeltis getula getula (Apalachicola,
Florida lowland variant)

151a Florida Kingsnake,
Lampropeltis getula floridana

151b Florida Kingsnake,
Lampropeltis getula floridana

151c Florida Kingsnake,
Lampropeltis getula floridana (juveniles)

R. D Bartlett

152a   Black Kingsnake,
Lampropeltis getula nigra

R. D Bartlett

152b   Black Kingsnake,
Lampropeltis getula nigra (hatchling)

M. J. Bowerman

153   Speckled Kingsnake,
Lampropeltis getula holbrooki

154a Desert Kingsnake,
Lampropeltis getula splendida

154b Desert Kingsnake,
Lampropeltis getula splendida (juvenile)

155a Eastern Milk Snake,
Lampropeltis triangulum triangulum

◀ **55b Eastern Milk Snake,**
Lampropeltis triangulum triangulum

155c Eastern Milk Snake,
Lampropeltis triangulum triangulum

155d Eastern Milk Snake,
Lampropeltis triangulum triangulum (Coastal Plains form)

156a Scarlet Kingsnake,
Lampropeltis triangulum elapsoides

56b Scarlet Kingsnake,
Lampropeltis triangulum elapsoides (hatchling)

156c Scarlet Kingsnake,
Lampropeltis triangulum elapsoides
(two color phases)

57 Red Milk Snake,
Lampropeltis triangulum syspila

M. J. Bowerman

158 Louisiana Milk Snake,
Lampropeltis triangulum amaura

159 Mexican Milk Snake,
Lampropeltis triangulum annulata

M. J. Allender

160a New Mexico Milk Snake,
Lampropeltis triangulum celaenops

160b New Mexico Milk Snake,
Lampropeltis triangulum celaenops

161a Central Plains Milk Snake,
Lampropeltis triangulum gentilis

161b Central Plains Milk Snake,
Lampropeltis triangulum gentilis (juvenile)

162 Pale Milk Snake,
Lampropeltis triangulum multistrata

163a Gray-banded Kingsnake,
Lampropeltis alterna (light-hued,
Blair color phase with orange saddles;
Val Verde County, Texas)

163b Gray-banded Kingsnake,
Lampropeltis alterna (light-hued,
Blair color phase; Terrell County, Texas)

M. J. Bowerman

63c Gray-banded Kingsnake,
Lampropeltis alterna (dark-hued Blair
color phase)

D. C. McIntyre

163d Gray-banded Kingsnake,
Lampropeltis alterna (hatchling; light-hued
alterna color phase; Val Verde County, Texas)

D. C. McIntyre

63e Gray-banded Kingsnake,
Lampropeltis alterna (light-hued alterna color
phase; Brewster County, Texas)

164   Florida Scarlet Snake,
Cemophora coccinea coccinea

M.J. Bowerman

165a   Northern Scarlet Snake,
Cemophora coccinea copei

165b   Northern Scarlet Snake,
Cemophora coccinea copei

65c **Northern Scarlet Snake,**
Cemophora coccinea copei

166 **Texas Scarlet Snake,**
Cemophora coccinea lineri

67a **Texas Long-nosed Snake,**
Rhinocheilus lecontei tessellatus

167b Texas Long-nosed Snake,
Rhinocheilus lecontei tessellatus

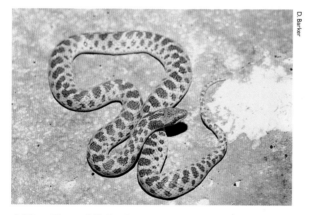

168a Texas Night Snake,
Hypsiglena torquata jani

168b Texas Night Snake,
Hypsiglena torquata jani (pale western form)

58c Texas Night Snake,
Hypsiglena torquata jani (hatchling)

169 Northern Cat-eyed Snake,
Leptodeira septentrionalis septentrionalis

70a Black-striped Snake,
Coniophanes imperialis imperialis

170b Black-striped Snake,
Coniophanes imperialis imperialis

M. J. Bowerman

171a Texas Lyre Snake,
Trimophodon biscutatus vilkinsonii

171b Texas Lyre Snake,
Trimophodon biscutatus vilkinsonii

71c Texas Lyre Snake,
Trimophodon biscutatus vilkinsonii (hatchling)

172a Eastern Coral Snake,
Micrurus fulvius fulvius

72b Eastern Coral Snake,
Micrurus fulvius fulvius

173 Texas Coral Snake,
Micrurus fulvius tener

174 Southern Copperhead,
Agkistrodon contortrix contortrix

175a Northern Copperhead,
Agkistrodon contortrix mokasen

75b Northern/Southern Copperhead Intergrade,
Agkistrodon contortrix contortrix

176a Osage Copperhead,
Agkistrodon contortrix phaeogaster

76b Osage/Northern Copperhead Intergrade,
Agkistrodon contortrix phaeogaster

177a Broad-banded Copperhead,
Agkistrodon contortrix laticinctus

177b Broad-banded/Southern Copperhead Intergrade, *Agkistrodon contortrix laticinctus*

178a Trans-Pecos Copperhead,
Agkistrodon contortrix pictigaster

178b Trans-Pecos/Broad-banded Copperhead Intergrade, *Agkistrodon contortrix pictigaster*

79a Eastern Cottonmouth,
Agkistrodon piscivorus piscivorus

179b Eastern Cottonmouth,
Agkistrodon piscivorus piscivorus

180a Florida Cottonmouth,
Agkistrodon piscivorus conanti

K. Love

180b Florida Cottonmouth,
Agkistrodon piscivorus conanti

180c Florida Cottonmouth,
Agkistrodon piscivorus conanti (juvenile)

81a Western Cottonmouth,
Agkistrodon piscivorus leucostoma

181b Western Cottonmouth,
Agkistrodon piscivorus leucostoma (juvenile)

82a Carolina Pygmy Rattlesnake,
Sistrurus miliarius miliarius (pale gray color phase)

182b **Carolina Pygmy Rattlesnake,**
Sistrurus miliarius miliarius (gray color phase, juvenile)

182c **Carolina Pygmy Rattlesnake,**
Sistrurus miliarius miliarius (dark gray color phase)

182d **Carolina Pygmy Rattlesnake,**
Sistrurus miliarius miliarius
(red color phase)

82e Carolina Pygmy Rattlesnake,
Sistrurus miliarius miliarius (red color phase, newborn)

83 Dusky Pygmy Rattlesnake,
Sistrurus miliarius barbouri

184   Western Pygmy Rattlesnake,
Sistrurus miliarius streckeri

185a   Eastern Massasauga,
Sistrurus catenatus catenatus

185b Eastern Massasauga,
Sistrurus catenatus catenatus (melanistic color phase, juvenile)

86 Western Massasauga,
Sistrurus catenatus tergeminus

187 Desert Massasauga,
Sistrurus catenatus edwardsii

R. D Bartlett

188a Timber Rattlesnake,
Crotalus horridus horridus (brown color phase)

188b Timber Rattlesnake,
Crotalus horridus horridus (newborn)

R. D Bartlett

188c Timber Rattlesnake,
Crotalus horridus horridus (dark color phase)

188d Timber Rattlesnake,
Crotalus horridus horridus

188e Timber Rattlesnake,
Crotalus horridus horridus (yellow color phase)

188f Timber Rattlesnake, *Crotalus horridus horridus*
(yellow color phase)

189a Canebrake Rattlesnake,
Crotalus horridus atricaudatus (large male, East Texas type)

189b Canebrake Rattlesnake,
Crotalus horridus atricaudatus (South Carolina coast type)

189c Canebrake Rattlesnake,
Crotalus horridus atricaudatus (central Florida type)

89d Canebrake Rattlesnake,
Crotalus horridus atricaudatus (newborn)

89e Canebrake Rattlesnake,
Crotalus horridus atricaudatus

189f Canebrake Rattlesnake,
Crotalus horridus atricaudatus (head-on-log posture)

190a Eastern Diamond-backed Rattlesnake,
Crotalus adamanteus

190b Eastern Diamond-backed Rattlesnake,
Crotalus adamanteus

191a Western Diamond-backed Rattlesnake,
Crotalus atrox

191b Western Diamond-backed Rattlesnake,
Crotalus atrox

191c Western Diamond-backed Rattlesnake,
Crotalus atrox

192a Northern Black-tailed Rattlesnake,
Crotalus molossus molossus

192b Northern Black-tailed Rattlesnake,
Crotalus molossus molossus

92c Northern Black-tailed Rattlesnake,
Crotalus molossus molossus

193a Prairie Rattlesnake,
Crotalus viridis viridis

93b Prairie Rattlesnake,
Crotalus viridis viridis (juvenile)

193c Prairie Rattlesnake,
Crotalus viridis viridis

M. J. Bowerman

194a Mojave Rattlesnake,
Crotalus scutulatus scutulatus

194b Mojave Rattlesnake,
Crotalus scutulatus scutulatus

95a Mottled Rock Rattlesnake,
Crotalus lepidus lepidus

195b Mottled Rock Rattlesnake,
Crotalus lepidus lepidus

5c Mottled Rock Rattlesnake,
Crotalus lepidus lepidus

195d Mottled Rock Rattlesnake,
Crotalus lepidus lepidus

195e Mottled Rock Rattlesnake,
Crotalus lepidus lepidus

195f Mottled Rock Rattlesnake,
Crotalus lepidus lepidus (juvenile)

196 Banded Rock Rattlesnake,
Crotalus lepidus klauberi

subspecies name means "dark pink") to vermillion-hued western coachwhips are common, while in Jeff Davis, Brewster, and Presidio counties, near the dark-reddish rhyolite formations of the Davis Mountains uplift, dark-reddish-pink *M. f. testaceus* are the prevailing color morph. Some truly spectacular "red racers" are even marked with wide alternating bands of pink and dark red or charcoal, though silvery-tan individuals also inhabit the western part of this area. The venter of all forms is gray, anteriorly marked by a double row of black spots. Juveniles are dimly crossbarred with brown on the tan anterior trunk.

Aside from the brilliant coloring of the Trans-Pecos population, however, the western coachwhips' most distinctive characteristic is the light and dark cross-hatch patterning of its tail. Since each dorsal caudal scale is two-toned (the forward portion is paler than its trailing edge) the posterior body of *M. f. testaceus* has the look of a braided rope or, to an earlier generation's eyes, a woven rawhide buggy whip. Yet these distinctive scales are actually quite smooth; they are arranged in 17 rows at midbody (in 13 rows just anterior to the vent) and a unique pair of lorilabial scales—the lower one very small—borders the anterior edge of the eye.

Similar snakes The **eastern coachwhip (101)** has uniformly blackish foreparts and a lighter-colored, dark- to light-brown midbody and tail. Other **whipsnakes (103–106)** are even wirier serpents than the coachwhip, with thin white lateral stripes, reddish undertails, and 15 midbody rows of dorsal scales.

Behavior This extreme termperature-tolerant reptile is often seen sliding across broiling pavement or rocky, barren ground in mid-summer when the temperature is above 100°F. No other serpent (except other whipsnakes, whose lean configuration is similarly resistant to heat and desiccation) can be active under such conditions. This ability to be active when a primary prey group, such as lizards, is most active, is a predatory advantage).

Conversely, western coachwhips are regularly seen abroad during mid-winter warm spells—even in mountainous areas of Trans-Pecos Texas—when no other snake is able to be abroad. Although invariably described in herpetological literature as being strictly diurnal, on a number of occasions the author has found western coachwhips foraging at night, particularly after an invasion of big lubber grasshoppers has left the Trans-Pecos countryside littered with their bodies.

Summer or winter, this animal's highly mobile daytime predatory style renders it vulnerable to predation by carnivorous birds: hawks are commonly seen perched on powerline poles feeding on coachwhips, and juveniles are preyed upon by roadrunners. (Vehicles also cause many coachwhip deaths, for *M. f. testaceus* is typically unwary of even heavily traveled highways.)

103 DESERT STRIPED WHIPSNAKE

Masticophis taeniatus taeniatus

Nonvenomous A nervous, fragile animal, *M. tae-niatus* flees rapidly from danger, but if cornered or seized may defend itself with several rapid nips.

Abundance Desert striped whipsnakes intergrade with the central Texas whipsnake from the western tip of Texas at least as far east as the Guadalupe Mountains; whether *M. t. taeniatus* exists as a pure subspecies anywhere within this area is in doubt.

Size See **Central Texas Whipsnake.**

Habitat *Masticophis taeniatus taeniatus* inhabits both gravel-floored succulent desert and evergreen montane woodland up to nearly 8,000 feet in elevation. Because the rocky faces of highway road-cuts constitute prime habitat for its lizard prey, desert striped whipsnakes are sometimes seen in these manmade canyons; here, trapped between the cuts' vertical faces they often fall victim to traffic, for it is not unusual to see road-killed *M. t. taeniatus* in such spots.

Prey The desert striped whipsnake feeds primarily on lizards and snakes—small western diamondback rattlers have been reported as prey—as well as rodents, nestling birds, and insects. Whipsnakes are not good constrictors, however, and typically simply pin prey animals to the ground while disabling them by biting their heads. See **Eastern Coachwhip.**

Reproduction Egg-laying. Like other whipsnakes, *M. t. taeniatus* lays clutches of 3 to 12 relatively large, granular-surfaced eggs. The 12- to 15-inch-long hatchlings—no thicker than a pencil and colored like their parents except that their pale nuchal marking is more pronounced—emerge in late summer or early autumn.

Coloring/scale form The desert striped whipsnake is descriptively named: below its rusty-brown dorsal ground color 3 prominent pale lateral stripes (*taeniatus* is "striped" in Latin) line its sides. The uppermost of these stripes is off-white, 2 scale rows in width, and longitudinally split by a blackish seam; this pale stripe's lower border is defined by a dark lateral stripe, and below this a second white stripe touches the outer edge of the belly. Ventral coloring is charcoal to mottled gray or white on the forebody, shading to coral beneath the tail. The dorsal scales are arranged in 15 rows at midbody.

Similar snakes   As with other whipsnakes, the desert striped whip-snake intergrades with any race of *M. taeniatus* whose range abuts its own; throughout the northern Trans-Pecos this merging involves the **central Texas whipsnake (104)**, which in typical form is distinguished by its black back, white neck patch, and the strip of elongate white dashes—sometimes compared to highway traffic lane dividers—that runs along its anterior sides.

Behavior   Whipsnakes are among the most radically shaped of serpents: their gracile configuration allows them speed and agility, but their wiry bodies are primarily an adaptation to resist heat and desiccation. This is vital for such diurnal, desert-living lizard-hunters because it allows *M. taeniatus* to forage during the midday activity peak of its lacertillian prey. (Another advantage of the whipsnake's narrow body is that it allows this wire-like reptile to almost disappear by freezing partially upright, transforming its thin profile into what appears to be an inconspicuous plant stem.)

104   CENTRAL TEXAS WHIPSNAKE

Masticophis taeniatus girardi

Nonvenomous   See **Desert Striped Whipsnake.**

Abundance   Common. Despite its geographically descriptive name, the central Texas whipsnake is probably seen more often in the Trans-Pecos portion of its range. It is likely to be equally abundant in the central hill country, but because of the thickly  vegetated juniper brakes it inhabits there, it is relatively unfamiliar even to rural residents of the area.

Size   Despite its considerable length—adult size is 28 to 72 inches—*M. t. girardi* is so slender that even the largest individuals have heads no bigger than a man's thumb: one healthy 3½-foot-long specimen captured by the author weighed but 5½ oz.

Habitat   In central Texas, oak-juniper evergreen woodland is this animal's favored habitat. In the Trans-Pecos, *M. t. girardi* is found in a wider range of environments: dry watercourses, both montane and low-lying desert canyons, rocky slopes up to nearly 8,000 feet in elevation, and evergreen mountain forest.

Prey Food animals include lizards, snakes, and small rodents. Newly caught central Texas whipsnakes are typically voracious, immediately taking several mice in succession; after settling into confinement their metabolisms slow, however, and settled captives eat no more than a mouse every week or two.

Reproduction Egg-laying. See **Desert Striped Whipsnake.**

Coloring/scale form *Masticophis taeniatus girardi* is named in honor of Charles Frederich Girard, French-born collaborator with Spencer Fullerton Baird in first naming some 24 southwestern ophidian species and subspecies.

Dorsal coloring varies to the extent that individuals from central Texas are grayish-black above, with whitish scales on the nape and a row of tiny white flecks on both the lowest dorsal scale row above the belly and the outer tips of the gray- and white-mottled ventral plates (posterior to the vent, these shade to pink). Chihuahuan Desert–living *M. t. girardi* may fit this description, have brownish dorsolateral crossbands, or be uniformly mahogany above, with charcoal anterior bellies. All color morphs have a white lateral stripe—made up of long white patches separated by dark intervening scales—that runs along the third and fourth scale rows above the belly. There are 15 midbody rows of smooth dorsal scales.

Similar snakes Throughout the northern Trans-Pecos, intergrades occur with the subspecies **desert striped whipsnake (103)**, which is distinguished by its brown to rusty dorsolateral color and its pair of mostly unbroken white lateral stripes. The uppermost of these stripes is longitudinally split by a blackish streak; the lower white stripe touches the outer edge of its venter. Along the southern edge of the Edwards Plateau, the **Schott's whipsnake (105)** is distinguished by its bluish to olive dorsolateral color, its pair of unbroken white lateral stripes, and the orange flecks often found on its neck and anterior sides.

Behavior Although few serpents in the wild live much beyond the prime of life, even among animals as high-strung as whipsnakes a few survive to old age. In Big Bend, D. Craig McIntyre came upon a 6-foot-long central Texas whipsnake that showed signs of age ordinarily seen only in captive serpents at the end of long lives in confinement. Drinking deeply from a stock tank, this individual was quite lethargic despite the warm weather, and made no attempt to escape when approached.

Nonvenomous See **Ruthven's Whipsnake.**

Abundance Named in honor of Arthur C. V. Schott, a surveyor with the 1852–53 Mexican Boundary Survey. *Masticophis schotti* is seasonally active in Texas' Duval, Brooks, Jim Wells, Webb, Kleberg, and Kenedy counties, but it is not numerous there.

Size Most adult Schott's whipsnakes are 40 to 56 inches long—the record is 66 inches—but even the largest adults are not much thicker than a fountain pen and weigh only a few ounces.

Habitat *Masticophis schotti* inhabits the coastal plain south of the Balcones Fault. Here, between the oak/juniper brakes of the hill country to the north (home of the central Texas whipsnake) and the Tamaulipan thorn brush to the south (where the Ruthven's whipsnake prevails), the predominant vegetation is mesquite/live oak/prickly pear savannah and the resident whipsnake species is the Schott's.

Prey Lizards are this species' principal prey, but rodents are also taken—captives typically eat mice immediately—as well as other snakes; cannibalism of its own kind by *M. schotti* is reported. The young probably feed largely on insects or small lizards.

Reproduction Egg-laying. Three Texas clutches reported by Howard Gloyd, laid in May and June, consisted of 3, 10, and 12 eggs. None hatched, but reproductive success was achieved during 1996 when a gravid Webb County female cared for by Kenny Wray of the University of Texas at Arlington laid 9 nearly two-inch-long, rough-surfaced eggs on May 1. Four were infertile, but 72 days later the remaining egg hatched into a 12¾-inch-long offspring whose brick-red cephalic wash and salmon-hued venter were quite different from the coloring of its parent (its photograph, the first ever taken of a hatchling *Masticophis schotti*, is included here).

Coloring/scale form Formerly known as *Masticophis taeniatus schotti*, the Schott's whipsnake has now been re-defined by James Dixon and others of Texas A & M University, as the separate species, *Masticophis schotti*. Its bluish- to greenish-gray back and sides contrast sharply with its pair of white lateral stripes and the reddish-orange scales scattered along its off-white lower neck. Its venter is cream-colored beneath the chin, stippled with bluish gray at mid-body, and deep yellow to salmon below its tail. Its smooth dorsal scales are arranged in 15 rows at midbody.

Similar snakes Along the southern Edwards Plateau, the adjacently ranging **central Texas whipsnake (104)** is gray-black, with a prominent white nuchal patch and a series of white dashes—sometimes likened to highway lane dividers—along its anterior sides; it lacks the Schott's pair of unbroken white dorsolateral lines. To the south, **Ruthven's whipsnake (106)** is greener, lacks distinct white lateral stripes, and has both gray or dark orange spots on its white or pale yellow throat and a bright red undertail.

Behavior Fast-moving small animals, especially lizards, instantly attract this diurnal reptile's attention. They are not hotly pursued, however, but instead are stalked, using a stop-and-go technique in which the whipsnake pauses while its quarry darts about. Then, when the lizard's attention is diverted by its own foraging, the whipsnake quickly advances a few inches, then a few more. Once grasped by the jaws, prey too large to be immediately engulfed is held down with a loop of the trunk and disabled by repeated bites to its head.

106   RUTHVEN'S WHIPSNAKE, *Masticophis ruthveni*

Nonvenomous *Masticophis ruthveni* is nervous and quick to flee danger, but if cornered it does not hesitate to nip in its own defense, after which it may quickly retract its head and neck, raking its teeth across its adversary's skin and leaving shallow scratches.

Abundance Formerly abundant. Ruthven's whipsnake is now common only near the scattered patches of uncut mesquite savannah and thorn woodland still found in Texas' Rio Grande valley; it is sometimes seen as a roadkill near the Cameron County Airport and is abundant on the Laguna Atascosa National Wildlife Refuge.

Size Most adults are 40 to 56 inches long; the record is 66⅛ in.

Habitat This semi-tropical whipsnake is native to—and one of the animals most typical of—Tamaulipan thorn woodland. Until mid-century this massive thorn thicket, named for Mexico's northeastern-most state, stretched from the Rio Grande almost halfway to San Antonio. Its tangle of catclaw acacia, paloverde, tamarisk, cenizo, and ocotillo was once among the United States' richest biotic communities in species diversity, but its lush vegetation grew on fertile, level land, and the agricultural boom of the 1950s leveled most of its native vegetation, decimating the tropical birds, mammals, and reptiles that historically ranged only as far north as this thorn-jungled tip of southern Texas.

Prey   See **Schott's Whipsnake.**

Reproduction   Egg-laying. See **Schott's Whipsnake.**

Coloring/scale form   The dorsum of adult Ruthven's whipsnakes is an unmarked bluish- to olive-green, with lighter-hued blue-green lower sides faintly marked behind the jaw with rusty orange spots. (The leading edge of some of the anterior vertebral scales is cream-colored, shading to olive or reddish gray toward the tail.) The pale yellow forebelly changes to blue-gray, lightly mottled with salmon on the middle third of the trunk, to pink around the vent, and deep red beneath the tail.

Juveniles have a faintly russet crown and nape and a black-edged pale side stripe on adjacent portions of the third and fourth scale rows above the belly; they generally lack the light anterior vertebral scale margins of adults, as well as most of their dark ventral stippling. The dorsal scales occur in 15 rows at midbody.

Similar snakes   Formerly classified as *Masticophis taeniatus ruthveni*, a subspecies of more northerly whipsnakes, Ruthven's whipsnake has now been defined as the separate species *Masticophis ruthveni* by James Dixon and others of Texas A & M University. The **Schott's whipsnake** (105) has much more conspicuous white lateral stripes, a paler forebelly and a deep yellow posterior venter shading to salmon beneath the tail.

Behavior   In his 1928 monograph, A. I. Ortenberger (who named this snake in honor of his teacher, Alexander Grant Ruthven, president of the University of Michigan) concluded that little was known of its ecology. Even brief field observation reveals, however, that like other whipsnakes *M. ruthveni* is a seemingly curious animal: with abrupt darting movements it investigates any unusual activity within its territory. Since most of its U.S. habitat has been lost to agricultural and residential development during the last 30 years, however, further information regarding its natural history will probably come from northern coastal Mexico. See **Schott's Whipsnake.**

RACERS
Genus Coluber

Northern Black Racer, *Coluber constrictor constrictor*
Southern Black Racer, *Coluber constrictor priapus*
Blue Racer, *Coluber constrictor foxii*
Everglades Racer, *Coluber constrictor paludicola*
Brown-chinned Racer, *Coluber constrictor helvigularis*
Black-masked Racer, *Coluber constrictor latrunculus*
Buttermilk Racer, *Coluber constrictor anthicus*
Tan Racer, *Coluber constrictor etheridgei*
Eastern Yellow-bellied Racer, *Coluber constrictor flaviventris*
Mexican Racer, *Coluber constrictor oaxaca*

Along with whipsnakes of the genus *Masticophis*, racers are part of the colubrine subfamily *Colubrinae*. An oviparous genus first scientifically described by Carolus Linneaus in 1758, members of the *coluber* group produce leathery eggs with roughly surfaced shells and a distinctively crimped, starburst pattern on their ends. Racers' scales are smooth, arranged in 17 rows at midbody (usually 15 rows just anterior to the vent), and their anal plate is divided. These serpents are notable for their alert demeanor, readiness to bite if molested, and considerable speed. They also climb well and spend a great deal of time in shrubs and low trees, but unlike other arboreal ophidian predators like the rat snakes, racers do not constrict their prey, despite the scientific species name "*constrictor*." Instead, these snakes simply grasp a food animal in their jaws and swallow the struggling creature alive.

At least twelve subspecies of *C. constrictor* are found from the Atlantic to the Pacific (ten of which are found east of the Rocky Mountains), while *Coluber* is absent from large parts of the southwestern and north-central United States as well as from the area along the continental divide. Adults of most of these races are solid black, gray, blue, or brownish-green above, but the dark ground color of two subspecies, the buttermilk, *C. c. anthicus*, and tan, *C. c. etheridgei*, racers is variably patterned with light-hued spots and blotches. (Hatchlings and juveniles of all races are strongly patterned with dark dorsal blotches or crossbars on a tan to light-brown or grayish ground color.)

NORTHERN BLACK RACER

Coluber constrictor constrictor

Nonvenomous This is a courageous animal that will bite if cornered or molested, but North American snakes typically have very weak jaws, and even a large racer can inflict only scratches. (If one of its tiny, thin teeth should break off in the wound it can be plucked out like a blackberry thorn.)

Size Most adults are 3 to 4 feet in length. This subspecies often attains 5 feet, however, and the largest individuals on record are much larger: one New York specimen killed in a road construction area was measured by Gerard T. Salmon at 81 inches.

Abundance The northern black racer is one of the most successful and abundant large snakes in the eastern United States. Its range extends inland from the Atlantic through northern South Carolina, Georgia, and Alabama, north through eastern Tennessee and Ohio to southern New York, Vermont, New Hampshire, and the southeastern coast of Maine.

Habitat *Coluber constrictor constrictor* is a habitat generalist which may be encountered in almost any well-vegetated terrestrial environment. Among the places it is often seen are suburban fencerows, rural gardens, fields, meadows and pastures, open woodlands, and rocky hillsides. It can be found on high ground or low, in dry areas and along the verges of ponds and swamps. While usually seen on the ground, the northern black racer also frequently ascends into shrubs and densely branched trees—where it may climb high above the ground.

Prey Frogs, lizards, smaller snakes, rodents, nestling birds, and even insects are eaten by the black racer. When hunting, racers may raise their heads above grass level in order to better visually search for prey—a tactic that lets them spot bird and mouse nests high in the branches of trees, which they are easily able to climb.

Reproduction Egg-laying. Each clutch contains from 5 to more than 20 roughly textured eggs, marked with a characteristic star-shaped crimp on their ends. These are deposited beneath or within moisture-retaining logs and debris. (Several females may lay their

WHIPSNAKES, RACERS, AND INDIGO SNAKES

eggs in a particularly suitable location.) Incubation varies from 48 to 65 days, depending on warmth, and at emergence the slender hatchlings are 10 to 12½ inches long.

Coloring/scale form As with all racers, ontogenetic changes in color and pattern are marked. Against a grayish ground color, hatchlings backs are patterned with a series of russet to brown vertebral blotches that are most sharply defined on the forebody. On both their sides and their grayish venters are small dark spots. With growth, the ground color quickly darkens, and the adult northern black racer is satiny black. Its chin may be white, and rarely the white may extend onto the anterior section of its throat, but otherwise its back, sides, and belly are evenly covered lustrous dark pigment. Its eye is usually dark, but may be yellowish brown.

Similar snakes The **southern black racer (108)** usually has more white on its chin and anterior venter and may have a dark-red eye, but it is difficult to distinguish from the northern race because the basis for their classification as separate subspecies is the subtly differing morphology of their respective hemipenes. The **black rat snake (134)** has keeled scales with a shiny, not satiny, luster; even as an adult it usually retains a trace of dorsal blotching.

Behavior Racers typically flee the approach of a larger creature with alacrity (the speed with which a startled black racer can disappear into cover can be startling), but an occasional individual may stand its ground and even advance toward a threat. Holding its head, neck, and forebody above the ground and noisily vibrating its tail in dried vegetation as it approaches is a formidable defensive technique which, combined with feinting bluff strikes, can be disconcerting even to those who understand snakes. While unusual, this sort of vigorous defensive display is often characteristic of a species, such as *Coluber constrictor*, which fills high-risk ecological niches exposed to attack by predators.

This lifestyle is sufficiently different from that of most snakes— it brings in additional prey calories, but its increased mortality and high-energy expenditures are difficult to offset—to prompt Plummer and Congdon (1994) to chart, using radio telemetry, the activity profile of *C. c. constrictor*. They found that thickets, which allowed northern black racers to climb to escape danger, were preferred habitat. Here, they were active on 3 out of 4 days during summer (their inactive periods were mainly devoted to shedding, during which most individuals hid in rodent burrows).

Home ranges usually covered several acres, but big racers had no larger territories than small ones (males, as well as females seeking egg-laying sites, traveled further than other racers), but in autumn all activity areas decreased significantly.

108   SOUTHERN BLACK RACER
Coluber constrictor priapus

Nonvenomous   Racers are comparatively high-strung snakes that will bite in self-defense. See **Northern Black Racer.**

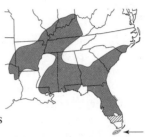

Abundance   *Coluber constrictor priapus* occurs throughout the Southeast, where, as a pure race, it can be found as far south as Lake Okeechobee, Florida, as far north as southern Indiana, and as far west as eastern Texas and Oklahoma. Like its northern subspecies, throughout most of this vast territory it is among the most successful and abundant large snakes.

Size   Most adults are 20 to 56 inches in length; the record is 72 in.

Habitat   Like other *Coluber*, the southern black racer is a habitat generalist which thrives in a variety of rural and even suburban areas. Its preferred environment, however, seems to be deciduous forest-meadowland interface—a vegetative transition zone characterized by the low-level shrubbery that racers favor.

Prey   This wide-spectrum predator takes whatever smaller creatures—including animals from insects and their larvae to vertebrates such as frogs, toads, lizards, snakes, birds and their eggs, and rodents—are most available within its range. In captivity (unlike many other serpents), racers' high metabolism requires them to eat every few days. See **Eastern Yellow-bellied Racer.**

Reproduction   Egg-laying. Seven to 18 granular-textured oval eggs, about 1 by 1⅛ inches and bearing characteristic star-like markings on their ends, are laid in a humid subsurface cavity (a few of these nests are communally used year after year). The 9- to 11-inch-long hatchlings emerge in July and August and, because they are otherwise defenseless, may feign death when handled.

Very different in coloring from the adults, young southern black racers are conspicuously patterned with chestnut-brown vertebral saddles, grayish lateral spots, and pale, often posteriorly pinkish bellies. They do not turn uniformly dark above until they reach about 22 inches in length.

Coloring/scale form   The southern black racer's dorsum is a satiny charcoal gray to jet black, with some white generally visible on its chin and throat; the remainder of its belly ranges from yellowish gray to as dark a charcoal as its back. (Individuals from the Cape Canaveral/Merrit Island region of Florida's Atlantic Coast are a blue-gray color dorsally.) This subspecies' slender body and elongate head follow the same configuration as those of other racers, but its eye is notable for its dark, orange-red iris.

Similar snakes   The subspecies **northern black racer (107)** has less white on its chin and throat and most often has a dark- to yellowish-brown eye. Its primary difference from the southern race, however, is the subtle dissimilarity in the morphology of their respective hemipenes, hence the Latin subspecies designation "priapus." The equally dark, but larger and longer-tailed **eastern coachwhip (101)** has a lighter-hued posterior body marked by dark-edged crosshatching; it also has a uniformly dark chin and throat and 13 rows of dorsal scales just anterior to its vent.

Behavior   One study found that, during spring and summer several *C. c. priapus* maintained small, well-defined home territories around the rocky outcroppings of grassy, oak-studded hillsides in Grayson County, Texas. Other southern black racers have been observed more than 10 feet up in trees, where they sought refuge after having eluded a pursuer on the ground; *C. c. priapus* tends to be far less wary when hidden in thick branches where, rather than flee, it is inclined to freeze, sometimes until actually touched. When preparing to shed, however, these animals most often seek the higher humidity of an animal burrow or shady shelter beneath either natural or manmade debris.

As reflected in its name "racer," *C. constrictor* is capable of maximum burst speed of about 12 mph, or 18 feet per second. Though exhaustion is reached in less than 30 minutes, short of the endurance of birds and mammals, this is, nevertheless, great stamina for a terrestrial reptile, and can only be achieved because of racers' sophisticated physiology. For example, Plummer and Congdon found that, among this race's northern subspecies, within 30 seconds of seizing a mouse a racer's heart rate can shoot up to 3 times its resting level. At the same time, its arterial blood pressure increases nearly fourfold, a rush of circulating blood that lets *C. constrictor* respond nearly as rapidly, from a resting state, as a bird or mammal. As field experience has repeatedly confirmed, a reptile need not be a warm-blooded dinosaur to make use of a quick reacting neuromuscular system, nor to sustain that system with considerable cardiovascular stamina.

Nonvenomous   Like other racers, specimens of this subspecies will bite vigorously and repeatedly in their own defense.

Abundance   Locally common. This animal's upper Midwest range connects the territories of North America's most widespread races of *Coluber constrictor*, and there is some basis for the theory that the blue racer is actually an intermediate color morph between the eastern yellow-bellied racer (with which it intergrades in eastern Iowa and Missouri) and the southern and northern black racers, with which it intergrades in southern Illinois, Indiana, northern Kentucky and southeastern Ohio.

Size   Similar to that of the subspecies southern black racer: the largest recorded specimens are slightly less than 72 inches long.

Habitat   A resident of open grassland, sparse woods, and sphagnum bogs, *C. c. foxii* is most abundant in the sand prairie country of the southern Great Lakes, where the type specimen was collected by the Reverend Charles Fox early in the 19th century. This territory includes southern Wisconsin (a small disjunct range occurs in the northeastern corner of this state) and, on the opposite of the Chicago metroplex, southern Michigan and a bit of Ontario. In this far northern range the blue racer is frequently encountered dead on roadways traversing its preferred habitat.

Prey   Racers are extremely generalized predators, taking whatever smaller creatures are most available, including insects, birds and their eggs, frogs, lizards, rodents, and other snakes. Prey is overpowered or pressed down with a loop of the body in order to subdue it.

Reproduction   See **Northern Black Racer.**

Coloring/scale form   This subspecies, found east of the Mississippi River, varies little from the eastern yellow-bellied racer and may be only a color phase of *C. c. flaviventris*. Its slender body and elongate head follow the same configuration as those of other racers, and the typical blotched pattern of juvenile *C. coluber* is lost at the same age as the blue racer's dorsum assumes the typical, unmarked gray-blue shade of the adult. Yet the dorsal coloring of adult *C. c. foxii* is highly variable individually—dark-hued specimens often have an even darker postocular patch. While most *C. c. foxii* are a rather dull blue-green, little different from that of the eastern yellow-bellied racer, an occasional individual manifests any shade of azure from a beautiful aquamarine to turquoise.

Similar snakes   The larger and longer-tailed **eastern coachwhip (101)** almost always has a lighter-hued posterior body with dark-edged caudal cross-hatching and 17 midbody rows of dorsal scales.

The **smooth green snake (99)** is bright green above and each nostril is centered within a single nasal scale; at the size of an adult smooth green snake the blue racer still retains its blotched juvenile patterning. The **black rat snake (134)** has keeled scales with a shiny, not satiny, luster; even as an adult it usually retains a trace of dorsal blotching.

Behavior   In the northern parts of its range the blue racer needs deep crevices below the frost line for winter hibernacula and in chilly springtime weather, when this animal is still cool and sluggish, sunny sanctuaries for thermoregulatory basking—an essential part of northern racers' metabolic cycle. In summer *C. c. foxii* is completely diurnal, and during the heat of the day individuals are alert and fast-moving. See **Southern Black Racer.**

110   EVERGLADES RACER

Coluber constrictor paludicola

Nonvenomous   Like other racers, *C. c. paludicola* is quick to flee when encountered in the field, but if cornered it is likely to strike in self-defense. (In this situation, racers typically vibrate their tails so rapidly that in dry grass they produce a sound somewhat like the caudal whir of a rattlesnake.)

Abundance   Endemic to Florida, the everglades racer is abundant from the Tamiami Trail south to Key Largo. Well to the north, in Brevard County, *C. c. paludicola* also occurs in a disjunct range not far from Cape Canaveral.

Size   Similar to that of its subspecies, the southern black racer, whose range entirely surrounds that of the Everglades racer.

Habitat   First scientifically described in 1955 by University of Florida Komodo dragon authority Walter Auffenberg, this racer's Latin subspecies name describes its presumably marshy native environment. Nevertheless, the Everglades racer is not a snake of the

Everglades' river of grass. Actually, it is only rarely found in inundated saw-grass swale, or any other true marsh, though it is common in the hardwood hammocks, pinelands, and drained agricultural fields now typical of the Everglades region. Elsewhere in south Florida, Everglades racers occupy a variety of habitats that include urban parks, canals bordering sugarcane fields, and stands of melaleuca, pine, and cypress.

Prey Racers are generalized predators, taking whatever smaller creatures are most available, including insects, birds and their eggs, frogs, lizards, rodents, and other snakes.

Reproduction A wild-caught female *C. c. paludicola* captured by D. Craig McIntyre just outside Everglades National Park laid 8 eggs on September 8. See **Southern Black Racer**.

Coloring/scale form The slender body and elongate head follow the same configuration as those of other racers, but the dorsum is grayish brown, sometimes with a bluish cast. Unlike the dark red iris of the southern black racer the Everglades subspecies' iris is a distinctive pale orange or yellow, and its venter is off-white, mottled with blue-gray. Juveniles resemble those of the southern black racer with a slightly more pinkish ground color and russet dorsolateral patterning.

Similar snakes The larger and longer-tailed **eastern coachwhip (101)** almost always has a lighter-hued posterior body with dark-edged caudal cross-hatching and 13 rows of dorsal scales just anterior to its vent.

Behavior See **Southern Black Racer**.

---

111 BROWN-CHINNED RACER

Coluber constrictor helvigularis

Nonvenomous When cornered, like other racers, *C. c. helvigularis* does not hesitate to coil, strike, and bite in self-defense. See **Northern Black Racer**.

Abundance Brown-chinned racers are common within their very restricted range, which principally involves the Apalachicola River basin in the Florida panhandle.

Size   Adult *C. c. helvigularis* are 26 to 62 inches in length.

Habitat   Racers can be found in nearly all terrestrial habitats, both rural and urban, but the brown-chinned racer is most often seen crossing sandy lumbering roads that traverse the pine flatwoods of the Apalachicola National Forest.

Prey   Despite the name *C. constrictor*, racers are not in fact constrictors. Small prey such as insects are snapped up and quickly swallowed, but when feeding on larger vertebrates—birds, frogs, lizards, snakes, and rodents are recorded—rather than suffocating a food animal by constriction, racers overpower it by using a coil of their muscular bodies to press their prey against the ground while they disable it by biting.

Reproduction   See **Southern Black Racer**.

Coloring/scale form   Coloring is similar to that of the subspecies southern black racer except for the light brown mottling of the lips, chin, and throat—a hue referred to by the latin subspecies name *helvigularis*.

Similar snakes   The **southern black racer (108)**, whose range entirely surrounds that of the brown-chinned racer, has whitish lips, chin and throat. The larger and longer-tailed **eastern coachwhip (101)** has 13 rows of dorsal scales just anterior to its vent and a lighter-hued posterior body marked by dark-edged scales which give its tail a cross-hatched look.

Behavior   See **Northern and Southern Black Racers**.

112   BLACK-MASKED RACER

Coluber constrictor latrunculus

Nonvenomous   Like other racers, if unable to flee *C. c. latrunculus* will coil, strike, and bite in self-defense. See **Northern Black Racer**.

Abundance   *Coluber constrictor latrunculus* is not uncommon within its small range, which is limited to the lower Mississippi River corridor. This floodplain range includes a bit of southeastern Arkansas, all of western Mississippi, northeastern Louisiana, and the entire Mississippi delta.

Size   See **Eastern Yellow-bellied Racer.**

Habitat   The black-masked racer is a subspecies with a very specialized habitat consisting of two quite different local regions. The first is the low-lying Mississippi delta, a boggy landscape traversed by myriad bayous, canals, flooded ditches, lakes, ponds, and marshes—terrain much wetter than that inhabited by any other racer except the Everglades form. Like its southern Florida relative, though, in true swampland the black-masked racer seems to favor islands of higher ground, especially patches of live oaks and stands of cypress surrounded by inundated forest.

The second region favored by *C. c. latrunculus* is just up-river. This is the heavily agriculturalized cotton and sorghum-farmed floodplain that makes up the western half of the state of Mississippi. Here, black-masked racers seek shelter in the microhabitat of hardwood-forested creekbed gullies, secluding themselves beneath logs, boards, or piles of leaves and brushy vegetation.

Prey   See **Eastern Yellow-bellied Racer.**

Reproduction   See **Buttermilk Racer.**

Coloring/scale form   The black-masked racer is appropriately named, for its most distinctive marking is the thin yet distinct black pre- and post-ocular line that runs like an outlaw's mask—*latrunculus* is Latin for "robber"—through its eyes and across its posterior cheeks. Otherwise, this animal's dorsal and ventral coloring is more or less intermediate between that of its neighboring subspecies, the southern black racer and the eastern yellow-bellied racer: the black-masked racer's dorsum is dusky gray or dark gray-green, its belly a murky, grayish-blue or -green.

Similar snakes   The adjacently ranging **southern black racer (108)**, whose range almost entirely surrounds that of the black-masked racer, is a considerably darker gray-black, both above and below; it has whitish lips, chin and throat. To the west, the **buttermilk racer (113)** has an anteriorly pale-spotted (with randomly dispersed whitish scales) gray-blue dorsum; it has yellowish lips and chin. To the southwest, the **eastern yellow-bellied racer (115)** is olive- to bluish-green above, with a bright yellow venter. None of these related racers has a distinct dark stripe through its eye.

Behavior   Racers' nervous temperament makes them restless captives that seldom do well in confinement. See **Northern and Southern Black Racers.**

113 BUTTERMILK RACER
Coluber constrictor anthicus

Nonvenomous Like other racers, *C. c. anthicus* will nip in self-defense, although even in distress these animals often bluff by striking open-mouthed and not biting down (even when they do bite, racers' jaws are not strong enough to inflict more than shallow scratches).

Abundance Common (during one week in mid-May, 9 buttermilk racers were found on the grounds of a Lake Houston golf course) within its small range. This unusually shaped territory encompasses most of non-coastal Louisiana and eastern Texas, with the exception of the heavily wooded Big Thicket areas of both states which occupies the center of this region and is home to the subspecies tan racer.

Size Most adults are 30 to 60 inches long; the record is 70 in.

Habitat The buttermilk racer favors brushy, forest-edge habitats: the borders of overgrown fields, meadows, and partially open areas where it is able to shelter in brier patches and undergrowth. This habitat preference has benefited *C. c. anthicus* because most of East Texas' old growth forest has been cut for timber, leaving a patchwork of such woodland-interface habitats at the edges of fields, residential subdivisions, and golf courses.

Prey In the single study of this subspecies' diet, mice were found in the stomachs of 25 adults, lizards were found in 8, frogs in 7, rats in 5, and 3 had eaten birds. (Racers are also noteworthy for the deep channels that line the sides of their snout in front of their eyes. These grooves give their large eyes an overlapping field of view directly ahead, thus providing the binocular vision and depth perception so important to a pursuit-oriented diurnal predator of fast-moving prey.)

Reproduction Egg-laying. During the breeding season in April and May, male racers become quite aggressive, with several sometimes courting a single female. Deposited during June, July, and early August in a variety of sites—within the tunnels of small burrowing mammals, beneath rotting boards or sheets of iron siding, in loose soil along the margins of plowed fields—the granular-surfaced eggs, notable for the distinctive star-burst pattern on their ends, measure up to 1⅜ inches in length.

Of 3 *C. c. anthicus* clutches deposited at the Houston Zoo in late May, 2 clutches were made up of 18 eggs, the third of 27. All these eggs hatched about 46 days later into 10- to 11-inch-long young whose off-white ground color was blotched with brown vertebral saddles and small lateral spots.

Coloring/scale form   Named for the supposed similarity of its pale-dappled dorsum to the light-hued droplets of fat sprinkled throughout old-time buttermilk, *C. c. anthicus* is notable among racers for its unique dorsolateral patterning. The ground color of its foreparts is dark bluish or greenish gray, which becomes lighter and browner to the rear (especially in Angelina, Polk, Tyler, and northern Jasper and Newton counties, where the buttermilk racer intergrades with its uniformly brownish gray subspecies, *C. c. etheridgei*, the tan racer).

Across this dark ground color the buttermilk racer's back and sides are (sometimes spectacularly) spattered with off-white scales, densely packed on some individuals, scattered and few in number on others (animals genetically influenced by the tan racer may exhibit only a white-spotted dark patch on the nape). The lips, chin, and lower sides of the neck are pale yellow, while the belly is gray, often with a few little yellow spots.

Similar snakes   The subspecies **tan racer (114)** is almost entirely light gray or brown above, although sometimes it is marked with a few white dorsolateral scales. Another subspecies, the **eastern yellow-bellied racer (115)**, is olive- to bluish-green above, with a bright yellow venter. (Young buttermilk racers' dark vertebral saddles, big, yellow-irised eyes, and 17 anterior rows of dorsal scales set them off from adults of the similar-sized burrowing serpents found in the same leaf-litter microenvironment.)

Behavior   Even in areas of sub-optimal habitat, buttermilk racers probably occupy ranges of no more than 25 acres; few have been known to travel as far as ¾ mile. See **Northern and Southern Black Racers.**

114   TAN RACER, *Coluber constrictor etheridgei*

Nonvenomous   See **Eastern Yellow-bellied Racer.**

Abundance   *Coluber constrictor etheridgei* is not uncommon within its very limited range.

Size   This subspecies has been recorded to nearly 6 feet in length. Most adults are 3 to 5 feet long, however, while hatchlings measure 8 to 12 inches.

Habitat   A habit-defining member of the heavily overstoried eastern Texas/western Louisiana longleaf pine/oak/sweetgum climax forest, the tan racer also occupies dense second-growth woodland. Yet, as even East Texas' previously lumbered pine forest has given way to fields, subdivisions, and golf courses, much of the tan racer's former Big Thicket territory has been usurped by the more open-clearing, woodland-edge-living buttermilk racer. First scientifically described by Larry David Wilson in 1970, this animal's subspecies name honors Richard Etheridge, a San Diego State University zoology professor who, as a high school student in 1946 (when much of East Texas' forest habitat still remained), collected the type specimen.

Prey   See **Eastern Yellow-bellied Racer.**

Reproduction   Egg-laying. The only data for this subspecies is that on May 28, a female from east of Woodville, Texas, deposited 30 eggs—a very high number for a racer, whose clutches generally number fewer than 20 eggs—each a little more than an inch in length.

Coloring/scale form   Although the individual pictured here is grayish, the tan racer's dorsolateral coloring is more often light brown (at first glance it resembles a western coachwhip with a scattering of pale dorsal scales). Sometimes there is a white-spotted patch of dark bluish or greenish gray on its nape, and its venter is unmarked light gray, with a few yellowish spots.

Similar snakes   East Texas' more widespread **buttermilk racer (113)** has a darker, generally gray-blue or gray-green back patterned with much more profuse off-white dorsolateral scales. (Intergrades between the two races are common. These animals usually exhibit the dark forebody of the buttermilk subspecies, but with fewer white dorsal scales, and the brownish tail of the tan racer.)

Hatchling racers are distinguished from other small terrestrial serpents with brown dorsolateral patterning by their dark vertebral saddles, proportionately large heads and big yellow eyes, as well as by their singular combination of a divided anal plate and 17 rows of smooth dorsal scales at midbody, 15 just ahead of the vent.

Behavior   As with other racers, *C. c. etheridgei* is most easily found in early spring while it is still lethargic, hiding beneath woodland ground cover or human detritus. (Later in the year when they are warm and active these racers are almost impossible to either find or capture in the dense forest they inhabit.)

Using the measure of individuals seen crossing pine woods logging roads, however, tan racers seem to be most active from May to July, perhaps retiring somewhat during the hottest and driest part of late summer, then emerging for another foraging peak in October (hunting is apparently divided mostly into morning and afternoon periods, especially when the temperature at those times is between 70 and 85 °F).

115 EASTERN YELLOW-BELLIED RACER
Coluber constrictor flaviventris

Nonvenomous   If cornered, *C. c. flaviventris* may vibrate its tail, and if restrained it is likely to snap with agility. Compared to even a tiny mammal, however, racers are unable to exert much pressure with their jaws, and pricks or scratches are all that result from a bite.

Abundance   The most widely distributed member of its genus, the eastern yellow-bellied racer occupies an enormous range that extends from the northwestern Gulf Coast and arid Trans-Pecos Texas, northwest as far as southern Alberta, and southeast across the Dakotas to Iowa and Missouri.

Size   Although reported to reach nearly 6 feet in length, adult *C. c. flaviventris* generally measure between 30 and 54 in.

Habitat   Although in the eastern part of its range the eastern yellow-bellied racer generally keeps to wooded cover and traverses overgrown fields mainly on hunting forays, in western parts of its range entire populations live in open grassland. Here, *C. c. flaviventris* is most often found in more vegetated areas such as brush-filled gullies or wooded riparian corridors, however, where it typically shelters under flat rocks, bushes, or clumps of bunchgrass. Derelict buildings with fallen boards and siding constitute another favored microhabitat.

Despite its name, the eastern yellow-bellied racer also inhabits arid deserts. One individual, found near Marathon by the author, was thought to be part of a relict population that had survived in a small mesic refuge remaining from the wetter West Texas of Pleistocene times, until a second specimen was discovered nearby in entirely waterless, rocky desert north of Sanderson.

Such animals have been linked with either the subspecies Mexican racer, *C. c. oaxaca*, or the far western subspecies, *C. c. mormon*, but both these Trans-Pecos individuals were phenotypically perfect eastern yellow-bellied racers, and their presence in the northern Chihuahuan Desert (like the presence of exactly similar individuals also found by the author near Miles City, Montana, in dry, northern Great Plains grassland not far from the Canadian border) simply broadens our perspective of the variety of environments in which this extraordinarily adaptable subspecies can survive.

Prey   Despite the name *C. constrictor*, racers are not constrictors. Small prey such as insects are simply snapped up, but when feeding on larger vertebrates—birds, frogs, lizards, other snakes, and rodents are recorded—rather than suffocating their prey by constriction, racers sometimes overpower these creatures by pinning them against the ground with a body coil, then disabling the animal by biting its head.

Like other racers, *C. c. flaviventris* will eat any smaller creature it can capture (the author found a 2-foot-long eastern yellow-bellied racer in a coop housing half-grown chickens far too large for it to swallow), including large insects. Cicadas are important prey for many woodland snakes, and during the periodic simultaneous emergence of tens of thousands of these big insects, eastern yellow-bellied racers feed on them almost exclusively.

Reproduction   Egg-laying. With the approach of their early summer parturition, female racers move to denser vegetation than they frequent at other times, subsequently hiding their eggs beneath litter or burying them under a layer of sandy soil. See **Buttermilk Racer**.

Coloring/scale form   Adult eastern yellow-bellied racers are a lovely, unmarked blue-gray-green above, with a bright yellow venter. The pale ground-colored young are dorsally blotched with brown, but during their second year, after reaching 16 to 18 inches in length, in an ontogenetic pattern change they start to lose their juvenile coloring, beginning on the tail. There are usually 7 upper labial scales.

Similar snakes   In the northeastern portion of its range, the eastern yellow-bellied racer's range abuts that of both the **northern** and **southern black racers (107, 108)**, whose backs are a satiny charcoal gray to jet black, with some white generally visible on the chin and throat. East Texas' subspecies **buttermilk racer (113)** has a darker, gray-blue or gray-green back and sides patterned with profuse off-white scales. In southwestern Texas the eastern yellow-bellied racer's territory overlaps that of the **Mexican racer (116)**, a more southerly and westerly subspecies with a slightly darker back and lighter sides, a greenish-yellow venter, and 8 upper labial scales. (Intergrades between adjoining racer subspecies are common.)

Behavior   Racers' comparatively advanced physiology is the primary factor that gives rise to a subtle quality one notices when handling these snakes. Unlike a majority of serpents, racers have an almost mammalian presence: they clearly take note of what is going on around them. A newly captured individual may seem to have settled down passively in one's hands but, in a way not seen among most other serpents, it typically continues to pay attention to its circumstances and, if a chance for escape arises, it is instantly ready to take advantage of the opportunity. See **Southern Black Racer.**

116   MEXICAN RACER, *Coluber constrictor oaxaca*

Nonvenomous   Like other racers, *C. c. oaxaca* is adept at self-defense. If cornered, it will strike energetically and bite repeatedly, although it is incapable of inflicting anything more than pricks and scratches.

Abundance   Uncommon even in undisturbed parts of its South Texas range, the Mexican racer seems to be most prevalent in the brush country of the lower Rio Grande valley. Yet occasional individuals have been found so far to the west of this primary territory that the true U.S. range of *C. c. oaxaca* may have not yet been adequately defined.

Size   Slightly smaller than other racers, most adult *C. c. oaxaca* measure 18 to 36 inches in length, and any individual over 40 inches long would be very large. Hatchlings are from 8 to 11 inches in length.

Habitat   In the United States, genetically pure examples of the Mexican racer are restricted to Texas' subtropical southern Gulf Coast—where it occurs in the grassy sand dunes, called lomas, which abut the saline Laguna Madre—and lower Rio Grande valley. Inland, *C. c. oaxaca* is a resident of shrubby fields, open woodlands and riverbanks. Tamaulipan thorn woodland is also a principal habitat, where this subspecies shelters in clumps of prickly pear or beneath boards and debris around unworked farms and stock tanks, but Mexican racers are also sometimes found in the suburban vacant lots and city parks.

Prey   Lizards and frogs seem to be the principal prey of adults, but small rodents, nestling birds, and insects are also taken. Juveniles feed on locusts, crickets, cicadas, and non-toxic caterpillars, but will also eat suitably sized lizards and frogs when they can.

In addition, an unusual and previously unrecorded prey species for *Coluber constrictor oaxaca* is reported by herpetologist Gus Renfro—an observer of these snakes for years—who has found that individuals captured in the coastal dunes often defecate the shell fragments of fiddler crabs.

Reproduction   Egg-laying. Little is known about the reproduction of the Mexican racer. Clutches probably vary from the 3 eggs produced by one small captive female to about a dozen.

Sometimes, though, deriving reproductive data for an uncommon animal like *C. c. oaxaca* can be an exercise in forensic science. For example, one freshly traffic-killed, 3-foot-long female discovered on June 25 by D. Craig McIntyre had milky skin and eye coverings. When she was found to be near the end of pregnancy, her epidermal condition meant that she was beginning her pre-egg-laying shed.

From this, a tentative copulation date sometime in mid-May could be deduced, using the gestation period of the Mexican racer's numerous subspecies. In addition, counting ahead the usual 15 days from the beginning of her pre-laying shed to egg deposition would give an expected laying date of around July 10, and since captive *Coluber constrictor* incubation times are 50 to 65 days, this particular Mexican racer's hatchlings would probably have emerged sometime in early to mid-September. (An attempt was made to salvage and incubate her 13 fully formed and shelled eggs, but since they were still in the oviduct—where serpents' eggs are supplied with oxygen by their mother's respiration—by the time the eggs were removed all the embryos had suffocated.)

Coloring/scale form   Adult *C. c. oaxaca* have a mostly unmarked olive-gray back which is only slightly darker along the spine, although some individuals appear to have a dusky vertebral stripe. Their sides are a faintly paler gray-green, greenish-brown, or greenish-yellow. Some specimens show dark blue or black skin between their scales—colors that may also appear on the forward (attached) margins of the scales themselves.

The upper and lower labial scales, the chin, and the venter are pale yellow, often with a pronounced greenish tinge; a few individuals have yellowish-pink throats. There are usually 8 upper labial scales.

Unlike the young of other racers, which generally have rounded brown vertebral saddles, juvenile *C. c. oaxaca*—which are tan to buff in ground color—are marked with jagged-edged dark bands across the forward part of their backs (these bands fade or disappear posteriorly). Brown flecks are scattered over their sides, while both the crown and the posterior back are grayish brown.

Similar snakes   The **eastern yellow-bellied racer (115)**, which to the northwest intergrades with the Mexican racer, is a slightly more robust race with 7 upper labial scales.

Behavior Mexican racers spend considerable time in shrubs and bushes, where their coloring serves as marvelous camouflage. They are alert to nearby movement and will often raise their heads above body level, apparently to better assess their circumstances. If approached, they may freeze, dart quickly away if touched, flee for several yards and then suddenly stop again—their lack of movement almost instantly blending their slim profiles into the surrounding foliage.

INDIGO SNAKES
Genus Drymarchon

Eastern Indigo Snake, *Drymarchon corais couperi*
Texas Indigo Snake, *Drymarchon corais erebennus*

Indigo snakes are large, racer-like, oviparous serpents whose genus, *Drymarchon,* first described by L. J. F. Fitzinger in 1843, is part of the colubrine subfamily *Colubrinae.* The classification of the single species within this genus is controversial, however, because some researchers believe the two races into which *Drymarchon corais* is divided are actually fully distinct species. (This is based on the long-term separation of their widely separated Florida and Texas ranges.) The author, however, continues to regard both eastern and Texas indigo snakes as races of a single species.

Both indigo snake subspecies are heavy-bodied reptiles that are good at defending themselves, partly because of their size: *Drymarchon corais* is among the largest colubrines (*archos* is Greek for "ruler"), and occasional individuals exceed 8 feet in length. In an impressive defensive display, provoked individuals may vibrate their tails noisily, hiss, flatten their necks vertically and bite vigorously with strong jaws that can produce deep lacerations.

Indigo snakes are also the widest-ranging terrestrial North American reptiles—behavior that brings them into conflict with people and their vehicles; faced with human population expansion, both races are in decline.

In the east, though the Florida race tends to be most active in moderately cool weather, it relies on the burrows of gopher tortoises for shelter; in the west, the similarly alert, fast-moving Texas indigo uses burrows vacated by armadillos to withdraw from both summer heat and winter cold.

The smooth, almost mirror-finished scales of both subspecies are arranged in 17 midbody rows and their anal plates are undivided.

117 EASTERN INDIGO SNAKE

Drymarchon corais couperi

Nonvenomous   First described by J. E. Holbrook in 1842, this beautiful reptile is perhaps the most spectacular of North American snakes. When encountered in the field, a large adult may hiss, vertically flatten its neck, and vibrate its tail in threat, but a majority of even the largest eastern indigo snakes allow themselves to be handled without aggression.

Abundance   Threatened. Federally protected since 1978, *D. c. couperi* is also legally protected by the state of Florida. Yet it is declining in numbers. In the past, collecting for the pet trade heavily impacted the eastern indigo snake population, but the most harmful factor in this animal's current ecological difficulty is deterioration of its habitat.

As an essentially tropical animal living at the northern limit of its biological capacity, *D. c. couperi* is unable to tolerate the winter freezes of northern Florida, Georgia, and Alabama without deep underground refuges. Due to the simultaneous decline of the gopher tortoise—also depleted by loss of habitat and commercial collecting—in whose burrows the eastern indigo formerly found shelter, such retreats are now very hard for it to find. (In addition, as Paul E. Moler of the Florida Game and Fresh Water Fish Commission has pointed out, the resinous wood industry's removal of thousands of the dead logging stumps beneath which indigos also found shelter has left these animals with greatly diminished opportunities to escape winter cold.)

Fragmentation of individual indigo snakes' home ranges is an even greater problem. Few indigenous serpents have suffered as much as *D. c. couperi* from the conversion of peninsular Florida's uplands to agriculture and residential subdivisions—where these big, unwary reptiles are quickly extirpated by landowners, dogs, and automobiles. Because of the eastern indigo snake's need for space—the warm-weather range of adults averages over 370 acres, with adult males covering even more territory on their breeding forays—to maintain a stable population this reptile requires larger areas of safe refuge than are available in most of the Southeast.

Nevertheless, Kevin Enge, who monitors the state's commercial reptile trade for the Florida Game Commission, says that to a limited extent

> Indigos are now making a comeback in some agricultural areas due to reduced collecting pressure: [reptile] hunters are seeing quite a few along . . . canefield irrigation canals.

Size Along with its similarly sized Texas subspecies, *D. c. couperi* is the largest nonvenomous snake in North America: adult males average 60 to 74 inches in length and 4 to 5½ pounds in weight; females average 60 to 72 inches and weigh about 3½ pounds. The record is 103½ in.

Habitat Although it was formerly numerous throughout the deep Southeast in environments ranging from grassy prairie to longleaf pine forest to coastal scrub to tidal mangrove swamp, *D. c. couperi* is now uncommon in even the richest natural habitats. Originally described by J. E. Holbrook in 1842, this subspecies' name honors James Hamilton Couper, who collected the type specimen in Georgia. Today, eastern indigo snakes appear most often in undisturbed pine flatwoods, brushy riparian corridors (including landowner-protected canal banks), sandhills, and wet prairie hammocks.

Adult eastern indigo snakes ordinarily only traverse the flooded saw-grass prairies of wetlands such as the Everglades when moving between elevated hardwood hammocks, but juveniles may prefer wetland edges to upland environments. Its microhabitat includes both tortoise and mammal burrows (including those of the nine-banded armadillo recently established in Florida), limestone solution holes, hollow logs, stump holes, and the deep cavities found beneath large live oaks and aged Australian pines.

Prey One of the few snakes large and active enough to be easily observed in its foraging, the eastern indigo patrols canal and pond banks, slides into and out of rodent burrows, then rapidly crosses open ground on its way to the next patch of cover. Prey can include any vertebrate big enough to attract its attention and small enough to be swallowed.

While not true constrictors, *Drymarchon* sometimes pin their prey to the ground with a muscular body coil, then immobilize it with bites from their powerful jaws. This tactic is effective in subduing even large pitvipers—whose venom seems to have no effect on the indigo—although more preferred prey is pig frogs and corn snakes, which even newly captured *Drymarchon* will often take directly from one's hands.

Reproduction Egg-laying. Breeding takes place in late fall and winter, when the territoriality of adult males waxes to the extent that they sometimes inflict 6-inch-long, razorlike fang cuts on each other's foreparts (copulation is almost as aggressive).

Like many other reptiles, female indigos retain sperm from these autumnal pairings until early spring fertilization. Following 70 to over 100 days of incubation, the 4 to 11 oblong whitish eggs (as much as 3 inches in length and 1⅓ inches in diameter, their leathery surface covered with fine pebbling) hatch into dorsally blotched young, 18 to 26 inches long.

Coloring/scale form   The adult eastern indigo's thick, blue/black dorsal scales are so glossy that, on newly shed individuals, they seem almost iridescent. Its chin and throat are usually russet, with reddish pigment sometimes extending onto the forebody, and occasionally a bit of white. Like their brownish Central American relatives, many individuals have dark facial striping. The venter exhibits a singular combination of cloudy orange and blue-gray.

Most of the 17 midbody rows of dorsal scales are smooth, but among *D. c. couperi*, scutellation is sexually dimorphic: as males reach sexual maturity at 55 to 60 inches in length they tend to develop partial keels on a few of their vertebral scale rows.

Similar snakes   The **eastern coachwhip (101)** is a much slimmer, longer-tailed snake with a two-toned, dark forebody–lighter posterior body color division, a cross-hatched tail, and a divided anal plate. The **southern black racer (108)** is also more slender and has 15 posterior scale rows and a divided anal plate.

Behavior   During the warmer months, the wide-ranging behavior of adult male *D. c. couperi* places them in jeopardy from encounters with human beings. In winter, both sexes maintain smaller ranges of less than 50 acres near residence dens where the same individuals, marked by clipping a subcaudal scale, have been recovered year after year.

Indigo snakes' dramatic appearance has created a huge demand for captives, but *Drymarchon* are much too restless to make a satisfactory adjustment to confinement. "Cage-trashers," as they are known by reptile-keepers, indigo snakes' high metabolism will not allow wild-caught individuals to settle into the lethargy that captivity requires, and these unfortunate animals tend to rub their snouts raw in constant efforts to pry out of their enclosures.

118   TEXAS INDIGO SNAKE

Drymarchon corais erebennus

Nonvenomous   A large adult *D. c. erebennus* is a strikingly beautiful animal when encountered in the field. Moreover, most individuals allow themselves to be handled without aggression— astonishing behavior in a reptile of the indigo's great size and power—for only rarely, when very warm and active, does one bite vigorously enough to inflict deep cuts.

Abundance   Threatened. Federally protected, and protected by the state of Texas. Despite receiving complete legal protection, the Texas indigo snake is slowly declining. The heavy collecting for the pet trade that formerly impacted the eastern indigo population has not occurred to a major extent with the Texas race, and this animal's current decline is almost entirely due to a loss of habitat.

The widespread conversion of its native terrain to agriculture has recently restricted *D. c. erebennus* to uncleared portions of South Texas' mesquite savannah and Tamaulipan thorn woodland, while another small population occupies desert terrain as far west as the eastern Trans-Pecos. (Here, Damon Salceies recently recorded a large adult in Sanderson Canyon, followed by D. Craig McIntyre's report of a vehicle-killed 2-foot-long adolescent in the same region, confirming at least sporadic breeding success by this lower Pecos River–area group).

Nevertheless, fragmentation of its home range by human incursion remains the central problems of the Texas indigo. Among adults, the requisite warm-weather hunting territory has been found to range up to hundreds of acres, and adult males cover even more terrain in search of receptive females. This means that only in the South Texas brush country and eastern Trans-Pecos is there enough non-human-occupied space to allow a viable population of these animals, for a breeding population's territorial needs are estimated at more than 2,500 acres.

Size   Along with its similarly sized eastern subspecies, *D. c. erebennus* is the largest nonvenomous snake in North America; individuals of the Texas race over 8½ feet in length are recorded.

Habitat   Although it occurs in environments ranging from grassy prairie to coastal sandhills to limestone-floored desert, *D. c. erebennus* is most plentiful in the thorn brush woodland and mesquite savannah of the coastal plain of southern Texas. Here, tree-filled riparian corridors constitute its favored habitat, while its microhabitat includes mammal burrows, especially those of armadillos. (These subterranean retreats are essential not only as protection from the brush country's host of large mammalian predators, but because in order to shed its skin the indigo snake requires a somewhat moist milieu—which in arid terrain it can find only in humid underground tunnels.)

Prey   In foraging, the Texas indigo moves rapidly through burrows and across the bare ground between patches of thorn thicket. It is a singularly unwary animal, and on these forays one can sometimes actually hear it sniffing for prey at the entrance of burrows, searching for any vertebrate big enough to attract its attention and small enough to be swallowed.

Not a true constrictor, *Drymarchon corais* typically seizes its prey with its jaws and, if it is not too large, thrashes it back and forth against the ground while biting its head. This tactic is effective in subduing even large pitvipers, to whose venom adult indigos seem to be immune (a rattlesnake seized at midbody by a big indigo will strike its assailant many times before being overpowered and swallowed).

The Texas indigo snake's preferred prey, however, is rodents—new captives immediately take rats—frogs, and nonvenomous snakes. A great many of these prey animals are taken, moreover: *D. c. erebennus* has such an active metabolism that warm and active adults may feed several times a week if prey is abundant, the young every 3 to 5 days.

Reproduction   Egg-laying. Breeding occurs in late fall, after which female indigo snakes retain sperm until early spring fertilization. (Sometimes, sperm are retained much longer: one female *Drymarchon* deposited fertile eggs after 4 years of isolation.)

Following 70 to over 100 days of incubation, the 4 to 11 pebbly surfaced, 3-inch-long, 1½-inch-wide eggs hatch into dorsally blotched young, 18 to 26 inches long. Sexual maturity is not reached until 3 years of age—the longest adolescence of any native serpent.

Coloring/scale form   The adult Texas indigo snake's dorsum is covered with big, predominantly smooth, glossy dark scales (both its species and subspecies names are drawn from the Greek for "black") that seem to have been freshly waxed. Even darker facial striping is evident on most individuals' slightly brownish foreparts. The venter is a cloudy, orange-mottled blue-gray; there are 17 midbody rows (14 on the posterior trunk) of generally smooth dorsal scales, though partial keels may occur on some of the vertebral scale rows of adult males.

Similar snakes   No other terrestrial serpent in southwest Texas has an entirely black back and sides.

Behavior   The Texas indigo snake is seasonally territorial. In spring and summer males roam for miles, but in winter both sexes remain near their residence dens, which they periodically leave during warm spells. (On their home terrain these animals seem to be familiar with every stick and bush, for if pursued they may make false runs in two or three different directions before doubling back toward their dens.)

Indigo snakes' dramatic appearance has created a demand for captives but, besides being illegal to capture, *Drymarchon* are so given to voiding musk and feces that handling them is usually an ordeal. Unlike arboreal snakes such as the boas, which are comfortable draped over one's limbs, the terrestrial indigo is ill at ease off the ground, and typically makes such efforts to be free of human contact that it is clear it should have been left in the wild.

SPECKLED RACERS
Genus Drymobius

Central American Speckled Racer, *Drymobius margaritiferus margaritiferus*

This tropical group of alert, fast-moving oviparous serpents—whose genus, *Drymobius*, is part of the colubrine subfamily *Colubrinae*—is represented in the United States by a single species restricted to the lower Rio Grande River valley. Its 17 rows of dorsal scales have apical pits and are weakly keeled along its spine, and its anal plate is divided.

Drymobius margaritiferus margaritiferus is also a uniquely colored snake: it has a flat black ground color, yet the spot of bright yellow on the center of each of its scales, coupled with a dab of blue on the scale's anterior edge, somehow gives a fast-moving individual (for these colors are most visible when the snake flexes its trunk) an almost glowing bluish-green cast.

119 CENTRAL AMERICAN SPECKLED RACER, *Drymobius margaritiferus margaritiferus*

Nonvenomous Its rarity and restricted habitat—as well as its speed and shyness—ensure that the Central American speckled racer seldom encounters human beings. If cornered, however, it is so agile that avoiding a nip is difficult.

Abundance **Endangered. Protected by the state of Texas.** The only member of its mostly tropical genus to inhabit the United States, *D. m. margaritiferus* reaches the northern limit of its range in the southernmost tip of the Rio Grande valley. Here, in Texas' Cameron and eastern Hidalgo counties, it is among the rarest reptiles in the country.

Size Most adults are 30 to 40 inches in length; the record is 50 in.

Habitat From southern Texas to the Yucatan Peninsula, *D. m. margaritiferus* occupies dense thickets or palm groves whose layered floor of decaying fronds is undisturbed, especially those near freshwater where its amphibian prey is plentiful. Because little of this native woodland is left north of the Rio Grande, the Central American speckled racer's continued existence here is in doubt, but among the few places it can sometimes still be found is the Audubon Society's 60-acre Palm Grove Sanctuary and the stands of Texas palms that remain in Cameron Couny Riparian woodland near Brownsville, as well as brushy Hidalgo County creekbeds have also been noted as habitat. See **Ruthven's Whipsnake.**

Prey Central American speckled racers are diurnal predators which most often feed on anurans: on a jungled Mexican riverbank, the author found a large *Drymobius* by following the shrill cries of a frog held in its jaws.

Reproduction Egg-laying. Between April and August Central American speckled racers typically deposit clutches of 2 to 8 non-adhesive, smooth-shelled eggs approximately 1⅛ inches in length by ⅝ inch in diameter. For the size of the parent, these are rather small, and after an incubation of some 8 weeks, their hatchlings are only 6 to 7 inches long.

Coloring/scale form The vividly patterned dorsum of *Drymobius margaritiferus* is evocative of oriental lacquer work: each dark dorsal scale bears a yellow-white, dart-shaped spot, a bluish margin near its anterior base, and a black perimeter. Hans Schlegle, who named this snake in 1837, described this patina of glossy dots by combining the Latin *margarita*, or "pearl," with *ferre*, which means "to carry." ("*Drymobius*" is Greek, and means "of the forest.")

The lower sides are yellowish-green, the neck washed with turquoise, and a black stripe runs from the eye across the posterior lemon-yellow labial scales—the sutures of which are edged with black.

Compared to adults, the young are even more vividly colored, for their pale yellow spots are larger in proportion to the size of their scales, although their backs are often overlaid with dark vertebral blotches or crossbands. Both adults and juveniles have greenish-yellow bellies, with ventral scales whose trailing edges are bordered, beneath the tail, with black.

Similar snakes No other snake within its U.S. range resembles the Central American speckled racer.

Behavior   In Southern Mexico, Guatemala, and Belize, *Drymobius margaritiferus* is abundant in thickly vegetated riparian milieus, where it constantly searches damp places for prey. In these countries speckled racers are also seen in both open savannah and woodland, as well as in overgrown fields and even village backyards.

BROWN-BLOTCHED TERRESTRIAL SNAKES

HOG-NOSED SNAKES
Genus Heterodon

Eastern Hog-nosed Snake, *Heterodon platirhinos*
Southern Hog-nosed Snake, *Heterodon simus*
Plains Hog-nosed Snake, *Heterodon nasicus nasicus*
Dusty Hog-nosed Snake, *Heterodon nasicus gloydi*
Mexican Hog-nosed Snake, *Heterodon nasicus kennerlyi*

This unusual group of oviparous, thick-necked serpents has so many bizarre habits, physical structures, and patterns of musculature that the genus *Heterodon* has been considered for classification as a separate family, apart from other colubrids. Currently, though, this genus remains classified in the colubrine subfamily *Xenodontinae*. All *Heterodon*, a term which means "different-toothed," are characterized by the enlarged teeth in the rear of the upper jaws, as well as by saliva which contains mild toxins.

Hog-nosed snakes are stout for their length, have a moderately to prominently upturned, dorsally keeled rostral scale, 23 to 25 rows of strongly keeled body scales, and a divided anal plate. In the United States, *Heterodon* cosists of three species, with only *H. nasicus*, the western hog-nose species, being divided into different races. Hog-nosed snakes tend to be active by day, but during the hottest weather the western hog-nose, which generally inhabits open, less-shady environments, switches to crepuscular or nocturnal foraging. The two more easterly species, *H. platirhinos*, the eastern hog-nose, and *H. simus*, the southern hog-nose, are specialist feeders on toads, while the western hog-nosed snake races also feed on lizards and small rodents.

The most distinctive behavioral attribute of *Heterodon*, however, is this genus' characteristic defensive strategy. Engaged in most often by the eastern hog-nose, a threatened individual may huff and puff, flatten its head like a viper and bluff-strike. Or it may spread its body, writhe, and if severely distressed, open its mouth to loll out its tongue and roll onto its back as if dead. At this point, nothing will make a hog-nose show any sign of life except turning it right side up, when it typically rolls upside down again.

120 EASTERN HOG-NOSED SNAKE

Heterodon platirhinos

Very mildly venomous, but harmless. *Heterodon platirhinos* has a pair of small, lance-shaped rear teeth, but these are located too far back in its mouth to be used in defense. Despite the threatening, viper-like gestures of its defensive behavior—which have given rise to the common name "spreading adder"—the eastern hog-nosed snake is harmless to humans.

Abundance Common. The eastern hog-nosed snake may be locally abundant in almost any area which favors its anuran prey (in most cases this means heavy ground cover and the moist, sandy soil in which both toads and hog-noses like to burrow) within its enormous and complexly bordered range.

For example, *H. platirhinos* is fundamentally an animal of both southeastern and midwestern woodland and most of the southeastern Great Plains. But along the western edge of the plains, as the easterly tall-grass prairie is replaced by its arid, short-grass counterpart, from almost the Mexican border to the Canadian this hog-nosed snake's territory extends upstream along the riparian corridors of a dozen or so rivers: Texas' Nueces, Colorado, Red, and Canadian; Nebraska's North and South Platte; the Missouri; and to the northwest, the Mississippi and its tributaries as far as northern Minnesota.

These riparian habitat extensions give the western boundary of *H. platirhinos*' range an intricate, multi-fingered configuration, while to the north, a series of broader territorial extensions reach into northern Minnesota, Michigan, and Manitoba. Another northward-extruding edge of the eastern hog-nose's range runs along the old glacial-boundary moraines that define the northern limit of the southern hill country, traversing central Indiana, Illinois, Ohio, Pennsylvania, and southern New England. The rest of the Southeast, to the Atlantic and western Gulf coasts, is populated with local groups of *H. platirhinos*.

Size   Adults are usually 20 to 33 inches in length; the record is 45½ in.

Habitat   *Heterodon platirhinos* inhabits a variety of usually sandy-substrate terrestrial environments, especially mixed hardwood and upland pine forest and forest/grassland boundaries. For some reason, these animals often turn up in recently disturbed areas such as flood-cut riverbanks.

Prey   This scent-hunting predator of amphibians locates the bulk of its prey beneath leaf litter and even layers of soil by their odor, then roots them out with the upturned, plowshare-like rostral scale for which it is named: in Greek, *platirhinos* means roughly "spade-nosed." Most of this prey is toads, which are abundant and unwary largely because few other predators can tolerate their toxic skin secretions. *Heterodon platirhinos* has become such a predatory specialist on toads, however, that it has evolved a refined set of adaptations that allow it to feed almost exclusively on these plentiful anurans.

Adaptations which help the eastern hog-nose physically overcome toads include enlarged posterior teeth hinged to the maxillary bone at the rear of its upper jaw. (After its flexible lower jaw has partially engulfed a toad and maneuvered it as far back into the mouth as possible, the hog-nose swings these long upper teeth forward to puncture the amphibian's swollen torso, for toads are themselves behaviorally adapted to ballooning their bodies with air to make themselves too large to swallow.) Through these puncture wounds the hog-nose introduces its stringy, opalescent saliva, whose neurotoxins soon leave a toad too limp to continue its struggle.

Another adaptation deals with metabolizing the amphibian's bufotoxin, heart-suppressing digitaloid compounds excreted by the toad's epidermal glands. To offset their effect and maintain its proper heart rate, *H. platirhinos* has developed huge adrenal glands, ¼ by 2 in. long in large adults, with a weight 10 times heavier, in proportion to their bodies, than the adrenals of other snakes.

Frogs are also a principal food of *H. platirhinos*, and lizards may occasionally be taken; in captivity hatchling hog-noses will accept crickets. This reptile also readily scavenges carrion (the author has seen an eastern hog-nosed snake trying to pull a road-killed leopard frog from the pavement), but since this species is disinclined to take the domestic mice that most captive snakes are fed, *H. platirhinos* was seldom maintained in confinement until it was discovered that many could be enticed to feed on mice by rubbing the rodents against a toad to impart its scent.

Reproduction   Egg-laying. Mating occurs March through May, followed by deposition of 4 to 61 (average 22) eggs in mid- to late summer. The eggs are 1¼ by ¾ inches, and they are more rounded in shape than those of most serpents. Hatchlings measure 6½ to 9½ inches in length and, in an unusual developmental pattern, typically experience their first shed while still in the process of emerging from the egg. See **Southern Hog-nosed Snake.**

Coloring/scale form *Heterodon platirhinos* varies enormously in dorsolateral coloring: individuals can have a khaki-green, yellowish-, or reddish-brown ground color, elaborately patterned with almost any combination of darker spots and splotches. Some eastern hog-nosed snakes are entirely black, but most individuals are yellowish in ground color, blotched with darker brown. (As *H. platirhinos* ages, many undergo an ontogenetic color change in which their bold juvenile patterning darkens so much that older adults are almost entirely dusky.)

Whatever its age or coloring, the eastern hog-nose almost always has a big, characteristic, darker blotch just behind its jaw, however—a blotch which extends posteriorly along the sides of its neck—and among all color morphs the underside of the tail is much lighter than the (occasionally orange-blotched) gray belly.

Yet because of this reptile's variability, it may be best to identify *H. platirhinos* by its configuration: stocky trunk, short head scarcely distinct from its wide neck, and upturned, pointed snout backed by a raised keel and flanked by sharp-edged labial ridges. Behind this turned-up rostral scute, the prefrontal scales touch and a prominent bulge over its little dark eyes is emphasized by a brown band that masks its forecrown.

Similar snakes The **southern hog-nosed snake (121)**, which shares the southeastern part of the eastern hog-nose's range, has a more markedly upturned rostral scute, its prefrontal scales are separated by smaller scales, and the underside of its tail is the same pale color as the rest of its venter. The westerly ranging **plains (122), dusty (123),** and **Mexican (124) hog-nosed snakes** have a sandy ground color more or less uniformly patterned with brown dorsolateral spots; their bellies and undertails are heavily pigmented with black. **Copperheads' (174–178)** dorsolateral bands completely cross their backs and sides; their slender, pitviper's neck is much narrower than their flat-crowned heads, while a dark pit is visible between the nostril and the large, pale, vertically slit-pupiled eye.

Behavior The strongly keeled dorsolateral scales of *H. platirhinos* give it tank tread-like traction to root through the earth, using its muscular trunk and wedge-like snout like a small plow to force loosened soil to the sides. In the open, this animal's deliberate pace makes it an easy target for predators, and in defense it has developed elaborate death-feigning behavior. This usually initially entails spreading its long nuchal ribs to flatten its neck into an approximation of a venomous serpent's foreparts (one common name is "spreading adder"), hissing, and making feinting pseudo-strikes.

Except that the hog-nose strikes with its mouth closed. In fact, unless one has recently handled a toad, even prodding its snout with a finger won't prompt *H. platirhinos* to bite.

If its antagonist persists, the hog-nose may conceal its head under its tightly spiraled tail and, presumably to make itself unappealing as a meal, it may then writhe convulsively, regurgitate, defecate, discharge musk from its cloaca, and turn belly-up, its tongue hanging loosely from its slackened jaw. If placed right side up some eastern hog-noses will even flop back over into their death-pose, righting themselves only after the danger has passed.

121   SOUTHERN HOG-NOSED SNAKE

Heterodon simus

Very mildly venomous, but harmless to humans. If threatened, *Heterodon simus* may hiss, flatten its head and neck, or occasionally feign death, but it does not bite humans.

Abundance   Uncommon to rare. Protected only in Alabama and Mississippi, *Heterodon simus* is occasionally locally common, but throughout the majority of its broad southeastern range (along both Gulf and Atlantic coastal plains from Mississippi to North Carolina), it is not an abundant animal.

Similar in its size, dorsal pattern, and strongly upturned rostral scale to the western hog-nose species, *H. nasicus*, the southern hog-nose is a relictual member of an ancient xeric-community fauna. (During glacial advances, when much of North America's freshwater was locked up in ice, this group of arid terrain–adapted animals occupied a dry, low-lying corridor that stretched along the northern Gulf of Mexico from the desert Southwest to the Florida peninsula).

Size   The smallest of the three North American *Heterodon*, adult southern hog-noses average only 20 to 21 inches in length, with females being slightly larger than males. The record is 24 in.

Habitat   The southern hog-nosed snake's old, desert dweller's orientation to silicaceous soil is still evident in its abundance in sandhill terrain—the only place it occurs in greater numbers than the generally more numerous and widespread eastern hog-nose.

In Florida and along the coast of Georgia and the Carolinas, another unique habitat is stabilized coastal sand dunes.

Inland, open scrub-brush is inhabited sporadically throughout the Southeast while (perhaps because it may be more fossorial than other hog-nosed snake species) *Heterodon simus* also appears in bulldozed, flood- or storm-ravaged terrain where sandy subterranean soil has been exposed.

Prey   Southern hog-nosed snakes are even more narrowly focused predators on toads and frogs than the eastern hog-nose: their principal prey species are spadefoot, southern, and oak toads, though lizards and small mammals are also occasionally taken. Bill Griswold of Spring Hill, Florida, an authority on these snakes, reports that in captivity squirrel- and green tree frogs, as well as mice scented with anuran skin secretions, are also accepted.

Reproduction   Egg-laying. No natural nests have been reported, but Griswold's records of captive reproduction among both *H. platirhinos* and *H. simus* document that courtship among southern hog-nosed snakes begins in early spring with the male nudging and caressing the female with his rostral scale. Copulation—which entails an extremely large hemipenal bulge and can last up to 3 hours—begins mid- to late-April and, unlike most other southeastern colubrids which breed between March 1 and early May, continues intermittently until August.

Among *H. simus*, the clutches of 6 to 14 (average: 8) non-adherent eggs are deposited between July and late September and, after 55 to 60 days of incubation in moist vermiculite, hatch into 6- to 7-inch-long young. Unlike eastern hog-nose neonates, which shed as they emerge from the egg, newborn southern hog-noses do not shed until they are 3 to 5 days old.

Coloring/scale form   Unlike the eastern hog-nose, most *Heterodon simus* are similar in dorsal color and pattern. Dark vertebral blotches are separated by smaller pale orange blotches on a yellowish-brown ground color; the tail is light- and dark-banded. Unlike the eastern hog-nosed snake, its undertail is the same sandy-gray hue as the anterior belly.

The prominent rostral scale is sharply upturned (*Heterodon* are anything but "hog" nosed), the prefrontal scales are separated by smaller scutes, and the keeled dorsal scales are usually arranged in 25 rows at midbody.

Similar snakes   The **eastern hog-nosed snake (120)** has a smaller and less upturned rostral, its prefrontal scales touch, the underside of its tail is a distinctly lighter gray than its dark venter, and it occurs in a host of colors (including mottled olive green, orange-brown, and black) not found among southern hog-nosed snakes. Many people mistakenly kill southern hog-nosed snakes, thinking they are **pygmy rattlesnakes (182–184)**. Besides having a small rattle, the pygmy rattler is grayish- or reddish brown, with a russet vertebral stripe and the characteristic pitviper configuration of narrow neck, flat crown, and dark pit between its nostril and large, slit-pupiled eye.

Behavior   Most active during early summer in early morning and evening when toads are abroad, the southern hog-nose is able to scent out anurans hidden beneath ground cover. Then, with its upturned rostral tool (*simus* is Latin for "upturned"), *H. simus* roots them from their buried nooks. Griswold reports that his captives refuse food during winter even when not in brumation, so between Thanksgiving and Valentine's Day he induces dormancy by keeping them at a constant temperature of 50 to 60°F.

122   PLAINS HOG-NOSED SNAKE

Heterodon nasicus nasicus

Very mildly venomous.   *Heterodon nasicus nasicus* does not ordinarily bite humans—its defensive behavior includes imitation strikes made with the mouth firmly shut. However, if it does happen to clamp onto a human finger (the only place it can gain a biting surface) either subspecies of western hog-nose may hang on with determination. One such bite, which occurred during the spring of 2002 to Joe Monahan, involved, after the snake had chewed on his finger for several minutes, a slight anti-coagulant effect, followed by mild swelling and numbness that after several hours reached almost to his elbow. No permanent damage occurred, however.

Abundance   Uncommon. *H. n. nasicus* is widely dispersed across a huge swath of short- and mixed-grass prairie on the western Great Plains. In a roughly 200-mile-wide north-south section reaching from southern Saskatchewan and Alberta to the Texas panhandle (south throughout central Trans-Pecos Texas this animal intergrades with the Mexican hog-nose) the plains hog-nosed snake occurs in mostly localized populations and appears to be nowhere abundant.

Size   Adults are some 15 to 25 inches long; the largest specimen on record, a male from Hale County, Texas, measured 35¼ in.

Habitat   The plains hog-nosed snake's macrohabitat is short- and mixed-grass western Great Plains prairie. Yet within this sweep of open, arid grassland, *H. n. nasicus* is most often found in broken terrain where canyons or large draws provide at least seasonal water, gravelly or sandy soil which allows burrowing, and leaf litter or ground cover where both this hog-nose and its prey can shelter.

Prey   See **Dusty Hog-nosed Snake.**

Reproduction   Egg-laying. Reproduction is similar to that of the dusty hog-nose, but the shorter foraging season of this race's more northerly range makes it more difficult for females to build the fat reserves necessary for annual pregnancy. Since many female *H. n. nasicus* examined in mid-summer are not gravid, for example, much of the population may breed only in alternate years.

This makes contact between males and the only periodically fecund females unusually important. But since hog-nosed snakes winter in scattered, solitary denning niches, males have less access to females than do communally wintering serpents, and during the first weeks after springtime emergence they must wander widely in search of mates. (Another brief period of copulation occurs in the fall, with spermatozoa from these pairings remaining viable in the female's cloaca throughout the winter.)

Coloring/scale form   The plains hog-nosed snake's sandy ground-colored back is marked with more than 35 brown dorsal blotches between snout and vent in males, more than 40 blotches in females. (Males can be identified by their thicker-based tails.)

Its sides are patterned with both large brown spots and similarly colored dots and speckles. The prominent brown band, or mask—typical of *Heterodon*—through the eyes and across the forehead is present, as is the western hog-nose's characteristic big darker brown nuchal blotch that reaches from the rear of the crown back onto the sides of its neck. (A few individuals—which may or may not be partial intergrades with the much differently marked Mexican hog-nose—with almost unmarked dorsums have been found in Val Verde County, however.)

Sections of the plains hog-nosed snake's mostly coal-black belly are edged with white, yellow, or pale orange, there are 9 or more small azygous scales separating the prefrontal plates of its forecrown, and there are 23 midbody rows of dorsal scales.

Similar snakes   Across the southwestern boundary of its range, the plains hog-nose intergrades with its southerly subspecies, the **dusty hog-nosed snake (123)**. In pure form, this race has fewer than 32 medium-sized brown dorsal blotches between snout and vent in males, fewer than 37 in females; like the plains hog-nose, there are 9 or more small azygous scales separating the prefrontal plates of its forecrown. Another subspecies, the **Mexican hog-nosed snake (124)**, with which the plains hog-nose intergrades sporadically throughout the central Trans-Pecos, is marked like the dusty race, but has an orange-bordered black belly and no more than 6 azygous scales between its prefrontal plates. (Jim Costabile, an authority on these snakes, reports that in Texas' northern Brewster and Jeff Davis counties all three subspecies' populations appear to intersect, with individuals typical of each form turning up only a few miles apart.)

Behavior   Field studies of *H. n. nasicus* in central Kansas show it to be most active morning and evening, sheltering at night and during cold weather by burrowing into sandy soil; on the surface it is often found submerged in leaf litter.

123   DUSTY HOG-NOSED SNAKE

Heterodon nasicus gloydi

Very mildly venomous, but harmless to humans.   *Heterodon* means "different-" or "multiple-toothed," in reference to this genus' combination of conventional anterior teeth and hinged upper rear fangs. Although mildly toxic to its small mammal, lizard, and amphibian prey, the seromucous parotid gland secretions in the saliva of *H. nasicus* pose no danger to humans because the tips of its long rear teeth lie so far back in the throat that they cannot be used for defense.

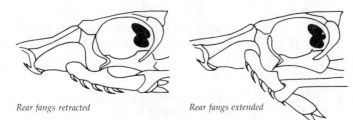

Rear fangs retracted   *Rear fangs extended*

Abundance Uncommon. *Heterodon nasicus gloydi* occurs in widely separated populations scattered throughout three distantly disjunct ranges. The largest of these separate ranges is a stretch of open prairie grassland that extends from Texas' Pecos River northward through Oklahoma into Kansas. A second range, quite different in habitat, encompasses the scattered woodland and bottomland pasture and crop fields along the Brazos River and its tributaries from the Gulf Coast inland almost as far as Texas' Edwards Plateau. A third entirely separate range, but one with a biotic community similar to that of the Brazos valley, is the mixed pasture and woodland of northeastern Texas.

Size Most adult dusty hog-nosed snakes are 17 to 25 inches; the record is nearly 3 feet.

Habitat *Heterodon nasicus gloydi* occupies a geographically diverse assortment of mostly sandy-soiled habitats: shortgrass prairie, grassy areas in rocky semi-desert, and pasture/pine/hardwood forest interface. On the upper coastal islands the dusty hog-nose lives both on salt-grass prairie and dunes and in residential areas.

Prey A generalized feeder, mainly on small mammals, *H. n. gloydi* is also reported to prey on amphibians, lizards, and smaller snakes—all subdued by its parotid salival secretions—as well as on reptile eggs and the young of ground-nesting birds. Carrion is also occasionally eaten.

Reproduction Egg-laying. Despite the long foraging season of this race's southern range, there is evidence that breeding may occur primarily in alternate years. Deposited between early June and August, the 4 to 23 eggs hatch after 52 to 64 days into young 6 to 7½ inches in length; sexual maturity is reached at 18 to 24 months.

Coloring/scale form In 1952 R. A. Edgren divided the western hog-nosed snakes—all of which have buff ground-colored backs blotched with big brown dorsal spots and smaller brown lateral patches—into the 3 subspecies recognized today. The dusty hog-nose race, *Heterodon nasicus gloydi*, is named for Howard K. Gloyd, author of *The Rattlesnakes, Genera Sistrurus and Crotalus*. It has fewer than 32 medium-sized brown dorsal blotches between snout and vent in males, fewer than 37 in females. (Males can be identified by their thicker-based tails.) This race's predominantly black belly has scattered yellowish-white blotches, it has 9 or more small azygous scales separating the prefrontal plates of its forecrown, and there are 23 midbody rows of dorsal scales.

Similar snakes The subspecies **plains hog-nosed snake (122)** (with which the dusty hog-nose intergrades in the northern part of its range) has more than 35 slightly smaller dorsal blotches in males, more than 40 in females and, like the dusty hog-nose, 9 or more small azygous scales separating the prefrontal plates of its forecrown. Another subspecies, the **Mexican hog-nosed snake (124)** is dorsolaterally marked like the dusty hog-nose but has an orange-bordered black belly and no more than 6 azygous scales between its prefrontal plates. The **eastern hog-nosed snake (120)** never has a pale tan ground color broken only by small brown vertebral and lateral splotches; its undertail is always much lighter in hue than its unmarked dark gray venter.

Behavior   See **Plains Hog-nosed Snake.**

124   MEXICAN HOG-NOSED SNAKE

Heterodon nasicus kennerlyi

Mildly venomous, but harmless.   See **Dusty Hog-nosed Snake.**

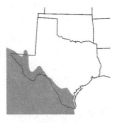

Abundance   Uncommon in pure form. *Heterodon nasicus kennerlyi* was formerly thought to occupy two widely separated parts of Texas: a primary range on the southern Gulf Coast and lower Rio Grande plain and a secondary habitat encompassing the state's Trans-Pecos region. Now, however, it appears that in the central part of the Trans-Pecos the Mexican hog-nose is replaced by its northern subspecies, the plains hog-nosed snake, *Heterodon nasicus nasicus*. Intergrades between thsee two races occur throughout the remaider of the region, with the Mexican form predominating in southwestern Presidio County (To further complicate the genetic picture, the hog-nose snakes living north of Alpine and Marathon and south of Interstate 10 appear to constitute a three-way intergrade population between the Mexican hog-nose, the more northerly plains race, and the eastern dusty hog-nose.)

In contrast, in the mesquite savannah and Tamaulipan thorn brush of South Texas the pure form of *Heterodon nasicus kennerlyi* is widespread but—perhaps because of its semi-fossorial lifestyle—seldom seen. Here, most records are of individuals found during damp weather in May and June, then again in September; at these times, over the course of a few days several individuals may turn up in places where no others have been seen for months.

Size   See **Plains Hog-nosed Snake.**

Habitat   In South Texas, Mexican hog-nosed snakes occur most often in grassland, including both inland pastures punctuated with mesquite and prickly pear and the drier milieu of grass-covered coastal sand dunes. Another, less-frequented habitat is the region's thorn woodland, where *H. n. kennerlyi* is frequently found near arroyos or watercourses where its anuran and small rodent prey is likely to be found.

Intergrades between the Mexican and plains hog-nosed snakes are most often found in the Trans-Pecos, in the shortgrass prairie of Presidio, and northern Brewster and Jeff Davis counties, although *H. n. kennerlyi* has occasionally been found in rocky, desert-like terrain along the Rio Grande.

Prey   See **Dusty Hog-nosed Snake.**

Reproduction   See **Dusty Hog-nosed Snake.**

Coloring/scale form   Coloring is somewhat similar to that of other western hog-nosed snake subspecies, but darker dorsally, with larger, chocolate-brown vertebral and lateral blotches. Prominent orange pigmentation occupies a good bit of the otherwise glossy black venter. In its genetically pure form, no more than 6 azygous scales separate the prefrontal plates of this race's forecrown.

Nevertheless, much of Texas' Trans-Pecos appears to be an intergrade zone for this animal, for while many individuals exhibit the dark dorsal color and pattern of the Mexican race, this is combined with the much smaller rostral of the plains hog-nose, the latter's only sparingly orange-marked venter, and the up to 10 small azygous scales that separate the prefrontal plates of the plains hog-nose's forecrown.

Similar snakes   A subspecies, the **dusty hog-nosed snake (123)** has fewer than 32 medium-sized brown dorsal blotches between snout and vent in males, fewer than 37 in females. (Males can be identified by their thicker-based tails.) In pure form, this race has 9 or more small azygous scales separating the prefrontal plates of its forecrown. Another subspecies, the **plains hog-nosed snake (122)**, has more than 35 slightly smaller dorsal blotches in males, more than 40 in females, and 9 or more small azygous scales separating its prefrontal plates. The **Mexican hook-nosed snake (145)** is a smaller serpent with 17 rows of dorsal scales and a shallow depression rather than a raised keel behind its tiny upturned snout.

Exhibiting almost the same dorsal coloring, size, and body shape as the Mexican hog-nose is the **desert massasauga (187)**; at night, in the beam of a flashlight, only by looking for the viper's rattle is it possible to tell at a glance which animal is at hand. (This is an interesting case of parallel habitat-selection, for this small pitviper shares both of the Mexican hog-nosed snake's widely separated ranges.)

Behavior Named for Caleb Kennerly, who collected the type specimen while medical officer of the 1855–60 Pacific Railroad Surveys, *H. n. kennerlyi* is fossorial for much of the year. Thus it is always a treat to come across a Mexican hog-nose on one of its sporadic forays, generally just before dark. Because this slow-moving little reptile is vulnerable on the surface to a host of predators—hawks and owls, bobcats, coyotes and foxes, raccoons, and bands of snake-eating javelinas—it is possible that the Mexican hog-nose is so adapted to the relative safety of fossorial life that it need not employ the defensive death-feigning of other hog-nosed snakes. Several individuals found by the author could not be induced to engage in this behavior even when first handled in the field.

PINE, GOPHER, AND BULL SNAKES
Genus Pituophis

Northern Pine Snake, *Pituophis melanoleucus melanoleucus*
Florida Pine Snake, *Pituophis melanoleucus mugitus*
Black Pine Snake, *Pituophis melanoleucus lodingi*
Louisiana Pine Snake, *Pituophis ruthveni*
Bullsnake, *Pituophis catenifer sayi*
Sonoran Gopher Snake, *Pituophis catenifer affinis*

Defined by John Edward Holbrook in 1842, the genus *Pituophis* means pine snake—*pitu* and *ophis* in Greek—a name which describes the pinewoods-living eastern species first seen by Europeans. A part of the colubrine subfamily *Colubrinae*, the members of this genus are large, oviparous snakes with heavily keeled dorsal scales and the ability to constrict powerfully. The rostral—the scale on the tip of the snout—is characteristically prominent among *Pituophis*, strongly convex, usually higher than it is wide, and extends upward between the internasal scales. All *Pituophis* covered here have four prefrontal scales; their dorsal scales are arranged in 29 or more rows at midbody, and the anal plate is undivided. (Despite having a somewhat different morphology, the genus *Pituophis* is closely related to rat snakes and kingsnakes, and captives of all three groups have interbred, producing viable, fertile young.)

Within this genus, pine snakes have proportionately narrow heads, while the heads of bull and gopher snakes are somewhat wider (it was long thought that there were but two species of *Pituophis*, the pine snakes, *P. melanoleucus*, and the bull- and gopher snakes, *P. catenifer* in the United States; the theory that the Louisiana pine snake, *Pituophis ruthveni*, is a separate species is now accepted by many authorities).

Because adult pine, bull- and gopher snakes are heavy-bodied and comparatively slow moving, when threatened they tend to rely on an assertive defense rather than flight. This most often entails a sort of mostly bluffing belligerence in which these species vibrate their tails like a pitviper, swell their necks and—helped by their unique glottal structure—hiss very loudly.

Although all *Pituophis* can climb, their lifestyle is primarily terrestrial (pine snakes are not arboreal, but take their name from the pine woods they inhabit). This genus' burrowing skill is essential to its pursuit of rodents such as the pocket gophers, on which some species are prey specialists, within their underground tunnels. Burrowing is also crucial to pine, bull- and gopher snakes' excavation of the deep subsurface chambers in which they deposit their relatively few, but comparatively large eggs (greater numbers of eggs are sometimes found in the same chamber since communal nesting is well documented among *Pituophis*). Hatchlings are correspondingly sizable, with some exceeding 20 inches as they emerge from their shells, and in late summer can be extremely numerous.

125   NORTHERN PINE SNAKE

Pituophis melanoleucus melanoleucus

Nonvenomous   Some northern pine snakes, surprised in the open, react so adversely to even a distant intruder that they draw attention to themselves by hissing and rattling their tails. (Air expelled from the lungs past a flap of tissue on the glottis produces the loud, wheezy hiss, while the distinct whirring sound they make—often mistaken for the caudal buzz of a rattlesnake—comes from vibrating their strong tails in dead leaves or grass.) If  closely approached, these animals may rear the anterior third of their body into an elevated "S" and strike, but their small heads and short teeth make *P. m. melanoleucus* a much less fierce adversary than its mostly bluffing defensive behavior would suggest.

Abundance Threatened. Although the northern pine snake is specifically protected as a threatened animal only by New Jersey and Tennessee, it is also protected in Georgia by that state's blanket prohibition against killing or capturing nonvenomous snakes. Perhaps always a spottily distributed animal, the northern pine snake occupies a range whose boundaries have always been something of a mystery. Despite the presence of a large historical human population over virtually all its territory, *P. m. melanoleucus* was not recorded in western North Carolina until 1946, in Alabama in 1955, and in western Tennessee in 1981. Today, it apparently exists primarily in relict populations scattered among pockets of residual habitat. (Among these sites are a Pine Barrens–living group which occurs far to the north in New Jersey, isolated colonies in north-central Virginia and central and western Kentucky.)

Size *Pituophis melanoleucus melanoleucus* is one of the largest eastern snakes: hatchlings are usually more than 18 inches long, and adults often attain 5½ feet. The largest individuals have been measured at more than 7 feet in length, with a proportionately heavier trunk than smaller specimens.

Habitat Its name notwithstanding, the northern pine snake is now a decidedly southern animal, with the majority of its remaining range falling below the Mason-Dixon Line. Here, *P. m. melanoleucus* is typical in sandy, well-drained upland pine or pine-oak woodland where it can burrow itself easily in loose soils, and is almost exclusively fossorial.

Prey *Pituophis melanoleucus melanoleucus* preys on a variety of small mammals and birds and their eggs (this subspecies is known to climb trees in search of birds' nests). Yet wherever its range overlaps that of the pocket gopher (*Geomys*), these burrowing rodents are its favored food; even neonates, which also take mice and lizards, are particularly attracted to pocket gophers, whose young they are big enough to eat.

Because pocket gophers almost never forage on the surface, hunting them means doing so in their underground warren of tunnels, where lack of space prevents the northern pine snakes from using its constricting coils. Instead, *P. m. melanoleucus* employs a specialized predatory technique, pressing rapidly through a series of *Geomys* burrows, forging past any gopher it encounters, then pinning the rodent against the wall of its tunnel with an arc of the pine snake's muscular trunk.

Reproduction   Most northern pine snakes produce 4 to 16 eggs per clutch (the record seems to be 27), but their eggs are so large that gravid females can develop an immense girth. The nesting burrow is typically dug into a sandy embankment, sometimes beneath boards or logs but usually not in a heavily shaded area. Clutches are deposited off the main tunnel in a side chamber hollowed from moist soil (some of these nest chambers may be used for years, since communal laying is well documented in this subspecies), where incubation lasts between 58 and 90 days. The 17- to 19-inch-long hatchlings have a paler ground color (rarely off-white or pale pink) than adults, with more sharply defined dorsolateral blotching.

Coloring/scale form   Within the Pine Barrens of New Jersey, *P. m. melanoleucus* is most contrastingly patterned by coloring reflected in its species name, *melanoleucus*, which is a combination of the Greek *melanin* for "dark" and *leukos* for "white." These northeastern Pituophis, the first to be seen be Europeans, may have a ground color that is nearly white, off-white, pale gray, yellowish or, rarely, reddish, marked with prominent dark brown, black, or charcoal-gray dorsal saddles. The posterior saddles contrast most sharply with the ground color, while the anterior third of the northern pine snake's body, especially its neck, is usually suffused with melanin. Both these saddles (which may contain some light-centered scales) and the similarly hued lateral spots are irregular in shape.

Among more southerly *P. m. melanoleucus* populations, ground color is likely to yellowish, with lighter brown dorsolateral blotches that contain more light-centered scales. Individuals from South Carolina are dingier yet, usually with an anterior suffusion of dusky or black pigment and still less-contrasting dorsolateral blotches, most of which contain light-centered scales.

The northern pine snake's crown, like that of most *Pituophis*, is distinctly lighter in color than the rest of the body; otherwise, its comparatively narrow head has some blackish pigment on the scale edges and tiny dark dots on the scales themselves. A dark brown or black interorbital line may also be present and, especially on southern specimens (among which the rostral scale is noticeably enlarged), dark pigment may appear on the sutures of the upper labial scales. The white, yellowish or, rarely, reddish, belly is unpatterned.

Similar snakes   **Eastern (120)** and **southern (121)** **hog-nosed snakes** are short, stout, and have a sharply upturned (rather than bulbous) rostral scale. **Yellow (135)** and **black (134) rat snakes** and the **corn snake (140)** have a divided anal plate, weakly keeled dorsal scales, and a more rounded snout.

Behavior   Because the northern pine snake is so secretive it is not yet known with certainty how rare it actually is, and how much of its apparent scarcity is due to its skill at remaining out of sight. Pine snakes are unquestionably the most fossorial of the East's large constricting serpents, however, and are poorly understood except in the Pine Barrens, where they have been studied extensively by Robert Zappalorti.

Although usually assumed to live only in old-growth forests, where its pocket gopher prey prevails, herpetologist Bart Bruno has recorded *P.m. melanoleucus* in disturbed habitat; one individual was found next to a peach orchard in Chesterfield County, South Carolina.

126   FLORIDA PINE SNAKE

Pituophis melanoleucus mugitus

Nonvenomous   Florida pine snakes are not likely to bite unless they are closely approached, when they may bite vigorously in self-defense. Before commercial sawmills moved into the deep South during the 1920s *P. m. mugitus* was common, and attracted written comment on both its formidable size and the dramatic display in which it rears its forebody off the ground while hissing loudly enough to be heard for yards. Although characteristic of all pine, bull-, and western gopher snakes, this aural threat is the source of the Florida pine snake's subspecies name, *mugitus*, Latin for "roar." See **Black Pine Snake: Behavior.**

Abundance   Rare. In Florida, *P. m. mugitus* is classified as a **threatened species of special concern,** while, like other nonvenomous reptiles, it is also protected in Georgia. According to herpetologist Robert Mount, it is also protected as a non-game animal in Alabama. As with other pine snakes, accurate population statistics are nonexistent. Even in favorable habitat pine snakes' retiring habits (rodent prey is captured in subsurface burrows, where these reptiles remain to digest their meal) allow the Florida pine snake to avoid contact with humans except when dispersing to new hunting areas or during males' annual search for females.

Nevertheless, it seems certain that Florida's rampant population growth has so fragmented the upland sandhill/pine/oak forest habitat once available to *P. m. mugitus* that it is now extirpated from much of its former range. See **Northern Pine Snake.**

Size   Most adults are 34 to 59 inches in length, but the record is 7½ ft.—a very sizable snake since *Pituophis* become proportionately more bulky with age.

Habitat   Florida pine snakes are more likely to inhabit open, pine-turkey oak woodland and abandoned fields than sandhill, scrub, or climax longleaf pine forest—the only other natural environments in which they regularly occur.

Prey   Like the northern pine snake, *P. m. mugitus* feeds on a host of mostly warm-blooded vertebrates. Its favored prey is pocket gophers, however, in whose underground colonies it has been found living, and where it even lays its eggs. See **Northern Pine Snake**.

Reproduction   See **Black Pine Snake**.

Coloring/scale form   Dorsal ground color is light tan, but dark pigment may obscure the margins of some of the anterior 25 to 31 dorsal blotches (juveniles have more distinctly blotched forebodies). The venter is gray, marked with varying amounts of black.

Similar snakes   See **Black Pine Snake**.

Behavior   In Richard Franz's northern Florida field study, *P. m. mugitus* had particularly large home ranges, with a mean size of 130 acres. Adult males utilized up to 247 acres—almost as much territory as that used by indigo snakes, the most wide-ranging of North American serpents. Franz's Florida pine snakes spent 85% of their time underground—mostly in gopher and tortoise burrows—but during droughts they moved into open areas adjacent to wetlands.

127   BLACK PINE SNAKE

Pituophis melanoleucus lodingi

Nonvenomous   When above ground (as is sometimes the case during the spring breeding season or after heavy rains) black pine snakes can be very adversarial and will not hesitate to bite if molested.

Abundance   Rare. *Pituophis melanoleucus lodingi* is one of the rarest of large eastern serpents. It was not formally described until 1924, by Frank Blanchard, who gave this race the name "lodingi" after Henry P. Loding, the collector who first presented this dark-hued southern pine snake to the scientific community. Even in the heart of its extremely restricted range in southwestern Alabama, southeastern Mississippi, and Washington Parish,

Louisiana, it is not common, but its apparent rarity may stem in part from the fact that the black pine snake's fossorial lifestyle means it is almost never encountered in the wild.

Nevertheless, this reptile's bold coloring, hardiness, and the ease with which it can be bred in confinement have led to its becoming a staple in the pet industry. Hundreds of baby black pine snakes are hatched each year by herpetoculturists, and it is quite possible that there are now more *P. m. lodingi* in captivity than exist in the entire wild population.

Size   Most adults measure 36 to 60 inches in length; the record is 89 in.

Habitat   Although they occasionally climb in search of nestling birds or eggs, pine snakes don't live in trees. Instead, most of the black pine snake's life is spent below ground, for these animals are fossorial residents of first- and second-growth longleaf pine forests and sandy-soiled pine and mixed hardwood communities. Here, like other *P. melanoleucus*, the black pine snake occupies stumpholes, rodent, armadillo, or gopher tortoise burrows, or excavates tunnels of its own making. These underground catacombs are used for hunting, summer refugia, and winter hibernacula—and, except during the spring breeding season when males may wander abroad in search of females, black pine snakes seldom if ever leave them.

Prey   Prey is primarily small vertebrates. Mice, birds and their eggs, reptile eggs, and young rabbits are reported as prey, but pocket gophers (*Geomys*) are pine snakes' principal, and favored, food species.

Reproduction   Little is known with certainty about the black pine snake's reproduction in the wild, except that copulation occurs in April and May, with 4 to 8 whitish eggs (almost the size of hen eggs) being deposited during June and July at the end of, or in chambers adjacent to, long subsurface tunnels. In September and October these hatch into 18- to 20-inch-long offspring.

Coloring/scale form   The adult dorsolateral color of this large, dramatically colored snake is an unmarked flat black. Its belly is whitish to dark gray, with scattered black pigment that becomes more profuse as the snake advances in age. (Intergrades with the Florida pine snake are usually very dark brown or gray above, and so suffused with black pigment toward the head that their anterior vertebral blotches are obscured.)

Like those of other pine snakes, hatchling *P. m. lodingi* are boldly blotched, and cannot be distinguished as to subspecies until they reach about 30 inches in length.

Similar snakes   Called pine snakes in the East, bullsnakes in the Midwest, and gopher snakes in the West, all members of the genus *Pituophis* are similar in body configuration, although the uniformly colored black pine snake departs from this genus' typical patterned dorsum. The **southern black racer (108)** is similarly colored, but is much more slender, has smooth scales with a satiny luster, and 2 prefrontals. The **eastern indigo snake (117)** also has but 2 prefrontals, 17 midbody rows (14 on the posterior trunk) of big, predominantly smooth, glossy black scales, an often partially russet-hued chin and a cloudy, orange-mottled blue-gray belly.

Behavior   Pine snakes are big, slow-moving terrestrial and subterranean foragers. During their rare forays above ground, they are ill-suited for either flight or concealment and, like other *Pituophis*, have instead evolved a dramatic tutelary display in which threatened individuals rear their forebodies off the ground and expend loud, threatening hisses.

The volume of this hiss is made possible by a unique physiological adaptation: at the base of its throat a flexible fin of cartilage protects the pine snake's glottal breathing tube from the passage of ingested prey, and during its monumental exhalations this flap buzzes loudly in the outgoing airstream.

128   LOUISIANA PINE SNAKE, *Pituophis ruthveni*

Nonvenomous   See **Northern Pine Snake.**

Abundance   **Endangered. Protected by the state of Texas.** In historical times the Louisiana pine snake's range was moderately large, and included most of west/central Louisiana as well as Texas' Big Thicket lowlands north of Harris County, Texas. Yet *Pituophis ruthveni* seems to have never been a common—or at least not commonly seen—animal, since its secretive subterranean life lets it avoid contact with humans.

But with the advent of large-scale timbering in this area's longleaf pine woodland, as well as the control of wildfires—which historically kept open the forest's interior savannahs where rodent prey was plentiful—*Pituophis ruthveni* lost most of its habitat. Louisiana pine snakes apparently suffered a radical decline in population, and until recently this species was known primarily from historical records and some 17 individuals preserved in museum collections. It was thought that only small populations of *Pituophis ruthveni* remained in existence, scattered throughout disjunct pockets of old-growth timber like the solitary stand in Wood County, Texas, where Neil Ford of the University of Texas at Tyler studied an isolated group of Louisiana pine snakes.

During the last three years, however, a federally funded study undertaken by Craig Rudolph of the Southern Forest Experimental Station has located more than a dozen additional specimens in East Texas and Louisiana National Forests and has begun to unravel the population dynamics of this very rare reptile.

Size Most adult Louisiana pine snakes are between 3 and 5 feet in length; the record is just under 6 ft.

Habitat Louisiana pine snakes don't live in trees: they are terrestrial/burrowing residents of Louisiana and East Texas' longleaf pine/hardwood forest. But as lumber industry–affiliated forest management has led to monoculture crops of slash pines for pulping into newspaper, this environment has become less suitable for the Louisiana pine snake's primary prey, the Baird's pocket gopher.

Prey Pocket gophers are such important prey to pine snakes that their population density is usually the most important factor determining the presence of *Pituophis ruthveni* in a climax forest. Pocket gophers have formidable defenses against predators; however, in order to feed on these rodents, the Louisiana pine snake has developed a pair of singular hunting techniques.

Unlike generalized ophidian predators like rat snakes, which are more tentative subsurface hunters, the Louisiana pine snake typically dives straight down gopher burrows. It has to move fast because gophers are rapid diggers and can quickly throw up a plug of dirt, blocking the burrow behind them. A creeping rat snake encounters a dead-end tunnel, but the pine snake, with its burrower's conical skull and muscular neck, is better adapted to overcome this defense: *P. ruthveni* observed in Rudolph's glass-walled subterranean chamber in Nacadoches promptly twisted their heads sideways and scooped this rapidly erected obstacle out of their path.

When the pine snakes' quarry was overtaken, since there was no room to constrict the gopher in the narrow confines of its tunnel, Rudolph reports *P. ruthveni* forcing past the gopher, pinning it against the side of its burrow and suffocating it with the pressure of a body coil.

Other recorded food animals include rodents and young cottontails as well as ground-nesting birds and their eggs, while the stomachs of three road-killed individuals examined in Louisiana contained only amphibian remains. *Pituophis ruthveni* drift-fence-trapped in Texas have contained no prey except for two that had fed on turtle eggs. (These animals were probably empty because they would have been unlikely to come to the surface except when moving from one feeding area to another, or during males' annual search for a female's pheromone scent.)

Reproduction   Egg-laying. Nothing is recorded for this race, but its reproduction is probably identical to that of other *Pituophis*. See **Bullsnake.**

Coloring/scale form   Fewer than 40 irregularly shaped chocolate dorsal saddles mark the posterior dorsal ¾ of most *P. ruthveni*, but a pair formerly maintained at the Lufkin Zoo varied markedly in coloring. The male, taken from the western edge of the range in the Angelina National Forest, had a light brown ground color, dark dorsal blotches and a black crossbarred tail, a grayish-tan crown, and a dark mask through its eyes and across its forehead. The female, no larger than the male although perhaps older, was captured in Newton County on the Louisiana border and was an almost uniformly brown serpent: her brownish dorsal mottling, which extended to both crown and tail, obscured almost all of her vertebral saddles and caudal bands.

Among a majority of Louisiana pine snakes the venter is creamy, with brown or black spots along its sides, the vertebral rows of the 28 or 29 midbody rows of dorsal scales are more heavily keeled than the lateral rows, and the slightly bulbous rostral scale is higher than it is wide.

Similar snakes   Called pine snakes in the East, bull snakes in the Midwest, and gopher snakes in the West, members of the genus *Pituophis* share similar configuration and ecology, yet their relationships are cloudy. The Louisiana pine snake's woodland habitat is certainly both geographically separate and ecologically distinct from the easternmost range of the bullsnake, *P. catenifer*, as is its smaller, lighter-skulled head and less heavily-scaled snout, and these animals seem to be validly different species.

An even larger geographic gap exists between the Louisiana pine snake's range and that of the three eastern races of *P. melanoleucus*, however. This, according to Steven Reichling (1995) along with the Louisiana pine snake's dissimilar dorsolateral coloring and lifestyle, indicates sufficient difference in their respective evolutionary trajectories to warrant classification of the Louisiana pine snake as the separate species *P. ruthveni*.

This volume's author disagrees in principle with division into species primarily by range map, and believes that until recent habitat alteration by Europeans, a single species of *Pituophis* may have occurred from the Atlantic to the Continental Divide—one which differed clinally in color, pattern, and configuration as one subspecies' range gradually merged with that of another. Yet the isolated locale and unique physiological characteristics of the Louisiana pine snake are sufficiently pronounced to support Reichling's separation of the Louisiana pine snake from the eastern races of *P. melanoleucus* races, leaving *P. ruthveni* as a probably valid distinct species.

Behavior Rudolf and his collegues have also documented the Louisiana pine snake's reliance on underground shelter to escape forest fires. Nine of his research group's transmitter-equipped *P. ruthveni*, all of them living in prescribed burn areas, avoided injury by retreating at the last minute into pocket gopher burrows. Three individuals that were observed as ground fires approached did not flee or respond in any way until flames were within a few feet, then rapidly sought burrow entrances, even when that meant moving toward the advancing fire.

129 BULLSNAKE, *Pituophis catenifer sayi*

Nonvenomous Named for Thomas Say—who collected the type specimen as chief zoologist on Major Steven H. Long's 1820s rocky mountain explorations—*Pituophis catenifer sayi* varies widely in temperament. Both because of the differences between individual snakes and variables such as temperature and hunger, some wild adults allow themselves to be picked up without distress while others rear their heads and forebodies into an elevated S-shaped curve, hiss, and attempt to bite. None will strike unless molested, however.

Abundance Very common. Along with the western diamond-backed rattlesnake, bull- and gopher snakes (the western race) are the most abundant large serpents in the Southwest, particularly in late summer when the year's neonates first appear.

If not as numerous in the northern part of its range, *P. c. sayi* is also common throughout most of an enormous swath of the Great Plains. This area stretches from the mouth of the Rio Grande to central Saskatchewan and Alberta—farther north than any other North American snake except two species of garter snakes, *T. sirtalis* and *T. radix*.

On an east-west axis, bullsnakes are found from roughly the historic western edge of the continent's eastern woodland—southern Minnesota and Wisconsin, central Illinois, northwestern Missouri and Oklahoma, and east-central Texas—to, in the southwest, the Pecos River and in the northwest, the Rocky Mountains' front range.

Size Most adult bullsnakes are from 4 to 6 feet in length, but *P. c. sayi* can grow much larger. The largest specimen ever taken is the 8-foot, 6½-inch-long Wichita County, Texas, giant captured by Dr. Robert Kuntz of San Antonio's Southwest Research Center.

Habitat One of the most widely distributed snakes of the central United States, *P. c. sayi* occupies every sort of mostly dry, open-country terrain from the sea-level Gulf coastal plain, along the western edge of the Great Plains—the foothills of the Rocky Mountians.

Prey *Pituophis catenifer sayi* feeds primarily on burrowing rodents, especially pocket gophers and ground squirrels. Although less fossorial than the eastern pine snakes, which live in much softer soils, the bullsnake's muscular neck, heavy skull, and enlarged rostral scale enable it to root through even gravelly strata in pursuit of these animals. Gophers are not helpless in such situations, however, and may push up a plug of soil to seal their tunnels behind them—sometimes successfully, for the author has seen a large bullsnake turn away from a burrow just backfilled by a frantically digging gopher. (This bullsnake's reluctance to dig may have been because, as a regular resident of the gopher colony, it may not have felt the need to press every predatory opportunity.)

In such situations, even a single *P. c. sayi* exerts a major predatory impact, and around crop fields where mice, cotton rats, or gophers proliferate an undisturbed population of bullsnakes can lower rodent numbers enough to eliminate the need for poisoning. Other prey, such as young rabbits and ground-nesting birds, are also usually warm-blooded, but the author has also observed other large snakes to be eaten opportunistically. Juveniles are reported to also take lizards, as well as insects.

Reproduction Egg-laying. Courtship involves males' springtime olfactory tracking along a female's pheromonal scent trace. Up to 24 eggs (the record number deposited by a robust, 6½-lb. female maintained by *Pituophis* enthusiast Jim Costabile) are deposited in loose soil during June and July.

These leathery, adhesive-shelled eggs, which measure from 2 to more than 3½ inches long, adhere to form a single large cluster. In late summer and early autumn the young appear in great numbers throughout the western plains, plateaus, and Rocky Mountain foothills (at up to 20 inches in length they are, along with neonate indigo snakes and diamond-backed rattlesnakes, the largest newborn North American serpents).

Coloring/scale form   Of native snakes, only *Pituophis catenifer* has a khaki-hued, brown-freckled crown much paler than its brown-blotched back. Patterned with more than 40 brown vertebral blocks, the bullsnake's back is very differently marked from its tail, where very dark brown crossbands stand out against a mustard ground color.

A slightly elevated transverse ridge—from which the bullsnake's common name is derived—crosses its forehead like the boss of a bull's horn; along it a dark band angles back through the eye and across the pale cheeks. This reptile's cephalic scalation is also unique: 4 small prefrontal scales back its enlarged rostral scale. Arranged in 29 to 37 rows (usually 33 at midbody), the dorsal scales have apical pits and are most strongly keeled along the spine, while the laterally speckled venter is off-white.

Similar snakes   The **Sonoran gopher snake (130)** is a slightly paler, perhaps faintly more reddish-brown-blotched subspecies whose rostral scale is a bit broader than that of the bullsnake (the bullsnake's rostral scale is narrower than it is wide). The Sonoran race intergrades with the bullsnake across Trans-Pecos Texas, ostensibly predominating genetically over most of this area.

Yet Terry Hibbitts, of the University of Texas at Arlington, reports finding that both sorts of rostral scales occur with about equal fre-

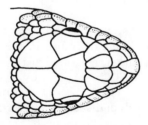

Prefrontal scales: bull, pine, and gopher snakes

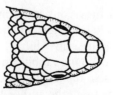

Prefrontal scales: glossy snakes

quency throughout the Trans-Pecos and everyone, including many herpetologists, still calls the *P. catenifer* living in this area bullsnakes.

The **Louisiana pine snake (128)** is darker and usually less distinctly patterned, with fewer than 40 non-rectangular vertebral blotches. Adult **Texas rat snakes (138)** have dark brown heads, 27 rows of dorsal scales, 2 prefrontal scales, and a divided anal plate. **Kansas (131)** and **Texas (132) glossy snakes** have a pale longitudinal line along their napes, a white venter, and 2 prefrontal scales.

Behavior   See **Sonoran Gopher Snake.**

130   SONORAN GOPHER SNAKE

Pituophis catenifer affinis

Nonvenomous   Some adults among this western race of *Pituophis catenifer* are docile and can be picked up without protest. Others assume a perfect replica of the pre-strike posture—raised forebody loop and lowered, flattened head, its posterior splayed wide to approximate a viper's triangular skull—characteristic of a large rattlesnake. See **Bullsnake.**

Abundance   Common throughout the western United States, *P. c. affinis* appears in Trans-Pecos Texas primarily as an intergrade with the more easterly ranging bullsnake.

Size   Most adults are between 3½ and 5 feet in length, although one very long, slender individual, found in the Davis Mountains by python breeder Dave Barker, measured just over 8 feet in length.

Habitat   The western Texas habitat of this subspecies includes short-grass prairie, shrub and succulent desert, and both barren and evergreen-wooded mountain slopes up to at least 7,000 ft. in elevation, where *P. c. affinis* has been found by the author.

Prey   This big snake's prey consists primarily of small burrowing mammals, especially pocket gophers and ground squirrels. In gopher and ground squirrel colonies, an adult *P. c. affinis* simply takes up residence in the burrows. Young rabbits and the eggs and nestlings of ground-living birds are also reportedly taken, and while other snakes are seldom mentioned as prey, the author has had this subspecies instantly devour an adult western black-necked garter snake with which it was momentarily placed in a collecting bag. Captive-born juvenile gopher snakes also take lizards and large insects.

Reproduction Egg-laying. C. M. Bogert and V. D. Roth (1966) report dominance rivalry among male Sonoran gopher snakes. In these contests, the combatant most successful in the pair's preliminary head-rearing skirmishes attempts to maintain its superiority by holding its forebody above that of its adversary for as much as an hour, from time to time dropping its anterior trunk onto the snake below. See **Bullsnake**.

Coloring/scale form Throughout eastern Trans-Pecos Texas, the Sonoran gopher snake intergrades with the **bullsnake (129)**. (In this area the gopher snake is lighter and sometimes very slightly more reddish in color; further west some individuals have a pinkish-tan cast, slightly more numerous rusty-brown vertebral rectangles, and a comparatively somewhat broader rostral scale.)

The Sonoran gopher snake's throat is white, shading to pale yellow at midbody; posteriorly, scattered dark spots tip the outer edges of its ventral scales. Like other *Pituophis*, four prefrontal scales border the rear of its enlarged rostral, and its 29 or more midbody rows of dorsal scales are heavily keeled, especially along the spine.

Similar snakes Of 15 Guadalupe Mountains *Pituophis catenifer*, 8 had comparatively taller, slightly narrower, bullsnake-type rostral scales, 5 were intermediate between the bullsnake and gopher snake, and 2 had the comparatively lower, broader rostral scale typical of the Sonoran gopher snake. See **Bullsnake**.

Behavior Diurnal as well as nocturnal, gopher snakes may be abroad at any hour. In the Trans-Pecos, where ground cover is sparse enough to observe a large snake's movements from a distance, the author has followed individual *P. c. sayi* for more than a quarter mile as they foraged across the desert. Most of the time these animals crept along slowly but deliberately. Foregoing lateral undulation in favor of energy-efficient concertina, or rectilinear, locomotion (inching the ventral scutes ahead in successive waves of belly-muscle contraction), they investigated every burrow and crevice by poking in their heads for up to thirty seconds, in what was probably a careful olfactory scrutiny, before proceeding on.

Because Sonoran gopher snakes cross roads with the same slow gait, they are vulnerable to being run over by traffic. Generally terrestrial, like its more easterly race, the bullsnake, *P. c. sayi* may scale trees both in search of nestling birds and as a last resort when pursued. Although generally diurnal, during hot weather gopher snakes may be active throughout the night.

GLOSSY SNAKES
Genus Arizona

Kansas Glossy Snake, *Arizona elegans elegans*
Texas Glossy Snake, *Arizona elegans arenicola*
Painted Desert Glossy Snake, *Arizona elegans philipi*

Arizona—a genus whose name means "dry land" due to this burrowing animal's preference for arid, sandy soils—is part of the colubrine subfamily *Lampropeltinae*. It contains but a single species, *Arizona elegans*, divided into several North American subspecies.

Glossy snakes are both oviparous and closely related to the pine, gopher, and bullsnakes. Like them, *A. elegans* has a relatively narrow head that is still distinct from its slender neck, but unlike these *Pituophis*, *Arizona* is characterized by the smooth, shiny dorsal scales from which its common name is drawn. These scales occur in as few as 25 or as many as 35 rows, there are two prefrontal scales and the anal plate is undivided.

Arizona elegans is an efficient burrower that emerges onto the surface only after dark to seek its prey of sleeping lizards and, sometimes, small rodents—both of which it may overcome by constriction. Although entirely nonvenomous, like both the pitvipers and the rear-fanged colubrids, in daylight, glossy snakes have semi-eliptical pupils—which in darkness enlarge to a circular shape.

131 KANSAS GLOSSY SNAKE
Arizona elegans elegans

Nonvenomous Large Kansas glossy snakes may bite if molested.

Abundance Uncommon. Like other glossy snake subspecies, the Kansas glossy's abundance seems to vary radically. In 1948, D. L. Jameson and A. C. Flury's exhaustive West Texas field work failed to yield a single Kansas glossy snake, yet *A. e. elegans* was more numerous than any other snake collected by Charles McKinney and R. E. Ballinger (1966) in the lower panhandle. In the shrub desert around the Guadalupe Mountains, an area included in Jameson and Flury's study that found this to be a rare snake, Frederick Gehlbach of Baylor University found Kansas glossies to be not uncommon.

Although Kansas glossy snakes are apparently unevenly distributed across their approximately 200 mile-wide range—which stretches from Texas' Big Bend to northern Kansas and northeastern Colorado—this subspecies' varying local abundnace is probably due more to its meteorologically determined above-ground forays than to a geographic or cyclical variation in its abundance. In fact, *A. e. elegans* may be both more fossorial and more common than the sporadic records of its presence would suggest, and in wet years it may even be common. During the summer rainstorms of 1999 these animals turned up throughout the southern Trans-Pecos where almost none had been seen in recent years.

Size   Slightly larger than other glossy snake races, adult *A. e. elegans* range from 20 to 47 inches in length.

Habitat   The Kansas glossy is a western plains and Northern Chihuahuan Desert subspecies whose habitat varies markedly. Throughout the drier parts of its range this animal is rarely found, and is equally uncommon in the intensively cotton- and sorghum-farmed Texas panhandle. Kansas glossy snakes are seen more often, however, in the better-watered, yet still sandy-soiled grasslands of north-central Texas, western Oklahoma, southern Kansas, and eastern Colorado.

Prey   While recent captives are somewhat more willing to feed on mice than are members of the more southerly Texas glossy snake race, the Kansas glossy snake's prey is, nevertheless, probably mostly lizards (kangaroo and pocket mice have been found in the same burrows as *A. e. elegans* and are likely to constitute at east intermittent prey).

Reproduction   Egg-laying. See **Texas Glossy Snake.**

Coloring/scale form   The Kansas glossy snake's definitive marking, like that of all *Arizona elegans*, is the pale vertebral line that runs along the neck just posterior to the skull (*elegans* refers to this animal's presumably elegant dorsolateral patterning). A brown band masks its eyes and crosses its cheeks, while its usual off-white dorsolateral ground color is off-white. This is marked, between snout and vent, by (41 to 69, average 55) large brown vertebral blotches with thin dark borders. (A slightly different color morph is reported by Abilene Zoo director Jack Joy, who has regularly found large Kansas glossy snakes with a faintly pinkish ground color and olive-brown dorsal blotches in Tom Green County, Texas.) Glossy snakes have uniformly white bellies, their smooth dorsal scales occur in 29 to 31 midbody rows, and there are 2 prefrontal scales.

Similar snakes   Southwest of a line through Del Rio, San Saba, and Gainesville, Texas, the Kansas glossy snake is replaced by its sub-species, the **Texas glossy snake (132)**, which has both statistically fewer dorsal blotches (41 to 60, average 50 between snout and vent) and fewer dorsal scale rows, 29 to 35 (average 32). The **bullsnake (129)** has a pale, speckled head, keeled dorsal scales, 4 prefrontal scales, and an enlarged rostral. It lacks the glossy snake's whitish vertebral line along the nape. The **great plains rat snake (141)** also lacks the glossy snake's light vertebral line just behind the head, while its venter is pigmented with dark gray and its anal plate is divided.

Behavior   See **Texas Glossy Snake.**

132   TEXAS GLOSSY SNAKE

Arizona elegans arenicola

Nonvenomous   See **Kansas Glossy Snake.**

Abundance   Endemic to Texas, *A. e. arenicola* is uncommon in the northeastern part of its range— an extended peninsula of sandy-soiled terrain that stretches from the state's central crosstimbers into its eastern pine forest—yet this race of glossy snake is one of the more abundant serpents encountered on warm spring and early summer nights almost everywhere on the Rio Grande plain south of Falfurrias and Hebbronville.

Size   Adults are most often 20 to 30 inches long, and rarely exceed 3 feet. *Arizona elegans arenicola* is recorded to 54⅝ inches in length, however.

Habitat   *Arizona* means "dry area" and *arenicola* is "sand-loving"—the primary siliceous habitat of glossy snakes. South of San Antonio this reptile is occasionally found in cropland, but it seems to be more abundant in Tamaulipan thorn woodland between Duval County and the Mexican border.

In the northeastern part of the Texas glossy's range, sandy-soiled terrain is often used as hay-growing pasture, and here the author has found this race in both Lee and Milam counties. Even further from its South Texas population center, *A. e. arenicola* has even been recorded east of the Trinity River by James Dixon of Texas A & M University, who defined this subspecies in 1960.

Prey   Based on the behavior of recent captives, *Arizona elegans* feeds mainly on lacertilian prey (whiptails, race runners, and spiny lizards are numerous in the Texas glossy's range), scented out after dark while they sleep. Small mammals are probably also sometimes taken, although few newly caught individuals accept mice as food.

Reproduction Egg-laying. Little reproductive data are recorded, but in September and early October up to 2 dozen young, 9½ to 11 inches in length, emerge from buried clutches of 2¾-inch-long eggs.

Coloring/scale form Dorsolateral ground color is off-white, marked, between snout and vent, by 41 to 60 (average 50) large brown vertebral blotches with very thin dark borders. Unique to glossy snakes, the Texas glossy's definitive marking, however, is the pale longitudinal line that runs along its spine just behind the crown. A brown band masks the eyes and crosses the cheeks, and the venter is uniformly white. The smooth dorsal scales, which reflect the nacreous patina suggested by the glossy's name, occur in 29 to 35 (average 32) rows at midbody, and there are 2 prefrontal scales. See **Illustration: Bullsnake.**

Similar snakes The Kansas glossy snake is distinguished from the Texas race by its slightly more numerous (41 to 69, average 55) vertebral blotches and its lower number (29 to 31) of midbody dorsal scale rows. See **Kansas Glossy Snake.**

Behavior All three of Texas' glossy snake races are thought to have once been members of an ancient, xeric-adapted fauna that occupied a dry corridor joining the desert Southwest to the Florida peninsula. After this arid-land community was fragmented by the cooler, wetter climate that prevailed along the Gulf Coast during the late Pleistocene, *A. e. arenicola* survived in relict populations living on sandy, desert-like soil well into the eastern part of Texas. Here, as in the southern part of its range, *A. e. arenicola* is almost never seen above ground except well after dark.

---

133 PAINTED DESERT GLOSSY SNAKE

Arizona elegans philipi

Nonvenomous See **Kansas Glossy Snake.**

Abundance Uncommon. Perhaps because of the very harsh terrain it inhabits *A. e. philipi* seems to be very unevenly distributed: like other races of glossy snake, its abundance varies radically from place to place.

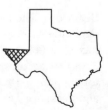

Size   See **Kansas Glossy Snake.**

Habitat   El Paso County and a bit of western Hudspeth County harbor animals found nowhere else east of the 100th meridian, because of this area's long stretch of sand dunes. This Sahara-like milieu harbors a biotic community that includes such xeric sand-adapted animals as the Apache pocket mouse and the most westerly of Texas' glossy snakes, *Arizona elegans philipi*. In places other than the West Texas dunes, the Painted Desert glossy snake's favored habitat consists of creosote- and blackbrush-covered sandy or gravelly slopes, sagebrush flats, and grassland.

Prey   See **Kansas Glossy Snake.**

Reproduction   Egg-laying. See **Texas Glossy Snake.**

Coloring/scale form   Like most arid-land reptiles, whose dorsolateral camouflage coloring must mirror the glaucous hue of the prevailing desert substrate, the Painted Desert glossy snake is paler than its eastern relatives, with its golden brown dorsal blotches often compressed over the spine into a waisted, hourglass shape. The white vertebral stripe along the neck typical of all glossy snakes is present, but the Painted Desert glossy snake is a seemingly sun-bleached version of its eastern subspecies (though it only emerges onto the surface long after dark). It also lacks their well-defined dark masks; however, a faint umber line running from its eye to the corner of its jaw suggests this marking.

Arizona elegans philipi differs from those more eastern glossy snake races by not only its paler coloring, but its higher number of body blotches (average 64.2), its slightly longer tail (about 15 percent of its total length), and a slightly lower average (27) number of dorsal scale rows.

Similar snakes   The subspecies **Kansas glossy snake (131)** has statistically less numerous dorsal blotches (41 to 69, average 55) and fewer dorsal scale rows (29 to 31, average 30). The **Sonoran gopher snake (130)** has a pale, speckled head, keeled dorsal scales, 4 prefrontal scales and an enlarged rostral scute, and lacks the glossy snake's whitish vertebral line along the nape.

Behavior   The Painted Desert glossy snake—the subspecies name honors Philip M. Klauber, whose father, Lawrence M. Klauber, defined this race in 1946—is similar in behavior to the state's two more easterly glossy snake subspecies: its activity cycle is one of exclusively nocturnal foraging on the surface and subterranean retreat during dawn, daylight, and dusk. See **Texas Glossy Snake.**

RAT SNAKES
Genus Elaphe

Black Rat Snake, *Elaphe obsoleta obsoleta*
Yellow Rat Snake, *Elaphe obsoleta quadrivittata*
Everglades Rat Snake, *Elaphe obsoleta rossalleni*
Gray Rat Snake, *Elaphe obsoleta spiloides*
Texas Rat Snake, *Elaphe obsoleta lindheimeri*
Baird's Rat Snake, *Elaphe bairdi*
Corn Snake, *Elaphe guttata guttata*
Great Plains Rat Snake, *Elaphe guttata emoryi*
Eastern Fox Snake, *Elaphe gloydi*
Western Fox Snake, *Elaphe vulpina*

The genus *Elaphe* is a member of the colubrine subfamily *Colubrinae*—a group of powerful, oviparous constrictors represented in the eastern United States by five species: *E. obsoleta*, which includes five races of the nominate black rat snake; *E. bairdi*, Baird's rat snake; *E. guttata*, the corn snake/great plains rat snake; and *E. gloydi* and *E. vulpina*, the two fox snake species. Adult *Elaphe* have weakly keeled dorsal scales and generally un-keeled lateral scales; juveniles lack scale keels. The number of dorsolateral scale rows varies by species as well as, to some extent, individually. The black rat snake races have from 25 to 33 rows, Baird's rat snake usually has 27 rows, corn/Great Plains rat snakes have 27 to 29 rows, and the fox snakes have 23 to 27 rows. The anal plate of all American *Elaphe* is divided.

Except for the fox snakes, American *Elaphe* undergo marked ontogenetic, or age-related, changes in color and pattern. At hatching juveniles are strongly blotched or crossbarred and are difficult to differentiate as to subspecies, but with age and growth many lose their contrasting juvenile pattern and become either more indistinctly marked above or, in the case of the yellow rat snake, strongly striped.

Because of their propensity for farms and barnyards, members of the genus *Elaphe* have received the official common name of rat snake, though they are more widely, and erroneously, known by the public as chicken snakes. (A foraging rat snake will eat an occasional baby chick or egg but it is the proliferation of their preferred rodent prey among piles of debris or within unused buildings that draws these reptiles to farmyards.)

With the exception of the fox snakes, rat snakes are also agile climbers that can ascend straight up moderately rough-barked tree trunks; with more difficulty they usually can climb even smooth-trunked trees. This ability is crucial to the ecological niche of American *Elaphe*, for arboreal refuge is central both to these animals' avoidance of predators and to the acquisition of their own prey: young rat snakes usually feed on small lizards and tree frogs, while adults consume rodents, juvenile rabbits, and birds. Most of these creatures are killed or immobilized by constriction, though where there is no room to wrap body coils around a victim—in the confines of narrow rodent burrows, for example—small prey is simply grasped in the jaws and swallowed.

134 BLACK RAT SNAKE, *Elaphe obsoleta obsoleta*

Nonvenomous The black rat snake exhibits a wide range and individual temperament. Many individuals seem to be easy-going, even lethargic, but others, if touched or otherwise provoked, will coil and strike in defense. Large individuals can deliver a painful bite, but this behavior is normally short-lived, and wild-caught specimens quickly lose their fear of humans.

Abundance *Elaphe obsoleta obsoleta* has the broadest range of any North American rat snake. It is found from northern Louisiana, Oklahoma and eastern Kansas and Nebraska across the entire north/central United States (it is quite common throughout Kentucky) as far east as the Atlantic seaboard from the Carolinas to Connecticut, and west through New York state to southern Michigan. Despite its size, even where it is common the black rat snake often escapes detection. This is partly due to the effective camouflage patterning of the young and to adults' tendency to rest inconspicuously high in trees, hidden crevices, or the darkness of deserted buildings.

Yet, according to Gerard T. Salmon,

> Black rat snakes are much more common in southern New Jersey, Delaware, Maryland, Virginia and the Carolinas than anywhere else in the East. [This race] is also fairly common in

Missouri and in Kansas . . . where its affinity is for wooded hills and bluffs—as opposed to open grassland. This is quite different from its habitat in the Appalachians and the Northeast, where its range is very fragmented [and it] chooses only inaccessible rocky areas with deep crevices [that in winter] allow it to get below the frost line.

Elaphe obsoleta obsoleta has also adapted to rural manmade environments such as farms and junkyards where it is sometimes observed in or around stone walls, broken concrete slabs and covered wells. Nevertheless, over much of its range the black rat snake is declining, especially wherever mankind has taken over most of the natural terrain.

Size   Adult black rat snakes measuring 4½ to 5½ feet in length are of average size; specimens more than 7 feet long are regularly reported and, at a record length of just over 100 inches, the largest black rat snakes are among the longest serpents in North America.

Habitat   This is a snake of deciduous and mixed woodland which is also often found in the proximity of human dwellings. Here, it favors infrequently used outbuildings, stone walls, trash heaps, and any other natural or manmade shelter that harbors rodents. Black rat snakes are also likely to be found in woodpiles and under boards (inland from the Atlantic coastal plain *E. o. obsoleta* inhabits seem to seek rocky outcroppings, talus slopes, or bluffs—often those adjacent to rivers or lakes).

Besides the shelter from predators this broken country offers, and the numerous feeding opportunities its nooks and crevices afford these agile climbers, the topographical intricacy of such areas also provides hibernacula, for in the northern parts of its range the black rat snake requires both recesses well below the frost line and inaccessible sunny ledges for thermoregulatory basking. In these rocky environs one or two *E. o. obsoleta* may den alongside a large number of timber rattlesnakes and copperheads, earning the black rat snake the local name "pilot blacksnake" because of the misguided belief that it leads its venomous relatives to the safety of their dens.

Prey   Black rat snakes prey primarily on rodents and birds and their eggs. Gerard T. Salmon reports one individual which, even after ingesting 10 quail eggs, was still sufficiently agile to climb high into a tree. Juveniles feed mostly on lizards and frogs, as well as on nestling birds and rodents. Both adults and juveniles are efficient hunters, which may engage in patient ambush predation, although when very hungry they more often actively search out prey.

Reproduction   Egg-laying. Depending on latitude, and therefore the date at which it emerges from winter brumation, *E. o. obsoleta* breeds in early to late spring. Six to 10 weeks afterward (for among most snakes spermatozoa are retained in the female's oviducts for varying periods prior to ovulation/fertilization), from May through early July a single clutch, averaging 8 to 20 adherent eggs, is deposited in a humid subsurface nest chamber or buried in decaying plant matter.

Large healthy females may deposit more than 24 eggs; one of Salmon's captives laid 32. The 12- to 14-inch-long hatchlings that emerge some 60 to 70 days later resemble the young of other *E. obsoleta*.

Coloring/scale form   *Elaphe obsoleta obsoleta* undergoes a dramatic ontogenetic color change from juvenile to adult. Hatchlings are boldly patterned with dark brown vertebral and lateral blotches on a light- to medium-gray dorsum. Below their dark-striped, lead-gray crowns, a solid-colored dark brown eye mask extends postocularly into a darker stripe that ends at the mouth line; their bellies are checked with black and white.

At 20 to 30 inches in length juvenile northern black rat snakes begin to lose their dorsolateral patterning as dark pigment starts to suffuse their pale ground color and their ventral checkerboard gradually fades. By the time they reach about 36 inches this process has transformed their dorsal appearance into the uniformly shiny black coloring of adults. Individuals from the northern, Atlantic coast, and montane portions of the range seem to be particularly dark-hued, while in other areas even fully mature individuals usually retain traces of their juvenile dorsal blotches (these blotches are especially evident when the scales separate as these reptiles' skins distend after a large meal). Small white, yellow, and red colored spaces between the dorsal and lateral scales are also present in most adult black rat snakes, among whom the tongue is black. (In a band stretching from near Georgia's Atlantic coast, across northern Florida and west into Alabama, the black rat snake intergrades with its southern subspecies, the yellow rat snake. The genetic mixing of these two races creates a distinctive and well-known dark-backed, yellowish-brown-sided, light brown-headed color morph found nowhere else).

The white or off-white forebelly of adults shades to dark gray a third of the way along the venter, sometimes marked with either squarish darker gray blotches while the underside of the tail tip is usually solid gray (ventral scales number 220 or more). There are 2 prefrontal scales and of the 27 (sometimes 25) midbody rows of dorsal scales, those along the spine are most strongly keeled.

Similar snakes As the black rat snake intergrades over wide zones with the **yellow rat snake (135)** in the Southeast, the **gray rat snake (137)** in the south-central states and the **Texas rat snake (138)** at the southwestern extreme of its range, almost any combination of patterns typical of each race may appear. Occasionally, pattern components may even show up in areas far from any mapped zone of genetic contact, as happened recently when an aged northern black rat snake found in Putnam County, New York, exhibited (faintly) the four longitudinal black stripes typical of the southeastern **yellow rat snake (135)**.

Eastern and **western fox snakes (142, 143)**, which as juveniles closely resemble the black rat snake, have fewer than 220 ventral scales, snout-to-vent. **Northern** and **southern black racers (107, 108)** differ in having smooth, flat or gunmetal-black scales; juveniles lack a dark postocular/temporal bar. The **black kingsnake (152)** is smooth scaled and has an undivided anal plate. Juvenile **corn snakes (141)** resemble young black rat snakes but have a dark-edged brown eye mask and postocular stripe that stretches onto the neck.

Behavior In the northern portions of its range, *E. o. obsoleta* is completely diurnal, and individuals are often observed sunning themselves during the heat of the day. Northern black rat snakes usually choose partially shaded areas for this thermoregulatory basking, and even when they are in plain sight often go unnoticed because they often arrange their dark bodies in a series of tight "S" shapes that help them disappear in the light and dark chiaroscuro of sunlight filtering through the woodland canopy above. In the South and West *E. o. obsoleta* is more crepuscular and after morning basking usually retreats to cooler areas by noon, remaining there until the ambient temperature decreases later in the day. Afternoon showers seem to prompt these animals into foraging, and during hot weather they remain active far into the night. According to Salmon, black rat snakes may be more oriented toward particular denning sites than other *Elaphe*, for— though most often this race winters singly—sometimes several individuals use the same large hollow tree as a permanent residence year after year.

YELLOW RAT SNAKE
Elaphe obsoleta quadrivittata

Nonvenomous In the wild, *E. o. quadrivittata* does not hesitate to strike at an aggressor, and if it makes contact, tends to hang on and chew. Yet, like other rat snakes (many of which are also known rurally as chicken snake), it tames readily and thrives in captivity, living up to 17 years with good care.

Abundance Common. The range of the yellow rat snake reaches southward along the Atlantic coastal plain from North Carolina's Pamlico Sound to the tip of the Florida peninsula. This snake is a common, dominant species throughout Florida, and although it is not abundant in the Florida Keys, *E. o. quadrivittata* has been able to adjust to life on what are essentially small Caribbean islands—as it has adapted to a variety of both wet- and dry-terrain mainland habitats. See **Everglades Rat Snake.**

Size Among this race, adults generally measure 40 to 70 inches in length. The record yellow rat snake, collected in 1993 by Kenneth Krysko near Lake Okeechobee, was almost 90 inches long.

Habitat Like other *E. obsoleta*, the yellow rat snake is seldom found in open terrain. Primarily a climber, it most often inhabits cypress groves, pinelands, hardwood hammocks, stands of melaleuca, and the margins of farms and other disturbed areas such as canal banks; its microhabitat includes hollows and holes in palm and pine trees, beneath loose tree bark, and the underpinnings of wooden trestles.

Prey As is the case with most rat snakes, either the scent or visual proximity of almost any smaller vertebrate can trigger a feeding response, but birds and their eggs, rodents, lizards, and frogs account for a large portion of the subspecies' prey.

Reproduction Egg-laying. Similar to other *Elaphe obsoleta*. (Juveniles have a gray dorsum with dark vertebral and lateral blotches.) See **Black Rat Snake.**

Coloring/scale form Throughout its broad range *E. o. quadrivittata* (its subspecies name is Latin for "four-striped") is a highly variable race. South of Lake Okeechobee—an area where the genetic influence of the now greatly diminished Everglades rat snake remains—yellow rat snakes may be almost orange in ground color, with muted dorsolateral stripes, a dark red-rooted tongue, (the tongues of other yellow rat snake color morphs are black), yellow to orange eyes, and a whitish chin. In a clinally varying progression individuals from peninsular Florida are also boldly colored, their yellow backs and sides streaked with four dark stripes (*quadrivittata* means "four lined"), while those living in southeastern Georgia are darker yellow. Specimens from coastal South and North Carolina are olive, with dark longitudinal stripes and dorsal blotches.

Yellow rat snakes from more inland parts of northern Florida are grayer in ground color, and often show the genetic influence of the gray rat snake in the form of dorsal blotches as well as dimly defined stripes.

Mangrove-living *E. o. quadrivittata* which occupy the upper Keys are for the most part a muddy yellow, with both dark stripes and dorsal blotches, but a rare and beautiful color morph, which also occurs on the north side of Card Sound, was once afforded the Latin name *E. o. deckerti*. This "Deckert's rat snake" inhabits both coastal mangroves and inland hardwood hammocks and is one of the region's rarest serpents. Most often, it has a golden brown to burnt orange back and sides with dark stripes and silver-edged scales.

Juvenile yellow rat snakes are as variably colored as the adults: northern individuals are dark gray with black dorsal blotches, while southern examples are light gray with charcoal dorsal blotches. Keys-living yellow rat snakes usually have a faded, yellow-orange ground color marked with brown dorsal blotches. The belly of all the yellow rat snake's color phases is usually pale yellow; there are 27 rows of weakly keeled dorsal scales.

Similar snakes Very similar as a hatchling, the subspecies **gray rat snake (137)** retains its dark juvenile dorsolateral blotches as it matures (a tendency termed neotenic); intergrades with the yellow rat snake displaying both stripes and blotches occur in northeastern Florida, southern Georgia, and Alabama. See **Black Rat Snake**.

Behavior In southern Florida, *E. o. quadrivittata* is often observed sunning itself—frequently just after a rain shower—on the dark-needled branches of canal-side Australian pines where its sometimes vivid yellow coloring makes it particularly conspicuous. See **Gray Rat Snake**.

Elaphe obsoleta rossalleni

Nonvenomous   Cornered *Elaphe obsoleta* of all races may raise their forebodies and strike in self-defense, but unless seized or molested they do not bite humans.

Abundance   Rare. Endemic to the state of Florida, the Everglades rat snake was abundant around Lake Okeechobee as recently as the 1970s, and ranged southward throughout the Everglades area to the tip of the mainland peninsula. It is thought that in this seasonally flooded region it was adapted to life in the hardwood hammocks too wet for the more widely distributed yellow rat snake.

Since that time, much of the northern Everglades has been drained and elevated roadway corridors have been built across its saw-grass marshes. This has allowed the more aggressive yellow rat snake to first invade, then take over virtually all the territory that was formerly the exclusive habitat of *E. o. rossalleni*. Aided by inadvertent human intervention, the yellow rat snake has genetically absorbed its more habitat-specialized subspecies to the extent that the old Everglades race of bright orange rat snakes has virtually disappeared as a subspecies, for the only rat snakes now found in the Everglades are intergrades with yellow rat snake.

Size   See **Yellow Rat Snake.**

Habitat   Orange Everglades rat snakes were never restricted to the seasonally inundated Everglades/Big Cypress drainage area (though they were good swimmers and were often found there). These animals also inhabited the Kissimmee prairie and were to be found throughout the broad river of submerged saw-grass and elevated hardwood hammocks that filled Lake Okeechobee's 100-mile-long floodplain. Here, *E. o. rossalleni* lived high in inundated stands of cypress, islands of native pine, and for a few decades, the Australian pines lining the region's newly built roads and canal banks.

Prey   Like all rat snakes, *E. o. rossalleni* was a powerful constrictor as well as a generalized predator on birds, rodents, lizards, and frogs; with good care it thrived in captivity, where individuals have been maintained for up to 22 years.

Reproduction   Egg-laying. Similar to that of other *E. obsoleta.*

Coloring/scale form Also known as the orange rat snake, adults of the beautiful pure *E. o. rossalleni*—named for antivenin collector, field researcher, and early Florida reptile showman E. Ross Allen—can be spectacularly vivid. Four dark dorsolateral stripes are usually present, but may be faint, or even absent over much of the otherwise dull- to bright-orange trunk; the belly is yellowish, the tongue (unlike that of the black-tongued yellow rat snake) is blood red, and even the eyes may be an intense orange. The 27 rows of dorsal scales are weakly keeled.

Similar snakes See **Yellow Rat Snake.**

Behavior Like the long, muscular yellow rat snake race that has largely absorbed it, *E. o. rossalleni* is a good burrower and swimmer—and a distinguished climber.

---

137 GRAY RAT SNAKE, *Elaphe obsoleta spiloides*

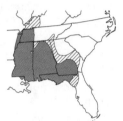

Nonvenomous This large and often beautiful serpent—known locally as "oak runner" or "white oak snake"—may bite to defend itself, but it seems to be somewhat less aggressive than its yellow rat snake subspecies.

Abundance Common. *Elaphe obsoleta spiloides* is common throughout the Florida panhandle and southern Georgia, almost all of Alabama and Mississippi, as well as north along the eastern Mississippi valley as far as St. Louis. Immediately after hatching in late summer, the young are frequently found in both residential and rural areas.

Size Most adults are 36 to 72 inches long; the record is 84¼ in.

Habitat Almost every wooded terrestrial environment within its range offers habitat for *E. o. spiloides*. Oak forest and pinelands, stands of cypress, and tree-lined riverbanks are typical macro-environments. Gray rat snakes also seem to be particularly oriented to exploiting the dense population of rodents that are often found in disturbed areas such as forest-bordered fields, farms, and stock ponds (even to humans, barns and sheds tend to smell of mice, and to scent-hunting *Elaphe*, such rural outbuildings are a magnet).

Prey Like other *Elaphe obsoleta*, gray rat snakes are agile climbers, powerful constrictors, and generalized predators on mostly vertebrate prey. Even hatchlings feed mainly on lizards in trees and frogs along pond margins, while adults prey mostly on rodents and birds and their eggs. This predation is not lost on the avian community because as one sure way to find a rat snake coiled high in the forest's branches is to locate a group of agitated jays.

Reproduction   Egg-laying. Breeding takes place from April to July, with 5 to 27 eggs being deposited in mid- to late summer. During September the pale gray, sharply brown-blotched hatchlings emerge.

Coloring/scale form   The most distinctive visual characteristic of the gray rat snake is that as an adult it resembles the young of most other races of *Elaphe obsoleta*. (Maintaining blotched juvenile patterning into adulthood is not limited to rat snakes and occurs among several of ophidian subfamilies, including *Natricinae*.) This means that its pale gray back remains boldly patterned with anteriorly elongate dark brown dorsal blotches separated by 4 or more paler-hued scale rows, its pale-gray crown retains the juvenile striping that forms a forward-facing spearpoint, below which another solid-chocolate-colored band masks its eyes and extends rearward only as far as the posterior upper labial scales.

Among *E. o. spiloides* another color phase, sometimes referred to as the "white oak" type, possesses a silvery ground color with dark brown or gray dorsolateral blotches. A third color morph, genetically influenced by the black rat snake with which the gray rat snake intergrades from northern Florida to Tennessee, has a dark brown back with blackish vertebral blotches.

In the southern part of the gray rat snake's range, the genetic influence of the yellow rat snake (which looks very similar as a hatchling) is seen among individuals with dark dorsolateral stripes as well as blotches. (Individuals of this type from north and northwestern peninsular Florida were once thought to represent a separate race known as the Gulf Hammock rat snake, *Elaphe obsoleta williamsi*.)

The venter of most gray rat snakes is a dingy off-white or pale gray, marked with both squarish darker gray blotches and a double row of black spots behind the vent. There are 2 prefrontal scales and the 25 (sometimes 27) midbody rows of dorsal scales are weakly keeled.

Similar snakes   The **corn snake (140)** is distinguished by the black-edged brown lines that form a forward-pointing V on its crown, by the black-edged brown stripe that runs across its snout, masks its eyes, and continues past its upper labial scales onto its neck, its black-edged dorsolateral blotches, and its laterally dark-striped undertail. The brown dorsal blotches of the entirely terrestrial **mole kingsnake (148)** are also usually edged with black, its dorsal scales are smooth, and its anal plate is undivided. Young water snakes (64–74) have strongly keeled dorsal scales and seldom leave aquatic environments.

Behavior Its adaptability to human-occupied areas and its wide-ranging search for rats and mice make *E. o. spiloides* the large terrestrial snake most likely to be found in southeastern U.S. suburbs: it is the source of the majority of calls police and fire departments receive about long, gray-brown serpents found in garage rafters, attics, abandoned automobiles, and machinery. Since these animals are usually cornered, their typical defensive feinting strikes (evolved only to startle an assailant long enough for them to escape) appear so aggressive that these gray rat snakes are often wrongfully killed.

Part of the arboreal agility that gets *E. o. spiloides* into these situations comes from rat snakes' adaptively stiffened ventral plates, whose backward-turned outer edges can be dug into furrowed tree bark like linemens' climbing spikes. By using both lateral undulation and concertina movement (inching the ventral scutes ahead in successive waves of belly-muscle contraction), *Elaphe obsoleta* is able to ascend almost straight up a rough-trunked oak or pine.

Once aloft, rat snakes are superlatively arboreal. Aided by some 50% more vertebrae than most terrestrial or aquatic serpents, they can stiffen their wirily muscled bodies enough to bridge branch-to-branch gaps more than half their own length, then calmly thread themselves through branches dozens of feet from the ground.

138 TEXAS RAT SNAKE, *Elaphe obsoleta lindheimerii*

Nonvenomous Texas rat snakes are vigorous in their own defense and if threatened often make several mostly bluffing, open-mouthed strikes. Pressed further, *E. o. lindheimerii* may defecate in fear, emit musk from its cloacal glands, and ultimately, bite—though the pressure of its jaws is slight and only scratches usually result.

Abundance Very common. One of the handful of truly abundant large terrestrial serpents, the Texas rat snake is the long, brown-mottled snake that most often appears in suburban neighborhoods throughout the eastern ⅔ of Texas and the southern ⅔ of Louisiana. It is likely to be found high in trees or, in human-populated areas, hidden in barns, henhouses, abandoned buildings and machinery. After the grayish young hatch in late summer, they are often found around both rural and suburban houses and, like the adults, nip when picked up.

Size   Adult Texas rat snakes are slender but long, averaging 42 to 72 inches—dimensions which in Louisiana has earned *E. o. lindheimerii* the nickname "piney woods python." The record is just over 7 feet.

Habitat   Abundant in both deciduous woods and pastureland, this reptile is named for pioneer naturalist Ferdinand Jacob Lindheimer, who collected the type specimen near his home in New Braunfels, Texas. This westernmost race of *Elaphe obsoleta* also occurs in almost every terrestrial and aquatic-margin environment from upland pine/hardwood forest to coastal prairie marsh.

Prey   Both juvenile and adult Texas rat snakes feed almost entirely on warm-blooded prey, especially birds and their nestlings— on which *E. o. lindheimerii* is a major predator. (A flock of blue jays and other passerines screaming at a Texas rat snake coiled high in the branches is a common woodland sight.)

Also called "chicken snake" for its attraction to the rodents (and sometimes eggs and chicks) to be found in henhouses, *E. o. lindheimerii* is equally likely to be seen by the usually shocked residents of wooded subdivisions who set out cage birds on their patios. Larger prey such as small mammals are overpowered by constriction.

Reproduction   Egg-laying. Hatchling Texas rat snakes are 12 to 14 inches long, with lead-gray crowns striped by a pair of solid chocolate lines that form a forward-facing spearpoint. Another chocolate-colored band masks the eyes and extends rearward only as far as the posterior upper labial scales. Juveniles' backs have a pale gray ground color, boldly patterned with darker-edged, irregularly shaped brown dorsal and lateral blotches which enlarge and, along with their ground color, darken as they mature.

Coloring/scale form   Adult Texas rat snakes' large, dark brown rectangular vertebral blotches are separated by smaller, yellowish brown transverse areas about 4 scale rows in width; reddish skin may be evident on the sides of the neck. Older adults are darker in color. The pale venter is blotched with dark squares partially obscured by a grayish overwash, while the underside of the tail tip is usually solid gray. Of the 27 midbody rows of dorsal scales, those along the spine are most strongly keeled.

Similar snakes   To the northeast, the subspecies **black rat snake (134)** is almost entirely an unmarked black above, with only traces of dark dorsal blotches; its chin and forebelly are off-white. Another rat snake, formerly classified as a subspecies but now accorded full species status, the **Baird's rat snakes** (139), is faintly striped above and lacks dorsal blotches; juveniles are grayer than young Texas rat snakes, with dark transverse vertebral bars. The similar-looking juvenile **Great Plains rat snake** (141) has a black-edged brown V on its pale crown. Another dark-edged brown band crosses its snout, masks its eyes, and extends posteriorly onto its neck, while a pale subcaudal midventral stripe is centered between dark distal borders. The **prairie kingsnake** (147) has smooth scales and an undivided anal plate.

Behavior The Texas rat snake's wiry musculature and sharp-edged belly scales make it an agile climber, but it also patrols creek banks from the water, and has been captured swimming across the middle of large lakes. See **Gray Rat Snake.**

139   BAIRD'S RAT SNAKE, *Elaphe bairdi*

Nonvenomous Although some Baird's rat snakes are entirely non-aggressive even when first picked up in the field, other individuals may hiss and nip if cornered.

Abundance Very uncommon. Native only to Texas and three or four small, disjunct ranges in northern Mexico, *Elaphe bairdi* seems to be spottily dispersed in even the best habitat. Although its primary range is the Trans-Pecos, it is also found on the western Edwards Plateau: back roads in the vicinity of Leakey, Vanderpool, and Barksdale are the site of a number of nocturnal sightings, especially after summer rainfall.

Size Adults are usually between 24 and 40 inches long; one enormous specimen measured 62 in.

Habitat *Elaphe bairdi* inhabits three very different primary environments: A. Both montane forest and lower elevation canyons throughout the Trans-Pecos; B. The very different oak/juniper-wooded limestone riparian corridors containing the central hill country's streams and rivers; and C. The barren, Cretaceous limestone canyons of the Pecos River drainage, where Baird's rat snakes are rare.

Although much of this range includes extremely arid terrain, most of this terrain is unsuitable habitat, for *Elaphe bairdi* occurs primarily in comparatively mesic canyon biomes (one small male taken just before shedding was unable to rid itself of its old skin until it had soaked in a pan of water for several days).

Prey   Like other rat snakes, *Elaphe bairdi* is a generalized predator on small vertebrates, constricting prey that includes birds and their eggs, lizards, rodents and other small mammals. Lizards and nestling rodents are probably the primary food of the young.

Reproduction   Egg-laying. Mating during May and early June results in the mid-summer deposition of usually fewer than 10, 1¾ by 1-inch-wide smooth-shelled eggs. Like the eggs of other rat snakes, the whole clutch usually adheres to form a single cluster that, after 70 to 85 days hatches into 11- to 13-inch-long gray, dorsally dark-barred offspring. As they mature, juveniles undergo an ontogenetic color and pattern change, losing their prominent dark brown cross-dorsal bands during their second year—bands which soon reappear—turned at right angles—as the longitudinal brown stripes of the adult.

Coloring/scale form   *Elaphe bairdi* is a subtly beautiful snake: beneath a translucent sheen, the forebody of adults is washed with a golden tint—the result of myriad tiny orangish crescents, one of which rims the forward margin of each dorsal scale. From the eyes to the rear of the skull the crown is dark mahogany, followed by a pair of moderately wide brown dorsolateral stripes. These stripes have a cross-hatched appearance because only part of each scale that makes them up is pigmented with brown.

A rare, yellowish-tan color phase dimly marked with gray stripes occurs to the west of Big Bend while an extraordinarily colored individual with rusty-hued cross-dorsal bands was found in the Chisos Mountains by former Big Bend National Park Superintendent Roland H. Wauer.

The lips and chin are light gray-brown to pale yellow, colors which continue beneath the forebelly, then darken to pale salmon, scalloped with gray, under the tail. The weakly keeled dorsal scales are arranged in 27 rows at midbody divided.

Similar snakes   The adult **Texas rat snake (138)** has an entirely dark brown head and neck and rectangular chocolate dorsal blotches along the length of its trunk.

Behavior   Like those of the Baird's sparrow and sandpiper, this animal's name honors Spencer Fullerton Baird.

As secretary of the Smithsonian Institution throughout the second third of the 19th century, Baird fueled much of the burst of zoological discovery that accompanied the opening of the West: often in partnership with Charles Frederich Girard, he first described some 24 southwestern snake species and subspecies.

Nonvenomous Occasionally a wild corn snake will rear and strike in its own defense, but this is almost always only a bluff because its small teeth are not capable of harming a large predator. Most *E. g. guttata* are docile, though, and as the most widely kept hobbyist's snake, thousands are bred in captivity every year. If given good care and gentle handling, virtually all remain tame throughout captive lives which can last as long as 22 years.

Abundance Very common. In a broad southeastern range that stretches from the Texas/Louisiana border to northern Tennessee, Virginia, and southern New Jersey, corn snakes can occur in almost any sort of wooded terrain, including suburban neighborhoods. (The rosy-hued *E. g. guttata* from the lower Florida Keys comprise a threatened population of special concern, however.)

Size A majority of adult corn snakes are between 18 and 44 inches long; the record is 72 inches.

Habitat Like other rat snakes, *E. g. guttata* can occur in almost any terrestrial habitat: pine/hardwood forest, elevated marshland hammocks, thickets of melaleuca and canal-bordering Australian pines in Florida, farmlands, evergreen-wooded Appalachian Mountains, and in and around bridges (especially old wooden railroad trestles) and human dwellings of all sorts.

Within these diverse macrohabitats, most corn snakes are found in constricted microenvironments: in rock piles, trash heaps, between dangling palm fronds, in the cavities typical of softwood trees like tupelo, red maple, and ash, and in the nooks and crannies of crumbling walls and buildings. During summer, newborns sometimes turn up in swimming pools.

Prey Corn snakes feed mostly on small vertebrates: rodents, lizards, birds, and frogs. The snakes themselves are a preferred prey of indigo snakes and coachwhips.

Reproduction Egg-laying. Breeding takes place April to June; 3 to 40 eggs are laid in mid-summer and hatch during July, August, and September. See **Great Plains Rat Snake**.

BROWN-BLOTCHED TERRESTRIAL SNAKES

Coloring/scale form   Named for the native American corn, or maize, whose harlequin ears the corn snake's variegated black-and-white belly suggests, most *E. g. guttata* are patterned with big, black-edge dorsal and lateral blotches (*guttata* is Latin for "splotched") on a yellow-brown ground color. Although corn snakes' contrasting hues stand out boldly against a solid-colored background, on a shade-dappled forest floor covered with reddish pine needles they function as sophisticated camouflage.

The most distinguishing marking of *E. g. guttata*, however, is the often black-edged brown V that points forward on its crown. A similar dark-edged yellow-brown stripe runs across its snout, masks its eyes, and continues rearward past its supralabial scales. On the underside of the corn snake's tail, its black-and-white checkered ventral pattern is replaced by a pair of dark distal stripes bordering a pale mid-line. The dorsal scales are weakly keeled, and usually arranged in 27 (sometimes 29) rows at midbody.

Because the Southeast's climax oak/longleaf pine woodland comprised most of the corn snake's original range, a majority of *E. g. guttata* living on the southern Atlantic coastal plain have a russet-orange or tan ground colors that match the prevailing hue of this woodland's understory leaf litter. Black-bordered russet vertebral blotches (usually separated by no more than 3 rows of the paler ground-color scales) pattern these animals' backs and sides, with the brightest red/boldest black-backed individuals being the famously vivid Okeetee corn snakes from South Carolina's coastal lowlands.

Besides southern pine- and hardwood forests, however, *E. g. guttata* is found in many other sorts of habitat, where it occurs in a number of different color phases—each probably having evolved as a cryptic accommodation to a particular locale. For example, corn snakes have developed a proliferation of color morphs in response to Florida's myriad habitat types. One variety, known as "Miami phase" corn snakes, occurs on the limestone-floored southeastern Florida coast and tends to have a light gray dorsolateral ground color and prominently black-edged dark red vertebral blotches.

To the northwest, extensive collecting near the southern end of Lake Okeechobee by Kenneth Krysko has shown that gray "anerythristic" corn snakes, entirely devoid of red pigment, make up some 20 percent of the local population, while elsewhere in peninsular Florida brightly colored orange-and-white "amelanistic" corn snakes completely lacking black pigment have also been found. At the opposite extreme, individuals from Louisiana, whose territory abuts that of the more open-country-living—hence more grayish ground-colored—western subspecies, the Great Plains rat snake, are patterned with dark gray-brown.

Another variant population is the remnant group of *E. g. guttata* living in the lower Florida Keys. Now threatened by human alteration of its limited island habitat, this highly variable population, often referred to as "rosy rat snakes," has reduced black borders lining its orange dorsal blotches, minimal ventral checkerboarding, a faint or absent cephalic spearpoint, and a slimmer body and more elongated head than mainland corn snakes.

Similar snakes   In early 2003, Joseph Collins, of the Center for North American Herpetology in Lawrence, Kansas, and Frank T. Burbrink of the College of Staten Island, proposed, based on Burbrink's molecular DNA analysis, that *Elaphe guttata* be divided into three species: the eastern corn snake (*Elaphe guttata*), Slowinki's corn snake (*Elaphe slowinskii*), the type found in western Louisiana and eastern Texas, and the western Great Plains rat snake (*Elaphe emoryi*). This is a radical new classification, which may or may not be accepted by the herpetological community. As a juvenile, the **gray rat snake (137)** is similar, but lacks the corn snake's black-edged brown cranial V. The brown band through its eyes stops at the corner of its mouth, its undertail is not usually distally dark-striped, and its brown vertebral blotches lack dark edges. The **mole kingsnake (148)** has smooth dorsal scales and an undivided anal plate.

Behavior   Primarily nocturnal, corn snakes are good burrowers, climbers, and swimmers (although they are seldom found in extensive wetlands). When not foraging, corn snakes tend to hide, and almost any penetrable crevice can provide refuge for even sizable *E. g. guttata*.

141   GREAT PLAINS RAT SNAKE
Elaphe guttata emoryi

Nonvenomous   Although a large individual may nip if picked up roughly, most wild Great Plains rat snakes are easily handled.

Abundance   Common in Texas and Oklahoma, *elaphe guttata emoryi* is much less abundant in other parts of its range, and is protected as a threatened species in Illinois and Colorado.

Size   Most adults are 2½ to 3½ feet long; the record is 60¼ in.

Habitat   A grayer, drier habitat-living race of the eastern corn snake, *E. g. emoryi* occupies terrain that varies from upland prairie to tidewater marsh to bottomland forest. In the western part of its range, an even grayer color morph with smaller dorsal blotches is found in both the arid northern Chihuahuan Desert and in Montane Forest several thousand feet in elevation.

Elaphe guttata emoryi is also more of a chthonic animal than is generally recognized, for not only is this snake a common inhabitant of fissured canyon walls, it also inhabits inaccessible rock crevices far below the surface: in places where big Great Plains rat snakes are almost never seen, very large individuals are sometimes flushed from deep subsurface haunts by flash flooding; Robert Webb (1970) reports one active individual found 60 feet underground.

During the warmer months some subterranean caverns provide food—*E. g. emoryi* is a regular predator on Mexican free-tailed bat nursery colonies—while in winter, caves, rock quarries, and abandoned building foundations offer temperate shelter. At this season Great Plains rat snakes have been found brumating alongside both Texas rat snakes and copperheads, while the cellar of one derelict farmhouse in Woods County, Oklahoma, served as a hibernaculum for 6 Great Plains rat snakes and 27 eastern yellow-bellied racers.

Prey   *Elaphe guttata emoryi* eats mostly warm-blooded animals which it kills by constriction. Rodents, as well as birds and their young, are its primary prey. (The author observed one Brewster County, Texas, Great Plains rat snake wedging its way up the furrowed bark of a cottonwood in whose lower branches a pair of vermillion flycatchers were frantically defending their nest.) Frogs and lizards are also sometimes preyed upon, but smaller snakes are not ordinarily taken.

Reproduction   Egg-laying. The first description of reproduction— of a typical clutch of 15—was published by John E. Werler in 1951:

> On June 14 . . . a 44¾-inch-long female from near Brownsville laid 5 smooth, adhesive eggs. Ten more were deposited the following day, averaging 1.8 inches in length, 1.1 inches in width. Slits first appeared in 2 of the eggs on Aug. 7, and these snakes emerged from their shells on August 8. Two additional snakes escaped from their shells on August 9, another on August 10, and the last two on August 12.

The record-sized clutch for *E. g. emoryi* is probably that of a Murchison County, Texas, female maintained by Gus Renfro of Brownsville.

She deposited 25 fertile eggs during the first week in July, and after 68 days her emerging hatchlings ranged from 11 to 15½ inches in length. The members of a smaller litter maintained by the author had grown to about 29 inches in length after 14 months; at 9 years of age one of these animals measured 44 inches and weighed just under 3 pounds.

Coloring/scale form   The Great Plains rat snake's most distinctive marking is the diamond-shaped brown arrowhead shape (whose point lies between the eyes) that patterns its crown; forward of this marking and below it a dark-edged brown mask crosses its snout, masks its eyes, and continues rearward past its supralabial scales. Like its eastern subspecies, the corn snake, the Great Plains rat snake's dorsolateral color and pattern vary according to geographic location. As the substrate—which snakes' dorsal camouflage must match—generally becomes lighter in color as one moves westward, a majority of *E. g. emoryi* display corresponding paler dorsolateral hues.

For example, most Great Plains rat snakes living in southwest Texas have a paler, grayer ground color than more easterly individuals, patterned with smaller, more numerous, and lighter-hued dorsal blotches.

Some authorities (Dixon, Werler, et al.) have defined this pale variant as *E. g. meahllmorum,* the southwestern rat snake. In the predominantly whitish, limesone-substrate portions of south and southwest Texas, light-hued *elaphe guttata* are likely to survive better than their darker-blotched kin.

E. g. emoryi from the northern part of this subspecies' range tend to have larger, darker brown vertebral blotches on a medium brown ground color, and Great Plains rat snakes from East Texas and Louisiana sometimes have a little dark orange pigment on their necks, suggesting the genetic influence of the Great Plains rat snake's easterly race, the russet and black-backed corn snake, which occurs at least as far west as Louisiana's Allen and Jeffereson parishes.

Among all geographic variants the belly is blotched with brown—more heavily in eastern specimens—while the underside of the tail has a pair of dark distal stripes bordering its pale midventral stripe. The 27 to 29 midbody rows of dorsal scales are weakly keeled along the spine.

Similar snakes   In early 2003, Joseph Collins, of the Center for North Herpetology in Lawrence Kansas, and Frank T. Burbrink of the College of Staten Island, proposed, based on Burbrinks molecular DNA analysis, that *Elaphe guttata* be divided into three species: the eastern corn snake (*Elaphe guttata*), Slowinki's corn snake (*Elaphe* *slowinskii*), the type found in western Louisana and eastern Texas, and the western Great Plains rat snake (*Elaphe emoryi*). This is a radical new classification, which may or may not be accepted by the herpetological community. Adult **Texas rat snakes (138)** have unmarked dark brown heads and necks and solid gray undertails; juveniles have a lead-gray crown and a solid chocolate eye mask. The **prairie kingsnake (147)** has smooth dorsal scales and an undivided anal plate. **Glossy snakes (131–133)** have a pale vertebral line along the nape, a white venter, and an undivided anal plate.

Behavior   This abundant but rather secretive reptile is named for William Hemsley Emory, the long-whiskered U.S. boundary commissioner who, in authorizing the initial mapping of the Texas-Mexican border, subsequently saw his name attached to a number of the plants (Emory oak) and animals (Emory's rat snake, *E. g. emoryi*) first described by members of his expeditions.

Extremely nocturnal, during its March to October activity period *E. g. emoryi* emerges from hiding only well after dark. When rainstorms drive terrestrial snakes to shelter, Great Plains rat snakes are typically among the first serpents to emerge again.

142   EASTERN FOX SNAKE, *Elaphe gloydi*

Nonvenomous   Although some individuals will bite in self-defense if molested, most are inoffensive even when first picked up in the wild.

Abundance   Uncommon. The eastern fox snake is now a **threatened species** protected throughout its very restricted range, which does not extend far beyond the western shore of Lake Ontario, the western and northern shores of Lake Erie, and the eastern and southern shores of Lake Huron.

Size   Hatchlings of this northern rat snake measure just over 11 inches in length, while most adults are from 3 to 5 feet long.

Habitat   The eastern fox snake is an eastern Great Lake species associated with the marshes, dunes and, occasionally, the open woodlands bordering the south-central and southeastern perimeters of these freshwater seas. *Elaphe gloydi* is also found in meadows, pastures, and farmlands some distance from these lakes, but nowhere does its ranges intersect that of the open prairie-living inland western fox snake.

Prey Adult eastern fox snakes prey largely on meadow voles and other wild mice, but probably also consume small ground-nesting birds and perhaps frogs. The diet of juveniles is less well known. The feeding behavior of captive-hatched *E. gloydi* indicates that wild individuals would certainly eat nestling rodents if they could find them, and it seems probable that frogs and salamanders are also dietary components. James Harding (1997) suggests that earthworms may also be taken in the wild.

Reproduction Little is known about the reproduction among wild *Elaphe gloydi*, but eastern fox snakes probably breed soon after emerging from hibernation in the spring. Captive males indulge in forebody-rearing dominance contests similar to those of many other ophidian species in which the individual least able to top the other's elevated head and neck becomes subordinate and the dominant male then copulates with any available female.

Starting in June or July, the eastern fox snake's buried nest chambers often contain 4 to 20 partially adherent eggs (the record verified clutch is 29). Hatchlings, which are paler than the adults and lack their coppery-colored heads, emerge 58 to 65 days after egg deposition. (Given the early onset of Great Lakes winters, this means that in many cases eastern fox snake hatchlings undergo hibernation without having time to find their first meal.) See **Western Fox Snake.**

Coloring/scale form First described in 1940 by Roger Conant, *E. gloydi*'s name honors Howard K. Gloyd, former emeritus professor of zoology at the University of Arizona. Although the two types of fox snake have sometimes been viewed as only races of a single species, current thinking considers each to be a separate species, for not only is there a 200-mile hiatus between the ranges of the eastern and western varieties, but their habitats are quite different.

The eastern fox snake, in particular, has a subdued beauty. Its yellowish, tan, or buff dorsolateral ground color (which is somewhat darker vertebrally than lower on its sides) is marked with 28 to 43 (average, 34) deep brown to black vertebral blotches, while on its sides, small lateral blotches alternate with these larger dorsal blotches—the anterior-most of which, on its nape, is elongate and may be shaped like an H or U whose open end faces forward. On each side of this species' neck its anterior-most lateral blotch is also elongate, while its crown and cheeks are often coppery red.

Juveniles and young adult eastern fox snakes have a temporal stripe extending from the eye to the back of the mouth, a dark bar across the top of the snout, a dark line along the trailing edge of the prefrontal scales, and another line running from below each eye to the lips. These fade with age, however, and the heads of older individuals may be devoid of all markings.

The yellowish belly is checkered with dark, rectangular spots which often extend to the first or first and second rows of lateral scales (among *E. gloydi* scale keeling is best defined on the vertebral dorsal scale rows).

Similar snakes   The **eastern milk snake (155)** has smooth scales and a single anal plate. Juvenile **blue** and **northern black racers (109, 107)** also have smooth scales and lack a dark temporal bar. Juvenile eastern fox snakes and juvenile **black rat snakes (134)** are similar in appearance, but (although it is difficult to count the number of belly scales on a live snake) snout-to-vent the fox snake has 216 or fewer ventrals, the black rat snake more than 220.

Behavior   The eastern fox snake is usually discovered during summer hidden beneath vegetation and logs; during cool weather it is most often found in burrows or stumpholes. It does not seem to climb much, but it swims well and may be met crossing open water some distance from shore.

---

143   WESTERN FOX SNAKE, *Elaphe vulpina*

Nonvenomous   Like its eastern counterpart, *Elaphe vulpina* is usually quiet and inoffensive, although frightened western fox snakes vibrate their tails and may nip if molested.

Abundance   Fairly common in some sections of its range, which includes parts of Michigan, Wisconsin, Minnesota, South Dakota, Nebraska, Iowa, Illinois, and Indiana, the western fox snake is nevertheless protected as a threatened species in Missouri.

Size   *Elaphe vulpina* is identical to its eastern relative in both length and girth: most adults are 3 to 4 feet long, occasionally reaching 5 ft.

Habitat   The western fox snake is much less specialized in habitat than the eastern species for, rather than being restricted to Great Lakes shore- and marshlands, *E. vulpina* also inhabits high ground and farmland, and is found in open woodland, prairie, hayfields and pastures from the western shore of Lake Michigan and the southern shore of Lake Superior to eastern South Dakota and Nebraska.

Prey   Unlike the eastern fox snake, which is a specialist feeder on voles, *Elaphe vulpina* accepts a wide variety of prey. Suitably sized rodents and lagomorphs are preferred, but ground-nesting birds are also taken (small animals are swallowed without constriction). Hatchling and juvenile *E. vulpina* prey on baby rodents, nestling birds, insects, lizards, frogs, and salamanders.

Reproduction   The reproductive biology of the eastern and western fox snakes is probably identical: breeding occurs soon after emergence from hibernation, with males entwining their raised anterior bodies in an effort to topple and suppress each other in dominance contests prior to copulation that are especially persistent if a female is nearby.

According to James Harding (1997) about a month after breeding female western fox snakes deposit between 4 and 27 often-adherent eggs in a moisture-retaining nest chamber usually located beneath natural or manmade litter, in a burrow or stumphole, or beneath a rock pile. Hatchlings, which are about 11 inches long, emerge after incubation lasting up to 65 days.

Coloring/scale form   The ground color of *E. vulpina* may be buff, yellowish, or off-white, with 32 to 52 (average, 41) well-defined but irregularly outlined dark brown to black dorsal blotches. The first blotch behind the head is often shaped like an elongate H or U whose arms are directed forward.

Dark lateral blotches are spaced between those reaching down from the center of the back, with the anterior-most being noticeably elongate. The western fox snake's head and tail may be either brighter or darker than its ground color, with olive, brownish, buff, copper, or even vivid orange pigmentation. (Young fox snakes have an interorbital bar across their crowns, another along the posterior edge of their prefrontal scales, and yet another from each eye to the back of the mouth. With advancing age these markings often fade, sometimes to invisibility.)

The cheeks of both young and adults are typically brighter in color than their crowns, and their yellowish bellies are checked with black. Keeling is strongest on the vertebral scale rows and, snout-to-vent, there are fewer than 217 ventral scales.

Similar snakes   Although characteristics of the two fox snake races overlap, the **eastern fox snake (142)** usually has less intricate dorsal patterning and fewer—28 to 43 (average, 32)—larger dorsal blotches. The very similar juvenile **black rat snake (134)** has more than 220 ventral scales, snout-to-vent, while juvenile **blue** and **eastern yellow-bellied racers (109, 115)** have smooth scales and lack a dark temporal bar. **Eastern** and **red milk snakes (155, 157)** and the **prairie kingsnake (147)** have smooth scales and undivided anal plates.

Behavior   Western fox snakes can climb and, because they inhabit a more wooded habitat than the eastern fox snake, occasionally do so; they are still predominantly terrestrial snakes, however. Most commonly encountered in areas with ample ground cover, *E. vulpina* is just as secretive as its eastern relative but is much more common than the less-adaptable *E. gloydi*, being both a habitat and prey generalist.

TRANS-PECOS RAT SNAKE
Genus Bogertophis

Trans-Pecos Rat Snake, *Bogertophis subocularis*

Bogertophis is a new genus defined in 1988 by H. G. Dowling and R. M. Price and named for Charles M. Bogert, head of herpetology at the American Museum of Natural History, as part of the colubrine subfamily *Colubrinae*.

It is an oviparous, primarily saxicolous desert and dry savannah-living genus whose most unique characteristic is the row of subocular scales that separates its eye from its upper labial scales (its 31 to 35 rows of dorsolateral scales are weakly keeled and its anal plate is divided). Despite being commonly termed "rat snake," some researchers consider this genus to be more closely related to the bull and gopher snakes, *Pituophis*, than to the rat snake genus *Elaphe*, from which *Bogertophis* was only recently separated. (This genus' slim, muscular body is more similar in configuration to that of the rat snakes than to the bull/gopher snakes, however, and is the reason its members were long considered to be *Elaphe*.)

Whatever its genetic affinity with related genera, *Bogertophis* is made up of only 2 species, one of which, the Trans-Pecos rat snake, occurs in the area covered here. This big-eyed, delicate nocturnal serpent has a somewhat flattened head, much broader than its slender neck and, at least toward humans, an extremely gentle, tolerant disposition. It typically constricts medium- and large-sized prey, but often chooses not to constrict smaller animals.

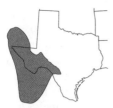

Nonvenomous   Trans-Pecos rat snakes almost never defend themselves against human beings.

Abundance   Uncommon. *Bogertophis subocularis* is among the numerous cryptic nocturnal Chihuahuan Desert serpents which, despite being widespread, are seldom seen by humans. For the most part "Subocs"—as these snakes are termed by reptile enthusiasts—are encountered on dark, humid nights between May and September on back roads through Texas' Val Verde, Terrell, Presidio, Brewster, and Jeff Davis counties (the author, however, once found a Trans-Pecos rat snake crossing busy U.S. Highway 90 between WalMart and Luby's in Del Rio). Other *B. subocularis* have been found as far north as the Guadalupe Mountains, but most of this species' range is northern Mexico, and its greatest concentration in the United States is probably along the Rio Grande's Big Bend.

Size   Adult *B. subocularis* measuring 30 to 48 inches long are most often seen in the wild—though Tennant found one 12¾-inch neonate with a fresh umbilical scar in Big Bend National Park late in September, and other juveniles turn up from time to time. Specimens have been recorded to 5½ feet in length.

Habitat   This arid land reptile's macrohabitat includes the northern Chihuahuan Desert's barren flats and slopes of ocotillo, lechugilla, and sotol cactus, as well as Trans-Pecos Texas' less xeric short-grass prairie and oak-juniper woodland at altitudes of more than 6,500 feet in Texas' Davis Mountains. Everywhere in its range the Trans-Pecos rat snake is found on and around rocky outcroppings and stony, heavily fissured road cuts.

Prey   Despite the preference for lacertillian prey shown by a majority of newly captured individuals, in its natural setting *B. subocularis* appears to be a generalized feeder on smaller vertebrates, with the exception of other snakes. The author once observed a well-fed Trans-Pecos rat snake coiled on a caveside ledge below a layer of flightless young Mexican free-tailed bats, while herpetologist Damon Salceies observed a rare instance of predation by this nocturnal hunter.

A wild adult *B. subocularis* which he had been watching from a distance with a flashlight flushed a crevice spiny lizard from its nighttime hiding place on a roadside rock ledge. Darting from beneath the

BROWN-BLOTCHED TERRESTRIAL SNAKES

411

thin layer of dirt that hid it from view, the lizard, as is typical, only ran a few feet, then paused and soon became drowsy, shutting one eye and then the other. Meanwhile, with the predatory concentration that characterizes all ophidian hunters, the Trans-Pecos rat snake crept gradually nearer its prey. Finally, holding its head and forebody motionless to avoid attracting the crevice spiny's attention, the rat snake drew its posterior body forward, gathering its coils behind its head. Then, belying the docile nature this species shows toward humans, the rat snake abruptly shot forward in a shower of flying dirt to pin the lizard in its open mouth, instantly encircling its prey with loops of its body.

Reproduction   Egg-laying. First accomplished by Jonathan Campbell at the Fort Worth Zoo during the 1960s, captive propagation of this species has since become widespread. Twenty-five pairings among *B. subocularis* maintained by D. Craig McIntyre reveal that only during a brief annual period of fertility will the female accept a mate, for nearly all these copulations took place between June 18 and 30.

Deposited during July, August, and September, the proportionately large eggs range from 3 to 11 per clutch and require a comparatively long incubation of up to 88 days. (Some *B. subocularis* clutches have taken more than 100 days to hatch, but since serpent embryos begin developing as soon as the egg is formed, longer incubation in the nest cavity may only mean that the mother has not retained her eggs for as long as females whose eggs hatch after shorter incubation.)

This species' long incubation and late-season breeding pattern—one road-killed Davis Mountains female was still gravid with unlaid eggs in late August, and the eggs of captives often hatch as late as Thanksgiving—means that the higher elevations of this animal's range have become quite cold by the time its young are ready to emerge from the egg. Therefore, rather than face this hostile time of year abroad, newborns may remain below ground until the following spring, perhaps emerging only rarely during their first year. (Another possibility, suggested by the presence of apparently fresh umbilical scars on neonate *B. subocularis* discovered in late spring, is that with the advent of cold weather this species' embryos may cease development within their eggs so that whole clutches may overwinter below ground, hatching only in the following year's warming temperatures.)

Delicate little creatures 11½ to 13 inches in length, hatchling *B. subocularis* are paler than the adults but share the same dorsal pattern. Sexual maturity is reached in 2 to 3 years, and fertility can last for at least an additional 13 seasons. (McIntyre's females have produced fertile eggs at more than 16 years of age, and one individual—which now holds the species' longevity record of 26 years—was captured as an adult in 1971 and has since laid more than 60 fertile eggs.)

Coloring/scale form   Against a soft, mustard-brown dorsolateral ground color a pair of parallel black lines, one on either side of the spine, are joined by 27 to 41 dark crossbars that form a series of H-shaped patterns along the spine. On the tail these crossbars become squarish saddles. (Pale yellow *B. subocularis* with no paravertebral stripes and only faint dorsal patterning also exist. In 1964 the first of these "blondes" was found in southern Brewster County by Dennie Miller of the Chihuahuan Desert Research Institute; since then other similarly colored individuals appear periodically from the lower Pecos River area to southern Presidio County. Some Trans-Pecos rat snakes from north of El Paso are also lighter-hued, but with a light gray ground color.)

The Trans-Pecos rat snake is unique among North American serpents in possessing 40 pairs of chromosomes instead of the usual 36 or 38, while its scalation is also unusual. A row of small subocular scales (from which the species' Latin name, *subocularis*, is derived) separates the scales of its upper lip from its eye.

The venter is a silky off-white on the throat that darkens to olive-buff by midbody; some individuals show dim undertail striping. Only the 7 vertebral rows of dorsal scales, which occur in 31 to 35 rows at midbody, are keeled.

Similar snakes   Classified with other North American rat snakes in the genus *Elaphe* until 1988, the Trans-Pecos rat snake has now been shown—by H. G. Dowling and R. M. Price—to be genetically distinct enough to warrant taxonomic placement in a new genus, *Bogertophis*. (This genus includes only one other species, the Baja California rat snake, *B. rosaliae*.) No other North American serpent shares either the Trans-Pecos rat snake's mustard-brown dorsolateral ground color or its distinctive dark, H-shaped vertebral pattern.

Behavior   Like many xeric-adapted reptiles, *B. subocularis* responds to the harsh climate of its Chihuahuan Desert range by restricting its movements on the surface to temperate summer nights. During the day, as well as for what may be as much as several months' winter brumation, it remains within this succulent-desert's subsurface labyrinth of creviced limestone. Living mostly in this sheltered milieu, the Trans-Pecos rat snake may have never needed to evolve strong fight-or-flight behavior for, illuminated by headlights, *B. subocularis* typically makes no attempt to escape, most often lying quietly when approached on foot, or to defend itself when picked up.

MEXICAN HOOK-NOSED SNAKE
Genus Ficimia

Mexican Hook-nosed Snake, *Ficimia streckeri*

The genus *Ficimia* is a member of the colubrine subfamily *Xenodontinae,* which, in the United States contains 2 genera (*Gyalopion* is the other) of the diminutive, minimally rear-fanged burrowing spider eaters known as hook-nosed snakes. Although these genera differ, their external characteristics are similar, with both resembling diminutive hog-nosed snakes. Both are oviparous, use similar defense mechanisms (writhing and popping the cloacal lining in and out, producing a snapping sound), and both have 17 rows of smooth dorsal scales and a divided anal plate. The crown of the Mexican hook-nose is largely devoid of a dark pattern, however, its enlarged rostral scale reaches all the way back to its frontal scale, and it is found only in the lower Rio Grande valley (the western hook-nosed snake lives in west-central Texas and the Trans-Pecos).

---

145 MEXICAN HOOK-NOSED SNAKE
Ficimia streckeri

Nonvenomous *Ficimia streckeri* does not bite human beings.

Abundance Common. Within its limited South Texas range, during May and June this primarily Mexican species is often seen at night on the back roads of Webb, Brooks, Jim Hogg, Duval, Zapata, and Starr counties.

Size Almost all Mexican hook-nose snakes are between 5½ and 9 inches in length, but the record is a comparatively huge 19 in.

Habitat Widely distributed throughout the Tamaulipan thorn brush biome of the Rio Grande plain, like most herpetofauna in this often dry country, *F. streckeri* is attracted to moisture and is most likely to be found in the vicinity of stock ponds and irrigation canals.

Prey Spiders are this reptile's preferred prey, but centipedes and other small invertebrates may also be taken. In an example of parallel evolution, this little snake has developed a hooked, upturned rostral scale which, along with its slightly bulbous forehead, closely resembles the cephalic configuration of the only distantly related western hook-nosed snake. (The upturned rostral of the much larger hog-nosed snakes is used both for digging for shelter and to root out hidden prey, but it is not clear whether the Mexican hook-nosed snake's similar-looking rostral is also directed toward uncovering hidden food animals—spiders are seldom fossorial—or whether its miniature snout-plow is used primarily for burrowing to evade predators.)

Reproduction Egg-laying. No other reproductive behavior is recorded for *F. streckeri*.

Coloring/scale form The Mexican hook-nosed snake's ground color is olive- to grayish-brown, patterned with 50 or more thin, dark, narrowly spaced vertebral crossbars which extend from its nape—where there is a single wider crossband—to its tail tip. Except for a large brown spot below its eye, its lips, throat, and lower sides are pale buff; its belly is off-white.

There are usually no internasal scales because this species' enlarged, upturned rostral scale, which has a surprisingly sharp point, occupies this area, separates the two prefrontal scales, and reaches all the way back to its frontal scale. (The Mexican hook-nosed snake's forehead exhibits the bulging brow characteristic of serpents which have evolved a hyper-developed rostral.) The otherwise smooth dorsal scales are pocked with tiny apical pits.

Similar snakes The **western hook-nosed snake (146)** has a smaller rostral scale that does not extend rearward as far as its frontal scale, leaving room for a conventional pair of internasal scales. Its crown is marked with a back-edged brown partial mask, and its similarly black-edged dorsal crossbands are wider than those of *F. streckeri*. The **Mexican hog-nosed snake (124)** has 23 rows of keeled dorsal scales and a proportionately larger rostral backed by a perpendicular reinforcing ridge.

Behavior *Ficimia streckeri*—whose name honors herpetologist John K. Strecker, former head librarian of Baylor University and the founding force behind its Strecker Museum—is also a slow-moving creature whose principal means of self-defense is its exceptional burrowing ability. When picked up, it vigorously noses downward through one's fingers; when set free it will disappear into soft earth within moments. The Mexican hook-nose's other defensive tactics include slowly weaving its miniature elevated head and forebody in a surprisingly adept approximation of the defensive posture of a pitviper, while a direly threatened individual may suddenly flip itself back and forth, making a sharp little popping sound by extending and retracting its cloacal lining through its vent.

WESTERN HOOK-NOSED SNAKE
Genus Gyalopion

Western Hook-nosed Snake, *Gyalopion canum*

First described in 1861 by pioneer paleontolgist Edward Drinker Cope, the genus *Gyalopion* is a member of the colubrine subfamily *Xenodontinae*. In the United States this subfamily contains 2 genera (*Ficimia* is the other) of the diminutive, minimally rear-fanged burrowing spider eaters known as hook-nosed snakes. Although these genera differ, their external characteristics are similar, with both resembling diminutive hog-nosed snakes.

Both genera are oviparous, burrowing snakes, widely distributed in northern Mexico, that emerge from burrows only after nightfall. Both feed primarily on spiders, both have 17 rows of smooth dorsal scales and a divided anal plate, and both use similar defense mechanisms: writhing and popping the cloacal lining in and out, producing a snapping sound.

Yet there are significant differences. In the United States *Gyalopion* is the more westerly of the 2 genera of hook-nosed snakes, occurring only in west-central Texas and the Trans-Pecos (the Mexican hook-nose is restricted to the Rio Grande valley). Its single species, *G. canum*, has a smaller rostral scale backed by the conventional pair of prefrontal scales, and its crown is strongly patterned with wide, black-edged brown bands.

146 WESTERN HOOK-NOSED SNAKE
Gyalopion canum

Nonvenomous   This little snake never bites humans.

Abundance   Fairly common. For nearly a century *Gyalopion canum* was thought to be extremely rare; now, due to increased reporting of observations, this species is known to occur widely over both Texas' Stockton Plateau and its Trans-Pecos region.

Size   Most western hook-nosed snakes are between 6½ and 11 inches in length; the record is a 17¼-inch-long Andrews County specimen found by Damon Salceies.

Habitat   *Gyalopion canum* is primarily an inhabitant of shortgrass prairie above 2,500 feet in elevation. After the summer rains have started it is often found in high meadows of the Davis Mountains. Western hook-nosed snakes also occur, although less frequently, at lower elevations on Texas' north-central plains and in the oak-juniper savannah of the western Edwards Plateau.

Its microhabitat on the surface is the shelter found beneath flat rocks and any sort of vegetative or manmade debris. This shelter's slightly enhanced humidity and damp earth substrate draw predatory spiders, centipedes, and scorpions in search of the smaller insects which find such conditions attractive. It is here that the western hook-nosed snake, in turn, discovers much of its arachnid and arthropod prey.

Prey   *Gyalopion canum* feeds on spiders, centipedes, and scorpions.

Reproduction   Egg-laying. All that is known about this species' reproduction is that in early July a captive female laid a single, pro-portionately large 1⅛-inch-long egg.

Coloring/scale form   The buff dorsolateral ground color of the western hook-nosed snake is both dark-speckled and crossed with black-edged brown or reddish brown, zigzag-edged vertebral bars. These taper to points just above its off-white venter. This little snake's bulbous forehead emphasizes the small depression, or in Greek, *gyalopion*, below. This prominent brow is crossed with a black-bordered brown band that partially masks the eyes and ex-tends posteriorly past the rear of its jaw. Above this band, rusty to dark brown bands and splotches, a pattern which varies from indi-vidual to individual, usually include a longitudinal brown patch on the rear of the skull and nape.

Yet the most distinctive characteristic of this stub-tailed little rep-tile is the tiny upturned hook formed by the enlarged rostral scale which tips its snout. This hyper-developed scale splits the internasal scales which lie just behind it and reaches back as far as the juncture of the prefrontal scales. The otherwise smooth dorsal scales are dot-ted with inconspicuous apical pits.

Similar snakes   The **Mexican hook-nosed snake (145)** is more olive-gray, has a darker, largely unpatterned crown and narrower, solid brown dorsolateral crossbands. There are usually no internasal scales because this species' enlarged rostral scale occupies their space and extends rearward between its prefrontals all the way to its frontal scale. The sympatrically ranging **dusty, Mexican,** and intergrade plains hog-nosed snakes (123, 124, 122) are more robust reptiles with 23 rows of keeled dorsal scales and a proportionately larger up-turned rostral scale with a raised keel along its anterior edge.

Behavior   Found at the surface mainly under rocks, this slow-gaited burrower emerges only after dark or, following summer rains, at dusk. Besides hiding, its primary protective strategy is to perhaps dis-comfit some predators by engaging in a series of sudden gyrations and producing distinct popping sounds by extending and retracting the lining of its cloaca through its vent.

KINGSNAKES, MILK AND SCARLET SNAKES
Genus Lampropeltis

The milk snake and kingsnake genus, *Lampropeltis*, is part of the colubrine subfamily *Lampropeltinae*. This subfamily includes both the rat and pine snake genera, *Elaphe* and *Pituophis*, respectively, to which *Lampropeltis* is more or less closely related since captives of all three genera have hybridized and produced viable offspring.

All *Lampropeltis* have scales so smooth they appear polished, and indeed *lampros* and *peltas* mean "shiny-scaled" in Greek. All *lampropeltis* have an undivided anal plate and are noted for their ophio-phagous inclination—predatory behavior aided by their great resis-tance to the venoms of the various pitvipers which share their habitat, and that sometimes leads them to cannibalize smaller mem-bers of their own species.

In the eastern and central United States there are four species of *Lampropeltis*, some arbitrarily called milk snakes and some kingsnakes, though there is no taxonomic difference between the two. Of these four species, only one, the gray-banded kingsnake, *L alterna*, is not subspeciated. A second species, *L. calligaster*, the prairie kingsnake, contains three subspecies, the south Florida mole kingsnake being of questionable validity. The third species, *L. getula*, the com-mon kingsnake, has five subspecies and several localized color morphs. The fourth species, *L. triangulum*, the milk snake, has eight formerly described subspecies and a problematic form, the Coastal Plains milk snake. (The prairie and mole kingsnakes have 21 to 27 dorsolateral scale rows, eastern representatives of the common kingsnake have 21 to 25 rows, the scales of milk snakes are arranged in 19 to 23 rows, and the scales of the gray-banded kingsnake occur in 25 rows.)

BROWN-BLOTCHED KINGSNAKES
Genus Lampropeltis

Prairie Kingsnake, *Lampropeltis calligaster calligaster*
Mole Kingsnake, *Lampropeltis calligaster rhombomaculata*
South Florida Mole Kingsnake, *Lampropeltis calligaster occipitolineata*

147 PRAIRIE KINGSNAKE
Lampropeltis calligaster calligaster

Nonvenomous   This mild-tempered reptile may vibrate its tail in fear, but even when picked up in the wild it seldom nips humans.

Abundance   Uncommon. Prairie kingsnakes are widely but sparsely distributed across a huge, primarily Great Plains (and its adjacent eastern woodlands) range. This extends from the western Gulf Coast north through central and eastern Texas and western Louisiana north across all of Oklahoma, eastern Kansas, all but northern Illinois, southern Indiana and western Kentucky. All *L. calligaster* are so secretive however, that in spite of being quite sizable snakes, they are only rarely seen even in open-country parts of the range.

Size   Adults average 2 to 3 feet in length; the record is 58⅛ in.

Habitat   As its common name implies, the prairie kingsnake is predominantly an inhabitant of grassland. This includes not only the dry tall-grass prairie of the upland plains but flood-prone salt-grass savannah and grassy barrier island dunes along the upper Gulf Coast—where piles of driftwood are a good microhabitat. Other areas where *L. c. calligaster* is often recorded includes the sheltered undersides of large flat rocks on stony hillsides, meadow/riparian woodland interface and, in the southeastern part of its range in northern Mississippi and southern Tennessee (where this race intergrades with its subspecies the mole kingsnake), hardwood forest.

Prey   Like other kingsnakes, *L. c. calligaster* is a powerful constrictor, but one more oriented toward warm-blooded prey than other kingsnakes: food animals include mice, rats, gophers, moles, and birds. Frogs and toads, lizards, and other snakes are also less frequently reported as prey.

Reproduction   Egg-laying. No natural nests are recorded, and hatchling *L. c. calligaster* evidently live deeply fossorial lives, for very few wild newborns have ever been observed. In captivity, clutches of 6 to 17 smooth-shelled eggs are deposited during late June and July, hatching into relatively small, 6- to 8-inch-long young (one such captive-hatched specimen has been maintained at the Oklahoma City Zoo for over 13 years).

Coloring/scale form   The prairie kingsnake's yellow- to light olive-brown dorsolateral ground color is usually patterned with 50 to 55 irregular brown vertebral saddles; its sides are marked with jagged brown spots. A short, yellow-brown vertebral stripe extends forward along the nape from its anterior back; the dark borders of this stripe widen, then come together on the forecrown to form a spearpoint-shaped marking; anterior to this spearpoint a dark stripe runs across the prairie king's snout, masks its eyes, and extends posteriorly past the rear of its jaw.

Lampropeltis calligaster calligaster also exhibits ontogenetic color variation, darkening with age and sometimes developing, from its dorsal blotches, four dimly defined dusky lengthwise stripes. Among very old prairie kingsnakes the entire dorsum may have darkened to a solid umber. The yellowish to cloudy gray venter—*calligaster* means "beautiful belly"—is checked with large, squarish, rusty-brown blotches, and the smooth dorsal scales occur in 25 to 27 midbody rows.

Similar snakes   The subspecies **mole kingsnake (148)** has a lighter, sometimes even whitish ground color patterned with slightly more numerous (an average of 57), more reddish-brown dorsal markings; it has only 21 to 23 midbody rows of dorsal scales. The **Great Plains rat snake (141)** has weakly keeled vertebral scales, a pale buff rather than olive-brown ground color, a dark-edged undertail tip and, unlike *Lampropeltis*, a divided anal plate. **Kansas** and **Texas glossy snakes (131, 132)** have a pale longitudinal line along the nape, at least 29 rows of dorsal scales, and an unmarked white belly.

Behavior   Prairie kingsnakes are secretive reptiles that seldom emerge from beneath rocks, clumps of grass, or the depths of small-mammal burrows (even in forested parts of its range *L. c. calligaster* is entirely terrestrial). John MacGregor has found the prairie kingsnake to be quite diurnal during spring in Kentucky, but in the more southerly part of its range foraging typically takes place at dusk in spring and fall, but occurs only well after dark during the hottest months. See **Mole Kingsnake.**

Lampropeltis calligaster rhombomaculata

Nonvenomous   Although mole kingsnakes are harmless to humans, some individuals will nip in self-defense.

Abundance   Rare. Widely distributed across the Southeast in a 150-mile-wide band stretching from the Mississippi Delta to Chesapeake Bay, *L. c. rhombomaculata* is seldom seen, even by herpetologists working in the field.

Size   Most adults are 30 to 40 inches long; the record is 47 in.

Habitat   Secretive in nature, *L. c. rhombomaculata* inhabits a variety of terrestrial milieus. These include upland pine/oak forest, its interface with pastures and agricultural areas, and both meadow and woodland in riparian corridors.

Prey   Prey includes most smaller vertebrates, especially reptiles.

Reproduction   Egg-laying. See **Prairie Kingsnake**.

Coloring/scale form   The mole kingsnake's off-white to buff dorsolateral ground color is patterned (more distinctly among juveniles, which also have a grayish crown), with an average total of 57 reddish-brown dorsal markings (vertebral blotches average 44, darker tail bands, 13). Occasionally, partial longitudinal striping is evident. Like other *L. calligaster*, a characteristic, Y-shaped rusty-brown marking is sometimes evident on the otherwise dark crown, but both the russet head and rusty-colored dorsal blotches of young adults become so much darker and less distinct with age that very old mole kingsnakes may be uniformly dusky brown. The pale, yellowish venter is checked or clouded with grayish brown—not particularly either beautiful or arranged in the rectangular spots indicated by the mole kingsnake's scientific names, "calligaster rhombomaculata." There are 21 to 23 midbody rows of dorsal scales.

Similar snakes   A northwestern subspecies, the **prairie kingsnake (147)**, has a more yellowish- to olive-tan dorsolateral ground color marked with slightly fewer (50 to 55) darker brown vertebral saddles; it has 25 to 27 midbody scale rows. On the other hand, the mole kingsnake's southerly race, the **south Florida mole kingsnake (149)**, has even more vertebral blotches: an average of 75 (body blotches average 58, dark tail bands, 17). Longitudinal dark lines may also streak its neck and the posterior sides of its head. The **corn snake (140)** has a dark-edged, not solid-colored spearpoint on its crown, some keeled dorsal scales, a divided anal plate, and a striped undertail.

Behavior A primarily fossorial animal, *L. c. rhombomaculata* is occasionally encountered crossing roads after heavy spring and summer rainfall—a time when the saturated soil forces many burrowing serpents to seek drier ground. Yet since 19 of 25 Alabama specimens collected in this way were males, most were probably searching, instead, for a reproductively receptive female's pheromone scent trail.

149 SOUTH FLORIDA MOLE KINGSNAKE
Lampropeltis calligaster occipitolineata

Nonvenomous This docile little snake does not bite humans.

Abundance Rare. Endemic to Florida, *L. c. occipitolineata* was only recognized as a subspecies in 1987, when it was described in the Bulletin of the Chicago Herpetological Society by Robert Price. Until recently, fewer than 20 of these animals were known, most from a smattering of locations in Brevard and Okeechobee counties. New records of 19 additional south Florida mole kingsnakes from Okeechobee, De Soto, Glades, and Hendry counties have considerably extended its known range, suggesting that rather than occurring only in disjunct, localized populations, *L. c. occipitolineata* may instead occupy much of the grassy floodplain that stretches more than 40 miles to the north, northwest, and west of Lake Okeechobee.

Size *Lampropeltis calligaster occipitolineata* is the same size as its northern subspecies, the mole kingsnake.

Habitat South Florida mole kingsnakes have been found in cattle pastures, in oak hammocks, and in abandoned fields. The periodically flooded grassland which formerly surrounded Lake Okeechobee is probably this small kingsnake's primary habitat, however, because most of the few *L. c. occipitolineata* that have been recorded came from this environment.

Prey According to Tim Walsh of the Central Florida Zoo, who has maintained this subspecies for 7 years, hatchling *L. c. occipitolineata* feed readily on anoles, ground skinks, and hatchling snakes; adults take either mice or snakes considerably smaller than themselves.

Reproduction Egg-laying. See **Mole Kingsnake.**

Coloring/scale form   The markings of this southern subspecies are similar to those of the more northerly mole kingsnake, except that they are somewhat neotenic in that adult *L. c. occipitolineata* retain the distinctly delineated reddish-brown dorsal blotches typical of juvenile mole kingsnakes of both races. *L. c. occipitolineata* averages 75 of these mid-dorsal blotches (body blotches average 58, tail bands, 17). Longitudinal dark lines also often streak the sides of this subspecies' head and anterior back, giving it the Latin name *occipitolineata*, or "eye-lined."

Similar snakes   The subspecies **mole kingsnake (148)** has an average total of 57 reddish-brown mid-dorsal markings (vertebral body blotches average 44, tail bands, 13). The **corn snake (140)** has a dark-edged rather than solid-colored spearpoint on its crown, some keeled dorsal scales, a divided anal plate, and a striped undertail.

Behavior   This rare reptile's burrowing lifestyle is so secretive and is so seldom encountered that Walsh was overjoyed to find the two specimens he located in the wild. As one of the few who has observed this subspecies in depth, he has become an authority on its captive behavior and husbandry.

PALE-SPECKLED KINGSNAKES
Genus Lampropeltis

Eastern Kingsnake, *Lampropeltis getula getula*
Florida Kingsnake, *Lampropeltis getula floridana*
Black Kingsnake, *Lampropeltis getula nigra*
Speckled Kingsnake, *Lampropeltis getula holbrooki*
Desert Kingsnake, *Lampropeltis getula splendida*

150   EASTERN KINGSNAKE
Lampropeltis getula getula

Nonvenomous   If they are threatened, eastern kingsnakes sometimes swell their necks and, using their robust neck and jaw muscles, bite with determination. If treated gently, however, they soon become entirely at ease while being handled unless one's hands smell of their prey, in which case they may try an exploratory nip.

Abundance   Common. Drawn by the proliferation of rodents in many human-altered environments, this beautiful, thick-bodied constrictor is

frequently encountered despite its secretive nature. From central New Jersey to north-central Florida it is widespread along the Atlantic seaboard as far inland as the foothills of the Appalachians. Eastern kingsnakes living on the Outer Banks of the Carolinas are both uncommon and somewhat unusual in appearance but—though this population is probably only a local color phase—an Outer Banks kingsnake, *L. g. sticticeps*, is listed as a species of special concern by the state of North Carolina.

To the south, another common, strongly divergent color variant inhabits the Apalachicola lowlands of the Florida panhandle. A third, apparently disjunct population eastern/Florida kingsnake intergrades occurs in the Okefenokee drainage of southeastern Georgia and adjacent Florida. Across northrn peninsular Florida the eastern kingsnake also intergrades with its subspecies the Florida kingsnake, and to the west in southern Mississippi the range of *L. g. getula* merges into that of its more westerly ranging subspecies, the speckled kingsnake.

Size   Neonates are 7 to 11½ inches in length, with about the diameter of a pencil; adult eastern kingsnakes are robust, cylindrically-bodied reptiles (whose head is often no thicker than the stout neck) usually 36 to 48 inches in length. The record is 82 in.

Habitat   Found in pine and hardwood forest, fields and meadows in the north (although generally not far from water), *L. g. getula* occurs in the southern parts of its range around hyacinth-filled ponds and canals, cypress strands and marshes. Eastern kingsnakes are especially likely to be found around or hidden beneath human-generated debris such as boards and discarded roofing metal. In a similar microenvironment these animals occur in the ruins of abandoned sawmills, houses and barns, trash piles and dumps, and at the base of crumbling stone walls. Old wooden railroad trestles, stump holes, and large fallen tree trunks also attract these big kingsnakes. Along thousands of miles of Atlantic and Gulf coastal shoreline this race of *L. getula* is also found on saline tidal flats and in reed-lined estuaries.

Prey   *Lampropeltis getula* is a primarily terrestrial scent hunter that preys on a variety of smaller vertebrates. Other snakes, including members of its own species, as well as venomous pitvipers, are overcome with a combination of the kingsnakes' great resistance to hematoxic venom and their ability to immobilize ophidian prey, including pitvipers nearly as long as themselves, with tireless constriction and the power of their muscular jaws. Small mammals, birds, fish, and frogs are also taken, while another favorite food is turtle eggs. In 1915, Wright and Bishop reported that rural people often told of finding a kingsnake waiting for a female turtle to deposit her eggs. Unlike many such folktales, this one proved true: J. L. Knight and R. K. Loraine (1986) described watching a South Carolina box turtle obliviously excavate her nest cavity while an adult eastern kingsnake, its head elevated for a better view, waited nearby.

This snake later regurgitated 4 previously eaten turtle eggs, then defecated pieces of at least 10 additional kinosternid eggs, indicating that it had robbed at least 3 different turtle nests. See **Black Kingsnake.**

Reproduction Egg-laying. Much more has been written about the reproduction of captive kingsnakes than is recorded concerning this animal's breeding habits in the wild, but courtship among free-ranging *L. g. getula* is known to follow the typical pattern for colubrid snakes. Breeding occurs between March and June, clutches of 3 to 29 eggs can be deposited at any time throughout the summer, and after 60 to 70 days of incubation the 7½- to 11-inch-long young emerge, often covered with a suffusion of rose- to orange-colored pigment which soon disappears.

Coloring/scale form Throughout most of its range the eastern kingsnake is characterized by a fairly uniform appearance: its ground color is black or very dark brown, overlaid with white to cream-colored crossbands which enclose 30 to 40 dark dorsal saddles, and on its sides separate to form a chain-like pattern. (Dorsally, the cross-links of this pale-hued "chain" are usually narrow, but among populations such as the eastern kingsnakes living in the Charleston area of South Carolina, the crosslinks may be quite wide.)

Lampropeltis getula getula found in Florida's Apalachicola low-lands vary even more widely. Some entirely lack crossbands and have only a dark vertebral stripe. These animals may exhibit a distinct, light-hued spot on each dorsolateral scale. Other individuals have only broken horizontal bars on their flanks with no dark vertebral stripe, while still others are marked with 20 to 25 light-spotted dark saddles separated by broad, 4- to 8-scale-wide pale dorsolateral bands. In the past many of these Apalachicola River basin variants were thought to be a separate race, "*L. g. goini*," but since most kingsnakes found in this area exhibit typical *L. g. getula* patterning it is now believed that these color/pattern types and the more typical kingsnakes that share the same range are all simply color variants of the eastern kingsnake, *L. g. getula.*

A similar situation is likely to prevail among the "Outer Banks kingsnakes" found on the barrier islands off the North Carolina coast. First described in 1942, this population was formerly referred to as "*L. g. sticticeps*," an ostensible subspecies defined by its reportedly enlarged, tapering rostral scale, its lighter ground color (made up of fewer than 35 white dorsolateral bars but with a great deal of white in its dark lateral areas), and 210 or fewer ventral scales.

In evaluating the validity of this race, however, William Palmer and Alvin Braswell (1995) re-counted several specimens' ventral scales and found that the original describers had erred. Additionally, all this form's other presumed differences from mainland kingsnakes also occur sporadically among *L. g. getula* living throughout its range, and the Outer Banks population is now thought to be only a local variant of the eastern kingsnake.

The venter of all color phases is usually heavily blotched with black, and most often there are 21 midbody rows of dorsal scales (though some individuals have 23 rows).

Similar snakes   The subspecies **Florida kingsnake (151)** has a reduced, or less-distinct pale dorsal pattern, with lighter-tipped dark scales frequently appearing within the dark vertebral rectangles separated by its more than 40 pale vertebral crossbands. This race usually has 23 midbody dorsal scale rows. See **Speckled Kingsnake.**

Behavior   *Lampropeltis getula getula* is a big, slow-moving serpent whose principal defense against predators is to retire into holes or rodent tunnels. Even in wooded terrain it is almost always encountered on the ground, although it also swims well and can even climb: M. W. Eichholz and W. D. Koenig (1992) found *L. getula* species from the western United States ascending trees to prey on hatchling bluebirds inside experimental nest boxes.

Because of this animal's vividly contrasting dorsal patterns, its docile disposition, willingness to breed in confinement, and the ease of feeding domestically bred young, *L. g. getula* is among the most popular captive reptiles, and eastern kingsnakes raised in confinement have lived nearly 23 years.

151   FLORIDA KINGSNAKE
Lampropeltis getula floridana

Nonvenomous   See **Eastern Kingsnake.**

Abundance   Common. Endemic to Florida and the most numerous of the state's kingsnakes, *L. g. floridana* is widespread from the central peninsula south to the tip of the mainland. Two researchers, R. M. Blaney, 1977, and Kenneth Krysko, 1995, delineate this subspecies' range with quite different northern and eastern borders, but it is clear that throughout central Florida, in a wide band stretching from Baker and

Duval counties in northeastern Florida south to Pinellas and Hernando counties on the Gulf Coast, eastern and Florida kingsnakes interbreed. (This sort of intergradation also occurs around Jacksonville as well as in the Apalachicola delta, with members of these intergrade populations showing combinations of the markings and scutellation of both races—or, in the case of Apalachicola kings, exhibiting coloration atypical of either eastern or Florida kingsnakes.)

Krysko also found that, probably due to habitat fragmentation from residential development and to hunting by commercial reptile collectors, populations of *L. g. floridana*, especially the lightest-colored animals living in the southernmost part of the state, have declined substantially. Yet, because of the Florida kingsnake's broad range and its abundance in particular areas such as the sugarcane fields around Lake Okeechobee, *L. g. floridana* is still not afforded legal protection; Krysko's solution would be "for the southern Dade Co. population to be managed by the state, prohibiting the collection of *L. getula* during March, April, and May, when breeding and egg-laying take place."

Size Florida kingsnakes are about the same size as their more northerly subspecies, the eastern kingsnake; the record length is somewhat shorter, however, at 69½ inches.

Habitat Habitat is similar to that of the eastern kingsnake, with the addition of the irrigation canal banks found only in south Florida.

Prey Like its northern and western subspecies, the Florida kingsnake is a predatory generalist. During an extensive study of both races of *L. getula*, Krysko identified in the natural diet of the Florida subspecies green water snakes, ribbon snakes, ring-necked snakes, black racers, five-lined skinks, juvenile cottontails, hispid cotton rats, and turtle eggs. Other rodents, lizards, birds and their eggs, greater sirens, and striped swamp snakes are also reportedly taken, as are smaller Florida kingsnakes and members of the Florida king's own species.

Kingsnakes have also long been noted for their relentless predation on venomous snakes. Venerable herpetologist Archie Carr recorded two such episodes: a Florida kingsnake eating an adult cottonmouth near a Lake County flatwoods pond and another *L. g. floridana* devouring a coral snake on the shore of Lake Virginia in Orange County. See **Black Kingsnake**.

Reproduction Egg-laying. Breeding among *L. g. floridana* begins a bit earlier in the year than does that of more northerly races—Krysko observed combat rituals between rival males in the wild as early as February, with breeding continuing until June.

Whatever their ultimate coloring, most newborn Florida kingsnakes hatch with shiny yellowish-white crossbands that separate darker vertebral rectangles; their dark-speckled sides are often suffused with orange. As these snakes mature, among pale color-phase individuals an ontogenetic change gradually lightens these dark areas until their pale dividing lines almost disappear. See **Eastern Kingsnake**.

Coloring/scale form   Members of this variably colored subspecies are characterized by each dorsolateral scale's yellowish base and brown tip. There are more than 40 pale vertebral crossbands dividing often only slightly darker, dimly defined rectangular areas— crossbands that are more distinct in young animals before ontogenetic lightening of their coloration has occured. (This age-related change to a paler color with maturation is most typical of *L. getula* living on the pale limestone substrate of southern Florida, a population once recognized as the subspecies *L. g. brooksi* by the academic community and called brooks kingsnakes in the pet trade, where the more separate types of kingsnakes one could offer for sale, the greater one's turnover.)

Individuals bearing very pale dorsolateral coloring are often found in the marshes and cane fields around Lake Okeechobee, and adult males from southern Dade and Monroe counties and western Collier and Lee counties are often lighter in color than adult females fom the same areas. Since this is an area rich in prey these kingsnakes also tend to be particularly robust animals.

The variably light-hued belly of the Florida kingsnake is to a greater or lesser degree blotched with black, and most often its dorsal scales are arranged in 23 midbody rows (though some individuals have only 21 rows).

Similar snakes   *Lampropeltis getula* living from the vicinity of Levy, Alachua, and Flagler Counties southward to Tampa Bay on the west coast and to Palm Beach County on the east coast are considered to be intergrades between the Florida and eastern kingsnake subspecies. These animals undergo a less dramatic ontogenetic change than pure Florida kingsnakes, and often retain much of their dark juvenile pigmentation and dorsolateral patterning throughout their lives. The pure **eastern kingsnake (150)** also has a shiny black to deep brown dorsum with less than 30 very narrow light-yellow crossbands that both enclose black vertebral rectangles and form a chain-like pattern on its sides; it usually has 21 midbody rows of dorsal scales. Juvenile **southern black** and **Everglades racers (108, 110)** have a divided anal plate and lack patterning on the upper side of their tails.

Behavior   Local reptile hunters believe that in the vicinity of Lake Okeechobee, Florida kingsnakes feed solely on turtle eggs, and while a number of adult *L. g. floridana* collected there and in southern Dade County by Krysko had recently eaten turtle eggs, in captivity these individuals also fed readily on mice. This may represent learned rather than instinctual predatory behavior, for ingestively naive neonate kingsnakes—which possess only innate, instinctual food preferences—from southern Florida wetlands often refuse to eat either nestling mice or small lizards. As Krysko discovered, their genetically determined feeding orientation is almost entirely ophiophagous: when presented with a sliver of Florida green water snake flesh these young kingsnakes, which previously refused small mammalian and lacertillian prey, vigorously gulped it down, then exhibited the same enthusiastic predatory response toward both small rat snakes and house geckos.

Such intense preferences show that individuals from certain areas have an inherited orientation toward certain food species. In this case, snakes are appropriate prey for *L. g. floridana* living in south Florida's marshlands since aquatic serpents are especially abundant there. Rodents and lizards are for the most part dry land–living creatures that in flooded marshes never match the biomass of aquatic reptiles such as the Florida green water snake, which annually deposits litters of up to 100 offspring at about the time young kingsnakes begin foraging.

Yet, unlike their predatorial-naive hatchlings, Krysko found that (in addition to numerous ophidian remains in their feces) adult *L. g. floridana* captured in this area also feed readily on mice. For instinctual snake-eaters this may constitute learned behavior—a broadening of their inbred vomeronasal images of the proper food species in order to take advantage of the newly available small mammal prey provided by the replacement of their original wetland habitat with agricultural fields able to support a large rodent population.

152 BLACK KINGSNAKE, *Lampropeltis getula nigra*

Nonvenomous   If aggressively confronted, *L. g. nigra* is not reluctant to strike and bite, and adult kingsnakes have jaws strong enough to cause a wound. (Even tame captives sometimes develop the disconcerting habit of first carefully smelling, then vigorously chewing on a finger).

Abundance   Locally common. In parts of its compact range, which encompasses southeastern Illinois, southern Indiana and Ohio, western West

Virginia, almost all of Kentucky and Tennessee, and northern Georgia and Alabama, this is a very abundant subspecies. In other areas well within its general distribution it is only infrequently encountered.

Size Although most black kingsnakes are adult at between 3 and 4 feet in length, occasional specimens reach almost 5 ft. Hatchlings measure about 10½ in.

Habitat The black kingsnake has the same habitat preferences as other eastern *L. getula*: moisture, ample hiding places, and a constant food supply seem to be the only circumstances this reptile requires. It inhabits open woodlands, forest clearings and edges, meadows, the margins of ditches and ponds, and the periphery of swamps, marshes, and impoundments, especially the sunny, grassy slopes of their retaining embankments or dikes. Within these macrohabitats, black kingsnakes utilize all manner of ground cover and are found, sometimes in numbers, beneath boards, roofing tin and other debris: dumps and trash piles are especially favored microhabitats.

Prey The *getula*-complex kingsnakes are dietary generalists. Individuals captured in the northern part of the range mostly eat mice, snakes, and lizards, refusing birds and amphibians, but those from the south sometimes show a preference for amphibians, smaller reptiles and their eggs (some populations seem to preferentially seek out turtle eggs and hatchling turtles).

Kingsnakes are also powerful constrictors, and are able to survive the venoms of the pitvipers with which they are sympatric in distribution, although marked swelling results, which can last up to a week. *L. getula* can overpower all but the largest pitvipers, but to say (as many popular articles maintain) that kingsnakes are the sworn enemies of venomous species is untrue, and after being bitten by a viper the kingsnake usually chooses not to eat it.

Reproduction Egg-laying. From 2 to 12 (rarely up to 15) eggs, which often adhere in an irregular cluster, are deposited in a moisture-retaining substrate. This may be beneath a board, log, mat of vegetation, or in a sawdust pile, stump hole, or decomposing log or stump. Depending upon temperature and ground moisture, incubation takes from 55 to 68 days.

Coloring/scale form This aptly named reptile is one of the least colorful of the eastern kingsnake races. Black pigment predominates, especially dorsally, with most individuals having a small but variable amount of yellow on their sides (in many cases the yellow chain pattern typical of the eastern kingsnake is at least weakly visible). On other snakes, especially old ones (for hatchlings are more contrastingly patterned), this chain-like pattern is nearly invisible, and only a few yellow-spotted lateral scales are apparent. The almost entirely black head is narrow for a kingsnake, the venter is predominantly black, with variable pale spots and bars, and there are usually 21 rows of smooth, shiny dorsolateral scales.

Similar snakes Northern and southern black racers (107, 108) lack yellow lateral spots and have only 17 midbody rows of satiny (not shiny) smooth dorsolateral scales and a divided anal plate. Juvenile gray and black rat snakes (137, 134) have lightly keeled scales and a divided anal plate, while the black pine snake (127) has heavily keeled scales, a strongly convex rostral, and 4 prefrontal scales. Black phase eastern hog-nosed snakes (120) have a sharp, upturned rostral scale and a stubby-appearing body. See **Speckled Kingsnake.**

Behavior Although essentially a terrestrial animal, the black kingsnake swims well and occasionally climbs. During cool weather it is primarily diurnal, sometimes sunning itself in exposed areas, but more often engaging in the thermoregulatory basking (so necessary for a snake with such a northerly range) while secluded beneath recumbent vines and grasses where its color and pattern meld magnificently with traceries of light and shadow. As the weather warms, *L. g. nigra* becomes more inclined to crepuscular foraging.

153   SPECKLED KINGSNAKE

Lampropeltis getula holbrooki

Nonvenomous If molested, the speckled kingsnake may swell its neck and bite with determination. If treated gently, however, it quickly becomes accustomed to handling, although if one's hands smell of its prey it may try an exploratory nip.

Abundance Fairly common. *Lampropeltis getula holbrooki,* which is named for the father of American herpetology, John Edwards Holbrook, occupies a mostly wooded range that stretches from the Gulf coasts of eastern Texas, Louisiana, Mississippi, and Alabama north along the Mississippi valley as far as southern Iowa. The speckled kingsnake's territorial influence is much broader than this, however, for as an intergrade with the eastern and black kingsnakes its range extends to the east as far as Alabama, central Tennessee, the western tip of Kentucky and southern Illinois; to the west *L. g. holbrooki* shares a huge zone of intergradation with its subspecies, the desert kingsnake, that reaches from the western Gulf Coast north across the black-land prairies of central Texas, Oklahoma, Kansas, and Nebraska—penetrating further north than any other kingsnake.

Size Recorded to 74 inches in length, adult speckled kingsnakes are robust, cylindrically bodied reptiles whose muscular necks are, among well-fed individuals, as large in diameter as their heads. Most adults are 18 to 36 inches long; hatchlings are 6 to 9 inches in length and about the thickness of a pencil.

Habitat Despite the extent of its northward distribution, *L. getula* kingsnakes are basically southern animals, and *L. g. holbrooki* is far more common in the South. Here, it occupies a variety of terrestrial and semi-aquatic environments, among them pine and deciduous woodland (where rotting logs and stumps are a favored microhabitat), grassy pastures, estuarine wetlands (including saline tidal flats), and salt-grass- and succulent-covered barrier beach dunes where speckled kingsnakes are found sheltering beneath driftwood.

During wet spring weather, along the upper Gulf Coast *L. g. holbrooki* occurs with some frequency in brackish and freshwater marshes, throughout inundated riparian bottomland, around abandoned farms, and along the edges of crop fields and drainage ditches where other snakes are likely to be found.

Prey Speckled kingsnakes are scent-oriented hunters which prey on a variety of smaller vertebrates. Other snakes, including members of their own species as well as venomous pitvipers, are also devoured. Although pitvipers are formidable adversaries that may strike and poison them repeatedly, kingsnakes are resistant to the effects of Crotalid venom and sometimes overcome these vipers by immobilizing them with constriction. Then the kingsnake's powerful neck and jaw muscles let it work its way forward to engulf the head of the viper although often after a viper's bite the kingsnake chooses not to consume its prey. Small mammals, birds, fish, and frogs are also taken; a favorite food is turtle eggs.

Reproduction Egg-laying. See **Desert Kingsnake.**

Coloring/scale form Each shiny black or dark brown dorsal scale bears a yellowish-white spot—creating, among adults, a uniformly pale-speckled patternless back and sides. (Juveniles are also profusely light-freckled, but many of their light-colored spots are clumped together in pale lines that cross the back, leaving dark intervening areas similar to those of the eastern and Florida kingsnakes.) The venter is predominantly yellow, checked or blotched with black; the glossy dorsal scales—*Lampropeltis* means "shining skin"—are arranged in 21 to 23 midbody rows.

Similar snakes   A western race, the **desert kingsnake (154)**, is distinguished by its predominantly black venter and crown, its 23 to 25 dorsolateral scale rows, and its large dorsal areas of predominantly black or dark brown scales. To the east, the **black kingsnake (152)** is predominantly black above, with only a few yellow-spotted scales on its sides, a narrow, almost entirely black head, and a mostly black venter. The **eastern kingsnake (150)** is usually patterned with less than 30 narrow, white or yellow dorsolateral crossbands that split, on its sides, to form a chain-like pattern. This race can exhibit almost any combination of pale cross-dorsal bands or even dark stripes, but only those from the Apalachicola River basin are likely to have a patternless dorsum like the speckled king.

Behavior   See **Eastern Kingsnake.**

154   DESERT KINGSNAKE

Lampropeltis getula splendida

Nonvenomous   Like other kingsnakes, *L. g. splendida* is for the most part a docile animal when approached (or even first handled) in the wild. Yet if badly threatened, even a small individual may put on a valiant defensive display: drawing its neck into an S-shaped curve, vibrating its tail tip, and striking open-mouthed. Big kingsnakes can bite with conviction, but most of these strikes are bluffs, and most frightened desert kings merely defecate and discharge odorous musk.

Abundance   Uncommon. This xeric-adapted race of *L. getula* is widespread in northwestern Mexico and western Texas. North of the U.S. border it is most numerous in the thorn brush community of the Rio Grande valley and the blackland prairie of central Texas, Oklahoma, and Kansas. In the eastern part of this prairie grassland, as an intergrade with its eastern race, the speckled kingsnake, *L. g. splendida* ranges north across the Great Plains as far as Nebraska—reaching a higher latitude than any other kingsnake.

Desert kingsnakes are also widely distributed throughout extensive montane areas west of the Pecos River, but they are not common there, or in the intervening low-lying Chihuahuan Desert, except in artificially watered areas like the irrigated fields around Balmorrhea, where this subspecies is abundant. (Elsewhere in northwestern Texas, even the largest desert kingsnakes may spend most of their lives as burrowers: after torrential rains in Andrews County had flooded many snakes from their subsurface haunts, Damon Salceies found a gravid female *L. g. splendida* almost 5 feet long.)

Size   Adults average 22 to 38 inches in length; the record is 60 in.

Habitat   *Lampropeltis getula splendida* may occur in any rural habitat in the western half of Texas. Yet—despite its common name—the desert king generally inhabits the more mesic parts of its range and is most often found near water tanks or within riparian corridors. Here, the soil is soft enough for burrowing (in the far west, for much of the year the desert king appears to be even more fossorial than its eastern relatives) and it is more likely to find its favored prey of other snakes and buried reptile eggs.

Prey   This arid land–living kingsnake feeds on other snakes, lizards, and small mammals, as well as on clutches of reptile eggs detected beneath the surface by smell. In part because of its resistance to pitviper venom, *L. g. splendida* is also able to prey on the young diamond-backed rattlesnakes which, in early autumn, are extremely common within its range (at this kingsnake's scent even huge western diamond-backs, far too big to fall prey to any *Lampropeltis*, instinctually edge backward, shielding their heads with a body coil).

Reproduction   Egg-laying. Courtship and copulation among desert kingsnakes take place between March and June. Clutches of 5 to 12 adhesive-surfaced eggs are deposited in late June or July, sometimes buried as deeply as a foot to prevent drying, in the extremely low humidity of their parent's western range, through their moisture-permeable shells. After about 60 days of incubation the 8½- to 10-inch-long hatchlings emerge, each weighing about ⅕ ounce.
  Brightly yellow-speckled with pale vertebral cross-lines and as shiny as porcelain figurines, hatchlings are marked with a row of big dark vertebral squares. As individuals from the eastern part of the range mature, these dark vertebral areas may be fragmented by encroaching yellow flecks; western specimens are more uniformly dark above.

Coloring/scale form   This beautiful kingsnake is notable for its glossy black or very dark brown dorsum, finely speckled with off-white or yellow. Some of these flecks may join to form narrow, pale yellow crossbands, between which large black or dark brown dorsal rectangles are only faintly pale-speckled. Light yellow scales usually predominate along the lower sides.

West of the Pecos River, even more strikingly-colored *L. g. splendida* make up a considerable percentage of the population. Posteriorly colored like individuals from the eastern part of the range, this Chihuahuan Desert color phase—called "sock-heads" by enthusiasts—has a jet black head and neck with only a bit of yellow labial scale edging. Other Trans-Pecos desert kings have such uniformly glossy black heads and forebodies that they look as if they had been dipped in black enamel.

The venter of both adult and young is mostly black or dark gray, with white or pale yellow blotches marking the ventral plates of the intergrade specimens found throughout the south-central Great Plains. The dorsal scales are arranged in 23 to 25 rows at midbody.

Similar snakes   An eastern subspecies, the **speckled kingsnake (153)**, is distinguished by its largely unmarked, more uniformly yellow- or white-speckled back, sides, and head, its predominantly yellow, black-blotched venter, and its 21 to 23 midbody rows of dorsal scales. Intergrades with the speckled kingsnake prevail in a wide band along the eastern portion of the desert king's range, where most individuals exhibit characteristics, such as partially pale cross-patterned dorsums and yellow-and-black bellies that combine the attributes of both races.

Behavior   See **Black Kingsnake.**

RED- AND BLACK-BANDED MILK AND KINGSNAKES
Genus Lampropeltis

Eastern Milk Snake, *Lampropeltis triangulum triangulum*
Scarlet King Snake, *Lampropeltis triangulum elapsoides*
Red Milk Snake, *Lampropeltis triangulum syspila*
Louisiana Milk Snake, *Lampropeltis triangulum amaura*
Mexican Milk Snake, *Lampropeltis triangulum annulata*
New Mexico Milk Snake, *Lampropeltis triangulum celaenops*
Central Plains Milk Snake, *Lampropeltis triangulum gentilis*
Pale Milk Snake, *Lampropeltis triangulum multistrata*
Gray-banded Kingsnake, *Lampropeltis alterna*

Lampropeltis triangulum triangulum

Nonvenomous Like other king-snakes (milk snakes are only set off by common name; there is no taxonomic difference), the disposition of *L. t. triangulum* is variable. This is based on temperature (cool snakes are more docile), recent hunting success (hungry snakes are more irritable), the degree to which the animal

has been disturbed, and innate individual differences in temperament. When nervous, some eastern milk snakes vibrate their tails, producing an audible whirring, yet can be handled with impunity even when first picked up in the wild. Others rear into a striking S at the slightest provocation, but all will bite if sufficiently provoked.

Abundance Occasionally locally abundant, but more often very uncommon, eastern milk snakes are secretive. As a group, despite their bright colors *L. triangulum* go mostly unnoticed due to their exceptional ability to hide in even minimal cover.

For example, in rural northwestern Massachusetts Richard D. Bartlett discovered about a dozen adult eastern milk snakes one spring morning beneath a single weathered sheet of plywood. Despite hours of searching, no other *L. t. triangulum* had been noted in the area, nor were any ever found there again.

Size Most adult *L. t. triangulum* measure between 24 and 40 inches in length; the record is 52 in.

Habitat *Lampropeltis triangulum triangulum* inhabits elevations from mountaintop to coastal plain, which covers a great variety of habitats. It is found on rocky hillsides (where individuals seek seclusion under rocks), along field and meadow edges (where mats of vegetation serve as shelters), and on road shoulders in damp lowlands (where its amphibian, reptile, and small rodent prey are both abundant and more easily captured in the open).

Eastern milk snakes are also occasionally seen around barnyard buildings, in deserted, tumble-down dwellings, or beneath manmade debris and litter at the edges of dumps or trash piles where mouse nests holding newborns are numerous.

Prey   Lizards and nestling rodents seem to be favored as prey, but in confinement large individuals accept adult mice and even juvenile rats as food; one such eastern milk snake maintained by Bartlett swallowed an adult spotted salamander, then spent a long time trying to wipe the salamander's skin secretions from its face and mouth. Other snakes and buried reptile eggs are also eaten by eastern milk snakes, while a wild-caught indiviual taken in Vinton County, Ohio, promptly regurgitated two nestling birds.

Reproduction   Egg-laying. From 6 to as many as 24 eggs are deposited within decomposing logs and stumps, mats of vegetation, burrows, stump holes, or beneath moisture-retaining surface debris. Incubation may take as few as 58 days or, if temperatures are cooler, up to 68 days. At more than 10 inches long, the hatchlings are comparatively sizable, but only as newborns do they show the bright colors—on a pale gray ground color, neonates have dark-edged red dorsal saddles alternating with red lateral spots—for which their species is known.

Coloring/scale form   As adults, most eastern milk snakes are brownish above. The pretty, highly contrasting colors of neonates are retained by only juveniles and a few adults because with growth, the bright red saddles of most juveniles dulls to maroon or russet-olive, sometimes with a brownish- olive-, or cinnamon-colored sheen, as the adult ground color darkens to olive- or dark gray. (This triangular arrangement of spots or small bars led to the Latin species name *triangulum*.) Intergradation with the Scarlet Kingsnake occurs to the east; with the red milk snake to the west. The tip of the snout is gray and a dark line extends posteriorly from the eye to the rear corner of the mouth. The grayish belly is variably checked with bluish-black—spots that sometimes extend onto the lowest row of dorsolateral scales, which are most often arranged in 21 midbody rows, but vary from 19 to 23 rows.

Similar snakes   Of the more than 25 milk snake subspecies that range from southern Canada to the mountains of northern South America, the eastern milk snake is among the least likely to be mistaken for the **eastern coral snake (172)** because it is not ringed with brilliant bands of red, black, and yellow. The **northern copperhead (175)**, for which the eastern milk snake is sometimes mistaken, has light-hued brown crossbands that are narrowest over its spine and a wide, coppery-colored head with big, pale, slit-pupiled eyes. The **prairie kingsnake (147)** can be confusingly similar to this milk snake, but is basically a medium brown snake blotched dorsally and laterally with darker brown; it is often initially difficult to distinguish, but lacks the milk snake's lighter-hued ground color, often reddish dorsal saddles, and pale-centered, reddish-bordered cranial spearpoint; its subspecies the mole kingsnake (148) has a darker olive-brown ground color, more widely separated dorsal saddles, and largely unmarked sides. The **corn snake (140)** has weakly keeled vertebral scales and a divided anal plate.

Behavior   Except when frightened, milk snakes move quite slowly. They swim well and are able to climb, but are basically a terrestrial species.

156   SCARLET KINGSNAKE
Lampropeltis triangulum elapsoides

Nonvenomous   Scarlet kingsnakes seldom bite when picked up in the field, although occasional individuals may defend themselves vigorously, nipping and hanging tenaciously. Commonly believed to be a coral snake mimic (though the biological validity of this assumption is uncertain) *L. t. elapsoides* is distinguished from the coral snake by both its red snout and cheeks and its black-bordered red dorsolateral bands: "Red touches black means friend of Jack."

Abundance   Fairly common. Once thought to be rare because its retiring, semi-subterranean lifestyle limited its exposure to humans, *L. t. elapsoides* is now known to be locally abundant and in spite of the myriad inroads into its habitat made by timbering and land-clearing, scarlet kingsnakes are widespread from southern Virginia south to the tip of mainland Florida, west to the Mississippi River and north as far as northeastern Kentucky. It is more spottily distributed in the Piedmont provinces of the southeastern states and western Tennessee.

In many areas where the range of the scarlet kingsnake abuts that of its subspecies the eastern and red milk snakes, this race does not seem to interbreed with these neighboring races, yet from Virginia north to New Jersey—as well as in montane parts of South Carolina, Georgia, and Alabama, intergrade individuals have been found. This is a difficult snake to define with precision because in contrast, John MacGregor reports that *L. t. elapsoides* occurs with *L. t. syspila* in western Kentucky without evidence of interbreeding. See **Coastal Plains Milk Snake.**

In south Florida, Richard Bartlett has found up to 8 scarlet kingsnakes in a single evening, and in the low country of South Carolina has encountered more than 30—all less that 17 inches in length—on a cold spring afternoon.

Especially at this time of year, when low-lying forest is often flooded (for *L. t. elapsoides* avoids saturated ground), scarlet kingsnakes may be found wedged beneath the loosened bark of pine stumps; later in the year they are primarily fossorial inhabitants of sandy loam, although they appear at the surface under logs and construction debris during rainy weather, at which time they may also be seen crossing roads or, in south Florida, ascending rough-barked trees. See **Eastern Milk Snake.**

Size   *Lampropeltis triangulum elapsoides* is among the smallest of the milk snakes. It has been recorded up to 28 inches in length, but most adults measure only 14 to 20 in.

Habitat   This small kingsnake is found in a huge variety of mostly wooded environments throughout the Southeast, from low-lying swamps and riparian bottomland to the lower montane elevations of the southern Appalachians. In the southernmost portion of its range, drift-fence surveys conducted by Florida Game and Fresh Water Fish Commission biologist Kevin Enge indicate that *L. t. elapsoides* is common only in pine flatwoods and wet prairie hammocks. In this area it occurs less frequently in bottomland, mixed hardwood, upland pine forest, sandhills and, along the Gulf Coast from the northern edge of the Everglades to the Mississippi delta, in the wind-pruned strip of stunted hardwoods, known as maritime hammock, that defines the border between marine-shore marsh and inland forest. In south Florida, scarlet kingsnakes are now often associated with the ubiquitous stands of introduced Australian pines.

Prey   Much of the scarlet kingsnake's diet consists of smaller snakes that, along with its secondary prey of skinks and other small lizards, share the forest-floor microhabitat of leaf litter that *L. t. elapsoides* occupies during its spring through autumn foraging period. Nestling rodents are also taken opportunistically, and captives occasionally accept small frogs.

Reproduction   Egg-laying. Breeding occurs from March to June, with the 2 to 9 elongate whitish eggs being deposited between May and August in decomposing logs, piles of sawdust, under moisture-retaining surface debris or (in south Florida), beneath the damp clumps of fallen needles collected in the crotches of Australian pines. After about 2 months' incubation, during late summer and early autumn these hatch into slender 3½- to 4½-inch-long young that, like other *Lampropeltis*, do not feed until after their first shed at about 10 days of age. Free-ranging juveniles reportedly feed mostly on earthworms and insects, but captive-hatched neonates do not respond to this sort of prey.

Coloring/scale form   The scarlet kingsnake's narrow head and pointed, orange-red snout are distinctive, as is its brilliant pattern of wide scarlet dorsolateral bands bordered by much narrower black bands separated from adjacent black bands by chrome-yellow rings (both its wide red bands and its narrow yellow rings touch only black bands, never each other). From time to time, aberrantly colored scarlet kingsnakes, such as the individual pictured here beside a normally marked specimen, turn up throughout this animal's range.

Juveniles may have whitish rings in place of the bold yellow bands of adults, but among all ages the scarlet kingsnake's dorsolateral bands encircle its entire body, including the venter. The glossy dorsal scales—the genus name *Lampropeltis* means "shining shield or skin"—are arranged in 19 rows at midbody.

Similar snakes   Unlike those of the scarlet kingsnake, the red and yellow bands of the **eastern coral snake (172)** touch. Coral snakes also have a stubby black snout, a yellow- and black-banded tail, and a divided anal plate. Among both **northern** and **Florida scarlet snakes (165, 164)** the red dorsolateral saddles do not reach the unmarked white venter. The least similar to any of its milk snake subspecies, *L. t. elapsoides* apparently intergrades primarily with the **eastern milk snake (155)** along the Atlantic seaboard, producing the intermediate coastal plains morph. (In contrast, all races of southwestern milk snakes interbreed freely with adjacently ranging subspecies, but along the northwestern border of its range the scarlet king apparently maintains its separate genetic identity from the subspecies **red milk snake (157)**; a similar genetic detachment occurs to the west with another subspecies, the **Louisiana milk snake (158)**.

Behavior   Everywhere in its range the scarlet kingsnake is associated with decomposing trees and stumps, and it is sometimes found beneath the bark or in the rotted interiors of stumps protruding from the saturated soil of bottomland hardwood forest, in the rafters of abandoned buildings, and among the supporting beams of old wooden railroad trestles; in Florida these little snakes also hide high above the ground in the dead fronds skirting palm tree trunks.

Scarlet kingsnakes are often abroad in cool weather, for *L. t. elapsoides* seems to suffer less inhibition of movement due to chilly temperatures than most other southern serpents. This enables it to forage later into the fall than competing species, as well as adapting it to hunt effectively during the cooler hours of darkness. Its nocturnal foraging, in fact, may be the reason for the scarlet kingsnake's bright coloring because, rather than mimicking the venomous coral snake's bold pattern in a presumed oposematic deception, the scarlet king's contrasting colors may function as nocturnal camouflage. Although in daylight its bright bands rivet human attention, red looks gray at night—the only time that *L. t. elapsoides* appears in the open. With its crimson bands inconspicuous to color-visioned predators such as owls, the scarlet kingsnake's alternating black and pale yellow crossbands may have evolved simply as a cryptic approximation of the light and dark shadows that dapple nighttime forest floor.

Indeed, this adaptation of a pattern which fragments a snake's distinctive serpentine image against the chiaroscuro patchwork of dark woodlands may have been the same evolutionary pathway followed by the coral snake. The protective function of these bright colors may have only come later, learned by predators that were able to associate boldly contrasting bands with a small but dangerous creature.

One measure of protective coloring, for example, is the number of predator attacks an animal suffers, and among snakes partial loss of the tail is a good measure of near-miss predation. Few tail injuries are seen among coral snakes and, in one recent study of predation-caused injury in a large group of nonvenomous colubrids, only brightly banded milk snakes and the scarlet kingsnake showed a similar absence of tail damage.

Whatever its function in the nighttime woods, to human eyes the scarlet kingsnake's vivid pigmentation makes it a very attractive reptile. Adults do well in confinement—the captive longevity record is over 16 years—but hatchlings' extremely small size makes them difficult to feed. Hatchlings from south Florida feed on greenhouse frogs and ground skinks, but because captive neonates ordinarily take only lizard tails or, occasionally, pieces of newborn mice, raising them is so much trouble that *L. t. elapsoides* is usually bred only by specialists.

157 RED MILK SNAKE

Lampropeltis triangulum syspila

Nonvenomous   See **Eastern Milk Snake.**

Abundance   The range of the red milk snake encompasses the heartland of the United States: all of Missouri, most of Iowa and Arkansas, southeastern North Dakota, eastern Kansas, northeastern Oklahoma, southern Illinois, southwestern Indiana, westernmost of Kentucky and Tennessee, and northwestern Louisiana.

Ecosystems vary enormously throughout this broad territory, and while scarce in peripheral habitats, *L. t. syspila* can be abundant in areas offering good cover, moist soil loose enough for burrowing, and abundant food animals.

Size   Hatchling red milk snakes are about 9¾ inches in length; they reach adulthood at from 20 to 30 inches, and the record size is 42 in.

Habitat   This secretive snake may be found in open woodlands, rocky hillsides and meadows, fallow fields, pastures, and farmlands. It has been found beneath all manner of natural ground litter, while decrepit buildings and trash piles, with their usual dense population of small rodents, constitute ideal artificial habitats.

Prey   Mice, lizards, smaller snakes, reptile eggs, and amphibians are all eaten by red milk snakes.

Reproduction   Egg-laying. Clutches normally consist of from 4 to 8 eggs, but occasionally more than 15 are deposited. These are typically laid in moisture-retaining sites beneath ground litter, in decomposing logs or stumps, in stump holes, or in unused rodent burrows. Incubation varies from 8 to 9 weeks.

Coloring/scale form   As its common name indicates, the red milk snake is a largely red-and-white serpent. It is a largely saddled rather than a ringed milk snake: on an off-white to pale gray ground color its thinly black-edged big red dorsal saddles may extend to its ventral plates, but unlike its completely ringed subspecies, do not cross its black-and-white checked belly. The top of its head is red; its snout is gray, and lateral spots are small or absent; the dorsal scales occur in either 21 or 23 rows.

Similar snakes   The red milk snake's southern and western subspecies, the **scarlet kingsnake (156)**, and the **Louisiana** and **Central Plains milk snakes (158, 161)** are distinctly white- or yellow-, black-, and red-ringed serpents with prominent black bands. Their dorsolateral bands completely or almost completely encircle their bodies, including the venter. To the northwest, the **pale milk snake (162)** is a less brightly colored race lacking bright red markings, while the **eastern milk snake (155)** is generally brownish above, but red and eastern milk snakes intergrade broadly across western Kentucky and Tennessee.

Behavior   Although most milk snake races are comparatively well adapted to cool weather, in the northern part of its range *L. t. syspila* spends the early spring engaged in thermoregulatory basking in locations so sheltered that at any given time only a single body coil may be exposed to the sun. Later in the year it forages diurnally, as it does in early fall, engaging in crepuscular and nocturnal activity only during the warmest nights of mid-summer.

158 LOUISIANA MILK SNAKE

Lampropeltis triangulum amaura

Nonvenomous   Louisiana milk snakes seldom bite even when first picked up in the wild. Like other members of the kingsnake family, occasional individuals may nip and hang on tenaciously, but most *L. t. amaura* are so small that these nips are inconsequential.

Abundance   Uncommon to rare. Louisiana milk snakes are widely but sparsely distributed throughout the pine forest and more open oak-greenbriar woodland of eastern Texas and Louisiana west of the Mississippi River, as well as bits of southern Oklahoma and Arkansas.

Rarely encountered because of their retiring, semi-subterranean lifestyle, the bright colors of most *L. triangulum* races have long been sought by reptile enthusiasts, and for years every milk snake sub-species was protected in Texas. Collectors' impact on the natural population is now thought to have been minimal, however, and de-spite the major incursions both logging and agricultural/residential land clearing have made into its original longleaf pine forest home, *L. t. amaura* is no longer classified as a threatened animal.

Size   Recorded to 31 inches in length, most adult Louisiana milk snakes are much smaller, averaging only 16 to 24 in. and attaining a girth no thicker than one's forefinger.

Habitat   The Louisiana milk snake is by no means principally an inhabitant of the state for which it is named and is, in fact, absent from the estuarine marshes of both its southwest coast and Mississippi delta. Further west along the Gulf shoreline *L. t. amaura* inhabits both sandy beach dunes and barrier islands, however, where it is found beneath driftwood, planks, and littoral debris marking the spring tide line. Inland, Louisiana milk snakes live in both pine and hardwood forest, where both fallen and still-upright dead trees standing in riparian bottomland seem to be a preferred microhabitat.

Here, in dry weather, Louisiana milk snakes are cryptic, fossorial inhabitants of thickly layered forest-floor detritus. When late winter rainfall makes this vegetative milieu too saturated for fossorial life, Louisiana milk snakes may wedge their tiny bodies into the narrow crevices beneath the loosening shingles of pine bark on either fallen or still-standing dead longleaf and loblolly pines or, for cold weather brumation, tunnel their way deep into these decaying trees' soft interiors.

Prey   Much of the diet of *L. t. amaura* consists of the small serpents that, along with its secondary prey of skinks and spiny lizards, share its forest-floor microhabitat of leaf litter and humus.

Reproduction   Egg-laying. See **Central Plains Milk Snake.**

Coloring/scale form   The typical Louisiana milk snake is characterized by a partially black snout—often so mottled with white that the animal seems to have been nosing into flour—while the posterior portion of its head is entirely black, followed by a pale collar. Broad red dorsolateral bands, ranging in number from 13 to 21 (average, 16), are spaced along its trunk, pinched in at the belly line by their narrower black borders.

Between these black rings are light-hued dorsolateral bands (considerably less broad than the Louisiana milk's red body bands), whose color varies from light yellow among more southerly ranging individuals subject to gene flow from the deep yellow-banded Mexican milk snake, to white among *L. t. amaura* living in the pine/oak woodland at the northeastern edge of the range. Many individuals living in this area are so heavily clouded with dark gray that the typical bright milksnake pigmentation is only dimly visible; it is from this color variant that the race's name, *amaura*, Greek for "dark," is drawn. Among each of the Louisiana milk snake's subtle color morphs, however, the belly is off-white or light gray along a central strip. Red and black pigment encroaches onto the outer portion of the ventral scales, while the dorsolateral scales are arranged in 21 rows at midbody.

(As this color variation suggests, southwestern milk snakes are difficult to define with precision because their ranges overlap so intricately. Not only are there broad zones of intergradation where the territories of adjacently ranging subspecies meet but Bern Tryon, formerly of the Houston Zoo, has pointed out that throughout the ranges of the Louisiana, Mexican, and New Mexico milk snakes, individuals typical of neighboring races can be found. For example, D. Craig McIntyre recently found a perfectly typical Louisiana milk snake in Texas' LaSalle County, deep within the range of the Mexican milk snake.)

Similar snakes   Milk snakes' red and pale yellow or white dorsal hues never touch as they do on the **Texas coral snake (173)**. Unlike *L. triangulum*, the coral snake's black body bands are as broad as its red ones, while it also has a divided anal plate. The darker red dorsolateral bands of the subspecies **Mexican milk snake (159)** seldom narrow at the belly line and are often suffused with black along the spine; it has a black-blotched midventral area and a black snout. Another subspecies, the **Central Plains milk snake (161)**, has even more profuse white flecks on its head and snout and a higher number—20 to 32 (average, 26)—of narrower, more orangish dorsolateral rings. The **Texas long-nosed snake (167)** is marked with roughly rectangular red and black vertebral saddles above black-speckled yellowish lower sides. It has 23 rows of dorsal scales, its unmarked venter is off-white, its elongate snout is tan, and under its tail is a single row of subcaudal scales unlike the double row characteristic of other nonvenomous snakes. The **northern scarlet snake (165)** has a pointed red snout, an unmarked white belly, 19 midbody rows of dorsal scales, and red dorsolateral saddles that do not reach its venter.

Behavior   Like other milk snakes, *L. t. amaura* seems to suffer less inhibition of movement from lowered temperatures than most other southern snakes. (In chilly conditions that render neighboring serpents so slow-moving that photographing them is easy, Louisiana milk snakes still present a fast-wriggling challenge—a trait which may enable *L. triangulum* to forage later into the fall, and begin breeding earlier in the spring, than competing species.)

It also adapts these animals to forage effectively during the cooler hours of darkness, to which their coloring is also suited, for milk snakes' contrasting dorsal hues appear to function as nocturnal camouflage. Although in daylight these bright colors instantly draw the attention of human eyes, at night—the only time Louisiana milk snakes are abroad—red looks gray to even color-visioned snake predators such as owls. (The mammalian carnivores that feed on small terrestrial serpents are largely color-blind.)

Moreover, by approximating dark shadows the milk snake's black crossbands break up the visual continuity of its serpentine shape, while its intervening pale dorsolateral rings further fragment its profile against the light-dappled patchwork of the nighttime forest floor. These contrasting body bands are either so effective in hiding from— and perhaps also deterring—carnivores that both coral snakes and milk snakes have a lower incidence of predator-caused injuries than do non-banded serpents. See **Scarlet Kingsnake**.

Lampropeltis triangulum annulata

Nonvenomous   Mexican milk snakes grow large enough to bite effectively in self-defense, but do so only if they are seized roughly.

Abundance   Uncommon. Found north of Mexico only in southern and south-central Texas, *L. t. annulata* is widespread throughout both the remaining brush country of the Rio Grande floodplain and the irrigated farmland which has replaced much of the area's native vegetation. According to most references' range maps, the Mexican milk snake also occupies much of the Edwards Plateau, but this seems to be largely a historical phenomenon, for milk snakes are virtually never found in this part of the state today.

Size   The largest North American milk snake, adult *L. t. annulata* average 20 to 32 inches in length, while the record is a truly huge 54 in.

Habitat   Mexican milk snakes are most often observed in the Tamaulipan thorn woodland of the lower coastal plain. (Named for Mexico's most northeastern state, this tangle of catclaw acacia, paloverde, tamarisk, cenizo, and ocotillo formerly stretched almost halfway from the Rio Grande to San Antonio. In species diversity, it was among the United States' richest biotic communities, but its dense vegetation grew on fertile, level land, and the agricultural boom of the 1950s leveled most of its thornbrush, eliminating the tropical birds, mammals, and reptiles that ranged only as far north as this jungle of spiny legumes and succulents.)

Another very different habitat, also characteristic of the Mexican milk snake, is the coastal barrier islands, where these animals are found under high-tide-deposited driftwood.

Prey   Like most *Lampropeltis*, milk snakes are powerful constrictors of other serpents, from rattlesnakes to smaller members of their own species. Other prey includes lizards and small mammals, both of which are usually immediately accepted as food by recent captives.

Reproduction   Egg-laying. See **Central Plains Milk Snake.**

Coloring/scale form   Fourteen to 20 (average, 18) broad, dark red dorsolateral bands, often peppered along the spine with black, cover the upper trunk. The lower edges of these reddish bands (*analata* is "ringed" in Latin) extend onto the otherwise pale gray belly scales, where they are cut off by blotchy strips of black pigment that occupy the midventral area. Narrower black body bands border each side of these red bands.

About as wide as the Mexican milk snake's black dorsolateral bands are its intervening yellow bands; a few light anterior labial spots sometimes mark its otherwise black head, and its smooth, glossy dorsolateral scales are small and arranged in 21 rows at midbody.

Similar snakes   Milk snakes' red and yellow (or white) body bands touch only black bands, never each other; in contrast, the **Texas coral snake (173)** has adjacent red and yellow bands. Unlike the milk snakes its body bands entirely encircle its trunk, its black bands are about as broad as its red bands, and its anal plate is divided. Where their ranges intersect, the Mexican and **Louisiana milk snake (158)** races show intermingled characteristics, while throughout both animals' ranges individuals typical of neighboring milk snake subspecies can be found. To the west, *L. t. annulata* merges with the **New Mexico milk snake (160)**, which is distinguished by its greater average number of red dorsal bands (22), black dorsolateral rings much thinner than its broad white (rather than yellow) pale body bands, and its distinctly light-hued midventral area. The **Texas long-nosed snake (167)** is distinguished by rectangular red and black vertebral saddles, predominantly yellowish- to cream-colored lower sides speckled with blackish scales, a long brown or pinkish snout, and 23 rows of dorsolateral scales. Its belly is whitish, with a single row of scales beneath its tail.

Behavior   As vividly tri-colored reptiles, milk snakes are anything but milky in appearance, their name apparently having stemmed from early attempts to explain their presence in dairy barns. These smallish kingsnakes were probably drawn there in search of nestling mice, but since all *Lampropeltis* are slow-moving serpents lacking the agility to capture adult rodents, it originally seemed likely that they could have subsisted in these barns only by twining up the legs of dairy cows after dark to suck milk from their udders.

160   NEW MEXICO MILK SNAKE

Lampropeltis triangulum celaenops

Nonvenomous   See **Louisiana Milk Snake.**

Abundance   Very rare. Although its range encompasses both Trans-Pecos Texas as far west as El Paso and, above the caprock formation, the western quarter of the Texas panhandle, the New Mexico milk snake is almost never seen. A majority

of the few recorded *L. t. celaenops* were encountered at night cross-ing Trans-Pecos ranch roads during May and June.

Size Most adults are between 14 and 22 inches in length; the largest of 7 Texas specimens measured 25¼ in.

Habitat In Texas' Trans-Pecos' intermittently montane terrain, one habitat in which the author has seen two individuals is ever-green/hardwood woodland. A similar environment, in which New Mexico milk snakes have also been found, is the handful of riparian corridors penetrating the Davis Mountains up to an altitude of nearly 6,000 feet. To the north, in a grassland milieu more typical of western *L. triangulum*, another New Mexico milk snake was re-cently found near Highway 176 in Andrews County.

An entirely different habitat—one seemingly impossibly inhos-pitable to a species whose other races live in well-vegetated milieus—is the waterless, stony northern Chihuahuan Desert. In this severely arid biome, *Lampropeltis triangulum celaenops* are found on both the rocky plateaus and bluffs north of Sanderson, Texas, as well as in the even harsher desert environment of the Big Bend's Black Gap Wildlife Management Area.

Prey The New Mexico milk snake feeds on primarily smaller snakes, lizards located by scent in the crevices where they retreat for the night, and burrow-dwelling rodents.

Reproduction Egg-laying. See **Central Plains milk snake.**

Coloring/scale form The 17 to 25 (average, 22) broad carmine dorsolateral bands are bordered by narrower black bands sepa-rated by equally narrow off-white bands; within the latter, scat-tered brown flecks give a grizzled appearance. The New Mexico milk snake's black body bands are often slightly wider over its posterior spine, its midbelly is largely without black pigment, and its black snout is flecked with white. Arranged in 21 rows at mid-body, its smooth dorsal scales have an enamel-like surface to which the genus' Latin name, *Lampropeltis*, or "shining skin shield," refers.

Similar snakes In the eastern part of its range the New Mexico milk snake shares the territory of the **Texas coral snake (173),** whose red and sulfur-yellow body bands touch (milk snakes' red dorsolateral bands are bordered only by black bands). Because their ranges over-lap so broadly, Texas' four milk snake races can be difficult to distin-guish, but the **Central Plains milk snake (161)** has narrower, more numerous (average, 26), orangish dorsolateral bands; along its ven-tral mid-line splotchy black pigment separates the lower edges of these bands. The **Mexican milk snake (159)** also has a black-pigmented midbelly, deep yellow body bands and fewer, wider red bands (average, 18). The **Texas long-nosed snake (167)** often has rectangular red and black vertebral saddles, 23 rows of dorsal scales, and an off-white venter whose undertail scales occur in a single row.

Behavior   In addition to winter dormancy milk snakes living in the western United States typically undergo a similar subsurface retirement, or aestivation, to escape the heat and aridity of July, August and September. Even during spring and fall these animals spend most of the daylight hours deep in subterranean crevices, however (the animal pictured here was found at dawn on a rocky Big Bend trail), where the humidity is higher and the temperature more constant than on the surface. They are seldom abroad, in fact, except on still nights of high humidity, when the preponderance of males suggests that most individuals have emerged not in search of prey but are, instead, seeking reproductively receptive females' pheromone scent trails.

161   CENTRAL PLAINS MILK SNAKE
Lampropeltis triangulum gentilis

Nonvenomous   See **Louisiana Milk Snake.**

Abundance   Generally very uncommon. Sparsely distributed across the central Great Plains from the eastern Texas panhandle north through central Oklahoma and Kansas to southern Nebraska, then west to the front range of Colorado's Rocky Mountains, to southeastern Nebraska, most of Kansas, central Oklahoma and northern Texas, *L. t. gentilis* can, nevertheless, sometimes be locally common during early summer in some places. Yet, because this primarily fossorial snake is seldom found at the surface—and then almost always beneath the cover of flat stones or other sheltering debris—it is rarely seen even in these areas.

Size   Most adult Central Plains milk snakes are 16 to 24 inches long; the record is just over 36 in.

Habitat   Little is recorded of this animal's natural life history. Although *L. t. gentilis* inhabits a wide sweep of basin and rangeland, its specific habitat preferences are largely unknown. It has been found both on brushy hillsides and in rolling, short- or tallgrass prairie, especially where the soil was slightly moist, broken with large rocks, and loose enough for burrowing, and while it is easy to see why such a conspicuous, slow-moving reptile would find it dangerous to expose itself on the surface of its largely coverless habitat, where it lives below ground and what behaviors it employs there remain a mystery.

Prey   Nothing is recorded of prey taken in the wild, but the young probably feed mainly on lizards, skinks, and miniature serpents such as blind snakes and *Tantilla*, as well as on earthworms and insects. In captivity, like other milk snakes adult *L. t. gentilis* readily constrict and feed on other snakes as well small rodents.

Reproduction   Egg-laying. The reproduction of captives indicates that after springtime breeding and gestation this race of milk snakes deposits clutches of up to 10 1¼- by ⅝-inch-long adhesive-shelled eggs. After 65 to 80 days' incubation these hatch into 7½- to 11-inch-long young whose colors are somewhat brighter than those of their often rather pallid parents.

Coloring/scale form   Among *L. t. gentilis* both dorsal pattern and color are highly variable, as is the appearance of its black snout and forehead, which are usually mottled to some extent with white. Individuals from the northern plains have less vividly colored reddish-orange dorsolateral bands than those from North Texas, however, which intergrade with more brightly colored southern subspecies, but in both areas the Central Plains milk snake's reddish dorsolateral bands are more numerous (20 to 40, average 26) than those of most other milk snakes, and are suffused with black scales over the posterior spine. These bands are bordered by narrow black rings that sometimes almost entirely encircle them low on the sides and outer belly, and with age may darken to russet-brown. The intervening yellowish-gray dorsolateral rings only intermittently cross the darkly pigmented midventer. There are 21 midbody rows of dorsal scales.

Similar snakes   Even the approximate distribution of western milk snake races is difficult to define because individuals typical of adjacently ranging races can be found throughout the territory of their neighbors. For example, the Central Plains subspecies intergrades with the **Louisiana milk snake** (158) as far south as Fort Worth, where the latter is distinguished by its fewer (average, 16), wider and brighter red dorsolateral bands, as well as by its at least partially pale midventral area. The **New Mexico milk snake** (160) also has fewer, wider, and brighter red body bands (average, 22), whitish pale bands, and a lighter-hued midbelly. The **Texas long-nosed snake** (167) has rectangular red and black dorsal saddles, black-speckled yellowish lower sides, and an unmarked off-white venter distinguished by its single row of subcaudal scales.

Behavior Perhaps because so much of its habitat consists of coverless grassland, like other milk snakes *L. t. gentilis* is an extremely fossorial animal which seldom risks emerging into the open: during cool weather, rather than basking to elevate its temperature it may seek warmth by coiling against the underside of sun-heated flat rocks. In an area known for this sort of semi-subterranean thermoregulation, during the spring of 1998 the first albino Central Plains milk snake ever recorded was found, in Kansas, on a rock-strewn prairie in one of the few places where a seasonally surfacing population of *L. t. gentilis* has been identified.

162 PALE MILK SNAKE

*Lampropeltis triangulum multistrata**

Nonvenomous Because of this races's small adult size, pale milk snakes are generally unable to nip humans hard enough to break the skin.

Abundance Uncommon to rare. *Lampropeltis triangulum multistrata* is by far the most northerly ranging of North American milk snakes, inhabiting a broad band stretching northwest from central Nebraska through western South Dakota into eastern Wyoming and southern Montana as far as the Rockies' front range. In this mostly open-country, often rugged stretch of basin and range (several "badlands" areas are included) the pale milk snake is, by all accounts, a very sparsely distributed animal.

Size Most adult *L. t. multistrata* are between 16 and 26 inches in length, but occasional individuals have measured just over 30 in.

Habitat As the most northerly race of *Lampropeltis triangulum*, an essentially temperate-zone species, the pale milk snake lives at the northern limit of its biological capacity. In this harsh environment *L. t. multistrata* is able to tolerate the climatic extremes of wide daily fluctuations in temperature and the region's exceptionally long, cold winters only by spending almost all its life in deep underground refugia.

*The original spelling for this race was "*L. t. multistrata*," a Latin term meaning "multiple striped," that is used in both Behler and King (1992) and in Baxter and Stone. "*Multistrata*" was also used in the first 2 editions of Conant (1958 and 1975), before an "*i*" was added in later editions, making the spelling "*multistriata*." This volume has followed the long-prevailing original spelling.

This makes either thick silicaceous soil loose enough for extensive burrowing or a deeply fissured substrate essential to its survival. At the surface, pale milk snakes have been found beneath flat rocks or other solar radiation-absorbing surface debris from whose underside *L. t. multistrata* can absorb enough heat to raise its temperature to the level necessary for seasonal foraging and digestion. These sites include open, stony woodlands, rock-strewn prairie and escarpments; here, pale milk snakes have been found beneath logs, inside rotting stumps, and behind loosened bark—as well as in the shelter of large flat stones and human-generated litter.

Prey   Although milk snakes in general tend to be partial to lizards and small snakes as prey, almost all *L. triangulum* also feed on small warm-blooded vertebrates (the name milk snake derives from this species' presence in dairy barns where, because they were not thought capable of catching fast-moving mice, these little kingsnakes were imagined to subsist by twining up the legs of cows to suck milk from their udders).

Almost no ophidian or lacertillian prey is available in the pale milk snake's northern haunts however, where mammalian and avian species are the predominant fauna, so mice, voles, and the flightless young of small ground-nesting birds constitute the pale milk snake's principal prey.

Reproduction   Egg-laying. *Lampropeltis triangulum multistrata* produces small clutches of 2 to 8 (rarely as many as 10) eggs whose incubation period, depending on temperature, ranges from 60 to just over 70 days. Neonates measure about 9 inches in length at hatching.

Coloring/scale form   While not as brilliantly colored as more southerly races of *L. triangulum*, the pale milk snake is still a subtly beautiful subspecies. Its light-hued body bands are grayish (rather than the white or yellow of other milk snakes) while its russet bands are muted orange- or dusty-red, thinly bordered with black. These bands do not completely encircle the pale milk snake's body, leaving its midventral area an unpatterned light gray. The top of its head is dark, its snout is orangish with scattered dark scales, and its dorso-lateral scales are arranged in 19 rows.

Similar snakes   No other reddish-banded serpents occur within the range of *L. t. multistrata*. To the south and southeast its territory borders only that of the subspecies **Central Plains** and **red milk snakes (161, 157)**, both of which are more brightly red-orange banded and have, in the case of the Central plains race, a darkly pigmented midbelly, and in the case of the red milk snake, a black-and white-checked venter.

Behavior   See **Central Plains Milk Snake**.

Lampropeltis alterna

Nonvenomous   When first picked up in the field, a large gray-banded kingsnake may give a single frightened nip, but unless severely mistreated it will never bite a second time.

Abundance   Widespread—the range of *L. alterna* is now known to include 15 Texas counties, adjacent Eddy County in New Mexico, and much of the northern Mexican state of Coahuila—but uncommon.

Because gray-banded kingsnakes are almost entirely fossorial for most of the year, they were traditionally thought to be extremely rare, and as a result, for decades this species was protected by the state of Texas. *Lampropeltis alterna* is no longer classified as threatened, however, since over 90 percent of its U.S. habitat occurs either on private ranchland or within state and national parks. (South of the Rio Grande, where ⅔ of the gray-banded kingsnake's range lies, it has even less contact with humans due to the mostly roadless terrain it inhabits.)

Nevertheless, to some extent *L. alterna* remains a controversial species. Influential magazine articles have maintained that it is disappearing, but the prevailing scientific view is that neither the 50 to 100 gray-banded kingsnakes taken from the Trans-Pecos every year by collectors nor those run over by traffic are ecologically significant. Moreover, these losses are unlikely to increase since *L. alterna* is largely inaccessible to the public except where road cuts and canyon bluffs border the few roads that cross thousands of square miles of its barren range.

Although long a little-studied animal, the gray-banded kingsnake's existence has been known for over a century: the type specimen was collected in the Davis Mountains by E. Meyenberg in 1901. This dark-hued specimen was formally described by A. E. Brown, who named it *Ophibolus alternus* for its alternating broad and narrow dark dorsolateral bands. For the next 47 years this species, re-renamed *Lampropeltis alterna* after it was found to be a true kingsnake, was known only from the Chisos, Davis, and Sierra Vieja mountains, from a single locality near Bakersfield in Pecos County, and from the Mexican state of Coahuila.

Then, in 1948, a pale, broadly orange-banded kingsnake unlike any previously reported from the Trans-Pecos was discovered 9 miles west of Dryden. This animal was thought to be a new species and was formally described by A. G. Flury, who named it *Lampropeltis blairi* after University of Texas herpetologist W. F. Blair. Flury's classification was in error, however, for some 20 years later Ernest Tanzer found both types of young kingsnakes emerging from a single clutch of eggs laid by a wild-caught female. This established that both wide-banded *L. blairi,* narrow-banded *L. alterna,* and pale-hued "*L. blairi*" were all a single species. The older scientific name prevails, so *Lampropeltis alterna* is the proper term for all Texas' gray-banded kingsnakes. (For a time, West Texas' gray-banded kingsnake was also thought to be a subspecies of the wide-ranging Mexican kingsnake *L. mexicana.* During this period it was known as *Lampropeltis mexicana alterna*, but in 1982 W. R. Garstka taxonomically separated the northern, gray-banded kingsnake from its Mexican relative.)

Herpetoculturalists now breed thousands of these beautiful snakes in captivity, but wild-caught specimens still carry some cachet, and the chance of capturing one attracts enthusiasts from all over the world to Trans-Pecos Texas during the gray-band's activity-and-breeding season in May and June.

Size Adult *L. alterna* average 28 to 34 inches in length, with those from the Chisos and Davis Mountains being slightly smaller, with narrower heads and more forward-pointing eyes. The record is a 57¾-inch-long male "Blair's phase" found 17 miles west of Rocksprings in Edwards County.

Habitat To avoid the harsh surface conditions of its northern Chihuahuan Desert range, the gray-banded kingsnake spends the majority of its life in a more sheltered enviroment beneath the surface. The limestone substrate that makes up the subterranean world in this region is penetrable by a large snake like *L. alterna* only where crevices caused by weathering and geologic uplifting permit subsurface movement, however, and graybands are therefore almost entirely restricted to broken, rocky habitat. In terrain ranging from stony low-lying flats adjacent to bluffs or arroyos to montane rock faces as high as 6,500 feet, canyons, craggy ridges, talus slopes and boulder piles are this animal's preferred microenvironment. The limestone faces of road cuts offer the same conditions, and until recently gray-banded kingsnakes were assumed to be exclusively saxicolous since virtually all reported sightings were from such rocky environs. Yet during the summer of 1999 the author found a young adult male alterna phase gray-band miles from the nearest rocky bluff in a grassland/yucca milieu midway between Marathon and Alpine, Texas.

Prey Moving slowly through the maze of interconnecting crevices that underlie the region's broken limestone topography, *L. alterna* is able to feed on the lizards that, at dusk, descend into its chthonic warren in search of shelter. On the surface, where it sometimes hunts, *L. alterna* uses its prominent ventral scales to grip rough-surfaced stone, inching its way across nearly vertical rock faces while searching every crevice for the side-blotched and spiny lizards that sleep there: Gerard T. Salmon observed an adult male gray-band trying to pull a crevice spiny lizard from a crack in a roadside rock cut where the lizard had wedged itself for the night. (In captivity, *L. alterna*—which is clumsy at conventional constriction—may immobilize its prey by pressing mice against the side of its enclosure.)

In addition to their usual lacertilion prey—the author found a desert side-blotched lizard in the stomach of one road-killed specimen—most wild-caught adults feed readily on small rodents, though the young are exclusively lizard eaters. Lizard and snake eggs are also reportedly eaten by *L. alterna,* while Ed Acuna and Dan Vermilya found a big female near Big Bend National Park filled with eggs that turned out to be those of scaled quail. Canyon treefrogs and other small amphibians are also taken on occasion, although ophiophagy—eating other snakes, which is common among most kingsnakes—is rare.

Reproduction Egg-laying. No reproductive behavior has been recorded for gray-bands in the wild, but extensive captive breeding of *Lampropeltis alterna*—successful propagation was first described by James Murphy of the Dallas Zoo—has led to the thorough documentation of its courtship and breeding.

Clutches of 3 to 13 eggs, 1¼ to 1⅝ inches in length, are deposited from late May to July. Following a 60- to 80-day incubation the young pip through their leathery eggshells but remain coiled within the eggs for another couple of days, peaking out from time to time while adsorbing the last of their yolk sacs. Well-fed *L. alterna* reach reproductive maturity in their second or third year (wild females may become gravid at as small as 24 inches), and in captivity can live more than 20 years.

Coloring/scale form The species name *alterna*, drawn from Latin, refers to the arrangement of the gray-banded kingsnake's dorsolateral bands. These bands are so widely spaced along its body that they were assumed to be only the alternate markings between a second set of invisible, yet genotypically present intervening bands.

The great variety of this species' color and patterning has made this animal the obsession of many herpetoculturists, among whom it is said that "no two *alterna* are exactly alike." This may not be entirely true, but gray-banded kingsnake populations are highly polytypic, and wild specimens seem to present an almost infinite variety of color and patterning.

Ground color varies from black to light gray, though two principal color phases prevail (the original terms *alterna* and *blairi* are still used to distinguish these color-types, despite the fact that many specimens are intermediate between them).

Individuals from the lower Pecos and Devil's river drainages are most often pale gray, with orange dorsal saddles delineated by narrow, sometimes thinly white-bordered black edges. Among the more northerly and westerly specimens known as *alterna* morphs, heavier pigmentation is likely, and thin black bands, sometimes narrowly split with red, are separated by still thinner intermediate, or "alternating" dark bands or vertical rows of small black spots.

These differences are loosely tied to the hue of the background rocks on which these populations live. In the southern part of the range where the paler "Blair's" form more often occurs, these snakes live on a chalky desert pavement of limestone or naviculite; at higher elevations to the north and west, more moisture allows lichens to encrust the dark, volcanic rhyolite, and here more heavily pigmented *alterna* morphs prevail. Because both sorts of young emerge from the egg clutches produced in both regions, natural selection determines which color phase is best camouflaged against the local background rock and is thus most likely to survive.

The gray-banded kingsnake's ventral coloring varies almost as much as that of its dorsum, ranging from off-white to, in the Davis Mountains, almost entirely black. There are 25 midbody rows of dorsal scales.

Similar snakes   The light-hued color phase of the **mottled rock rattlesnake (195)** is almost identical in pigmentation to pale-phase *L. alterna*. The heads of both species are somewhat triangular, but rattlesnakes have both a rattle and a dark, distinctly depressed heat-sensing pit midway between the nostril and the slit-pupiled eye (like other subterranean or nocturnal serpents, gray-banded kingsnakes have bulging eyes with prominent round pupils).

Behavior   The gray-banded kingsnake's movement on the surface is sporadic, fluctuating according to both season and weather: most of its infrequent forays occur on warm spring and early summer nights with low or falling barometric pressure, especially when rainfall has recently occurred and the humidity is higher than normal. During times of extreme drought, even these desert-adapted animals are stressed by lack of water. In the very dry summer of 2000 one was photographed, after having ascended a set of stone steps, drinking water from a puddle on the porch of a house in Terlingua Ranch, Big Bend, Texas.

Surprisingly, the sometimes gaudy colors of *Lampropeltis alterna* are difficult to see at night except in the beam of a spotlight: red looks gray after dark, and the variegated dorsolateral patterning of *L. alterna* masks its serpentine shape against shadowy rock faces. See **Scarlet Kingsnake.**

SCARLET SNAKES
Genus Cemophora

Florida Scarlet Snake, *Cemophora coccinea coccinea*
Northern Scarlet Snake, *Cemophora coccinea copei*
Texas Scarlet Snake, *Cemophora coccinea lineri*

Cemophora is part of the colubrine subfamily *Lampropeltinae*, establishing its member species as close relatives—as one would expect from their glossy scalation, subterranean lifestyle, and bright dorsolateral colors—of both the milk snake/kingsnake group and the southwestern long-nosed snakes. Like the latter group, *cemophora* have a hard, pointed rostral scale, presumably to help them unearth their buried food. This characteristic is the source of this animal's species name: Greek for *phoros* ("having"), and *cemo* (or "snout").

Unlike both king and long-nosed snakes, however, scarlet snakes are specialist feeders on reptile eggs that only when driven from their burrows by heavy rains, or on warm, humid evenings emerge from their burrows to move about on the surface. This oviparous, monotypic genus consists of a single species, *C. coccinea*, a beautiful burrower of the southeastern and western Gulf Coastal plains whose back and sides are marked with bands or saddles of red, black, and white or yellow; the yellow and red bands are separated by bands of black. This species' head is narrow and not overly distinct from its neck, its pointed snout is red, its belly an unmarked off-white, its smooth dorsolateral scales are arranged in 19 rows and its anal plate is undivided.

FLORIDA SCARLET SNAKE

Cemophora coccinea coccinea

Nonvenomous *Cemophora coccinea coccinea* does not bite humans.

Abundance From Marion County south to the tip of peninsular Florida *C. c. coccinea*, which is entirely endemic to Florida, is common in pine flatwoods, dry prairie, maritime hardwood hammocks, and sandhill habitats, but it is rarely seen because of its extremely secretive nature.

Size Adults are 14 to 32 inches in length.

Habitat As a relict member of an ancient, xeric-adapted fauna that, during the glacial period of lowered sea-level stretched from the desert southwest to Florida via a sandy Gulf Coast corridor, *C. c. coccinea* still inhabits similarly dry, silicaceous soil, although it is also sometimes found in the crevices of the limestone-sided irrigation canals that cross saw-grass prairies.

Prey Florida scarlet snakes prey on smaller snakes, lizards, and newborn rodents but, like other *Cemophora*, their dietary preference seems to be reptile eggs.

Reproduction Egg-laying. Breeding occurs from March to June, with oviposition occurring between May and August. The 3 to 8 eggs, 1 to 1¼ inches in length, hatch from July to October into 5½- to 6-inch-long young that are colored differently from the adults. (An ontogenetic color progression takes place over the course of the scarlet snakes' life: neonates are off-white with pinkish snouts and dorsal saddles, whose lower edges are flecked with black. As they grow older, these black flecks merge into prominent black bands that form the lower borders of their dorsal saddles.)

Coloring/scale form Among adults, the black-bordered dorsolateral bands (which number up to 32) have lost the pinkish hue typical of juveniles and darkened to crimson, while the snout has become orange-red. These broad dorsolateral bands are also the source of the scarlet snakes' species name; *coccinea* is red in Latin. The anterior-most pair of black dorsolateral rings are very thin, and the furthest forward usually does not touch the parietal scales of the head. The venter is uniformly pale and there are usually 7 supralabial scales.

Similar snakes The subspecies **northern scarlet snake (165)** usually has 6 supralabial scales and its anterior-most black dorsal band touches its parietal scales. The **eastern coral snake (172)** has a round black snout, adjacent red and yellow bands that circle its belly, a yellow- and black-banded tail, and an undivided anal plate. The **scarlet kingsnake (156)** has dorsolateral/ventral bands that also encircle its venter.

Behavior   Scarlet snakes are primarily burrowers seen above ground only well after dark; in summer, newborns are sometimes found in suburban swimming pools. In captivity, due to its strong preference for whole reptile eggs *C. c. coccinea* is difficult to feed (typically refusing raw egg in a dish) and fares poorly except in the hands of a resourceful keeper: the longest-lived captive was maintained for over 6 years by D. Craig McIntyre, who syringe-fed it 2 to 3 cc of stirred chicken egg every 2 weeks.

165   NORTHERN SCARLET SNAKE

Cemophora coccinea copei

Nonvenomous   It is almost impossible to induce the northern scarlet snake to bite.

Abundance   Fairly common. Yet, despite the fact that during May and June northern scarlet snakes are sometimes abundant on East Texas back roads, this subspecies is nevertheless **protected by the state of Texas.**

Cemophora coccinea copei is widespread throughout a broad range that stretches from Maryland and Delaware (a small, disjunct population occupies New Jersey's sandy-soiled pine barrens) south to northern Florida and west, except for the Appalachian highlands, to northern Kentucky, Arkansas, and central Oklahoma. Within this broad sweep of mostly wooded terrain, northern scarlet snakes may be locally abundant in pine flatwoods, wet prairies, bottomland forest and both coastal and inland sandhill habitat. In most of these environments drift fence surveys regularly catch *C. c. copei* on late spring and early summer nights.

Size   Adult scarlet snakes are 16 to just over 32 inches in length; the slim, rarely seen hatchlings are 4½ to 6 in. long.

Habitat   A primarily fossorial inhabitant of sandy-soiled pine, hardwood, and mixed forest environments, *C. c. copei* also evidently frequently forages abroad, for it is sometimes found in open terrain some distance from woodland. Here, it occurs most often along the borders of swamps and stream banks and in agricultural fields.

In the wetter southern part of its range too much water may be a problem, though, for Jim Ashcraft reports that in riparian forest near Beaumont, Texas, during minor flooding caused by heavy rainfall northern scarlet snakes are sometimes found on white pine-wooded sandy ridges that rise above intervening boggy ground covered with baygall and magnolia.

Prey   Reptile eggs are this animal's preferred food—in search of which *C. c. copei* apparently forages widely on the surface. (To puncture the leathery shells of eggs too large to swallow whole it has developed enlarged upper posterior teeth.) Northern scarlet snakes may also take small lizards, snakes, and nestling rodents.

Reproduction   Egg-laying. See **Florida Scarlet Snake**

Coloring/scale form   Adult *C. c. copei* have a grayish or yellowish-white ground color, with up to 32 broad red dorsal saddles prominently bordered with black. Their lower sides are flecked with brown and their elongate snouts are orange-red, as is the crown, which is sometimes capped by a circular marking edged with black. The anterior-most black vertebral band usually touches the parietals, there are usually 6 supralabial scales, and the unmarked venter is white.

Yet this appearance is only one manifestation of the scarlet snake's lifelong ontogenetic change in appearance. Both this reptile's pattern and coloring alter so much during the course of its life that hatchlings, adults, and very old individuals look like different species. Hatchlings are off-white, their pink dorsal saddles extend only a short way down their sides, where they are surrounded by black lateral flecks. As northern scarlet snakes grow older these flecks coalesce to form the dark lower borders of steadily reddening dorsal blotches, which eventually develop a broad, solid black edging. Among very old *C. c. copei*, the red vertebral color dulls, their once-carmine saddles fade to mahogany and their formerly white intervening spaces become tarnished with tan or gray.

Similar snakes   The subspecies **Florida scarlet snake (164)** usually has a whiter ground color, its anterior-most black dorsal band does not touch its parietal scales and it has 7 supralabial scales. The **Louisiana milk snake (158)** usually has a white-flecked black nose, dorsolateral bands that extend onto its red, white, and black ventral scales, and 21 rows of dorsal scales.

Both **eastern** and **Texas coral snakes (172, 173)** have red and yellow dorsolateral bands that border one another and extend unbroken across their bellies; the coral snake's stubby, rounded snout is jet black, its anal plate divided.

Behavior *Cemophora coccinea copei*'s subspecies name honors Edward Drinker Cope, professor of geology, minerology, zoology, and comparative anatomy at the University of Pennsylvania. One of the most deeply subterranean of serpents, the northern scarlet snake seldom appears in the open except on late spring and early summer nights. Yet, in search of buried reptile eggs, from time to time it evidently forages furtively abroad. Its only defense during these excursions is to dig its way out of sight as rapidly as possible, and in the loose, sandy soil it favors, the northern scarlet snake can disappear with surprising rapidity. It presses its tapered snout into the ground at a shallow angle and wagging its head from side to side, rooting up a pair of little earthen berms that quickly collapse inward over its foreparts.

Thus partially concealed, *C. c. copei* discontinues its sideways cephalic motions and forces its head almost straight down into the ground. There, it may continue to move forward like a big earthworm, or seek out subterranean crevices or the tunnels of small mammals, but during building excavation northern scarlet snakes have been uncovered as much as 6 feet beneath the surface.

166 TEXAS SCARLET SNAKE
Cemophora coccinea lineri

Nonvenomous See **Northern Scarlet Snake.**

Abundance **Threatened. Protected by the state of Texas.** Endemic to this state and widely separated in range from any other member of its species, the Texas scarlet snake is a very rare animal. Only a handful of specimens have been recorded, including the type specimen discovered in Kenedy County by tireless Texas and Mexico field researcher Ernie Liner. This southwestern-most scarlet snake's scarcity has given it such mystique that a myth has sprung up among enthusiasts that *C. c. lineri* is a descendant of Florida scarlet snakes accidentally transported to South Texas in a load of oil field drilling pipe.

Size This race of scarlet snake grows to a length of at least 26 inches.

Habitat Almost the only habitat in which *C. c. lineri* has been observed is a narrow band of sand-floored baygall thicket adjacent to

Texas' Laguna Madre, and a three-county inland extension of this coastal vegetative zone into the Tamaulipan thorn woodland of the Rio Grande plain.

Prey Although evidently a sometime constrictor—small lizards and snakes are probably taken—*C. c. lineri* seems to feed largely on reptile eggs, which it punctures with the slightly enlarged teeth located in the rear of its upper jaw. One newly captured individual brought to the Houston Zoo drank nearly a quarter of the contents of a hen's egg from a shallow dish and, over the next 8 days, consumed 9 Texas spiny lizard eggs. Then for months it refused both eggs and small snake and lizard prey; another captive *C. c. lineri* lived nearly a year in captivity feeding solely on fresh hen's egg yolks while refusing both living and dead lacertillians and small serpents. (Jim Ashcraft, who has elicited feeding responses among northern scarlet snakes which were reluctant to feed by providing them with deep soil in which to burrow, suggests that exposure in an open cage may have inhibited the feeding of both these specimens.)

Reproduction Egg-laying. See **Northern Scarlet Snake.**

Coloring/scale form Basic color, pattern, and scutellation are similar to those of the northern scarlet snake, *Cemophora coccinea copei*—from which this subspecies was formally distinguished in 1966 by Kenneth Williams, Bryce Brown, and Larry David Wilson.

Both the northern and Texas races have an off-white dorsolateral ground color, although at all stages of maturity the Texas race's ground color is less grayish, 17 to 24 heavily black-bordered carmine to mahogany-red vertebral saddles, and an elongate orange-red snout. Like its northeastern subspecies, the Texas scarlet snake's anterior-most black vertebral band usually touches its parietals, but its crown and cheeks, including its eye, are wrapped in a glossy jet black cap, marked only with a tiny white post-cranial bar; there are 6 supralabial scales; and its venter is uniformly white.

Similar snakes Scarlet snakes typically exhibit ontogenetic variation, their pale, pinkish young growing first redder and then darker and more brownish with age, but among Texas scarlet snakes a black cap replaces the red crown typical of other scarlet snake races, and the black border below its vertebral saddles does not join across their lower edges, as it does in the subspecies **northern scarlet snake (165)**. There is no geographic or recent genetic connection with the **Florida scarlet snake (164)**, whose anterior-most black dorsal band does not touch its parietal scales, whose crown is unmarked pinkish-orange except for a thin (sometimes absent) brownish line between its supraocular scales, and whose supralabial scales number 7.

The **Texas coral snake (173)** has a rounded black snout, adjacent red and bright yellow dorsolateral bands that cross its venter, and a divided anal plate. The **Mexican milk snake (159)** also has a black, sometimes white-speckled nose, a red, white, and black venter, and 21 midbody rows of dorsal scales. The **Texas long-nosed snake (167)** usually has rectangular black dorsolateral saddles, black-speckled yellowish lower sides, 23 rows of dorsal scales, and a single row of undertail scales (unlike the double row typical of every other harmless snake).

Behavior   Few observations of Texas scarlet snakes have been made in the wild, but the activity cycle of *C. c. lineri* is probably similar to that of its two subspecies. Captives remain buried in the loose sand of their cage bottoms during the day, emerging only at night, when their bright colors, by visually breaking their serpentine outline, may function primarily as nocturnal camouflage. See **Scarlet Kingsnake.**

LONG-NOSED SNAKES
Genus Rhinocheilus

Texas Long-nosed Snake, *Rhinocheilus lecontei tessellatus*

The genus *Rhinocheilus* (whose name is taken from the Greek *rhinos* for "nose" and *cheilo* for "lip" for its extended rostral scale) is part of the colubrine subfamily *Lampropeltinae*, within which its related genera include those of the similarly glossy-scaled, brightly colored scarlet, milk, and kingsnakes. *Rhinocheilus* are oviparous, characterized by slender heads, a long, pointed snout, smooth dorsolateral scales arranged in 23 rows, and an undivided anal plate. These beautiful, busily patterned tri-colored snakes, of which only one subspecies is native to central North America, are associated with arid- and semi-arid grasslands, where they are secretive, capable burrowers. By day, long-nosed snakes may be found hidden amid sheltering rocks, in crevices and rodent burrows, or under debris, but by evening they often prowl widely on the surface, especially during or following rains. Like their milk snake relatives, long-nosed snakes seem to be more tolerant of cool weather than most snakes, foraging later into the crisp early morning hours than their ophidian competitors; even in the higher altitudes of Texas' Davis Mountains the author has found the Texas race, *R. l. tessellatus*, abroad at dawn on decidedly chilly roadway pavement.

If threatened, the long-nosed snake may hide its head beneath a body coil, or even autohemorrhage, spontaneously bleeding a drop or two from its cloaca. Nasal hemorrhaging has also been noted, but the biomechanics of this presumably defensive maneuver remain unknown. An occasional individual may rear into an elevated S posture and bluff-strike if provoked, but its nosed's mouth remains firmly shut—at least if it is an adult, since juveniles, for some reason, are apt to nip if picked up.

Rhinocheilus lecontei is an efficient constrictor of larger prey but consumes small food animals without constricting them. Lizards seem to be this species' preferred food, but individuals from southern parts of the range also take small rodents immediately after capture; flightless young ground-nesting birds are reportedly eaten as well.

167 TEXAS LONG-NOSED SNAKE

Rhinocheilus lecontei tessellatus

Nonvenomous Adult *R. l. tessellatus* almost never bite, even if picked up suddenly, but an occasional individual defecates and writhes in agitation, sometimes discharging blood, musk and feces from its vent.

Abundance Uncommon. Sparsely distributed in both central Texas and the state's Stockton Plateau, the Texas long-nosed snake is more often found in Trans-Pecos and New Mexico grassland, and it may be fairly numerous on the prairies of the Texas and Oklahoma panhandles and southern Kansas. *Rhinocheilus lecontei tessellatus* is probably most abundant, however, in grassy parts of the Tamaulipan thorn brush savannah of the Rio Grande plain.

Size Most adults are 16 to 30 inches long; the record is 41 in.

Habitat A burrower—and rooter for hidden prey—living in the dry, gravelly soils of prairie and thorn brush grassland, the Texas long-nosed snake is sometimes found near the moisture of stock tanks and intermittently flowing streams. It also occurs in the northern Chihuahuan Desert, however, for the author has found this animal in Trans-Pecos Texas' harshest desert biomes, including the arid, rocky slopes of the Black Gap Wildlife Management Area.

Prey Despite its enlarged rostral, the Texas long-nosed snake is not primarily a fossorial animal: instead it uses its sharply pointed snout to root lizards from beneath the layer of soil beneath which desert-living lacertilians shelter for the night: in 1966 Charles McKinney and R. E. Ballinger found only lizard remains in 14 *R. l. tessellatus* taken in the panhandle. (Much too swift to be captured by the slow-moving long-nosed snake during the day, open plains- or rock-living lizards are vulnerable to scent-hunting snakes at night when they sleep wedged into crevices or buried beneath a layer of sand.) Abilene Zoo Director Jack Joy reports observing a Texas long-nosed snake using its pointed snout to root out sleeping racerunner lizards.

Rodents are also taken by some populations—perhaps preferentially. Captives from southern Texas' LaSalle and McMullen counties refused reptilian food but immediately recognized small mammals as prey. Although no more than ½ inch in diameter, these *R. l. tessellatus* had no difficulty in constricting adult mice with a loop of their muscular trunks. Yet the long-nosed snake's small mouth limits it to prey animal smaller than those eaten by similarly sized serpents like young rat and bullsnakes.

Reproduction   Egg-laying. Four to 9 eggs are deposited in an underground nest. After 2 to 2½ months, the 6½- to 9½-inch-long young emerge, pallidly marked with pink dorsal saddles and dark-speckled whitish sides.

Coloring/scale form   Its elongated rostral scale is the source of both this creature's common and scientific names: *rhino* is Greek for "nose" and *cheil* means "lip." (*Lecontei* honors John Eatton Leconte, an army engineer who, after organizing the defense of Savannah during the War of 1812, devoted himself to herpetology.) In reference to the long-nosed snake's multi-hued, mosaic-like dorsolateral patterning, *tessellatus* is Latin for "tiled."

Although the coloring of all *R. l. tessellatus* tends to darken and intensify with age, separate populations vary in both hue and marking. Specimens from South Texas have equally sized vertebral blocks of red and black, lightly black-speckled yellow sides, and white bellies. In the northern Trans-Pecos, Texas long-nosed snakes may resemble those from the southern part of the range or have larger red dorsal rectangles separated by (sometimes hourglass-shaped) wide black dorsolateral bands. Among this population there is less yellow, and the pale venter may be dark-splotched. The 23 midbody rows of dorsal scales are smooth, the anal plate is undivided and, as in no other nonvenomous serpent in North America, the scales beneath the long-nosed snake's banded tail usually occur in a single row like that of the pitvipers.

Similar snakes   Each of the four races of **milk snake** (158, 159, 160, 161) that occur within the range of the Texas long-nosed snake has a stubby snout, narrow black dorsolateral crossbands, a vividly colored venter marked with black, pale gray, and red, 21 rows of dorsolateral scales; and a double row of scales under its tail.

Behavior   In 1967, McCoy and Gehlbach established that some *R. l. tessellatus* employ defensive behavior in which bloody fluid mixed with anal gland musk is discharged through the cloaca. If more severely stressed, such an auto-hemorrhagic individual may hang limply, presumably imitating a moribund carcass. Alternatively, with its head buried in its coils for safety, the Texas long-nosed snake may elevate its curled tail tip, then wave it about in a threatening pose thought to evoke the similarly banded, about-to-strike head of the coral snake.

MILDLY VENOMOUS REAR-FANGED SNAKES

NIGHT SNAKES
Genus Hypsiglena

Texas Night Snake, *Hypsiglena torquata jani*

The genus *Hypsiglena* is classified within the colubrine subfamily *Xenodontinae*, a category containing a host of rear-fanged (or "differently-toothed") snakes, some of which also have mildly toxic saliva. Like dangerously-venomed serpents such as the pitvipers, night snakes also have the vertical pupils to which, in Greek, *hypsiglen ı* refers. Most of the *Xenodontinae,* including the Texas night snake, *H. t. jani,* are harmless to humans, however, due to their diminutive size and/or non-aggressive temperaments.

To the west, the species *H. torquata*, which is the only night snake species found in North America, is divided into several races that can be difficult to differentiate. All share small size, a variable, earth-toned ground color with an elongate dark brown blotch on each side of the neck, smooth dorsolateral scales arranged in from 19 to 21 rows, a divided anal plate, and the vertically elliptical pupils typical of snakes possessing at least weakly toxic saliva.

Among *H. torquata* this saliva is toxic only to tiny prey species (small lizards are adults' preferred food, but some individuals also take small frogs), however, and these quiet, cryptic animals emerge, as their common name indicates, from hiding only as daylight wanes, are active far into the hours of darkness, and do not attempt to bite large assailants. Primarily terrestrial, they may be common in areas where numerous flat rocks provide surface cover.

168   TEXAS NIGHT SNAKE, *Hypsiglena torquata jani*

Mildly venomous   Although its mildly toxic saliva has a paralytic effect on its diminutive reptile, insect, and annelid prey, the Texas night snake does not bite larger creatures. In self-defense it does, however, threaten to do so, raising its slightly triangular head and making abrupt little imitation strikes.

Abundance   Variable, sometimes locally common. This widespread though seldom seen reptile inhabits a variety of dry, terrestrial environments within a large range that includes a narrow strip immediately adjacent to the southern Gulf Coast, all of Texas west of the Edwards Plateau and crosstimbers and most of western Oklahoma; a small, disjunct population of Texas night snakes lives in northeastern Texas.

Uncommon (except along the Texas Gulf Coast) east of the Great Plains and central hill country, *H. t. jani* is sometimes fairly abundant in this central oak/juniper savannah, in the Tamaulipan thorn brush of the Rio Grande plain, and in the Trans-Pecos where its pale color morph is one of the most common snakes. *Hypsiglena torquata jani* is also found in considerable numbers in the grasslands of the Oklahoma and Texas panhandles.

Size   Most adults are 10 to 14 inches in length, but *H. t. jani* is recorded to 20 in.

Habitat   Its favored microhabitat is sandy or gravelly ground broken by rocky bluffs or overlaid with flat stones and fallen branches. In South Texas this race is often found in the neighborhood of stock tanks and irrigation ditches. In the Trans-Pecos, as well as in the Oklahoma and Texas panhandles it occurs in both short-grass prairie and around rocky outcroppings—in the Davis Mountains, Texas State Parks biologist Linda Hedges has found *H. t. jani* at more than 6,000 ft. in elevation.

Prey   Lizards, smaller snakes, worms, and insects have been reported as prey. Neonates probably also feed largely on invertebrates.

Reproduction   Egg-laying. In northern Tom Green County Abilene Zoo Director Jack Joy observed a copulating pair of Texas night snakes on May 10. Other records are of clutches of 4 to 6 proportionately large eggs—up to 1⅛ inches in length and ½ inch in diameter. These were found between early April and late June beneath stones, decaying vegetation and/or other debris.

John E. Werler (1951) reported an incubation period of 54 days, after which the

> 5.7-inch to 6-inch young emerged and, 13 days after hatching, ate newly hatched rusty lizards but refused the small anole lizards that were offered from time to time. Most of the day the snakes remained hidden beneath the sand in their cage, coming to the surface to prowl only after dark.

Another gravid female found in a rock cut 9 miles north of Sanderson by Alpine, Texas reptile breeder Jim Costabile deposited two similarly sized, torpedo-shaped eggs on June 1. These hatched on July 31 into 5½-in. long young which showed no interest when presented with the scent of locally common toads, a chirping frog, and a tiger salamander. Interest, but no feeding behavior, was elicited by the scent of whiptail, earless, spiny, and canyon lizards, as well as by that of a Texas banded gecko and ground and five-lined skinks. Long-nosed and ground snake scent prompted some aggression, but only the odor of invertebrates—beetle larvae and pin-headed crickets—produced an immediate feeding response.

Coloring scale/form   Dorsolateral ground color is beige, marked with 50 or more irregular brown vertebral blotches and numerous small dark lateral spots. (Along the Rio Grande from east of Big Bend to the Quitman Mountains in southern Hudspeth County, much lighter-hued night snakes prevail. Probable intergrades with the more westerly spotted night snake subspecies, *H. t. ochrorhyncha*, these animals are smaller and slimmer than their more easterly ranging relatives and have only little light brown dorsolateral spots separated by much larger areas of off-white ground color.)

Night snakes' most distinctive characteristic, however, is their large coppery eyes, slit by a vertical hairline pupil reminiscent of the similar eyes of pitvipers. The big, chocolate-brown blotches that mark the nape and sides of night snakes' necks are also definitive, and are the source of this species' Latin name, which means "neck-ringed." The venter is white with a faint silvery sheen. Except for slightly ridged vertebral scales above the anal region of adult males, the 21 midbody rows of dorsal scales are smooth and the anal plate is divided.

Similar snakes Their tiny upturned snouts distinguish **western** and **Mexican hook-nosed snakes (146, 145)**, which have but 17 rows of dorsal scales, round-pupiled dark eyes, and lack very large, dark brown nuchal blotches.

Behavior Active between April and late October, *H. t. jani* has an elliptical pupil whose vertical aperture protects the eye's light-sensitive optic rods in daylight, yet allows for more radical expansion after dark than a circular pupil. North of the Rio Grande, this configuration is shared only with the pitvipers and other rear-fanged colubrids. Ordinarily entirely terrestrial, the Texas night snake also sometimes forages up into low vegetation: north of Sanderson, Texas, Connie McIntyre found an adult *H. t. jani* 4 feet off the ground in thorny shrubbery.

CAT-EYED SNAKES
Genus Leptodeira

Northern Cat-eyed Snake, *Leptodeira septentrionalis septentrionalis*

The subtropical genus *Leptodeira*—"thin-necked" in Greek—is classified within the colubrine subfamily *Xenodontinae*. It is oviparous, and its members have smooth scales arranged in 21 to 23 rows, and a divided anal plate. South of the Rio Grande several other species of cat-eyed snakes, as well as subspecies of *L. septentrionalis*, are common, but only this nominate race of a single species, which is restricted to the lower Rio Grande valley and the adjacent Gulf Coast, occurs in the United States.

The northern cat-eyed snake's tropical affinities are evident, for it resembles Central and South American vine snakes. Its large, coppery-gold eyes have the vertically elliptical pupils characteristic of rear-fanged, weakly venomed colubrid snakes, and its broad head, slim neck, and slender body follows the configuration of rear-fanged tropical colubrids.

Although *L. septentrionalis* is often found in the rushes and sedges of water's edge habitats, like vine snakes it is principally arboreal. It is also a mostly nocturnal hunter, which becomes more active when rainy periods bring out concentrations of small frogs and result in aggregations of their eggs and tadpoles. By day, *L. s. septentrionalis* secrets itself in surface debris, stump holes, beneath fallen logs, and in the leaf crowns of bromeliads or climbing vines. Its venom quickly immobilizes frogs and lizards; what effect these toxins have on humans remains unknown.

169 NORTHERN CAT-EYED SNAKE

Leptodeira septentrionalis septentrionalis

Mildly venomous   The longitudinal grooves scoring this slender colubrid's pair of slightly enlarged rear teeth enable *L. s. septentrionalis* to channel its mildly toxic saliva into small prey, which is quickly immobilized by its narcotic effect.

Abundance   Endangered. Protected by the state of Texas. This tropical serpent is northern (*septentrion* in Latin) only in relation to its Mexican and Central American relatives. It inhabits the United States nowhere but at the southern tip of the Rio Grande valley and along the lower Gulf Coast. Here, because little of its native thorn brush and riparian woodland habitat remains intact, it is one of the rarest reptiles in the country.

Size   Adults average 14 to 32 inches in length (females are slightly longer), with bodies no thicker than a forefinger among even the largest individuals.

Habitat   Principally a Mexican species, the northern cat-eyed snake inhabits the jungle of coastal thorn brush, known as Tamaulipan woodland, whose remnants can still be found along the Gulf Coast from Tampico to Texas' Kleberg County (At one time this mass of catclaw acacia, paloverde, tamarisk, cenizo, and ocotillo harbored an entire tropical ecosystem—of which *L. s. septentrionalis* was a part— a biotic community comparable to East Texas' "Big Thicket" in species diversity. But during the 1950s an agricultural boom leveled most of this native subtropical vegetation, and a majority of the Mexican birds, mammals, and reptiles that historically ranged only as far north as the Tamaulipan thorn brush now remain as relictual, diminishing populations isolated in a handful of the Rio Grande floodplain's widely separated preserves.)

In what remains of this subtropical thicket, the northern cat-eyed snake's favored microhabitat is dense vegetation bordering ponds and watercourses, where this reptile's arboreal agility affords it an effective means of flight from danger.

Prey   Predominantly pond and tree frogs. In much of its Latin American range, *L. s. septentrionalis* feeds heavily on the red-eyed treefrog. This amphibian's eggs and tadpoles are simply swallowed, but the adult frogs are envenomed using the cat-eyed snake's long rear teeth, which introduce its somewhat paralytic salival toxins.

Captive *L. s. septentrionalis* will also feed on smaller snakes, minnows, and mice, and an array of such diminutive vertebrates probably constiute most of its prey north of the Rio Grande.

Reproduction   Egg-laying. Incubation periods of several clutches deposited by Mexican females has varied from 79 to 90 days; except for their bolder dorsal patterning, the 9-inch-long young resemble adults.

Coloring scale/form   The northern cat-eyed snake's slender dorsum is alternately crossbarred with rectangular khaki and dark brown blocks; its light-hued crown bears a distinctive darker oval with a rearward-pointing apex. But it is the bulging golden eyes that are this animal's signature. Shared with other rear-fanged, mildly venomed colubrids, as well as with the pitvipers, the irises of *L. s. septentrionalis*—which are the source of its common name—are slashed with sharply defined, cat-like vertical pupils.

The pale underchin and throat shade to light orange at midbody and salmon beneath the tail, while the outer ends of many of the belly scales, which have a slightly darkened posterior border, are peppered with brown speckling. The 21 to 23 midbody rows of dorsal scales are predominantly smooth, although some are pocked by tiny apical pits.

Similar snakes   None. No other serpent within its range is likely to be mistaken for the northern cat-eyed snake.

Behavior   As might be inferred from its big, cat-like eyes, *L. s. septentrionalis* is an exclusively nocturnal reptile. Like the lyre snake, a similarly rear-fanged desert-dwelling colubrid, the northern cat-eyed snake has pursued an evolutionary strategy very different from that of the thick bodied, sedentary pitvipers (whose toxins are pre-digestive agents often injected into large, hard-to-swallow prey to partially break down its body and ease its passage down their throats).

Instead, cat-eyed snakes have developed toxins only as potent as they need to subdue their diminutive, mostly anuran prey, while maintaining a slender, agile body that allows them to both hide effectively in thick branches and adeptly evade predators.

BLACK-STRIPED SNAKES
Genus Coniophanes

Black-striped Snake, *Coniophanes imperialis imperialis*

The rear-fanged genus *Coniophanes* is contained in the colubrine subfamily *Xenodontinae*; its members have toxic saliva that allows them to overcome the lizards, small snakes, amphibians, and nestling rodents on which they prey. These toxins have caused fairly severe local inflamation in humans, while internal bleeding has been associated with bites by the related Mexican genus *conophis*. Black-striped snakes' heads are moderately distinct from the neck, their scales are smooth and arranged in 19 rows, and the anal plate is divided.

Coniophanes imperialis is the only species in this primarily subtropical Latin American genus to live north of the Mexican border, where, in Texas' lower Rio Grande valley, it is a rare and secretive snake that is occasionally encountered abroad after dark, though it is more often found hidden beneath moisture-retaining surface litter.

170 BLACK-STRIPED SNAKE

Coniophanes imperialis imperialis

Mildly venomous The longitudinally grooved rear teeth for which *C. imperialis* is noted allow it to introduce salivary toxins into its small vertebrate prey. Yet its small size and calm temperament mean that it is unlikely to bite a human being—in whom its saliva has produced severe local inflammations but no lasting effects.

Bryce C. Brown (1939), who as a young man allowed a black-striped snake to bite him on the hand as an experiment, reported that the sharp initial pain was similar to a bee sting but lasted much longer. Within an hour the discomfort had reached his elbow and his slightly swollen hand had grown temporarily numb, a condition that remained for several days, though Brown eventually recovered and went on to pursue a successful career in herpetology at Baylor University.

Abundance Threatened. Protected by the state of Texas. *Coniophanes imperialis imperialis* is a predominantly Mexican reptile known in the United States only from Cameron, Hidalgo, and Willacy counties where, before World War II, it was quite numerous. Today, because elimination of the Rio Grande valley's native thorn woodland by agricultural and residential clearing has devastated much of the area's wildlife, black-striped snakes are seldom encountered.

Size Adult *C. i. imperialis* are 12 to 18 inches in length; the record is 20 in.

Habitat   The Tamaulipan thorn thicket—particularly its riparian arroyos and seasonally filled watercourses and resacas—was the black-striped snake's original home. This tangle of catclaw acacia, paloverde, tamarisk, cenizo, and ocotillo, named for Mexico's most northeastern state, formerly covered the lower Gulf coastal plain with one of the United States' richest biotic communities, harboring tropical fauna like *C. i. imperialis* which ranged no further north than the Rio Grande valley.

In what is left of this thorn brush, the semi-fossorial black-striped snake's microhabitat on the surface consists of natural or manmade debris (on the outskirts of Harlingen, black-striped snakes are edificial, turning up around buildings beneath long-discarded trash and construction material). See **Northern Cat-eyed Snake.**

Prey   This reptile's prey is mostly small frogs and toads, lizards, and smaller snakes.

Reproduction   Egg-laying. In Chiapas, Mexico, clutches have been found to number up to 10 eggs that in the area's tropical heat and humidity can reportedly require as few as 40 days to hatch into 6½-inch-long young.

Coloring scale/form   This slender colubrid is notable for both its small head, hardly distinct from its neck, and for the three dark dorsolateral stripes—a single prominent black vertebral line and a wider dark longitudinal stripe low on each side—that run the length of its medium brown body. In contrast, the black-striped snake's venter shades from orange to pink, with a bright red undertail.

Similar snakes   None. No other serpent within its range is likely to be mistaken for the black-striped snake.

Behavior   This secretive, semi-tropical serpent typically forages from late evening to early morning, avoiding daytime activity by burrowing into sandy soil or hiding under cacti, fallen palm fronds, or logs. Like other snakes with brightly hued undertails, *C. i. imperialis* typically everts this part of its belly when harassed.

With its foreparts lowered, it may then wave its elevated tail tip back and forth in a gesture presumed to approximate the threatening head of a venomous reptile such as the coral snake. Unlikely as this seems, the technique may work, for Frederick R. Gehlbach (1981) found fewer tail injuries among species like the coral, long-nosed, and black-striped snakes that raise and wave their colorful undertails, than among species that did not employ this defensive technique.

LYRE SNAKES
Genus Trimorphodon

Texas Lyre Snake, *Trimorphodon biscutatus vilkinsonii*

The rear-fanged genus *Trimorphodon*—a term that means "three forms of teeth—is characterized by dentition unique among North American snakes. Behind conventional, inward-curved teeth located in the front of the mouth, a set of barely visible small teeth is present. These are followed, far to the rear of the jaw, by the pair of enlarged, grooved fangs with which members of this genus envenomate their small prey. As a result, *trimorphodon* has been placed in the colubrine subfamily *Xenodontinae*, or "differently-toothed." Ranging from sea-level to over 7,000-foot elevations throughout Central America, lyre snakes—whose common name is derived from the dark, ostensibly lyre-shaped marking on their crowns—inhabit the United States only along the Rio Grande in West Texas, as well in southern New Mexico, Arizona, Nevada, and California.

Texas lyre snakes have been found in scrubby deserts, rocky hills and mountains, and wooded canyons. Their preferred macrohabitat, however, is exposed rock faces and boulder piles where they emerge early in the evening from crevices in weathered and split granite and other secluded hiding places, and remain active far into the night.

According to herpetologist Augustus Rentfro, who has studied all three races of lyre snakes,

> These medium-sized colubrids average about thirty inches
> in length but [especially among the western subspecies]
> can grow to nearly four feet in length.

The lyre snake's slim neck and broad head, which allows room for its enlarged salivary glands, as well as its elliptical pupils suggest its status as a rear-fanged serpent. Yet, despite its copious, mildly toxic saliva and the sizable, very slender and supple body of large individuals, *Trimorphodon biscutatus* rarely bites and poses no threat to humans if carefully handled.

This lyre snake race is the only southwestern snake with both a vertically elliptical pupil and a lorilabial scale between its loreal and its paired labial scales. This pair of labial scales is what the name *biscutatus* references—the Greek *bi* or "two," and *scutatus* or "scale." The Texas lyre snake has from 21 to 27 rows of smooth dorsolateral scales and an anal plate that may be either divided or undivided.

Lizards are their preferential prey, but nestling birds, rodents, and smaller snakes may also be taken.

171 TEXAS LYRE SNAKE

Trimorphodon biscutatus wilkinsonii

Mildly venomous Vertically slit hairline pupils mark *T. b. wilkinsonii* as a mildly venomous serpent whose posterior upper jaw carries a pair of slightly enlarged, grooved teeth.
This rare snake poses little danger to humans, however, for unlike the vipers it cannot inject muscle-pressurized venom. Instead, after a bite the lyre snake engages its rear fangs, down whose lengthwise furrows its toxic saliva is squeezed by contractions of its jaw. Though the Texas lyre snake is typically reluctant to bite, if restrained it tends to thrash about wildly, and large individuals are big enough to bite with conviction and deposit considerable painful saliva into a wound.

Abundance Threatened. Protected by the state of Texas. First described by E. D. Cope in 1886, from a specimen collected in Mexico's Sierra Madre occidental by Edward Wilkinson, *T. b. wilkinsoni* was known from only three other specimens at the time of L. M. Klauber's review of the genus in 1940. Yet Texas lyre snakes seem to be broadly, if spottily, distributed across the northern Chihuahuan Desert, for these secretive animals turn up every summer in widely separated locales across Trans-Pecos Texas.
Often, these sites are hidden nooks in the granite bluffs along the River Road west of Big Bend National Park. Although years pass in which no one sees a single *T. b. wilkinsonii* in this area, at other times these reptiles can seem to be almost abundant. Marty and John Walmsley—who chanced to venture out during a period when lyre snakes were active—found 5 individuals during the 3-day Easter weekend of 2001, then another 2 on the same May night. All were seen between Tornillo Creek, Fresno Canyon, and Ivey's Spring west of Lajitas, except a single individual found in a never-before-reported habitat high in the Chisos Mountains near the national park's basin campground. This animal—a male like all the others and therefore almost certainly abroad in search of female pheromone scent—was found in a drizzling, 60°F rain.
The decision by Texas Department of Parks and Wildlife to make illegal the possesssion and captive reproduction of this race has proven to be less important in maintaining its numbers than

regulating automobile traffic through its critical habitat would be. Before the human population of the El Paso area exploded, Texas lyre snakes were encountered regularly, and in some numbers, on the Trans-Mountain road which bisects the Franklin Mountains, where they are now very rare.

Size Most adults are 24 to 36 inches in length; the record is 41 in.

Habitat This slim saxicolous reptile is most often found in jumbles of fallen boulders or along fissured bluffs. Like most chthonic, arid land–living serpents, it leaves its creviced daytime retreats only well after dark. Earl Turner, who has spent decades hunting snakes in the Trans-Pecos, has observed *T. b. vilkinsonii* in a variety of habitats, including on barren desert flats, in Presidio County's Pinto Canyon, and at the mouth of Santa Elena Canyon on the Rio Grande, where he discovered a small female on a rock ledge overhanging the river.

Prey The Texas lyre snake probably feeds on any smaller vertebrate, but herpetologist Dave Barker found only lizard remains in the feces of several newly caught *T. b. vilkinsonii*, and while spiny lizards and skinks are accepted as food animals by captive lyre snakes, Rentfro reports that they greatly prefer racerunners.

The way in which Texas lyre snakes capture this lacertillian prey became evident when Dallas herpetologists Dave Blody and James Murphy observed one large individual methodically searching a stony arroyo wall for the several lizard species that had squeezed into its crevices for the night. Warm-blooded prey is also taken, and may even be preferred, for Shaw and Campbell (1974) propose that, rather than lizards, lyre snakes' primary prey is actually bats.

After reading this, Rentfro, searching for a way to fatten his prospective breeding stock, but fearing "acquiring some dreadful disease" from bats, turned to the hyper-abundant food source of nestling English sparrows—which his lyre snakes "enthusiastically accepted.

Reproduction Egg-laying. This enthusiastic feeding allowed Rentfro's females to quickly gain weight, and

> in late June . . . frequent copulation was observed. The females rapidly vibrated their tails when courted by the males [but] courtship and breeding was mild by the standards of some colubrids: no biting or wrestling was seen.

In late July one 28-inch-long female deposited 7 adhesive-shelled oval eggs, averaging 1⅛ inches in length and ⅝ inch in diameter. After a 77-day incubation period these hatched into 8-inch-long young dramatically different in appearance from their subdued gray-brown parents. They were

> a startling soft silver-grey with 25 white-edged neat black bands (exclusive of the tail). The trademark lyre-shaped head marking [was] absent. Only two irregular black spots [could] be seen on their otherwise unmarked heads. [After shedding] the young fed readily on small spiny and racerunner lizards.

The only hatchling *T. b. vilkinsonii* ever seen in the wild was found in Brewster County, Texas, on Pepper's Hill between Lajitas and Terlingua by Damon Salceies in October 1997. Mired in newly laid road tar, this thin, 7-inch-long neonate—whose photograph is included here—had a recent umbilical scar that indicated it had hatched only a few weeks previously; wild-born Texas lyre snakes may remain mostly below ground for their first several foraging seasons. (It may not be necessary for juveniles—or females—to venture beyond the shelter of their residential rock piles because Texas lyre snakes are probably able to capture much of their lacertillian prey without leaving the creviced warrens where desert lizards retire for the night.)

Coloring scale/form   The adult Texas lyre snake's ground color is medium brown, with 17 to 24 very widely spaced, triangularly shaped dark brown dorsolateral saddles (so widely spaced that Hobart M. Smith has suggested that some unique genetic suppression obscures what would be expected to be intervening dark-hued markings between them).

Broadest over the spine and outlined by an irregular yellowish border, each of these brown triangular saddles has a paler, cinnamon-hued center and tapers to a point no more than a single scale in width at the belly line; across the tail these saddles become narrow brown bands. The Texas lyre snake's wiry neck supports a wide oval head notable for the big, pale, slit-pupiled eyes associated with the development of a rudimentary venom system.

Among more westerly subspecies, the dark, somewhat lyre-shaped cephalic marking (that is the source of this reptile's common name) is evident, but the crown of Texas specimens shows little more than a trio of chocolate smudges. The anterior venter is yellowish or pinkish-brown, becoming buff on its posterior third. A small facial scale called a lorilabial is located between the loreal and upper labial scales, the dorsal scales are smooth, usually arranged in 23 rows at midbody, and the anal plate may be either divided or undivided, usually the former.

Similar snakes   None. No other serpent in the Trans-Pecos shares the Texas lyre snake's slim configuration and widely spaced triangular vertebral saddles.

Behavior   Exclusively nocturnal in the wild, Texas lyre snakes may have less innate aversion to bright light than other night-hunting reptiles because according to Barker captives are willing to emerge in the evening to explore even a well-lit room, using the distinctive gait—head held high off the ground—typical of *Trimorphodon*.

Wild Texas lyre snakes usually restrict their rare appearances in the open to early-to-mid-summer, especially during periods of elevated humidity following rainfall. Yet Blody and Murphy have also observed *T. b. vilkinsonii* moving about on a rainy night in March, while L. M. Klauber, speaking of western subspecies, noted that *T. biscutatus* seemed to be very tolerant of low temperatures, foraging abroad on nights too cold for other nocturnal species.

CORAL SNAKES
Family Elapidae

The family *Elapidae* is comprised of predominantly neurotoxically venomed snakes, including the cobras, mambas, kraits, and their allies. All elapids have enlarged, frontally grooved (*proteroglyphous* in Greek) anterior fangs. In most species, including the American coral snakes, these grooves are folded over to make an enclosed tube, at whose lower, forward end is the discharge/injection orifice. At its upper end, each fang—no more than a millimeter or two long in most coral snakes—is connected to a small venom gland located at the rear of the jaw. The jaw muscles compress both this gland and the cells that secrete the coral snake's complex and potent yet minuscule quantity of neurologically destructive venom. (This is why corals typically seize their prey, then hold on, chewing, until it has been immobilized.)

Elapids are of exclusively old-world distribution except for 3 genera of North and South American coral snakes; *micrurus* is the only member of the family *Elapidae* in eastern/central North America.

CORAL SNAKES
Genus Micrurus

Eastern Coral Snake, *Micrurus fulvius fulvius*
Texas Coral Snake, *Micrurus fulvius tener*

In the eastern United States, the genus *Micrurus* has but a single species, *M. fulvius*, sometimes called the Harlequin coral sake, which is divided into two races, the eastern coral snake, *M. f. fulvius*, and its western subspecies, the Texas coral snake, *M. f. tener*. Both races are ringed with red, yellow, and black, with only the two warning colors of a traffic signal—red and yellow—touching. (In this country, all nonvenomous red-, yellow-, and black-banded snakes have their red and yellow bands separated by a black band, though this does not hold true in Latin America.)

Coral snakes are also shaped differently from other red-, yellow-, and black-banded North American snakes: the head is flattened, with a rounded black snout, and there are both 15 rows of smooth dorsolateral scales and a divided anal plate.

The harlequin coral snake can be a dangerous reptile, in part because its temperament is so unpredictable. As it is with all reptiles, highly variable behavior is based on a number of factors, among them temperature (cool snakes are more docile), recent hunting success (hungry snakes are more irritable), and the degree to which the animal has been disturbed. Coral snakes' mercurial behavior is also a function of the diversity between the individual temperaments of particular snakes . . . and some *M. fulvius* seem to be innately inclined to suddenly and reflexively bite sideways in response to even a gentle touch.

Because coral snakes have short, immovable fangs and a comparatively small mouth, a myth has arisen that it can only nip the tip of a finger or toe, and then must chew deliberately to administer venom. Actually, while *M. fulvius* is not able to make the long, lunging strikes of large pitvipers, or to inject pressurized venom deeply into muscle tissue, it does not need to, because coral snakes are perfectly capable of biting an arm, leg, foot—or your side, if you happen to roll on one in the grass. A single quick bite, moreover, one that just penetrates the skin, is all this animal needs to mortally envenomate its reptilian prey, and the same is true of a human adversary.

Another erroneous belief is that one can safely lift a coral snake by its tail, but *M. fulvius* can rapidly change ends by adroitly climbing its own dangling body. (Like other snakes, *M. fulvius* tend to do this only if they are dangled; if their forefparts are allowed to touch the earth they generally forget about climbing their own bodies and resume merely trying to crawl away.)

Yet, because of its its tendency to whip its foreparts from side to side, biting anything against which it bumps its head, despite its initially seemingly docile nature, an aroused coral snake can be an aggressive creature. Its first response is often the decoy maneuver of raising its tail like an about-to-strike head—then suddenly snapping outward with its previously hidden jaws.

Harlequin coral snakes inhabit open woodlands, hammocks and fields, as well as suburban backyards. Here, they hide under fallen tree trunks, beneath discarded litter, in mats of vegetation or the recumbent stems of lawn grasses. Yet *M. fulvius* is seldom seen, in spite of being common throughout most of its range, because it has such a secretive nature.

172   EASTERN CORAL SNAKE

Micrurus fulvius fulvius

Venomous   If "Red touches yellow, Kill a fellow" is usually too extreme a prognosis, it is still the best way to quickly identify a coral snake. *Micrurus fulvius fulvius*, the eastern race, is the only red-, black-, and yellow-banded snake in the Southeast whose red and yellow bands adjoin.

Despite the threatening rhyme hardly anyone is harmed by coral snakes, however, because for the most part *M. f. fulvius* is a shy burrower living beneath leaves and logs, and if unmolested it is so non-aggressive toward humans that it poses almost no danger to anyone who has not handled or stepped barefoot on it. Moreover, because the coral's rigid little fangs (no more than ⅛ inch in length), are too short to penetrate shoe leather, many *M. fulvius* bites result in no envenomation at all: only about 1 percent of the venom poisonings in North America involve coral snakes.

Yet, anywhere it can make contact with bare flesh *M. f. fulvius* has no trouble biting a larger animal or human, because the coral snake's mouth can gape open to form a wide biting surface that enables its strong jaws to pinch out and easily puncture a fold of skin anywhere on one's body. In addition, as hollow hypodermic needles, coral snake fangs are designed to instantly inject venom, and a restrained coral snake can twist suddenly sideways and in a flash deposit several drops of venom onto a pinning stick.

Since this venom consists almost entirely of neurotoxically destructive peptides, the toxins of *M. f. fulvius* are more virulent than those of any snake in eastern North America. Approximately equal in potency to cobra venom, a lethal dose for a human adult is estimated to consist of as little as 5 to 10 milligrams, while the largest eastern coral snakes have been milked of up to 20 mg.

Immediate pain usually accompanies a bite by *M. fulvius*, but the real danger of coral snake toxins is their suppression of the central nervous system—a process that may not manifest symptoms for several hours. In the case of every coral snakebite, therefore, antivenin should be ready well before the possible onset of neurological problems, because once symptoms appear it is often difficult to prevent further decline. See **Venom Potency Table**.

Abundance   Common. *Micrurus fulvius fulvius* is, with the exception of a small population found in the highlands of Alabama, a coastal plain–living subspecies. Its range extends along, and about a hundred miles inland from, the northern Gulf Coasts of Louisiana, Mississippi, Alabama, and Florida, north along the Atlantic seaboard as far as central North Carolina.

As a small, cryptic reptile the eastern coral snake is not averse to human habitation, and especially during its activity peak in cool fall and spring weather it is often encountered in human-inhabited areas. This is not true of its seldom-seen nocturnal look-alikes, the milk snakes, scarlet snakes, and scarlet kingsnakes, all of which prefer natural terrain. For example, in their study of 93 Florida *M. f. fulvius* Dale Jackson and Richard Franz found that in suburban sites

> the red-, yellow-, and black-banded snakes found crossing driveways or crawling in yards . . . without exception proved to be eastern coral snakes.

Size   *Micrurus fulvius fulvius* grows larger than most people expect: the record is 51 inches. The biggest eastern coral snakes are almost always female, for the two sexes parallel each other in size during their first 3 years. The growth rate of males then declines. Females continue to grow at the rapid juvenile rate through at least their fourth year, and among 125 individuals, females' mean length (despite their proportionately shorter tails) was 35 inches, that of males, 27 in.

Habitat   Eastern coral snakes live primarily in dry, wooded terrain: oak/hardwood forest, stands of longleaf or loblolly pines, both upland and seasonally flooded bottomland woods, and even in arid scrub, though coral snakes are rare or absent in extensive wetlands. Thick ground cover of leaf litter, fallen logs, and pine or palmetto stumps is important both as a hiding place and as habitat for the smaller snakes and lizards on which coral snakes prey.

Prey   Coral snakes prey chiefly on other snakes which, in the wild, they have been observed actively scent-tracking. Tennant discovered a 26-inch-long female *M. fulvius*, in the field, which was in the process of envenoming a young rat snake (*E. obsoleta*). The rat snake was first immobilized and then, very gradually, swallowed. That evening, as coral snakes often do when captured, this animal disgorged the rat snake—which turned out to be just slightly longer than the coral itself. Slender-bodied lizards (especially snake-like glass lizards and skinks), as well as small amphisbaenians, are also consumed, though much less frequently than ophidian prey. Cannibalism among *M. fulvius* has also been reported, which means that males much smaller than their prospective mates approach them only at the risk of being eaten.

Reproduction   Egg-laying. Dale R. Jackson and Richard Franz found that male and female *M. f. fulvius* follow seasonally differing sexual cycles. Females undergo early spring vitellogenesis, developing their eggs between March and May, while males' testicular enlargement and spermatogenesis occur in autumn.

Yet, because viable sperm is stored by males throughout the year, breeding most often occurs during the female's most fertile period, in late spring. The single clutch of up to 13 (though usually less than 8) white, sausage-shaped eggs, 1½ by ⅔ inch in diameter, are deposited between late may and the end of July. Some 2 months later the 6½- to 7½-inch-long young emerge, identical to the adults, fully equipped with venom, and capable of biting at once. Neonate *M. f. fulvius* are very rarely seen in the wild, however, apparently because during their first year or two juveniles are apparently almost exclusively fossorial; each fall, small coral snakes in perhaps their second year of life are often found.

At this time, adult female eastern coral snakes are engaged in a seasonal activity peak, foraging heavily to replace the fat stores depleted by their summertime egg-laying, and during this period they may breed with young, newly sexually mature males which—unlike most older males—are also active during this cooler season.

Coloring/scale form   The eastern coral snake's 12 to 18 equally broad red and black bands are separated by bright yellow rings. Black speckles, spots, or large black blotches are often present within its red bands—while an aberrant color morph distinguished by very wide red bands is well known (its black bands are of normal width). On both color phases only black and yellow bands occur on the tail and forward of the nape. All the bright dorsolateral bands of *M. f. fulvius* are made up of 15 midbody rows of smooth dorsal scales; they also encircle its venter, whose subcaudal scales occur in a double row, and its anal plate is divided.

Similar snakes   Among both races of **scarlet snakes (164, 165)**, as well as in the **scarlet kingsnake (156)**, red bands occur all the way to the tail tip, black crossbands adjoin yellow ones ("Red touches black, venom lack"), and the elongate snout is orange.

Behavior   Whether the coral snake's bold dorsolateral patterning functions as a warning signal remains an area of controversy.

Certainly these vivid hues are inconspicuous to the largely color-blind nocturnal mammalian carnivores that feed on small terrestrial serpents but the coral snake's tail-raising threat behavior seems to deter some predators: opossums, which ordinarily feed on snakes, usually hesitate before a tail-waving coral snake.

As a primarily diurnal reptile, however, *M. f. fulvius* is seldom active during the nocturnal foraging period of these mammalian carnivores. In contrast, Jackson and Franz found that during all weather conditions eastern coral snakes' above-ground activity peaked in late morning and again in the afternoon. This means that most of its predators are diurnal birds of prey, to whom the coral snake's bright dorsolateral pigment is plainly visible. Yet among various hawks and falcons—which typically decapitate ophidian prey—sucessful predation on *M. f. fulvius* is well known.

Nevertheless, as Frederick Gehlbach pointed out in 1972, among snakes, partial loss of the tail is a good measure of near-miss predatory attempts, and overall both coral snakes and other nonvenomous, brightly banded snakes evidently suffer fewer predatory attacks than non-banded species, venomous or not. For example, only two of 134 *M. f. fulvius* examined by Jackson and Franz were missing parts of their tails, while of 26 other nonvenomous colubrid species only the scarlet kingsnake, a brightly banded possible mimic of *M. f. fulvius*, showed a similar lack of tail damage.

---

173   TEXAS CORAL SNAKE, *Micrurus fulvius tener*

Venomous   Since its venom is primarily made up of neurotoxically destructive peptides, *Micrurus fulvius* (along with the Mojave rattlesnake) is the most virulently toxined snake in North America. The lethal dose for a human adult is estimated to be as little as 5 to 10 milligrams of venom, which is approximately the same potency as the toxins of most cobras. Immediate pain usually accompanies a coral snakebite, but since nervous system impairment may not manifest symptoms for several hours, antivenin should be ready before the onset of neurological problems.

Yet few people are harmed by coral snakes. If unmolested, *M. fulvius* is so non-aggressive toward people that virtually everyone bitten has first touched or handled the animal. Moreover, many coral snakebites result in no envenomation at all (partly because at only about an ⅛ inch in length the coral's tiny, rigidly fixed fangs are too short to penetrate shoe leather or thick clothing), and only about 1 percent of North American venom poisonings involve coral snakes.

Nevertheless, *Micrurus fulvius* is adept at biting a large adversary. Its mouth can gape open to form a surprisingly wide biting surface, and its strong jaws can easily pinch out a fold of skin anywhere on the human body. In addition, as hollow hypodermic needles, coral snake fangs are designed to both puncture skin and rapidly inject venom. Janis Roze, the world's leading authority on coral snakes, has observed that *Micrurus* also typically releases a small additional amount of venom from glands located in its lower jaw. The common myth is that *M. fulvius* must chew deliberately to infuse its venom, and though coral snakes certianly bite-and-chew, agitated individuals do so with vigor and can instantly deposit their toxins onto a pinning stick or inject them deep into a thick leather handling glove. In confined areas *Micrurus fulvius* can also move very quickly, suddenly twisting its head to snap sideways. See **Venom Potency Table**.

Abundance   Common. Throughout western Louisiana and the eastern third of Texas, *M. f. tener* inhabits mostly wooded environments, either pine forest—where it is uncommon—or more open oak-hickory woodland, including both crosstimber hillsides and riparian bottomland. To the west these riparian corridors allow the Texas coral snake to range across a wide expanse of oak-juniper savannah on Texas' central Edwards Plateau, and to even penetrate the arid eastern reaches of the state's northern Chihuahuan Desert. Here, if even a bit of terrestrial leaf litter, fallen grass, or other vegetative detritus offers shelter for its small ophidian prey, *M. f. tener* is sometimes found in virtually waterless basin, range and canyon milieus.

The Texas coral snake is also entirely at home in residential areas where stone walls and densely landscaped shrubbery provide both cover and a habitat for the ground, ringneck, brown, and earth snakes on which it feeds (as a largely diurnal forager, *M. f. tener* is far more likely to be seen in suburban areas than its nocturnal look-alikes, the milk snakes, which are rare to nonexistent in cities. The author has often been called to suburban backyards and even porches to remove Texas coral snakes—sometimes quite early in the spring since this is a comparatively cool-weather-adapted snake.

Size   Texas coral snakes are larger than commonly thought: 74 adult females averaged 26½ inches in snout-vent length, 93 males just over 24 inches. The record is a 47¾-inch-long specimen from Brazoria County, Texas.

Habitat   *Micrurus fulvius tener* occupies a variety of dry terrestrial milieus, generally at least partially wooded. These include the eastern pine forest of Texas and Louisiana, Texas' central oak-juniper brakes, and the thorn brush woodland of the Rio Grande plain. Either rock-crevice cover or thick plant litter is important, both as a hiding place and as habitat for the semi-subterranean serpents on which coral snakes prey.

Prey   Coral snakes feed largely on other snakes, but lizards—especially slender, snake-like lizards such as skinks—are reportedly also taken, although captive coral snakes of both eastern and Texas races are often reluctant to feed, no matter what prey is offered.

The food of hatchling coral snakes in the wild is unknown, but 1 captive brood raised by the author fed sporadically on small earth and brown snakes, and 3 of the 6 reached adulthood.

Reproduction   Egg-laying. "No other North American snake has been reported to breed from late summer to late spring, then lay its eggs in midsummer," wrote herpetologist Hugh Quinn in 1979. The 3 to 8 white, sausage-shaped eggs—1⅛ inch in length by ⅜ in. in diameter—are laid during June and July, hatching 2 months later into 6½- to 7½-inch-long young.

Identical to the adults in color and marking, in the wild these neonates evidently lead almost entirely fossorial lives, perhaps for years, since they have only rarely been seen; neonates cared for by the author virtually never emerged from a deep layer of cage-bottom litter, even to feed.

Coloring/scale form *Micrurus fulvius tener* is the only black-, red-, and yellow-banded serpent in Louisiana and Texas whose red and yellow bands touch. "Red against yellow, kill a fellow" seldom turns out to be the case, but it is a good phrase to use in quickly identifying a coral snake. The Texas coral snake's trunk is completely encircled with 14 to 20 equally broad red and black bands separated by much narrower yellow rings. Both its head and tail are banded only with black and yellow; the nape and posterior crown are marked with a wide yellow band. Partially albino coral snakes have also been found, with white bands replacing normal individuals' black pigmentation. (This very rare color morph has ordinary red and yellow bands, however.)

Whatever its color, the Texas coral snake's bright dorsolateral bands continue unbroken across its belly, while its undertail has a double row of scales like that of most nonvenomous snakes. There are 15 midbody rows of smooth dorsal scales and its anal plate is divided.

Similar snakes   Among both **milk snakes (155–162)** and **scarlet snakes (164–166)** the red and pale (yellow or white) crossbands do not touch—black dorsolateral rings separate them: "Red against black, venom lack." Unlike coral snakes, whose tails are entirely black and yellow, milk and scarlet snakes' red crossbands occur all the way to their tail tips. The **Texas long-nosed snake (167)** may have a few red and creamy yellow scales that touch, but only in the speckled edging of its dorsal saddles. Its venter is mostly white, its protruding snout light brown or orange.

Behavior   Judged against the behavioral norms of other North American snakes (all colubrids and crotalids), coral snakes are somewhat strange. Like other elapids such as the cobras—which exhibit a wide range of behavioral flexibility—coral snakes do surprising things: during the sumer of 2002, Connie McIntyre was called to rescue a texas coral snake from a suburban back yard. This individual seemed lethargic until it was touched, when it began *Micrurus fulvius'* typical thrashing and sideways snapping, then made a dash for shelter. As it squeezed under a rock, McIntyre took hold of its about-to-disappear tail and pulled it out—only to find that in the second or two its foreparts had been out of sight, the coral snake had discovered and seized a rough earth snake, Virginia *valeria striatula*, which it held wriggling in its jaws.

To what degree coral snakes' bold patterning functions as a warning has long been an area of controversy. To realize their defensive potential, however, the coral's bright body bands may need to be combined with its distinctive threat behavior. For example, opossums confronted with both artificial replicas and dead coral snakes were not frightened. Only when live *Micrurus fulvius* actively raised and slowly wagged their yellow- and black-banded tail tips (presumably in a threatening imitation of their similarly patterned heads) did the opossums hesitate. See **Louisiana Milk Snake**.

PITVIPERS
Family Viperidae

This group of dangerously venomous, lengthily front-fanged snakes contains two subfamilies, *Viperinae* (true vipers) and *Crotalinae*, or pitvipers. The latter subfamily consists, in the eastern and central part of North America north of Mexico, of the genera *Agkistrodon*, or copperheads and cottonmouths, and *Crotalidae, Sistrurus, and Crotalus,* or rattlesnakes. (Pitvipers' common name is derived from the well-defined heat-sensing pits, one of which deeply indents on each side of the snout between eye and nostril.)

These heat-sensitive facial organs not only let pitvipers pick out warm-blooded prey against a kaleidoscope of generally less-warm background temperatures, but the sensitivity and positioning of these pits allows them to strike almost unerringly even in complete darkness. The strike is particularly effective because a pair of long, hollow fangs, each attached to a rotatable maxillary bone within a distal socket, is located at each front corner of the upper jaw. When the pitviper lunges toward its prey each maxilla is rotated anteriorly to direct its fang almost straight forward to jab its victim; when the snake closes its jaws the maxilla rotates posteriorly to fold its fang against the roof of the mouth.

Each of these fangs (if either breaks off it is quickly replaced by the anterior-most in a row of proto-fangs lined up just behind it) intersects a hollow, tubular duct against which its upper opening is sealed by sphincter-like muscles. Each of these paired ducts leads, in turn, to a venom gland, or lumen, set in the outer rear third of the skull. (In conjunction with the contracting musculature that surrounds it, these big lumens broaden the rear of the pitviper's head into the distinctive, triangular viperid shape.) *Crotalinae* also share a vertically elliptical pupil with the mildly venomous North American colubrids, but unlike most nonvenomous snakes, pitvipers have a single row of subcaudal scales.

Pitvipers' control of both their fangs and their venom glands is highly evolved, allowing these animals to choose both the depth of its fangs' penetration and the amount of venom expended during a strike. Because of this element of choice on the snake's part many purely defensive bites are "dry," meaning no venom is injected, since the snake is trying to merely deter rather than kill its attacker.

Actually, even where prey is involved, pitviper venom is only partially a killing device. The primary function of pitvipers' toxic mixture of cell-destroying proteases is to pre-digest food animals. *Viperidae* are able to ingest larger, more calorically valuable prey animals because their cell-destroying venom has rendered these creatures' lumpy carcasses into softened masses of partially digested tissue. Like everything else about pitvipers, the action of their venom is far from random: from inside envenomed prey, cell-dissolving enzymes disintegrate the dying animal's skin and muscle; then, after it is swallowed, opening its viscera and finally exposing its skeleton to further digestive disintegration. (The simpler, less elaborately evolved venom of elapids is much more lethal.)

COPPERHEADS AND COTTONMOUTHS
Genus Agkistrodon

Southern Copperhead, *Agkistrodon contortrix contortrix*
Northern Copperhead, *Agkistrodon contortrix mokasen*

Osage Copperhead, *Agkistrodon contortrix phaeogaster*
Broad-banded Copperhead, *Agkistrodon contortrix laticinctus*
Trans-Pecos Copperhead, *Agkistrodon contortrix pictigaster*
Eastern Cottonmouth, *Agkistrodon piscivorus piscivorus*
Florida Cottonmouth, *Agkistrodon piscivorus conanti*
Western Cottonmouth, *Agkistrodon piscivorus leucostoma*

The viperine subfamily *Crotalinae* contains all North American members of the genus *Agkistrodon*, commonly known as copperheads (**or highland moccasins**) and cottonmouths (**or water moccasins**). These common names are highly descriptive, for copperheads have unmistakable coppery- to russet-colored crowns while a glimpse of the pinkish-white interior of a frightened cottonmouth's gaping oral cavity makes clear the reason for its common name. Likewise, its scientific designation *Agkistrodon* is drawn either from the Greek *ankistron* or "fish hook," and *odon* or "tooth," which describes these pitvipers' long, curved, fishhook-like fangs.

Agkistrodon feed on a variety of both endothermic and ectothermic prey—animals which range from grasshoppers and cicadas to amphibians, ground-dwelling birds, and mammals up to the size of muskrats. Both copperheads and cottonmouths give birth to live young, often only every second year among northern copperheads, and perhaps also among cottonmouths from the more northerly parts of the range. Both species' neonates have a pale yellowish or greenish tail tip which they use, probably subconsciously, as a wriggling, worm-like decoy to lure small prey within striking range (excited adult copperheads and cottonmouths exhibit the same instinctive tail-whirling, and despite lacking a rattle can produce an audible buzzing sound as their tail tips vibrate against dried vegetation).

174 SOUTHERN COPPERHEAD

Agkistrodon contortrix contortrix

Venomous   While poisoning by any race of *A. contortrix* could be fatal to a small child, records of the Antivenin Institute of America show that throughout the United States, regardless of the kind (or lack) of treatment, over a 10-year period not a single death resulted from 308 copperhead bites. This is largely because *A. con-*

tortrix seldom strikes unless it is stepped on or handled, because it has short (⅜ in. maximum length) fangs, and because its toxins are only about half as destructive to tissue as those of an equal quantity of most rattlesnake venom. Even animals as small as cats, which are often bitten due to copperheads' prevalence in wooded parts of suburban neighborhoods, usually survive *A. contortrix* envenomation, although they typically experience substantial tissue loss and skin-sloughing. See **Venom Potency Table.**

Abundance   Common. In much of the Southeast—from South Carolina across central Georgia, southern Alabama, all of Mississippi and Louisiana through Arkansas to eastern Oklahoma and Texas—*A. c. contortrix* is the most numerous venomous snake. An entirely typical example is the experience of Gerry Salmon: while working as a naturalist in a South Carolina state park campground, Salmon was called to identify the remains of at least two southern copperheads among the camp's several hundred tent sites every morning. Though these animals were invariably killed when discovered by campers and employees, no diminishment in their numbers was evident over the course of an entire summer. Three hundred and fifty miles to the south, however, in Florida's Gadsden County, *A. c. contortrix* is a **threatened animal** afforded **state protection.**

Size   The largest of the copperhead subspecies, individual *A. c. contortrix* from the southeastern United States have reached a record size of 52 inches. Most individuals are much smaller, however, with a majority of adults measuring 24 to 36 in.

Habitat   Southern copperheads are almost always found in tree-shaded areas where fallen leaves, logs, and branches afford these terrestrial ambush-foragers a complexly patterned background against which their dark-edged dorsolateral crossbands provide amazingly cryptic coloration.

Heavy vegetative ground cover also shelters the southern copperhead's small forest-floor-living prey which, if it is numerous, can support as many as 6 or 7 adult copperheads on a single acre. In one North Texas study plot, for example, a majority of intergrade southern/broad-banded copperheads marked and subsequently recovered were found within 100 yards of where they were released a year earlier.

Prey   Copperheads ordinarily take whatever small prey is most seasonally available. Deer mice and white-footed mice are probably the principal food source of *A. c. contortrix*—followed by anurans (in spring, large numbers of puddle-spawning frogs are taken). Large insects such as cicadas can also be a major food source as they emerge en masse from underground. When excited by nearby prey, young copperheads slowly twitch their yellowish- or grayish-green tail tips in a subconscious but tantalizing imitation of a wriggling caterpillar—a maneuver which may lure small frogs and toads within striking range.

Reproduction   Live-bearing. See **Broad-banded Copperhead.**

Coloring/scale form   This eastern subspecies' most distinctive characteristic is its pale beige, sometimes almost pinkish ground color. This is marked with 13 to 20 pale-centered, dark-bordered reddish brown dorsolateral bands. Often, the right and left sides of these bands do not line up along the spine, where they are cinched, or contorted, into an hourglass configuration—a shape which gave rise to the Latin name *contortrix*.

The tan, wedge-shaped crown bears a pair of dark posterior spots, while the prominent supraocular plates are part of a sharply angled intersection between the crown and the flat, undercut cheeks. Posterior to its slit-pupiled, coppery-colored eyes the southern copperhead's cheeks (supralabial scales) are marked with a pale, reward-pointing V whose upper border is defined by a dark line leading from the eye to the rear of its jaw; just below and behind its nostril is the pitviper's dark heat-sensing pit.

The southern copperhead's whitish venter is only slightly mottled along its mid-line; distally, it is marked with large brown ovals. The 23 to 25 midbody rows of dorsal scales are weakly keeled, there is a single row of ventral scales beneath the tail tip, and the anal plate is undivided.

Similar snakes   Where the ranges of the southern and **broad-banded copperhead (177)** races meet along a broad strip stretching from the Gulf Coast to central Oklahoma, individuals intermediate in pattern between these subspecies prevail. The western broad-banded race can be distinguished, however, by its more darkly mottled venter, the absence of dark borders on its reddish-tan dorsolateral bands, and the almost equal width of these bands at the belly line and along the spine. To the north, the southern copperhead intergrades through northern Oklahoma, Arkansas, and southern Missouri with its subspecies the **Osage copperhead (176)**. This race is more brownish in ground color, and the left and right sides of its thinly white-edged dorsolateral bands meet symmetrically along its spine. In a 1,000-mile-long band from southern Iowa down the Mississippi through Illinois and Tennessee, then across Mississippi, Alabama, Georgia, the Carolinas and Virginia to Delaware, the southern copperhead intergrades with the **northern copperhead (175)**. This race has a coppery-red ground color and unmarked crown, with broad, dark brown edges outlining its medium brown dorsolateral bands. In a dark brown area at least 3 scale rows in width the right and left halves of these bands are joined across the spine. Rounded dark paravertebral spots may occur in the light-colored parts of the sides, while a dark spot is often present in the center of each dorsolateral band (these may be better defined in young specimens). Dark ventrolateral spots encroach on the outer edges of the ventral scales, which are lighter than the dorsum but heavily smudged with dark pigment.

The nonvenomous serpent most commonly mistaken for the southern copperhead is the **eastern hog-nosed snake (120)**, especially in its coppery color phases. Sometimes similarly patterned, these short, heavy-bodied, snakes inhabit the same tree-shaded suburban neighborhoods as the southern copperhead, and like it often show little fear of humans. But the hog-nose's raised forehead, round-pupiled dark brown eyes, comparatively thick neck, and prominently upturned snout are distinctive, as is its divided anal plate and the double row of scales beneath its tail. As a juvenile, the **western cottonmouth (181)** resembles the young southern copperhead, but it is a dusky gray-brown with dark dorsolateral bands. Newborn *A. p. leucostoma* also have a wide, dark band across their cheeks and are seldom found away from water in the copperhead's dry woodland habitat.

Behavior Most often abroad at dawn or dusk between March and October, copperheads are low-energy-budget predators. Because they may eat no more often than once every 3 weeks even during the months in which they are most active, *Agkistrodon contortrix* often lives virtually alongside small mammal populations: during late spring and summer both snakes and rodents may be simultaneous residents of the sheltered microhabitats beneath logs and human debris such as sheets of plywood or metal siding. The author has found nests of baby mice within a few feet of a coiled, quiescent copperhead whose lethargy had failed to excite the parent mouse into moving her brood.

Although normally entirely terrestrial, after floods southern copperheads have been seen on sloping boughs above high water, and in

Lee County, Texas, the author once discovered an intergrade *A. c. contortrix* coiled inside a dead stump protruding from several inches of standing water.

175 NORTHERN COPPERHEAD

Agkistrodon contortrix mokasen

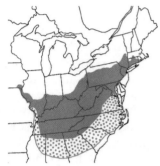

Venomous   Northern copperheads often occur in suburban neighborhoods adjacent to creeks and woodlands. Yet serious injuries from this animal are rare. Sherman Minton (1953, 1974) estimated the lethal venom dose for a healthy human adult at well over 150 mg, but since the largest copperheads can be milked of only 40 to 70 mg (and no viperid can inject more than a third of its milkable capacity in a single bite), *A. c. mokasen* is considerably less dangerous than timber or eastern diamond-backed rattlesnakes. In past years, however, when medical treatment was less effective copperhead envenomations occasionally caused the loss of a digit and a severe bite could still be fatal to a small child. See **Venom Potency Table**.

Abundance   Generally uncommon, although in wooded, hilly terrain it may often be the most abundant rodent-eating snake, especially near its wintering dens. See **Broad-banded copperhead**.

Size   Most adult *A. c. mokasen* (copperheads were once known as "highland moccasins") are between 26 and 34 inches in length and of moderately heavy girth. The record is 53 inches, while John MacGregor and Andy White measured a female northern copperhead taken in Ohio at 51 inches.

Habitat   Northern copperheads occur in varied habitats. These include rocky denning sites—vulnerable wintering spots copperheads may share with a number of other snake species. One such den in Scioto County, Ohio, held 13 *A. c. mokasen* and a single (threatened) timber rattlesnake; other copperhead dens have also harbored black racers, black rat snakes, and numerous other, smaller species. See **Timber Rattlesnake**.

After emerging from brumation in the spring, these animals descend first into talus beds on the lower slopes of their denning mountains for thermoregulatory basking, then disperse further into the surrounding deciduous and mixed woodlands as advancing seasons bring additional warmth.

In New York and northern New Jersey, *A. c. mokasen* follows a pattern much like those in Massachusetts, while in western North Carolina, at the southern edge of its range, *A. c. mokasen* is active in deciduous forest by early April, apparently already partially engaged in its springtime dispersal. During summer *A. c. mokasen* forages in open woodlands, woodland clearings, swamp edges, rocky slopes, overgrown fields, and even suburban lots filled with manmade debris. (Here, it often hides beneath discarded sheets of roofing metal and pieces of plywood.)

In natural environments this reptile's remarkable dorsolateral camouflage means that if quietly coiled in dead leaves or grass most copperheads will be completely overlooked by people—and, in areas of human activity, sometimes stepped on, causing the frightened copperhead to strike rapidly and forcefully.

Prey   The catholic feeding habits of this adaptable pitviper allow it to prey on animals that vary from cicadas and caterpillars to lizards and amphibians, smaller snakes, birds, and rodents.

Reproduction   Live-bearing. Northern copperheads produce small litters of live young. Up to 10 neonates have been borne by big North Carolina females, but most litters are closer to the 4 to 6 young reported from several Ohio parturitions by D. Craig McIntyre. Further north, Massachusetts females observed by Richard Bartlett deposited as few as 2 offspring. Such low fecundity, combined with northern pitvipers' slow maturation and the difficulty for females of gaining enough fat to give birth more often than every third or fourth year means these animals are particularly susceptible to human predation—especially attacks directed at their vulnerable den sites.

Young *A. c. mokasen* are generally between 8 and 9 inches in length at birth, which occurs in late summer or early autumn. Many neonates, which are paler than the adults and have a yellow to greenish-yellow tail tip, have also been found at denning sites only days prior to the group's entering their hibernacula for the winter.

Coloring/scale form   The northern copperhead's dorsolateral ground color is variable from tan to brownish, or even a rich russet.

It lightens at the edge of the hourglass-shaped brown crossbands, which are darkest at their edges. In this race, these crossbands are usually complete across the back, though some may be staggered or even discontinuous over the spine, where their dark junctures are at least 3 scales wide. Rounded dark spots may occur in the lighter-hued areas between these bands, and a dark lateral spot, most clearly defined among juveniles, is often present in the center of each band.

The head is distinctly broader than the neck, but only assumes the radically "triangular" shape (often erroneously thought to be diagnostic of a pitviper) when it is flattened in fear. The slightly darker coloring of the northern copperhead's unmarked crown is separated from its lighter-hued labial scales by a thin dark line that runs from its snout, through its eye to the back of its jaw. Dark ventrolateral spots are present at regular intervals along the belly line and encroach on the outer edges of the light gray ventral scutes, which are heavily smudged with dark pigment.

The 23 or 25 midbody rows of dorsal scales are weakly keeled, and the subcaudal scales are arranged either in a single row or undivided anteriorly and divided posteriorly. The anal plate is also undivided.

Similar snakes   Where their ranges abut, the northern copperhead intergrades with both the southern and Osage copperheads, and intermediate individuals can be confusingly similar. See **Southern Copperhead.**

Boldly patterned juvenile **eastern** and **western cottonmouths (179, 181)** are often mistaken for copperheads, but young cottonmouths are darker brown than grayish-tan juvenile copperheads and have a broad dark eye stripe where the northern copperhead has a pale eye stripe. The **eastern hog-nosed snake (120)** has an enlarged, pointed, upturned rostral scale.

Behavior   *Agkistrodon contortrix mokasen* is an ambush predator that may remain in exactly the same spot for days or even weeks. This spot is most often adjacent to a rodent pathway, beside an outline-masking rock or limb, and almost always on the ground for although they can climb, copperheads are basically terrestrial snakes.

For a northern pitviper, *A. c. mokasen* is also comparatively warmth-loving, and in the higher latitudes of its range is among the first snakes to return in autumn to its hibernaculum; in spring it seems to be among the last to disperse. (Rather than basking in the open like a water snake, copperheads typically thermoregulate, or draw warmth from the sun, by concealing themselves next to a heat-radiating rock or by coiling under lightly shadowed branches.) Although essentially diurnal in cool weather, during the warmest nights of summer northern copperheads engage in extensive nocturnal activity, especially just after gentle rainfall.

176   OSAGE COPPERHEAD

Agkistrodon contortrix phaeogaster

Venomous   See **Northern Copperhead.**

Abundance   Uncommon. Within a roughly circular range that encompasses northeastern Oklahoma, eastern Kansas, and almost all of Missouri the Osage copperhead can vary from rare to fairly common. Copperheads tend to occur in pockets like this because individual snakes seldom travel far, and if they find enough food to survive, young copperheads remain near the site of their birth. For example, after tracking radio-transmitter-equipped Osage copperheads in eastern Kansas, Henry S. Fitch (1971) found that some females spent their entire lives within an acre or two. Most of Fitch's population occupied home ranges of between 8 and 25 acres, however, with males maintaining the largest territories.

The Osage copperhead is found only as far north as the southeast corners of Nebraska and Iowa; in the latter state *A. c. phaeogaster* is listed as **endangered,** though it is not protected by any of the other states in which it occurs.

Size   *Agkistrodon contortrix phaeogaster* is a moderately sized race of copperhead, with any individual more than 30 inches long being a large adult; 40 in. is the record length.

Habitat   This northwesternmost copperhead subspecies is most often associated with rocky hillsides and fields, open woodlands, second-growth brush and timber, stream banks and the edges of swamps. It is often found beneath manmade debris, especially around deserted buildings that harbor rodents.

Prey   See **Southern Copperhead.**

Reproduction   Live-bearing. Three to 9 offspring, each about 8¾ inches in length, seems to be an average range in litter size for this race. See **Broad-banded Copperhead.**

Coloring/scale form Although very similar to the northern copperhead in appearance, *A. c. phaeogaster*, named for its darkly mottled belly (*phaios* and *gaster* in Greek), differs in its generally somewhat lighter ground color, its lighter-centered, narrowly white-outlined brown dorsolateral bands, and its lack of dark paravertebral spots in the light-hued ground-colored spaces between these bands. Adults are somewhat neotenic, retaining the greenish tail tip of juveniles throughout their lives. (Newborns are paler and have a yellow tail tip.) As with all copperheads, the dorsolateral scales are weakly keeled, the anterior subcaudal scales are undivided, and the anal plate is undivided.

Similar snakes Within broad stretches of the Midwest the range of *A. c. phaeogaster* overlaps that of its subspecies the northern, southern, and broad-banded copperheads. Here, intergrades are common. The pure **broad-banded copperhead (177)**, with which the Osage race interbreeds in northeastern Oklahoma, can be distinguished by its more reddish overall coloring, its more darkly mottled venter, the absence of dark borders inside thin white edging along the fringes of its russet dorsolateral bands, and the fact that these bands do not narrow significantly over its spine. To the south, in northern Arkansas and southern Missouri the Osage copperhead intergrades with the **southern copperhead (174)**. This race is paler, sometimes with a pinkish-brown hue; its prominently dark-edged, pale-centered dorsolateral bands are either joined by thin dark lines across its spine; or its left and right sides fail to line up symetrically and thus do not meet at all over the spine. In a 200-mile-long band along the Mississippi between Missouri and Illinois the Osage copperhead intergrades with its subspecies, the **northern copperhead (175)**. This race is usually a much darker coppery-red—especially on its unmarked crown—with broad, dark brown borders (and no white edging) defining its medium brown dorsolateral bands. Unlike the Osage race, a dark spot is often present in the center of each of its dorsolateral bands and dark ventrolateral spots encroach on the outer edges of its ventral scales, which are heavily smudged with dark pigment.

Behavior Unlike rattlesnakes, which are usually quickly eliminated from urbanized areas, copperheads readily adapt to the presence of man, and unless molested do well in wooded suburbs, where they prey on the resident mice. Here, *A. contortrix* is most often seen at dawn or dusk, but this small pitviper is generally so non-aggressive that unless it is stepped on, the shock of unexpectedly finding a copperhead in a woodpile or trash heap is usually the only trauma that results.

Agkistrodon contortrix laticinctus

Venomous   Although all pitvipers will bite if sufficiently provoked, copperheads of all races are singularly docile, and when found around suburban houses can be gently picked up with a stick, placed in a trash can or other large container, and easily moved to safety. See **Southern Copperhead**.

Abundance   Very common. *Agkistrodon contortrix laticinctus* is confined to the central parts of Texas and Oklahoma. Along the eastern side of its range, in a broad north-south band it intergrades with its subspecies the southern copperhead while, to the west, from Del Rio, Texas, north along the Pecos River the broad-banded copperhead intergrades with its westerly Trans-Pecos race.

Although this animal's range includes a great deal of open country, in these areas *A. c. laticintus* is mostly confined to riparian corridors, for its ideal microenvironment is mesic woodlands with plentiful ground cover. Since this description also fits many tree-shaded urban neighborhoods, throughout the eastern part of its range the broad-banded copperhead is sometimes abundant in the suburbs. Readily adapting to the presence of humans, *A. c. laticinctus* does well in creek bottoms and vacant woodlots among housing developments as long as it is not molested by humans, cats, or dogs.

Size   The record length for this race is just over 37 inches. See **Osage Copperhead**.

Habitat   Almost everywhere in its range the broad-banded copperhead occurs in either riparian or upland woods on a carpet of fallen oak leaves or pine needles—against which its russet dorsal patterning makes it almost invisible. This reptile is also locally abundant in the live oak/cedar brake bottomland of Texas' Edwards Plateau.

Prey   Primarily small rodents, nestling ground birds, spiny lizards, frogs, and large insects. Newly metamorphosed cicadas, which periodically emerge in swarms numbering thousands per acre, at times account for a large percentage of this reptile's prey, but deer and white-footed mice are the staple diet of most copperheads.

Like other copperheads, *A. c. laticinctus* is also successful in surviving within a small area—thus avoiding the exposure to predation that extensive foraging entails. This success is a result of 2 sets of extraordinary predatory adaptations. First, pitvipers have good night vision, heat-sensing facial pits, sophisticated venom, and delicately

COPPERHEADS AND COTTONMOUTHS

manipulable fangs that require only a short, rapid thrust to kill a majority of the small prey animals that come within striking range. Second, as mostly ambush hunters, they use comparatively little energy, and the slow metabolism this lifestyle permits allows copperheads to thrive on as little as 1 kill every 3 or 4 weeks.

Reproduction   Live-bearing. Courtship begins with the male advancing to touch the female with his snout and, if she does not move away, rubbing her back with his chin. If she is receptive she will remain stationary, often flattening her body, waving or vibrating her tail and, as a preliminary to mating, eliminating waste from her cloaca.

Copulation is initiated only when she opens her cloaca to receive the male's hemipenes, after which the pair can remain linked for several hours. Although prior breeding by the female tends to deter subsequent mating attempts by other males, spring copulation by a female carrying sperm from a previous autumn pairing can probably produce a litter sired by 2 males. Born during the latter part of July and all of August, broad-banded copperhead litters number 4 to 8, with most neonates—which have paler pigmentation than their parents—measuring 7½ to 10 inches in length.

Coloring/scale form   *Agkistrodon contortrix laticinctus* is defined by its light brown ground color and its 11 to 17 reddish-tan dorsolateral bands—almost equally wide at the belly line and along the spine, for which it is named *laticinctus* for "broad-banded." To accommodate this pitviper's large venom glands the rear of its skull broadens to more than 3 times the width of its narrow neck; ahead of its eyes and slightly below the level of its nostrils lie its dark, heat-sensing pits. The pale venter is mottled with reddish brown. Arranged in 23 (occasionally 25) rows at midbody, the dorsal scales are weakly keeled, and under the tail the belly plates are arranged in a single row behind the vent; the anal plate is undivided.

Similar snakes   The **southern copperhead (174)** is typically a light, sometimes almost pinkish-tan subspecies noted for its hourglass-shaped, chocolate-bordered dorsolateral bands that narrow to solid brown bars across its spine; its buff-colored venter is only laterally splotched with large brown ovals. In northern Oklahoma the **Osage copperhead (176)** is a more grayish subspecies with white-edged, brown-bordered dorsolateral bands that are also both constricted and often asymmetrically aligned along its spine. To the west, the **Trans-Pecos copperhead (178)** is distinguished by its chestnut to near-black belly, interrupted by pale lateral intrusions. Its dorsolateral crossbands often bear a pale central aura around a dark mahogany spot just above the belly line, as well as a whitish bordering wash, while the area between these bands may be almost white. On the average, there are more undertail scales (52 to 59 to the broad-banded's 40 to 54).

Seen from above, **hog nose snakes (120–124)** have a proportionately thicker neck than any pitviper, beady little eyes with round pupils, a bulbous forehead, and a markedly upturned snout; they also lack the copperhead's grayish tail tip, have a divided anal plate, and a single row of undertail scales. Newborn copperheads are distinguished from young **cottonmouths (179–181)** by the pale, rearward-facing V that marks the copperheads' cheeks; neonate cottonmouths have blackish cheeks and, unlike the copperhead, seek shelter in water.

Behavior   Copperheads and cottonmouths are the only North American members of the genus *Agkistrodon*, which apparently originated in Asia during early Miocene times, then spread to the New World over the Bering land bridge. Here, these ancestral pitvipers gradually gave rise to the more highly evolved rattlesnakes.

Like most temperate-zone reptiles, copperheads' activity patterns vary considerably throughout the year. After early spring emergence from winter denning, *A. c. laticinctus* seeks an optimal temperature of 78 to 84°F. by basking during the sunniest hours and hiding beneath woodland debris at other times. As midday temperatures climb, copperheads grow largely crepuscular, foraging mostly at dawn and at twilight except on overcast days or when soil and vegetation are damp; in the hottest weather of mid-summer they are abroad mainly at night.

Among the least agile of snakes—its only capacity for rapid motion is in the darting jab of its strike—the copperhead's predatory forays characteristically involve little more than deliberate travel from one ambush site to another, although sedentary prey such as nestling birds and rodents are sought by scent. If threatened, *Agkistrodon contortrix* may both emit musk from a pair of anal glands flanking its vent and vibrate its tail in agitation.

178   TRANS-PECOS COPPERHEAD

Agkistrodon contortrix pictigaster

Venomous   See **Southern Copperhead.**

Abundance   Uncommon. Confined, in the United States, to Trans-Pecos Texas, *A. c. pictigaster* also inhabits wooded montane parts of northern Chihuahua, Mexico. In both regions, however, the Trans-Pecos copperhead is essentially a

xeric-adapted race of an eastern woodland serpent, living here at the limit of its biological capacity.

How this came to be is illustrative of the slow but unending changes that occur to all habitats, and of the struggle their plants and animals continually face in trying to continue living there. For example, because the northern Chihuahuan Desert is of more recent origin than much of its resident wildlife, a number of species—including *A. c. pictigaster*—persist in relict populations confined to the vicinity of the scattered permanent springs and streams remaining from the wetter climate of the late Pleistocene.

Yet, even in these areas of presumably prime habitat Trans-Pecos copperheads are hard to find and—perhaps because these routes are driven so frequently by gray-banded kingsnake hunters—most *A. c. pictigaster* sightings occur not around desert springs but in the dry, canyon-laced country north of Langtry in Val Verde and Crockett counties, Texas.

Size   Most adults are 18 to 26 inches in length; the record is 32⅞ in.

Habitat   Although most of the U.S. copperheads are associated with moist bottomland, this species' westernmost race is found throughout Trans-Pecos Texas—where springs and seasonally moist canyons are thought to be its favored habitat. Yet *A. c. pictigaster* has also been found on the xeric, creosote-shrub plains of Terrell County, while biologist Kelly Bryant reports frequently seeing this race in the very arid terrain of Big Bend Ranch State Park but has yet to see a single Trans-Pecos copperhead in several years' field work in the far more mesic Davis Mountains uplands—though records exist of this subspecies' presence there at over 6,000-ft. elevations.

Prey   Both West Texas' canyonlands and shrub desert are heavily populated with the small rodent species that copperheads feed on everywhere in their range—as well as a host of abundant, and possibly-preyed-upon lizard species. See **Broad-banded Copperhead**.

Reproduction   Live-bearing. See **Broad-banded Copperhead**.

Coloring/scale form   Some individuals of this strikingly colored subspecies are distinguished by an off-white or even silvery ground color unlike that of any other copperhead. The back and sides of all *A. c. pictigaster* are patterned with 13 to 19 broad, cinnamon-bay to seal brown dorsolateral bands, however, each of which usually bears a pale aura just above the belly line, centered with a mahogany spot. (Juveniles tend to be somewhat lighter-hued, with more contrasting colors, while large adults have usually darkened into a medium brown ground color.)

The heavily mottled belly, typically mahogany to black, but interrupted with pale lateral intrusions, is unique to this subspecies and is the source of the Trans-Pecos copperhead's scientific name: *picti* means "painted" and *gaster* is "stomach." The tail is gray-brown above, with thin, grayish or greenish crossbands, while a single row of subcaudal plates lines its posterior tip. The 21 to 25 midbody rows of dorsal scales are weakly keeled and the anal plate is undivided.

Similar snakes The **broad-banded copperhead (177)** is less reddish above, generally has more uniformly colored, lighter brown body bands, a much less heavily mottled belly, and a lower average number of subcaudal scales (37 to 54 vs. 52 to 59 among *A. c. pictigaster*). In the field such distinctions are largely meaningless, however, because southern, broad-banded, and Trans-Pecos copperhead subspecies only gradually diverge into their pure forms across an east-west sequence of gradual clinal variation.

Behavior As part of a basically mesic-adapted species, this race of copperhead's ability to thrive in a region now much drier than at any time in recent history is due partly to its general ophidian capacity for enduring long periods of hostile conditions—heat, drought, or cold—as long as some portion of the year allows active foraging.

Yet few other moist-climate snakes are found in the harsh Chihuahuan biome. Energy conservation is this species' edge. The minimal caloric expenditure which lets ambush-hunting pitvipers like *A. c. pictigaster* thrive on a single kill per month even during its primary activity period in the Trans-Pecos' brief, late-summer rainy season is a major factor in its survival.

179 EASTERN COTTONMOUTH

Agkistrodon piscivorus piscivorus

Venomous The eastern cottonmouth is similar in both defensive behavior and venom toxicity to its subspecies the Florida cottonmouth.

Abundance Common. Along the Atlantic coastal plain from southern Virginia to central Georgia (where it begins to intergrade with its Florida subspecies) *A. p. piscivorus* is abundant

in marshes, riparian corridors of all sorts and sizes, wooded bottomland, and even the saline marine verges of offshore barrier islands.

Size   Similar in size to the Florida cottonmouth.

Habitat   Almost any heavily vegetated, aquatic or brackish still-water environment unoccupied by humans can serve as habitat for *A. p. piscivorus*.

Prey   Like both its southern and western subspecies, the eastern cottonmouth will feed on any vertebrate small enough to swallow; for large individuals this means prey up to the size of adult swamp rabbits.

Reproduction   Live-bearing. Reproduction follows the typical pitviper pattern of slow growth, delayed maturation, and low reproductive frequency. This is true to a slightly lesser extent than with many terrestrial *Crotalinae*, however, because the more favorable foraging opportunities of their aquatic milieu afford female cottonmouths better odds of acquiring the body fat needed for pregnancy, and a number of female *A. p. piscivorus* are able to breed annually.

Coloring/scale form   The white interior mouth is the source of the cottonmouth's common name, while *Agkistro* is either a mistranslation of *ancil* meaning "forward," or of *ankistro* for "fishing hook." *Odon*, "tooth," refers to the cottonmouth's fangs; and *piscivorus* means "fish-eating." (In this aquatic pitviper's scientific designation, therefore, *Agkistrodon piscivorus* is a forward-fanged fish eater.) The adult eastern cottonmouth has a more yellowish ground color than its Florida subspecies, with narrower dark dorsolateral bands and less distinct whitish facial markings. From southeastern Georgia to southern Alabama, eastern and Florida cottonmouths occur only as intergrades, and individuals morphologically typical of either race are sympatric with specimens showing intermediate characteristics of both subspecies. Very old animals of both races may be entirely black or dark gray.

There are 25 rows of keeled dorsal scales at midbody, the majority of the subcaudal scales occur in a single row, and the anal plate is undivided.

Similar snakes   For similarities with water snakes, see **Florida cottonmouth (180)**. The juvenile **southern copperhead (174)** is lighter brown and has dark-edged beige cheeks unlike the cottonmouth's dark labial scales.

Behavior   See **Florida Cottonmouth**.

Agkistrodon piscivorus conanti

Venomous   Despite the cottonmouth's formidable reputation, very few people are bitten by them: the mortality rate for the entire United States is less than 1 person per year. Envenomation by *Agkistrodon piscivorus* can be serious in terms of tissue death, however, for while its toxins are less lethal than those of most rattlesnakes—Sherman Minton estimates the lethal dose of cottonmouth venom for a healthy human adult as about 150 mg—their hemorrhagic effects are pronounced.

Cottonmouths can also be huge snakes, with proportionately wide jaws, up to ¾-inch-long fangs, and venom-storage lumens which have yielded, from the largest individuals, over 1000 mg of venom. See **Venom Potency Table.**

Abundance   Confined, as a pure race, to the state of Florida, until recently *A. p. conanti* was extremely abundant: old-time hide hunters sometimes took over 300 in a single night's collecting in the Everglades or west of Lake Okeechobee. Although its numbers have been drastically reduced by this state's exploding human population, the Florida cottonmouth is still common in undeveloped areas, and where thick vegetation stifles the humid air above small, leutic bodies of water its unique musky scent is sometimes noticeable.

Size   The record Florida cottonmouth measured 74½ inches in length. The proportionately massive trunk of large cottonmouths would have made that animal enormous, but most *A. p. conanti* are much smaller; the majority of adults attain no more than 38 inches in length.

Habitat   *Agkistrodon piscivorus conanti* may be found almost anywhere in Florida except inside large towns and cities. Although cottonmouths generally remain within ½ mile of permanent fresh, brackish, or saltwater, they are sometimes also found in dry forest and grassland, while in springtime, flooded prairies are a prime foraging site.

Salt marshes and the low-lying salt marsh islands bordering peninsular Florida are also good cottonmouth habitat, and *A. p. conanti* occurs there in very high densities. Yet cottonmouths are absent from the lower Keys south of Grassy Key, and even on the mainland their populations tend to vary, with large areas of apparently prime habitat being entirely devoid of these reptiles.

COPPERHEADS AND COTTONMOUTHS

Prey Frogs are probably the Florida cottonmouth's most frequent prey, but *A. piscivorous* is an indiscriminate feeder whose diet alters with the availability of different food animals. At times these include fish, hatchling alligators, cottontail and swamp rabbits, water birds, and sizable water snakes—as well as smaller cottonmouths.

Game fish such as largemouth bass and bluegills are generally too fast for the cottonmouth to capture, and only sick or dead specimens are taken (like other aquatic serpents, *A. piscivorous* feeds readily on carrion and is consequently drawn to injured or dead fish dangling from fishermen's stringers).

Reproduction Live-bearing. Courtship follows the pattern of most *Crotalinae* as the adult male initiates contact by following a female's pheromone scent trail. If he encounters another male engaged in the same pursuit, dominance competition—in the form of both animals rearing their forebodies in an attempt to force their opponent to the ground—is likely. Injury-producing agonistic behavior almost never occurs among rival snakes, however. Courtship involves dorsal tongue-flicking by the male, as well as rubbing his chin on the female's back before attempting copulation. The 3 to 12 young are born during August and September, with neonates being so stoutly proportioned that gravid females average only 5 to 6 offspring per litter; similarly sized water snakes, in comparison, deposit dozens of much more slender young.

Juvenile cottonmouths are more brownish in ground color than adults, and are clearly patterned with distinct dark dorsolateral bars and lateral blotches. Their tails have grayish-green tips which, in a predatory technique shared with their relatives the copperheads, are used (probably unconsciously) as wriggling, worm- or caterpillar-like decoys to attract frogs and lizards.

Coloring/scale form Sometimes displayed in open-jawed threat, the white interior mouth is the source of the cottonmouth's common name. *Agkistro* is probably a mistranslation of *ancil* meaning "forward"; *odon* refers to the cottonmouth's front teeth, or fangs; and *piscivorus* means fish-eating. In this aquatic pitviper's scientific designation, therefore, *Agkistrodon piscivorus conanti* is a forward-fanged fish eater, whose Florida race is also named *conanti* in honor of eminent herpetologist Roger Conant.

Adult Florida cottonmouths are dark gray-brown, with broad, usually dimly defined paler lateral bands. These animals' apparently dull dorsal coloring sometimes results from a film of water-deposited sediment and algae, however: clean-water-living cottonmouths have more distinct dorsolateral patterning and lighter brown lower sides.

Very old individuals are almost entirely dark gray or black, yet even among obscurely patterned specimens the Florida cottonmouth's slightly paler upper labial scales and the light longitudinal line between its crown and the sides of its head are noticeable.

There are 25 rows of keeled dorsal scales at midbody, and the scales beneath its tail occur in a pattern by which *Agkistrodon* can be identified even from their shed skins: for ⅔ of the tail's length the subcaudal scales occur in a single row. (The remaining ⅓ of the undertail has a double row of scales like that of nonvenomous snakes.) The anal plate is undivided.

Similar snakes   The dark, heavy bodies and aquatic habitat of **large water snakes (66, 68, 70–73, 75–78, 91–93)** often cause them to be mistaken for cottonmouths, but water snakes lack the cottonmouth's darkly sunken, heat-sensing facial pit between eye and nostril and have clearly visible round pupils. *Agkistrodon piscivorus* also behaves differently from water snakes. Most individuals flee when approached, although on land some hold their ground and gape open-mouthed, twitching their tail tips; threatened water snakes neither gape nor nervously twitch their tails. Also unlike water snakes, the cottonmouth swims in a leisurely way, its whole body floating buoyantly with its head held high, although it dives quickly when threatened. In contrast, water snakes squirm along comparatively rapidly, with their posterior bodies drooping below the surface, especially when they stop.

Behavior   Although big cottonmouths can be pugnacious when annoyed, *A. piscivorus* is not nearly as ferocious as it is popularly envisioned. Can a cottonmouth bite underwater? Of course, that's how they catch fish. Apparently its only fish, though, mostly captured in the shallows. In deep water, cottonmouths swim away if annoyed; they do not remain in place, as they often do on land, to gape in threat. (Generated by the force of its own strike, water resistance against a swimming cottonmouth's wide-spread mouth would press it backward, making a long, aggressive underwater strike impossible.)

This is all more or less hypothetical, though, because unlike water snakes *A. piscivorus* is not a true aquatic animal and seldom forages underwater: in observation tanks cottonmouths take fish by cornering them in shallow water or (rarely) by seizing them with a short lateral grab as the trapped fish accidentally brush against the cottonmouth's sides. But *A. piscivorus* spends very little time submerged; mostly it forages along banks and shorelines, basks on floating vegetation, and swims slowly across the surface—diving, briefly, only if it is attacked.

Agkistrodon piscivorus leucostoma

Venomous   Despite the cottonmouth's formidable reputation, very few people are bitten by this reptile, and even fewer are seriously injured: only about 7 percent of Texas' snakebites involve cottonmouths, and throughout the United States the mortality rate is less than 1 person per year. Envenomation by *Agkistrodon piscivorus* may result in substantial tissue death, however, because these big aquatic vipers have up to ⅜-inch-long fangs and venom-storage lumens which, from the largest individuals, can yield hundreds of mg., dry weight, of venom. While its toxins are less potent than those of most large *Crotalus*-genus rattlesnakes—Sherman Minton estimates the lethal dose for a healthy human adult as about 150 mg—the hemorrhagic effects of cottonmouth venom are pronounced. See **Venom Potency Table**.

Abundance   Locally very common. Although the majority of presumed "cottonmouth" sightings are actually of *natricine* water snakes, western cottonmouths are extremely numerous in some places, especially on the Gulf coastal plain. Near Sinton, Texas, as well as 100 miles to the north, as on ricefield levees around Egypt, the author has seen a basking cottonmouth every few hundred yards. Dense populations of this big pitviper can even make themselves known by scent: in the still air of forest-enclosed woodland ponds in East Texas the musky smell of *Agkistrodon piscivorus* can sometimes be detected.

Size   The record *A. p. leucostoma*, taken on East Texas' Neches River by George O. Miller, was a fraction of an inch over 5 feet in length. Most western cottonmouths are much smaller, however: of 306 recorded individuals, only a few males—which grow larger than females—were longer than 3 feet, and the great majority measured between 20 and 30 inches.

Habitat   Although western cottonmouths are generally found within ½ mile of permanent water, they are not limited to aquatic environments (all cottonmouth races favor leutic microhabitats primarily because of the more plentiful prey and better cover available there, but they do quite well in entirely dry milieus). Dry forest, grassland, and even cornfields are also occupied; in spring, a flooded prairie is a prime foraging site. Salt marshes and the low-lying saline barrier islands bordering the Gulf coast also constitute good territory for western cottonmouths, yet the density of *A. p. leucostoma* populations tends to vary widely, with large areas of apparently perfect wetland habitat being almost entirely devoid of these reptiles.

Prey The western cottonmouth may feed on any vertebrate small enough to swallow. Frogs are probably this pitviper's most frequent prey, but *A. p. leucostoma* (its Greek-derived subspecies name means "white-mouthed") is an indiscriminate feeder whose diet alters with the availability of different food species. Water birds, smaller snakes—including copperheads and even other cottonmouths—are also reported, as are a variety of fish species, although game fish are generally too fast for cottonmouths to capture. Like other aquatic serpents, *A. piscivorus* also feeds on carrion and is consequently drawn to wounded and dying fish dangling from fishermen's stringers.

Reproduction Live-bearing. Reproduction follows the usual viperid pattern of slow growth, delayed maturation, and low reproductive frequency. But the enhanced foraging opportunities afforded by their rich aquatic habitat give female cottonmouths a better chance than terrestrial vipers of acquiring the increased body fat necessary for successful pregnancy. (Unlike terrestrial viperids, many of which require two years' hunting to acquire enough fatty tissue to nourish their large, well-developed young, female *A. piscivorus* may breed every year.)

During early spring courtship adult male cottonmouths typically follow a female's pheromone scent trail, sometimes even across lily pads. If they encounter another male engaged in the same pursuit, dominance behavior is likely to ensue, with each combatant attempting to force down the other's foreparts. Pairing initially involves tongue-flicking of the female's back by the male, followed by rubbing his chin along her spine, after which copulation may last several hours.

Because gestation among snakes is not as uniformly timed as among birds and mammals, fertilization may be delayed for weeks while sperm remain viable in the cloaca. Up to several months after copulation, the 8- to 11-inch-long young are born during August, September, and early October. They are so stoutly proportioned that gravid females bear only 3 to 12 offspring per litter (while similarly sized water snakes typically deposit dozens of much more slender young).

Newborn western cottonmouths are both more brownish and more clearly patterned than adults, with dark dorsal bars and lateral blotches. Their tails have gray-green tips which, in a predatory technique shared with their relatives the copperheads, are instinctively flicked back and forth in the excitement of seeing prey, thus unconsciously imitating the movements of a worm or caterpillar and reportedly sometimes luring small frogs and toads within striking range.

Coloring/scale form   See **Florida Cottonmouth**. Adult western cottonmouths are dark gray-brown, with broad, dimly defined lateral banding. (Some individuals' dull dorsal coloring results from a film of water-deposited sediment and algae: clean-water-living cottonmouths show more distinct patterning.) Very old cottonmouths, however, may be entirely dark gray or black.

In daylight, the pupils of the large, grayish eyes are vertical black slits easily discernible from a safe distance; at night in the beam of a flashlight they are oval or rounded for the few moments it takes them to close against the glare. Definitive but less evident is the dark orifice of the heat-sensing pit located between the eye and nostril and the pronounced taper from the thick posterior trunk to the cottonmouth's attenuated little tail; especially among females the tail seems out of proportion to the thickset trunk. The male's tail contains its hemipene and is somewhat larger.

The keeled dorsal scales occur in 25 rows at midbody, while the subcaudal scutes display a unique pattern by which even from their shed skins *Agkistrodon* can be identified: behind the undivided anal plate a single row of belly-wide scale plates occupies the under-tail tip.

Similar snakes   The dark, heavy bodies and aquatic habitat of **large water snakes (64, 68–71, 74–76, 79–81, 90, 92)** often cause them to be mistaken for the western cottonmouth. All water snakes lack the cottonmouth's heat-sensing pit between eye and nostril, however, and have clearly visible round pupils.

Agkistrodon piscivorus also behaves differently from water snakes, which neither gape in threat nor vibrate their tails in agitation. Also unlike water snakes, the cottonmouth swims in a leisurely way, its whole body floating buoyantly, with the head held high. Water snakes swim by squirming rapidly along, their bodies drooping below the surface when they stop. Juvenile **copperheads (174, 176, 177)** are lighter brown and have dark-edged beige cheeks unlike the cottonmouth's dark labial scales.

Behavior   The most widespread story about the cottonmouth concerns the water-skier purportedly killed by a flurry of bites after tumbling into a "nest" of these reptiles. For years various re-tellings of this fictitious event have circulated in boating circles, and an even more absurd fantasy about a cowboy killed by western cottonmouths while crossing a river on horseback appeared in the television special *Lonesome Dove*.

All such episodes are untrue: no water-skier or river-fording horseman has ever suffered multiple *A. piscivorus* envenomation. These scary myths originate in people's observations of the large number of harmless water snakes that, during late summer, become concentrated in drying creeks and stock tanks, where they are mistaken for nests of cottonmouths.

Cottonmouths do not "nest," however, and packed groups would last no longer than it took the larger *A. piscivorus* to swallow their smaller relatives. Further, in the water cottonmouths quickly dive and flee even when approached stealthily—much less when confronted with the churning bow wave of a 1,000-pound mustang. On land, an occasional western cottonmouth will hold its ground and gape open-mouthed, but none attack en masse. (In fact, the cottonmouth's notorious gape is actually a comparatively passive defense gesture, for such wide-jawed *A. piscivorus* often fail to strike even when prodded with a boot.)

RATTLESNAKES
Genera *Sistrurus* and *Crotalus*

Carolina Pigmy Rattlesnake, *Sistrurus miliarius miliarius*
Dusky Pigmy Rattlesnake, *Sistrurus miliarius barbouri*
Western Pigmy Rattlesnake, *Sistrurus miliarius streckeri*
Eastern Massasauga, *Sistrurus catenatus catenatus*
Western Massasauga, *Sistrurus catenatus tergeminus*
Desert Massasauga, *Sistrurus catenatus edwardsi*
Timber Rattlesnake, *Crotalus horridus horridus*
Canebrake Rattlesnake, *Crotalus horridus atricaudatus*
Eastern Diamond-backed Rattlesnake, *Crotalus adamanteus*
Western Diamond-backed Rattlesnake, *Crotalus atrox*
Northern Black-tailed Rattlesnake, *Crotalus molossus molossus*
Prairie Rattlesnake, *Crotalus viridis viridis*
Mojave Rattlesnake, *Crotalus scutulatus scutulatus*
Mottled Rock Rattlesnake, *Crotalus lepidus lepidus*
Banded Rock Rattlesnake, *Crotalus lepidus klauberi*

All rattlesnakes (as well as copperheads and cottonmouths) are contained in the viperine subfamily *Crotalinae*, which includes both the pigmy and massasauga rattlesnake genus *Sistrurus* and the generally larger and more widespread genus *Crotalus*.

PIGMY RATTLESNAKES AND MASSASAUGAS
Genus Sistrurus

Carolina Pigmy Rattlesnake, *Sistrurus miliarius miliarius*
Dusky Pigmy Rattlesnake, *Sistrurus miliarius barbouri*
Western Pigmy Rattlesnake, *Sistrurus streckeri*
Eastern Massasauga, *Sistrurus catenatus catenatus*
Western Massasauga, *Sistrurus catenatus tergeminus*
Desert Massasauga, *Sistrurus catenatus edwardsii*

Two of the three species of *Sistrurus* (a name drawn from the Latin *sistrum* for "rattle" and the Greek *oura* for "tail") occur in the United States, where both *S. miliarius* and *S. catenatus* are divided into three subspecies. These are generally small, excitable rattlesnakes with slender tails and rattles so attenuated that their whirring warning can be difficult for a human to hear. Although in Florida the dusky pigmy rattlesnake can at times be present in immense numbers, the other two races of pigmy rattlesnake, and all three races of massasauga, are uncommon even in suitable habitat.

Sistrurus are quite different from members of the genus *Crotalus*. The latter have much smaller crown scales, while *Sistrurus* are characterized by a set of 9 large, unbroken cephalic scale plates that resemble those of both nonvenomous snakes and the copperheads and cottonmouths from which rattlesnakes are thought to be descended. (Both pigmy and massasauga *Sistrurus*-genus rattlesnakes are believed to belong to an ancient group of pitvipers similar to those from which the more highly developed *Crotalus* evolved.) Although venom potency among *Sistrurus* is quite high, as small pitvipers their venom gland capacity is not large and their fangs are relatively short.

The dorsolateral scales of pigmy and massasauga rattlesnakes are keeled, both the anal plate and subcaudal scales are undivided and, like all pitvipers, the pupil is vertically elliptical. The head is distinctly wider than the neck, but not nearly as broad, proportionately, as that of rattlesnakes belonging to the genus *Crotalus*.

Sistrurus miliarius miliarius

Venomous   Although its venom is quite toxic, the small size of this rattlesnake and the correspondingly low yield of its venom storage lumens means that most bites sustained by a healthy adult are not life-threatening.

Abundance   *Sistrurus miliarius miliarius* is uncommon in much of its range which, east of the Appalachians, extends from central North Carolina to northeastern Georgia (where the Carolina pigmy rattlesnake intergrades with both its southern race, the dusky pigmy, and its western pigmy subspecies). Rare in places, *S. m. miliarius* is protected in North Carolina, but not in any of the other states in which it occurs.

Size   *Sistrurus miliarius miliarius* is adult at from 14 to 20 inches long, yet has a record length of only 25 inches.

Habitat   The Carolina pigmy rattlesnake occurs well beyond the confines of the Carolinas, ranging from coastal central North Carolina, across almost all of South Carolina, then westward through central Georgia to northwestern Alabama. Intergrades with the dusky pigmy rattlesnake occur along the southern boundary of this territory and with the western pigmy rattlesnake along the western edge of the range.

On the Atlantic coastal plain this race is a pinewoods/scrub oak inhabitant of sandy substrates. In the Piedmont and elsewhere, it inhabits both pine and open, mixed woodlands, occurring both near watersources and in dryer areas.

In bygone years Richard D. Bartlett found this snake near transient sawmills, where it was formerly numerous among and within sawdust piles and mounds of bark slabs. It also occurs in suburban and rural areas, especially where litter offers cover, and along the edges of dumps. Sometimes, *S. m. miliarius* may be seen crossing country roadways on warm evenings.

Prey   The small adult size of the Carolina pigmy rattlesnake restricts its prey to correspondingly diminutive species. This includes primarily frogs, lizards, and mice, while the nestlings of ground-nesting bird species are occasionally taken. Young pigmy rattlesnakes of all races have yellowish tail tips which are used in the caudal luring of prey. See **Western Pigmy Rattlesnake.**

RATTLESNAKES

Reproduction   Although litters of the more southerly ranging dusky pigmy rattlesnake can number up to two dozen, those of the Carolina pigmy rattler are considerably smaller, with 11 being the largest litter recorded. Most broods number between 2 and 8, however, with the neonates—born from mid- to late-summer—measuring about 6¼ inches in length. These juveniles are usually more intensely colored and boldly patterned than the adults and have a yellowish-green tailtip.

Coloring/scale form   *Sistrurus miliarius miliarius* is the most variably colored of the United States' three pigmy rattlesnake subspecies. In the mixed woodlands of east-central and coastal North Carolina the ground color of most individuals is pinkish, light reddish-brown, or russet. Against this base color, well-defined dark brown to dark reddish-brown dorsal blotches are well separated from a row of lateral blotches usually narrowly—sometimes very narrowly—bordered with light pigment.

In more southerly parts of the range the ground color is a distinctive grayish-lavender (sometimes very light gray) and the sharply contrasting dorsal and lateral blotches are dark brown to black. In other places intermediately marked and colored individuals occur.

A several-scale-wide orange vertebral stripe, most intensely pigmented anteriorly, is usually visible between the dark blotches of all three color phases. An elongate pair of dark blotches runs from the supraocular scales to the nape, while a dark blotch extends from each eye to the rear of the head. The venter is paler than the dorsum and bears paired, variably shaped dark blotches.

Similar snakes   In central Georgia and Alabama the Carolina pigmy intergrades with its southern subspecies, the **Dusky pigmy rattlesnake (183)**, which is distinguished by its thoroughly stippled back and sides, often ill-defined posterior dorsal and lateral blotches, its three rows of dark lateral spots, and its dark-blotched venter. Otherwise, throughout its range the Carolina pigmy rattlesnake is the only small rattler (water snakes and copperheads lack a rattle) with 9 large crown scales.

Behavior   In temperament, *S. m. miliarius* varies as much as it does in color. Some individuals are quiet, others are nervous and irritable and when alerted, will often coil loosely, facing their adversary, and twitch their heads nervously. A few pigmy rattlers even begin striking—presumably as an advance warning or threat—while their perceived offender is still far beyond range.

Sistrurus miliarius barbouri

Venomous   Despite the fact that many pigmy rattlesnakes are pugnacious, quick-to-strike little serpents with fairly potent venom, *S. miliarius* is far less dangerous to humans than larger rattlesnake species. (Because *S. miliarius* has such a miniscule rattle—no longer than the width of its head—a myth has arisen of the rattle-less ground rattlesnake.)

Its diminutive fangs—no more than 5⁄32 inch across the curve—limit *S. miliarius* to superficial penetration of the human body, and even when its venom glands are artificially milked to depletion, a large pigmy rattler yields no more than 35 milligrams (dry weight) of venom. (This is why envenomation by a pigmy rattler seldom causes the extensive tissue necrosis characteristic of envenomation by *Crotalus*-genus rattlesnakes.)

This is also why it has long been thought that envenomation by *S. miliarius* could be fatal only to a small child. Yet Florida herpetologist Craig Trumbower recently found himself hospitalized in intensive care from what he initially judged to be an insignificant dusky pigmy rattlesnake bite, but which almost immediately produced severe systemic shock. See **Venom Potency Table**.

Abundance   *Sistrurus miliarius barbouri* is named for Harvard Comparative Anatomy Museum curator Thomas Barbour, author of *Zoogeography of the West Indies*, who collected the type specimen near Miami. This small rattlesnake is common throughout Florida and southern Georgia and Alabama. In biologically generous marsh/palmetto grassland environments—in particular, the Everglades—it can be one of the most numerous serpents. Yet *S. m. barbouri* is less often encountered than its numbers would suggest, since these small pitvipers generally remain well hidden beneath ground cover.

Size   Adult dusky pigmy rattlesnakes are short, plump, and seldom more than 20 inches long. The record is 31 inches.

Habitat   Primary habitat includes both wet and dry areas. Mesic pine flatwoods, bottomland hardwood forest, wet saw-grass and marl prairies are occupied along with drier, elevated hardwood hammocks, xeric sandhills and upland scrub brush environments.

Prey   Like other viperids, rattlesnakes typically employ a sit-and-wait, ambush-predation strategy, and *S. m. barbouri* is no exception. Yet much of the warm-blooded prey taken by larger vipers is

RATTLESNAKES

too big for pigmy rattlers. Therefore, the typical food of most juvenile crotalids—amphibians, lizards, small snakes, and even insects—constitutes much of the diet of adult *S. miliarius*. For example, 13 dusky pigmy rattlesnakes from southern Georgia contained 4 large centipedes, 3 ground skinks, 1 six-lined racerunner, 1 ringneck snake, and 2 deer mice.

Reproduction   Live-bearing. Pitvipers tend to have slow rates of growth and maturation, as well as low overall levels of reproduction. This means that female rattlesnakes living in cooler climates with short seasonal activity periods are seldom able to marshal sufficient resources to give birth every year, but even pigmy rattlers active year-round in subtropical southern Florida follow this alternate-year reproductive cycle. (As Terrence Farrell and Melissa Pilgrim report, only about half of adult Florida females become gravid every summer.)

Primarily autumn breeders, after winter-long sperm storage by the female, over 90% of *S. m. barbouri* births in the southern part of the range take place during August. A few weeks prior to parturition, females stop feeding and move to the sunniest parts of their territories to bask, thereby elevating their body temperature and accelerating development of their young. (Like other pitvipers, pigmy rattlesnakes have proportionately large neonates: 26 litters of *S. m. barbouri* ranged from 2 to 11.)

Coloring/scale form   The brisk movement of the dusky pigmy rattler does not suggest a conventional, heavy-bodied rattlesnake, nor does its black-spotted gray dorsum lined with a russet vertebral stripe. Most often its back and sides are so heavily stippled with pigment—giving this race its name "dusty"—that its posterior vertebral and lateral blotches are largely obscured.

The dusky pigmy rattlesnake's sides are spotted with three rows of small dark blotches above its stippled or dark-blotched venter, more whitish anteriorly, but sometimes solid dark gray-brown toward its tail. Its strongly keeled dorsal scales are arranged in 23 to 25 rows at midbody, its crown is covered with 9 large scale plates, and its anal plate is undivided.

Similar snakes   In central Georgia and Alabama the dusky pigmy intergrades with its northern subspecies, the **Carolina pigmy rattlesnake (182)**, which is distinguished by its more cleanly defined dorsal and lateral blotches, its two rows of dark lateral spots, and its less heavily pigmented belly. In western Alabama and southern Mississippi this race also interbreeds with the **western pigmy rattlesnake (184)**, a grayish race with short, dark dorsal crossbars, rather than blotches, and a more reddish vertebral stripe. Except as newborns, both **timber (188)** and **eastern diamond-backed rattlesnakes (190)** are much larger. Small scales cover the center of their broad crowns, while the timber has a black tail and jagged, dark brown dorsal chevrons; the diamondback's dorsum is marked with white-edged diamonds. The **southern hog-nosed snake (121)** is sometimes mistaken for the pigmy rattler, but it lacks a rattle and has both a sharply upturned snout and small, dark eyes with round pupils.

Behavior   Entirely terrestrial and seldom seen in the open, dusky pigmy rattlesnakes frequently rattle their tails from beneath ground cover or fallen palmetto fronds. If exposed, they may flatten their bodies and if touched, snap sharply sideways without coiling. The strike never spans more than a few inches, though, since *S. miliarius* does not raise its forebody into the elevated defensive posture that lets larger rattlesnakes strike up to half their body length.

184   WESTERN PIGMY RATTLESNAKE
Sistrurus miliarius streckeri

Venomous   See **Dusky Pigmy Rattlesnake.**

Abundance   Uncommon. The western pigmy rattlesnake is widely dispersed throughout its broad eastern Texas and Oklahoma to southern Missouri, Tennessee to the Louisiana Delta range (most of the lower Mississippi River flood plain is not inhabited). Yet, *S. m. streckeri* is seldom encountered even by those working in the heart of its range since it is an extremely cryptic animal which spends the day hidden beneath ground cover.

Size   Adults usually measure 14 to 20 inches in length; the record is 25⅛ inches.

Habitat   Favored habitat includes loblolly/longleaf pine forest, riverbottom hardwoods, wet saw-grass prairie, and palmetto lowlands. (*Sistrurus miliarius streckeri* also occurs in the riparian corridor of sycamore, pecan, black willow, and mustang grape that traces the Trinity and Red River systems northwestward, allowing this fundamentally eastern-forest animal to penetrate an extensive dry, upland area.)

Along the upper Gulf Coast, *S. m. streckeri* was formerly found in most places where there was both heavy vegetation and abundant surface water. Such sites recently included low-lying woodland in the Alvin/Liverpool/Angleton section of Texas' Brazoria County, the swampy portion of Matagorda County between Cedar Lane and the coast, and the seaward verges of the entire Mississippi Delta. Extensive urbanization and agricultural development have eliminated a majority of this animal's Texas habitat, however, and only the latter area retains enough natural cover to support a substantial population of pigmy rattlesnakes.

Prey   Small reptiles, amphibians, and insects constitute most of the diet of adult *S. miliarius*. For the first several months of their lives the young have yellowish tail tips (just anterior to their rattles) that involuntarily twitch with excitement when prey is nearby, therefore functioning as wriggling, worm- or caterpillar-like decoys to attract frogs, lizards, or other small animals. See **Dusky Pigmy Rattlesnake.**

Reproduction   Live-bearing. Primarily autumn breeders—males have been observed in combat at this season—*S. miliarius* typically gives birth in early summer after winter-long sperm storage by the female. A captive pair maintained at the Fort Worth Zoo bred repeatedly throughout September, with the female giving birth some 8½ months later to 3, ⅒-ounce, 5⅓-inch-long young with pale yellow tail tips. See **Dusky Pigmy Rattlesnake.**

Coloring/scale form   *Sistrurus miliarius streckeri*—*Sistrurus* was coined in 1883 by S. Garman from the Greek for "rattle" and "tail," while the subspecies name honors herpetologist John K. Strecker, for whom the Mexican hooknose snake, a chorus frog, and Baylor University's Strecker Museum are also named—also has unusual coloring for a rattlesnake. Its gray dorsum is widely spotted with black and marked with a russet-tan vertebral stripe, while its lower sides bear a double row of dark spots that may overlap onto the whitish, faintly stippled venter.

This little rattlesnake's head is proportionately narrower than that of larger rattlers, and boldly black-striped on both its crown and cheeks, where its large, slit-pupiled eyes are obscured by a dark mask. The strongly keeled dorsal scales are arranged in 23 to 25 rows at midbody, the crown is capped with 9 large scale plates, and the anal plate is undivided.

Similar snakes   In southern Mississippi and western Alabama *S. m. streckeri* intergrades with its eastern subspecies, **the dusky pigmy rattlesanke (183)**, a darker, more heavily mottled and pigmented (both dorsally and ventrally) race with 3 rows of dark lateral spots. The **western massasauga (186)** has larger, more closely spaced brown dorsolateral blotches; it lacks a distinct vertebral stripe and has 25 rows of dorsal scales at midbody. It is rarely found in the pigmy rattlesnake's woodland/wetland habitat.

Behavior   Entirely terrestrial, *S. m. streckeri* may rattle its tail from beneath ground cover, although its rattle is so minuscule that the sound is difficult to hear. (No longer than the width of its head, the western pigmy's inconspicuous little rattle has given rise to the myth of the rattle-less ground rattler.)

If exposed in its hiding place, this little pitviper does not raise its forebody into the defensive posture that enables *Crotalus*-genus rattlesnakes to strike up to half their body length. Instead, threatened *S. m. streckeri* may flatten its trunk and if touched, snap without coiling—though its strike never extends more than a few inches.

185   EASTERN MASSASAUGA

Sistrurus catenatus catenatus

Venomous   Although bites from this medium-sized pitviper are rare, its venom is apparently quite potent, particularly in regard to its anticoagulatory hematoxicity. During the summer of 2002, a 13-year-old girl, bitten by *S. c. catenatus* during a canoe trip in Ontario, Canada, was treated with the newly released Crofab anitvenin. However, after her release she was forced to return to the hospital 3 times in successive weeks because of the venom's residual effect in suppressing her blood's clotting level. See **Western Massasauga**.

Abundance   Eastern massasaugas are found in Ontario, Michigan, Wisconsin, Iowa, Illinois, Indiana, Ohio, and western Pennsylvania and New York. In each of these states *S. c. catenatus* is diminishing in numbers—since massasaugas are still on high ground during the late summer haying season, they are often injured or killed during mechanized hay baling—and is listed as threatened, endangered, or a species of special concern. As this species becomes increasingly rare throughout its range, it is important that even problem massasaugas be humanely moved to suitable habitat in refuges, preserves or parks.

Size   Eastern massasaugas reach adulthood at from 20 to 26 inches in length. Individuals rarely exceed 34 inches, and the record is 39½ in.

Habitat   Bogs, marshes, swamps, and damp meadows and prairies are among the primary habitats utilized by massasaugas. In autumn, *S. catenatus* seek rodent, crayfish and stump holes for brumation, sometimes descending nearly to the level of ground water (Harding

1997). After vernal emergence from these hibernacula, massasaugas seek sunny, elevated spots for basking, often climbing to the tops of grass clumps and low shrubs and, in marshy areas, beaver and muskrat lodges.

Prey   Although massasaugas occasionally prey on frogs and lizards, rodents comprise the majority of their prey—among which voles seem to be the most favored species, with other mice being taken opportunistically.

Reproduction   *Sistrurus catenatus catenatus* probably produces off-spring only every second year, in late summer. Its litters number up to 18 young, each about 8½ inches long, which, soon after parturition, begin seeking their winter hibernating grounds.

Coloring/scale form   Named *catenatus* from the Latin for its chain-like dorsal blotches, the eastern massasauga occurs in 2 very different color morphs. The ground color of the lighter phase varies from tan to medium gray, with dark brown to black dorsal saddles often narrowly outlined with light gray or white. The anterior-most blotches of this phase (which begin immediately posterior to the large head scales and extend onto the nape) are elongate, while a broad, often light bordered dark line extends rearward from the eye to the back of the head. Dark, rounded lateral blotches, usually also narrowly edged with light pigment, are evident, and the belly is predominantly black but may have a smudged appearance.

The darker color phase's melanistic pattern suggests rich, black humus soil (as opposed to the more brownish earth tones of the paler color phase), and with increasing age its patina of suffused dark pigment increases until, in an old melanistic massasauga, any dorsal pattern may be difficult to discern. The rattle of this species is easily seen, and unless the snake is a newborn or has broken the rattle, it is also easily heard.

Similar snakes   The **timber rattlesnake (188)**—whose cephalic scales are small and numerous—is the only other pitviper within the eastern massasauga's range that has a rattle.

Behavior   *Sistrurus catenatus catenatus* varies widely in its defensive behavior, depending on the circumstances. If approached, a coiled massasauga will often remain quiescent while a crawling individual will freeze—both responses being good ways of avoiding detection through camouflage. If molested or injured, however, the same snake will often strike repeatedly, with great accuracy.

Sistrurus catenatus tergeminus

Venomous Few envenomations by *Sistrurus cate-natus tergeminus* take place in the wild (the great majority of snake venom poisonings occur while handling captives) because western massasaugas are retiring animals which avoid human-inhabited areas. In addition, this snake's nocturnal habits— out of 60 recorded field observations, not a single instance of daytime activity was noted—further restrict its chance of encounters with humans.

Massasauga envenomation itself is likely to be less serious than that of larger, *crotalus*-genus rattlesnakes because this reptiles's fangs are usually no more than ⅜ inch in length, while its venom capacity is also comparatively low. Only 15 to 45 milligrams (dry weight) can be obtained even by artificial milking; a bite lethal to a healthy human adult (for whom a probable lethal dose would be 30 to 40 milligrams) is unlikely. Despite some serious envenomations (see **eastern massasaguaga**), many massasauga bites resemble those suffered by Rick Pratt, former director of Houston's Armand Bayou Nature Center, and Jack Joy of the Abilene Zoo, both of which caused no permanent damage.

Abundance Uncommon throughout a broad, north-south swath of Great Plains grassland stretching from Texas' Gulf Coast through Oklahoma and Kansas into parts of Nebraska, Iowa and Missouri.

Here, the western massasauga has probably always occurred in somewhat localized populations, where they were formerly sometimes numerous. According to John E. Werler (1978):

> This reptile was very abundant in some parts of the state more than 50 years ago. In the early 1900s one Armstrong County, Texas farmer . . . killed 50 or 60 during one wheat season.

Even as late as the mid-1970s it was not unusual to find concentrations of western massasaugas: both the author and Jonathan Campbell of the University of Texas at Arlington remember seeing as many as 40 of these animals in a night's road cruising on the prairie west of Fort Worth. Yet this localization has made *S. c. tergeminus* vulnerable to human expansion. For example, intensive crop cultivation has depleted Texas and Oklahoma panhandle populations, while residential real estate development and the destruction of their wintering dens have all but eliminated the western massasaugas living between

RATTLESNAKES

Fort Worth and Weatherford, as well as those living along the now heavily populated Gulf Coast.

Size   Most adult *S. c. tergeminus* are about 2 feet in length; the record is 34¾ inches.

Habitat   The western massasauga is primarily a prairie animal. That habitat once meant a 200-mile-wide band of grassland running from the Gulf to eastern Nebraska, but little of that original Great Plains ecosystem has escaped human alteration. Yet, where the big bluestem and Indian grass remain, *S. c. tergeminus* is still sometimes present, spending the daylight hours hidden either below ground or in clumps of prickly pear or bunchgrass.

Prey   *Sistrurus catenatus tergeminus* is an opportunistic predator on a variety of small vertebrates: 18 stomachs contained 9 pocket and harvest mice, 3 whiptail and rusty lizards, 2 ground snakes, 1 lined snake, 2 leopard frogs, and a shrew.

Reproduction   Live-bearing. Breeding occurs both spring and fall, with a courtship that begins, as Joseph Collins (1974) writes, when:

> The male crawls along beside the female with quick, jerk-
> ing movements of his body. His tail bends beneath her un-
> til their cloacal openings meet and copulation occurs.

Sperm from the autumn pairings remains viable in the female's cloaca throughout the winter, fertilizing her developing eggs only in spring. Pregnancy lasts 15 to 16 weeks, with litters of 5 to 13 young, 7 to 9 inches long, being born during July and August.

Coloring/scale form   *Sistrurus* are thought to be similar to the first rattlesnakes to branch from their moccasin-like ancestors, for they retain the 9 large forecrown scale plates of the copperheads and cotton-

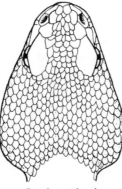

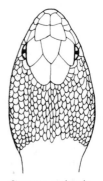

Crotalus *rattlesnake*   Sistrurus *rattlesnake*

mouths. The western massasauga's 38 or more big brown vertebral splotches are closely spaced along its gray-brown dorsum; below its narrow, almost oval, brown-striped crown a white-edged chocolate mask hides its pale, vertically-pupiled eyes and stretches back across its cheeks. Its venter is mottled with gray. Arranged in 25 rows at midbody, the dorsal scales are keeled; the anal plate is undivided.

Similar snakes The **desert massasauga (187)** is a slightly smaller, paler, arid-land race formally distinguished—though these distinctions do not hold true for many individuals of intermediate parentage living in areas where the ranges of these two races overlap—by its fewer (35 to 37) dorsal blotches on a creamy ground color, its uniformly white venter, and its 23 midbody rows of dorsolateral scales. The **western pigmy rattlesnake (184)** is found in eastern woodland and along the Gulf Coast and is distinguished by its gray dorsolateral ground color, its widely spaced blackish dorsal bars or blotches, and its russet-tan vertebral stripe. It has but 21 rows of dorsal scales and a diminutive rattle.

All other rattlesnakes living within the western massasauga's range have crowns covered with small scales.

Behavior In cool weather this nocturnal reptile sometimes thermoregulates by seeking the heat-retaining asphalt of little-traveled roads. Here, unlike more active serpents intercepted as they cross pavement on hunting or breeding forays, *S. c. tergeminus* typically coils quietly at the edge of the asphalt, soaking up its warmth.

Yet western massasaugas are also very sensitive to elevated temperatures: Dmi'el (1972) reports diminished activity above 93°F, and few massasaugas are seen on the roads after hot weather begins. By July, even in areas where it was abundant in late spring *S. c. tergeminus* seems to be almost nonexistent, although the first cool, damp autumn weather always draws a few individuals back to the sun-warmed pavement before they enter winter dormancy.

187 DESERT MASSASAUGA

Sistrurus catenatus edwardsii

Venomous No record exists of human envenomation by this retiring rattlesnake race, but the potency of its toxins is almost certainly the same as those of its subspecies, the western massasauga.

Abundance Very uncommon. Although distributed over a large range, the desert massasauga is unevenly dispersed and is extremely difficult to find even during its late spring activity period.

Size *Sistrurus catenatus edwardsii*'s subspecies name honors Dr. L. A. Edwards, who—for Charles Girard's and Spencer Baird's subsequent scientific description—collected the type specimen of this southwesternmost massasauga in northern Mexico. Adults average less than 18 inches in length, while the record specimen measured only 20½ in.

Habitat This misleadingly named reptile is not a true desert-dweller and only occasionally occurs in Texas' arid northern Chihuahuan biotic province. Here, individuals have been found north of the Christmas Mountains and on arid flats near Hen Egg peak, but most often, in both the panhandle and the Trans-Pecos, *S. c. edwardsii* inhabits dry, shortgrass prairie. In South Texas, its distribution is very fragmented: one localized population occurs in mesquite/prickly pear savannah near Norias in Kenedy County, while a few other desert massasaugas have been found among grass-covered dunes along the inland side of the Laguna Madre.

Prey *Sistrurus catenatus edwardsii* captured in the thorn brush of the lower Gulf Coastal plain typically choose laboratory mice as prey over small reptiles or amphibians, but two adults taken in Texas' Presidio County grassland fed only on whiptail lizards.

Reproduction Live-bearing. A pair of long–term captives maintained by Tim Cole bred during the second week in April; three 8-inch-long young were born 95 days later to the very plump, 18-inch-long female. After their first shed at 9 or 10 days of age, these newborns immediately began to feed on nestling mice. See **Western Massasauga.**

Coloring/scale form This little pitviper is a xeric conditions-adapted race of the western massasauga, which it resembles except for its paler dorsal coloring, its fewer (35 to 37) dorsal blotches on a creamy ground color, its uniformly whitish venter, and its 23 midbody rows of dorsal scales. See **Western Massasauga.**

Similar snakes The desert massasauga is the only rattlesnake within its range whose head is capped with the 9 large scale plates typical of its *Sistrurus* genus. The **western diamond-backed rattlesnake (191)** has a mottled grayish back patterned with white-edged vertebral diamonds, a distinctly black-and-white-ringed tail, and 25 to 27 dorsal scale rows at midbody. The **prairie rattlesnake (193)** is browner in ground color and also has 25 to 27 rows of dorsal scales at midbody, as well as numerous small cephalic scales between the large supraocular scales that flank its broad, triangular crown.

Exhibiting eerily similar dorsolateral coloring, size, and body shape is the **Mexican hog-nosed snake (124)**; at night, in the beam of a flashlight it takes a close look, checking for the viper's rattle, to be sure whether a desert massasauga or Mexican hog-nose is at hand. (This is an interesting case of parallel evolution—in configuration, coloring, and habitat selection—among unrelated snakes, for the Mexican hog-nose shares both of the desert massasauga's geographically separated ranges, favoring the same, sandy-subsoiled shortgrass prairie on the western plains and mesquite savannah in southern Texas.)

Behavior   Almost entirely nocturnal, *S. c. edwardsii* is almost never seen except shortly after dark during its late spring/early summer activity period, when individuals appear coiled along the edges of roads.

RATTLESNAKES
Genus Crotalus

Timber Rattlesnake, *Crotalus horridus horridus*
Canebrake Rattlesnake, *Crotalus horridus atricaudatus*
Eastern Diamond-backed Rattlesnake, *Crotalus adamanteus*
Western Diamond-backed Rattlesnake, *Crotalus atrox*
Northern Black-tailed Rattlesnake, *Crotalus molossus molossus*
Prairie Rattlesnake, *Crotalus viridis viridis*
Mojave Rattlesnake, *Crotalus scutulatus scutulatus*
Mottled Rock Rattlesnake, *Crotalus lepidus lepidus*
Banded Rock Rattlesnake, *Crotalus lepidus klauberi*

This evolutionarily advanced genus is exclusively of new-world derivation and distribution, with numerous species occurring from southwestern Canada and central New Hampshire south to Argentina. In the United States, this genus is best represented west of the Mississippi River: east of the Mississippi, only two *Crotalus* species occur, the timber and the eastern diamond-backed rattlesnakes.

The rattlesnakes of this genus have large, well-developed rattles—a characteristic for which, from the Greek *krotalon* or "rattle," the genus is named. The rattle is a connected string of enlarged, interlocking hollow scales which, like a too-long fingernail, breaks off periodically.

What primarily distinguishes *Crotalus*-genus rattlesnakes from those in the genus *Sistrurus*, however, are the many small scales covering the center of their broad crowns. (Both *Sistrurus* and the *Agkistrodon* pitvipers and nonvenomous North American snakes have 9 large scale plates covering the tops of their heads.)

Crotalus-genus rattlesnakes have a pair of long fangs, each attached to a rotatable maxillary bone. As these fragile, tubular teeth break off during hunting—or are simply shed (rattlesnake fangs generally function for less than 2 months during the activity season)—they are replaced by the forwardmost fang in the row of developing proto-fangs waiting just behind. In order to accommodate such radically enlarged dentition, when the rattler's mouth is closed, its fangs lie folded against the roof of its mouth. When its mouth is opened widely, the fangs can be voluntarily erected, and in striking they are directed almost straight forward. Penetration of their target's skin, followed by venom injection, occurs in a fraction of a second, with the amount of venom expended regulated by the snake. The venom itself is a complex combination of enzymes and proteins which varies both among species and within populations of a single species.

Like a majority of pitvipers, *Crotalus*-genus rattlesnakes are wait-and-ambush hunters. Using chemosensory testing, they are able to position themselves along active small mammal trails . . . then when a rodent scampers past, suddenly strike and release it. The animal is often able to dash away but, after allowing its venom time to immobilize its stricken prey, the rattler typically sets off to trail it by scent—a process in which experiments have shown that rattlesnakes are able to differentiate between the trails of non-envenomated and envenomated animals of the same species.

188   TIMBER RATTLESNAKE

Crotalus horridus horridus

Venomous   As its name suggests, *Crotalus horridus horridus* is a dangerously venomous snake. Although many individuals lie quietly, this is not always the case, for the timber rattlesnake's temperament is variable. When approached by humans or their pets, others individuals coil and vibrate their tails, producing an audible whirring, and rear into a striking S.

The potency of the timber rattlesnake's toxins is at least as variable. More than 20 years ago Sherman Minton took venom samples—one of which was 5 times as powerful as the other—from a pair of gravid *C. h. horridus* captured on the same day on a single hilltop. This subspecies' toxins are much less destructive to tissue, however, than those of the eastern diamond-backed rattlesnake, which shares the southern part of the timber's range. For example, the largest *C. h. horridus* produce no more than 100 to 400 mg. of venom (the snake might be able to inject 30% to 40% of that amount on its own), while an average lethal dose for a human adult is estimated by Minton to be about 100 mg. See **Venom Potency Table**.

Abundance   Threatened. "Timber rattlesnakes were once prominent predators in the forests of eastern North America," writes Harry Greene (1997). "John Smith mentioned them in 'A Map Of Virginia.'" On Revolutionary War flags these creatures epitomized the underdog colonists' "Don't Tread On Me" determination. Widely exterminated by later generations of the same Americans who once respected their wild and truculent nature, today's diminished timber rattler populations—still an indicator of untouched northeastern woodland—are protected in most eastern states, with the exception of Pennsylvania, where most *Crotalus horridus* dens are on the brink of extinction. A better example has been set by the state of New York, where in late 2000, the state supreme court ruled that a stone-mining firm violated state conservation laws by building a buried wire-mesh fence that prevented timber rattlesnakes, including pregnant females, from traveling between their feeding grounds and two dens located near the company's mine.

At the same time, collecting for the pet and hide trades—including the summertime capture of pregnant females, the least expendable segment of the population—has diminished whole regional communities of this slow-reproducing species.

Size   Most adult *C. h. horridus* are 34 to 48 inches long. Where food is plentiful, however, some very old individuals reach 5 feet, and the record just exceeds 6 ft.

Habitat   The range of the timber rattlesnake extends southward from central New England, southern Ohio, and southeastern Minnesota to northern Georgia, western Kentucky, and northeastern Texas.

In the central and northeastern United States the timber rattler is an upland animal of wooded, rocky ridges, bare but fissured mountaintops, ledges and escarpments with southerly exposures, and talus slopes. Yet in New Jersey *C. h. horridus* is associated with both the state's northern uplands and its low-lying southeastern Pine Barrens.

Prey   *Crotalus horridus horridus* prefers endothermic prey. Most adults seem to be partial to large rodents such as squirrels and rats, as well as rabbits. The diet of juveniles is restricted to mice, nestling rats, and both the nestlings and adults of ground nesting birds; some timber rattlesnakes include amphibians and lizards in their diet.

Because *C. h. horridus* feeds primarily on alert rodents, it is vital for them to maximize close contact with these highly mobile creatures beyond chance encounters on the forest floor. Fallen logs are important byways for small woodland mammals, and timber rattlers have been observed moving from one log to another, apparently investigating them (by repeated tongue-flicking along the logs' upper surface) for evidence of prey animals' scent trails.

Quickly passing over trunks lacking strong rodent scent, both northern and southern subspecies of *Crotalus horridus* typically rest their heads on the upper surface of a log whose scent identifies it as a currently used small mammal avenue, where it can survey both directions along its prey's line of travel. At the same time, this pitviper's sensitive throat can detect even the miniscule vibrations of a white-footed mouse's approaching footsteps.

Only actively hunting timber rattlers engage in this kind of ambush predation, however. Heavily gravid females—which have no room in their bellies for prey and have thus foregone feeding—do not coil with their chins on logs.

Reproduction   Live-bearing. Like other northern pitvipers, the timber rattlesnake has very low fecundity. Females begin breeding late in life, at ages—which vary somewhat by geographic region, body weight, and length—of between 4 and 8 years.

Moreover, most females only produce young every second, third or fourth year, and their litters are not large. In his study of 51 gravid female *C. h. horridus*, L. M. Klauber (1972) recorded a range of 5 to 17 unborn young, with an average brood numbering about 10. This extremely limited reproductive rate—typical of northern pitvipers adapted to a short acivity season—means that female timber rattlesnakes may only reproduce 3 or 4 times in their entire lives, usually in specific birthing areas used in concert with other parturitional females. This is a sustainable rate for a large predator defended from enemies by formidable venom, but it is not a viable replacement rate for animals whose dependence on a handful of easily located winter den sites makes them vulnerable to humans. This includes hunters, park administrators and wildlife personnel who have also destroyed many such sanctuaries, and paving and building construction crews.

Born in late summer, neonates range in size from 9 to 13½ inches in length, averaging about 11 in. They are similar in pattern to, but paler in coloration than adults (at birth it is difficult to tell whether the snake will be a dark or yellow color phase, for the neonate ground color of both is most often a light olive-gray or green).

Coloring/scale form   In the northeastern part of its range, the timber rattlesnake occurs in both a blackish and a quite different yellowish color phase. The ground color of the former is very dark brown or blackish, that of the latter either bright yellow or dark gold tinged with olive.

Among both color phases a suffusion of dark pigment becomes prominent about ⅔ of the way along on the trunk, darkening toward the tail until its posterior patterning is obscured. On the dark color phase, a blackish-brown band—which usually remains weakly visible throughout the animal's life—angles downward from the eye past the rear corner of the mouth. This marking is typically absent, however, on the pale, yellow-brown head of yellow color phase males. A rust to olive-colored vertebral stripe is most visible anteriorly on both color phases, but is especially evident among dark-phase southern individuals—on other *C. h. horridus*, it is often poorly defined and sometimes occurs only between the dark dorsal blotches.

Both color phases have 15 to 34 broad, dark dorsal markings, which on the foreparts are more likely to be expressed in vertebral blotches, with separate lateral markings; the rear half of the body is more likely to be dorsolaterally banded.

The timber rattlesnake's ventral coloration reflects that of its dorsal ground color, but is stippled and smudged along its edges with dark pigment. Northern and western timber rattlesnakes have 23 midbody rows of keeled dorsal scales (among southeastern timber rattlers, more individuals have 25 rows), and the anal plate is undivided.

Similar snakes   The timber is the only large rattlesnake in the northeast with numerous small scales covering its crown.

The **eastern** and **western massasaugas** (185, 186) are also smaller animals whose proportionately narrower crowns are striped with chocolate and capped with 9 large scale plates. The **eastern diamond-backed rattlesnake** (190), whose range overlaps that of the timber rattler along the southern Atlantic plain, is also distinguished by its light-hued cheek stripes, white-edged brown vertebral diamonds, and brown-banded tail.

Across the South, however, differences with the timber rattlesnake's southern subspecies, the **canebrake rattlesnake** (189), are less clear. Taxonomic uncertainties have long plagued the systematics of *Crotalus horridus*, and herpetological opinion is divided over whether the southern form of the timber rattlesnake constitutes a subspecies, the canebrake rattlesnake, *C. h. atricaudatus*. One view is that the canebrake is merely a variant color phase (although a geographically specific color phase often defines a subspecies). Both "canebrake" and "northern-form" timber rattlesnakes—the latter have solid blackish posterior bodies—occur together in eastern Kansas and Missouri, however (canebreaks do not have a melanistic form) leaving those who define the canebrake as a separate subspecies to do so on the basis of its pale pinkish ground color, its 25 rows of dorsal scales and, in the South, its distinctly different microhabitat.*

Behavior   This reptile's dens—around which its spring and fall congregations are famous—are, according to a new telemetry study conducted by Bill McMahon of the Louisvile Zoo, more prevalent in the northern part of the range. In the southern part of the range most timber rattlers brumate singly or in small groups, or in dens, usually situated in exposed, elevated areas facing south. As daily temperatures rise during spring, the timber rattlesnake extends its diurnal activity into the late afternoon and evening hours, but until early summer it generally remains in the neighborhood of its den.

Then, during truly warm weather, timber rattlers disperse widely into the surrounding woodlands, sometimes moving several miles from their wintering area. By late summer many seem to be slowly retracing their paths to the den-site, however, and gravid females—who give birth at this time—sometimes deposit their litters virtually at their den's entrance.

189   CANEBRAKE RATTLESNAKE
Crotalus horridus atricaudatus

Venomous   Like other *Crotalus*-genus rattlesnakes, this large and potentially dangerous rattlesnake is of variable disposition. If startled while moving, some canebrake rattlesnakes freeze motionless but remain stretched out and silent, while other individuals coil and begin

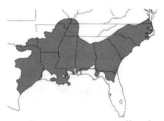

rattling while a potential threat is still some distance away; still others lie quietly until actually jostled, then either attempt a headlong dash for safety, rattle buzzing furiously, sporadically, or not at all, or strike suddenly, with or without rattling.

---

*In 1973, George Pisani et al. compared the characteristics that had traditionally separated the timber from the canebrake rattlesnake and found the two were subspecifically different. Nevertheless, largely because many of this study's comparison specimens were from the western part of the range where intergradation of the two types of *C. horridus* was obvious, a number of researchers concluded that subspeciation was unwarranted. Therefore, in 1986 Brown and Ernst repeated the 1973 study, adding average adult size and average pattern differences. Because this study dealt with specimens from the East, where the two forms are easily differentiated, Brown and Ernst's conclusion was that taxonomic separation was indeed proper.

The venom is geographically variable, being predominantly haemolytic throughout much of the range, but highly neurotoxic and dangerously potent in animals from both the Gulf and Atlantic coastal plains. Laboratory studies as well as field evidence suggest that the venom of some *C. h. atricaudatus* from South Carolina and Florida eastward to Texas may contain a much larger percentage of neurotoxically active peptide components than the venom of the subspecies timber rattlesnake of the northern and central United States. Immediate systemic collapse has occurred after canebrake envenomation in the Southeast, and the same sort of immediate shock and near-lethal systemic failure has also occurred in East Texas. See **Venom Potency Table.**

Abundance   Threatened. Canebrake rattlesnakes range southward along the Atlantic coastal plain and eastern Piedmont from southeastern Virginia to north-central Florida, then westward to central Texas; northward, this race occurs in the Mississippi valley as far as southern Illinois. In most of this broad area, *C. h. atricaudatus* has suffered massive habitat loss to human development, however, and in most places it is uncommon near human-populated areas. (In Florida, it is found on a regular basis in the Osceola National Forest and in Texas it is fairly common inland in Lee and Burleson counties, as well as along the Gulf Coast in Matagorda and adjacent counties.)

Overall, the canebrake seems to be withstanding the pressures caused by human expansion more successfully than its northern relative, the timber rattlesnake, and where prime habitat remains, we have found *C. h. atricaudatus* to persist in both farming communities and wooded parks and preserves.

Size   This southern race of the timber rattlesnake is adult at from 44 to 54 inches in length. Historically, adult female canebrakes averaged about 48 inches in length, males somewhat larger. Populations not impacted by human-caused mortality are now very rare, however. Since both the largest individuals and adult males—which tend to wander furthest and spend the most time exposed to human predation—are now reduced in most wild populations, samples seem to indicate a recent demographic shift among canebrake rattlesnakes toward a younger and more female-dominated population. Nevertheless, where humans are scarce even contemporary *C. h. atricaudatus* regularly attains 60 inches in length, with the largest individuals slightly exceeding 72 in.

Habitat   Throughout the southeastern states, *C. h. atricaudatus* is found most often in low-lying deciduous forest, where it seems to especially favor the dense, but unflooded thickets of moist riparian corridors. (Here, during the latter part of the 18th century it came to be known as the canebrake rattlesnake for its prevalence in the impenetrable cane reed thickets, or brakes, which historically matted every damp clearing in this southeastern woodland.)

Almost all the old cane brakes are gone now, and the closest remaining habitat is dense undergrowth, although in Florida, cypress swamps and wet prairie habitats are also occasionally occupied. In west-central North Carolina, canebrake rattlesnakes enter the lower Appalachians in Stokes and nearby counties; in Texas, undisturbed upland oak-hickory forest sometimes constitutes good habitat.

In extensive natural areas, radio-telemetry-equipped *C. h. atricaudatus* have maintained home ranges that varied from the 10 or fewer acres utilized by quiescent gravid females to as many as several hundred acres covered by wide-roaming adult males. Like those of other large snakes, however, timber rattlers' territories are now largely defined by the presence of man, as these pitvipers occasionally stray (usually fatally) into suburban yards and parking lots.

Prey Prey is almost entirely warm-blooded, and primarily mammalian. Juvenile *C. h. atricaudatus* take mostly white-footed mice—even newly born canebrakes are large enough to eat adult mice—as well as, occasionally, amphibians and lizards. The stomachs of 30 large individuals collected in Louisiana contained 10 rabbits, 8 mice, 6 rats, and 1 fox squirrel.

Yet there are exceptions to this preference for mammalian prey. Spiny lizards are readily taken by captive canebrakes, and cannibalism of its own kind has also been observed. A different, and exclusive, prey orientation was exhibited by a three foot long *C. h. atricaudatus* captured by D. Craig McIntyre. After this individual had refused small mammal prey for weeks, McIntyre was about to release it for fear it would starve when he accidentally discovered its sole food requirement was birds—a diet on which it then thrived for years. (Research suggests that pitvipers can acquire this sort of exclusive prey preference by successfully killing a particular food animal early in life.) See **Timber Rattlesnake.**

Reproduction Because its seasonal activity period is longer than that of the more northerly timber rattlesnake race, canebrake rattlers may attain sexual maturity somewhat earlier in life than the late-maturing timber, although their fecundity is still low because most females produce young only once every two to four years. Parturition occurs in mid- to late summer, with litters varying from 3 to 19 (between 6 and 10 is the usual number of offspring). Neonates, which average 13½ inches in length, are similar in pattern to adults, but are paler, with a light gray ground color.

Coloring/scale form The black tail, cinnamon vertebral stripe, and 21 to 29 dark dorsolateral bands—usually in the form of anteriorly directed chevrons—are definitive. The russet vertebral stripe is strongest anteriorly. It fades toward the tail, where dark pigment prevails (in Latin, *atri-caudatus* means "black-tailed").

In the Southeast, the canebrake's ground color varies from yellowish-gray through pale brown to buff or, rarely, a dull pink or lavender. Further west, this snake tends to be duller and in Texas can have a medium brown to olive ground color, often with lighter areas outlining its dark bands.

In all cases, the posterior third of the body becomes progressively suffused with black pigment until the posterior of the trunk is so dark that any pattern is difficult to discern. The crown is much paler than the dorsum, and on the sides of the head the big, slit-pupiled eyes are hidden in the pitvipers' characteristic dark mask. The dull yellowish venter may be smudged along its edges with patches of darker pigment, and usually reflects the dorsal ground color, darkening toward the tail.

Both ontogenetic variation and sexual dimorphism—the latter rare among snakes—occurs in *C. h. atricaudatus*. As this pitviper ages, its body darkens, obscuring the contrast between its creamy youthful ground color, black dorsolateral chevrons, and rusty vertebral stripe. Males are grayer than females, so the oldest and largest males—one of which is pictured here—are far less colorful than young females.

Among southern *C. horridus*, more individuals have 25 midbody rows of keeled dorsal scales than among northern and western populations, where 23 rows are most common. Like that of other rattlesnakes, the anal plate is undivided.

Similar snakes The **prairie rattlesnake (193)** and both the **eastern** and **western diamond-backed rattlesnakes (190, 191)** have light lines on the sides of their heads and light-and-dark banded tails. **Pigmy rattlesnakes** and **Massasaugas (182–187)** have 9 large scale plates crowning their heads.

Behavior This is a more secretive and less flamboyant rattlesnake than the eastern diamond-backed rattler, and as such, despite its invariably being killed on sight, *C. h. atricaudatus* persists in areas of human habitation more successfully than the diamond-back. This is partly due to the generally quieter temperament of this sedentary, nocturnal forager, but it also reflects how well *C. h. atricaudatus* blends into even a little background debris. A few fallen leaves, a stick or two, and a patch of dark soil will render a coiled 4-foot-long canebrake virtually invisible. For example, in one farming area of north-central Florida, canebrake rattlesnakes can be seen crossing roads in the evening with some regularity, but they are very difficult to find during the day because these snakes not only coil on top of the forest floor's carpet of leaves, but also slide beneath such cover, showing only the tip of the nose and eyes.

Therefore, in both southern Georgia and the low country of southeastern South Carolina, after decades of persecution that have noticeably lessened populations of the eastern diamond-backed rattlesnake, canebrakes remain fairly common in large wooded tracts. Although *C. h. atricaudatus* is not often seen here, before spring foliage has cut visibility in the woodland understory an occasional individual is sometimes to be found basking in a patch of sunlight at the base of a tree or next to a fallen log.

On one cold but sunny early March day, for example, 5 huge canebrake rattlers were found sunning near a stump hole above a woodland swamp in southern South Carolina. Thirty feet further up the forested slope, at the top of the hill, was a well-tilled, soybean field. This huge crop field had been farmed for years, and it seems probable that these big snakes had spent their entire lives in the vicinity—a case of satisfactory, but precarious, coexistence unsuspected by either landowner or farmworkers.

190 EASTERN DIAMOND-BACKED RATTLESNAKE, *Crotalus adamanteus*

Venomous   The most dangerous venomous snake in the eastern United States, *C. adamanteus* sometimes holds its ground when threatened. In Greek, *adamenteus* means "fierce" or "unyeilding." Yet a majority of eastern diamondbacks do not behave aggressively, even when closely approached. (While radio-tracking *C. adamanteus* in northern Florida, biologist Walt Timmerman made 743 visits to locate his transmitter-bearing snakes, often accidentally stepping very close to their hiding places. Yet in only 9 instances did such a close approach trigger a rattle, and none of the snakes struck.) Another factor affecting the eastern diamond-backed rattlesnake's comparatively few hostile encounters with human beings is the fact that these animals are now abundant primarily in undisturbed wilderness, where they spend a great deal of time below ground in rodent and gopher tortoise burrows.

On the exceptional occasions when this pitviper does behave aggressively toward a human intruder, however, the great size and agility of the largest adults give them a striking range that can exceed 3 feet. Moreover, their broad heads (which allow room for big venom glands), as well as their proportionately long fangs, let eastern diamond-backs deliver a large quantity of venom well below the surface. Feeding on sizable prey like rabbits (which if not dropped quickly may run so far that their bodies are difficult for the rattlesnake to find) may also accustom large *C. adamanteus* to delivering a substantial amount of venom: among smaller prey animals death often occurs within 60 seconds of the strike.

In addition to its hemorrhagic properties, eastern diamond-back venom contains a significant proportion of neurotoxically active peptide fractions which, even in creatures the size of human beings, can result in systemic failure. The lethal dose is probably somewhat less than 100 mg for a healthy human adult, with the largest eastern diamond-backs sometimes being milked, in the old reptile-show days, of nearly 900 mg. Pitvipers can deliver less than ⅓ their total venom capacity in a bite, but even this amount constitutes more than the amount needed for a deadly envenomation: almost all the Southeast's rarely-ocurring snakebite fatalities (seldom more than 1 per year) are the result of bites by *Crotalus adamanteus*. See **Venom Potency Table.**

Abundance   Increasingly uncommon. Eastern diamond-backed rattlesnakes still occur in southern Mississippi, Alabama, Georgia, and the Carolinas, as well as throughout Florida, including its saline offshore keys, yet *C. adamanteus* is now in serious decline. Its decline initiated, decades ago, by human predation. This began on a major scale with rattlesnake roundups, and though the eastern diamond-back was never as abundant as the western diamond-back, *Crotalus atrox*, on which Texas' and Oklahoma's huge reptile carnivals are based, the Florida and Georgia roundups obtained their sacrificial snakes in the same way: pumping gasoline into "gopher holes." Besides flushing out poisoned though still-living rattlesnakes, this practice decimated a variety of burrow-living wildlife, including the protected gopher tortoises which originally dug the tunnels. Tunnel-gassing is now illegal in Florida but still occurs in Georgia and Alabama.

Current human predation on *C. adamanteus*, however, is prompted primarily by the commercial trade in rattlesnake skins. For over a quarter of a century the Ross Allen Reptile Insititute shipped eastern diamond-backed rattlesnakes (more than 50,000 in all) out of the state, and a network of hide hunters and commercial collection points still exists in Florida, Georgia and Alabama. (Although *C. adamanteus* is far less numerous today, between 1990 and 1992 the state's largest snakeskin dealer delivered some 10,000 eastern diamond-back hides each year.)

The major problem now facing *C. adamanteus* is much more serious than exploitation by hide hunters, however, which is loss of its native habitat to residential development. Small reptiles such as ringneck and brown snakes can burrow unharmed in the soft soil of neighborhood lawns, garter snakes thrive in suburban plantings, and cryptic nocturnal species like corn snakes adapt well to disturbed environments—but big, dangerous serpents like the eastern diamond-back are quickly exterminated in human-occupied areas. These areas are expanding so rapidly everywhere in the Southeast that the occasional *Crotalus adamanteus* which turns up on the fringes of urban areas has simply been overtaken by the asphalt glacier of human commerce.

Size A beautiful and impressive reptile at any size, most eastern diamond-backed rattlesnakes now seen in the wild are considerably smaller than in the recent past, presently averaging 32 to 48 inches in adult length. Earlier samplings of this animal's wild populations cited adult females as averaging about 51 inches in length (Means), 54½ inches (Martin), and 56 in. (Diemer-Berish, Van Horn); in all three studies, adult males averaged slightly larger.

Yet today, a 6-foot-long eastern diamond-backed rattler is a real rarity. This is because all large, venomous North American snakes are now experiencing such heavy mortality from mankind's activities that in any population many fewer of the largest and oldest animals remain alive, leaving neonates, juveniles, and subadults to comprise a larger proportion of the group sampled in the field.

Given sufficient time and undisturbed space, eastern diamond-backed rattlesnakes can still grow very large, however: old male *C. adamanteus* are the biggest snakes in North America. The record specimen measured 8 feet, 3 inches in length, with a midbody diameter of 4½ inches and a crown 3¼ inches wide.

Habitat Eastern diamond-backs can occur almost anywhere in still-wild parts of its range, but its prime habitat is upland pine forest, pine-palmetto flatwoods, sandhills, and coastal maritime hammocks.

Prey Large pitvipers tend to be generalized predators on a variety of warm-blooded animals. Adult *Crotalus adamanteus* reportedly favor cottontails and marsh rabbits as prey, but squirrels, gophers, and cotton rats, as well as quail and other birds, are also taken.

Like other large rattlesnakes, the eastern diamond-back is both an active forager and a sit-and-wait ambush predator. At times it employs the same hidden-site hunting tactics as the timber rattlesnake, but because this technique typically produces no more than a dozen meals a year, *C. adamanteus* is adapted to long non-feeding periods between kills. Newborns are off to a good start, for example, if they manage to kill a single mouse between their late-summer birth and their first winter dormancy, for even this seemingly meager amount of food is sufficient to sustain them until spring.

Reproduction   Live-bearing. The low reproductive capacity of large pitvipers such as the eastern diamond-back is partially a result of these creatures' slow growth. *Crotalus adamanteus* requires at least 2 years to reach reproductive maturity, and most females are unable to acquire the body fat necessary for pregnancy more often than every other year.

Part of the reason these big viperids lack the ability to reproduce more frequently may be that gestation of their large, well-developed young requires gravid female *C. adamanteus* to forego hunting by moving to optimally warm basking sites with low prey availability. This can occur many weeks before parturition, and may cause post-partum female eastern diamond-backs to feed for a year or more to rebuild the fat reserves consumed by giving birth.

Such intense effort makes for great parental investment in the 7 to 24 (mean: 14) plump, 7- to 10-inch-long offspring, however, and there are accurate accounts of at least the appearance of maternal protection. Born in late summer, neonate *Crotalus adamanteus* typically remain near their birth site—typically a tortoise or rodent burrow whose humid interior minimizes the dessication to which they are prone. At the entrance to these burrows an adult female, presumably the mother, has been observed remaining for days in succession.

After their first shed at about 10 days of age the young are less vulnerable to drying and venture away from their natal shelter, but during their first week their mother's nearby presence—even if she is only resting from parturition—probably affords them enhanced odds of surviving early predation by small mammals.

Coloring/scale form   Less-vividly patterned than eastern diamond-backs from the Carolinas, Florida *C. adamanteus* have more gray than yellow in their ground color, but display the same white-edged chocolate vertebral diamonds. These diamonds fuse into brown crossbands on the posterior trunk and tail, the latter being brown to olive, ringed with black.

There is a white-edged dark postocular stripe, the venter is pale yellow, and the crown is capped with small scales between its lateral postocular plates. The 27 to 29 midbody rows of dorsal scales are keeled and the anal plate is undivided.

Aberrantly colored *C. adamanteus* are also well known. Leucistic (white) individuals are periodically found west of Gainesville, Florida, and for years "Snowflake," one of these snow-white leucistic eastern diamond-backs, was the showpiece of Glades Herp. in Ft. Myers.

Similar snakes   The **timber rattlesnake (188)** has a tan crown, a rusty mid-dorsal stripe, blackish dorsolateral chevrons, and a black tail. Even the largest **pigmy rattlesnakes (182–184)** are only the size of a juvenile diamond-back, with a tiny rattle, small dark dorsal and lateral blotches on a gray ground color, and a dark-striped crown capped with 9 large scales unlike the small-scaled crown of the eastern diamond-back.

Behavior   Young eastern diamond-backs are preyed upon by raptors, mammalian carnivores, hogs, and ophiophagous king and indigo snakes, but adult *C. adamanteus* need only fear man. Even in the wild they are reported to reach 10 years in age, an extremely long life for a wild snake, and captives have lived nearly 23 years.

191   WESTERN DIAMOND-BACKED RATTLESNAKE, *Crotalus atrox*

Venomous   Nearly all of the most serious cases of snakebite treated in Oklahoma and Texas hospitals are inflicted by *Crotalus atrox*, the heaviest serpent in the Southwest and statistically the most likey to inflict serious harm (*atrox* is Latin for "frightful" and indeed, many western diamond-backs are quick to coil, rattle, and strike if approached too closely). This large reptile's venom contains roughly 17% neurologically active peptide components, 30% tissue-digestive proteases, and 53% blood-targeted toxic enzymes. Injection of this complex (and constantly subtly changing) mixture is characterized by immediate severe pain, swelling, weakness, sweating and chills, faintness or dizziness, elevation or depression of pulse, nausea, vomiting, and swelling of the regional lymph nodes.

   The western diamond-back is a dangerous reptile because, like many other venomous snakes, its temperament is unpredictable. This wide range in behavior is based, to some extent, on temperature (cool snakes are more docile), recent hunting success (hungry snakes are more irritable), and the degree to which the animal has been disturbed. It is also a function of the animal's innate individual temperament, and some *Crotalus atrox* seem to be inherently far more agressive than others.

Yet few people die from western diamond-backed rattlesnake bites. Widely available care at hospital facilities accustomed to combating hypovolemic shock has cut the fatality rate to less than 10 percent even among heavily envenomated patients; those who succumb are mostly children, whose body fluid volume is too small to accommodate the plasma leakage brought about by the venom toxins' perforation of their capillaries. In cases of heavy envenomation, peripheral morbidity, including the loss of digits and even limbs, is still fairly high, however, especially when aggravated by ill-advised first-aid procedures. See **Venom Potency Table**.

Abundance   Very common. *Crotalus atrox* is by far the most numerous and widespread venomous snake in south-central Oklahoma and the western ¾ of Texas. Because of its bold temperament and frequently diurnal foraging pattern, it is also the most likely pitviper to be noticed, both in remote areas and around farm buildings that shelter rats and mice.

Size   Adults average 3 to 4 feet in length, yet because newborns are so numerous in early autumn, at this time of year the majority of *C. atrox* are less than 20 inches long. Huge western diamond-backs also occur. These are always males, since pitviper males are the larger gender. Among diamond-backs, the largest males weigh as much as 20 percent more than the biggest females.

Several recorded western diamond-backs have measured from 7 to just under 7½ feet in length. (Such animals have usually been stretched by their own great weight—their heads can be as wide as a man's spread hand and their maximum diameter up to 5 inches—since they are almost invariably hung up for photographs after death. This stretching can add 20% to a big snake's length, making the true size of these individuals difficult to determine.)

Extremely large *Crotalus atrox* like these are not simply very old snakes, but true genetic giants. For example, many western diamond-backs have spent long lives in confinement—the record is nearly 26 years—without reaching remarkable size. Moreover, most record-sized *Crotalus atrox* come from particular local areas uniquely suited to produce populations of big crotalids. The gene pool of Texas' Starr, Hidalgo and Willacy counties regularly produces western diamond-backs over 5 feet in length (in this area naturalist Greg Lasley observed a copulating pair, both of which were more than five feet long), while other giant western diamond-backed rattlesnakes have been found in the equally rich agricultural region along the Texas/New Mexico border near Carlsbad.

Habitat   At one time or another *Crotalus atrox* can be found in nearly every terrestrial habitat within its range (it is especially abundant on the Gulf's coastal barrier islands, in South Texas' Tamaulipan thorn woodland, and in the northern part of Big Bend National Park).

Compared to other rattlesnakes which share its range, and are to a greater degree oriented toward specific habitat niches, *Crotalus atrox* is a generalist—an animal whose microhabitat overlaps, to the east, that of the mesic-bottomland, dense-cover-preferring timber and pigmy rattlesnakes. To the northwest, the western diamond-back inhabits large portions of the prairie and massasauga rattlesnakes' grassland range, and to the west it occurs throughout most of the rock and black-tailed rattlesnakes' mountainous/saxicolous environs. To the southwest, the western diamond-back also occupies the creosote desert and mesquite-tarbush zone typical of the arid-adapted Mojave rattlesnake. In these desert areas, *C. atrox* seems to be at the edge of its adaptive capacity, especially during years of severe drought. Under such conditions, the author has found diamondbacks so thirsty that when doused with water to move them off a highway, instead of fleeing or coiling as they would ordinarily do, they turned their heads upward to drink from the stream.

Prey   *Crotalus atrox* feeds mostly on mammals. Newborns swallow full-grown mice without hesitation while, among the largest adults, squirrels, prairie dogs, cottontails, and even young jackrabbits are possible prey species; ground-living birds are also taken, but very small rodents are apparently sometimes ignored.

Reproduction   Live-bearing. Photographs of large *Crotalus atrox* engaged in dominance combat—agonisitic encounters usually provoked when two similarly sized adult males meet along a receptive female's pheromone scent trail—are common post card fodder. Copulation is prolonged, sometimes occurring without interuption for more than 24 hours, depending on both geography and elevation. Litters avergage 9 to 14, with most newborns measuring between 9 and 13½ inches in length. Shortly after their birth in late August, September, and early October, small western diamondbacks are often encountered by humans because they are both abundant and, naively unwary, engaged in dispersing across unfamiliar terrain.

Coloring/scale form   Dorsolateral coloring is dark-speckled gray-brown, vertebrally patterned with the big, light- and dark-edged "diamonds" for which the species is named. On the posterior back these

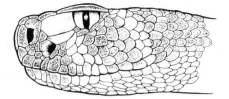

Western diamond-back rattler

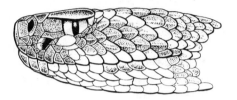

Prairie and Mojave rattlers

markings become obscure, but dorsal pigmentation is less helpful in quickly identifying *Crotalus atrox* than is its boldly black-and-white-banded "coon tail." (Dorsal ground color varies considerably among *C. atrox*, in part because this species' population is so large; the author has seen one nearly all-black individual, an almost pattern-less specimen, and large, rusty-red red individuals occur near Monahans, Texas. (The author has also seen one nearly all-black wild diamond-back, as well as almost patternless specimens, all of which seem to be female, taken from old barns in central Texas. This region is also home to albino/leucistic *C. atrox*—including one pale, but dark-eyed hypomelanistic individual. Both pale color morphs are now bred in capivity by Tim Cole of Austin.)

A chocolate-gray band, its anterior and posterior edges lined with white, diagonally masks each check, partially camouflaging the big, pale, slit-pupiled eye. The light-hued lower border of this band intersects the upper lip midway along its length, while the white posterior edge of the dark cheek stripe runs from behind the eye straight to the rear corner of the mouth. The venter is unmarked yellowish white, the heavily keeled dorsal scales are arranged in 25 to 27 rows at midbody, and only 2 internasal scales intersect the rostral. Like that of all pitvipers, the anal plate is undivided.

Similar snakes The **prairie rattlesnake (193)** has rounded brown vertebral blotches, which on its posterior trunk elongate into narrow crossbands. More than 2 internasal scales intersect its rostral, while the white posterior border of its dark subocular cheek band curves backward above the corner of its mouth. The **Mojave rattlesnake**

(194), found only in Texas' central and southwestern Trans-Pecos region, has 2 or 3 longitudinal rows—the diamond-back has several much smaller rows of scales—of large, roughened cephalic scales between the supraocular plates of its anterior crown. See **Mojave Rattlesnake for illustration**. The Mojave rattler's white tail bands are also sometimes noticeably wider than its black caudal rings, its more cleanly defined vertebral diamonds elongate on the posterior third of its back into crossbands like those of the prairie rattler, and its white postocular line curves backward above the posterior corner of its mouth.

The **canebrake rattlesnake (189)**, with which the western diamond-back shares a crosstimbers and southeastern Oklahoma range, has an entirely dark tail, a russet vertebral stripe, and black, chevron-shaped crossdorsal bands. **Rock rattlesnakes (195, 196)** lack diamond-shaped vertebral markings and have only 23 midbody rows of dorsal scales. The crowns of both southwestern **massasaugas (186, 187)** are dark-striped and capped with 9 large scale plates.

Behavior   Most western diamond-backed rattlesnakes follow seasonally structured activity patterns. By late May or June, this reptile's predatory forays have split into early morning and evening periods, while during July and August high temperatures limit its foraging to the coolest part of the day, long after dark.

In winter, most *C. atrox* seek shelter in communal dens, although sometimes for relatively brief periods, for on the Rio Grande plain and coastal islands a majority of individuals are fully active during mid-winter warm spells. (Even in cooler parts of its broad range some *C. atrox* venture abroad at midday during winter, although they remain very close to their dens from late November through March.)

In spring, this concentrated population enhances males' chances of mating with emerging females before they disperse—for *C. atrox* may move as far as 3 miles to its summer ranges—but it renders the emerging snakes vulnerable to predation by humans. (In their attempts to flush wintering *Crotalus atrox* from brumation dens, participants in the Southwest's annual Rattlesnake Roundups inadvertently kill hundreds of other animals. Banned by most states for the ecologically destructive practice of pumping of gasoline fumes into rock crevices and earthen burrows, these roundups remain popular springtime carnivals in both Texas and Oklahoma.)

Large roundups such as those promoted by Sweetwater, Texas, and Albuquerque, New Mexico, as well as the many roundups held at smaller venues, unfortunately continue to operate without intervention by state fish and game departments. More progressive policies in Louisiana and Florida now prohibit using gasoline to collect wildlife.

192 NORTHERN BLACK-TAILED RATTLESNAKE, *Crotalus molossus molossus*

Venomous So few bites are recorded that the specific pathology of black-tail venom has been little known. At roughly 79% the lethality of western diamond-backed rattlesnake venom, black-tail toxins are quite potent and were thought to have a primarily anti-coagulant action. Yet a recent envenomation—a bite on the finger of a healthy adult male by a 3-foot-long black-tail—brought about severe systemic shock within 15 minutes.

Abundance Uncommon. Found only occasionally on the western part of Texas' Edwards Plateau, black-tailed rattlesnakes are more numerous in the deserts, mountains, and canyons of this state's Trans-Pecos region. Here, especially during rainy periods following long droughts, *C. m. molossus* can be temporarily abundant. The enhanced scent-carrying capacity of humid air can send individuals in search of prey as well as mates (in the case of pheromone-seeking males), and at the mouths of rhyolite-walled canyons south of Alpine, Texas, human residents may re-locate one or more black-tails from their yards every day after heavy rains.

Size Although adult *C. m. molossus* are generally less than 32 inches in length, the largest black-tail on record is the 52-inch-long male captured and measured by the author on the edge of a rocky Davis Mountains arroyo in September 1995.

Habitat *Crotalus molossus molossus* occurs all over West Texas, but it is most common in broken terrain: canyons, vegetated gullies, and wooded mountainsides. On the western Edwards Plateau, black-tails live in brushy limestone canyons; west of the Pecos River they are found at lower elevations, in desert terrain broken by rocky bluffs and canyons. In the pine-oak forests of montane far West Texas, black-tailed rattlesnakes go up as far as the land itself: the author has found dark-hued individuals at over 7,000 feet on the Chisos Mountains' south rim.

Prey   Adult *c. m. molossus* feed mostly on small mammal prey. Wood rats are abundant in the westernmost parts of black-tails' montane habitat and probably constitute this species' major prey species there, for black-tails are often found near the rats' runways and burrow entrances. (Nevertheless, unlike most other large crotalids, newly captured black-tails are often reluctant to accept domestic mice as food.)

Reproduction   Live-bearing. Two females from Texas' Brewster County found while gravid deposited litters of 7 and 8 young (all of which measured between 8 and 10¼ inches in length) in late July.

Coloring/scale form   Calling to mind the jagged, light-dark patterning of Navajo blankets, the dark band running along the black-tailed rattlesnake's spine is inlaid with patches of pale scales. In Texas, this reptile's ground color ranges from brownish- to silver-gray, with boldly contrasting patches of off-white, tan, or faintly olive vertebral scales. (Black-tails from the Chiricahua and Huachuca Mountains in southern Arizona often have beautiful lemon-hued dorsal patches and nearly golden lower sides.) The dark-hued posterior crown is speckled and spotted, the forecrown covered by a wide black band that hides both the heat-sensing viperid pit and the slit-pupiled eyes and tapers rearward to a point just above the posterior corner of the jaw. As its common name indicates, this animal's tail is a uniformly sooty black.

A majority of Texas' black-tailed rattlesnakes have 27 midbody rows of keeled dorsal scales, but individuals vary between 25 and 29 rows. The pale venter may have a yellowish cast, clouded and mottled in places with gray; the anal plate is undivided.

Similar snakes   No other rattlesnake in the Southwest has a black forecrown and tail and creamy vertebral scales enclosed by dark pigment.

Behavior   *Crotalus molossus molossus* seldom emerges from shelter until evening, and may forage in comparatively cool weather. Despite temperatures near 60°F, three Kerr County, Texas, individuals were abroad as late as December 12; other black-tails have been found in the Trans-Pecos as early as mid-February.

Like other large crotalids—pitvipers that in predation orient on the body heat of their predominantly endothermic prey—black-tails are unbelievably sensitive to even faint vibrations of warmth. The heat-sensing pits between eye and nostril let one individual in the author's experience accurately track the movements of a lighted cigarette from more than a foot away, even through the thick glass wall of its cage front.

Venomous   Findlay E. Russell's work with the toxins of *Crotalus viridis* (1980) indicates that prairie rattler toxins have only about ½ the tissue-necrotizing effect, and less than ⅓ the blood-destroying potency of western diamond-backed rattlesnake venom (the type most often treated in Texas and Oklahoma). Yet, due to its large complement of neurotoxically active peptide components the prairie rattlesnake's overall venom potency is slightly greater than that of the western diamond-back.

Most prairie rattlesnakes are much smaller than adult diamond-backs, however. Besides having shorter fangs, their average venom capacity is only 35 to 110 mg. (dry weight)—the largest diamond-backs produce 175 to 600 mg. capacity—and as a result the prairie rattler's potential threat to humans is considerably less than that of the western diamond-back. See **Venom Potency Table.**

Abundance   Along gully and canyon drop-offs, or in places where agriculture has not plowed under native grassland, *C. v. viridis* may be locally abundant anywhere—on the western Great Plains east of the Rockies—from the Texas panhandle north to the Canandian border of North Dakota where, because northern pitvipers both reproduce and mature slowly, *crotalus viridis* have a very low replacement rate. South of the Texas panhandle, *C. v. viridis* is uncommon on the Stockton Plateau and in the Trans-Pecos, but a resident population inhabits the rich pastureland southwest of the Davis Mountains.

Size   Although this slender pitviper reaches a maximum of 4½ feet in length, the majority of adults are between 2 and 3 ft.

Habitat   The prairie rattlesnake, like the three races of massasauga, is a grassland animal: in undisturbed areas *C. v. viridis* may be found throughout the long sweep of open country that stretches from southeastern Alberta and Saskatchewan to northern Chihuahua. Because this prairie environment offers little cover, the prairie rattlesnake probably spends more time in small mammal burrows than any other western pitviper; on these windswept grasslands, gopher, ground squirrel, and prairie dog tunnels are often the only shelter available—and at times *C. v. viridis* shares them with not only its resident rodents, but with burrowing owls, toads, and a host of invertebrates.

RATTLESNAKES

Prey An ambush specialist, like a majority of pitvipers *Crotalus viridis* is adept at making the most of the few hiding places its rangeland habitat provides, coiling inconspicuously beside any outline-masking bush or rock shadow. Yet it is a more active forager than strictly sit-and-wait predators like the rock rattlesnakes, having been described by *Crotalid* authority Harry Greene as a "mobile ambusher." This means that *C. viridis* maximizes its chances of encountering prey by seeking out and patrolling sites, such as gopher colonies and prairie dog towns, where food animals are most concentrated. Other prey reportedly includes baby rabbits, ground-nesting birds, and among the young, lizards.

Reproduction Live-bearing. The prairie rattlesnake's interrupted reproductive schedule is an example of the adaptations typical of pitvipers living in northern ranges. Because the foraging season there is too brief to build up in a single year the reserves of body fat necessary to nourish developing offspring, females typically give birth as infrequently as every third or fourth year. Because in such populations female prairie rattlesnakes are only periodically receptive, it is imperative for as many as possible of them to be found by males during their bi-annual fertile periods. Communal denning, therefore, is an important part of this animal's reproductive strategy, for as the denning group simultaneously emerges from winter brumation all the sexually receptive females available in any particular year find themselves surrounded by a host of males ready to breed.

In the northern environment where many prairie rattlesnakes live, it is also important for gestating females to observe an energy-conserving regimen of nocturnal sheltering beneath the earth and midday basking, often on sun-warmed stones. Devoting all their hard-won reserves of body fat to the final development of their young, gravid female *Crotalus viridis* move about very little and feed rarely if at all during their final weeks of gestation. Because *Crotalus viridis* is the only rattlesnake to range far into Canada, gravid females may also bask together near communal birthing sites, sharing the brief sunlight available at these highter latitudes—while perhaps also benefiting, as a group, from reduced vulnerability to predators. Birth of the 8½- to 11-inch-long offspring occurs in August on the northern Great Plains, as late as October in southwestern Texas. See **Banded Rock Rattlesnake**.

Coloring/scale form Thirty-five to 55 oval brown blotches line the center of the prairie rattlesnake's tan dorsum. (This animal's Latin species and subspecies names seem a sort of misnomer, for *viridis* means "green"—though prairie rattlers from the northern Great Plains are occcasionally reported with a faintly greenish ground color.) Frequently waisted over the spine anteriorly, these blotches elongate into crossbands on the posterior ⅓ of the trunk. *Crotalus viridis* is also unique in having more than 2 internasal scales touching its rostral scale, while along its cheeks a pair of thin white seams—the higher of which curves backward above the corner of the mouth—border a dark ocular band. Arranged in 25 to 27 rows at midbody, the dorsal scales are keeled, the unmarked venter is yellowish white, and the anal plate is undivided.

Similar snakes   The **western diamond-backed rattlesnake (191)** has bold black and white bands around its tail (the prairie rattler's tail is ringed with brown), diamond-shaped, dimly white-edged anterior vertebral blotches, 2 internasal scales intersecting its rostral, and a white upper cheek stripe that runs straight to the posterior corner of its mouth. The **Mojave rattlesnake (194)** may have even wider white caudal bands than the diamond-back, separated by black rings, and more sharply defined white-edged vertebral diamonds. Two internasal scales touch its rostral, and a distinctive double or triple row of large, rough scales lines the center of its crown (here, the prairie rattler has 4 or more rows of much smaller scales). The **rock rattlesnakes (195–196)** lack the prairie rattlesnake's brown vertebral ovals and white cheek lines. These little reptiles have 23 rows of dorsal scales, and only 2 internasal scales touch the rostral.

Behavior   Prairie rattlers are most likely to forage abroad between 80 and 90°F. In the northern portion of their range this makes for a short annual activity period, yet this snake's adaptation to life below ground (including months-long winter denning) combined with its ability to exploit the rich bird and small mammal life of the Great Plains enable it to range farther into Canada than any other serpent except the bullsnake, hog-nose, and garter snakes.

194   MOJAVE RATTLESNAKE
Crotalus scutulatus scutulatus

Venomous   *Crotalus scutulatus* is probably the most dangerous serpent living north of Mexico. This is due to its combination of quick-striking defensive behavior and extremely potent venom. (This extreme potency is characteristic both of *C. scutulatus* native to California's Mojave Desert and to most individuals living in Arizona, whose venom is referred to as Type A Mojave. This venom's lethal dosage for a human adult is reportedly no more than 10 to 15 milligrams (dry weight), toxicity which approaches that of the cobras, and a large specimen can be milked of up to 90 milligrams. (Although pitvipers can typically deliver only about ⅓ of this milked volume, in the of Mojave Type A venom, that is still more than double a lethal human dose.) New Mexico and West Texas' *C. s. scutulatus* populations, however, reportedly carry the less virulent toxins of Type A Mojave venom. See **Venom Potency Table.**

Abundance   In Texas, *C. s. scutulatus* occurs primarily in Brewster, Presidio, Jeff Davis, Terrell, and Pecos counties. The author has found both adult and young Mojaves to be not uncommon here, both in arid, low-lying environments and in montane situations such as the high meadows of the Davis Mountains and the slopes of Elephant Butte south of Alpine; in both milieus, after late summer rainfall *C. s. scutulatus* can outnumber the region's ubiquitous western diamond-backed rattlesnakes.

Size   Mojave rattlesnakes are relatively slender, with a majority of adults measuring less than 32 inches. The record is just over 54 inches.

Habitat   Most of the range of *C. s. scutulatus* is windswept Mexican tableland at 2,000- to 6,800-foot elevations. According to Frederick Gehlbach (1981), along the Trans-Pecos' Mexican/U.S. border:

> The Mojave rattlesnake prefers the shortest grass and fewest shrubs at lowest elevations. . . . Overlap between the diamondback and Mojave in the mesquite-tarbush zone is [perhaps a result of] an invasion by the Mojave over the last hundred years. . . . The most logical scenario evokes the all-too-familiar theme of desertification: as grassland is degraded into desert shrubland, the [dry-adapted] Mojave rattler moves in.

In Texas, this desert biome includes creosote bush flats along the Rio Grande west of Big Bend, as well as parts of the arid Christmas Mountains. *Crotalus scutulatus scutulatus* is also present, but less common, in the rolling grasslands around Marfa. According to Thomas Van Devender and C. H. Lowe (1977), it is uncommon here because it faces strong competitive interaction with the prairie rattlesnake, *C. v. viridis*: Mojave rattlesnakes do not enter into more than the southwestern fringes of the Great Plains communities occupied by the prairie rattlesnake [although in] the absence of *C. viridis*, [the Mojave] inhabits both plains grassland and oak woodland communities.

The latter community includes the evergreen forested Davis Mountains, where the author has also found this species.

Prey   Little is reported, but the Mojave rattlesnake's prey probably consists primarily of rodents.

Reproduction   Live-bearing. One brood of *C. s. scutulatus* conceived, after copulation on October 2, at the Fort Worth Zoo, was born 9 months later on July 23.

Coloring/scale form   The distinctive scalation that occupies the top of its head conclusively distinguishes the Mojave rattler from the several other species it resembles. Between its supraocular plates—the big flat scales that cap its eyes—the mid-section of the Mojave rattlesnake's crown is capped with a double or triple row of enlarged, roughened scales. (It is from these unique scales, or scutes, that the Mojave receives both its Latin species and subspecies name, *scutulatus*.)

Crotalus scutulatus scutulatus is also unusual in that individuals living in different parts of its range differ not only in overall color—a common trait among snakes—but in pattern as well. In some areas, such as the Rio Grande's Black Gap region, the anterior part of the local Mojaves' back closely resembles that of the western diamond-backed rattlesnake (there is even speculation of hybridization with *Crotalus atrox*). These Mojaves' posterior backs, however, are patterned with brown dorsolateral crossbands that resemble the posterior back markings of the prairie rattlesnake.

In contrast, *C. s. scutulatus* from the Christmas Mountains area of southern Brewster County are well known for their paler, almost silvery ground color and white-edged dark dorsal markings, which are much more sharply defined than those of the diamond-back. (Unlike the vertebral diamonds of more easterly Mojave populations, these vertebral markings share the ovoid form of prairie rattlers' anterior dorsal blotches.)

A third variation is seen among Mojave rattlesnakes living on the dark rhyolitic substrate of Texas' Brewster and Ft. Davis counties. These animals characteristically display the diamond-shaped vertebral forebody patterning of their more easterly relatives, combined with much darker coloring. Their crowns are solid charcoal to chocolate (almost as dark as that of a black-tailed rattlesnake), while both their dorsal blotches and lateral stippling are a similar rich brown, but little of the pale edging that outlines the vertebral blotches in other populations is evident. Finally, some grassland-living mojaves show dusty greenish dorsolateral tones.

Among all these groups, narrow black and—usually—wider white bands encircle the tail, the pale venter may be darkly smudged along its edges, and the lower half of the basal rattle segment may have a yellowish hue. The diagonal white line bordering the rear of the Mojave

Mojave rattler

Western diamond-back rattler

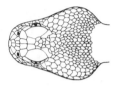

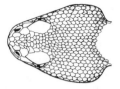

rattlesnake's brown ocular mask passes (again, like that of the prairie rattler) well above the posterior corner of its mouth.

Arranged in 25 rows at midbody, the dorsal scales are keeled, more than 2 of its internasal scales touch its rostral, and its anal plate is undivided.

Similar snakes   The very similar-looking **western diamond-backed rattlesnake (191)** is distinguished by the 4 or more rows of very small scales that cover its forecrown and by its more mottled, less cleanly defined vertebral diamonds. These fade posteriorly, but do not elongate into brown crossbands on the rear of its trunk as do those of the Mojave. The western diamond-back also has nearly equally wide black and white tail bands, and its upper postocular white line directly intersects the posterior corner of its mouth, although in the eastern part of the Mojave's range these differences become blurred.

The **prairie rattlesnake (193)** is unique in that more than 2 of its internasal scales touch its rostral scale. The center of its forecrown, unlike the Mojave's, is evenly covered with 4 or more rows of little scales, and along its spine its foreparts are patterned with rounded brown blotches, usually white-edged vertebral blotches or diamonds. **Rock rattlesnakes (195, 196)** have heavy dorsolateral speckling, irregular dark crossbands, and lack the Mojave rattler's characteristic row of enlarged mid-crown scales.

Behavior   In Texas, adult Mojave rattlesnakes are typically small but very hot-tempered. When mildly threatened, individuals may lower their heads, raise their tails, and slowly flick their rattles from side to side like a metronome—a particularly menacing gesture in light of their extremely toxic venom. Pressed further, *C. s. scutulatus* is, as cowhands put it, "a bitin' fool." Throughout its range, the author has seen angry but un-assaulted Mojaves strike out, over and over in quick succession, at thin air.

MOTTLED ROCK RATTLESNAKE

Crotalus lepidus lepidus

Venomous Because deep penetration is not necessary to kill its diminutive prey, *Crotalus lepidus* has very small fangs. According to L. M. Klauber (1956), these seldom measure more than ¼ inch across their curve. The rock rattlesnakes' venom, however, contains a high percentage of potent neurotoxic peptide components. Except for reptile fanciers and zoo personnel, there is little danger of being bitten by one of these little pitvipers, though, because rock rattlesnakes' inaccessible mountain and desert habitat, as well as their inclination to withdraw into crevices at the first vibration of human footsteps, make accidental encounters unlikely.

Abundance Uncommon. In areas of suitable habitat mottled rock rattlesnakes are thinly distributed over much of the southwestern quarter of Texas, but even in their favored Davis Mountain canyons these animals are not abundant.

Size The smallest of West Texas' rattlesnakes, *C. l. lepidus* averages under 2 feet in length; the record length is 32½ inches.

Habitat Mottled rock rattlesnakes occupy a great range of environments, but two quite different primary habitats prevail. In the northwestern part of its range this almost exclusively rock-dwelling animal inhabits igneous canyon ledges and bluffs and evergreen mountain woodland at altitudes above 4,500 feet. To the southeast, in a less exclusively saxicolous milieu, a population of much paler *C. l. lepidus* lives on the barren sandy mesas and within the shallow Cretaceous limestone canyons of Terrell, Crockett, and Val Verde counties.

Prey *Crotalus lepidus lepidus* evidently feeds primarily on lacertilian prey: there are reports of desert side-blotched, rusty, and spiny lizards taken in the wild. Smaller snakes, mice, and occasional amphibians are also probably eaten, as are large *Scolependra* centipedes.

One avergage-sized adult *C. l. lepidus* attacked these 9- or 10-inch-long chilopods just as it would a large rodent or lizard: striking 2 or 3 times in rapid sucession, then withdrawing into a defensive coil to

RATTLESNAKES

wait for its venom to take effect. After the *S. heros*—whose sizable fangs and the most toxic venom of any native centipede enable it to kill and feed on snakes nearly its own size (Easterla, 1975)— succumbed, it was swallowed headfirst like any other prey.

Reproduction   Live-bearing. Its small litters and probable alternate-year reproductive cycle mean that *Crotalus lepidus* has the same low fecundity—and therefore heightened vulnerability to human predation or disturbance—as northern pitvipers contending with short activity seasons. The 2 to 4 young are born in late summer or early autumn, 9 to 11 months after mating. The earliest account of parturition came from John Werler (1951):

> A 20.15-inch-long female [taken on] the Blackstone Ranch in Texas' Terrell County . . . gave birth to three young on July 21. The newborns averaged 8½ inches in length and differed from their pale, indistinctly banded parent in being more vividly colored, with dark gray crossbands. Food taken includes young rusty lizards . . . and newborn mice.

Another pair, from the Chinati Mountains in far southwestern Texas, bred early in October but, like other high-altitude, desert-living crotalids, did not produce young until the following September.

Coloring/scale form   *Crotalus lepidus lepidus* is folklore's celebrated "pink" and "little blue" rattlesnake. While not ever really blue (although certainly sometimes quite pink), by matching its background coloring the mottled rock rattlesnake's highly variable dorsal hues offer camouflage from both its lizard quarry and its similarly color-visioned avian predators. For example, mottled rock rattlesnakes from the Davis Mountains, where brownish-maroon granite is prevalent, have numerous dark primary blotches on a mottled, muddily russet—or, less often, pinkish buff—ground color. In contrast, *C. l. lepidus* living along the Rio Grande, as well as those from the Stockton and western Edwards Plateaus, live on pale limestone and have ground colors of chalk to faintly bluish gray. Their dark cross-dorsal bars occur mostly on the posterior body, where there is also considerable dark speckling.

Among all rock rattlesnakes the wedge-shaped head is much wider than the wiry neck and crowned with small scales. The slit-pupiled eyes are often masked by a dark stripe, there is a dark, heat-sensing pit posterior to the nostril, and 2 internasal scales touch the rostral. The 23 midbody rows of dorsal scales are keeled and the anal plate is undivided.

Similar snakes   Against a predominantly pale, un-speckled ground color, the **banded rock rattlesnake (196)** has distinctly defined, jagged-edged blackish crossbands throughout its length. Adult *C. l. klauberi* also usually lack a dark postocular stripe, and the rear of their crowns is likely to be marked with a pair of large brown spots absent in the mottled race. The **desert massasauga (187)** is a grassland serpent distinguished by its 9 large cephalic scale plates and the pair of brown stripes which band its crown. The **black-tailed rattlesnake (192)** has an entirely sooty black tail and dark vertebral pigmentation patched with jagged clumps of pale scales.

Behavior   Texas' rock rattlesnakes may be the only serpents easier to hear than to see: while walking across Davis Mountain talus slopes it is not unusual to hear these little reptiles buzzing their rattles from rocky niches beneath the shingles. Yet *Crotalus lepidus* may also have a characteristic curiosity, for in order to watch—and rattle at—an intruder, individuals will withdraw into crevices less deeply than they might for their own protection.

During spring and fall, as well as on overcast days, rock rattlesnakes engage in extensive diurnal foraging, especially after thunderstorms when individuals emerge onto the still-moist rocks. At these times *Crotalus lepidus* is more often abroad in early morning and around sunset, avoiding the midday heat by coiling (in the Guadalupe and Davis Mountain highlands) against tree trunks or, in the low desert of Val Verde and Terrell counties, under rock overhangs or low bushes. Although seemingly inactive at these times, these little pitvipers are fully alert and poised to strike any lizard that darts through their patch of shade.

196   BANDED ROCK RATTLESNAKE

Crotalus lepidus klauberi

Venomous   See **Mottled Rock Rattlesnake.**

Abundance   Uncommon. *Crotalus lepidus klauberi* is almost unknown as a pure race in Texas, for this predominantly Mexican subspecies' genetic influence occurs only in the state's most western county.

Size   See **Mottled Rock Rattlesnake.**

Habitat   The banded rock rattlesnake is named for Lawrence M. Klauber, chairman of the board of the San Diego Gas and Electric

Co. and author of the two-volume *Rattlesnakes: Their Habits, Life Histories, and Influence on Mankind*. For the most part, this small, usually inconspicuous reptile inhabits saxicolous montane terrain from 3,500 to over 7,000 ft. in elevation. In Texas its range includes the Franklin Mountains north of El Paso (where the male pictured here was found).

Prey   See **Mottled Rock Rattlesnake.**

Reproduction   Live-bearing. Among the *C. l. klauberi* observed in Chihuahua, Mexico, during September, Barry Armstrong and James Murphy (1979) note that courtship began as "the male directed rapid head bobs onto the dorsum of the female. Tongue-flicking occurred at the same speed."

Unlike most autumn-breeding snakes, which simply retain viable spermatozoa throughout the winter to permit springtime fertilization, female *Crotalus lepidus* evidently become gravid immediately after fall copulation and experience a true 9- to 10-month gestation period protracted by winter dormancy. First propagated in captivity in 1975 by Dave Barker of the Dallas Zoo, breeding pairs of banded rock rattlesnakes were initially only seasonally cooled to elicit the dormancy of their normal winter brumation.

But San Antonio Zoo Reptile Supervisor Jozsef Laszlo and Curator Alan Kardon found that, in addition to the mild chill of a simulated winter, *C. l. klauberi* fared better if kept year-round at temperatures—76 to 80°F during the day, 67 or 68°F at night—considerably cooler than those preferred by lowland serpents.

Yet at these temperatures, the reproductively delicate gravid females tended to either re-absorb their developing fetuses or give birth to malformed offspring. Finally, it was discovered that in addition to maintaining banded rock rattlers in a comparatively cool environment all year, a "winter" of up to 14 weeks at even lower temperature was desirable after a pair's autumn copulation—but only if the newly gravid female had access to an electrically heated "hot rock" on which to bask. This artificially warmed ceramic surface mimicked the radiated heat of the sun-warmed rocks and ledges of banded rock rattlesnakes' high-desert habitat, which pregnant females seek out on warm winter days. (The result of this temperature manipulation was regularly produced litters of healthy, 7½- to 8-inch-long neonates with bright yellow tail tips, most of which weighed just over ¼ ounce at birth.)

Coloring/scale form   In Texas, *C. l. klauberi* with silvery dorsums patterned solely by sawtooth-edged black crossbands have been just north of El Paso. An occasional male from Arizona has a beautiful pale green ground color (the "green rattler" of southwestern folklore is *C. l. klauberi*) while female banded rock rattlers from the same area are grayish—a type of sexual dimorphism known primarily from old-world snake species such as the European adders and African boomslangs.

Similar snakes   See **Mottled Rock Rattlesnake.**

Behavior   See **Mottled Rock Rattlesnake.**

GLOSSARY

adhesive-shelled eggs Eggs with a sticky surface that causes them to adhere in a cluster when laid (the shells soon dry out, but the eggs remain stuck together).

aestivation The hot-weather-induced dormancy of many reptiles and amphibians.

allopatric Having a separate or discrete range.

amelanistic Color phase almost entirely lacking black pigment.

amphiuma Large, eel-like aquatic salamander with small legs and no external gills.

anal plate Scale covering the cloacal vent.

anaphylaxis Antigen-antibody reaction caused by sensitivity to a foreign protein such as antivenin; capable in extreme cases of producing severe shock, respiratory impairment, coma, and death.

anchor coil The lowermost loop of the body of a coiled snake; this serves the animal as a foundation from which to strike.

anerythristic Color phase almost entirely lacking red pigment.

annelid Segmented worm or leech; most commonly the earthworm.

anterior Toward the head.

antibody A globulin produced in reaction to the introduction of a foreign protein.

antiserum The fluid portion of the blood of an animal previously infused with a reactive foreign protein.

antivenin Crystallized serum produced from the antibodies of animals infused with venom; able to partly neutralize venom's effects on the victim's tissue by blocking the toxic enzymes' access to their target cells.

Antivenin Index A compendium of antivenins is available in the United States (including those for non-indigenous snakes) from the Arizona Poison Center at the University of Arizona Medical School in Tucson. Antivenin for indigenous North American pitviper and coral snake venoms is produced by Wyeth Laboratories in Philadelphia.

anuran Frog or toad.

aposematic   Warning signal: sound, posture, coloration, etc.

arachnid   Eight-legged invertebrate: spiders, scorpions, mites, and ticks.

arthropod   Segmented invertebrate with jointed legs: insects, arachnids, and crustaceans.

azygous scale   A single scale (that is, not one of a bilateral pair).

belly line   The horizontal line of intersection between the venter, or belly, and the lower sides of the body.

brumation   The winter dormancy of reptiles and amphibians.

caudal   Pertaining to the tail.

cephalic   Pertaining to the head or crown.

chemoreception   The perception of chemical signals such as scent particles by the smell/taste mechanism of olfactory and veromonasal glands. See **Jacobson's organ.**

chin shields   The central scales on the underside of the lower jaw.

chthonic   Below or within the earth.

cloaca   Lower chamber of the digestive, urinary, and reproductive systems of birds, reptiles, and amphibians, which opens to the outside through the anus, or vent.

colubrid   A member of the largest worldwide family of snakes, *Colubridae*; most North American species are harmless.

compartment syndrome   The pressure of extreme edema, which after severe envenomation may rarely cut off blood flow to a limb, causing the death of its tissue. Some authorities believe this to be a cause of local necrosis that warrants surgical alleviation by fasciotomy; most maintain that necrosis is due almost exclusively to the enzymatic, digestive action of the venom itself.

congeneric   Within the same genus. (Species belonging to the same genus are congeneric.)

conspecific   Within the same species. (Subspecies, or races, of a single species are conspecific.)

corticosteroid   Steroid (often used to treat venom poisoning) which originates in the adrenal cortex and whose effects include the enhancement of protein replacement, the reduction of inflammation, and the suppression of the body's immune responses.

crepuscular   Active at dusk or dawn.

crossband   Among snakes, a pigmented strip running from side to side across the back.

crotalid   A pitviper; a member of the family *Viperidae*, subfamily *Crotalinae*. In the United States: rattlesnakes, cottonmouths, and copperheads.

cryotherapy   Treatment of an injury with cold. Dangerous when a snakebitten extremity is radically chilled, since this can cause tissue death. (A cold pack on the wound may slightly reduce pain; another on the forehead may help to offset the nausea that often accompanies pitviper poisoning.)

cryptic Serving to conceal or camouflage.

debridement The surgical removal of (venom-saturated) tissue.

depauperate Diminished in species-diversity.

dichromatism The presence of two or more color phases within a species or subspecies.

diel Daily or daytime.

disjunct Geographically separate.

distally Toward the periphery, or sides, of the body.

diurnal Active during the day.

DOR Initials of **Dead On Road**, an abbreviation for vehicle-slain wildlife: a rough but useful indicator of the presence of fauna in an area.

dorsal Pertaining to the back.

dorsolateral Pertaining to the back and sides, usually the entirety of the back and sides.

dorsum The back and upper sides.

Duvernoy's gland A gland that produces some of the venom of rear-fanged colubrid snakes; named for the French anatomist D. M. Duvernoy, who first described it.

ecdysis The shedding of a reptile's outer skin. See **exuviation**.

ecotone Transition zone between differing biological communities, such as the border between forest and meadow.

ectotherm Animal whose temperature is almost entirely determined by its environment.

edema Swelling of tissue due to the release of fluids (primarily from the vascular and lymphatic systems) into the interstitial tissue spaces.

elapid A rigidly front-fanged, venomous serpent of the family *Elapidae*, such as the coral snake. Elapids are characterized by a large proportion of neurotoxically active peptide venom fractions.

endemic Only found in a particular area.

endotherm Internally heat-regulating animal.

envenomation Infusion of venom.

enzyme Organic agent capable of producing the metabolic breakdown of tissue into its component proteins.

exuviation A shed: the sloughing of the entire outer covering, or *stratum corneum*, of a snake's body. This process first occurs soon after birth, then takes place every few weeks to months (more often if the snake has been injured; less often as the snake grows older) throughout the animal's annual foraging period. This process can occupy from ten minutes to several hours. Rattlesnakes add a new basal rattle segment with each exuviation; the terminal segments are periodically broken off.

fasciotomy Surgical incision into the fascial band enclosing a muscular compartment. This is usually done in an attempt to prevent tissue destruction from excessive hydraulic pressure caused by the fluid released by the venom's perforation of the capillary walls and pumped into the tissues by the heart. Fasciotomy is of questionable value except as an emergency measure to save a limb in immediate danger of general necrosis due to vascular constriction.

form Subspecies or race.

fossorial Adapted to burrowing; subterranean.

frontal scale(s) Scale(s) located on the crown, or top of the head between the eyes.

genotype Genetic makeup of an individual.

gravid Pregnant.

hemotoxic Destructive to blood, blood cells, or the vascular system.

hemipenis The bi-lobed, therefore Y-shaped, penis of serpents and lizards.

herpetoculture The breeding of reptiles in captivity.

hibernation Dormancy during winter.

holotype The specimen from which the description of a species or subspecies is derived.

hydric Well watered.

hydrophytic Plant life adapted to living in standing freshwater.

hypovolemic shock Due to a loss of fluid from the circulatory system. In snakebite, this occurs when the arteriole and venule walls are perforated by venom enzymes.

infralabial scales The scales which line the lower jaw.

indigenous Native to an area; not introduced.

infrared perception Apprehension of the infrared band of the light spectrum.

intergradation The gradual genetic alteration of one subspecies into another across a geographical continuum.

intergrade Intermediate individual or population which often exhibits some combination of the characteristics of two or more species or subspecies.

internasal scales Scales just posterior to the rostral scale on top of the snout, anterior to the prefrontals.

Jacobson's organ Double-sided sensory organ located in the roof of the mouth of serpents and some lizards into which the tips of their forked tongues are pressed. When a snake flicks it tongue, molecules that adhere to its sticky surface are carried into the mouth when the tongue returns to its sheath, then placed in ducts in the roof of the mouth. These ducts lead to veromonasal epithelia containing the chemosensory neurons which have evolved highly specific, inherited selective recognition of the chemical signature of appropriate prey species.

keel   Small longitudinal ridge creasing the centerline of a dorsal scale.

labial scales   Large scales lining the outer edges of the upper and lower jaws (**supralabial scales** line the upper jaw; **infralabial scales** line the lower jaw).

lacertilian   Pertaining to lizards.

lateral   Pertaining to the sides.

lecithotrophy   Yolk-nourished embryos.

leucistiphosis   The nourishment of embryos by means of an egg yolk.

leutic   Still, non-flowing water.

linear constriction   Pressing a prey animal against a stationary object such as the side of a burrow or rock crevice to immobilize it.

ligature   Binding a limb with a circulation-impairing band such as a tourniquet.

littoral   Pertaining to the margins of bodies of water; shoreline.

live-bearing   Reproduction by means of fully-formed young born in membranous sheaths which are immediately discarded.

loreal scale   Scale between the preocular and nasal scales.

lumen   Venom-generating and storing gland.

lysis   The breakdown or metabolism of cells or tissue by a peptide or enzyme.

matrotrophy   Nourishment of embryos by nutrient exchange from the mother's blood.

maxillary bones   Paired bones at the front of the upper jaw that in anterior-fanged venomous snakes carry the fangs. Among pitvipers the maxillary bones are able to rotate outward separately, swinging each fang tip forward independent of the other.

mesic   Moderately watered; moist.

midventral   The center of the belly.

milieu   Environment or habitat.

morph   Short for morphological; of variant appearance. For example, a color phase.

morphological   Pertaining to an animal's appearance (as opposed to its genetic makeup).

natricine   Large water snakes of the genus *Nerodia*.

nare   Reptilian nostril.

nasal scales   Scales through which the nostrils open.

necrosis   Death of bone or soft tissue.

neotenic   Retention of the juvenile form or coloring into adulthood.

non-indigenous   Not native to an area: therefore, introduced.

neurotoxic   Destructive primarily by impairing neuromuscular function. Among the most dangerous effects of ophidian neurotoxins is the blockage of acetylcholine receptor sites in the upper spinal ganglia.

nuchal   Pertaining to the neck.

ocular   Pertaining to the eye.

ocular scale   Scale covering the eye.

ontogenetic   A change in morphology due to aging.

ophidian   Pertaining to snakes.

ophiophagous   Feeding on snakes.

oviparous   Egg-bearing or laying: producing young by means of eggs that hatch outside the body.

oviposition   Egg-laying.

ovoviviparous   Live-bearing. Producing young by means of membranous eggs, whose membrane-encased embryos remain within the mother's body until hatching, at which time they are deposited as fully developed offspring.

paraphyletic   Genus or species-level groups of organisms which, due to significantly differing habits, morphology or physiology, now exist alongside their progenitors in slightly different niches.

parietal scales   Pair of large scales located on the rear of the crown.

parotid gland   Organ that secretes saliva in mammals and most of the venom in pitvipers and elapids.

parthenogensis   Reproduction by the development of an unfertilized egg.

phenotype   Physical characteristics of an organism.

pheromone   Primarily hormone-derived chemical substance released by an animal that influences the behavior of others of the same species. Ophidian pheromones include both general scents used for locating the retreats, hiding places, or microhabitat of other individuals of the same species and male-attracting scents excreted by breeding-condition females.

placentophosis   Nourishment of embryos by nutrient exchange from the mother's blood.

plate   Large scales covering the crown, or top of the head, as well as the venter, or belly.

polyvalent antivenin   An antivenin produced from a combination of anti-bodies and therefore useful against the venom of a genus or related group of venomous snakes. Wyeth's polyvalent antivenin is a single crystallized serum developed to treat the bites of all North American pitvipers: rattlesnakes, copperheads, and cottonmouths.

posterior   Toward the tail.

postocular scales   Scales bordering the posterior edge of the eye.

preocular scales   Scales bordering the anterior edge of the eye.

primary band   A snake's more distinct and complete dorsolateral cross-bands (as opposed to the irregular, broken markings which may occur between them).

proteinase   Proteolytic, or tissue-dissolving, enzyme.

proteolysis   Destruction of tissue due to the inability of venom-weakened cell walls to withstand their internal fluid pressures.

race   Subspecies.

range   The area thought to be the entire geographic distribution of an organism.

relict population   Contemporary remnant group of a species formerly found over a broader range.

riparian   The banks or bottomland along streams or rivers.

rostral scale   Scale covering the tip of the snout, frequently enlarged among burrowing species.

ruderal   Agricultural

saxicolous   Rock-living

scute   Scale plate.

scutellation   Scalation: the arrangement of scales.

serosanguinous   Swollen with blood.

sexual dimorphism   A morphological difference (in coloring, pattern, size, configuration, or other trait) according to gender.

siren   Large aquatic salamander shaped like an eel but possessing forelegs and external gills.

spermatogenesis   Generation of spermatozoa.

Squamata   The Order of Classification comprising snakes and lizards.

subcaudal scales   The scales lining the undersurface of the tail posterior to the cloacal opening.

subocular scales   Small scales separating the lower edge of the eye from the supralabial scales.

subspecies   A group or cluster of local populations that, to a significant degree, differs taxonomically from adjacent groups or clusters.

supralabial scales   The scales which line the upper jaw.

supraocular scales   The scales on the sides of the crown above the eyes.

sympatric   Overlapping or corresponding ranges; occurring in the same area.

syntopic   Overlapping or corresponding microhabitats; occurring in the same pond or beneath the same log.

temporal scales   Scales along the side of the head behind the postocular scale(s) and between the parietal scales and the supralabial scales.

terminal segment   Among *Sistrurus* and *Crotalus*, the last, or posterior-most, rattle segment. Because rattles break off periodically, there are rarely more than eight or ten segments in a series no matter how old the snake. See **exuviation**.

thermoregulation   Control of body temperature—usually by an ectotherm—by moving toward or away from warmer or cooler areas.

variant   Individual or population difference—most often in color or pattern—not judged to be of sufficient genetic magnitude to warrant recognition as a subspecies or race.

venom fractions   The approximately three dozen discrete toxic proteins—principally peptides and enzymes—that make up reptile venoms. Most of these fractions can be isolated from the venom mix by electrophoresis and dialysis.

vent   The posterior opening of the cloaca.

venter   The belly.

ventral   Pertaining to the belly.

ventral scales   The transversely elongate scale plates, or scutes, that line the underbody of most snakes.

ventrolateral   On the outer edge of the venter and the lower sides of the body.

vertebral   Along the spine.

vitellogenesis   Generation of ova.

viviparous   Live-bearing. Among snakes this means retaining the developing young (in their membranous egg-sacs) within the body cavity of the mother until their birth/hatching, which occur simultaneously.

vomeronasal organ   The primary chemical sense that snakes use to both orient themselves in their environment and to detect prey is vomerolfaction, which is the perception of scent particle carried into the mouth by the tongue, then placed in the vomeronasal, or Jacobson's organ, located in the roof of the mouth. See **Jacobson's organ**.

xeric   Arid.

BIBLIOGRAPHY

Abell, Joseph M. Jr., M.D. 1974. Snakebite: Current treatment concepts. *University of Michigan Medical Center Journal* 1 (40):29–31.

Abrahamson, W. G., and D. C. Hartnett. 1990. R. L. Myers and J. J. Ewell, eds. *Ecosystems of Florida*. Orlando: Central Florida University Press.

Aldridge, Robert D. 1992. Oviductal anatomy and seasonal sperm storage in the southeastern crowned snake (*Tantilla coronata*). *Copeia* (4):1103–1106.

Aldridge, Robert D. and Raymond D. Semlitsch. 1992. Female reproductive biology of the southeastern crowned snake (*Tantilla coronata*). *Amphibia-Reptilia* 13:209–218.

———. 1992. Male reproductive biology of the southeastern crowned snake (*Tantilla coronata*). *Amphibia-Reptilia* 13:219–225.

Adler, Kraig. 1979. *A Brief History of Herpetology in North America before 1900*. Society for the Study of Reptiles and Amphibians.

Allen, E. R., and W. T. Neill. 1950. The coral snake. *Florida Wildlife* 5 (5): 14–15.

———. 1953. The short-tailed snake. *Florida Wildlife* 6 (11):8–9.

Allen, Frederick M., M.D. 1938. Mechanical treatment of venomous bites and wounds. *Southern Medical Journal* 31 (12):1248–1253.

———. 1939. Observations on local measures in the treatment of snake bite. *American Journal of Tropical Medicine* 19:393–404.

Allen, William B. 1992. The snakes of Pennsylvania. Pottsville: *Reptile and Amphibian Magazine*.

Anderson, Paul K. 1961. Variation in populations of brown snakes, genus *Storeria*, bordering the Gulf of Mexico. *American Midland Naturalist* 66 (1):235–247.

Arnold, S. J. 1972. Species densities of predators and their prey. *American Naturalist* 106: 220–236.

Armstrong, Barry L., and James B. Murphy. 1979. *The Natural History of Mexican Rattlesnakes*. Lawrence: University of Kansas Press.

Ashton, Ray E., Jr., Stephen R. Edwards, and George R. Pisani. 1976. *Endangered and Threatened Amphibians and Reptiles in the United States*. Lawrence, Kansas: Society for the Study of Amphibians and Reptiles, Herpetological Circular no. 5.

Ashton, Ray E. Jr., and Patricia S. Ashton. 1988. *Handbook of Reptiles and Amphibians of Florida. Part 1: The Snakes.* Miami: Winward Publishing, Inc.

Assetto, R. Jr. 1978. Reproduction of the gray-banded kingsnake, *Lampropeltis mexicana alterna. Herpetelogical Review* 9 (2):56–57.

Auffenberg, W. 1955. A reconsideration of the racer, *Coluber constrictor,* in the eastern United States. *Tulane Zoological Studies* 2 (6):89–155.

———. 1963. The fossil snakes of Florida. *Tulane Zoological Studies* 10 (3): 131–216.

Axtell, R. W. 1951. An additional specimen of *Lampropeltis blairi* from Texas. *Copeia* (4):313, pl. 1.

———. 1959. Amphibians and reptiles of the Black Gap wildlife management area, Brewster County, Texas. *Southwestern Naturalist* 4 (2):88–109.

———. 1978. Ancient playas and their influence on the recent herpetofauna of the northern Chihuahuan Desert. In R. W. Wauer and D. H. Riskind, Transactions of the symposium on the biological resources of the Chihuahua Desert Region, United States and Mexico. National Park Service Trans. Proc. Ser., (3):493–512.

Baker, R. S., G. A. Mengden, and J. J. Bull. 1972. Karyotypic studies of thirty-eight species of North American snakes. *Copeia* 257–265.

Ballinger, R. E., and J. D. Lynch. 1983. *How to Know the Amphibians and Reptiles.* Dubuque, Iowa: William C. Brown Publishers.

———. 1981. Florida environments and their herpetofaunas. Part I: Environmental characteristics. Florida State Museum, Florida Herpetology no. 2.

Bartlett, Richard D. 1988. *In Search of Reptiles and Amphibians.* New York: E. J. Brill.

———. 1993. Herping Texas: The Guadalupe River and Langtry. Parts 1 and 2. *Notes from Noah* 20 (4):7–10.

———. 1999. *A Field Guide to Florida Reptiles and Amphibians.* Houston: Gulf Publishing.

———. 1999. *A Field Guide to Texas Reptiles and Amphibians.* Houston: Gulf Publishing.

———, and Alan Tennant. 2000. *Snakes of North America, Western Region.* Houston: Gulf Publishing.

Bechtel, Bernard H. 1978. Color and pattern in snakes. *Journal of Herpetology* (April 1978):521–532.

———. 1980. Geographic distribution of two color mutants of the corn snake, *Elaphe guttata guttata. Herpetelogical Review* 11 (2):30–40.

Bechtel, Bernard H., and E. Bechtel. 1989. Color mutations in the corn snake (*Elpahe guttata guttata*): Review and additional breeding data. *The Journal of Heredity* 80 (4):272–276.

———. 1995. *Reptile and Amphibian Variants: Colors, Patterns, and Scales.* Malabar, Florida: Krieger Publishing Company.

Behler, John L., and F. Wayne King. 1979. *The Audubon Society Field Guide to North American Reptiles and Amphibians.* New York: Alfred A. Knopf Inc.

Bellairs, Angus. 1970. *The Life of Reptiles.* 2 vols. New York: Universe Books.

Bellairs, Angus, and John Attridge. 1975. *Reptiles.* London: Hutchinson.

Bellairs, Angus, and C. B. Cox, eds. 1976. *Morphology and Biology of Reptiles.* London: Academic Press.

Bellairs, Angus, and Garth Underwood. 1951. The origin of snakes. *Biological Reviews of the Cambridge Philosophical Society* 26:193–237.

Bernardino, Jr., Frank S., and George H. Dalrymple. 1992. Seasonal activity and road mortality of the snakes of the Pa-hay-okee wetlands of Everglades National Park, USA. *Biological Conservation* 62: 71–75.

Blair, W. F. 1949. The biotic provinces of Texas. *Texas Journal of Science* 2 (1):93–117.

Blanchard, F. N. 1920. Three new snakes of the genus *Lampropeltis.* Occ. Papers Mus. Zool. Univ. Michigan (81):1–10.

———. 1920. A synopsis of the king snakes, genus *Lampropeltis* Fitzinger. Occ. Papers Mus. Zool. Univ. Michigan, (87):1–7.

———. 1921. A revision of the king snakes, genus *Lampropeltis.* Bulletin United States Natural Museum (114): 1–260.

———. 1924. The snakes of the genus *Virginia.* Papers of the Michigan Academy of Arts, Science, and Letters 3 (3):343–365.

———. 1936. Eggs and natural nests of the eastern ringneck snake, *Diadophis punctatus edwardsii.* Papers of the Michigan Academy of Science, Arts, and Letters 22:521–532.

———. 1937. Data on the natural history of the red-bellied snake, *Storeria occipitomaculata,* in Northern Michigan. *Copeia* 151–162.

———. 1938. Snakes of the genus *Tantilla* in the United States. Field Museum of Natural History (Zoology) 20 (28):369–376.

———. 1942. The ring-neck snakes, genus *Diadophis.* Bulletin of the Chicago Academy of Science 7 (1):1–142.

Blaney, R. M. 1971. An annotated checklist and biogeographic analysis of the insular herpetofauna of the Apalachicola Region, Florida. *Herpetologica* 27:406–430.

———. 1977. Systematics of the common kingsnake, *Lampropeltis getulus* (Linnaeus). *Tulane Stud. Zool. Bot.* 19 (3–4):47–103.

Blem, Charles R., and Leann B. Blem. 1990. Lipid reserves of the brown water snake (*Nerodia taxispilota*). *Comparative Biochemistry and Physiology* 97A (3):367–372.

Bloom, F. E. 1981. Neuropeptides. *Scientific American* 245 (October 1981):148–168.

Bogert, C. M. 1949. Thermoregulation in reptiles, a factor in evolution. *Evolution* 3:195–211.

Bogert, C. M., and V. D. Roth. 1966. Ritualistic combat of male gopher snakes, *Pituophis melanoleucus affinis*. *American Museum Novitiates* 2245:1–27.

Bonilla, C. A., and M. K. Fiero. 1971. Comparative biochemistry and pharmacology of salivary gland secretions. II: Chromatographic separation of the basic proteins from North American rattlesnake venoms. *Journal of Chromatography* 56:253.

Boulenger, G. A. 1973. *Contributions to American herpetology: Collected papers*. Facsimile Reprints (Index 1977). New York: Society for the Study of Amphibians and Reptiles.

Bowler, J. Kevin. 1977. Longevity of reptiles and amphibians in North American collections. New York: Society for the Study of Amphibians and Reptiles, Herpetological Circular no. 6.

Boxall, J. 1982. Pressure/immobilization first aid treatment of snake bite. *Medical Journal of Australia* 1:155.

Bragg, A. N. 1960. Is *Heterodon* venomous? *Herpetologica* 16:121–123.

Braswell, A. L., and W. M. Palmer. 1984. *Cemophora coccinea copei*. *Herpetological Review* 15 (2):49.

Brattstrom, B. H. 1955. The coral snake "mimic" problem and protective coloration. *Evolution* 9:217–219.

———. 1964. Evolution of the pit vipers. Transactions of the San Diego Society of Natural History 13:185–265.

———. 1965. Body temperature of reptiles. *American Midland Naturalist*. 376–422.

Brinton, D. G. 1968. *Myths of the New World*. 3rd ed. New York: Haskell House.

Brisbin, I. L., and C. Bagshaw. 1993. Survival, weight changes, and shedding frequencies of captive scarlet snakes, *Cemophora coccinea*, maintained on an artificial liquid diet. *Herpetological Review* 24 (1):27–29.

Brodie, E. D. III, and Peter K. Ducey. 1989. Allocation of reproductive investment in the redbelly snake *Storeria occipitomaculata*. *The American Midland Naturalist* 122(1):51–58.

———. 1993. Differential avoidance of coral snake banded patterns by free-rangingavian predators in Costa Rica. *Evolution* 47:227–235.

Brodie, E. D. III, A. J. Moore, and F. J. Janzen. 1995. Visualizing and quantifying natural selection. *Trends in Ecology & Evolution* 10:313–318.

Brown, A. E. 1901. A new species of *Ophibolus* from western Texas. Proceedings of the Academy of Natural Science, Philadelphia, 53:612–613, pl. 34.

Brown, B. C. 1950. An annotated check list of the reptiles and amphibians of Texas. Waco, Tex: Baylor University Studies.

Brown, William S. 1993. Biology, status, and management of the timber rattlesnake (*Crotalus horridus*): A guide for conservation. SSAR Herpetological Circular no. 22, 1–78.

Burden, S. J., H. C. Hartzell, and D. Yoshikami. 1975. Acetylcholine receptors at neuromuscular synapses: Phylogenetic differences detected by snake a-neurotoxins. Proc. Nat. Acad. Sci. USA 72:3245–3249.

Burger, Joanna, R. T. Zappalorti, J. Dowell, Tino Georgiadia, Jacques Hill, and Michael Gochfeld. 1992. Subterranean predation on pine snakes (*Pituophis melanoleucus*). *Journal of Herpetology* 26(3):259–263.

Burghardt, G. M. 1970. Chemical perception in reptiles. In: J. W. Johnson, Jr., D. G. Moulton, and A. Turk, eds. *Advances in Chemoreception Communication by Chemical Signals*, 241–308. New York: Appleton-Century-Crofts.

Burkett, Ray O. 1966. Natural history of the cottonmouth moccasin, *Agkistrodon piscivorus*. Univeristy of Kansas. Publications of the Museum of Natural History 17 (9):435–491.

Butler, Joseph A., Todd W. Hull, and Richard Franz. 1995. Neonate aggregations and maternal attendance of young in the eastern diamondback rattlesnake, *Crotalus adamanteus*. *Copeia* (1):196–198.

Calhoun, G. 1995. The gray-banded kingsnake. *The Forked Tongue* 20 (7–8):5.

Campbell, H. W., and S. P. Christman. 1982. The herpetofaunal components of Florida sandhill and sand pine scrub associations. N. J. Scott, Jr., ed. Herpetological Communities. U.S. Fish and Wildlife Service, Wildlife Resources Report no. 13.

Campbell, Jonathan A., and Edmund D. Brodie Jr., eds. 1992. *Biology of the Pitvipers*. Tyler, Texas: Selva.

Carmichael, Pete, and Winston Williams. 1991. *Florida's Fabulous Reptiles and Amphibians*. Florida: World Publications.

Carpenter, Charles C. 1979. A combat ritual between two male pigmy rattlesnakes (*Sistrurus miliarius*). *Copeia* (4):638–642.

Carr, Archie F. 1940. A contribution to the herpetology of Florida. University of Florida Publications, Biol. Ser. 3(1).

———. 1963. *The Reptiles*. Life Nature Library. New York: Time-Life.

Carr, Archie F., and C. J. Goin. 1959. *Guide to the Reptiles, Amphibians and Freshwater Fishes of Florida*. Gainesville: University of Florida Press.

Chenowith, W. L. 1948. Birth and behavior of young copperheads. *Herpetologica* 4:162.

Chiszar, David, Charles W. Radcliffe, and Roy Overstreet. 1985. Duration of strike-induced chemosensory searching in cottonmouths (*Agkistrodon piscivorous*), and a test of the hypothesis that striking prey creates a specific search image. *Canadian Journal of Herpetology* 63:1057–1061.

Christman, S. P. 1980. Patterns of Geographic Variation in Florida Snakes. Bull. Fla. Sta. Mus. 25 (3):157–256.

———. 1988. Endemisn in Florida's interior sand pine scrub. Florida Game and Fresh Water Fish Commission, Nongame Wildlife Program Final Report.

Clark, Donald R. 1974. The western ribbon snake (*Thamnophis proximus*): Ecology of a Texas population. *Herpetologica* 30:372–379.

Clark, Donald R., and Robert R. Fleet. 1976. The rough earth snake (*Virginia striatula*): ecology of a Texas population. *Southwestern Naturalist* 20 (4):467–478.

Clausen, H. J. 1936. Observations on the brown snake, *Storeria dekayi*, with especial reference to habits and birth of young. *Copeia* 1936: 98–102.

Cloudsley-Thompson, J. L. 1971. *The Temperature and Water Relations of Reptiles*. London: Merrow Publishing.

Cohen, P., W. H. Berkley, and E. B. Seligmann Jr. 1971. Coral snake venoms: In vitro relation of neutralizing and precipatating antibodies. *American Journal of Tropical Medical Hygiene*. 20:646–649.

Cohen, Wayne R., Warren Wetzel, and Anna Kadish. 1992. Local heat and cold application after eastern cottonmouth moccasin (*Agkistrodon piscivorus*) envenomation in the rat: Effect on tissue injury. *Toxicon* 30 (11):1383–1386.

Cole, Charles J., and Lawrence M. Hardy. 1981. Systematics of North American Colubrids Related to *Tantilla planiceps* (Blaineville). Bulletin of the American Museum of Natural History, vol. 171 (3): 201–284, New York.

Collins, Joseph T. 1990. *Standard Common and Current Scientific Names for North American Amphibians and Reptiles*. 3rd ed. Lawrence: University of Kansas, Museum of Natural History.

———. 1993. *Amphibians and Reptiles in Kansas*. 3rd. ed. Lawrence: University of Kansas, Museum of Natural History.

Collins, Joseph T., and Suzanne L. Collins. 1993. Reptiles and Amphibians of Cheyenne Bottoms. U.S. Fish and Wildlife Service.

Conant, Roger, and Clay W. Conant. 1937. A new subspecies of waternsake from the islands in Lake Erie. Occasional papers of the University of Michigan Musem of Zoology 346:1–9.

———, and A. Downs Jr. 1940. Miscellaneous notes on the eggs and young of reptiles. *Zoologica* 25:33–48.

———. 1956. A review of two rare pine snakes from the Gulf coastal plain. *American Museum Novitiates* 1781:17–21.

——. 1963. A reassessment of the taxonomic status of the Lake Erie water snake. *Herpetologica* 19:179–184.

——, 1975. *A Field Guide to Amphibians and Reptiles of Eastern and Central North America.* 2nd ed. Boston: Houghton Mifflin Co.

——, and J. T. Collins. 1991. *A Field Guide to Amphibians and Reptiles of Eastern and Central North America.* 3rd ed. Boston: Houghton Mifflin Co.

——, and J. T. Collins. 1998. *A Field Guide to Amphibians and Reptiles of Eastern and Central North America.* 3rd ed., expanded. Boston: Houghton Mifflin Co.

Cook, D. G., and F. J. Aldridge. 1984. *Coluber constrictor priapus. Herpetological Review* 15 (2):49.

Cook, F. R. 1964. Communal egg laying in the smooth green snake. *Herpetologica* 20:206.

Cooper, William E. Jr., Donald G. Buth, and Laurie J. Vitt. 1990. Prey odor discrimination by injestively naive coachwhip snakes (*Masticophis flagellum*). *Chemoecology* 1:86–89.

Coote, J. 1978. Spotlight on a Species: The Gray-banded Kingsnake (*Lampropeltis mexicana alterna*). *Herptile* 3 (2):6–7.

Coote, J., and R. J. Riches. 1978. Captive Reproduction in North American Colubrids of the Genera *Lampropeltis* and *Elaphe*. Rep. Cotswold Herp. Symposium. 6–15.

Coulter, A. R., J. C. Cox, S. K. Sutherland, and C. J. Waddell. 1978. A new solid-phase sandwich radioimmunoassay and its application to the detection of snake venom. *Journal of Immunological Methodology* 23: 241–252.

Cowles, R. B., and R. L. Phelan. 1958. Olfaction in rattlesnakes. *Copeia*: 77–83.

Craighead, F. C. 1974. *Hammocks of South Florida.* Gleason, P. J., ed. Environments of South Florida: present and past II. Miami Geol. Soc. Mem. no. 2, Coral Gables, Fla.

Crews, David, and William R. Gartska. 1982. The ecological physiology of a garter snake. *Scientific American* 247 (5):158–168.

Cunningham, E. R., et al. 1979. Snakebite: role of corticosteroids as immediate therapy in an animal model. *American Surgery* 45 (12):757–759.

Curtis, Lawrence. 1949. The snakes of Dallas County, Texas. *Field and Laboratory* 17 (1):1–13.

——. 1952. Cannibalism in the Texas coral snake. *Herpetologica* 8:27.

Curtis, Lawrence., T. M. Steiner, R. Nodell and F. S. Bernardino Jr. 1992. Seasonal activity of the snakes of Long Pine Key, Everglades National Park. *Copeia* 1991: 294–302.

Dalrymple, G. H., F. S. Bernardino Jr., T. M. Steiner, and R. J. Nodell. 1991. Patterns of species diversity of snake community assemblages, with data on two Everglades snake assemblages. *Copeia* 1991: 517–521.

Danzig, L. E., and G. H. Abels. 1961. Hemodialysis of acute renal failure following rattlesnake bite, with recovery. *Journal of the American Medical Association* 175: 136.

Degenhardt, William G., and G. E. Steele. 1957. Additional specimens of *Trimorphodon vilkinsonii* from Texas. *Copeia* 1957: 309–310.

——, Charles W. Painter, and Andrew H. Price. 1996. *Amphibians and Reptiles of New Mexico*. Albuquerque: University of New Mexico Press, 1–431.

DeGraaf, Richard M, and Deborah D. Rudis. 1983. *Amphibians and Reptiles of New England*. Amherst: University of Massachusetts Press.

Ditmars, R. L. 1936. *The Reptiles of North America*. Garden City, N.Y.: Doubleday and Co., Inc.

Dixon, J. R. 1987. *Amphibians and Reptiles of Texas: With Keys, Taxonomic Synopses, Bibliography, and Distribution Maps*. College Station: Texas A & M University Press, 1–434.

Dodd, C. K. Jr. 1992. Biological diversity of a temporary pond herpetofauna in north Florida sandhills. *Biodiversity and Conservation* 1:125–142.

——. 1993. Population structure, body mass, activity, and orientation of an aquatic snake (*Seminatrix pygaea*) during a drought. Can. J. Zool. 71:1281–1288.

Dodd, C. K. Jr., and B. G. Charest. 1988. The herpetofaunal community of temporary ponds in north Florida sandhills: Species composition, temporal use, and management implications. Pp. 87–97 in R. C. Szaro et al., tech. coords. Proc. Symp. Manage. Ambhibs., Reptiles, and Small Mammals in N. Am. USDA For. Serv. Gen. Tech. Rep. RM-166.

Donald, J. A., and J. E. O'Shea. 1990. Neural regulation of the pulmonary vasculature in a semi-arboreal snake, *Elaphe obsoleta*. *Journal of Comparative Physiology* B. 159:677–685.

Dowling, H. G. 1950. Studies of the black swamp snake, *Seminatrix pygaea* (Cope), with descriptions of two new subspecies. Museum of Zoology, University of Michigan miscellaneous publication no. 76.

——. 1951. A proposed standard system of counting ventrals in snakes. *Bri. J. Herpetol.* 1:97–99.

——, and Linda R. Maxon. 1990. Genetic and taxonomic relations of the short-tailed snakes, genus *Stilosoma*. *Journal of Zoology* 221:77–85.

——, and R. M. Price. 1988. *Journal, "snake"* 20:52, 53.

Drummond, H. 1983 Aquatic foraging in garter snakes: A comparison of specialists and generalists. *Behaviour* 86:1–30.

———. 1985. The role of vision in the predatory behavior of natricine snakes. *Animal Behavior* 33:206–215.

Duellman, W. E., and A. Schwartz. 1958. Amphibians and reptiles of southern Florida. Bulletin of Florida State, Museum of Biological Sciences 3:181–324.

Dundee, Harold A., and M. Clinton Miller III. 1968. Aggregative behavior and habitat conditioning by the prairie ringneck snake, *Diadophis punctatus arnyi*. *Tulane Studies in Zoology and Botany* 15 (2):41–58.

———, and Douglas A. Rossman. 1989. *The Amphibians and Reptiles of Louisiana*. Baton Rouge: Louisiana State University Press.

Dunn, E. R. 1954. The coral snake mimic problem. *Evolution* 2: 97–102.

Dyrkacz, S. 1982. Striped pattern morphism in the prairie kingsnake, *Lampropeltis c. calligaster*. *Herpetological Review* 13(3): 70–71.

Easterla, David A. 1975. Giant desert centipede preys upon snake. *Southwestern Naturalist* 20: 41.

Edgren, Richard A. 1948. Notes on a litter of young timber rattlesnakes. *Copeia* 1948: 132.

———. 1952. A synopsis of the snakes of the genus *Heterodon*, with the diagnosis of a new race of *Heterodon nasicus*. Chicago Academy of Sciences, Natural History Miscellanies, no. 112.

———. 1955. The natural history of the hognosed snakes, genus *Heterodon*: A review. *Herpetologica* 11: 105–117.

———. 1957. Melanism in hog-nosed snakes. *Herpetologica* 13: 131–135.

Eichholz, M. W., and W. D. Koenig. 1992. Gopher snake attraction to birds' nests. *The Southwestern Naturalist* 37 (3): 293–298.

Ernst, Carl H., and Roger W. Barbor. 1989. *Snakes of Eastern North America*. Fairfax, Va.: George Mason University.

Emery, J. A., and F. E. Russell. 1961. Studies with cooling measures following injection of *Crotalus* venom. *Copeia* 1961: 322–326.

Enge, Kevin M. 1991. Herptile exploitation: Annual performance report. Florida Game and Freshwater Fish Commission, Tallahassee.

———. 1992. The basics of snake hunting in Florida. *Florida Wildlife* 46(1): 2–8.

———. 1993. Herptile use and trade in Florida. Florida Game and Fresh Water Fish Commission, Nongame Wildlife Program final performance report, Tallahassee.

———. 1996. Habitat occurrence of Florida's amphibians and reptiles. Technical report. Nongame wildlife program. Florida Game and Fresh Water Fish Commission, Tallahassee.

Ernst, Carl H., and Roger W. Barbor. 1989. *Snakes of Eastern North America*. Fairfax, Va.: George Mason University Press.

———. 1992. *Venomous Reptiles of North America*. Washington, D.C.: Smithsonian Institution Press.

Etheridge, R. E. 1950. Color Variants in Snakes from the Southeastern United States. *Copeia* (4):321.

Farrell, Terrence M., Peter G. May, and Melissa A. Pilgrim. 1995. Reproduction in the rattlesnake, *Sistrurus miliarius barbouri*, in central Florida. *Journal of Herpetology* 29 (1):21–27.

Fearn, H. J., C. Smith, and G. B. West. 1964. Capillary permeability responses to snake venom. *Journal of Pharmaceutical Pharmacology* 16: 79–84.

Fischer, F. J., H. W. Ramsey, J. Simon, and J. F. Gennaro Jr. 1961. Antivenin and antitoxin in treatment of experimental rattlesnake venom intoxication (*Crotalus adamanteus*). *American Journal of Tropical Medicine* 10: 75–79.

Fitch, Henry S. 1960. Autecology of the copperhead. University of Kansas Museum of Natural History Publication, 3 (4): 85–288.

———. 1963. Natural history of the racer *Coluber constrictor*. University of Kansas Museum of Natural History Publication 5 (8): 351–468.

———. 1970. Reproductive cycles of lizards and snakes. University of Kansas Museum of Natural History Miscellaneous Publication 42: 1–247.

Fitch, Henry S., and H. W. Shirer. 1971. Radio telemetry studies of spatial relations in some common snakes. *Copeia* 1: 118–128.

———. 1975. A demographic study of the ringneck snake (*Diadophis punctatus*) in Kansas. University of Kansas Museum of Natural History Miscellaneous Publication no. 62.

———. 1982. Resources of a snake community in prairie-woodland habitat of northeastern Kansas. N. J. Scott Jr., ed. Herpetological communities. U.S. Fish and Wildlife Service, Wildlife Resources Report no. 13.

———. 1985. Variation in clutch and litter size in New World reptiles. University of Kansas Museum of Natural History Miscellaneous Publication no. 76.

———, and R. R. Fleet. 1970. Natural history of the milk snake *Lampropeltis triangulum* in north-eastern Kansas. *Herpetologica* 26: 387–395.

Florida Natural Areas Inventory. 1990. Guide to the natural communities of Florida. Florida Department of Natural Resources, Tallahassee.

Foley, George W. 1971. Perennial communal nesting in the black racer (*Coluber constrictor*). *Herpetological Review* 3: 41.

Ford, Neil B. 1978. Evidence for species specificity of pheromone trails in two sympatric garter snakes. *Herpetological Review* 9: 10.

———. 1979. Aspects of pheromone trailing in garter snakes. Ph.D. dissertation, Miami University (Ohio).

———. 1981. Seasonality of pheromone trailing in two species of garter snakes. *Southwestern Naturalist* 26 (4): 385–388.

Flury, A. 1950. A New Kingsnake from Trans-Pecos, Texas. *Copeia* (3): 215–217.

Foley, George W. 1971. Perennial communal nesting in the black racer (*Coluber constrictor*). *Herpetological Review* 3: 41.

Force, Edith R. 1935. A local study of the opisthoglyph snake *Tantilla gracilis*. Papers of the Michigan Academy of Arts and Letters 20: 645–659.

Ford, Neil B. 1979. Aspects of pheromone trailing in garter snakes. Ph.D. dissertation, Miami University (Ohio).

———. 1981. Seasonality of pheromone trailing in two species of garter snakes. *Southwestern Naturalist* 26 (4): 385–388.

Fox, W., and H. C. Dessauer. 1962. The single right oviduct and other urogenital structures of female *Typhlops* and *Leptotyphlops*. *Copeia* 1962: 590–597.

Frank, Norman, and Erica Ramus. 1996. *A Complete Guide to Scientific and Common Names of Reptiles and Amphibians of the World*. Pottsville, Pa.: N. G. Publishing.

Franz, R., C. K. Dodd Jr., and A. M. Bard. 1992. The non-marine herpetofauna of Egmont Key, Hillsborough County, Florida. *Florida Scient.* 53(3): 179–183.

Frazer, James G. 1892. *The Golden Bough*. New York: Macmillan.

Funderburg, J. B., and D. S. Lee. 1968. The amphibian and reptile fauna of pocket gopher (*Geomys*) mounds in central Florida. *Journal of Herpetology* 1: 99–100.

Gamow, R. I., and John F. Harris. 1973. The infrared receptors of snakes. *Scientific American* 228 (5): 94–102.

Gans, Carl. 1970. How snakes move. *Scientific American* 222 (6): 82–96.

Gans, Carl., T. Krakauer, and C. V. Paganelli. 1968. Water loss in snakes: interspecific and intraspecific variability. *Comparative Biochemical Physiology* 27: 757–761.

———, and F. Billet, eds. 1970–present. *Biology of the Reptilia*. New York: John Wiley & Sons.

Garfin, S. R., et al. 1979. Role of surgical decompression in the treatment of rattlesnake bites. *Surgical Forum* 30: 502–504.

Garton, S. G., E. W. Harris, and R. A. Brandon. 1970. Descriptive and ecological notes on *Natrix cyclopion* in Illinois. *Herpetologica* 26: 454–461.

Garstka, W. R. 1982. Systematics of the *mexicana* species group of the colubrid genus *Lampropeltis*, with an hypothesis of mimicry. Breviora, Mus. Compl. Zool. (466): 1–35.

Gehlbach, Frederick. R. 1967. *Lampropeltis mexicana*. Cat. Amer. Amphib. Rept.: 55.1–55.2.

Gehlbach, Frederick. R., and J. K. Baker. 1962. Kingsnakes allied with *Lampropeltis Mexicana*: Taxonomy and natural history. *Copeia* (2):291–300.

———, and C. J. McCoy Jr. 1965. Additional observations on variation and distribution of the gray-banded kingsnake, *Lampropeltis Mexicana* (Garman). *Herpetologica* 21 (1):35–38.

———. 1970. Death-feigning and erratic behavior in leptotyphlopid, colubrid, and elapid snakes. *Herpetologica* 26: 24–34.

———, Julian F. Watkins II, and James C. Kroll. 1971. Pheromone trail-following studies of typhlopid, leptotyphlopid, and colubrid snakes. *Behavior* 40 (pts. 3–5): 282–294.

———. 1972. Coral snake mimicry reconsidered: The strategy of self-mimicry. *Forma et Functio* 5: 311–320.

———. 1981. *Mountain Islands and Desert Seas: A Natural History of the U.S.-Mexican Borderland.* College Station: Texas A & M University Press.

Geiser, S. W. 1948. *Naturalists of the Frontier.* Dallas: Southern Methodist University Press.

Gill, K. A. Jr. 1970. The evaluation of cryotherapy in the treatment of snake envenomation. *Southern Medical Journal* 63: 552–556.

Gillingham, J. C. 1976. Reproductive behavior of the rat snakes of eastern North America, *Elaphe. Copeia* 1979: 319–331.

———. 1976. Early egg deposition by the southern black racer, *Coluber constrictor priapus. Herpetological Review* 7(3): 115.

Gingrich, W. C., and J. C. Hohenadel. 1956. Standardization of polyvalent antivenin. In E. E. Buckley and N. Proges, eds., *Venoms*, 381–385. American Association of Advanced Science, Washington, D.C.

Githens, T. S., and N. O'C. Wolff. 1939. The polyvalency of crotalid antivenins. III. Mice as test animals for study of antivenins. *Journal of Immunology* 37:47–51.

Glass, Thomas G. Jr. 1969. Cortisone and immediate fasciotomy in the treatment of severe rattlesnake bite. *Texas Medicine* 65:41.

———. 1976. Early debridement in pit viper bites. *Journal of the American Medical Association* 235:2513.

Glenn, James L., and Richard C. Straight. 1977. The midget faded rattlesnake (*Crotalus viridis concolor*) venom: Lethal toxicity and individual variability. *Toxicon* 15:129–133.

——— and ———. 1978. Mojave rattlesnake *Crotalus scutulatus scutulatus* venom: Variation in toxicity with geographic origin. *Toxicon* 16:81–84.

——— and ———. 1982. *Rattlesnake Venoms: Their Action and Treatment.* New York: Marcel Dekker.

Gloyd, Howard K., and Roger Conant. 1934. Taxonomic status, range, and natural history of Schott's racer. Occasional papers of the Museum of Zoology, University of Michigan, 1–17.

Gloyd, Howard Kay. 1940. *The rattlesnakes, genera sistrurus and crotalus.* Chicago Academy of Science special publication 4:1–266.

———. 1944. Texas Snakes. *Texas Geogr.*, 8:1–18.

Gloyd, Howard Kay, and Roger Conant. 1990. *Snakes of the Agkistrodon Complex*. Oxford, Ohio: Society for the Study of Amphibians and Reptiles.

Godley, J. S. 1980. Foraging ecology of the striped swamp snake, *Regina alleni*, in southern Florida. *Ecological Monographs* 50: 411–436.

———. 1982. Predation and defensive behavior of the striped swamp snake (*Regina alleni*). *Florida Field Naturalist* 10 (2):31–36.

Goin, C. J. 1943. The lower vertebrate fauna of the water hyacinth community in Northern Florida. *G. Proc. Fla. Acad. Sci.* 6 (34):143–153.

Goldstein, R. C. 1941. Notes on the mud snake in Florida. *Copeia* 1941: 49–50.

Gotch, A. F. 1996. *A Guide to the Scientific Classification of Reptiles, Birds, and Mammals*. New York: Baker & Taylor, Brodart.

Green, N. Bayard, and Thomas K. Pauley. 1987. *Amphibians and Reptiles in West Virginia*. Pittsburgh: University of Pittsburgh Press.

Greene, Harry W. 1973. The food habitats and breeding behavior of New World coral snakes. Master's thesis, University of Texas at Arlington.

———, and Roy W. McDiarmid. 1981. Coral snake mimicry: Does it occur? *Science* 213: 1207–1212.

———. 1992. The ecological and behavioral context for pitviper evolution. In *Biology of the Pitvipers*. J. A. Campbell and E. D. Brodie Jr., eds. Tyler, Tex.: Selva.

———. 1997. *Snakes: The Evolution of Mystery in Nature*. Berkeley: the University of California Press.

Grobman, Arnold B. 1978. An alternative solution to the coral snake mimic problem. *Journal of Herpetology* 12 (1): 1–11.

Groves, F. 1960. The eggs and young of *Drymarchon corais couperi*. *Copeia* 1960: 51–53.

———, and R. J. Assetto. 1976. *Lampropeltis triangulum elapsoides*. *Herpetological Review* 7(3): 115.

Grudzien, Thaddeus A., and Paul J. Owens. 1991. Genic similarity in the gray and brown color morphs of the snake *Storeria occipitomaculata*. *Journal of Herpetology* 25(1): 90–92.

Haast, William E., and Robert Anderson. 1981. *Complete Guide to Snakes of Florida*. Miami: Phoenix Publishing.

Hahn, D. E., T. E. Megers, and J. W. Goetz. 1972. The status of *Elaphe guttata* (Serpentes: Colubridae) in central and northwestern Louisiana. *Southwestern Naturalist* 17 (2): 208–209.

Hakkila, M. 1994. An assessment of potential habitat and distribution of the gray-banded kingsnake (*Lampropeltis alterna*) in New Mexico. Unpubl. Rept. submitted to NM Dept. Gam & Fish., Santa Fe, N.M. 12 pp. + 3 maps.

Hall, H. P., and J. F. Gennaro. 1961. The relative toxicities of rattlesnake (*Crotalus adamanteus*) and cottonmouth (*Agkistrodon piscivorous*) venom for mice and frogs. *Anat. Rec.* 139:305–306.

Hall, P. M. 1993. Reproduction and behavior of western mud snakes (*Farancia abacura reinwardtii*) in American alligator nests. *Copeia* 1:210–222.

Haller, R. 1971. The diamondback rattlesnakes. *Journal of Herpetology* 5 (3):141–146.

Hamilton, W. J. Jr., and J. A. Pollack. 1955. The food of some crotalid snakes from Fort Benning. Georgia Natural History Miscellanies, no. 140.

Hammerson, Geoffrey A. 1986, second printing. *Amphibians and Reptiles in Colorado*. Colorado Division of Wildlife Publ. no. DOW-M-I-3-86.

Harding, James H. 1997. *Amphibians and Reptiles of the Great Lakes Region*. Ann Arbor: University of Michigan Press.

Hardy, David L. 1981. *Rattlesnake Envenomation in Southern Arizona*. Tuscon: Arizona Poison Control System, University of Arizona Health Sciences Center.

———. 1982. Overview of rattlesnake bite treatment. Address given November 5–6, 1982, at the Second Annual Southwestern Poison Symposium, Scottsdale, Arizona.

Harvey, Alan L. 1991. *Snake Toxins*. New York: Elsevier Science Publications.

Hawthorne, K. 1972. Rat snakes: Genus *Elaphe*. *Herpetologica* 9:11–16.

Heatwole, H. 1977. Habitat selection in reptiles. In C. Gans and D. W. Tinkle, eds., *Biology of the Reptilia*, vol. 7, 137–155. New York: Academic Press.

Heckman, C. W. 1960. Melanism in Storeria dekayi. *Herpetologica* 16:213.

Hellman, R. E., and S. R. Telford Jr. 1956. Notes on a large number of red-bellied mudsnakes, *Farancia a. abacura*, from northcentral Florida. *Copeia* 1956:257–258.

Hillis, David M., and Stephen L Campbell. 1982. New localities for *Tantilla rubra cucullata* (Colubridae) and the distribution of its two morphotypes. *Southwestern Naturalist* 27 (2):220–221.

Holman, J. A. 1962. A Texas Pleistocene herpetofauna. *Copeia* 1962: 255–162.

Holman, J. A., and W. H. Hill. 1961. A mass unidirectional movement of *Natrix sipedon pictiventris*. *Copeia* 1961: 498–499.

———. 1964. Pleistocene amphibians and reptiles from Texas. *Herpetologica* 20: 73–83.

———. 2000. *Fossil Snakes of North America*. Bloomington: Indiana University Press.

Huheey, J. E. 1959. Distribution and variation in the glossy water snake, *Natrix rigida*. *Copeia* 1959: 303–311.

Iverson, J. B. 1979. Reproductive notes on Florida snakes. *Florida Scientist* 41: 201–207.

Jackson, Dale R., and Richard Franz. 1981. Ecology of the eastern coral snake (*Micrurus fulvius*) in northern peninsular Florida. *Herpetologica* 37:213–228.

Jackson, Dudley. 1929. Treatment of snake bite. *Southern Medical Journal* 22:605–608.

———. 1931. First aid treatment for snake bite. *Texas State Journal of Medicine* 23: 203–209.

Jameson, D. L., and A. G. Flury. 1949. The reptiles and amphibians of the Sierra Vieja range of Southwestern Texas. *Texas Journal of Science*, 1 (2): 54–77.

Jayne, Bruce C. 1985. Swimming in constricting (*Elaphe g. guttata*) and non-constricting (*Nerodia fasciata pictiventris*) Colubrid Snakes. *Copeia* (1):195–208.

Jayne, Bruce C., and J. D. Davis. 1991. Kinematics and performance capacity for the concertina locomotion of a snake (*Coluber constrictor*). *The Journal of Experimental Biology* 1991(156): 539–556.

Johnson, Tom R. 1987. *The Amphibians and Reptiles of Missouri*. Jefferson City: Missouri Department of Conservation.

Jones, J. M., and P. M. Burchfield. 1971. Relationship of specimen size to venom extracted from the copperhead, *Agkistrodon contortrix*. *Copeia* 1971: 162–163.

Jones, K. B., W. G. Whitford. 1989. Feeding behavior of free-roaming *Masticophis flagellum*: An efficient ambush predator. *Southwestern Naturalist* 34:460–467.

Justice, D. W., and R. E. Herrington. 1988. Life history notes: *Elaphe guttata* (corn snake). *Herpetological Review* 19:35.

Kapus, Edward J. 1964. Anatomical evidence for *Heterodon* being poisonous. *Herpetologica* 20:137–138.

Kardong, Kenneth V. 1975. Prey capture in the cottonmouth snake. *Journal of Herpetology* 9 (2): 169–175.

Keenlyne, K. D. 1972. Sexual differences in feeding habits of *Crotalus horridus horridus*. *Journal of Herpetology* 6 (3–4): 234–237.

Kennedy, J. P. 1959. A minimum egg complement for the western mud snake, *Farancia abacura reinwardti*. *Copeia* 1959: 71.

———. 1965. Territorial behavior in the eastern coachwhip, *Masticophis flagellum*. *Anatomical Record* 1965: 151–499.

Kiester, A. R. 1971. Species density of North American amphibians and reptiles. *Systematic Zoology* 20:127–137.

King, Richard B. 1986. Population ecology of the Lake Erie water snake, *Nerodia sipedon insularum*. *Copeia*: 757–772.

———. 1987. Color pattern polymorphism in the Lake Erie water snake, *Nerodia sipedon insularum*. *Evolution* 41: 241–255.

———. 1992. Lake Erie water snakes revisited: Morph- and age-specific variation in relative crypsis. *Evolutionary Ecology* 6: 115–124.

———. 1993. Determinants of offspring number and size in the brown snake, *Storeria dekayi*. *Journal of Herpetology* 27(2): 175–185.

———. 1993a. Color pattern variation in Lake Erie water snakes: Inheritance. *Canadian Journal of Zoology* 71: 1985–1990.

———. 1993b. Color pattern variation in Lake Erie water snakes: prediction and measurement of natural selection. *Evolution* 47: 1819–1833.

———. 1993c. Microgeographic, Historical, and Size-correlated variation in water snake diet composition. *Journal of Herpetology* 27(1): 90–94.

———, and Robin Lawson. 1995. Color pattern variation in Lake Erie water snakes: The role of gene flow. *Evolution* 49 (5): 885–896.

———, and ———. 1997. Microevolution in island water snakes. *BioScience* 47 (5): 279–286.

Klauber, Laurence Monroe. 1956. *Rattlesnakes: Their Habits, Life Histories and Influence on Mankind*. 2 vols. Los Angeles: University of California Press.

———. 1972. *Rattlesnakes: Their Habits, Life Histories and Influence on Mankind*. 2 vols. Revised ed. Berkeley: University of California Press.

Klemens, Michael W. 1993. *Amphibians and Reptiles of Connecticut and Adjacent Regions*. Hartford: State Geological and Natural History Survey of Connecticut. Bulletin no. 112.

Knight, J. L., and R. K. Loraine. 1986. Notes on turtle egg predation by *Lampropeltis getulus* (Linnaeus)(Reptilia: Colubridae) on the Savannah River Plant, South Carolina.

Knight, R. L., and A. W. Erickson. 1976. High incidence of snakes in the diet of Red-tailed Hawks. *Raptor Res.* 10: 108–111.

Kofron, C. P. 1978. Foods and habitats of aquatic snakes (Reptilia, Serpentes) in a Louisiana swamp. *Journal of Herpetology* 12: 543–554.

———. 1979a. Female reproductive biology of the brown snake, *Storeria dekayi*, in Louisiana. *Copeia* 1979: 463–466.

———, and J. R. Dixon. 1980. Observations on aquatic colubrid snakes in Texas. *Southwestern Naturalist* 25: 107–109.

Kroll, James C. 1976. Feeding adaptations of hognose snakes. *Southwestern Naturalist* 20 (4): 537–557.

Krysko, Kenneth L. 1995. Resolution of the controversy regarding the taxonomy of the kingsnake, *Lampropeltis getula*, in southern Florida. Master's thesis, Florida International University.

Krysko, Kenneth L., and John Decker. 1996. *Tantilla oolitica* (rim rock crowned snake): Range extension. *Herpetological Review* 27 (4):215.

———, L. E. Krysko, and B. Dierking. 1997. *Lampropeltis getula floridana* (Florida kingsnake): Combat ritual. *Herpetologica* 20: 137–138.

LaDuc, T. J., D. Lannutti, M. Ross, and D. Beamer. 1996. *Lampropeltis getula splendida* diet. *Herpetological Review* 27: 25.

Lawler, H. E. 1977. The status of *Drymarchon corais couperi* (Holbrook), the eastern indigo snake, in the southeastern United States. *Herpetological Review* 8: 76–79.

Lawson, Robin, Albert J. Meier, Philip G. Frank, and Paul E. Moler. 1991. Allozyme variation and systematics of the *Nerodia fasciata-Nerodia clarkii* complex of water snakes (Serpentes-Colubridae). *Copeia* (3): 638–659.

———, and R. B. King. 1996. Gene flow and melanism in Lake Erie garter snake populations. *Biological Journal of the Linnean Society* 59: 1–19.

Laszlo, Jozsef. 1977. Notes on thermal requirement of reptiles and amphibians in captivity: The relationship between temperature ranges and vertical climate (life) zone concept. Proceedings from the American Association of Zoological Parks and Aquariums Regional Conference, Wheeling, West Virginia.

Layne, James M., and Todd M. Steiner. 1984. Sexual dimorphism in occurrence of keeled dorsal snakes in the eastern indigo snake (*Drymarchon corais couperi*). *Copeia* 1984(3): 776–778.

Lazell, Jr., James D. 1976. *This Broken Archipelago, Cape Cod and the Islands, Amphibians and Reptiles*. New York: Quadrangle/The New York Times Book Company, 1–260.

Lazell, J. D. Jr. 1989. *Wildlife of the Florida Keys: A Natural History*. Covelo, Calif.: Island Press.

Levell, John P. 1995. *A Field Guide to Reptiles and the Law*. Excelsior, Minn.: Serpent's Tale Natural History Book Distributors.

———. 1997. *A Field Guide to Reptiles and the Law*. 2nd ed. Excelsior, Minn.: Serpent's Tale Natural History Book Distributors.

Lipske, Michael. 1995. Observations on scarlet snakes, *Cemophora coccinea*. *Tropical Fish Hobbyist* 43 (7):128.

———. 1995a. The private lives of pitvipers. *National Wildlife* 33(5): 14–21.

Loennberg, E. 1984. Notes on the Reptiles and Batrachians Collected in Florida in 1892 and 1893. Proceedings of the U.S. National Museum 17:317–339.

Lovich, J. E., and E. O. Wilson. 1967. *The Theory of Island Biogeography*. Princeton, N.J.: Princeton University Press.

Lowe, Charles H., Cecil R. Schwalbe, and Terry B. Johnson. 1986. *The Venomous Reptiles of Arizona*. Phoenix: Arizona Game and Fish Commission.

Maldonado, Jose V. 1998. *Scolependra*. Unpublished Master's thesis, University of Texas at El Paso.

Mara, W. P. 1992. The eastern indigo snake: One of nature's finest. *Tropical Fish Hobbyist* 41 (2):164.

———. 1993. *Venemous Snakes of the World*. New York: TFH Publications.

———. 1995. Observations on scarlet snakes, *Cemophora coccinea*. *Tropical Fish Hobbyist* 43 (7):128.

Markel, Ronald G., and R. D. Bartlett. 1995. *Kingsnakes and Milksnakes*. New York: Barron's.

Markel, R. G. 1990. *Kingsnakes and Milk Snakes*. Neptune City, N.J.: T. F. H. Publications, Inc., 1–144.

Markel, R. G., and R. D. Bartlett. 1995. *Kingsnakes and Milk Snakes*. Hauppauge, N.Y.: Barron's Educational Series, Inc., 1–94.

Martin, William F., and R. B. Huey. 1971. The function of the epiglottis in sound production (hissing) of *Pituophis melanoleucus*. *Copeia* 1971: 752–754.

Martof, B. S., W. M. Palmer, J. R. Bailey, and J. R. Harrison III. 1980. *Amphibians and Reptiles of the Carolinas and Virginia*. Chapel Hill: University of North Carolina Press.

Marvel, Bill. 1972. A feeding observation on the yellow-bellied water snake—*Nerodia erythrogaster flavigaster*. Bulletin of the Maryland Heropetological Society 8 (2):52.

Mattison, C. 1988. *Keeping and Breeding Snakes*. London: Blanford Press.

McAdoo, J. 1995. Why keep locality *alternas*? *SEOSH News* 2 (2):2.

McCollough, N. E., and J. R. Gennaro, Jr. 1963. Evaluation of venomous snake bite in the southern United States. *Journal of the Florida Medical Association* 49: 959–972.

McDowell, S. B., and C. M. Bogert. 1954. The systematic position of *Lanthanotus* and the affinities of the anguinomorphan lizards. Bulletin of the American Museum of Natural History 105:1–142.

McEachern, Michael J. 1991. *A Color Guide to Corn Snakes Captive-Bred in the United States*. Lakeside, Calif.: Advanced Vivarium Systems, Inc.

McIntyre, D. Craig. 1977a. Reproductive habits of captive Trans-Pecos rat snakes *Elaphe subocularis*. *Journal of the Northern Ohio Association of Herpetology* 3 (1): 20–22.

———. 1977b. First report of double embryos in *Elaphe subocularis*. *Journal of the Northern Ohio Association of Herpetology* 3(2): 29.

———. 1978. The NOAH Breeder's Corner. Notes from NOAH 6(2): 9.

McKinney, Charles, and R. E. Ballinger. 1966. Snake Predators of Lizards in Texas. *Southwestern Naturalist* 11 (2): 410–442.

Meade, George O. 1934. Feeding *Farancia abacura* in captivity. *Copeia* 1934: 91–92.

———. 1935. The egg-laying of *Farancia abacura*. *Copeia* 1935: 190–191.

———. 1937. Breeding habits of *Farancia abacura* in captivity. *Copeia* 1937: 12–15.

———. 1940. Maternal care of eggs by *Farancia*. *Herpetologica* 2:15.

———. 1941. The natural history of the mud snake. *Science Monthly* 63 (1): 21–29.

Means, D. B. 1977. Aspects of the significance to terrestrial vertebrates of the Apalachicola River drainage basin, Florida. *Fla. Mar. Res. Publ.* 26: 37–67.

———. 1985. Radio-tracking the eastern diamondback rattlesnake. *National Geographic Society Res. Rep.* 18: 529–536.

———. 1992. Eastern common kingsnake, *Lampropeltis getula "goini"* (Apalachicola population). In *Rare and Endangered Biota of Florida. Volume III: Amphibians and Reptiles.* Gainesville: University Press of Florida.

Mecham, J. S. 1979. The Biographical Relationships of the Amphibians and Reptiles of the Guadalupe Mountains. Natl. Park Serv. Trans Proc. Ser. (4): 169–179.

Mecham, J. S., and W. W. Milstead. 1949. *Lampropeltis alterna* from Pecos County, Texas. *Herpetologica* 5 (6):140.

Mehrtens, J. M. 1987. *Living Snakes of the World.* New York: Sterling Publishing Co., Inc., 1–480.

Meier, Albert J. and Julian White (eds). 1995. *Handbook of Clinical Toxicology and Animal Poisons.* Basel, Switzerland: Parthenon.

Merker, G., and W. Broda Jr. 1993. Poster: Geographic Variation in the Gray-banded Kingsnake, *Lampropeltis alterna.* Broda-Merker Enterprises, Pacific Grove.

Merker, G., and C. Merker. 1996. The mystical gray-banded: Gem of North American kingsnakes. *Reptiles* 4 (7): 60–8.

Mertens, Robert. 1960. *The World of Amphibians and Reptiles.* London: George C. Harrap & Co; New York: McGraw Hill.

Meshaka, Walter E. Jr. 1994. Clutch parameters of *Storeria dekayi* Holbrook (Serpentes: Colubridae) from southcentral Florida. *Brimleyana* 21: 73–76.

Miller, D. A., and Henry R. Mushinsky. 1990. Foraging ecology and prey size in the mangrove water snake, *nerodia fasciata compressicauda.* *Copeia* 1990:1099–1106.

Miller, D. J. 1979. A life history study of the gray-banded kingsnake, *Lampropeltis mexicana alterna*, in Texas. M. Sc. thesis at the Sul Ross State University, Chihuahuan Desert Res. Inst. Cont., Alpine (87): 1–48.

Milstead, W. W., J. S. Mecham, and H. McClintock. 1950. The amphibians and reptiles of the Stockton Plateau in northern Terrell County, Texas. *Texas J. Sci.* 2 (4): 543–562.

Minton, Sherman A. Jr. 1953. Variation in venom samples from copperheads (*Agkistrodon contortrix mokeson*) and timber rattlesnakes (*Crotalus horridus horridus*). *Copeia* 1953: 212–215.

———. 1954. Polyvalent antivenin in the treatment of experimental snake venom poisoning. *American Journal of Tropical Medicine and Hygiene* 3: 1077–1082.

———. 1956. Some properties of North American pit viper venoms and their correlation with phylogeny. In E. E. Buckley and N. Porges, eds., *Venoms*, 145–151. American Association for the Advancement of Science, publication no. 44.

———. 1957. Snakebite. *Scientific American* 196 (1): 114–122.

———. 1959. Observations on amphibians and reptiles of the Big Bend region of Texas. *Southwest. Natur.*, 3: 28–54.

———. 1972. *Amphibians and Reptiles of Indiana*. Indianapolis, Indiana: Indiana Academy of Science (3):1–346.

———. 1974. *Venom Diseases*. Springfield, Ill.: Thomas.

———, and M. R. Minton. 1969. *Venomous Reptiles*. New York: Charles Scribner's Sons.

———, and S. K. Salanitro. 1972. Serological relationships among some colubrid snakes. *Copeia* 1972: 246–252.

———, and D. Simberloff. 1987. The peninsula effect: habitat-correlated species declines in Florida's herpetofauna. *Journal of Biogeography* 14: 551–568.

Mitchell, Joseph C. 1994. *The Reptiles of Virginia*. Washington, D.C.: Smithsonion Institution Press.

Moler, Paul E., ed. 1992. *Rare and Endangered Biota of Florida. Vol. III: Amphibians and Reptiles*. Gainesville: University Press of Florida.

Morafka, D. J. 1977. A biogeographical analysis of the Chihuahuan Desert through its herpetofauna. *Biogeographica* 9: 1–313.

Mount, Robert H. 1975. *The Reptiles and Amphibians of Alabama*. Auburn, Ala.: Auburn University Agricultural Experimental Station.

Mullin, Stephen J. 1994. Life history characteristics of *Nerodia clarkii compressicauda* at Placido Bayou, Florida. *Journal of Herpetology* 28 (3): 371–372.

Mullin, Stephen J., and Henry R. Mushinsky. Foraging ecology of the mangrove salt marsh snake, *Nerodia clarkii compressicauda*: Effects of vegetational density. *Amphibia-Reptilia* 16 (2): 167–175.

Murphy, James B., W. Tryon, and B. J. Brecke. 1978. An inventory of reproduction and social behavior in captive gray-banded kingsnakes, *Lampropeltis mexicana alterna* (Brown). *Herpetologica* 34 (1): 84–93.

———, and Barry L. Armstrong. 1978a. *Maintenance of Rattlesnakes in Captivity*. Lawrence: University of Kansas Press.

———, L. A. Mitchell, and J. A. Campbell. 1979. Miscellaneous notes on the reproductive biology of reptiles. *Journal of Herpetology* 13 (3):373–374.

Murray, L. T. 1939. Annotated List of Amphibians and Reptiles from Chisos Mountains. Contr. Baylor Mus., 24: 4–16.

Mushinsky, Henry R. 1984. Observations of the feeding habits of the short-tailed snake, *Stilosoma extenuatum*, in captivity. *Herpetological Review* 15 (3): 67–68.

Mushinsky, Henry R., and J. J. Hebrard. 1977. Food partitioning by five species of water snakes in Louisiana. *Herpetologica* 33:162–166.

———, and Brian W. Witz. 1993. Notes on the Peninsula crowned snake, *Tantilla Relicta*, in periodically burned habitat. *Journal of Herpetology* 27 (4): 468–470.

———, and D. E. Miller. 1993. Predation on water snakes: ontogenetic and interspecific considerations. *Copeia*: 660–665.

Myers, C. W., 1961. An exceptional pattern variant of the coral snake, *Micrurus fulvius* (Linnaeus). *Quarterly Journal of Florida Academy of Science* 24: 56–58.

———, 1965. Biology of the ringneck snake, *Diadophis punctatus*, in Florida. Bulletin Florida State, Museum of Biological Sciences 10: 43–90.

———, 1967. The pine woods snake, *Rhadinea flavilata* (Cope). Bulletin Florida State, Museum of Biological Sciences 11: 47–97.

Neill, W. T., and E. R. Allen. 1949. A new kingsnake (genus *Lampropeltis*) from Florida. *Herpetologica* 5: 1–12.

———, and E. R. Allen. 1955. Metachrosis in snakes. *Quarterly Journal of the Florida Academy of Sciences* 18 (3):207–215.

———. 1956. Secondarily ingested food items in snakes. *Herpetologica* 12: 172–174.

———. 1964. Rainbow Snake. *American Midland Naturalist* 71 (2).

Newman, Eric A., and Peter H. Hartline. 1982. The infrared "vision" of snakes. *Scientific American* 246 (3):116–127.

Nybakken, Oscar E. 1959. *Greek and Latin in Scientific Terminology.* Ames: Iowa State University Press.

Odum, W. E., C. C. McIvor, and T. J. Smith III. 1982. The ecology of the mangroves of south Florida: A community profile. U.S. Fish and Wildlife Services Office of Biological Services. FWS/OBS-81/24.

Oldham, Jonathon C., and Hobart M. Smith. 1991. The generic status of the smooth green snake, *Opheodrys vernalis*. Bulletin of the Maryland Herpetological Society 27 (4): 210–215.

Owen, J. E., and J. R. Dixon. 1989. An ecogeographic analysis of the herpetofauna of Texas. *Southwest Naturalist* 34(2):165–180.

Oxer, H. F. 1982. Australian work in first-aid of poisonous snakebite. *Annals of Emergency Medicine* 11:228.

Painter, C. W., P. W. Hyder, and G. Swinford. 1992. Three species new to the herpetofauna of New Mexico. *Herpetological Review* 23 (2):64.

Palmer, T. 1992. *Landscape with Reptile: Rattlesnakes in an Urban World.* New York: Ticknow and Fields.

Palmer, William M. 1971. Distribution and variation of the Carolina pigmy rattlesnake, *Sistrurus miliarius miliarius*. *North Carolina Journal of Herpetology* 5 (1):39–44.

Palmer, William M., and Alvin L. Braswell. 1995. *Reptiles of North Carolina*. Chapel Hill: University of North Carolina Press.

Parker, H. Wildman, and A. G. C. Grandison. 1977. *Snakes: A Natural History*. London: British Museum of Natural History; Ithaca, N.Y.: Cornell University Press.

Parker, W. S., and W. S. Brown. 1980. Comparative ecology of two colubrid snakes, *Masticophis t. taeniatus* and *Pituophis melanoleucus deserticola*, in north Utah. Milwaukee Public Museum Publication, *Biological Geology* 7, 104 pp.

Parmley, D. 1990. Late Pleistocene snakes from Fowlkes Cave, Culberson County, Texas. *Journal of Herpetology* 24 (3):266–274.

Parrish, Henry M. 1963. Analysis of 460 fatalities from venomous animals in the United States. *American Journal of Medical Science* 245 (2):35–47.

———. 1966. Incidence of treated snakebites in the United States. Public Health Reports 81:269–276.

———. 1980. *Poisonous Snakes in the United States*. New York: Vantage Press.

Parrish, Henry M., and M. S. Khan. 1967. Bites by coral snakes: Report of eleven representative cases. *American Journal of Medical Science* 253: 561–568.

Peam, J., J. Morrison, N. Charles, and V. Muir. 1981. First-aid for snakebite. *Medical Journal of Australia* 2: 293–295.

Perkins, C. B. 1940. A key to the snakes of the United States. Bulletin of the Zoological Society of San Diego, no. 16.

Perlowin, David. 1994. *The General Care and Maintenance of Garter Snakes and Water Snakes*. Lakeside, Calif.: Advanced Vivarium Systems, Inc.

Perz, Stephen G. 1994. Optimal foraging by patch and prey selection in *Thamnophis Sirtalis Similis*. *Journal of General Psychology* 121 (2): 121–130.

Peters, James A. 1964. *Dictionary of Herpetology*. New York: Hafner Publishing.

Pinou, Theodora, Carla Ann Hass, and Linda R. Maxon. 1995. Geographic variation of serum albumin in the monotypic snake genus *Diadophis* (*Colubridae:Xenodontinae*). *Journal of Herpetology* 29 (1): 105–110.

Pisani, G. R., J. T. Collins, and S. R. Edwards. 1973. A re-evaluation of the subspecies of *Crotalus horridus*. *Kansas Academy of Sciences* 75 (3):255–263.

Platt, Dwight R. 1969. Natural history of the eastern and western hognose snakes *Heterodon platyrhinos* and *Heterodon nasicus*. University of Kansas, Publications of the Museum of Natural History 18 (4): 253–420.

Plummer, Michael V. 1981. Habitat utilization, diet, and movements of a temperate arboreal snake (*Opheodrys aestivus*). *Journal of Herpetology* 15 (4): 425–432.

Plummer, Michael V. 1983. Annual variation in stored lipids and reproduction in green snakes (*Opheodrys aestivus*). *Copeia* (3):741–745.

———. 1990. Nesting movements, nesting behavior, and nest sites of green snakes (*Opheodrys aestivus*) revealed by radiotelemetry. *Herpetologica* 46:190–195.

Plummer, Michael V., and Howard L. Snell. 1988. Nest site selection and water relations of eggs in the snake (*Opheodrys aestivus*). *Copeia* (1):58–64.

———, and Justin D. Congdon. 1994. Radiotelemetric study of activity and movements of racers (*Coluber constrictor*) associated with a Carolina Bay in South Carolina. *Copeia* (1):20–26.

Porras, L. 1992. Gray-banded kingsnake, *Lampropeltis alterna*, predation. *Intermontanus* 1 (4): 3.

Porter, K. R. 1972. *Herpetology*. Philadelphia: W. B. Saunders Co.

Pough, F. H. 1964. A coral snake "mimic" eaten by a bird. *Copeia* 1964: 223.

Quinn, Hugh R. 1979. Reproduction and growth of the Texas coral snake (*Micrurus fulvius tenere*). *Copeia* 1979: 453–463

Raun, G. G. 1965. *A Guide to Texas Snakes*. Texas Memorial Museum, University of Texas, Austin, Museum Notes no. 9: 1–85.

Rawat, Sophia, Gavin Laing, Damon C. Smith, David Theakston, and John Landon. 1993. A new antivenom to treat eastern coral snake (*Micrurus fulvius fulvius*) envenoming. *Toxicon* 32 (2): 185–190.

Raymond, L. R., and L. M. Hardy. 1983. Taxonomic status of the corn snake, *Elaphe guttata* (Linnaeus) (Colubridae), in Louisiana and eastern Texas. *Southwest Naturalist* 28 (1): 105–107.

Reddell, J. R. 1971. A checklist of the cave fauna of Texas. 6. Additional Records of Vertebrata. *Texas J. Sci.* 22 (2–3): 139–158.

Redi, Francesco. 1664. *Osservazioni Intorno Alle Vipere*. Florence.

Reichling, Steven B. 1995. The taxonomic status of the Louisiana pine snake (*Pituophis melanoleucus ruthveni*) and its relevance to the evolutionary species concept. *Journal of Herpetology* 20 (2):186–198.

Riches, Robert J. 1976. *Breeding Snakes in Capativity*. St. Petersburg, Fla.: Palmetto Publishing.

Richmond, Neil D. 1952. *Opheodrys aestivus* in aquatic habitats in Virginia. *Herpetologica* 8:38.

———. 1954. The ground snake, *Haldea valeriae*, in Pennsylvania and West Virginia, with description of new subspecies. Ann Carnegie Museum 33:251–60

Riemer, W. J. 1957. The snake *Farancia abacura*: An attended nest. *Herpetologica* 13:31–32.

Robertshaw, D. 1974. *Environmental Physiology*. Baltimore: University Park Press.

Rogers, James S. 1976. Species density and taxonomic diversity of Texas amphibians and reptiles. *Systematic Zoology* 25: 26–40.

Romer, A. S. 1966. *Vertebrate Paleontology*. 3rd ed. Chicago: University of Chicago Press.

——. 1967. Early reptilian evolution reviewed. *Evolution* 21: 821–833.

Rosenberg, Martin J. 1981. *Medical Treatment of Venomous Snakebite*. Cleveland: Cleveland Museum of Natural History.

Rossi, John V. 1992. *Snakes of the United States and Canada: Keeping Them Healthy in Captivity. Vol. 1. Eastern Area*. Florida: Krieger Publishing Co.

Rossi, John V., and Roxanne Rossi. 1993. Notes on the captive maintenance and feeding bahavior of a juvenile short-tailed snake (*Stilosoma extenuatum*). *Herpetological Review* 24 (3):100–101.

——, and ——. 1995. *Snakes of the United States and Canada: Keeping Them Healthy in Captivity. Vol. 2. Western Area*. Florida: Krieger Publishing Co.

Rossman, Douglas A. 1962. *Thamnophis proximus*: A valid species of garter snake. *Copeia* 741–748.

——. 1963. The colubrid snake genus *Thamnophis*: A revision of the *sauritus* group. Bulletin of the Florida State Museum of Biological Sciences 7 (3):99–178.

Rossman, Douglas A., and Robert L. Erwin. 1980. Geographic variation in the snake *Storeria occipitomaculata* (Serpentes: Colubridae) in southeastern United States. *Brimleyana* 4:95–102.

Rossman, Douglas A., Neil B. Ford, and Richard Seigel. 1996. *Garter Snakes: Evolution and Ecology*. Norman: University of Oklahoma Press.

Roze, Janis A. 1996. *Coral Snakes of the Americas: Biology, Identification, and Venoms*. Malabar, Fla.: Krieger Publishing Co.

Ruben, John A. 1977. Morphological correlates of predatory modes in the coachwhip (*Masticophis flagellum*) and rosy boa (*Lichanura roseofusca*). *Herpetologica* 33:1–6.

Rubio, Manny. 1998. Rattlesnake: Portrait of a Predator. Washington, D.C.: Smithsonian.

Rudolph, D. Craig, S. J. Burgdorf, John C. Tull, Marc Ealy, Richard N. Conner, Richard R. Schaefer, and Robert R. Fleet. 1998. Avoidance of Fire by Louisiana Pine Snakes. *Herpetological Review* 29 (3).

Russell, Findlay E. 1961. Injuries by venomous animals in the United States. *Journal of the American Medical Association* 177:903–907.

——. 1966. Shock following snakebite. *Journal of the American Medical Association* 198:171.

———. 1967. Pharmacology of animal venoms. *Clinical Pharmacology Therapy* 8: 849–873.

———. 1969. Treatment of rattlesnake bite. *Journal of the American Medical Association* 207: 159.

———. 1980. *Snake Venom Poisoning*. Philadelphia: J. B. Lippincott.

Russell, Findlay E., and J. A. Emery. 1959. Use of the chick in zootoxicologic studies on venoms. *Copeia* 1959: 73–74.

———, R. W. Carlson, J. Wainschel, and A. H. Osborne. 1975. Snake venom poisoning in the United States: Experiences with 550 cases. *Journal of the American Medical Association* 233: 341.

Salmon, Gerard T., William F. Holmstrom Jr., Bern W. Tryon, and Gerold P. Merker. 1997. Longevity records for the gray-banded kingsnake, *Lampropeltis alterna*. Bulletin of the Chicago Herp. Soc. 32, No. 7.

Schmidt, Karl P., and D. D. Davis. 1941. *Field Book of Snakes of the United States and Canada*. New York: G. P. Putnam's Sons.

———. 1953. *A Check List of North American Amphibians and Reptiles*. Chicago: University of Chicago Press.

———, and D. W. Owens. 1944. Amphibians and reptiles of northern Coahuila, Mexico. *Zool. Ser. Field Mus. Nat. Hist.* 26 (6): 97–115.

Scudday, J. F. 1965. Another *Lampropeltis alterna* in Brewster County, Texas. *Southwestern Naturalist* 10 (1): 77–78.

Secor, S. M. 1990. Reproductive and Combat Behavior of the Mexican Kingsnake, *Lampropeltis mexicana*. J. Herp. 24 (2): 217–221.

Seigel, Richard A., and H. S. Fitch. 1984. Ecological patterns of relative clutch mass in snakes. *Oecologia* 61: 293–301.

Seigel, Richard A., and Joseph T. Collins, eds. 1993. *Snakes: Ecology and Behavior*. New York: McGraw-Hill, Inc.

Semlitsch, R. D., and Gary B. Moran. 1984. Ecology of the redbelly snake (*Storeria occipitomaculata*) using mesic habitats in South Carolina. *American Midland Naturalist* 111:33–40.

———, J. H. K. Pechmann, and J. W. Gibbons. 1988. Annual emergence of juvenile mud snakes (*Farancia abacura*) at aquatic habitats. *Copeia* 1988:243–245.

Sexton, Owen J., Peter Jacobson, and Judy E. Bramble. 1992. Geographic variation in some activities associated with nearctic pitvipers. In *Biology of the Pitvipers*. Jonathan A. Campbell and Edmund D. Brodie, eds. Tyler, Texas: Selva Press.

Shaw, C. E., and S. Campbell. 1974. *Snakes of the American West*. New York: Alfred A. Knopf Publishing.

Sievert, Gregory, and Lynette Sievert. 1993. *A Field Guide to Reptiles of Oklahoma*. Oklahoma City: Oklahoma Department of Wildlife Conservation, 1–96.

Slavens, Frank L. 1992. *Inventory of Live Reptiles and Amphibians in North American Collections*. Seattle: Frank L. Slavens.

Smith, Charles. 1992. Rattle length in *Crotalus horridus atricaudatus*. Bulletin of the Maryland Herpetological Society 28(3):77.

Smith, Hobart M. 1941a. *Lampropeltis alterna* from Mexico. *Copeia* (2): 112.

——. 1941b. A review of the subspecies of the indigo snake (*Drymarchon corais*). *Journal of the Washington Academy of Sciences* 31 (11):466–481.

——. 1944. Snakes of the Hoogstraal Expedition to northern Mexico. *Zool. Ser. Field Mus. Nat. Hist.* 29 (8): 135–152.

Smith, Hobart M., and W. L. Buechner. 1947. The influence of the Balcones escarpment on the distribution of amphibians and reptiles in Texas. Bulletin, Chicago Academy of Science, 8 (1):1–16.

——, and E. H. Taylor. 1950. Type localities of Mexican reptiles and amphibians. Univ. Kansas Sci. Bull. 33: 313–379.

——, and Fred N. White. 1955. Adrenal enlargement and its significance in the hognose snakes (*Heterodon*). *Herpetologica* 11:137–144.

——, D. Chizar, J. R. Staley II, and K. Tepedelen. 1994. Populational relationships in the corn snake *Elaphe guttata* (Reptilia: Serpentes). *Texas J. Sci.* 46(3): 259–292.

Smith, N. G. 1969. Avian predation of coral snakes. *Copeia* 1969: 402–404.

Smith, Philip W. 1961. *The Amphibians and Reptiles of Illinois*. Urbana: State of Illinois, Natural History Survey Division, Bulletin vol. 28, article 1.

Smith, R. L. 1977. *Elements of Ecology and Field Biology*. New York: Harper & Row.

Smith, S. M. 1975. Innate recognition of coral snake pattern by a possible avian predator. *Science* 187: 759–760.

Snyder, C. C., J. E. Pickins, R. P. Knowles, et al. 1968. A definitive study of snakebite. *Journal of the Florida Medical Association* 55: 330–338.

Stewart, James R. 1989. Facultative placentotrophy and the evolution of squamate placentation: Quality of eggs and neonates in *Virginia striatula*. *American Naturalist* 133 (1): 111–137.

——. Development of the extraembryonic membranes and histology of the placentae in *Virginia striatula* (Squamata: Serpentes). *Journal of Morphology* 205 (1): 33–43.

Stinner, J. N., and D. L. Ely. 1993. Blood pressure during routine activity, stress, and feeding in black racer snakes (*Coluber constrictor*). *American Journal of Physiology* (264).

Strecker, John K. 1915. Reptiles and amphibians of Texas. Baylor University Bulletin 18 (4):82.

——. 1926. On the habits of some southern snakes. Contributions of the Baylor University Museum, no. 4.

———, 1927. Chapters from the life history of Texas and amphibians. Part 2. Contribution of the Baylor University Museum, no. 10.

Sutherland, Struan K. 1977. Serum reactions, an analysis of commercial antivenoms and the possible role of anticomplexity activity in de novo reactions to antivenoms and antitoxins. *Medical Journal of Australia* 1: 613–615.

Sutherland, Struan K., Alan R. Coulter, and R. D. Harris. 1979. Rationalization of first-aid measures for elapid snakebite. *Lancet* 1: 183–186.

———. 1980. Venom and antivenom research. *Medical Journal of Australia* 2: 246–250.

———. 1981. When do you remove first aid measures from an envenomed limb? *Medical Journal of Australia* 1: 542–544.

———, and Alan R. Coulter. 1981. Early management of bites by eastern diamondback rattlesnakes (*Crotalus adamanteus*): Studies in monkeys. *American Journal of Tropical Medicine and Hygiene* 30 (2): 497–500.

Switak, K. H. 1984. The Life of Desert Reptiles and Amphibians. Produced by Karl H. Switak, P.O. Box 27141, San Francisco, Calif. 94127, 1–32.

Tanzer, E. C. 1970. Polymorphism in the *mexicana* complex of kingsnakes, with notes on their natural history. *Herpetologica* 26 (4):419–428.

Teather, Kevin L. 1991. The relative importance of visual and chemical cues for foraging in newborn blue-striped garter snakes (*Thamnophis sirtalis similis*). *Behaviour* 117 (3–4): 255–261.

Telford, S. R. Jr. 1948. A large litter of *Natrix* in Florida. *Herpetologica* 4:184.

———. 1955. A description of the eggs of the coral snake, *Micrurus f. fulvius*. *Copeia* 1955: 258.

Tennant, Alan. 1984. *The Snakes of Texas*. Austin: Texas Monthly Press, Inc.

———. 1985. *A Field Guide to Texas Snakes*. Austin: Texas Monthly Press, Inc.

———. 1997. *A Field Guide to Snakes of Florida*. Houston: Gulf Publishing Co.

———. 1998. *A Field Guide to Texas Snakes*. 2nd ed. Houston: Gulf Publishing Co.

———. 2000. *Snakes of North America: Eastern and Central Regions*. Houston: Gulf Publishing Co.

Thomas, R. G., and F. H. Pough. 1979. Effects of rattlesnake venom on digestion of prey. *Toxicon* 17 (3): 221–228.

Thompson, Stith. 1936. *Index of Folk Literature*. Bloomington: Indiana University Press.

Tinkle, Donald W. 1957. Ecology, maturation and reproduction of *Thamnophis sauritus proximus*. *Ecology* 38 (1): 69–77.

———. 1960. A population of *Opheodrys aestivus*. *Copeia* 1960: 29–34.

Timmerman, W. W. 1989. Home range, habitat use and behavior of the eastern diamondback rattlesnake. Master's thesis, University of Florida.

——, 1994. Big snakes in trouble. *Florida Wildlife* 48(5): 12–14.

Trapido, H. 1940. Mating time and sperm viability in *Storeria*. *Copeia* 1940: 107–109.

Truitt, J. O. 1968. *A Guide to the Snakes of South Florida*. Miami: Hurricane House Publishers, Inc.

Tryon, B. W. 1979. An unusually patterned specimen of the gray-banded kingsnake, *Lampropeltis mexicana alterna* (Brown). *Herp. Review* 10 (1): 4–5.

Tyron, B. W., and J. B. Murphy. 1982. Miscellaneous notes on the reproductive biology of reptiles. Thirteen varieties of the genus *Lampropeltis*, species *mexicana*, *triangulum* and *zonata*. *Trans Kansas Acad. Sci.* 85 (2): 96–119.

——, and R. K. Guese. 1984. Death-feigning in the gray-banded kingsnake *Lampropeltis alterna*. *Herpetological Review* 15 (4): 108–109.

Turner, Earl H. 1977. Colorful Kingsnake of the Trans-Pecos. Texas Parks and Wildlife, 35 (1):10–11.

Tyning, Thomas F. 1990. *A Guide to Amphibians and Reptiles*. New York: Little, Brown and Company.

Underwood, G. 1957. *Lanthanotus* and the anguinomorphan lizards: a critical review. *Copeia* 1957: 20–30.

——. 1967. *A Contribution to the Classification of Snakes*. London: British Museum of Natural History.

Van Devender, Thomas R., and R. D. Worthington. 1977. The herpetofauna of Howell's Ridge Cave and the paleoecology of the northwestern Chihuahuan Desert. In R. H. Waver and D. H. Riskind, eds., Trans. Symp. Resources Chihuahuan Desert, U.S. and Mexico, 16–41. U.S. Natl. Park Serv. Trans. Proc. Ser. no. 13. Washington, D.C.

——, and C. H. Lowe, Jr. 1977. Amphibians and reptiles of Yepomera, Chihuahua, Mexico. *Journal of Herpetology* 11 (1): 41–50.

——, and J. I. Mead. 1978. Early Holocene and late Pleistocene amphibians and reptiles in Sonoran Desert packrat middens. *Copeia* 1978(3): 464–475.

Van Hyning, O. C. 1931. Reproduction of some Florida snakes. *Copeia* 1931: 59–60.

Van Mierop, L.H.S. 1976. Poisonous snakebite: A review. *Journal of the Florida Medical Association* 63:191–209.

Vaughan, R. K, J. R. Dixon, and R. A. Thomas. 1996. A re-evaluation of populations of the corn snake *Elaphe guttata* (Reptilia: Serpentes: Colubridae) in Texas. *Texas J. Sci.* 48 (3): 175–190.

Vermersch, Thomas G., and Robert E. Kuntz. 1986. *Snakes of South-Central Texas*. Austin, Tex.: Eakin Press.

Visser, John, and David S. Chapman. 1978. *Snakes and Snakebite*. London: Purnell & Son.

Vogt, Richard C. 1981. *Natural History of Amphibians and Reptiles in Wisconsin*. Milwaukee: Milwaukee Public Museum.

Vosjoli, Philippe de. 1995. *Basic Care of Rough Green Snakes*. Santee, Calif.: Advanced Vivarium Systems, Inc.

Wade, D., J. Ewel, and R. Hofstetter. 1980. Fire in south Florida ecosystems. U.S. Dep. Agric. For. Serv., Gen. Tech. Rep. SE-17, Southeast. For. Exp. Stn., Asheville, N.C., 125 pp.

Ward, R., F. G. Zimmerman, and T. L. King. 1994. Environmental correlates to terrestrial reptilian distributions in Texas. *Texas J. Sci.* 46 (1):21–26.

Watt, Charles H. Jr. 1978. Poisonous snakebite treatment in the United States. *Journal of the American Medical Association* 240:654.

Webb, R. 1961. A new kingsnake from Mexico, with remarks on the *mexicana* group of the genus *Lampropeltis*. *Copeia* (3): 326–333.

———. 1970. *Reptiles of Oklahoma*. Norman: University of Oklahoma Press.

Weinstein, Scott, Clement DeWitt, and Leonard A. Smith. 1992. Variability of venom-neutralizing properties of serum from snakes of the colubrid genus *Lampropeltis*. *Journal of Herpetology* 26 (4): 452–461.

Werler, John E. 1948. *Natrix cyclopion cyclopion* in Texas. *Herpetologica* 4:148.

———, and James R. Dixon. 2000. *Texas Snakes*. Austin: University of Texas Press.

Wharton, C. H. 1960. Birth and behavior of a brood of the cottonmouth, *Agkistrodon piscivorus leucostoma*, with notes on tail-luring. *Herpetologica* 16: 125–129.

———. 1966. Reproduction in the cottonmouths, *Agkistrodon piscivorous*, of Cedar Keys, Florida. *Copeia* 1966: 149–161.

———. 1969. The cottonmouth moccasin on Sea Horse Key, Florida. Bulletin of Florida State, Museum of Biological Sciences 14: 227–272.

Williams, Kenneth L. 1970. The racer, *Coluber constrictor*, in Louisiana and eastern Texas. *Texas Journal of Science* 22 (1): 67–85.

———. 1978. Systematics and natural history of the American milksnake, *Lampropeltis triangulum*. Milwaukee Public Museum, Publications in Biology and Geology (2): 1–258.

———. 1988. Systematics and natural history of the American milksnake, *Lampropeltis triangulum*, second revised ed. Milwaukee Public Museum, Publications in Biology and Geology 1–176.

Williams, Kenneth L., Bryce C. Brown, and Larry David Wilson. 1966. A new subspecies of the colubrid snake *Cemophora coccinea* (Blumenbach) from southern Texas. *Texas Journal of Science* 18 (1):85–88.

——, and Larry David Wilson. 1967. A review of the colubrid snake genus *Cemophora*. *Tulane Studies in Zoology and Botany* 13 (4):103–124.

Williamson, M. A., P. W. Hyder, and J. S. Applegarth. 1994. *Snakes, Lizards, Turtles, Frogs, Toads and Salamanders of New Mexico: A Field Guide*. Santa Fe: Sunstone Press, 1–176.

Wilson, Larry David, and L. Porras. 1983. The ecological impact of man on the south Florida herpetofauna. University of Kansas, Museum of Natural History, Special Publication no. 9.

Wingert, W. A., T. R. Pattabhiraman, R. Cleland, P. Meyer, R. Pattabhiraman, and F. E. Russell. 1980. Distribution and pathology of copperhead *Agkistrodon contortrix* venom. *Toxicon* 18:591–601.

Winstel, A. 1996. Experience with a difficult feeder—*Lampropeltis alterna*. *The Forked Tongue* 21 (4):3.

Witwer, Mark T., and Aaron M. Bauer. 1995. Early breeding in a captive corn snake (*Elaphe guttata guttata*). *Herpetological Review* 26 (3):141.

Wolfe, S. H., J. A. Reidenauer, and D. B. Means. 1988. An ecological characterization of the Florida panhandle. U.S. Fish and Wildlife Services Biological Report 88 (12).

Wolfenden, R. Norris. 1886. On the nature and action of the venom of poisonous snakes. *Journal of Physiology* 7:327.

Worthington, R. D. 1976. Herpetofauna of the Franklin Mountains, El Paso County, Texas. In D. V. LeMone and E. M. P. Lovejoy, El Paso Geological Society Symposium on the Franklin Mountains. El Paso Geol. Soc. Quinn Mem. Vol., 205–212.

Worthington, R. D., and E. R. Arvizo. 1974. Western Records of the Davis Mountains Kingsnake, *Lampropeltis mexicana alterna*, in Texas. *Southwestern Nature*, 19 (3):330–331.

Wright, Albert Hazen, and W. D. Funkhauser. 1915. A biological reconnaissance of the Okefenokee Swamp in Georgia. Proceedings of the Academy of Natural Science Philadelphia:107–195.

——, and Anna Allen Wright. 1957. *Handbook of Snakes of the United States and Canada*. 2 vols. Ithaca, N.Y.: Comstock Publishing.

——, and ——. 1979. *Handbook of Snakes of the United States and Canada*. Vol. 3: Bibliography. Ithaca, N.Y.: Comstock Publishing.

Ya, P. M., T. Guzman, and J. F. Perry Jr. 1961. Treatment of bites of North American pit vipers. *Southern Medical Journal* 52 (2):134–136.

Young, Robert A. 1992. Effects of Duvernoy's gland secretions from the eastern hognose snake, *heterodon platirhinos*, on smooth muscle and neuromuscular junction. *Toxicon* 30 (7):775–779.

Zegel, J. C. 1975. Notes on collecting and breeding the eastern coral snake, *Micrurus fulvius fulvius*. Bulletin of the Southeastern Herpetological Society 1 (6):L10.

Zug, D. A., W. A. Dunson. 1979. Salinity preference in fresh water and estuarine snakes (*Nerodia sipedon* and *N. fasciata*). *Florida Science* 42:1–8.

Zug, George R. 1993. *Herpetology, and Introductory Biology of Amphibians and Reptiles*. London: Academic Press.

Zweifel, Richard G., G. R. Zug, C. J. McCoy, D. A. Rossman, and J. D. Anderson, eds. 1963–present. *Catalogue of American Amphibians and Reptiles*. New York: Society for the Study of Amphibians and Reptiles.

INDEX

Trumbower, Craig, 513
Tryon, Bern, 444
Tyning, Tom, 100
type, 62, 66, 84, 114, 121, 163, 185, 335, 342, 377, 453, 513
Typhlopidae, 9, 30

urban, 102, 108, 119

Vaughan, R. Kathryn, 53
venom, 14, 18, 20, 487, 498, 501, 513, 524, 537, 543, 545
Venom Potency Table, 29
vestigial, 34, 35, 44
vine snake, 469
Viperidae, 487
Virginia, 67–74, 486; *striatula*, 67, 72-74; *valeriae elegans*, 67, 71–72; *valeriae pulchra*, 67, 69–70 *valeriae valeriae*, 67, 68–69
vomeronasal, 5

Wakulla, 101
wandering garter snake, 96, 108–9
water snakes, 130–65; Atlantic salt marsh snake, 130, 152-53; banded water snake, 130, 146–48; blotched water snake, 130, 144–46; Brazos water snake, 130, 162-64; broad-banded water snake, 130, 148–49; brown water snake, 130, 158–60; Carolina water snake, 130, 137–38; Concho water snake, 130, 164–65; copper-bellied water snake, 130, 140–42; diamond-backed water snake, 130, 160–62; Florida green water snake, 130, 155–56; Florida water snake, 130, 149–51; gulf salt marsh snake, 130, 151–52; Lake Erie water snake, 130, 133–36; Mangrove salt marsh snake, 130, 154–55; midland water snake, 130, 136–37; Mississippi green water snake, 130, 157–58; northern water snake, 130, 131–33; red-bellied water snake, 130, 138–40; yellow-bellied water snake, 130, 142–44
Webb, Robert, 404
Werler, John, 404, 405, 468, 519, 550
western rattlesnake, 29, 509, 523, 543–45
whipsnakes, 8, 198–203, 324–30; Central Texas, 198, 325–26; desert striped whipsnake, 198, 324–25; eastern coachwhip, 198, 199–202; Ruthven's whipsnake, 198, 328–29; Schott's whipsnake, 198, 327–28; western coachwhip, 198, 202–3;
"white oak" phase, 275, 396
Williams, Kenneth, 462
Wilson, Larry David, 342
Wisconsin glacial period, 114
worm snakes, 86–90; eastern worm snake, 86–87; midwestern worm snake, 86, 88; western worm snake, 86, 89–90
Wyeth, 25, 28

Xenodontinae, 38, 74, 84, 90, 184, 355, 414, 416, 466, 469, 474
xeric, 93, 201, 411, 413, 513, 522

yellow rat snake, 387, 392–93
yellow-bellied water snake, 130, 142–44

Zappalorti, Robert, 371

ABOUT THE AUTHOR

Alan Tennant is an award-winning writer, wildlife lecturer, wilderness guide, and herpetologist. He is the author of many articles and books including Gulf's *Field Guide to Texas Snakes, Second Edition.* Tennant's *Field Guide to Snakes of Florida* is a National Outdoor Book Award winner.

He has received numerous awards. Among them, W. F. Blair Award: Outstanding Contribution to Texas Herpetology, Texas Medical Association Anson Jones Award Snake Venom Poisoning, and The Wildlife Society Annual Public Award *When Lizards Lost Their Legs: The Evolution of Snakes.*